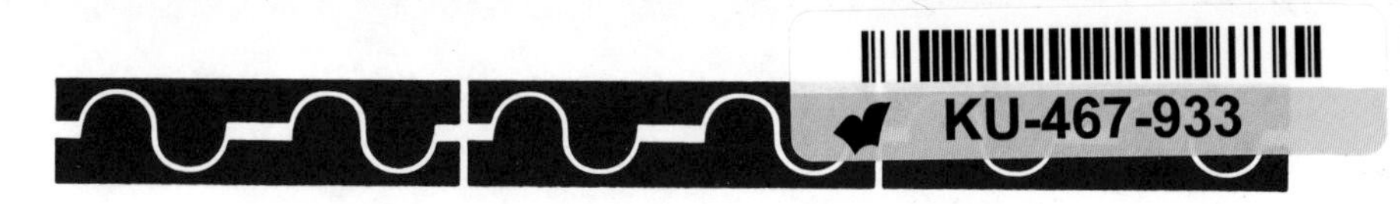

STRESS AND COPING

An Anthology

THIRD EDITION

EDITED BY ALAN MONAT
AND RICHARD S. LAZARUS

Columbia University Press New York

Columbia University Press
New York Chichester, West Sussex

Library of Congress Cataloging-in-Publication Data

Stress and coping : an anthology
edited by Alan Monat and Richard S. Lazarus. — 3rd ed. p. cm.
Includes bibliographical references and index.
ISBN 0231-07456-5
ISBN 0-231-07457-3 (pbk.)
1. Stress (Psychology) 2. Adjustment (Psychology)
I. Monat, Alan, 1945–
II. Lazarus, Richard S.
BF575.S75S77 1991 155.9—dc20 90-20507
CIP

Casebound editions of Columbia University Press books are printed on permanent and durable acid-free paper.

Printed in the United States of America

c 10 9 8 7 6 5 4 3 2
p 10 9 8 7 6 5

Stress and Coping: An Anthology

To Murline and Ian, Ron and Jeff, my parents,
Tillie and Harold, and to Lucy, Ernie, and Julie, and my many other supportive family members and friends.

AM

To Bunny, David and Mary, Nancy and Rick, Jessica, Adam, Maiya, and Ava, with love.

RSL

CONTENTS

ACKNOWLEDGMENTS xi

PREFACE TO THE THIRD EDITION xv

PREFACE TO THE SECOND EDITION xvii

PREFACE TO THE FIRST EDITION xix

Introduction: Stress and Coping—Some Current Issues and Controversies 1

I STRESS AND SOME OF ITS EFFECTS 17

1. History and Present Status of the Stress Concept 21
   HANS SELYE

2. Specificity and Stress Research 36
   JEROME E. SINGER and LAURA M. DAVIDSON

3. Anatomy of an Illness (As Perceived by the Patient) 48
   NORMAN COUSINS

4. Health Psychology: The Science and the Field 62
   SHELLEY E. TAYLOR

II STRESS AND THE ENVIRONMENT 81

5. The Living World 87
   RENE DUBOS

6. Toxins, Technology, and Natural Disasters 97
ANDREW BAUM

7. Stress, Coping, and the Meaning of Work 140
EDWIN A. LOCKE and M. SUSAN TAYLOR

8. Uplifts, Hassles, and Adaptational Outcomes in Early Adolescents 158
ALLEN D. KANNER, S. SHIRLEY FELDMAN, DANIEL A. WEINBERGER, and MARTIN E. FORD

III THE CONCEPT OF COPING 183

9. The Concept of Coping 189
RICHARD S. LAZARUS and SUSAN FOLKMAN

10. Coping and Emotion 207
SUSAN FOLKMAN and RICHARD S. LAZARUS

11. Measurement of Coping 228
FRANCES COHEN

12. The Development of Hardiness 245
SALVATORE R. MADDI and SUZANNE C. KOBASA

13. Gender Differences in the Social Moderators of Stress 258
DEBORAH BELLE

14. The Type A Behavior Pattern and Coronary Artery Disease: Quest for the Active Ingredients and the Elusive Mechanism 275
LOGAN WRIGHT

IV COPING WITH THE STRESSES OF LIVING AND DYING 301

15. The Response to Overwhelming Stress in Children: Some Introductory Comments 307
E. JAMES ANTHONY

16. Life Strains and Psychological Distress Among Adults 319
LEONARD I. PEARLIN

17. Some Modes of Adaptation: Defense 337
DAVID MECHANIC

18. Uncertainty and the Lives of Persons with AIDS 352
ROSE WEITZ

19. Two Decades of Research on Dying: What Do We Know About the Patient? 370
RICHARD SCHULZ and JANET SCHLARB

20. The Myths of Coping with Loss 388
CAMILLE B. WORTMAN and ROXANE COHEN SILVER

V STRESS MANAGEMENT 407

21. Stress Management: A New Approach to Treatment 411
ETHEL ROSKIES

22. Intervention Strategies 432
RICHARD H. COX

23. Out of the Habit Trap 475
STANTON PEELE

24. Healthy People—Healthy Business: A Critical Review of Stress Management Programs in the Workplace 483
KENNETH R. PELLETIER and ROBERT LUTZ

References 499

Index 573

ACKNOWLEDGMENTS

The editors would like to thank the following publishers for permission to reprint materials used in this book. It should be noted that, to achieve uniformity, we have in some cases slightly altered the original reference and/or footnote formats to conform with the author-date method of citation used throughout this book. It was also necessary to make some minor editorial changes appropriate to an anthology of this kind.

1. "History and Present Status of the Stress Concept" by Hans Selye: Reprinted with permission of the Free Press, a Division of Macmillan, Inc. from *Handbook of Stress: Theoretical and Clinical Aspects* by Leo Goldberger and Shlomo Breznitz, eds. Copyright © 1982 by the Free Press.

2. "Specificity and Stress Research" by Jerome E. Singer and Laura M. Davidson: Reprinted with permission of Plenum Publishing Corporation and authors from *Dynamics of Stress: Physiological, Psychological and Social Perspectives*, Mortimer H. Appley and Richard Trumbull, eds. 1986.

3. "Anatomy of an Illness (As Perceived by the Patient)" by Norman Cousins: Reprinted by permission of *The New England Journal of Medicine* (1976), 295:1458–63.

4. "Health Psychology: The Science and the Field" by Shelley E. Taylor: From the *American Psychologist* (1990), 45:40–50. Copyright © 1990 by the American Psychological Association. Reprinted by permission of the publisher and author.

5. "The Living World" by Rene Dubos: From *Man Adapting* by Rene Dubos: Copyright © 1965 by Yale University. Used with permission of Yale University Press.

6. "Toxins, Technology, and Natural Disasters" by Andrew Baum: From *Cataclysms, Crises, and Catastrophes: Psychology in Action* edited by G. R. VandenBos and B. K. Bryant, published by the American Psychological Association, 1987. Used with permission of Andrew Baum.

7. "Stress, Coping, and the Meaning of Work" by Edwin A. Locke and M. Susan Taylor: From *The Meaning of Work* edited by W. Nord and A. Brief. Copyright © 1990 by D. C. Heath & Company. Adapted with permission of the publisher and authors.

8. "Uplifts, Hassles, and Adaptational Outcomes in Early Adolescents" by Allen D. Kanner, S. Shirley Feldman, Daniel A. Weinberger, and Martin E. Ford: From the *Journal of Early Adolescence* (1987), 7:371–94. Copyright © 1987 by Sage Publications. Reprinted by permission of Sage Publications, Inc. and the authors.

9. "The Concept of Coping" by Richard S. Lazarus and Susan Folkman: From *Stress, Appraisal, and Coping* by Richard S. Lazarus and Susan Folkman. Copyright © 1984 by Springer Publishing Company, Inc., New York 10012. Adapted by permission of the publisher and authors.

10. "Coping and Emotion" by Susan Folkman and Richard S. Lazarus: From *Psychological and Biological Approaches to Emotion* edited by N. Stein, B. Leventhal, and T. Trabasso. Copyright © 1990 by Lawrence Erlbaum Associates, Inc. Reprinted with permission of the publisher, Lawrence Erlbaum Associates, Inc., and the authors.

11. "Measurement of Coping" by Frances Cohen: From *Stress and Health: Issues in Research Methodology* edited by S. V. Kasl and C. L. Cooper. Copyright © 1987 by John Wiley & Sons, Ltd. Adapted with permission.

12. "The Development of Hardiness" by Salvatore R. Maddi and Suzanne C. Kobasa: From *The Hardy Executive: Health Under Stress* by S. R. Maddi and S. C. Kobasa. Copyright © 1984 by Wadsworth, Inc. Reprinted by permission of Brooks/Cole

Publishing Company, Pacific Grove, California 93950, a division of Wadsworth, Inc.

13. "Gender Differences in the Social Moderators of Stress" by Deborah Belle: Reprinted with permission of the Free Press, a Division of Macmillan, Inc. from *Gender and Stress* by Rosalind Barnett, Lois Biener, Grace Baruch. Copyright © 1987 by Rosalind Barnett, Lois Biener, Grace Baruch.

14. "The Type A Behavior Pattern and Coronary Artery Disease: Quest for the Active Ingredients and the Elusive Mechanism" by Logan Wright: From the *American Psychologist* (1988), 43:2–14. Copyright © 1988 by the American Psychological Association. Reprinted by permission of the publisher and author.

15. "The Response to Overwhelming Stress in Children: Some Introductory Comments" by E. James Anthony: From *The Child in His Family: Perilous Development: Child Raising and Identity Formation Under Stress,* vol. 8, edited by E. J. Anthony and C. Chiland. Copyright © 1988 by John Wiley & Sons. Used with permission.

16. "Life Strains and Psychological Distress Among Adults" by Leonard I. Pearlin: From *Themes of Work and Love in Adulthood* by N. J. Smelser and E. H. Erikson, eds., Harvard University Press, 1980.

17. "Some Modes of Adaptation: Defense" by David Mechanic: From *Students Under Stress: A Study in the Social Psychology of Adaptation* by David Mechanic. The University of Wisconsin Press, © 1962, 1978 by David Mechanic. Used with permission of David Mechanic.

18. "Uncertainty and the Lives of Persons with AIDS" by Rose Weitz: From the *Journal of Health and Social Behavior* (1989), 30:270–81. Copyright © 1989 by the American Sociological Association. Used with permission of the publisher and author.

19. "Two Decades of Research on Dying: What Do We Know About the Patient?" by Richard Schulz and Janet Schlarb: From *Omega* (1987–88), 18:299–317. Copyright © 1988 by Baywood Publishing Co., Inc., 26 Austin Avenue, P.O. Box 337, Amityville, New York 11701. Used with permission of the publisher and authors.

20. "The Myths of Coping With Loss" by Camille B. Wortman and Roxane Cohen Silver: From the *Journal of Consulting and Clinical Psychology* (1989), 57:349–57. Copyright © 1989 by the American Psychological Association. Reprinted by permission of the publisher and authors.
21. "Stress Management: A New Approach to Treatment" by Ethel Roskies: *From Stress Management for the Healthy Type A* by Ethel Roskies. Copyright © 1987 by The Guilford Press. Used with permission of the publisher and author.
22. "Intervention Strategies" by Richard H. Cox: From Richard H. Cox, *Sport Psychology: Concepts and Applications,* 2d ed. Copyright © 1990 Wm. C. Brown Publishers, Dubuque, Iowa. All Rights Reserved. Reprinted by permission.
23. "Out of the Habit Trap" by Stanton Peele: *American Health Magazine* © 1983, Stanton Peele.
24. "Healthy People—Healthy Business: A Critical Review of Stress Management Programs in the Workplace" by Kenneth R. Pelletier and Robert Lutz: Copyright, 1988, *American Journal of Health Promotion,* Volume 2, Number 3. Reprinted with permission.

PREFACE TO THE THIRD EDITION

We feel quite fortunate to have the opportunity to put together yet another edition of *Stress and Coping: An Anthology.* As previously, finding appropriate material has been challenging and informative. Sifting through the literature and making final selections were agonizing endeavors as we inevitably had to make difficult choices as to what to include and what not to include. As always, our sincere apologies to those authors we have overlooked in assembling this edition and our genuine appreciation to those who have given us permission to use their works.

While the organization of this edition is similar to its predecessors, its content is mostly new. We have included articles on issues and applications that were largely neglected in our earlier editions. For example, selections now address stress and coping more directly with regard to: gender differences, developmental perspectives, health psychology, methodological issues, and applications to work and sport psychology. As before, we have attempted to select materials appropriate to the undergraduate student, though graduate students and professionals will also find many of the articles demanding, as well as engaging.

Our thanks once again to Columbia University Press for its continued support of this project. Particularly helpful on this edition have been Ann Miller (assistant executive editor), Amelie Hastie (editorial assistant), and Jonathan Director (manuscript editor). Also, several colleagues, including Diane Beeson, Eleanor Levine, Lee Schore, Joan Sieber, and Betty Wenz, furnished valuable suggestions along the way. The computer assistance generously provided by Professor Arnold Stoper and Richard Webster is most appreciated.

PREFACE TO THE SECOND EDITION

In the eight years since our anthology first appeared, the stress and coping field has continued to expand at an incredible pace. Courses and seminars on stress and coping are now commonplace; almost routinely, newspaper articles, radio talk shows, and television specials are devoted to topics relevant to stress and coping; and it is fashionable for corporations, police agencies, and even athletic teams to hire stress management consultants to teach "employees" more effective means for coping with stress.

Because the field has been expanding and evolving so rapidly, a second edition of our anthology is quite appropriate. Like the first edition, the present one is intended by and large for undergraduate students in a variety of disciplines. This second edition is organized much like the first and is similarly characterized by a cognitive perspective. The content of this edition has been significantly revised and updated; e.g., over 75 percent of the articles are new additions. Readers familiar with our earlier anthology will note a greater emphasis in the present edition on illness and stress management.

We are grateful for the wide acceptance of the first edition of *Stress and Coping*. The largely positive and constructive comments of many readers and reviewers have been most helpful as well as reassuring. We hope the present edition proves as useful as the first and gains similar acceptance.

We would like to thank the many authors and publishers who have consented to have their works reprinted here. Our thanks also to Columbia University Press for its support of this project throughout the years and to Columbia's Susan Koscielniak, Theresa Yuhas, and Anne McCoy for their fine efforts.

PREFACE TO THE FIRST EDITION

For many years the research literature pertaining to stress and coping has been proliferating. General interest in this body of knowledge and ideas has also increased dramatically, partially due, no doubt, to its relevance to our personal lives. Yet, paradoxically, there are few texts or readers offering a systematic presentation of the major issues or findings in this field. While many technical books containing conference papers on the topic have recently appeared, there is currently no general book of readings in the stress and coping area based upon a broad sampling of available writings, theoretical and empirical in nature, and geared primarily to the undergraduate student. Such a book would be highly appropriate not only to courses related directly to stress and coping, but also to those concerned with psychological adjustment and health. This book is designed to help remedy this omission.

Certain considerations were given prime importance in its design. First, readings dealing primarily with humans were given top priority. Although there has been much significant animal research, studies conducted with humans are generally more engaging to the student, and we believe they are ultimately the most relevant for understanding the struggles of humans to cope with the problems of living. Second, the current trend toward naturalistic studies is a healthy and strong one and also deserves emphasis. Third, because of the vast amount of available material, we decided to concentrate primarily upon articles written within the last ten years or so; however, a few earlier articles such as those by Cannon, Lindemann, Menninger, and Selye were included because of their strong and persisting impact. Fourth, while methodological issues, including those pertaining to physiological processes, are represented, they are not emphasized; these topics tend to bore or perplex most students, particularly those who are not yet prepared to grasp their significance. We think the important issues of method need to be dealt with by instructors in other ways, perhaps through lectures or organized commentaries about the readings.

The book begins with an introductory chapter, written by the editors, which systematically presents some of the major issues relevant to the concepts of stress and coping—for example, problems of definition, relationships between stress and illness, etc. This chapter does not summarize the selections in the book but rather provides the reader with a basic and fundamental background for approaching the selections.

At the start of each section of the book we have provided summaries and, often, critical evaluations of the readings. Our comments present what we see as the author's main points and in many cases clarify and elaborate upon theoretical biases, relationships with other research and, to a lesser extent, methodological problems.

The core of the book is divided into five sections, the first two dealing primarily with the concept of stress and the latter three with the nature of coping. The division of stress and coping into separate sections is of course somewhat artificial, as the concepts are intertwined. We found it useful, however, for purposes of organization and clarity of emphasis.

As might be expected, we were faced with a number of critical problems and decisions regarding the organization of this book. First of all, while many would understandably prefer rather narrow working definitions of "stress" and "coping," such a task seems to us to be unnecessarily restrictive here. Though adopting a broad perspective may preserve a certain amount of ambiguity in these terms, we believe a broad approach is more instructive for two reasons: (1) particularly valuable contributions are being made by investigators in fields as diverse as psychology, medicine, anthropology, and sociology, and (2) our understanding of the complex and urgent issues relevant to stress and coping is just only beginning to emerge. Thus, we do not try to give a restrictive definition of the field but treat stress and coping as broad rubrics. In line with this, articles examining stress and coping from many perspectives were selected. Secondly, choice of articles posed a most difficult and distressing problem because of the tremendous variety of interesting and outstanding works. We would have liked to include additional readings but this was prohibited by space limitations.

We express our appreciation to the many authors and publishers who gave us permission to reprint their works and our regrets to the many other investigators whose fine works we were unable to include. John Moore and David Diefendorf of Columbia Press have been most supportive and helpful throughout this project and we thank them sincerely for their efforts and encouragement. Also helpful have been the comments and suggestions of many colleagues and friends including Frances Cohen, Reuven Gal, Murline Monat, and Neil Weinstein. In addition, two anonymous reviewers provided valuable critiques of an earlier draft of the book but, in all fairness, we must assume full responsibility for the final product.

We hope our efforts provide the prospective reader with an accurate, representative, and exciting picture of current theory and research in the stress and coping field.

Introduction

Stress and Coping—Some Current Issues and Controversies

■

War, pollution, unemployment, natural disasters, divorce, discrimination and prejudice, "getting ahead," and illness all make us painfully aware of our daily struggles with adversities. Whether we master these stressors and prosper or become their victim, there is little question that they provide the scientist (and layperson) with vital and abundant material for the observation and systematic study of human adaptation.

Interest in the stresses and strains of "modern" life and how we cope with them has increased in recent years. The tremendous popularity of the stress and coping field can be seen by the steady outpouring of rather technical theoretical, empirical, and applied reports (e.g., Appley and Trumbull 1986; Field, McCabe, and Schneiderman 1988; Kasl and Cooper 1987), and of relevant books for the general public (e.g., Charlesworth and Nathan 1984; Friedman and Ulmer 1984). Many professional journals are also heavily devoted to research and theory in the stress and coping field.

The present edition of our anthology, as did its predecessors (Monat and Lazarus 1977, 1985), pulls together and organizes representative studies to give interested readers a sound and basic introduction to contemporary thought in a field so relevant to everyone's concerns about successful living. (A summary and evaluation of each of the readings included in this book can be found in the introduction to the various parts.)

The Concept of Stress

Definitions

Three basic types of stress are typically delineated: systemic or physiological, psychological, and social. *Systemic stress* is concerned primarily with the disturbances of tissue systems (e.g., Cannon [1929] 1953; Selye [1956] 1976b), *psychological stress* (with cognitive factors leading to the evaluation of threat (e.g., Lazarus 1966), and *social stress* with the disruption of a social unit or system (e.g., Smelser 1963). While many believe the three types of stress are related, the nature of this relationship is far from clear (Mason 1975a). Perhaps most surprising (and confusing) is the lack of agreement on a definition of "stress" among those researchers closest to the field. As Mason stated:

> Whatever the soundness of logic may be in the various approaches to defining "stress," however, the general picture in the field can still only be described as one of confusion. The disenchantment felt by many scientists with the stress field is certainly understandable when one views two decades in which the term "stress" has been used variously to refer to "stimulus" by some workers, "response" by some workers, "interaction" by others, and more comprehensive combinations of the above factors by still other workers. Some authorities in the field are rather doubtful that this confusion over terminology is correctable in the near future. (1975b:29)

The reasons investigators have been unable to reach any general agreement on a definition of "stress" are undoubtedly complex but revolve largely around the problems inherent in defining any intricate phenomenon. For example, a response-based definition of stress (e.g., one that looks at increased physiological activity as an indicator of stress) suffers from, among other things, the fact that the same response pattern (such as increased blood pressure or heart rate) may arise from entirely different stimulus conditions, for example, from heavy exercise or extreme fright. And, of course, the psychological meanings of these conditions are typically quite different (McGrath 1970). Likewise, stimulus-based definitions are incomplete because any situation may or may not be stressful, depending on characteristics of the individual and the meaning of the situation for him or her.

Because of these problems some have suggested abandoning the term "stress" (Hinkle 1974; Mason 1975b) while others have argued for using "stress" as a general label for a large, complex, interdisciplinary area of interest and study:

> It seems wise to use "stress" as a generic term for the whole area of problems that includes the stimuli producing stress reactions, the reactions themselves, and the various intervening processes. Thus, we can speak of the field of stress, and mean the physiological, sociological, and psychological phenomena and their respective concepts. It could then include research and theory on group or individual disaster, physiological assault on tissues and the effects of this assault, disturbances or facilitation of adaptive functioning produced by conditions of deprivation, thwarting or the prospects of this, and the field of negatively toned emotions such as fear, anger, depression, despair, hopelessness, and guilt. *Stress is not any one of these things; nor is it stimulus, response, or intervening variable, but rather a collective term for an area of study.* (Lazarus 1966:27)

To elaborate, the stress arena refers to any event in which environmental demands, internal demands, or both *tax* or *exceed* the adaptive resources of an individual, social system, or tissue system. However one chooses to define or study stress, to avoid confusion it is critical that the concepts and procedures employed in a specific study be made explicit—i.e., the antecedent conditions used to induce "stress," the response patterns measured as indices of "stress," and, finally, the intervening processes believed responsible for the nature of the responses should be indicated.

Other Stress-Related Concepts

When one thinks of stress, other concepts often come to mind and these need to be distinguished from stress and from each other. *Frustration* or psychological harm refers to blockage or delay in progress toward some goal. It implies something that is ongoing or has already happened. *Threat,* like frustration, also involves a harm of some kind, only it is one that has not yet happened. The harm is anticipated, however, on the basis of present cues. The person recognizes, somehow, or believes that future harm portends. The reason this distinction between past or present harm and anticipated harm is so important is that these two types of stress situations require different forms of coping. Harm that has already happened cannot be prevented, so it allows the person only to try to compensate for the damage, make restitution for it, tolerate or accept it, or give up any investment in what he or she has lost (as in the readjustments taking place in grief). On the other hand, future harm might be prevented or prepared for, so threat provides a warning that invites the person to take preventive steps or to do what he or she can to mitigate the impending harm.

Empirically, the importance of anticipation of harm in the production of stress reactions (physiological and psychological) is well supported. For instance, Shannon and Isbell (1963) have demonstrated that anticipation of a dental anesthetic injection results in the same amount of physiological stress reaction (increases in serum hydrocortisone) as the actual physical injection. Epstein (1967) has indicated that sport parachutists exhibit marked physiological and psychological stress reactions prior to a jump. In the laboratory, Birnbaum (1964) and Nomikos et al. (1968) have shown that unpleasant motion pictures elicit anticipatory physiological stress reactions. Moreover, considerable research has been done on antecedent conditions which may affect the appraisal of threat and the resulting stress reactions such as past experience (Breznitz 1984; Epstein 1967), availability of response options (Averill and Rosenn 1972; Elliott 1965; Pervin 1963), personality dispositions (Baum, Singer, and Baum 1981; Hodges and Spielberger 1966; Kobasa 1979; Lazarus and Alfert 1964; Lazarus and Folkman 1984b), and uncertainty (D'Amato and Gumenik 1960; Janis and Mann 1977; Monat 1976; Monat, Averill, and Lazarus 1972).

It might be noted, as an aside, that accurate assessment of harm and threat is, of course, crucial to the study of psychological stress and typically four classes of response variables are used to infer their presence (Lazarus 1966): negatively toned affect, motor-behavioral reactions, alterations of adaptive functioning, and/or physiological reactions. Unfortunately, each response class is characterized by inherent limitations and problems and, hence, it is desirable to rely upon the simultaneous measurement of several indices of threat (e.g., within and/or between response modalities) whenever feasible. (For a review of many of these measurement problems, the reader should consult Averill and Opton 1968; Brown 1967; Lacey et al. 1963; Lazarus 1990; Sternbach 1966; Venables and Martin 1967; Weinstein et al. 1968; and Wong in press.)

Finally, *conflict* involves the presence simultaneously of two incompatible goals or action tendencies, and so in conflict, frustration or threat of some sort is virtually inevitable. This makes it of great importance in human adaptation. Goals or action tendencies may be incompatible because the behavior and attitudes necessary to reach one such goal are contrary to those necessary to reach the other. If one spends now for enjoyment, saving up for future pleasure is negated. If one goal is attained, the other must be frustrated. Hence, conflict is a major source of psychological stress in human affairs and is a lifelong problem requiring much adaptive effort if one is to achieve a successful and rewarding life.

Summary

The concept of stress has received considerable theoretical and empirical attention in recent years, yet much "confusion and controversy" remain. Attempts have been made to integrate various points of view (e.g., Mikhail 1981; Singer and Davidson 1986) and further efforts along these lines may be forthcoming. Nevertheless, finding consensus among definitions of stress and related concepts (such as frustration, threat, and conflict) is still likely to remain a difficult endeavor.

The Concept of "Coping"

Definitions and Classification Systems

While stress and its damaging effects have been studied extensively, less systematic attention has been devoted to the ways in which humans respond to stress positively. More recently, however, there has been a rapid growth of curiosity and concern among researchers about coping and "adaptation" (e.g., Coelho, Hamburg, and Adams 1974; Krantz, Grunberg, and Baum 1985; Moos 1976).

Perhaps because of its common lay usage (there is even a drug named "Cope"), the term "coping" has accrued a variety of meanings. Nevertheless, there seems to be growing agreement among professionals (e.g., Lazarus, Averill, and Opton 1974; Lazarus and Folkman 1984a, 1984b; Murphy 1962, 1974; White 1974) that *coping* refers to an individual's efforts to master demands (conditions of harm, threat, or challenge) that are appraised (or perceived) as exceeding or taxing his or her resources.

An adequate system for classifying coping processes has yet to be proposed, although initial efforts along these lines have been made (e.g., Cohen 1987; Haan 1969, 1977; Hamburg, Coelho, and Adams 1974; Lazarus 1966, 1975; Mechanic [1962] 1978b; Menninger 1963; Murphy 1974). For example, Folkman and Lazarus (1980) have suggested a taxonomy of coping which emphasizes two major categories, problem-focused and emotion-focused modes. *Problem-focused* coping refers to efforts to improve the troubled person-environment relationship by changing things, for example, by seeking information about what to do, by holding back from impulsive and premature actions, and by confronting the person or persons responsible for one's difficulty. *Emotional-focused* (or palliative) coping refers to thoughts or actions whose goal is to relieve the emotional impact of stress (i.e., bodily or psychological disturbances). These are apt to be mainly palliative in the sense that such strategies of coping do not actually alter the threatening or damaging conditions but make the person feel better. Examples are avoiding thinking about the trouble, denying that anything is wrong, distancing or detaching oneself as in joking about what makes one feel distressed, or taking tranquilizers or attempting to relax. Some modes of emotion-focused coping deploy attention from stressful circumstances (as in thinking about last summer's romance rather than studying for the "big" exam or, as in meditating, relaxing, or jogging), while others alter the meaning or significance of what has happened, or is happening, in order to feel better about it. The latter are similar to strategies traditionally referred to as defense mechanisms.

The above classification in no way implies that we use one kind of coping process or another exclusively. Rather, all of us employ complex combinations of problem-focused and emotion-focused methods to cope with stress. The conditions determining our coping methods in particular situations are undoubtedly complex and largely unknown at this time but likely depend upon the conditions being faced, the options available to us, and our personality.

Coping Outcomes

An issue that frequently emerges in discussions of coping is whether some coping processes are more effective than others. Unfortunately, any answer to this problem must be prefaced with a long string of qualifiers due to inherent value questions (Smith 1961), levels of analysis (i.e., physiological, psychological, or sociological), points in time (i.e., short- vs. long-run), and particular situations (Cohen 1975). For instance, behavior which might be effective from, say, the physiological perspective might have devastating consequences for the psychological or sociological domains. Moreover, within any one domain, what is an optimal response in one situation at a particular point in time may be damaging in some other situation or at a different point in time.

For example, denial may be effective (in the physiological domain in terms of lowered secretions of stress-related hormones) for parents of terminally ill children prior to the child's death (Wolff et al. 1964) but may prove ineffective after the child dies, i.e., stress-related hormones then increase dramatically (*see* Hofer et al. 1972). It is clear that what is considered to be an optimal or beneficial response is highly dependent upon one's perspective and judgments.

Traditionally, emotion-focused modes of coping (particularly defense mechanisms such as denial) have been viewed as pathological or maladaptive. This view is often supported in studies where defensive behaviors (such as denial that a suspicious lump in the breast might be cancerous) have actually endangered the lives of individuals (e.g., Katz et al. 1970). On the other hand, denial can initially serve a positive function (cf. Hamburg and Adams 1967; Lazarus 1983; Visotsky et al. 1961) in preventing a person from being overwhelmed by a threatening situation where the possibilities for direct actions are limited and/or of little use (e.g., the person who has suffered severe burns or polio). Cohen states the matter as follows:

> Thus we see that denial has been found a useful defense in many situations, lowering physiological response levels and helping the person avoid being overwhelmed by negative life circumstances. However, its usefulness seems most apparent on a short-term basis, in particular situations (such as situations where the person would be otherwise overwhelmed by the unpleasant reality, where the likelihood of threats occurring is small, where there is nothing the individual can do to prepare for the potential threatening event, or where a hopeful attitude prevents feelings of giving up). Further studies must be done to determine the usefulness of denial in other situations and determinations of both long- and short-run consequences of this behavior must be made. (1975:14–15)

In general, then, emotion-focused modes of coping may be damaging when they prevent essential direct actions but may also be extremely useful in helping a person maintain a sense of well-being, integration, or hope under conditions otherwise likely to encourage psychological disintegration (*see* Lazarus 1983 and Taylor 1983 for a fuller discussion of the positive side to defenses and illusions).

Coping Disposition versus Strategies

Two different approaches to the study of coping have been pursued by various investigators. On the one hand, some (e.g., Byrne 1964; Goldstein 1973) have emphasized general coping traits, styles, or dispositions, while others (e.g., Cohen and Lazarus 1973; Katz et al. 1970; Wolff et al. 1964) have preferred to study active, ongoing coping strategies in particular stress situations. The former approach, often used by researchers interested in the study of personality, assumes that an individual will utilize the same type of coping (such as repression or sensitization) in most stressful situations. It is for him or her a stable pattern or style. A person's coping style or disposition is typically assessed by personality tests, not by actual observation of what the person says or does in a particular stress situation. Whether the person actually behaves under stress as predicted by the test depends largely on the adequacy of the personality assessment, the generality of the trait being measured, and the myriad internal and external factors affecting the person's actions and reactions in any given situation. It should be noted that many psychological traits, including coping styles, show very limited generality (cf. Cohen and Lazarus 1973; Mischel 1968) and, hence, are poor predictors of behavior in any given situation.

In contrast, those concentrating on active coping strategies prefer to observe an individual's behavior as it occurs in a stressful situation and then proceed to infer the particular coping processes implied by the behaviors. This approach has been largely neglected in the study of coping. Recent research by Folkman and Lazarus (1980, 1985, 1988a) has centered on a process approach to the assessment of coping. Although subjects are not observed in stressful situations, they are asked to reconstruct them and then to provide information about what they actually thought, did, and felt, using the "Ways of Coping Questionnaire" (Folkman and Lazarus 1988b). The coping items to be endorsed (or not) by the person include problem-focused varieties such as "Tried to get the person responsible to change his or her mind" and "Talked to someone to find out more about the situation," and emotion-focused varieties such as "Didn't let it get to me," and "I came out of the experience better than I went in." Increasingly, other researchers (e.g., Collins, Baum, and Singer 1983; Mitchell, Cronkite, and Moos 1983; Stone and Neale 1984) have been using this approach or modified versions of it to describe and measure the actual coping processes people use in the stressful encounters in their lives. We think that assessing coping processes, while time-consuming and often costly, will produce valuable information often unobtainable with the dispositional emphasis.

Summary

While the concept of coping is intimately tied to that of stress, it has been largely neglected by researchers until rather recently. Today much more interest is being expressed in the classification and measurement of coping processes, and the study of their causes and effects. A highly pertinent issue is the "adaptive" value of various coping processes—i.e., are some processes more effective or ineffective than others? There is a growing conviction that all coping processes, including those traditionally considered undesirable (i.e., defense mechanisms), have both positive and negative consequences for an individual, and that any evaluation of coping and adaptation must take into account diverse levels of analysis (physiological, psychological, sociological), the short versus long-term consequences, and the specific nature of the situation in question. Our understanding of how people cope with specific stress situations will probably be advanced further by assessing coping *in vivo* as well as by generalized trait measurements. With increased interest in the psychology of coping, we shall, no doubt, see rapid advances in our understanding of how people cope with the stresses of living, how their coping patterns are shaped by situational and personality factors, and how these patterns change during the course of development.

Stress, Coping, and Physical Illness

The excitement many find in the study of stress and coping is often attributable to an interest in the biological, psychological, and sociological factors believed to contribute to the development of physical and mental disorders. Although the issues and literature in this area are far too vast to cover here (*see* Cohen 1975, 1981; Coleman, Butcher, and Carson 1984), we would like to point out some basic theoretical positions relating stress and physical illness.

Possible Links Between Stress, Coping, and Illness

There are three main ways in which stress might lead to somatic illness (Holroyd and Lazarus 1982). The first is by the disruption of tissue function through neurohumoral influences under stress. In other words, under stress there are major outpourings of powerful hormones creating dramatic alterations in bodily processes many of which we sense as in the case of a pounding heart, sweating, trembling, fatigue, etc. A second way is by engaging in coping activities that are damaging to health, for example, by trying to advance occupationally or socially by means of a pressured style of life (e.g., Type A behavior), by taking minimal rest, by poor diet, heavy use of tobacco or alcohol, etc. Intrinsically noxious styles of living can increase the likelihood of disease by damaging the tissues of the body. A third way stress and coping might lead to disease is by psychological and/or sociological factors which consistently lead the person to minimize the significance of various symptoms or to fail to comply with treatment programs. A person, for instance, may frequently interpret pain or illness symptoms in such a way as to neglect to seek medical aid when it is crucial. Avoidance of doctors or of medical regimens can come about as a defense mechanism, for example, denial, or merely because the individual is a member of a culture or subculture that values stoicism (Mechanic 1978a; Zborowski 1969). Such avoidance can be fatal in certain instances, as in the case of heart attack victims who delay seeking medical attention, thereby decreasing their chances of survival (Hackett and Cassem 1975).

Concern with the role of stress and coping in the development or exasperation of physical illness has led in part to the emergence of a number of professional fields—particularly health psychology and psychoneuroimmunology. Workers in these and related areas are exploring the many facets of stress and coping as they pertain to becoming ill or remaining healthy. *Health psychology* is concerned with the "scientific study of those behaviors that relate to health enhancement, disease prevention, and rehabilitation" (Feist and Brannon 1988:11). Some of the interests of health psychologists may be illustrated by topics mentioned in a recent review of the field: behavioral factors in cardiovascular disorders, cigarette smoking and tobacco use, obesity and eating disorders, compliance with health care regimens, and prevention of disease and promotion of health (Krantz, Grunberg, and Baum 1985:359–76).

Psychoneuroimmunology is an interdisciplinary field interested in the effects of stress (and other factors such as emotions, personality, etc.) on immune system functioning. Because of the complexities in researching interrelationships among the nervous, endocrine, and immune systems, to date there is very little understanding of the ways psychological factors influence the immune system. Nevertheless, animal and human studies do suggest definite links (e.g., Ader 1981; Asterita 1985; Hall 1989; *Newsweek* 1988). Regarding the excitement psychoneuroimmunology has generated among researchers, Jemmott notes:

> Psychoneuroimmunology represents a major shift in thought about immunologic processes because traditionally the immune system has been viewed as largely autonomous, unaffected by the central nervous system. Interestingly though, the seeds of the new field were around as long ago as 1936, when Hans Selye introduced the *general adaptation syndrome.* Selye described a triad of morphological changes in response to noxious stimulation. It included deep, bleeding ulcers of the stomach and duodenal lining, adrenal cortical enlargement, and damage to immunologic functions, atrophy of the thymus and other lymphatic structures. Unfortunately, not given systematic attention were the possibilities, intimated by Selye's work, that stress might influence susceptibility to certain diseases by altering immunologic functioning and, more broadly, that there may be important relationships between the central nervous system and the immune system. But with the ascendancy of psychoneuroimmunology many researchers are considering these possibilities. (1985:498)

To illustrate, let us consider one of the most frightening illnesses, cancer. Cancer, of course, is really not one disease, but a complex array of various kinds of diseases. One in four people will develop cancer sometime in their lives, with cancer at certain sites having higher mortality rates than others (e.g., mortality rates for lung cancer are particularly high). At this time, and despite heroic efforts by many, the causes of cancer are not fully understood. But some risk factors apparently have been identified. For example, there seems to be a clear genetic factor or predisposition for certain kinds of cancer. But, more importantly, it has been estimated that unhealthy behaviors and lifestyles contribute significantly to most cancers (Whelan 1978). Smoking, diet, alcohol, ultraviolet light, and certain sexual behaviors have received much of the attention by researchers in recent years. Yet personality and emotional factors also have been implicated. Internalized anger and aggression, or more generally, the suppression of emotions (a condition likely to define a person low in neuroticism—e.g., *see* Eysenck 1984) may play a contributing role in cancer. Stressful life events, high levels of depression and anxiety, and denial are also among the suspected culprits.

Without elaborating on the quality of the research (much of it is tainted with controversy related to methodological concerns and the inability to replicate findings), it is fair to ask how psychosocial factors such as stress and personality could actually translate into cancer, or at least contribute to its development. Research in psychoneuroimmunology has often suggested that the outpouring of certain bodily chemicals associated with stress may actually end up suppressing vital immune functions. For example, generated under stress, perhaps certain chemi-

FIGURE 1. A theoretical model of how psychosocial stress and personality may influence the production of tumors. (Rice 1987:103. Used with permission.)

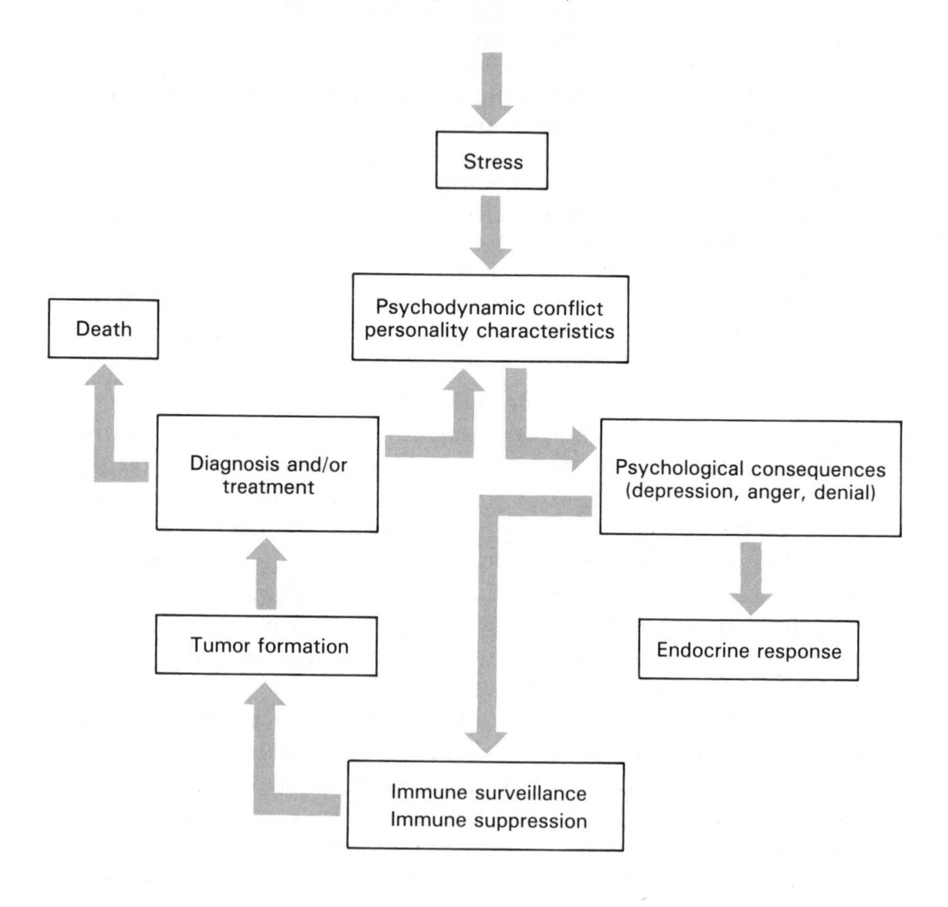

cals (e.g., cortisol) interfere with immune surveillance, the process whereby our bodies constantly seek out and destroy cancerous cells. If this were to happen, tumors could develop readily. Figure 1 diagrams some of these relationships.

Summary

While more research certainly is needed before definitive conclusions can be drawn about the relationships between stress, coping, and illness, theoretical and empirical advances have been progressing rapidly. In a basic sense, it is believed that stress and coping may contribute to illness in one or another of the following ways: (1) short- or long-term disruption of stress hormones on bodily processes; (2) unhealthy coping activities, such as substance abuse to reduce anxiety and tension; and (3) the potentially damaging consequences of psychological or social values which lead to poor compliance with medical regimens or which minimize the significance of bodily symptoms. There is much to be learned about each of these possibilities and controversy abounds.

Stress Management

It is now commonly believed that all illness is, in part, stress-related (Davison and Neale 1990). Given this widespread belief, it is not surprising that a new, multi-billion dollar stress management industry (mainly in the form of consulting firms and self-help manuals) has emerged to help contain the menacing "stress bug." As noted by Roskies, "It would be un-American to accept a new cause for disease without seeking to cure or control it" (1983:542).

Stress management typically attempts to reduce stress and its harmful effects (like excessive, chronic levels of catecholamines and steroids) by advocating either the use of a particular technique or a potpouri of techniques. There are three general (and somewhat overlapping and arbitrarily defined) categories of such stress management techniques: (1) alterations of environment and/or lifestyle; (2) alterations of personality and/or perception; and (3) alterations of biological responses to stress. Table 1 lists examples of each category (cf. Girdano, Everly, and Dusek 1990; Greenberg 1990).

Two points should be made about the stress management field. First, its growth has been largely the result of perceived need and demand rather than the availability of empirically supported "cures." There unfortunately have been rather weak efforts to determine clearly the effectiveness of the various techniques for different stress-related disorders or for different kinds of people. While practicing thought stopping, breathing exercises, etc., may usually not be harmful, one could (and should?) legitimately ask whether such techniques actually do any

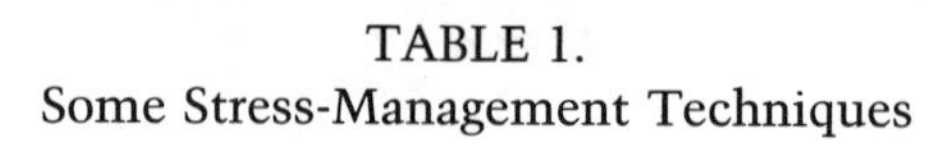

TABLE 1.
Some Stress-Management Techniques

Environment/Lifestyle	*Personality/Perceptions*	*Biological Responses*
Time Management	Assertiveness Training	Progressive relaxation
Proper nutrition	Thought stopping	Relaxation response
Exercise	Refuting irrational ideas	Meditation
Finding alternatives to frustrated goals	Stress inoculation	Breathing exercises
Stopping smoking, drinking, etc.	Modifying Type A behavior	Biofeedback
		Autogenics

Discussion of these and other stress-management techniques may be found in Davis, Eshelman, and McKay (1988), Girdano, Everly, and Dusek (1990), Greenberg (1990), Schafer (1987), and Steinmetz et al. (1980).

Note that one could easily place some of the techniques in more than one of the above categories. For example, exercise may be seen as a technique altering one's biological responses to stress, as well as a change in one's lifestyle (if exercise has indeed been absent).

good, and about the conditions under which they might help or harm people. With some exception (e.g., stress inoculation or biofeedback), there have been woefully few research efforts along these lines.

A second point is whether or not by offering "ready-made" and overly simplistic cures, we "trivialize" distress. Are professionals not mocking the victims of distress or illness when they rather patly provide (or prescribe) techniques of unproven validity or which fail to acknowledge individual differences and life agendas? As noted by Lazarus:

> It would also be well for professionals, of all people, not to fall into the trap of popularization that now plagues media treatment of stress, coping and adaptation, and programs of stress management. When professionals take their simplistic formulas for intervention too seriously and oversell their product, they encourage the public to think in terms of mechanical solutions that fail to address the most important sources of distress, and they help create a culture in which distress is trivialized, or at the least, encourage public acceptance of an already existing pattern of trivialization. The goal of realizing effective intervention requires more sophisticated thought than presently exists and a deeper respect for the person who receives professional help. (1984b:141)

Overview: A Look at This Book

In the following sections of our book, we have assembled articles capturing the flavor of the issues and controversies currently dominating the stress and coping field—many of which were highlighted in this introduction. The articles are organized into five parts: Stress and Some of Its Effects, Stress and the Environment, The Concept of Coping, Coping With the Stresses of Living and Dying, and Stress Management. It is our intention that the present collection of readings not only stimulates your interest, but also fosters a critical outlook on the stress and coping field.

I

Stress and Some of Its Effects

The readings in part 1 present divergent and controversial viewpoints about the stress concept, including its possible relationship with disease processes. The first article, written by Hans Selye (1982), is a succinct introduction to the history of the stress concept and to its current status. Selye describes briefly his own stress theory, and also presents his philosophical views about living a healthy life. Note that Selye discusses several psychological and behavioral stress-management techniques that the general public might use (without professional assistance) to combat the negative effects of stress. Selye's attention to psychology and philosophy (an apparent shift in his professional interests as he grew older) should not lead one to overlook the fact that his theory of stress is essentially a biologically based one.

Until the last several years, Selye's work was widely accepted and largely unchallenged. Then, several researchers (e.g., Lazarus 1974; Mason 1971, 1975a, 1975b) began criticizing aspects of Selye's position, particularly his total commitment to the concept of the physiological nonspecificity of the stress response. Selye distinguishes

> between the *specific* effects induced by a stressor agent and the effects induced by such stimulation which are *not* specific to it. Thus he observes that whereas one stimulus (e.g., cold) may produce a vasoconstriction and a second stimulus (e.g., heat) a vasodilation, both (or either), if applied intensely or long enough, produce(s) *effects in com-*

> *mon* and therefore not specific to either stimulus. These common changes, taken together, constitute the stereotypical response pattern of systemic stress. Selye "operationally" defines stress as *"a state manifested by a syndrome which consists of all nonspecifically induced changes in a biologic system."* (Cofer and Appley 1964:442)

Mason and Lazarus have offered theoretical viewpoints and presented empirical evidence which strongly suggest Selye overstated the role of nonspecificity, particularly in the production of illness. Mason (1975b) suggests that the pituitary-adrenal cortical system (the physiological system emphasized by Selye's stress theory) is remarkably sensitive and responds easily to emotional stimuli. This is important, for many laboratory situations designed to study physical stressors very often elicit discomfort or pain. Therefore, what would happen to the general adaptation syndrome (the stress response as it unfolds or evolves over time) if psychological factors were minimized?

> When special precautions are taken, however, to minimize psychological reactions in the study of physical stimuli, such as heat, fasting, and moderate exercise, it now appears that the pituitary-adrenal cortical system is *not* stimulated in nonspecific fashion by these stimuli which are generally regarded as "noxious," "demanding," or as appreciably disturbing to homeostatic equilibrium. . . . [In] heat studies with both human and monkey subjects, it appears heat *per se* either does not change or actually *suppresses* adrenal cortical hormone levels when measures are taken to avoid such factors as novelty or extremely sudden or severe temperature changes. (Mason 1975b:24)

These findings are important, for they imply that physical illness may depend on quite specific reactions to specific stressors. As Lazarus points out, the role of specificity in illness creates more varied options, since

> the nature and severity of the stress disorder could depend on at least three factors: (1) the formal characteristics of the environmental demands, (2) the quality of the emotional response generated by the demands, or in particular individuals facing these demands, and (3) the process of coping mobilized by the stressful commerce. (1974:327)

It may be too early to evaluate adequately the role(s) of nonspecific and specific factors in the etiology of illness, but clearly there is a growing belief in the importance of the latter.

Singer and Davidson's (1986) article extends the above discussion by highlighting the point that stress research has tended to fall into one of two categories: physiological or transactional. The physiological tradition, exemplified by Selye's research, emphasizes a reactive organism and follows in the footsteps of customary animal-based medical investigations, with their minimal interest in cognition. The transactional tradition or model, on the other hand, emphasizes the importance of appraisal processes. Stress in this approach is based on an understanding of the complex interactions and processes involved in any encounter between the individual and his or her environment. The work in this tradition is largely human-based and relies heavily on psychological measures, though physiological ones are also used. Singer and Davidson discuss at length some of the implications of Selye's notion of nonspecificity. The importance of individual differences for the transactional approach to stress is also substantially addressed.

In their overview of the stress field, Singer and Davidson have provided an excellent platform for viewing some of the most basic issues currently being struggled with by stress theorists and researchers. Singer and Davidson would like to see the physiological and transactional traditions merged to offer a more comprehensive understanding of stress. As an example, they note that in the area of stress and heart disease, "physiological and psychological theories have evolved separately. But it is becoming clear that the two perspectives cannot be separated and that an integrative approach provides the most information."

Norman Cousins' bout with a life-threatening disease is described in our next selection. In this influential paper, Cousins (1976) details his efforts at directing his own treatment procedure and course of recovery. Believing that his illness was stress-related, Cousins attempted to halt the spread of his collagen disease by inducing positive emotions. He watched, for example, old comedy classics to help him laugh vigorously. This "treatment," along with massive doses of vitamin C and a strong will to live, was largely responsible for Cousins' remarkable recovery—at least that is Cousins' belief.

As fascinating and encouraging as Cousins' account is, we will never know the exact cause (or causes) for his cure—*see* Holden (1981) for an overview of some criticisms of Cousins' conclusions. Nevertheless, Cousins has greatly spurred the holistic health movement and today's trend of patients playing a greater role in their own recovery procedures. Cousins' views provide an important source of optimism in the treatment (and perhaps in the prevention) of stress-related diseases. A fuller account of Cousins' experiences may be found in his 1979 book, *Anatomy of an Illness as Perceived by the Patient.* Cousins' more recent books (1983, 1989) give further expression to his views of the importance of a patient's role in the treatment of illness.

Our final selection in part 1 is an overview of the health psychology field. In this article, Taylor (1990) notes the importance of a current assumption among health care workers, that biological, psychological, and social factors all play vital roles in health and illness. This assumption, sometimes referred to as the *biopsychosocial model,* is today at the core of health psychology and suggests that Singer and Davidson's plea for an integration of viewpoints (noted above) is being heeded by many.

As indicated by Taylor, health psychology has devoted considerable attention to issues related to stress and coping. Some of these issues, particularly those pertaining to the development of illness, are clearly discussed and critiqued. For example, current work on life events has attempted to go beyond the demonstration of a relationship between life changes and disease and to pinpoint the dimensions of events that are most likely to lead to stress and disease. Taylor notes that these dimensions include *uncontrollability, unpredictability,* and *ambiguity.* Taylor's article provides an excellent introduction to, and survey of, health psychology, as well as a concise summary of how stress and coping have been investigated by health psychologists (and related health care personnel).

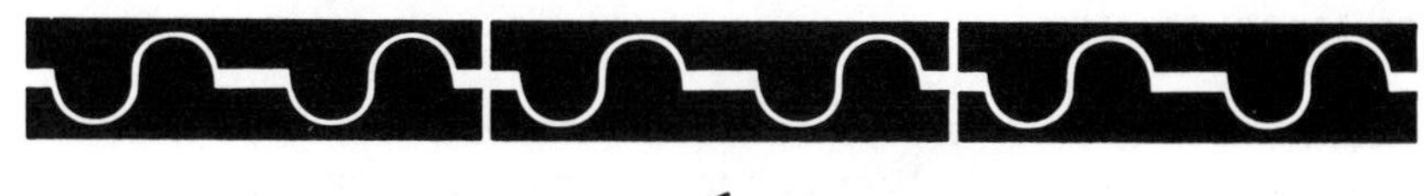

1

History and Present Status of the Stress Concept

■

HANS SELYE

Nowadays, everyone seems to be talking about stress. You hear about this topic not only in daily conversation but also on television, via radio, in the newspapers, and in the every increasing number of conferences, centers, and university courses devoted to stress. Yet remarkably few people define the concept in the same way or even bother to attempt a clearcut definition. The businessperson thinks of stress as frustration or emotional tension; the air traffic controller, as a problem in concentration; the biochemist and endocrinologist, as a purely chemical event; and the athlete, as muscular tension. This list could be extended to almost every human experience or activity, and, somewhat surprisingly, most people—be they chartered accountants, short-order cooks, or surgeons—consider their own occupation the most stressful. Similarly, most commentators believe that ours is the "age of stress," forgetting that the caveman's fear of attack by wild animals or of death from hunger, cold, or exhaustion must have been just as stressful as our fear of a world war, the crash of the stock exchange, or overpopulation.

Ironically, there is a grain of truth in every formulation of stress because all demands upon our adaptability do evoke the stress phenomenon. But we tend to forget that there would be no reason to use the single word "stress" to describe such diverse circumstances as those mentioned above were there not something common to all of them, just as we could have no reason to use a single word in connection with the production of light, heat, cold, or sound if we had been unable to formulate the concept of energy, which is required to bring about any of these effects. My definition of *stress* is the *nonspecific* (that is, common) *result of any demand upon the body,* be the effect mental or somatic. The formulation of this definition, based on objective indicators such as bodily and chemical changes that appear after any demand, has brought the subject (so popular now that it is often referred to as "stressology") up from the level of cocktail party chitchat into the domain of science.

One of the first things to bear in mind about stress is that a variety of dissimilar situations—emotional arousal, effort, fatigue, pain, fear, concentration, humiliation, loss of blood, and even great and unexpected success—are capable of producing stress; hence, no single factor can, in itself, be pinpointed as the cause of the reaction as such. To understand this point, it is necessary to consider certain facts about human biology. Medical research has shown that while people may face quite different problems, in some respects their bodies respond in a stereotyped pattern; identical biochemical changes enable us to cope with any type of increased demand on vital activity. This is also true of other animals and apparently even of plants. In all forms of life, it would seem that there are common pathways that must mediate any attempt to adapt to environmental conditions and sustain life.

Historical Development

Even prehistoric man must have recognized a common element in the sense of exhaustion that overcame him in conjunction with hard labor, agonizing fear, lengthy exposure to cold or heat, starvation, loss of blood, or any kind of disease. Probably he soon discovered also that his response to prolonged and strenuous exertion passed through three stages: first the task was experienced as a hardship; then he grew used to it; and finally he could stand it no longer. The vague outlines of this intuitive scheme eventually were brought into sharper focus and translated into precise scientific terms that could be appraised by intellect and tested by reason. Before turning to contemporary science, it will be helpful to review some of the intervening developments that laid the foundation for the modern theory of stress.

In ancient Greece, Hippocrates, often considered the "father of medicine," clearly recognized the existence of a *vis medicatrix naturae,* or healing power of nature, made up of inherent bodily mechanisms for restoring health after exposure to pathogens. But early investigations were handicapped by the failure to distinguish between distress, always unpleasant, and the general concept of stress, which also encompasses experiences of intense joy and the pleasure of self-expression.

The nineteenth-century French physiologist Bernard enormously advanced the subject by pointing out that the internal environment of a living organism must remain fairly constant despite changes in the external environment: "It is the fixity of the *milieu intérieur* which is the condition of free and independent life" (1879:564). This comment had enormous impact; indeed, the Scottish physiologist Haldane was of the opinion that "no more pregnant sentence was ever framed by a physiologist" (1922:427). But this influence was due largely to various meanings that subsequently were read into Bernard's formulation. Actually, inanimate objects are more independent of their surroundings than are living beings. What distinguishes life is adaptability to change, not fixity. Bernard's more enduring legacy was the stimulation of later investigators to carry forward his pioneering studies on the particular adaptive changes by which the steady state is maintained.

The German physiologist Pflüger crystallized the relationship between active adaptation and the steady state when he noted that "the cause of every need of a living being is also the cause of the satisfaction of that need" (1877:57). The Belgian physiologist Fredericq expressed a similar view: "The living being is an agency of such sort that each disturbing influence induces by itself the calling forth of compensatory activity to neutralize or repair the disturbance" (1885:34).

In this century, the great American physiologist Cannon suggested the name "homeostasis," from the Greek *homoios,* meaning similar, and *stasis,* meaning position, for "the coordinated physiologic processes which maintain most of the steady states in the organism" ([1939]1963:333). Homeostasis might roughly be translated "staying power." Cannon's classic studies established the existence of many highly specific mechanisms for protection against hunger, thirst, hemorrhage, or agents tending to disturb normal body temperature, blood pH, or plasma levels of sugar, protein, fat, and calcium. He particularly emphasized the stimulation of the sympathetic nervous system, with the resulting hormonal discharge from the adrenal glands, which occurs during emergencies such as pain or rage. In turn, this autonomic process induces the cardiovascular changes that prepare the body for flight or fight.

It was against this cumulative background that, as a medical student, I eventually was drawn to the problem of a stereotyped response to any exacting task. The initial focus of my interest was what I thought of as the "syndrome of just being sick." In my second year of training I was struck by how patients suffering from the most diverse diseases exhibited strikingly similar signs and symptoms, such as loss of weight and appetite, diminished muscular strength, and absence of ambition. In 1936, the problem presented itself under conditions suited to analysis. While seeking a new ovarian hormone, co-workers and I at McGill University injected extracts of cattle ovaries into rats to see whether their organs would display unpredictable changes that could not be attributed to any known hormone. Three types of changes were produced: (1) the cortex, or outer layer, of the adrenal glands became enlarged and hyperactive; (2) the thymus, spleen, lymph nodes, and all other lymphatic structures shrank; and (3) deep, bleeding ulcers appeared in the stomach and upper intestines. Being closely interdependent, these changes formed a definite syndrome.

It was soon discovered that all toxic substances, irrespective of their source, produced the same pattern of responses. Moreover, identical organ changes were evoked by cold, heat, infection, trauma, hemorrhage, nervous irritation, and many other stimuli. Gradually, I realized that this was an experimental replica of the "syndrome of just being sick," which I had noted a decade earlier. Adrenal enlargement, gastrointestinal ulcers, and thymicolymphatic shrinkage were constant and invariable signs of damage to a body faced with the demand of meeting the attack of any disease. These changes became recognized as objective indices of stress and furnished a basis for developing the entire stress concept.

The reaction was first described in *Nature* as "a syndrome produced by diverse nocuous agents." Subsequently it became known as the *general adaptation syndrome* (GAS) or *biologic stress syndrome* (Selye 1936). In the same report, I also suggested the name "alarm reaction" for the initial response, arguing that it probably represented the somatic expression of a generalized call to arms of the body's defensive forces.

The General Adaptation Syndrome

The alarm reaction, however, was evidently not the entire response. After continued exposure of the organism to any noxious agent capable of eliciting this reaction, a stage of adaptation or resistance ensues. In other words, a state of alarm cannot be maintained continuously. If the agent is so drastic that continued exposure becomes incompatible with life, the animal dies during the alarm reaction (that is, within the first hours or days). If the organism can survive, this initial reaction is necessarily followed by the *stage of resistance.* The manifestations of this second phase are quite different from, and in many instances the exact opposite of, those that characterize the alarm reaction. For example, during the alarm reaction, the cells of the adrenal cortex discharge their secretory granules into the bloodstream and thus become depleted of corticoid-containing lipid storage material; in the stage of resistance, on the other hand, the cortex becomes particularly rich in secretory granules. In the alarm reaction, there is hemoconcentration, hypochloremia, and general tissue catabolism, whereas during the stage of resistance there is hemodilution, hyperchloremia, and anabolism, with a return toward normal body weight.

Curiously, after still more exposure to the noxious agent, the acquired adaptation is lost. The animal enters into a third phase, the *stage of exhaustion,* which inexorably follows as long as the demand is severe enough and applied for a sufficient length of time. It should be pointed out that the triphasic nature of the general adaptation syndrome gave us the first indication that the body's adaptability, or *adaptation energy,* is finite, since, under constant stress, exhaustion eventually ensues. We still do not know precisely what is lost, except that it is not merely caloric energy: food intake is normal during the stage of resistance. Hence, one would think that once adaptation had occurred and ample energy was available, resistance would go on indefinitely. But just as any inanimate machine gradually wears out, so does the human machine sooner or later become the victim of constant wear and tear. These three stages are reminiscent of childhood, with its characteristic low resistance and excessive response to any kind of stimulus, adulthood, during which the body has adapted to most commonly encountered agents and resistance is increased, and senility, characterized by loss of adaptability and eventual exhaustion, ending with death.

Our reserves of adaptation energy might be compared to an inherited bank account from which we can make withdrawals but to which we apparently cannot make deposits. After exhaustion from excessively stressful activity, sleep and rest can restore resistance and adaptability very close to previous levels, but complete restoration is probably impossible. Every biologic activity causes wear and tear; it leaves some irreversible chemical scars, which accumulate to constitute the signs of aging. Thus, adaptability should be used wisely and sparingly rather than squandered.

Mechanisms of Stress

Discoveries since 1936 have linked nonspecific stress with numerous biochemical and structural changes of previously unknown origin. There has also been considerable progress in analyzing the mediation of stress reactions by hormones. However, the carrier of the alarm signals that first relay the call for adaptation has yet to be identified. Perhaps they are metabolic by-products released during activity or damage, or perhaps what is involved is the lack of some vital substance consumed whenever any demand is made upon an organ. Since the only two coordinating systems that connect all parts of the body with one another are the nervous and the vascular systems, we can assume that the alarm signals use one or both of these pathways. Yet, while nervous stimulation may cause a general stress response, deafferented rats will show the classic syndrome when exposed to demands; so the nervous system cannot be the only route. It is probable that often, if not always, the signals travel in the blood.

The facts that led us to postulate the existence of the alarm signals would be in agreement with the view that the various cells send out different messengers. In that case the messages must somehow be tallied by the organs of adaptation. Whatever the nature of the *first mediator,* however, its existence is assured by its effects, which have been observed and measured. The discharge of hormones, the involution of the lymphatic organs, the enlargement of the adrenals, the feeling of fatigue, and many other signs of stress can all be produced by injury or activity in any part of the body.

Through the first mediator, the agent or situation disruptive of homeostasis eventually excites the hypothalamus, a complex bundle of nerve cells and fibers that acts as a bridge between the brain and the endocrine system (see figure 1.1). The resulting nervous signals reach certain neuroendocrine cells in the median eminence (ME) of the hypothalamus, where they are transformed into corticotrophic hormone releasing factor (CRF), a chemical messenger that has not yet been isolated in pure form but is probably a polypeptide. In this way, a message is relayed to the pituitary, causing a discharge into the general circulation of adrenocorticotrophic hormone (ACTH).

ACTH, reaching the adrenal cortex, triggers the secretion of corticoids, mainly glucocorticoids such as cortisol or corticosterone. Through gluconeogenesis these compounds supply a readily available source of energy for the adaptive reactions necessary to meet the demands made by the agent. The corticoids also facilitate various other enzyme re-

FIGURE 1.1. Principal pathways of the stress response.

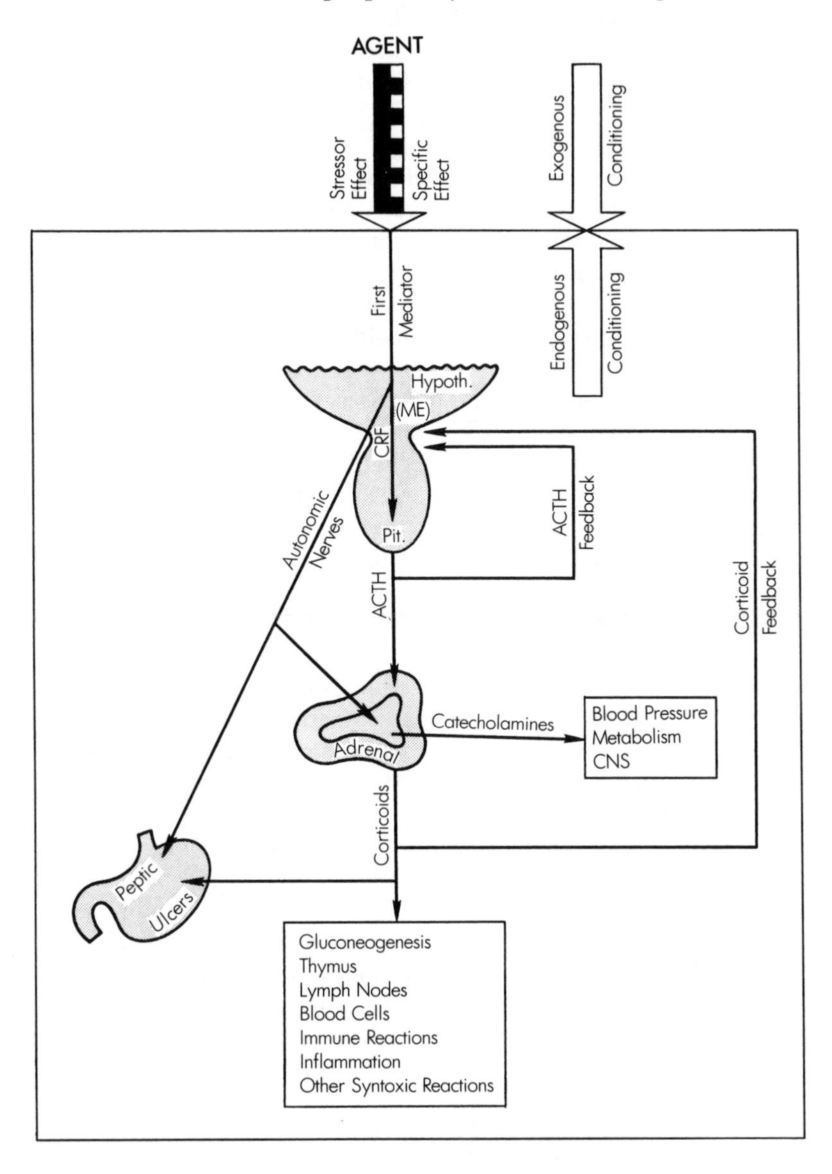

sponses and suppress immune reactions and inflammation, thereby helping the body to coexist with potential pathogens.

Usually secreted in lesser amounts are the pro-inflammatory corticoids, which stimulate the proliferative ability and reactivity of the connective tissue, enhancing the *inflammatory potential*. Thus, they help to build a strong barricade of connective tissue through which the body is protected against further invasion. Because of their prominent effect upon salt and water metabolism, these hormones have also been referred to as *mineralocorticoids* (e.g., desoxicorticosterone and aldosterone). The somatotrophic hormone (STH), or growth hormone, of the pituitary likewise stimulates defense reactions.

This chain of events is cybernetically controlled by several feedback mechanisms. For instance, if there is a surplus of ACTH, a short-loop feedback returns some of it to the hypothalamus-pituitary axis and this shuts off further ACTH production. In addition, through a long-loop feedback, a high blood level of corticoids similarly inhibits too much ACTH secretion.

Simultaneously with all these processes, another important pathway is utilized to mediate the stress response. Hormones such as catecholamines are liberated to activate mechanisms of general usefulness for adaptation. Adrenaline, in particular, is secreted to make energy available, to accelerate the pulse rate, to elevate the blood pressure and the rate of blood circulation in the muscles, and to stimulate the central nervous system (CNS). The blood coagulation mechanism is also enhanced by adrenaline, as a protection against excessive bleeding if injuries are sustained in the state of affairs eliciting stress.

Countless other hormonal and chemical changes during stress check and balance the body's functioning and stability, constituting a virtual arsenal of weapons with which the organism defends itself. The facts known today may lead us to believe that the anterior pituitary and the adrenal cortex play the cardinal role in stress, but this view probably reflects the active part endocrinologists have taken in elucidating the syndrome. Also, the techniques required to investigate the role of the nervous system are much more complex than those heretofore used. It is considerably easier, for example, to remove an endocrine gland and substitute injected extracts for its hormones than it is to destroy minute nervous centers selectively and then restore their function to determine the role they may play.

Syntoxic and Catatoxic Responses

In the course of human evolution, the body has developed two basic mechanisms for defense against potentially injurious aggressors, whether of external or internal origin. These two types of reactions, on which homeostasis mainly depends, are known as *syntoxic*, from *syn*, meaning together, and *catatoxic*, from *cata*, meaning against. The former help us put up with the aggressor while the latter destroy it. Syntoxic stimuli, acting as tissue tranquilizers, create a state of passive tolerance, which permits peaceful coexistence with aggressors. In the case of catatoxic agents, chemical changes, mainly the induction of destructive enzymes, generate an active attack on the pathogen, usually by accelerating its metabolic degradation.

Corticoids, substances produced by the adrenal cortex, are among the most effective syntoxic hormones. Of these, the best known are the anti-inflammatory group, including cortisone, and related substances that inhibit inflammation and many other defensive immune reactions such as the active rejection of grafted foreign tissues, that is, hearts or kidneys.

The main purpose of inflammation is to prevent the spread of irritants into the bloodstream by localizing them within a barricade. However, when the foreign agent is itself innocuous and causes disease only by inciting an exaggerated defense reaction, the suppression of inflammation is advantageous. Thus, anti-inflammatory corticoids have proved effective in treating diseases whose major complaint is inflammation of the joints, eyes, or respiratory passages.

On the other hand, when the aggressor is dangerous, the defensive reaction should be increased above the normal level. This is accomplished by catatoxic substances carrying a chemical message to the tissues to fight the invader even more actively than usual.

Stressors

The agents or demands that evoke the patterned response are referred to, quite naturally, as *stressors*. Something is thus a stressor to the same degree that it calls forth the syndrome. Stressors, it should be noted, are not exclusively physical in nature. Emotions—love, hate, joy, anger, challenge, and fear—as well as thoughts, also call forth the changes characteristic of the stress syndrome. In fact, psychological arousal is one of the most frequent activators. Yet it cannot be regarded as the only factor, since typical stress reactions can occur in patients exposed to trauma, hemorrhage, etc., while under deep anesthesia. Anesthetics themselves are commonly used in experimental medicine to produce stress, and stress of anasthesia is a serious problem in clinical surgery.

Stress and Disease

In general, the nervous and hormonal responses outlined above aid adaptation to environmental change or stimuli. Sometimes, however, they are the cause of disease, especially if the state of stress is prolonged or intense. In the latter case, the body passes through successive stages of the GAS, described earlier.

As we have seen, a fully developed GAS consists of the alarm reaction, the stage of resistance, and the stage of exhaustion. Yet it is not necessary for all three stages to develop before we can speak of a GAS; only the most severe stress leads rapidly to the stage of exhaustion and death. Most of the physical or mental exertions, infections, and other stressors that act upon us during a limited period produce changes corresponding only to the first and second stages. At first the stressors may upset and alarm us, but then we adapt to them.

Normally, in the course of our lives we go through these first two stages many, many times. Otherwise we could never become adapted to all the activities and demands that are man's lot. Even the stage of exhaustion does not always need to be irreversible and complete, as long as it affects only parts of the body. For instance, running produces a stress situation, mainly in our muscles and cardiovascular system. To cope with this, we first have to limber up and get these systems ready for the task at hand; then for a while we will be at the height of efficiency in running; eventually, however, exhaustion will set in. This sequence could be compared with an alarm reaction, a stage of resistance, and a stage of exhaustion, all limited primarily to the muscular and cardiovascular systems; yet such an exhaustion is reversible—after a good rest we will be back to normal.

It nevertheless remains true that the adaptive response can break down or go wrong because of innate defects, understress, overstress, or psychological mismanagement. The most common stress diseases—the so-called diseases of adaptation—are peptic ulcers in the stomach and upper intestine, high blood pressure, heart accidents, and nervous disturbances. This is a relative concept, however. No malady is just a disease of adaptation. Nor are there any disease producers that can be so perfectly handled by the organism that maladaptation plays no part in their effects upon the body. Such agents would not produce disease. This haziness in its delimitation does not interfere with the practical utility of our concept. We must put up with the same lack of precision whenever we have to classify a disease. There is no pure heart disease, in which all other organs remain perfectly undisturbed, nor can we ever speak of a pure kidney disease or a pure nervous disease in this sense.

The indirect production of disease by inappropriate or excessive adaptive reactions is well illustrated by the following example drawn from everyday life. If you meet a loudly insulting but obviously harmless drunk, nothing will happen if you take the syntoxic attitude of going past and ignoring him. But if you respond catatoxically, by fighting or even only preparing to fight, the outcome may be tragic. You will discharge adrenalinelike hormones that increase blood pressure and pulse rate, while your whole nervous system becomes alarmed and tense. If you happen to be a coronary candidate, you might end up with a fatal brain hemorrhage or cardiac arrest. In that case, your death will have been caused by your own biologically suicidal choice of the wrong reaction.

The Present Status of Research

In this short chapter, it is impossible to give a meaningful sketch of all that has been learned about the structure of stress hormones, the nervous pathways involved, the medicines that have been developed to combat stress, and the diagnostic aids that this approach has offered. Nevertheless, the medical, chemical, and microscopic approaches to the problem have all been extremely fruitful. Since the very first description of the GAS, the most important single discovery was made only recently: the brain produces certain simple chemical substances closely related to ACTH. These substances have morphinelike, painkilling properties, and since they come from the inside *(endo)*, they have been called *endorphins.* (I am especially proud that one of my former students, Dr. Roger Guillemin, was one of the three American scientists who shared the 1977 Nobel Prize for this remarkable discovery, although it was made at the Salk Institute quite independently of me.) The endorphins have opened up an entirely new field in medicine, particularly in stress research. Not only do they have antistress effects as painkillers, but also they probably play an important role in the transmission of the alarm signal from the brain to the pituitary, and their concentration is especially high in the pituitary itself. Thus, they may shed some light on the nature of the first mediator.

Significant breakthroughs have also been made with the discovery of tranquilizers and psychotherapeutic chemicals to combat mental disease. These have reduced the number of institutionalized mental patients to an unprecedented low. Also worth mentioning are the enormously potent anti-ulcer drugs that block the pathways through which stress ulcers are produced.

However, all these purely medical discoveries are applicable only by physicians, and the general public cannot use them in daily life without constant medical supervision. Furthermore, most of these agents are not actually directed against stress but rather against some of its morbid manifestations (ulcers, high blood pressure, or heart accidents). Therefore, increasing attention has been given to the development of psychological techniques and behavioral codes that anybody can use, after suitable instruction, to adjust to the particular demands made by his life.

Among these not strictly medical approaches are the relaxation techniques. We should spend a little time each day at complete rest, with our eyes closed and our muscles relaxed, breathing regularly and repeating words that are either meaningless or heard so often that they merely help us not think of anything in particular. This is the basis of Transcendental Meditation, Benson's relaxation technique, and an infinite variety of other procedures. These practices should not be underestimated merely because science cannot explain them; they have worked for so long and in so many forms that we must respect them.

More recently, biofeedback has added a great deal to the psychological approach. A number of highly sophisticated instruments have been developed that inform the user constantly about body changes characteristic of stress, for example, in blood pressure, pulse rate, body temperature, and even brain activity. We do not yet have a scientific explanation for biofeedback, but if people learn to identify, instinctively or through instrumentation, when they are under stress, they can automatically avoid, or at least reduce, their responses.

A Scientific Ethics

The drunk illustration I used earlier shows how certain well-known facts about the demands of everyday life can make clearer some of the principles involved in the unconscious, wired-in stress responses mediated by the neurohumoral system. Yet it is also true that the latter can refine our knowledge of the former. Laboratory observations on the body's methods for fighting distress have already helped us to lay the foundations for a biologically justifiable code of behavior, one designed to achieve the pleasant stress of fulfillment (known technically as *eustress*—from the Greek *eu* meaning good, as in euphemia and euphoria) without the harmful consequences of damaging stress, that is, *distress* (Selye 1974).

At first it seems odd that the laws governing life's responses at such different levels as the cell, the whole person, and even the nation should be so essentially similar. Yet this type of uniformity is true of all great laws of nature. For example, in the inanimate world, arrangement of matter and energy in orbits circulating around a center is characteristic of the largest celestial bodies, as well as of individual atoms. Why is it that on these opposite levels, the smallest and the largest, the satellites circling a huge planet and the minute electrons around an atomic nucleus, should go around in orbits? We find comparable similarities in the laws governing living matter. Countless phenomena run in cycles, such as the periodically recurring needs for food, water, sleep, and sexual activity. Damage is unavoidable unless each cycle runs its full course.

In formulating a natural code of behavior, these thoughts have fundamental importance. We must not only understand the profound biological need for the completion and fulfillment of our aspirations but also know how to handle these in harmony with our particular inherited capacities. Not everybody is born with the same amount of adaptation energy.

Work: A Biological Necessity

Most people consider their work their primary function in life. For the man or woman of action, one of the most difficult things to bear is enforced inactivity during prolonged hospitalization or after retirement. Just as our muscles degenerated if not used, so our brain slips into chaos and confusion unless we constantly use it for work that seems worthwhile to us. The average person thinks he works for economic security or social status, but at the end of a most successful business career—when he finally has achieved this goal—there remains nothing to fight for. There is no hope for progress and only the boredom of assured monotony. The question is not whether we should or should not work, but what kind of work suits us best.

In my opinion, today's insatiable demand for less work and more pay does not depend so much on the number of working hours or dollars as on the degree of dissatisfaction with life. We could do much, and at little cost, by fighting this dissatisfaction. Many people suffer because they have no particular taste for anything, no hunger for achievement. These, and not those who earn little, are the true paupers of mankind. What they need more than money is guidance.

Without the incentive to work out his role as *homo faber,* a person is likely to seek destructive, revolutionary outlets to satisfy the basic human need for self-assertive activity. Man may be able to solve the age-old problem of having to live by the sweat of his brow, but the fatal enemy of all utopias is boredom. What we shall have to do after technology makes most "useful work" redundant is to invent new occupations. Even this will require a full-scale effort to teach "play professions," such as the arts, philosophy, crafts, and science, to the public at large; there is no limit to how much each man can work on perfecting himself and on giving pleasure to others.

"Earn Thy Neighbor's Love"

Each person must find a way to relieve his pent-up energy without creating conflicts with his fellow men. Such an approach not only insures peace of mind but also earns the goodwill, respect, and even love of our neighbors, the highest degree of security and the most noble status symbol to which the human being can aspire.

This philosophy of hoarding a wealth of respect and friendship is merely one reflection of the deep-rooted instinct of people and animals to collect—a tendency as characteristic of ants, bees, squirrels, and beavers as of the capitalist who collects money to put away in the bank. The same impulse drives entire human societies to build systems of roads, telephone networks, cities, and fortifications, which they view as necessary ingredients of their future security and comfort.

In man, this urge first manifests itself when children start to amass matchboxes, shells, or stickers; it continues when adults collect stamps or coins. This natural proclivity is not artificial. By collecting certain things, one acquires status and security in the community. The guideline of earning love merely attempts to direct the hoarding instinct toward what I consider the most permanent and valuable commodity that man can possess: a huge capital of goodwill that protects him against personal attacks by others.

To live literally by the biblical command to "love thy neighbor as thyself" leads only to guilt feelings because this teaching cannot be reconciled with the laws of objective science. Whether we like it or not, egoism is an inescapable characteristic of all living beings. But we can continue to benefit by the wisdom of this time-honored maxim if, in the light of modern biological research, we merely reword it. Let our guide for conduct be the motto "Earn thy neighbor's love."

2

Specificity and Stress Research

■

JEROME E. SINGER AND
LAURA M. DAVIDSON

There are a number of different ways in which the psychological and physiological aspects of behavior have been interrelated. The connection between the two domains is fundamental. It is the distinction between them that is artificial. Yet there is some administrative virtue in partitioning the unitary responses of a human being or an animal into components that follow disciplinary lines. Each discipline—physiology, endocrinology, psychology, anthropology, and so forth—tends to focus on its aspect of the integrated biobehavioral response with its own set of questions and investigative concepts and techniques. This chapter discusses one of the most common and important of the biobehavioral responses, namely, stress. The perspective will be psychological, and the question to be examined will be the source of individual differences in the diverse factors believed to enter into the stress system.

The term *stress* has evolved, over the past several decades, to encom-

The opinions or assertions contained in this chapter are the private ones of the authors and are not to be construed as official or reflecting the views of the Department of Defense or the Uniformed Services University of the Health Sciences.

pass a large variety of phenomena and is used in a number of different ways. In general, however, research on stress falls into one of two broad categories. The first of these categories is essentially *physiologically* defined. It is the original notion of stress formulated by Selye (1936) in his paper in *Nature. Stress here is defined as the reaction of the organism to some sort of outside threat.* The organism is reactive and little cognition is involved in the model. In later formulations, Selye attempted to build in a broader concept of stress, making it applicable to a wider range of human situations, but at heart it remained a reactive model. Research done with this conceptualization was of the sort that followed the medical tradition of animal models, using physical or physiological stressors, and measuring physiological and endocrinological changes as indications of stress.

In contradistinction, a second tradition of stress research can be considered to be *transactional;* that is, *stress is defined as the outcome of interactions between the organism and the environment.* The general approaches taken by Lazarus (1966) and Leventhal (1970) are examples of this type of work. In the transactional model, an event in the environment is considered to be a stressor only if the organism's appraisals of it, and of its own resources, suggest that it is threatening or disturbing. Research done in this tradition tends to be human-oriented and uses psychological measures, both for how the subject evaluates the stress and in terms of the subject's reactions to it. Although the model is said explicitly to apply to physiological and physical stimuli as well as to psychological ones, most of the work done within this framework has been on psychological or nonphysical environmental stimuli.

Pathogen Reaction Model

Selye (1976a, [1956] 1976b) outlined the nature of the pathogen reaction model in a number of different publications. His description of the general adaptation syndrome, with three stages of alarm, resistance, and exhaustion, is now well known. The emphasis throughout his explication of the system is that stress consists of the nonspecific consequences of any stressor. In this context (although Selye goes to great pains to make clear what he means), the term *nonspecific* is slightly confusing. Selye means that every stressor produces certain reactions specific to that stressor as well as nonspecific changes that result from all stressors. In the pathogen reaction model, if an organism or an animal were to break a leg, the consequence of the leg breaking would be specific and local—the fracture of the bone, the tissue damage in that area, the disruption of the blood supply, the edema, and all other consequences brought about precisely by the breaking of the leg would be the specific reaction. The nonspecific reaction to the leg breaking would be the increased output of the adrenal cortical steroids and a variety of other endocrine changes that precede and react to the increased adrenal output (Mason 1968, 1975c; Selye 1976a, [1956] 1976b). Although it is possible to be precise about these nonspecific changes, they are called nonspecific because the same steroid output occurs in response to each stressor or pathogen. If the same organism or animal at some later time, after the leg had healed, were to acquire a dose of food poisoning, it would have specific effects of the food poisoning in the gastrointestinal (GI) tract. In addition, it would have the same nonspecific effects from the food poisoning that occurred from the broken leg—primarily increased cortical steroid output. Because the more or less precisely defined neuroendocrinological changes occur to any stressor or pathogen, they acquired the name nonspecific. Some confusion can be avoided if it is realized that nonspecific does not mean unspecified but rather occurring in response to every stressor.

Cumulative Stress Effects

There are several implications of this notion of nonspecificity. First, it implies that the effects of stress are cumulative, such that each episode leaves behind a residue that may add up across stressful exposures. Such consequences are relatively easy to see when the stress is chronic. Daily hassles, for example, are chronic low-intensity threats that may accumulate over time (Lazarus and Cohen 1977). Each exposure to such a stressor poses little threat to the individual, but severe consequences may ensue if the stressor persists or if adaptive abilities are low. When animals are chronically exposed to noise, heat, crowding, hemorrhagic shock, or blood loss, they will continue to suffer the debilitation of nonspecific stress effects. Indeed, Selye's formulation of the general adaptation syndrome suggests that the model is best tested with a chronic stressor. The stress is ever present; the animal continually reacts to it and, after a certain amount of continued resistance, exhaustion ensues. When exhaustion is reached, the animal can no longer cope with the stress and ultimately expires. The model is less explicit and more ambiguous when the stressor is cyclic or episodic. If the stressor occurs at intervals (and at this point it does not matter whether it occurs cyclically at regular intervals or episodically at irregular ones), the effects can be considered the same as for a chronic stressor if the new stressor begins before the organism has returned to baseline from previous stress responses.

The model is unclear, and the research is equivocal about what happens when periodic stressors occur far enough apart so that the nonspecific responses of the organism do return to baseline. For example, there are any number of things that create stress in human beings and that are toxic in large doses, but are tolerated, and in many cases sought after, in small doses. Throughout life, many individuals ingest caffeine, nicotine, or alcohol. These substances have specific effects that are cumulative. For example, damage to the lung tissue from ingesting cigarette smoke, damage to the cardiovascular system from caffeine, and damage to the liver from alcohol are cumulative and specific effects of those stressors. But the extent to which any of those agents or toxins has nonspecific stress components that accumulate is unknown. In addition, there are other substances that have specific toxic effects in large amounts, but, taken cyclically, seem to have no specific debilitating effects. For example, spinach contains oxalic acid, a chemical that would be lethal if sufficient quantities were ingested. It is not known if there are nonspecific stress effects from small amounts of spinach or how much spinach one would have to eat at a sitting in order for it to be a toxicant. Whether everything that needs to be detoxified is a stressor remains to be explored for episodic and cyclic stressors. Also, the circumstances under which nonspecific cyclic or episodic stress reactions cumulate, and the relationship between the cumulation of the specific effects and the nonspecific effects, need to be explored.

Selye's model, in which all stressors have the same nonspecific effects, or in which stress is the nonspecific effect common to all stressors, implies that stress cumulates over stressors. Thus, the pathogen reaction model would argue that if an animal breaks a leg and, a short time later, eats contaminated food, the nonspecific effects of both of these stressors would be additive. The leg break or the contaminated food alone would not cause the animal to go from resistance to exhaustion, but both together could deplete the resistive powers. It is an unsolved question whether a potential stressor may be potentiated by occurring along with another stressful event. For example, a person who eats spinach before getting in a traffic jam might find that a previously nonbothersome dose of spinach now has a stressful consequence.

Counting the Cumulative Effects of Stress

Considerations of both cumulation over periodic stressors and cumulation across different stressors raise a set of questions and generate research issues. One question concerns how the organism keeps track of stressors. Thus, if some of the nonspecific stress effects are irreversible, the organism must have some mechanism to keep track of the dosage level and the cumulation of stress effects. For example, it is possible that after an organism successfully resists a nonchronic stressor and returns to baseline, there will be no apparent damage or permanent harm caused by the stressor. But, when stressors occur repeatedly, the organism may develop harmful consequences, even though nonspecific responses have returned to baseline after each stressor occurs.

Counting mechanisms do seem to exist in other systems of the body, and, by using adipose tissue to draw an analogy, it becomes more clear how such a mechanism may exist for stress. Hirsch and his colleagues (Hirsch and Knittle 1970) have suggested that the number of adipocytes remains constant, even though the person's weight may fluctuate and the amount of fat stored in each cell may change. The curious aspect of this is that although lipectomy (the surgical removal of fatty tissue) decreases the number of adipocytes by mechanical excision, new adipocytes grow, bringing the number present back to the baseline or the number that existed before the lipectomy. There is no way to determine whether "back to baseline" means the exact same number of adipose cells, but roughly the same magnitude will return. This growth occurs even though that same person would probably not generate new adipose cells without the lipectomy. Also, since the storage capacity of each adipocyte varies greatly, the new cells would not, strictly speaking, be necessary in order to return to the baseline levels of fat deposits. The point is that somewhere within the system something must be keeping count of the number of adipocytes, the adipocyte activity, the amount of product that each adipocyte puts out, or some other indicator to suggest what this baseline number should be. In the same way, if multiple stressors, each of which does not appear to be toxic, result in some kind of cumulation of toxicity, then some mechanism may exist in order for the body of the human to keep track of what is happening.

Causal Stress Models

Not knowing the counting mechanisms for stressors may compound the establishment of retrospective causal stress models. Thus, although it is common to hear clinical statements such as "this is a stress-related disorder," it becomes impossible, in the absence of knowing the counting or cumulation mechanism, to discern what stressors were responsible for the disorder. Even though research indicates that clusters of life changes may be associated with illness episodes in the following year (e.g., Rahe 1975) many of the so-called stress disorders develop over a time span, perhaps up to 20 years. Such diseases as atherosclerosis or several of the types of cancer require at least 20 years for incubation (Herbst et al. 1974; Julius 1977). The logical, let alone empirical, task of stating what stressors, toxicants, or irritants may have initiated or facilitated the pathophysiology of these diseases is very difficult.

The difficulty in establishing causal models may be illustrated by considering noise as a stressor. There is some evidence that noise has cardiovascular effects and that continued exposure to it, chronically or cyclically, may bring about an elevation in blood pressure (Cohen et al. 1981; Peterson 1979; Welch 1979). These findings come from both epidemiological studies and from animal models. Nevertheless, the research is not conclusive about the circumstances under which noise will produce such effects, but suggests that, under some circumstances, the effects will be of clinical significance. Consider the situation of a person suffering from cardiovascular disease who has been exposed to a noxious and noisy environment. The question is whether it is possible to claim that the noise in the person's immediate environment caused the cardiovascular changes; the answer is not simple. Such a question is often the basis for court cases, and it turns out that it is impossible to prove that cardiovascular disease has been caused by a noise stressor. It could have been a response to any number of other cardiovascular irritants. On the other hand, it is impossible to prove that the noise was not at least a precipitating factor in the development of the disease. In short, the problem is one of the burden of proof, and the side of the issue that has the burden of proof is at a disadvantage, because the mechanisms of cumulation of stress and of its specificity cannot be established.

Transactional Model

The transactional model is not so much in opposition to the pathogen reaction model but addresses different issues or incorporates the reaction model as a special subclass. Thus, in the transactional model, a stressor is any potential threat in the environment. The emphasis is on the word *potential* because in the transactional model nothing by itself is considered to be a stressor. Rather, any stimulus, no matter how noxious or how pleasant, can be viewed as either desired, interesting, nonthreatening, or nonharmful and, if it is so appraised, it will not be considered a stressor (e.g., Lazarus 1966). For the transactional model, physical or physiological stressors will only produce stress responses after they have been defined as threatening by human beings. Unlike the pathogen reaction model, the transactional model does not assume that life threat or harm are inevitably stressful.

Appraisal

Indeed, the key issue in the transactional model is appraisal, which may occur repeatedly following introduction of a stressor. First, the potential stressor is evaluated in terms of its capacity to do harm. Subevaluations are then made about novelty, certainty, and predictability. Importantly, the stressor is construed as a threat or challenge. Having appraised a stressor, the individual appraises its own ability to handle this stress or challenge and the strategy most likely to reduce the potential harm (e.g., Appley 1967). These appraisals are not unitary judgments but rather are like iterative computer programs. It is as if the organism were to handle a stressor by the use of an algorithm: for example, appraise the stressor, appraise own capacities, decide on coping strategy, meet the stressor, reevaluate stressor, reevaluate own capacities, decide on coping strategy again, and so forth. This procedure suggests that circumstances once thought of as benign or challenging may become stressful as appraisals and coping are modified. Similarly, threatening stressors can become merely challenges, or even can become sought after, as the individual has experience with them and modified appraisals of both its own capabilities and the environmental challenges.

The transactional models are very important because they bring into play a full panoply of human cognitive activities. Also, they enable stress researchers to understand and explain a number of situations that are difficult to comprehend in the pathogen reaction model. For example, in physiological studies of the pathogen reaction model, one of the laboratory techniques is hemorrhagic shock. An experimental animal, such as a dog, will be placed on an operating table and have 10 percent of its blood supply withdrawn. Aside from the specific effects of withdrawing the blood, this induces a nonspecific stress response. The animal's reactions, in terms of cardiovascular, kidney, and gastrointestinal functioning, can all be assessed during the stress to see what the nonspecific consequences are. One prominent physiological researcher has reported that although stress reactions to hemorrhagic shock are as large and significant as stress reactions to any other physiological stressor, the single largest reaction ever obtained from an experimental dog occurred after the dog had been strapped to the operating table and a new dog was brought into the room. This was done prior to anesthetization and blood withdrawal. The stress reaction to the threat of a strange dog under these circumstances was more potent than the hemorrhagic shock. Although it would be difficult to explain this situation using the pathogen reaction model, the transactional model can more adequately handle such kinds of stressors.

Individual Differences

Although the transactional model does take account of more situations and handles a number of issues, such as the ability of people to withstand stress under seemingly heavy physical loads and how a person escalates a minor physical demand into a rather stressful environment, there are problems inherent to the system. Chief among these problems is the price that the transactional model exacts for being able to handle a number of situations and to impose several layers of human cognitive appraisal on the environment. The price is that it raises a host of individual difference measures that need not be considered in the stress pathogen model. For example, individuals may be exposed to different amounts of stress. This difference may occur in terms of the number, the frequency, or the patterning of stress exposures.

Second, when stress is examined using the transactional model, people may be viewed as differing in the extent to which they are stress-seeking. Almost all who study stress do not regard it as unalloyed harm in the environment, but rather consider it as a natural and unavoidable consequence of the real world. To some extent, people may view stress as providing relief from what would be humdrum monotony. Indeed, there are a number of people who seem to seek stress exposure (Zuckerman 1979). Participation in sports, such as race car driving, ski jumping, parachuting, and the like, indicates that people may seek what could be regarded as extremely potent stressors. Often, sport parachutists or ski jumpers report that they appraise their activity as stressful, particularly at the beginning of the season or at the start of a new exposure to it. Nevertheless, their enjoyment eventually overshadows the stress that they feel. Therefore, this is not a question of people necessarily regarding something as pleasurable, which others regard as stressful, but rather acknowledging the stress and still seeking it out. Clearly, there are individual differences in the extent to which this occurs.

The third, individual difference variable, which results from the transactional perspective, is that people differ greatly in their interpretation of stressful situations. This interpretation can determine whether the potential stressor is viewed as a threat or as a challenge. Lazarus (1966; Lazarus and Launier 1978), among others, argued that stressful consequences are engendered only if the potential threat is perceived as such. If, on the other hand, it is perceived as a challenge, those same circumstances will evoke a different kind of response and have different consequences. In addition, people will differ not just in how they appraise the stressor, but in how they appraise their own resources and capabilities. Whether these differences in appraisals are based on differences in actual experience, knowledge, and practice, or whether they are due to individual differences in self-esteem and perceived self-competence, is not known. Cognitive mediation comes into play in handling other aspects of the stress response. There is a large literature, and considerable debate, on the extent to which a person can have cognitive mediation of physiological consequence, that is, the extent to which emotion, mood, and their physiological and neuroendocrine concomitants can be influenced by, or determined by, the cognitions and labels that are attached to them (Schachter and Singer, 1962). Rather than view cognitive manipulations of physiological states as an all-or-nothing phenomenon, it is perhaps best to think of that as yet one other individual difference barrier.

Fourth, people differ in their choice of coping styles, and there are any number of ways to categorize coping styles. Lazarus (1966) described problem and emotional forms of coping. Using problem-focused coping, the person tries to manipulate the environment, confront the source of stress, and change the potential stressor itself. For example, coming in out of the rain is problem-focused coping. This form can be contrasted to a style that attempts to work on the emotional or the physiological responses directly. Tap dancing and whistling in the rain are emotion-focused coping. Even within these two broad categories, there are any number of other subvarieties of coping styles, like denial, meditation, and avoidance. All of these coping styles will be used differentially by people.

Fifth, people are placed in different circumstances, and the circumstances will determine how stress is moderated. For example, studies have shown that stressors that are predictable have less of an impact than stressors that are unpredictable (Glass and Singer 1972). The predictability can come about either because of a signal that indicates the stressor is going to occur or because of a timing or a periodicity that enables one to predict when the stressor is going to occur. Similarly, perceived control (i.e., a person's perception that he or she can modify a stressor) has also been shown to be a potent moderator of the stressor response (Baron and Rodin 1978; Glass and Singer 1972). The extent to which people differ in their ability or their willingness to attribute causality to controllable events, to infer predictability, or to be in circumstances that confer either predictability or controllability upon them will determine the amount of stress that they experience.

The sixth and final class of individual differences comes about from ancillary measures that are not present on a firm theoretical basis. Nevertheless, these differences have been shown to be of importance in stress reduction; social support is a suitable example of this. There has been a long debate about whether social support is a mediator or a moderator of stress. As a mediator, social support would be a benefit under all circumstances. Unstressed people with social support would be in better shape than unstressed people without social support, and stressed people with social support would be in better shape than stressed people without social support. Research in this area indicates that better health is associated with social support (Cassel 1976). In conceiving of it as a moderator, social support is viewed as a factor that ameliorates the effects of stress, although it has no effect when stress is not present (Cohen and McKay 1984). The evidence for social support either mediating or moderating stress is confusing at best. In studying social support, it is difficult to determine whether social support should be measured objectively or subjectively. If measured objectively, it would be assessed by counting the number of support groups, like groups of people, spouses, children, and the like (e.g., Berkman and Syme 1979). If measured subjectively, social support should be viewed as a perceived variable, irrespective of how many groups, family members, or friends a person has (e.g., Caplan, Cobb, and French 1975). The perception of support when needed is counted as the major consideration.

Some Additional Considerations

Overall, the net effect of these models has been to keep two different sets of variables separated. The pathogen reaction model deals primarily with physiological endocrine measures. The transactional model deals primarily with cognitive personality factors. In recent years, there have been a number of studies that have sought to view stress as an integrated biosocial phenomenon. Such research groups as Frankenhaeuser and her colleagues (Frankenhaeuser 1975; Frankenhaeuser et al. 1971); Mason (1975c), in differentiating endocrinological patterns to different stress responses; Baum and his associates, in studies of Three Mile Island (Baum, Gatchel, and Schaeffer 1983; Davidson, Baum, and Collins 1982); and many others have sought to look at stress from a transactional perspective while taking biological indicators and markers to see to what extent the neuroendocrine system correlates and covaries with the psychological cognitive system. Increasingly, these studies have shown that the two systems are really aspects of the same unitary process.

The further importance of combining physiological and psychological approaches may be illustrated using coronary heart disease (CHD) as an example. Traditional risk factors for CHD, such as age, diet, serum cholesterol, obesity, and so forth, are mainly physiological determinants of the disorder (Krantz et al. 1981). But, the majority of new cases of heart disease cannot be predicted using these factors along (e.g., Mann 1977). Psychological factors, including threat perceptions and coping styles, may also play key roles in the pathogenesis of CHD. By combining physiological and psychological perspectives, researchers have been better able to understand a disorder that accounts for almost half of all deaths in the United States (Krantz et al. 1981). Unfortunately, in areas of study like stress and heart disease, physiological and psychological theories have evolved separately. But it is becoming clear that the two perspectives cannot be separated and that an integrative approach provides the most information.

. . .

Conclusion

The study of stress has been benefited by two separate approaches: a physiologically oriented reactive one and a psychologically oriented transactional one. There has emerged an integrative, biobehavioral approach to the field that builds on the physiological and the psychological contributions. The integrative view has been hindered, to some extent, by confusion over terminology. Although there has come to be some shared definition of the meaning of stress and stressor, terms such as variability, reactivity, and specificity have been confusing.

3

Anatomy of an Illness (As Perceived by the Patient)

■

NORMAN COUSINS

Ever since the publication of Adam Smith's much-talked-about *Powers of the Mind* some months ago, people have written to ask whether his account of my recovery from a supposedly incurable illness was accurately reported (Smith 1975:11–14). In particular, readers have been eager to verify Mr. Smith's statement that I "laughed" my way out of a crippling disease that doctors believed to be irreversible.

I have not written until now about my illness, which occurred in 1964, largely because I was fearful of creating false hopes in other persons similarly afflicted. Moreover, I knew that a single case has small standing in the annals of medical research. I had thought that my own episode might have anecdotal value—nothing more. However, since my case has surfaced in the public press, I feel justified in providing a fuller picture than was contained in Mr. Smith's account.

In August 1964, I flew home from a trip abroad with a slight fever. The malaise, which took the form of a general feeling of achiness, rapidly deepened. Within a week it became difficult to move my neck, arms, hands, fingers, and legs. I was hospitalized when my sedimentation rate hit 80 mm per hour. The sedimentation rate continued to rise until it reached 115.

There were other tests, some of which seemed to me to be more an assertion of the clinical capability of the hospital than of concern for the well-being of the patient. I was astounded when four technicians from four different departments took four separate and substantial blood samples on the same day. That the hospital didn't take the trouble to coordinate the tests, using one blood specimen, seemed to me inexplicable and irresponsible. When the technicians came the second day to fill their containers with blood for processing in separate laboratories, I turned them away and had a sign posted on my door saying that I would give just one specimen every three days and that I expected the different departments to draw from it for their individual needs.

I had a fast-growing conviction that a hospital was no place for a person who was seriously ill. The surprising lack of respect for basic sanitation, the rapidity with which staphylococci and other pathogenic organisms can run through an entire hospital, the extensive and sometimes promiscuous use of x-ray equipment, the seemingly indiscriminate administration of tranquilizers and powerful painkillers, more for the convenience of hospital staff in managing patients than for therapeutic needs, and the regularity with which hospital routine takes precedence over the rest requirements of the patient (slumber, when it comes for an ill person, is an uncommon blessing and is not to be wantonly interrupted)—all these and other practices seemed to me to be critical shortcomings of the modern hospital.

Perhaps the hospital's most serious failure was in the area of nutrition. It was not just that the meals were poorly balanced; what seemed inexcusable to me was the profusion of processed foods, some of which contained preservatives or harmful dyes. White bread, with its chemical softeners and bleached flour, was offered with every meal. Vegetables were often overcooked and thus deprived of much of their nutritional value. No wonder the 1969 White House Conference on Food, Nutrition, and Health made the melancholy observation that the great failure of medical schools is that they pay so little attention to the science of nutrition.

My doctor did not quarrel with my reservations about hospital procedures. I was fortunate to have as a physician a man who was able to put himself in the position of the patient. Dr. William Hitzig supported me in the measures I took to fend off the random sanguinary assaults of the hospital laboratory attendants.

We had been close friends for more than twenty years, and he knew of my own deep interest in medical matters. We had often discussed articles in the medical press, including the *New England Journal of Medicine* and *Lancet*. He felt comfortable about being candid with me about my case. He reviewed the reports of the various specialists he had called in as consultants. He said there was no agreement on a precise diagnosis. There was, however, a general consensus that I was suffering from a serious collagen illness. I had considerable difficulty in moving my limbs and even in turning over in bed. Nodules appeared on my body, gravel-like substances under the skin, indicating the systemic nature of the disease. At the low point of my illness, my jaws were almost locked.

Dr. Hitzig called in experts from Dr. Howard Rusk's rehabilitation clinic in New York. They confirmed the general opinion, adding the more particularized diagnosis of ankylosing spondylitis.

I asked Dr. Hitzig about my chances for full recovery. He leveled with me, admitting that one of the specialists had told him I had one chance in 500. The specialist had also stated that he had not personally witnessed a recovery from this comprehensive condition.

All this gave me a great deal to think about. Up to that time, I had been more or less disposed to let the doctors worry about my condition. But now I felt a compulsion to get into the act. It seemed clear to me that if I was to be that "one case in 500" I had better be something more than a passive observer.

I asked Dr. Hitzig about the possible cause of my condition. He said that it could have come from any one of a number of causes. It could have come, for example, from heavy-metal poisoning, or it could have been manifested by the aftereffects of a streptococcal infection.

I thought as hard as I could about the sequence of events immediately preceding the illness. I had gone to the Soviet Union in July 1964 as chairman of an American delegation to consider the problems of cultural exchange. The conference had been held in Leningrad, after which we went to Moscow for supplementary meetings. Our hotel was in a residential area. My room was on the second floor. Each night a procession of diesel trucks plied back and forth to a nearby housing project in the process of round-the-clock construction. It was summer, and our windows were wide open. I slept uneasily each night and felt somewhat nauseated on arising. On our last day in Moscow, at the airport, I caught the exhaust spew of a large jet at point-blank range as it swung around on the tarmac.

As I thought back on that Moscow experience, I wondered whether the exposure to the hydrocarbons from the diesel exhaust at the hotel and at the airport had anything to do with the underlying cause of the illness. If so, that might account for the speculations of the doctors concerning heavy-metal poisoning. The trouble with this theory, however, was that my wife, who had been with me on the trip, had no ill effects from the same exposure. How likely was it that only one of us would have reacted adversely?

There were two possible reasons, it seemed to me, for the different responses. One had to do with individual allergy. The second was that I was probably in a condition of adrenal exhaustion and I was less apt to tolerate a toxic experience than someone whose immunologic system was fully functional.

Was adrenal exhaustion a factor in my own illness?

Again, I thought carefully. The meetings in Leningrad and Moscow had not been casual. Paper work had kept me up late nights. I had ceremonial responsibilities. Our last evening in Moscow had been, at least for me, an exercise in almost total frustration. A reception had been arranged by the chairman of the Soviet delegation at his dacha, located 50 to 65 kilometers outside the city. I had been asked if I could arrive an hour early so that I might tell the Soviet delegates something about the individual Americans who were coming to dinner. The Russians were eager to make the Americans feel at home, and they had thought such information would help them with the social amenities.

I was told that a car and driver from the government automobile pool in Moscow would pick me up at the hotel at 3:30 P.M. This would allow ample time for me to drive to the dacha by 5:00 P.M., when all our Russian conference colleagues would be gathered for the social briefing. The rest of the American delegation would arrive at the dacha at 6:00.

At 6:00, however, I found myself in open country on the wrong side of Moscow. There had been a misunderstanding in the transmission of directions to the driver, the result being that we were some 130 kilometers off course.

We didn't arrive at the dacha until 9:00 P.M. My host's wife looked desolate. The soup had been heated and reheated. The veal was dried out. I felt pretty wrung out myself. It was a long flight back to the States the next day. The plane was overcrowded. By the time we arrived in New York, cleared through the packed customs counters, and got rolling back to Connecticut, I could feel an uneasiness deep in my bones. A week later I was hospitalized.

As I thought back on my experience abroad, I knew that I was probably on the right track in my search for a cause of the illness. I found myself increasingly convinced, as I said a moment ago, that the reason I was hit hard by the diesel and jet pollutants, whereas my wife was not, was that I had had a case of adrenal exhaustion, lowering my resistance.

Assuming this hypothesis was true, I had to get my adrenal glands functioning properly again and to restore what Walter Cannon, in his famous book *The Wisdom of the Body* ([1939] 1963), called homeostasis.

I knew that the full functioning of my endocrine system—in particular, the adrenal glands—was essential for combating severe arthritis or, for that matter, any other illness. A study I had read in the medical press reported that pregnant women frequently have remissions of arthritic or other rheumatic symptoms. The reason is that the endocrine system is fully activated during pregnancy.

How was I to get my adrenal glands and my endocrine system, in general, working well again—both physically and emotionally?

I remembered having read, ten years or so earlier, Hans Selye's classic book, *The Stress of Life* ([1956] 1976b). With great clarity, Selye showed that adrenal exhaustion could be caused by emotional tension, such as frustration or suppressed rage. He detailed the negative effects of the negative emotions on body chemistry. He wrote, for example, about the increase of hydrochloric acid in the stomach. He also traced changes in corticoids and anticorticoids under conditions of emotional stress.

The inevitable question arose in my mind: What about the positive emotions? If negative emotions produce negative chemical changes in the body, wouldn't the positive emotions produce positive chemical changes? Is it possible that love, hope, faith, laughter, confidence and the will to live have therapeutic value? Do chemical changes occur only on the downside?

Obviously, putting the positive emotions to work is nothing so simple as turning on a garden hose. But even a reasonable degree of control over my emotions might have a salutary physiologic effect. Just replacing anxiety with a fair degree of confidence would be helpful.

A plan began to form in my mind for systematic pursuit of the salutary emotions, and I knew that I would want to discuss it with my doctor. Two preconditions, however, seemed obvious for the experiment. The first concerned my medication. If that medication were toxic to any degree, it was doubtful whether the plan would work. The second precondition concerned the hospital. I knew I would have to find a place somewhat more conducive to a positive outlook on life.

Let's consider these preconditions separately.

First, the medication. The emphasis had been on painkilling drugs—aspirin, phenylbutazone (Butazolidin), codeine, colchicine, sleeping pills. The aspirin and phenylbutazone were anti-inflammatory and thus were therapeutically justifiable. But I wasn't sure they weren't also toxic. With Dr. Hitzig's support, we took allergy tests and discovered that I was hypersensitive to virtually all the medication I was receiving. The hospital had been giving me maximum dosages: 26 aspirin tablets a day; and 3 phenylbutazone tablets four times a day. No wonder I had hives all over my body and felt as though my skin was being chewed up by millions of red ants.

It was unreasonable to expect positive chemical changes to take place so long as my body was being saturated with, and toxified by, painkilling medications. I had one of my research assistants at the *Saturday Review* look up the pertinent references in the medical journals and found that drugs like phenylbutazone and even aspirin levy a heavy tax on the adrenal glands. I also learned that phenylbutazone is one of the most powerful drugs being manufactured. It can produce bloody stools, the result of its antagonism to fibrinogen. It can cause intolerable itching and sleeplessness. It can depress bone marrow.

The hazards of phenylbutazone are explicit. Aspirin enjoys a far more auspicious reputation, as least with the general public. The prevailing impression of aspirin is that it is not only the most harmless drug available but also one of the most effective. When I looked into research in the medical journals, however, I found that aspirin is quite powerful in its own right and that it warrants considerable care in its use. The fact that it can be bought in unlimited quantities without prescription or doctor's guidance seemed indefensible. Even in small amounts, it can cause internal bleeding. Articles in the medical press reported that the chemical composition of aspirin, like that of phenylbutazone, impairs platelet function. Did the relation between platelets and collagen mean that both drugs do more harm than good for some sufferers from arthritis?[1]

It was a mind-boggling train of thought. Could it be, I asked myself, that aspirin, so universally accepted for so many years, was actually harmful in the treatment of collagen illnesses (Sahud and Cohen 1971)?[2]

The history of medicine is replete with instances involving drugs and modes of treatment that were in use for many years before it was recognized that they did more harm than good. For centuries, for example, people believed that drawing blood from patients was essential for rapid recovery from virtually every illness. Then, midway through the nineteenth century, it was discovered that bleeding serves only to weaken the patient. King Charles II's death is believed to have been caused in large part from administered bleedings. George Washington's death was also hastened by the severe loss of blood resulting from this treatment.

Living in the second half of the twentieth century, I realized, confers no automatic protection against unwise or even dangerous drugs and methods. Each age has had to undergo its own special nostrums. Fortunately, the human body is a remarkably durable instrument and has been able to withstand all sorts of prescribed assaults over the centuries, from freezing to animal dung.

Suppose I stopped taking aspirin and phenylbutazone? What about the pain? The bones in my spine and practically every joint in my body felt as though I had been run over by a truck.

I knew that pain could be affected by attitudes. Most people become panicky about almost any pain. On all sides they have been so bombarded by advertisements about pain that they take this or that analgesic at the slightest sign of an ache. They are largely illiterate about pain and so are seldom able to deal with it rationally. Pain is part of the body's magic. It is the way the body transmits a sign to the brain that something is wrong. Leprous patients pray for the sensation of pain. What makes leprosy such a terrible disease is that the victim usually feels no pain when his extremities are being injured. He loses his fingers or toes because he receives no warning signal that he is being injured.

I could stand pain so long as I knew that progress was being made in meeting the basic need. That need, I felt, was to restore the body's capacity to halt the continuing breakdown of connective tissue.

There was also the problem of the severe inflammation. If we dispensed with the aspirin, how would we combat the inflammation? I recalled having read in the medical journals about the usefulness of ascorbic acid in combating a wide number of illnesses—all the way from bronchitis to some types of heart disease. Couldn't it also combat inflammation? Did vitamin C act directly, or did it serve as a starter for the body's endocrine system—in particular, the adrenal glands? Was it possible, I asked myself, that ascorbic acid had a vital role to play in "feeding" the adrenal glands?

I had read in the medical press that vitamin C helps to oxygenate the blood (Hamburger 1962; Kinderlehrer 1974; Klenner 1971). If inadequate or impaired oxygenation was a factor in collagen breakdown, couldn't this circumstance be another argument for ascorbic acid? Also, according to some medical reports, people suffering from collagen diseases are deficient in vitamin C (Sahud and Cohen 1971). Did this lack mean that the body uses up large amounts of vitamin C in the process of combating collagen breakdown?

I wanted to discuss some of these ruminations with Dr. Hitzig. He listened carefully as I told him of my speculations concerning the cause of the illness, as well as my layman's ideas for a course of action that might give me a chance to reduce the odds against my recovery.

Dr. Hitzig said it was clear to him that there was nothing undersized about my will to live. He said that what was most important was that I continue to believe in everything I had said. He shared my sense of excitement about the possibilities of my recovery and liked the idea of a partnership.

Even before we had completed arrangements for moving out of the hospital, we began the part of the program calling for the full exercise of the affirmative emotions as a factor in enhancing body chemistry. It was easy enough to hope and love and have faith, but what about laughter? Nothing is less funny than being flat on our back with all the bones in your spine and joints hurting. A systematic program was indicated. A good place to begin, I thought, was with amusing movies. Allen Funt, producer of the spoofing television program "Candid Camera," sent films of some of his "CC" classics, along with a motion-picture projector. The nurse was instructed in its use.

It worked. I made the joyous discovery that ten minutes of genuine belly laughter had an anesthetic effect and would give me at least two hours of pain-free sleep. When the painkilling effect of the laughter wore off, we would switch on the motion-picture projector again, and, not infrequently, it would lead to another pain-free sleep interval. Sometimes, the nurse read to me out of a trove of humor books. Especially useful were E. B. and Katherine White's *A Subtreasury of American Humor* (1962) and Max Eastman's *The Enjoyment of Laughter* (1971).

How scientific was it to believe that laughter—as well as the positive emotions in general—was affecting my body chemistry for the better? If laughter did in fact have a salutary effect on the body's chemistry, it seemed at least theoretically likely that it would enhance the system's ability to fight the inflammation. So we took sedimentation-rate readings just before as well as several hours after the laughter episodes. Each time, there was a drop of at least five points. The drop by itself was not substantial, but it held and was cumulative.

I was greatly elated by the discovery that there is a physiologic basis for the ancient theory that laughter is good medicine.

There was, however, one negative side effect of the laughter from the standpoint of the hospital. I was disturbing other patients. But that objection didn't last very long, for the arrangements were now complete for me to move my act to a hotel room.

One of the incidental advantages of the hotel room, I was delighted to find, was that it cost only about one-third as much as the hospital. The other benefits were incalculable. I would not be awakened for a bed bath or for meals or for medication or for a change in the bed sheets or for tests or for examinations by hospital interns. The sense of serenity was delicious and would, I felt certain, contribute to a general improvement.

What about ascorbic acid and its place in the general program for recovery? In discussing my speculations about vitamin C with Dr. Hitzig, I found him completely open-minded on the subject, although he told me of serious questions that had been raised by scientific studies. He also cautioned me that heavy doses of ascorbic acid carried some risk of renal damage. The main problem right then, however, was not my kidneys: it seemed to me that, on balance, the risk was worth taking. I asked Dr. Hitzig about previous recorded experience with massive doses of vitamin C. He ascertained that at the hospital there had been cases in which patients had received up to 3 g by intramuscular injection.

As I thought about the injection procedure, some questions came to mind. Introducing the ascorbic acid directly into the bloodstream might make more efficient use of the vitamin, but I wondered about the body's ability to utilize a sudden massive infusion. I knew that one of the great advantages of vitamin C is that the body takes only the amount necessary for its purposes and excretes the rest. Again, there came to mind Cannon's phrase—the wisdom of the body ([1939] 1963).

Was there a coefficient of time in the utilization of ascorbic acid? The more I thought about it, the more likely it seemed to me that the body would excrete a large quantity of the vitamin because it couldn't metabolize it that fast. I wondered whether a better procedure than injection would be to administer the ascorbic acid through slow intravenous drip over a period of three or four hours. In this way we could go far beyond the 3 g. My hope was to start at 10 g and then increase the dose daily, until we reached 25 g.

Dr. Hitzig's eyes widened when I mentioned 25 g. This amount was far beyond any recorded dose. He said he had to caution me about the possible effect not just on the kidneys but on the veins in the arms. Moreover, he said he knew of no data to support the assumption that the body could handle 25 g over a four-hour period, other than by excreting it rapidly through the urine.

As before, however, it seemed to me we were playing for bigger stakes: losing some veins was not of major importance alongside the need to combat whatever was eating at my connective tissue.

To know whether we were on the right track, we took a sedimentation test before the first intravenous administration of 10 g of ascorbic acid. Four hours later, we took another sedimentation test. There was a drop of nine full points.

Seldom had I known such elation. The ascorbic acid was working. So was laughter. The combination was cutting heavily into whatever poison was attacking the connective tissue. The fever was receding, and the pulse was no longer racing.

We stepped up the dosage. On the second day we went up to 12.5 g of ascorbic acid, on the third day, 15 g, and so on until the end of the week, when we reached 25 g. Meanwhile, the laughter routine was in full force. I was completely off drugs and sleeping pills. Sleep—blessed, natural sleep without pain—was becoming increasingly prolonged.

At the end of the eighth day I was able to move my thumbs without pain. By this time, the sedimentation rate was somewhere in the 80s and dropping fast. I couldn't be sure, but it seemed to me that the gravel-like nodules on my neck and the backs of my hands were beginning to shrink. There was not doubt in my mind that I was going to make it back all the way.

Two weeks later, my wife took me to Puerto Rico for some sustained sunshine. On the first day, friends helped support me in the breaking surf. Within a few days I was standing up by myself. At first the soles of my feet were so sensitive that I felt as though I were standing on my eyeballs. But walking in the sand was the best possible therapy, and within a week I was able to jog—at least for a minute or two.

The connective tissue in my spine and joints was regenerating. I could function, and the feeling was indescribably beautiful.

I must not make it appear that all my infirmities disappeared overnight. For many months I couldn't get my arms up far enough to reach for a book on a high shelf. My fingers weren't agile enough to do what I wanted them to do on the organ keyboard. My neck had a limited turning radius. My knees were somewhat wobbly, and, off and on, I had to wear a metal brace.

But I was back at my job at *Saturday Review* full time again, and this was miracle enough for me.

Is the recovery a total one? Year by year the mobility has improved. During the past year I have become fully pain free, except for my knees, for the first time since I left the hospital. I no longer feel a sharp twinge in my wrists or shoulders when I hit a tennis ball or golf ball, as I did for such a long time. I can ride a horse flat out and hold a camera with a steady hand. And I have recaptured my ambition to play the Tocata and Fugue in D Minor, though I find the going slower and tougher than I had hoped. My neck has a full turning radius again, despite the statement of specialists as recently as 1971 that the condition was degenerative and that I would have to adjust to a quarter turn.

It was seven years after the onset of the illness before I had scientific confirmation about the dangers of using aspirin in the treatment of collagen diseases, which embrace the various forms of arthritis. In its May 8, 1971 issue, *Lancet* published a study by Drs. M. A. Sahud and R. J. Cohen (1971) showing that aspirin could be antagonistic to the retention of vitamin C in the body. The authors said that patients with rheumatoid arthritis should take vitamin C supplements since it has often been noted that they have low levels of the vitamin in their blood. It was no surprise, then, that I had been able to absorb such massive amounts of ascorbic acid without kidney or other complications.

What conclusions do I draw from the entire experience?

The first is that the will to live is not a theoretical abstraction, but a physiological reality with therapeutic characteristics. The second is that I was incredibly fortunate to have as my doctor a man who knew that his biggest job was to encourage to the fullest the patient's will to live and to mobilize all the natural resources of body and mind to combat disease. Dr. Hitzig was willing to set aside the large and often hazardous armamentarium of powerful drugs available to the modern physician when he became convinced that his patient might have something better to offer. He was also wise enough to know that the art of healing is still a frontier profession. And, though I can't be sure of this point, I have a hunch he believed that my own total involvement was a major factor in any recovery.

People have asked what I thought when I was told by the specialists that my disease was progressive and incurable.

The answer is simple. Since I didn't accept the verdict, I wasn't trapped in the cycle of fear, depression and panic that frequently accompanies a supposedly incurable illness. I must not make it seem, however, that I was unmindful of the seriousness of the problem or that I was in a festive mood throughout. Being unable to move my body was all the evidence I needed that the specialists were dealing with real concerns. But deep down I knew I had a good chance and relished the idea of bucking the odds.

Adam Smith, in *Powers of the Mind* (1975), says he discussed my recovery with some of his doctor friends, asking them to explain why the combination of laughter and ascorbic acid worked so well. The answer he got was that neither laughter nor ascorbic acid had anything to do with it and that I probably would have recovered if nothing had been done.

Maybe so, but that was not the opinion of the specialists at the time.

Two or three doctors, reflecting on the Adam Smith account, have commented that I was probably the beneficiary of a mammoth venture in self-administered placebos.

Such a hypothesis bothers me not at all. Respectable names in the history of medicine like Paracelsus, Holmes, and Osler have suggested that the history of medication is far more the history of the placebo effect than of intrinsically valuable and relevant drugs. Physicians in the past who favored such modalities as bleeding (in a single year, 1827, France imported 33 million leeches after its domestic supplies had been depleted); purging through emetics; physical contact with unicorn horns, bezoar stones, mandrakes or powdered mummies—the physicians prescribing such treatments no doubt regarded them at the time as specifics with empirical sanction. But today's medical science recognizes that whatever efficacy these treatments may have had—and the records indicate that the results were often surprisingly in line with expectations—was probably related to the power of the placebo.

I have wondered, in fact, about the relative absence of attention given the placebo in contemporary medicine. The literature on the subject is remarkably sparse considering the primacy of the placebo in the history of medicine. The late Henry K. Beecher (1955) and Arthur K. Shapiro (1964) are among the small number of contemporary medical researchers and observers who have done any noteworthy thinking and writing about this phenomenon. In connection with my own experience, I was fascinated by a report citing Dr. Thomas C. Chalmers (Blake 1976), of the Mount Sinai Medical Center in New York, which compared two groups that were being used to test the theory that ascorbic acid is a cold preventive. "The group on placebo," says Dr. Chalmers, "who thought they were on ascorbic acid had fewer colds than the group on ascorbic acid who thought they were on placebo."

I was absolutely convinced, at the time I was deep in my illness, that intravenous doses of ascorbic acid could be beneficial—and they were. It is quite possible that this treatment—like everything else I did—was a demonstration of the placebo effect. If so, it would be just as important to probe into the nature of this psychosomatic phenomenon as to find out if ascorbic acid is useful in combating a high sedimentation rate.

At this point, of course, we are opening a very wide door, perhaps even a Pandora's box. The vaunted "miracle cures" that abound in the literature of all the great religions, or the speculations of Charcot and Freud about conversion hysteria, or the Lourdes phenomena—all say something about the ability of the patient, properly motivated or stimulated, to participate actively in extraordinary reversals of disease and disability. It is all too easy, of course, to raise these possibilities and speculations to a monopoly status—in which case the entire edifice of modern medicine would be reduced to little more than the hut of an African witch doctor. But we can at least reflect on William Halse Rivers' statement, as quoted by Shapiro, that "the salient feature of the medicine of today is that these psychical factors are no longer allowed to play their part unwittingly, but are themselves becoming the subject of study, so that the present age is serving the growth of a rational system of psychotherapeutics" (1964).

What we are talking about essentially, I suppose, is the chemistry of the will to live. In Bucharest in 1972, I visited the clinic of Ana Aslan, described to me as one of Rumania's leading endocrinologists. She spoke of her belief that there is a direct connection between a robust will to live and the chemical balances in the brain. She is convinced that creativity—one aspect of the will to live—produces the vital brain impulses that stimulate the pituitary glands, triggering effects on the pineal glands and the whole of the endocrine system. Is it possible that placebos have a key role in this process? Shouldn't this entire area be worth serious and sustained attention?

If I had to guess, I would say that the principal contribution made by my doctor to the taming, and possibly the conquest, of my illness was that he encouraged me to believe I was a respected partner with him in the total undertaking. He fully engaged my subjective energies. He may not have been able to define or diagnose the process through which self-confidence (wild hunches securely believed) was somehow picked up by the body's immunologic mechanisms and translated into anti-morbid effects. But he was acting, I believe, in the best tradition of medicine in recognizing that he had to reach out in my case beyond the usual verifiable modalities. In so doing, he was faithful to the first dictum in his medical education: *primum non nocere.* He knew that what I wanted to do might not help, but it probably would do little harm. Certainly, the threatened harm being risked was less, if anything, than the heroic medication so routinely administered in extreme cases of this kind.

Something else I have learned. I have learned never to underestimate the capacity of the human mind and body to regenerate—even when the prospects seem most wretched. The life-force may be the least understood force on earth. William James (1948) said that human beings tend to live too far within self-imposed limits. It is possible that those limits will recede when we respect more fully the natural drive of the human mind and body toward perfectibility and regeneration. Protecting and cherishing that natural drive may well represent the finest exercise of human freedom.

NOTES

1. I realize, of course, that the implications here are not entirely negative in view of the fact that the same properties of aspirin that prolong bleeding also prevent clotting. Aspirin is therefore useful to some patients with cardiac disease and those for whom clotting is a danger.

2. The scientific verification that aspirin can be harmful in the treatment of collagen diseases came in 1971 and is discussed later in this article (Sahud and Cohen 1971).

4

Health Psychology

The Science and the Field

■

SHELLEY E. TAYLOR

Health psychology is defined as the "educational, scientific, and professional contributions of the discipline of psychology to the promotion and maintenance of health, the prevention and treatment of illness, the identification of etiologic and diagnostic correlates of health, illness, and related dysfunction, and the improvement of the health care system and health policy formation" (Matarazzo 1980:815). As such, its mission is broad, involving all branches of psychology in virtually every aspect of the health enterprise.

As a field, health psychology has made substantial contributions to the understanding of healthy behaviors and to the comprehension of the myriad factors that undermine health and often lead to illness. Much of the strongest work has involved providing theoretical and conceptual frameworks that elucidate the (non)practice of health behaviors, the role of stress in affecting illness and illness behavior, the

Preparation of this article was supported by two grants from the National Institute of Mental Health (MH 42152 and MH 42258) and by a Research Scientist Development Award from the National Institute of Mental Health (MH 03311).

representations that people hold regarding their health and illness, and the ways in which people cope with illness and the determinants of their adjustment to it.

These theoretical conceptualizations constitute major contributions inasmuch as they are often lacking in traditional medicine and medical practice. They provide a basis for making sense of otherwise isolated and confusing bits of data. For example, it is difficult for physicians to understand why 93 percent of patients fail to adhere to certain aspects of their treatment regimens; social psychological models not only make sense of these data but suggest ways of ameliorating them. Theoretical models also suggest new directions for research that might otherwise remain elusive and left as isolated observations. Finally, such models often point directly to interventions that can improve the practice of health behavior and adjustment to stress or illness. As such, these interventions constitute both rests and applications of the theories.

Research in behavioral medicine and, correspondingly, in health psychology has taken the position that biological, psychological, and social factors are implicated in all stages of health and illness, ranging from those behaviors and states that keep people healthy to those that produce severe, long-term, and debilitating disease. This position is termed the *biopsychosocial model* and is a guiding framework for both research and practice (Engel 1977; Schwartz 1982). This article will emphasize its guiding role for basic research.

Recent Scientific Developments in Health Psychology

If one asks where the field of health psychology is going, there would be no simple answer. As a microcosm of both psychology and the interdisciplinary endeavor of behavioral medicine, the field is pulled and pushed in many directions simultaneously. In this article, I first attempt to characterize some of the recent scientific developments that illustrate the trends in the field generally. I then focus on some of the major directions and forces affecting the future of the field as a whole. Although an exhaustive analysis of health psychology's contributions is precluded here, a focus on some of the more recent and exciting research developments is instructive in illustrating the progress of the field. For more comprehensive reviews, the reader is referred to overviews of the field (e.g., Friedman and DiMatteo 1989; Taylor 1986) and to the *Annual Review of Psychology* chapter by Rodin and Salovey (1989).

Health Promotion and Health Habit Modification

Health promotion and primary prevention have been of increasing concern to researchers and practitioners because of changing patterns of illness. In the past 80 years in the United States, the prevalence of acute infectious disorders such as influenza, tuberculosis, measles, and polio has declined while what have been termed the "preventable" disorders have increased, including lung cancer, cardiovascular disease, drug and alcohol abuse, and vehicular accidents (Matarazzo 1982).

The role of behavioral factors in the development of these diseases and disorders is increasingly clear. For example, 25 percent of all cancer deaths and approximately 350,000 premature deaths from heart attack could be avoided each year by modifying just one risk factor: smoking (American Heart Association 1988). A 10 percent weight reduction in men aged 35 to 55 through dietary modifications and exercise would produce an estimated 20 percent decrease in coronary artery disease (American Heart Association 1984a, 1984b; Ashley and Kannel 1974); it would also lower the degree of degenerative arthritis, gastrointestinal cancer, diabetes, stroke, and heart attack. The percentage of the gross national product that goes for health care has been climbing steadily, in part because the diseases that are currently most prevalent are chronic in nature and thus require continual treatment and monitoring. Successful modification of health behaviors may help to reduce both the numbers of deaths and the incidence of preventable disease as well as make a dent in the more than $400 billion spent yearly on health and illness (cf. Matarazzo 1982).

The desire to keep people healthy rather than wait to treat them after they become ill has been the impetus for much work on the development of the healthy lifestyle and the modification of faulty health habits. Although a number of conceptual models have been developed both to explain existing health practices and as impeti for changing faulty ones, there is now considerable convergence on the beliefs that contribute to a given health practice. Specifically, we now know that people are most likely to practice a good health measure or to change a faulty one when (1) the threat to health is severe; (2) the perceived personal vulnerability and/or the likelihood of developing the disorder is high; (3) the person believes that he or she is able to perform the response that will reduce the threat (self-efficacy); and (4) the response is effective in overcoming the threat (response efficacy) (Bandura 1986; Janz and Becker 1984; Rogers 1984). These four elements borrow heavily from distinct theoretical models—specifically, Bandura's self-efficacy framework, Rogers' protection/motivation theory, and the health belief model—but in practice, most researchers now make efforts to conceptualize and measure all four components.

Conceptual convergence has helped to clarify the difficulty and complexity of actually modifying health behaviors. Health habits predict each other only modestly, and their interrelations may decline with age (*see* Mechanic 1979). One of the reasons for this is the fact that each health habit has a complex pattern of etiology, maintenance, change, and relapse (*see* Jessor and Jessor 1982; Leventhal and Cleary 1980 for discussions of smoking). For example, although peer group influence and issues of personal identity may be bound up in the practice of faulty health habits in adolescence, these factors are less important in considering health habits in adulthood (Botvin and Eng 1982; Evans et al. 1978). Consequently, it is often difficult to develop intervention programs that will appeal to a broad segment of the population to change some targeted health habit. Whereas individualized appeals often have the greatest impact on behavior, such methods are intensive and expensive and affect only a limited portion of the population at a time. Mass-media appeals, however, sometimes change attitudes about health problems but may produce only modest behavior change (Lau et al. 1980; Leventhal, Meyer, and Nerenz 1980). How best to combine the advantages of the two methods is a problem on which much recent attention has been focused, and efforts to tailor interventions to designated communities have been one method used (Multiple Risk Factor Intervention Trial Research Group 1982; *see* Matarazzo et al. 1984 for a review).

Perhaps the most important problem for future research is that of preventing relapse (Marlatt and Gordon 1985), the often-observed phenomenon that, after successfully altering a health practice on their own for weeks or even months, many individuals revert to their former behaviors (Brownell et al. 1986). In this context, it becomes essential to consider not only the short-term effects of interventions designed to modify health habits but also their long-range effectiveness, focusing especially on factors that undermine long-term maintenance of short-term change.

Do Psychological States Cause Illness?

For centuries, philosophers and scientists have speculated about the role that personality factors and coping styles may play in the development of illness. In the 1930s and the 1940s, Flanders Dunbar (1943),

Franz Alexander (1950), and their associates developed specific personality profiles of those prone to hypertension, coronary artery disease, cancer, ulcers, rheumatoid arthritis, and other specific disease states. Until recently, however, theory outstripped methodology, so that convincing evidence regarding such relationships was lacking (e.g., Fox 1978). Several recent research developments have improved this situation.

Early research relating personality factors to disease states focused on whether personality states were related to a host of diseases (the general model) or whether particular personality traits could be related to specific diseases (the specificity model). Research continues to investigate both kinds of links. Recent research using meta-analysis suggests that a general negative affective style marked by depression, anxiety, and, to a lesser extent, hostility may be associated with the development of a broad range of diseases, including coronary artery disease, asthma, headache, ulcers, and arthritis (Friedman and Booth-Kewley 1987). Repression, as a coping style, may also be implicated in this cluster (Weinberger in press). These findings suggest the possibility of a general disease-prone personality, although at present the exact causal nature of the relationship is uncertain. Although negative emotional states certainly result from illness, longitudinal studies also suggest the validity of the reverse direction of causality. The links through which such relationships occur have drawn considerable attention (Matthews 1988). A negative emotional state may produce pathogenic physiological changes; it may lead people to practice faulty health behaviors; it may produce illness behavior (such as visiting a physician) but no underlying pathology; or it may be associated with illness via other factors in some as-yet-undetermined manner.

These developments have been paralleled by increasing attention to specific models of personality–disease relationships. Chief among these have been the exploration of the Type A behavior syndrome, characterized by competitive drive, impatience, hostility, and rapid speech and motor movements, in the development of coronary heart disease (CHD). Compared to earlier work, recent research has reported weaker links between Type A behavior and CHD (Matthews 1988), although researchers concur that the structured interview assessment technique shows a stronger relationship to CHD than other measures (Friedman and Booth-Kewley 1988; Matthews 1988). The emphasis on negative emotional states has prompted researchers investigating the role of Type A behavior in the etiology of CHD to focus most closely on hostility as the potential culprit (Dembroski and Costa 1987; Friedman and Booth-Kewley 1987). Other components of the Type A behavior syndrome, such as competitiveness and time urgency, do not seem to be as lethal. Such discoveries lay the groundwork for more sophisticated interventions to modify the Type A behavior syndrome in the hope that those susceptible to it may avoid the development of disease (e.g., Suinn 1982; Thoresen et al. 1982). Research to date suggests that interventions to reduce Type A behavior can be successful (Friedman et al. 1986).

For many years, researchers have suspected links between a passive, acquiescent, or repressed personality style and the development or progression of cancer. Although research relating personality variables to the development of cancer is lacking, in large part because such studies are difficult to design (Fox 1978), some evidence for the role of an acquiescent, repressed personality style in the rapid progression of cancer has accumulated (e.g., Derogatis, Abeloff, and Melasaratos 1979; Levy et al. 1987; Levy et al. 1985). The increasingly sophisticated efforts to relate personality variables to the onset or progression of cancer have been plagued by methodological difficulties: inasmuch as cancers grow over a long period, it is difficult to establish causality unambiguously (Fox 1978).

Research on the health significance of negative emotional states is fueled by related discoveries in other fields. Research in psychoimmunology using quasi-experimental studies of samples exposed to stress documents declines in certain indicators of immune activity, such as natural killer cell activity and lymphocyte proliferation in response to mitogenic stimulation (*see* Kiecolt-Glaser and Glaser in press; Stein, Keller, and Schleifer 1985 for reviews). Although direct links to disease have usually not been established, such results are useful in identifying potential biobehavioral mechanisms whereby psychologic states may exert adverse effects on health. The psychologic factors implicated to date in immunocompromise are the stressful event of bereavement, the state of depression, and stressful events involving the lack or loss of perceived control (*see* Kiecolt-Glaser and Glaser in press; Stein, Keller, and Schliefer 1985). For example, animal studies have suggested a causal chain linking uncontrollable stress to cancer in susceptible animals (Laudenslager et al. 1983), although the relationship appears to be moderated by the temporal course of the stressor in as yet unpredictable ways. This knowledge is now being applied to the effort to understand the role of psychosocial factors in the development of the acquired immunodeficiency syndrome (AIDS) following exposure to the human immunodeficiency virus (HIV) (Kemeny et al. 1989).

Increasingly, researchers are focusing on the potentially protective role of positive emotional states and coping styles in the development of illness. Chief among these are optimism (e.g., Scheier and Carver 1985) and perceived control. Optimists appear to experience fewer physical symptoms (Scheier and Carver 1985), and they may show faster or better recoveries from certain illnesses (Scheier et al. in press; *see also* Peterson, Seligman, and Vaillant 1988). The importance of self-efficacy beliefs in the practice of health behaviors (Bandura 1986) and the health benefits of control (e.g., Langer and Rodin 1976; Rodin 1986) are well established.

Of the many issues meriting further exploration, a chief concern is whether these psychological variables represent predisposing (or protective) personality states or whether they exert their impacts on health in interaction with situational variables such as stress. For example, whereas some researchers have regarded the Type A constellation as a predisposing personality factor for CHD, others have considered it to be a behavioral syndrome elicited by certain circumstances and not others (*see* Matthews 1982). Good cases for particular causal paths have not yet been made. This issue is part of the larger question regarding the pathways by which psychologic factors are involved in the etiology of health and illness, a concern that will guide research in the coming years.

The additional question arises as to whether the literature linking psychosocial factors to the etiology of illness provides any basis for intervention studies. Should we be intervening with people who show pronounced negative affect (Friedman and Booth-Kewley 1988) or a pessimistic explanatory style (Peterson, Seligman, and Vaillant 1988) with the goal of improving their health farther down the line? The effect sizes in these relationships are typically small, and it is not yet clear whether such interventions would have an identifiable impact on health. The possibility of using such relationships to develop interventions, however, remains a prospect for future research.

Cognitive Factors in Health and Illness

Just as emotional factors are involved in the experience of health and illness, cognitive factors influence how people appraise their health and cope with the threat of illness. Several researchers (e.g., Jemmott, Croyle, and Ditto 1988; Lau, Bernard, and Hartman 1989; Leventhal, Meyers, and Nerenz 1980; Millstein and Irwin 1987; Turk, Rudy, and Salovey 1985) have argued that people hold articulated general conceptions of illness against which particular symptoms or disorders may be evaluated. These so-called common-sense representations of illness include several dimensions: identity (the label of the illness and its symptoms), cause, consequences, time frame, and cure (e.g., Leventhal, Meyers, and Nerenz 1980). When people make appropriate matches of symptoms to their preexisting representations of illness, they may show appropriate illness behavior such as seeking treatment promptly and demonstrating effective follow-through; however, the improper match of symptoms to illness conceptions may account for delay behavior, the faulty practice of certain health behaviors, poor adherence to health recommendations, and other adverse effects on health (Baumann and Leventhal 1985; Turk, Rudy, and Salovey 1984).

Cognitions have also been examined in the context of coping with chronic disease and disability. In particular, researchers have focused on the causal attributions that people make for their chronic conditions and on the perceptions of control that they generate regarding the current course of their disorder and/or its daily symptoms, treatments, and side effects. Attributions for the cause of a chronic illness appear to be commonly made (e.g., Taylor, Lichtman, and Wood 1984a), and a relatively high percentage are made to the self. Some have regarded self-attribution as potentially destructive, whereas others have considered it indicative of efforts to assert control over the illness (*see* Bulman and Wortman 1977). Results concerning self-blame or self-responsibility for illness have been inconclusive (Miller and Porter 1983), perhaps because causality, blame, and responsibility have been used somewhat interchangeably in this literature (Shaver and Drown 1986). Attributions for an illness made to another person (such as an ex-spouse for causing stress), however, have been uniformly associated with poor psychological adjustment to chronic conditions (e.g., Bulman and Wortman 1977; Taylor, Lichtman, and Wood 1984a). A factor that appears to promote positive adjustment is perceived control. Those who believe they can control either the course of their illness or their day-to-day symptoms appear to be better adjusted to their disorders (Affleck et al. 1987; Taylor, Lichtman, and Wood 1984a).

Stress and Illness

Conceptual work on stress began with the fight-flight reaction described by Cannon ([1939] 1963). Early work on stress largely ignored psychological factors, perhaps because much of it was conducted with animals. Human research spearheaded by Lazarus and his associates (e.g., Lazarus 1966; Lazarus and Folkman 1984b), however, identified psychological appraisal as a crucial mediating process in the experience of stress. Events are judged to be positive, negative, or neutral in their implications, and if judged negative, they are further evaluated as to whether they are harmful, threatening, or challenging.

Early efforts to identify stressful events in humans focused on the amount of change that was required to deal with these events, that is, the life events approach. The measurement of stress involved checking off whether particular stressful events (e.g., death of a spouse, arguments with family members) had occurred within a given time period (e.g., six months) and then relating them to disease at later points in time. Such studies established modest but reliable relationships to illness.

More recent and sophisticated work has enabled researchers to identify the dimensions of events that are most likely to produce stress. Events appraised as negative, uncontrollable, unpredictable, or ambiguous are typically experienced as more stressful than those not so appraised. Research identifying the significance of these dimensions has come both from well-controlled laboratory studies (e.g., Glass 1977a) and from opportunistic studies of people undergoing major stressful events such as unemployment (Fleming et al. 1987) or crises such as the Three Mile Island catastrophe (Fleming et al. 1982). Of the factors implicated in stress, controllability may be especially important. In studies involving stressful events, when those events were under the control of the organisms studied, those organisms showed physiological profiles similar to those of organisms undergoing no stress at all, whereas organisms experiencing the event without the experience of control showed physiological reactions indicative of anxiety and arousal (Hanson, Larson, and Snowden 1976; Laudenslager et al. 1983).

In this context, it is useful to distinguish explicitly between illness behavior and illness inasmuch as the two only partially overlap. Illness behavior refers to the steps people take when they believe they are experiencing symptoms of illness (such as going to the doctor, taking days off from work). Illness itself involves documented pathology. The distinction is important because illness behaviors do not necessarily implicate underlying pathology, and the psychologic and biologic pathways responsible for the two types of outcomes are often totally different (cf. Cohen 1988). Much of the research implicating psychosocial factors in illness looks primarily at illness behaviors as the outcome points, rather than at pathology verified through such sources as physician records (*see* Kasl 1983). Extensions of these relationships to documented illness are needed.

Until relatively recently, research examining the role of stress in illness behavior and the development of illness focused on major stressful events and the impact these often extreme and dramatic conditions can have on health. More recently, research has investigated the day-to-day process of coping with minor stressful events such as daily hassles (Kanner et al. 1981). Unfortunately, the measurement of day-to-day stress sometimes confounds stress with psychological and physical symptoms, and it has been difficult to disentangle cause and effect (Dohrenwend et al. 1984). Whether minor stressors will ultimately prove to be important predictors of psychological distress and illness remains to be seen.

Just as recent efforts to relate personality variables to illness have focused on potential pathways, so research relating stress to illness has focused on the pathways by which such developments may occur. Of particular concern have been the patterns of physiological reactivity produced by stressful events. Initially, work was guided by Selye's ([1956] 1976b) general adaptation syndrome, which maintained that people develop patterned physiological reactions to stress which they then exhibit across a wide variety of stressful situations. More recent evidence, however, suggests that there is some physiological specificity in response to particular kinds of stressful events (e.g., Mason 1974) and emotional reactions (Smith 1989). Other pathways explored include the likelihood that stressful events erode health habits, such as smoking, drinking, and appropriate eating and sleeping patterns (*see* Krantz, Grunberg, and Baum 1985), or change illness behaviors without necessarily affecting health.

Understanding Coping

Coping has been defined as the process of managing external or internal demands that are perceived as taxing or exceeding a person's resources (Lazarus and Folkman, 1984b). Coping may consist of behaviors and intrapsychic responses designed to overcome, reduce, or tolerate these demands (Lazarus and Launier 1978). Until recently, research on coping was in disarray, characterized in one report as a "three-car garage filled to the rafters with junk" (Taylor 1984:2313). The reason was that researchers studied the same phenomena in different ways using idiosyncratic concepts, measures, and methods. The rise of health psychology as a field has ameliorated this situation in one important way by providing avenues and forums for communication. This has moved researchers toward greater awareness of the need for commonality in the definition of concepts and issues in the study of coping.

Other important developments include advances in the conceptualization and measurement of coping (e.g., Folkman et al. 1986; Holahan and Moos 1987; Stone and Neale 1984). For example, as conceptualized by Lazarus and his associates, coping is initiated by an appraisal process secondary to the assessment of circumstances as harmful, threatening, or challenging. In this view, a person judges his or her resources, such as time or money, assesses his or her coping skills and abilities, and then determines whether or not they will be sufficient to overcome the threat or challenge posed by a stressful event. Several measures of coping now exist. They include the Ways of Coping instrument, which is based on the Lazarus group's work and which identifies the specific actions, thoughts, and reactions that people have to stressful events; Stone and Neale's (1984) measure of daily coping, specifically designed for use in longitudinal studies; and the COPE measure (Carver, Scheier, and Weintraub 1989). Increasingly, too, researchers have found that coping measures targeted to particular populations experiencing particular stressors may be more useful than more general coping measures. For example, in this context, Wills (1986) has designed a coping measure for use with adolescents.

There are many ways in which coping responses can be grouped (Billings and Moos 1982). Two general categories of coping strategies are problem-solving efforts and strategies aimed at the regulation of emotions (Lazarus and Folkman 1984b). Although both sets of strategies are brought to bear on most stressful events, problem-solving efforts are especially useful for managing controllable stressors, and emotional-regulation efforts are well-suited to managing the impact of uncontrollable stressors. A distinction among coping strategies that overlaps with but does not perfectly correspond to the problem-solving/emotional-regulation distinction is that between active coping (behavioral or cognitive efforts to manage a stressful event directly) and avoidance (attempts to avoid dealing with the problem or reduce tension through escapist behaviors). Although most negative life events appear to elicit both types of coping strategies, people with more personal and environmental resources may rely more on active coping and less on avoidance coping (Holahan and Moos 1987). A long-standing issue in the individual-differences perspective is whether avoidant/repressive responses to stressful events are more adaptive or whether more vigilant/confrontational coping methods are superior. Avoidant responses may be more effective for managing short-term threats, but for long-term threats vigilant coping may manage stress more effectively (Suls and Fletcher 1985). These findings, too, will no doubt prove to be contingent on the nature of the stressful event (*see* Taylor and Clark 1986 for a review).

This emphasis on individual differences has shifted somewhat with the findings that most people appear to use a variety of coping strategies to deal with any given stressor (e.g., Folkman et al. 1986b). Successful coping may depend more on a match of coping strategies to the features of the stressful event than on the relative efficacy of one strategy over another (Folkman et al. 1986). This may explain the observation that the use of multiple coping styles may be most adaptive in managing at least some stressful events (e.g., Collins, Taylor, and Skokan 1989).

Many issues in coping remain to be investigated. In particular, the relationship between ongoing self-regulatory activities (such as mentally simulating potential stressful events; Taylor and Schneider 1989) and the initiation of specific coping activities to deal with specific stressors has received relatively little attention. Coping researchers are also investigating some of the costs of coping, such as the energy expenditure and physiologic arousal that may be required when people must be vigilant in response to threatening events (Cohen et al. 1986b).

Social Support

Coping research has also focused on coping resources, most particularly on social support. A substantial amount of research documents the psychological and physical benefits of social support and shows how those with social support adjust better psychologically to stressful events, recover more quickly from already-diagnosed illness, and reduce their risk of mortality from specific diseases (House, Landis, and Umberson 1988). Findings concerning the impact of social support on the likelihood of developing illness have been mixed (Holahan and Moos 1986; Sarason and Sarason 1984; Wallston et al. 1983). Certain of the positive effects of social support appear to occur whether an organism is under stress or not (direct effects), whereas other salutary effects of social support appear largely to exert a buffering effect such that they are protective primarily when people are under high degrees of stress (Cohen and McKay 1984). In particular, studies that have measured social support in terms of social integration or social networks have tended to report direct effects, whereas studies that have focused on aid, resources, and emotional support from specific network members have tended to uncover buffering effects (Cohen and Wills 1985).

Time and additional data have produced a more differentiated view of support. For example, research now examines different kinds of social support, such as emotional support, information and advice, tangible assistance, and appraisal support, identifying which types of support are perceived to be helpful for which types of events (Cohen 1988; Dunkel-Schetter, Folkman, and Lazarus 1987). A question that arises in this context is whether social support may actually be an individual-difference resource such that some people have better skills for making effective use of potential social support than others (Dunkel-Schetter, Folkman, and Lazarus 1987).

Research also addresses the fact that social support is sometimes not forthcoming to those under stress (Wortman and Dunkel-Schetter 1979) and that some efforts to provide social support misfire and aggravate stressful circumstances (Coyne, Wortman, and Lehman 1988). Social support researchers are also increasingly turning their attention to the problems that providers experience in their attempts to provide social support, as in trying to care for an ill family member (*see,* e.g., Coyne, Wortman, and Lehman 1988; Kiecolt-Glaser et al. 1987; Schulz et al. 1987). Other outstanding issues in the field include how best to measure social support (e.g., Heitzmann and Kaplan 1988) and the need to identify the psychologic and biologic pathways by which different aspects of social support affect health (Cohen 1988).

Interventions to Improve Coping With Stressful Events

Health Psychology became Division 38 of the American Psychological Association in 1978; the division has approximately 3,000 members, roughly 65 percent of whom are involved in clinical practice, 55 percent in research activities, and 50 percent in teaching and supervision (Houston 1988).

Reflecting the composition of the division, intervention has been a major concern of health psychology since the inception of the field. Indeed, successful interventions with patients undergoing noxious medical procedures such as surgery actually predated sophisticated models of stress and coping (*see* Janis 1958). Psychological control has been the conceptual focus of much of this intervention work. Those who believe that they can exert some controlling behavior in response to a stressful event, whether behavioral or cognitive, appear to adjust better to those stressful events than those without such feelings of control. Research documents the coping benefits of being told in advance what sensations to expect and why, being alerted to the specific procedures to be undertaken, and being given cognitive or behavioral coping strategies to use during the noxious procedure (Taylor and Clark 1986; Thompson 1981). More recently, similar interventions have been undertaken successfully with children awaiting noxious medical procedures (e.g., Melamed 1986).

This is not to suggest that control is a panacea for stressful events, whether naturally occurring or induced during treatment. Manipulations designed to enhance feelings of psychological control may produce feelings of responsibility or blame instead (Krantz and Schulz 1980; Rodin 1986), and in many circumstances, they may aggravate negative consequences and lead to increased stress and worry (Burger 1989; Rodin 1986). Thus the potential benefits of the concept of psychological control and interventions based on it must be tempered by knowledge of its potential psychological costs as well.

Some interventions have focused on the regulation of emotional and physiologic states through relaxation and guided imagery (Burish and Lyles 1979), whereas others have encouraged more confrontational coping methods, such as training in swallowing to ease the passage of a tube in an endoscopic examination (Johnson and Leventhal 1974). Some intervention procedures use avoidant techniques such as cognitive distraction, whereas others enlist vigilant coping, as in inducing a person to reinterpret a stressful experience as a positive one. Although all of these types of interventions appear to be successful in reducing stress, those involving relaxation, avoidance, and cognitive restructuring have been the most commonly used, perhaps because many noxious medical procedures are typically only minimally conducive to direct patient intervention. Indeed, the psychological technology of relaxation has proven to have wide applicability to a variety of issues relating to health and illness, including its use as an accompanying intervention in efforts to modify health habits such as obesity or smoking (*see* Rodin and Salovey 1989); its application to stress management (Suinn 1982); its widespread use in the management of pain (Turner and Chapman 1982a); and its impact on coping with chronic disease and its treatments (Taylor, Lichtman, and Wood 1984b).

Aided self-help is another low-cost effective intervention technique that psychologists and health practitioners have implemented across a broad array of health problems. Programs designed to help smokers quit on their own using manuals provided by the American Cancer Society and other organizations are a reasonably effective and cost-effective way of inducing people to quit (e.g., Cummings et al. 1988). Self-help telephone lines (Ossip-Klein, Shapiro, and Stiggins 1984) also provide support for those who are attempting with difficulty to maintain behavior change over time, such as not smoking.

Conclusion

This brief overview of the health psychology field may be significant less for what it has included than for what it has left out. The field is now so diverse and productive that no one article can easily cover all of the significant trends. For example, the review touched only briefly on the enormous and important areas of health promotion and health behavior modification, areas in which health psychologists have made consistent and exceptional contributions. Research on substance abuse is not addressed at all, nor the complex question of ethnic, socioeconomic, gender, and racial patterns in health and illness (*see* Rodin and Salovey 1989 for a discussion of these issues). Only a passing nod was given to the huge problem of nonadherence to medical treatment regimens (Meichenbaum and Turk 1987), which can be as high as 95 percent for some health care recommendations. Pain mechanisms and pain management received little mention. There is also little coverage of the problems and issues associated with particular chronic diseases, including the most common ones of coronary artery disease, cancer, stroke, and diabetes (Burish and Bradley 1983). And finally, research investigation on biobehavioral pathways to disease was alluded to only briefly (for examples of this work in the areas of CHD and hypertension, *see* Cinciripini, 1986a, 1986b; Krantz and Manuck 1984).

Despite the gaps in this review, certain commonalities in the field may be highlighted. Research that examines whether or not psychological and social factors are involved in health and illness has largely made its point. More recent investigations have gone beyond the demonstration of such simple relationships to an attempt to specify the models and pathways whereby psychological and social factors can be integrated into the biology of health and illness in multifactorial causal chains. This trend is evidenced in research on health promotion, stress and illness, personality and disease, coping, social support, and the factors affecting recovery. These investigations have addressed the direct impact of stress and other psychological states on physiological processes, the impact of psychological and social factors in risky health practices, and the impact of psychological and social factors on how people respond to potential illness states, such as whether or not they engage in appropriate illness behavior. As such, the field has advanced to an unprecedented level of complexity in research investigations.

Yet simultaneously the field has also succeeded in identifying certain broad principles of behavior that seem to cut across specific diseases and specific issues of health and illness. For example, the importance of feelings of personal control emerges in whether people practice particular health behaviors, whether they experience stress, whether their pain control efforts are successful, and how they adapt to chronic disease and disability. Relaxation training, a psychological intervention that requires little training and expense, can be applied in a wealth of settings, as noted earlier. Thus, unlike medicine, which is highly specialized and organized around particular diseases, health psychology affords the opportunity to look beyond particular disorders to the broad principles of thought and behavior that cut across specializations of diseases or problems studied to elucidate more fundamental psychosocial mechanisms.

Trends Affecting Health Psychology

In the past ten years, I have had the opportunity to comment on the developing field of health psychology on four prior occasions. What seems to distinguish the present occasion from prior ones is an increasing sense that health psychologists are now better integrated into the health enterprise. No longer acting primarily as consultants, statistical advisors, or peripheral members of research teams, health psychologists now number heavily among the chief architects framing the research questions, providing the conceptual structure, developing the research designs, and carrying the projects to fruition. In the early days of research in this field, we often worked alone or with a few students, seeking each other's counsel concerning how best to reach practitioners, obtain samples, and convince medical establishments of the value of our enterprise. That has changed. We seem no longer to need each other so much, as many of us are well integrated into the collaborative arrangements we have engineered with other health professionals. In so doing, we have come face to face with some of the major issues facing the health enterprise.

One of the major forces facing health psychology, as well as every other disciplinary contributor to behavioral medicine, is the growing cost of health care services and the accompanying mounting pressures to contain costs. Fueled by the spiraling expense of high-tech medicine and the increasing costs of malpractice cases and insurance, health care now costs roughly $400 billion a year in the United States alone. The growing specter of the AIDS crisis threatens to push costs even further, simultaneously putting affordable health care and insurance out of reach of increasing numbers of people.

This unhappy reality is relevant to health psychologists in several respects. It nudges us to keep an eye on the bottom line in research and intervention. Although effective health care interventions are an important goal of the field, the likelihood of their being integrated into medical practice will be influenced by their cost-effectiveness. Subtly, the pressures of cost containment push us in the direction of research questions designed to keep people out of the health care system altogether. On the clinical practice side, interventions increasingly examine the benefits and liabilities of self-help groups, peer counseling, self-management programs such as those for hemodialysis (Kirschenbaum, Sherman, and Penrod 1987), and other inexpensive ways to provide service delivery to those who might otherwise not receive care. Research suggesting that the stress-reduction and pain-amelioration benefits of expensive biofeedback equipment and training can be achieved by simple, less expensive techniques of relaxation (e.g., Blanchard et al. 1988; Turner and Chapman 1982a, 1982b) is consistent with this viewpoint. On the research side, the emphasis on cost containment draws researchers heavily into primary prevention activities designed to keep people healthy with the goal of reducing the use of health care services. By identifying the risks of smoking and drinking and the health benefits of exercise, stress management, and a proper diet and by developing programs that best help people to achieve a healthy lifestyle, psychology contributes to the larger endeavor that attempts to keep people healthy with the ultimate goal of containing health care costs. Whether this implicit goal is a pipe dream remains to be seen. Research examining the efficacy of health behavior interventions in reducing disease and lowering health costs has so far not been very encouraging (Kaplan 1984). To date, however, the evidence has only slightly tempered the idealistic goal.

There are benefits and risks attached to the formidable role that economic exigencies play in the field. On the one hand, health psychology cannot afford to pursue its scientific and clinical mission without at least some regard to cost. To do so would produce an ivory-tower isolation that would render its results of limited use. On the other hand, cost-containment issues can compromise the scientific and practical mission of the field by choking off prematurely areas of inquiry that do not immediately appear to be cost-effective. The relative lack of attention to issues of rehabilitation, in contrast to the heavy preponderance of research in primary prevention activities, can be regarded as one casualty of these pressures. Just as we must keep an intermittent eye on the bottom line to avoid putting our science and practice out of financial reach, we must also watch the bottom line to be sure that it does not come to dictate the nature of the field as a basic scientific enterprise.

The emphasis on primary prevention, both in medicine and in health psychology, will likely increase, especially as medicine itself becomes more oriented toward preventive health activities. Although the incidence of heart disease, stroke, and infectious disease is decreasing, the incidence of cirrhosis, lung cancer, and automobile deaths is still increasing. Our high-frequency illnesses and growing health problems continue to be tied directly to behavioral pathogens or life-style factors (Matarazzo 1984). Consequently, there will be a continuing role for health psychologists in this endeavor. As medicine and health psychology pay increasing attention to risky health behaviors, the at-risk role may become a more important construct (e.g., Allen et al. 1987). Individuals who are identified early as at risk for particular disorders need to be trained in how to change any modifiable risk-relevant behaviors as well as in how to cope psychologically with their risk status.

Health psychologists may serve the effort toward primary prevention even further by refocusing health efforts on ways to keep people from developing problematic health habits initially. This trend represents part of an increasing emphasis within health psychology on optimizing health rather than on preventing illness (Evans 1988). At present, the concept of a healthy lifestyle has clear media appeal but less applicability to the general population. Because health habits are only modestly intercorrelated, bringing about integrated lifestyle change essential in the prevention of certain disorders, such as coronary artery disease, is difficult. At least some of the emphasis on health habit change should go to developing methods designed to modify more than one health habit simultaneously, such as smoking, diet control, and exercise among individuals at risk for CHD.

Because there is an applied component to the field, health psychology is necessarily responsive to social problems and issues, including those within medicine. One need not be clairvoyant to appreciate certain developments that can be expected as a result. Increasingly, the field will be called on to address concerns of aging, including the problems of living with chronic disability and disease, the problems of adjustment to bereavement and geographic relocation (Rowe and Kahn 1987), and psychological changes associated with aging.

This point illustrates a larger concern of health psychology—namely, the need to monitor changing patterns of illness and disease and their implications. To the extent that we can successfully anticipate health- and illness-related problems of the future, we can begin to anticipate now how we must prepare for them. With respect to the elderly, for example, we need to identify the kinds of living situations these increasing numbers of people will have and what kinds of economic resources will be available to them. These factors in turn will influence their health habits, their levels of health, and their need to seek treatment, all of which will require advance planning.

Foretelling the future is never an easy task. Some trends are obvious and have relatively clear implications for the field; others are not so easily anticipated, and thus their implications for health psychology are still elusive. The foregoing set of issues represents a mere fraction of the ways in which health psychology will be shaped and molded by the changing dimensions of medicine and medical practice.

Only one prediction regarding the future of health psychology can be generated with confidence—namely, that articles like this one will gradually disappear from the literature. The diversity of issues studied and the complexity and sophistication of the models and designs used to explore them will preclude simple statements about the major empirical directions and developments of the field. Asking, "What's new in health psychology?" will be like asking "What's new in psychology or in medicine?," queries that can be answered in only the most general and superficial ways. Those of us who have regularly taken the temperature and pulse of the field and confidently offered diagnoses and prognoses will be out of business, for whatever trends could be culled from the myriad and diverse directions in the field will be dwarfed in significance by the divergences.

II
Stress and the Environment

There is currently a great deal of interest in the ways environmental factors determine and influence our behavior. Appropriately, the selections in Part II deal with the ways in which two broad classes of environmental stimuli, physical and social, operate in the production of stress reactions.

In the selection by biologist Dubos (1965), the stresses of overpopulation are discussed. As may be seen from Dubos' analysis, much of our knowledge about the harmful effects of crowding is based on animal studies (e.g., Calhoun 1962) and may or may not be relevant to humans. Dubos makes an important distinction (*see also* Stokols 1978), one often overlooked by others, between population density and crowding. *Density* is defined in terms of objective physical or spatial conditions (e.g., number of people per acre), while *crowding* is a psychological or experiential state in which the individual is troubled by the spatial conditions. While density and crowding may go together sometimes, it is surely not always the case. A packed gymnasium is a highly dense setting, but one in which most do not feel crowded. Understanding the effects of "crowding" on human behavior is extremely difficult, especially in comparison with animals, because the effects are so strongly determined by cultural, social, contextual, and psychological factors. (For additional studies and information on crowding and stress, *see* Baum and Valins 1977; Freedman 1975; Holahan 1982.)

In our next selection, Baum (1987) compares and contrasts natural and humanmade disasters. Acute and chronic effects are detailed, and Baum argues that while humanmade (technological) and natural catastrophes may share many features, they nevertheless tend to be quite distinct on several dimensions. Furthermore, the literature on natural disasters may be inadequate for understanding the impact of technological disasters. For example, the Three Mile Island accident in 1979 (*see* Fleming et al. 1982) involved the release of unknown amounts of radioactive gases and required the evacuation of over 100,000 people. This technological catastrophe produced measurable levels of stress and psychological disturbances in many of the local residents. Some research has indicated that the stress reactions were not just short-lived but actually chronic, lasting for at least five years after the accident—a period of time that is relatively long compared with the typical impact of natural disasters. At any rate, technological disaster, especially when involving toxic substances, may produce stress effects that linger and impair for lengths of time we had not previously envisioned.

The study of stress and its relationship with work has been a lively topic. Much of this research has focused almost exclusively on factors in the workplace that may lead to stress in workers. For example, guided by the establishment of the National Institute for Occupational Safety and Health (NIOSH) in 1970, many researchers began looking for job or work conditions which created or contributed to stress in employees. Typical findings (e.g., *see* Hurrell 1987) have included factors such as: *job/task demands* (e.g., excessive workloads, shift work, lack of control), *organizational factors* (e.g., role ambiguity and conflict, management styles not allowing worker participation in decision making, interpersonal relationships with colleagues, supervisors, and subordinates), and *physical conditions* (e.g., excessive noise, heat or cold, inadequate lighting).

Our next selection, by Locke and Taylor (1990), looks at work and stress from a slightly different perspective. Locke and Taylor argue that individuals seek to derive certain values from work (e.g., material, a sense of purpose, enhancement of one's self-concept). When the work environment conflicts with the individual's attainment of these values, stress is experienced. For example, individuals who base their self-concepts on the attainment of more and more money may experience stress when they fail to get an expected promotion or raise, or when they realize that the attainment of monetary goals was achieved at the expense of other important values, such as family relationships.

Locke and Taylor go beyond an emphasis on environmental forces in the workplace causing stress to an emphasis on how individuals interact and cope with such environmental forces. Meaning in life depends greatly on the achievement of important values, many of which we seek in the workplace. "Stress, Coping, and the Meaning of Work" provides a thoughtful, as well as interesting, look at how the workplace can help or hinder the pursuit of such values.[1]

One of the strongest traditions in the stress field has been the study of relatively major life changes and their relationship with physical illness and psychological distress. For instance, Holmes and Rahe (1967b) reported evidence that illnesses of all kinds increase following periods of "stressful" life changes because of the major coping activities such changes require. Both positive *and* negative changes, such as marriage and divorce, are considered to be stressful by Holmes and Rahe because they all presumably demand adjustments by the individual to a new lifestyle or pattern. To measure these life changes, Holmes and Rahe (1967a) developed a self-administered questionnaire, the Social Readjustment Rating Scale (SRRS), which the person uses to report whether any of the indicated life changes have occurred during the past few months or years (usually the preceding one- or two-year period) (see table II.1). Each change is assigned a life change unit (LCU) score and a total LCU score for each person is then obtained. Numerous studies (e.g., Rahe 1972; Rahe, McKean, and Arthur 1967; *see* reviews by Holmes and Masuda 1974; Rahe 1974) have demonstrated that the likelihood of future illness (and even accidents and athletic injuries) increases when a person experiences a considerably high number of life change units within a relatively brief time.

Many have found this traditional approach to life change and disease to be inadequate. The reasons for this are varied but include several theoretical and methodological weaknesses (e.g., *see* Dohrenwend and Dohrenwend 1974, 1978; Rabkin and Struening 1976; Sarason, de Monchaux, and Hunt 1975). To illustrate, many people undergo considerable changes in their lives without becoming ill. Moreover, the relationship between life change and illness is statistically quite small. For these, and other reasons, some researchers have begun to explore daily hassles, or the "microstressors" of ordinary life (Rowlison and Felner 1988), and how they relate to health and illness.

Our next selection is an example of this relatively new perspective exploring everyday hassles and stress. Kanner et al. (1987) present a study of 12-year-olds and how hassles, and uplifts, affect their levels of anxiety, depression, and distress—and other variables as well. The authors define *hassles* as "the irritating, frustrating, distressing demands that to some degree characterize everyday transactions with the environment," and *uplifts* as "positive experiences such as the joy

TABLE II.1
The Social Readjustment Rating Scale

	Life Event	*Mean Value*
1.	Death of spouse	100
2.	Divorce	73
3.	Marital separation from mate	65
4.	Detention in jail or other institution	63
5.	Death of a close family member	63
6.	Major personal injury or illness	53
7.	Marriage	50
8.	Being fired at work	47
9.	Marital reconciliation with mate	45
10.	Retirement from work	45
11.	Major change in the health or behavior of a family member	44
12.	Pregnancy	40
13.	Sexual difficulties	39
14.	Gaining a new family member (e.g., through birth, adoption, oldster moving in, etc.)	39
15.	Major business readjustment (e.g., merger, reorganization, bankruptcy, etc.)	39
16.	Major change in financial state (e.g., a lot worse off or a lot better off than usual)	38
17.	Death of a close friend	37
18.	Changing to a different line of work	36
19.	Major change in the number of arguments with spouse (e.g., either a lot more or a lot less than usual regarding child-rearing, personal habits, etc.)	35
20.	Taking out a mortgage or loan for a major purchase (e.g., for a home, business, etc.)	31
21.	Foreclosure on a mortgage or loan	30
22.	Major change in responsibilities at work (e.g., promotion, demotion, lateral transfer)	29
23.	Son or daughter leaving home (e.g., marriage, attending college, etc.)	29
24.	Trouble with in-laws	29
25.	Outstanding personal achievement	28
26.	Wife beginning or ceasing work outside the home	26
27.	Beginning or ceasing formal schooling	26
28.	Major change in living conditions (e.g., building a new home, remodeling, deterioration of home or neighborhood)	25
29.	Revision of personal habits (dress, manners, associations, etc.)	24

	Life Event	*Mean Value*
30.	Trouble with the boss	23
31.	Major change in working hours or conditions	20
32.	Change in residence	20
33.	Changing to a new school	20
34.	Major change in usual type and/or amount of recreation	19
35.	Major change in church activities (e.g., a lot more or a lot less than usual)	19
36.	Major change in social activities (e.g., clubs, dancing, movies, visiting, etc.)	18
37.	Taking out a mortgage or loan for a lesser purchase (e.g., for a car, TV, freezer, etc.)	17
38.	Major change in sleeping habits (a lot more or a lot less sleep, or change in part of day when asleep)	16
39.	Major change in number of family get-togethers (e.g., a lot more or a lot less than usual)	15
40.	Major change in eating habits (a lot more or a lot less food intake, or very different meal hours or surroundings)	15
41.	Vacation	13
42.	Christmas	12
43.	Minor violations of the law (e.g., traffic tickets, jaywalking, disturbing the peace, etc.)	11

Source: T. H. Holmes and R. H. Rahe, "The Social Readjustment Rating Scale," *Journal of Psychosomatic Research* (1967), 11:213–18. Used with permission of Pergamon Press.

derived from manifestations of love, relief at hearing good news, the pleasure of a good night's rest, and so on" (see Lazarus and Folkman 1989, and the Children's Hassles and Uplifts Scales at the end of Kanner et al. 1987).

The 1987 article by Kanner and colleagues is of interest for several reasons. First, it not only examines the impact of daily hassles but also of uplifts. There has been a tendency to ignore uplifts in the literature and Kanner et al. attempt to remedy this omission. Second, only a few studies of daily hassles and uplifts have included children or adolescents. Thus, much of our information in this arena is based on studies of adults. Kanner et al. provide an excellent description of the hassles and uplifts characterizing a group of Bay Area adolescents. Third, they investigate gender differences with regard to hassles and uplifts. For example, they note that although the same number of hassles and uplifts were reported by adolescent girls and boys, girls reported the hassles as "bad" more often than did the boys. Moreover, for boys there was a negative correlation between uplifts and anxiety; while for girls, the correlation was positive.[2]

NOTES

1. *See* articles in this volume by Pearlin (1980) and Pelletier and Lutz (1988) for further discussions of work and stress.
2. For further research by these authors on uplifts and hassles and how they interact with perceived control, *see* Kanner and Feldman (n.d.).

5

The Living World

■

RENE DUBOS

The word "crowd" has unpleasant connotations. It evokes disease, pestilence, and group-generated attitudes often irrational and either too submissive or too aggressive. Congested cities call to mind unhealthy complexions and harassed behavior; city crowds are accused of accepting despotic power and of blindly engaging in acts of violence. In contrast, rural areas and small towns are thought to foster health and freedom. The legendary Arcadia and the Utopias of all times are imagined as comfortably populated by human beings enjoying vast horizons. The nature and history of man are far too complex, of course, to justify such generalizations, but there is some truth nevertheless in the belief that crowding generates problems of disease and behavior. However, these problems are poorly understood and their formulation is rendered even more difficult by a number of oversimplified and erroneous concepts inherited from the late nineteenth century.

During the Industrial Revolution, the crowding in tenements, factories, and offices was associated with tremendous increases in morbidity and mortality rates. Along with malnutrition, the various "fevers" were the most obvious causes of ill health. Epidemic outbreaks and chronic forms of microbial disease constituted the largest medical problems of the late nineteenth century because they were extremely prevalent, not only among the economically destitute but also among the more favored classes. The new science of microbiology that developed during that period provided a theory that appeared sufficient at first sight to explain the explosive spread of infection. The germ theory made it obvious that crowding facilitates the transfer of microbes from one person to another, and this led to the reasonable conclusion that the newly industrialized communities had been caught in a web of infection, resulting from the increase in human contacts.

The expression "crowd diseases" thus became, and has remained ever since, identified with a state of affairs conducive to the rapid spread of infective agents, particularly under unsanitary conditions. Epidemiologists have built their science on the hypothesis that the pattern of microbial diseases in a given community of animals or men is determined by the channels available for the spread of microbes. In reality, however, the rise and fall of animal populations, both in confined environments and in the field, present aspects that cannot be entirely accounted for by these classical concepts of epidemiology. The reason, as we shall now see, is that crowding has several independent effects. On the one hand, it facilitates the spread of infective agents; on the other hand, it also modifies the manner in which men and animals respond to the presence of these agents and thereby increases indirectly the prevalence and severity of microbial disease. In fact, crowding affects the response of the individual and social body, not only to infection, but also to most of life's stresses.

In many species, the numbers of animals increase continuously from year to year until a maximum population density is reached; then suddenly an enormous mortality descends. This phenomenon, known as "population crash," has long been assumed to be caused by epidemics corresponding to those which have been so destructive in the course of human history, for example plague or yellow fever. Indeed, several different kinds of pathogens have been found to attack animal populations at the time of the crash. Pasteurellae and salmonellae are among the bacterial organisms that used to be most commonly incriminated; two decades ago a particular strain of *Mycobacterium muris* (the vole bacillus), isolated from field mice in England, was thought for a while to be responsible for population crashes in these rodents. Now that viruses have taken the limelight from bacteria, they in turn have been made responsible for occurrences of widespread mortality in several animal species.

It has become apparent, however, that the relation between population crashes and microbial diseases is far less clear than was once thought. On the one hand, several different types of pathogens can be associated with crashes in a given animal species. On the other hand, there are certain crashes for which no pathogen has been found to account for the pathological picture. These puzzling observations have led to the theory that the microbial diseases associated with population crashes are but secondary phenomena, and that the primary cause is a metabolic disturbance. . . .

Food shortages, or at least nutritional deficiencies, were long considered as a probable cause of drastic population decline. It is well known, in fact, that when wild animals multiply without check under natural conditions they exhaust their food supply, lose weight, and bear fewer young; this occurs for example when their predators are eliminated. However, a poor nutritional state can hardly account alone for population crashes. Its effect is rather to limit reproduction, either by failure of conception or by abortion; the overall result is an automatic adjustment of population size to the food supply instead of a massive crash. In fact, drastic population declines commonly occur even when the food supply is abundant.

The trend during recent years has been to explain population crashes by a "shock disease" related in some obscure way to overactivity of the adreno-pituitary system. A notorious example of this type of crowd disease is the mass migration of the Norwegian lemmings from the mountaintops of Scandinavia. According to an ancient Norwegian belief, the lemmings periodically experience an irresistible "collective urge" either to commit suicide or to search for their ancestral home on the lost Atlantic continent, and consequently they march unswervingly into the sea. In reality, such migrations take place whenever the lemmings become overcrowded, a situation that occurs every third or fourth year, as each mating pair produces 13 to 16 young annually. The migration of Norwegian lemmings was so massive in 1960–61 that a steamer entering the Trondheim Fjord took one hour to pass through a two-mile-long pack of swimming and sinking rodents!

Although the nature of the initial stimulus that prompts the lemmings to migrate is not understood, crowding is almost certainly one of its aspects. As the rodents become more and more crowded they fall victim to a kind of mass psychosis. This results in a wild scrambling about that, contrary to legend, is not necessarily a march toward the sea but merely random movement. The animals die, not by drowning, but from metabolic derangements associated with stress; lesions are commonly found in the brain and the adrenals.

Profound changes have also been observed to occur at more or less regular intervals in the population of snowshoe hares. According to a classical description, these animals observed in Minnesota during periods of crash

> characteristically died in convulsive seizures with sudden onset, running movements, hind leg extension, retraction of the head and neck, and sudden leaps with clonic seizures upon alighting. Other animals were typically lethargic or comatose. . . . This syndrome was characterized primarily by decrease in liver glycogen and a hypoglycemia preceding death. Petechial or ecchymotic brain hemorrhages, and congestion and hemorrhage of the adrenals, thyroid, and kidneys were frequent findings. (Deevey 1960)

Interestingly enough, many of the signs and symptoms observed in wild animals dying during population crashes have been reproduced in the laboratory by subjecting experimental animals to crowding and other forms of stress. Voles placed for a few hours a day during a month in cages containing another pair of aggressive voles eventually died, but not of wounds. The main finding at necropsy was a marked increase in the weight of their adrenals and spleen and a decrease in the weight of the thymus. Similar findings have been made on captive and wild rats.

Crowding can act as a form of stress in most species of experimental animals. In chickens, mice, rats, and voles, it causes an enlargement of the adrenals chiefly through cellular hyperplasia in the cortical areas; in addition it interferes with both growth and reproductive function.

Crowding affects many other biological characteristics of animal population; for example, the reproducibility of the response to various abnormal states, such as barbiturate anesthesia, is affected by population density. The toxicity of central nervous system stimulants such as amphetamine is remarkably enhanced when the animals are placed in a crowded environment; central depressants protect to some degree against this aggregation effect. The experimental hypertension produced in rats bearing regenerating adrenals is increased by crowding, and coronary arteriosclerosis develops more rapidly and more intensely in chickens that are grouped than in animals kept isolated.

Field studies of voles in England have revealed the puzzling fact that their population continues to fall the year after the crash. It would appear, therefore, that the reduced viability responsible for the crash is transmitted from one generation to another. This finding is compatible with other observations which indicate that crowding of the mother affects the physical development and behavior of the offspring.

The response to almost any kind of stimulus can be modified by crowding, as is illustrated by the production of experimental granuloma. Cotton pellets impregnated with turpentine were introduced subcutaneously into groups of mice that were then either caged individually or in groups. The granulomas that developed in the grouped mice weighed 19 percent less than in the other animals, a result probably due to the fact that the greater adrenocortical activity in the grouped mice had exerted a suppressive effect on the inflammatory reaction.

It is probable that the effect of crowding on tissue response accounts for the decrease in resistance to infection. In order to put this hypothesis to the test, mice were infected with a standardized dose of *Trichinella* and then were either isolated in individual jars or caged in groups immediately after infection. When these mice were sacrificed fifteen days later, it was found that all the grouped animals had large numbers of worms (15 to 51) in their intestines, whereas only 3 out of 12 of the isolated animals showed any sign of infection. Although exposure to infection had been identical, crowding had therefore increased the ability of trichinella to invade the intestinal wall, probably by decreasing the inflammatory response to the parasite. Analogous observations have been made with regard to infantile diarrhea of mice. The incidence of clinical signs of this disease remains small or is nil when the population density in the animal room is low, but it increases as the colony approaches peak production. The infection is endemic in most colonies, but the disease does not become overt until the animals are crowded.

The grouping of several organisms of one given species has certainly many physiological consequences more subtle than those mentioned above. One such curious effect has been observed in male ducks kept constantly either in the dark or exposed to artificial light for periods of over two years. In both cases, these abnormal conditions of light exposure resulted in marked disturbances of the sexual cycles, which were no longer in phase with the seasonal rhythms. However, the animals within each group exhibited a remarkable synchronism of testicular evolution, thus revealing a "group effect" on sexual activity that was independent of light, of season, and of the presence of animals of the opposite sex.

Territoriality, Dominance, and Adaptation to Crowding

As we have just seen, the epidemiology of "crowd" diseases involves factors other than those affecting the spread of infectious agents. Association with other living things modifies the total response of the organism to the various environmental forces and thereby affects susceptibility to a multiplicity of noxious influences, including infection.

A quantitative statement of population density is not sufficient, however, to forecast the effects of crowding on human beings or animals. Even more important than numbers of specimens of a given species per unit area is the manner in which each particular person or animal responds to the other members of the group under a given set of conditions. The response to population density is determined in large part by the history of the group and of its individual members; furthermore, it may be favorable or unfavorable, depending upon the circumstances.

Many types of rodents, such as laboratory rats and mice, prefer to be somewhat crowded. In fact, individually housed rats and mice usually behave in a more "emotional" or "frightened" manner than their group-housed counterparts; they are also less able to adapt to a variety of experimental procedures such as food restriction, food selection, or cold stress. Isolated mice are less able than grouped mice to overcome the disturbances in intestinal ecology caused by anti-microbial drugs and other physiological disturbances (unpublished observations). . . . The practice of mutual cleaning accelerates wound healing in many animal species, and isolation has unfavorable effects on the behavior and personality structure of animals and man.

In most animal species, probably in all, each group develops a complex social organization based on territoriality and on a social hierarchy comprising subordinate and dominant members, the so-called pecking order. The place of each animal in the hierarchy is probably determined in part by anatomical and physiological endowments and in part by the history of the group. In any case, the behavioral differences that result from the pecking order eventually bring about anatomical and physiological differences far more profound than those initially present. For example, the dominant animals usually have larger adrenals than the subordinates and they grow more rapidly because they have more ready access to food. It appears also that in rhesus monkeys the young males issued from females with a high social rank have a better chance than other males to become dominant in the colony.

Under a given set of conditions, the relative rank of each individual animal is fairly predictable. Social competition is often restricted to the male sex, the reproductive fortunes of the female being determined by the status of the male which selects her. Females associated with subordinate males in experimental populations may entirely fail to reproduce. However, the pecking order is valid only for well-defined environmental conditions. For example, each canary bird is dominant in the region near its nest; and similarly chickens in their home yard win more combats than strangers to that yard. The successes of animals on their own territorial grounds bring to mind the better performance of baseball teams on their home fields.

Successful competition within the group naturally confers advantages. The despot has first choice with regard to food and mates, and its position may even increase its resistance to certain forms of stress such as infection. In a particular experiment involving tenches, one fish in the group was found to dominate the whole territory and to be the first one to feed. This dominance had such profound physiological consequences that when all the tenches were infected with trypanosomes, the infection disappeared first from the dominant fish. When this fish was removed from the tank, fighting started among those remaining; the fish that became dominant in the new grouping in its turn had first access to the food, and soon got rid of its trypanosome infection.

The phenomenon of dominance has a social meaning which transcends the advantages that it gives to the dominant individuals. Acceptance of the hierarchical order reduces fighting and other forms of social tensions and thus provides a stability that is beneficial to the group as a whole. In an undisturbed organized flock of chickens, for example, the individual animals peck each other less frequently and less violently, eat more, maintain weight better, and lay more eggs than do chickens in flocks undergoing social reorganization through removal of some animals or addition of new ones. Furthermore, the subordinate animals do not suffer as much as could be expected from their low rank in the pecking order. There is no direct competition for food or for mates in the well-organized group; the subordinates readily yield their place to the dominants at the feeding box; they exhibit no sexual interest, often behaving as if they were "socially castrated." Thus, the establishment of an accepted hierarchy in a stable group of animals almost eliminates the stresses of social tension and results in a kind of social homeostasis.

Needless to say, there are limits to the protective efficacy social organization can provide against the dangers created by high population density. Excessive crowding has deleterious effects even in the most gregarious rodents. When laboratory rats are allowed to multiply without restriction in a confined space, an excess of food being available at all times, they develop abnormal behavior with regard to mating, nest building, and care of the young as soon as the population becomes too dense. However, such conditions of life are extremely artificial. Under the usual conditions of rodent life in the wild, animals migrate or are killed when the population becomes too large for the amount of food available.

Although man is a gregarious animal, sudden increases in population density can be as dangerous for him as they are for animals. The biological disturbances created during the Industrial Revolution by lack of sanitation and by crowding in tenements and factories were aggravated by the fact that most members of the new labor class had immigrated from rural areas and were totally unadapted to urban life. In contrast, the world is now becoming more and more urbanized. Constant and intimate contact with hordes of human beings has come to constitute the "normal" way of life, and men have eagerly adjusted to it. This change has certainly brought about all kinds of phenotypic adaptations that are making it easier for urban man to respond successfully to situations that in the past constituted biological and emotional threats.

There may be here an analogy with the fact that domesticated animals do not respond to various types of threatening situations in the laboratory as do wild animals of the same or related species. In any case, the effects of crowding on modern urban man are certainly very different from those experienced by the farmer and his family when they were first and suddenly exposed a century ago to the city environment of industrialized societies.

The readiness with which man adapts to potentially dangerous situations makes it unwise to apply directly to human life the results of experiments designed to test the acute effects of crowding on animals. Under normal circumstances, the dangerous consequences of crowding are mollified by a multiplicity of biological and social adaptations. In fact, crowding per se, i.e., population density, is probably far less important in the long run even in animals than is the intensity of the social conflicts, or the relative peace achieved after social adjustments have been made. As already mentioned, animal populations in which status differences are clearly established are likely to reach a greater size than those in which differences in rank are less well defined.

Little is known concerning the density of population or the intensity of stimulation that is optimum in the long run for the body and the mind of man. Crowding is a relative term. The biological significance of population density must be evaluated in the light of the past experience of the group concerned, because this experience conditions the manner in which each of its members responds to the others as well as to environmental stimuli and trauma.

Laying claim to a territory and maintaining a certain distance from one's fellow are probably as real biological needs in man as they are in animals, but their expressions are culturally conditioned. The proper distance between persons in a group varies from culture to culture. People reared in cultures where the proper distance is short appear "pushy" to those coming from social groups where propriety demands greater physical separation. In contrast, the latter will appear to the former as behaving in a cold, aloof, withdrawn, and standoffish manner. Although social anthropologists have not yet adequately explained the origin of these differences, they have provided evidence that ignorance of them in human relations or in the design of dwellings and hospitals can have serious social and pathological consequences.

The problems posed by crowding in human populations are thus more complex than those which exist in animal populations because they are so profoundly conditioned by social and cultural determinants. Indeed, there is probably no aspect of human life for which it is easier to agree with Ortega y Gasset that "man has no nature. What he has is a history." Most experimental biologists are inclined to scorn discussions of mob psychology and related problems because they feel that the time is not yet ripe for scientific studies on the mechanisms of collective behavior. Yet the phrase "mob psychology" serves at least to emphasize that the response of human beings to any situation is profoundly influenced by the structure of the social environment.

The numerous outbreaks of dancing manias that occurred in Europe from the fourteenth to sixteenth century constitute a picturesque illustration of abnormal collective behavior; such an event was witnessed by Breughel the Elder and became the subject of one of his most famous paintings, *The Saint Vitus Dancers,* now in Vienna. Even today, revivalists, tremblers, and shakers often outdo the feats of the medieval performers during the dancing manias. And millions of people can still be collectively bewitched by the antics of a Hitler or other self-proclaimed prophet, to whom they yield body and soul. What happens in the mind of man is always reflected in the diseases of his body. The epidemiology of crowd diseases cannot be completely understood without knowledge of mob psychology.

REFERENCES

Allee (1951); Barnett (1960, 1963, 1964); Barrow (1955); Benoit, Assenmacher, and Brard (1955, 1956); Bernardis and Skelton (1963); Bronson and Eleftheriou (1965a, 1965b); Calhoun (1949, 1962); Carpenter (1958); Chitty (1958); Christian and Davis (1956); Christian, Flyger, and Davis (1960); Christian and Williamson (1958); Curry-Lindahl (1963); Davis and Read (1958); Deevey

(1960); Ellis and Free (1964); Elton (1958); Etkin (1964); Flickinger and Ratcliffe (1961); Greenwood (1935); Hall (1959, 1964); Hediger (1950); Hinde (1960); Keeley (1962); Koford (1963); Lasagna (1962); Mackintosh (1962); McDonald, Stern, and Hahn (1963); McKissick, Flickinger, and Ratcliffe (1961); Mason (1959); Siegal (1959); Thiessen (1963); Tinbergen (1953); Washburn and Devore (1961); Welty (1957); Zeuner (1963).

6

Toxins, Technology, and Natural Disasters

■

ANDREW BAUM

Research on disasters has been uneven. One reason for this is that the study of disasters is complicated by methodological problems associated with field research that are exacerbated, in part, by the nature of disaster events. Baseline data are rarely available; because disasters are unpredictable and infrequent in any one locale, assessment of preimpact behavior and health is difficult. Large prospective study of an area that subsequently experiences a disaster can provide predisaster data when circumstances permit, but this is unusual (e.g., Robins et al. 1986). Assessments of predisaster mental and physical health can be made by assessing subjects' medical records, but data in these files are often incomplete and difficult to use (Baum et al. 1986). Lack of preimpact data increases the need for adequate control groups, but this too can be problematic. Finding individuals who are comparable to victims but unaffected by the disaster can be difficult, and more often research-

The author would like to thank India Fleming, Martha M. Gisriel, and Joan Ballard for their help in preparing this chapter.

ers must settle for comparisons of victimized and less affected groups. Selection of subjects is also difficult, because many traditional methods of sampling to ensure representativeness or eliminate potential biases are often inappropriate or impossible (Drabek 1970).

When acute response is of interest, it is necessary to begin data collection soon after the event occurs. Funding structures typically do not allow for rapid funding of research, and maintenance of quick-response teams that can get to an affected area quickly requires conditional funding or strong institutional support. When researchers arrive in disaster areas, they may find a chaotic environment in which normal amenities are not available. Telephone surveys are not effective when large numbers of victims are made homeless and have no access to a phone, and face-to-face interviews must be conducted under conditions of disruption and ongoing activity. In addition, temporary "removal" of subjects from a disaster for the purposes of data collection will alter their experience of the disaster, resulting in potential misinterpretation of findings.

Most studies of disaster have relied on descriptive data, and the study of response was begun soon after the event (Drabek 1970). Problems with sampling, numbers of subjects, consistency of measures, and inclusion of appropriate control groups are common. Many studies have focused on organizational or social group effects; fewer have considered individual response or both together. Research has taken (1) the approach of clinical-descriptive studies, documenting the nature of symptoms of disaster victims; (2) an epidemiological orientation in which rates of impairment and disasters following a disaster are measured; and (3) a quasi-experimental field research approach focusing on psychological variables as mediators of response and subsequent effects. The first and second approaches do not typically consider individual differences in stress and experience (Gleser, Green, and Winget 1981). Some laboratory simulations of "disaster exercises" have been reported but have not been frequent (Drabek 1970). Studies of long-term response following a disaster and investigations of chronic physical and mental health effects of disasters are less common than are examinations of short-term effects and mental health consequences (e.g., Trainer and Bolin 1976). Follow-up and longitudinal studies of disaster impact have not been reported very often, and when they have been done, their results have often been difficult to interpret.

In this chapter, methodological problems and limitations will not specifically be considered. Almost all of the studies reported suffer from one or more of the problems already noted, and this accounts for some inconsistencies among studies and for limits on conclusions from the extant literature (*see* Green 1982). Regardless, much can be learned about responses to extreme stress and victimization by evaluating this literature and relating it to research on related issues or stressors.

In this chapter, I will discuss issues concerning definition and characterization of disasters, typical responses to such disasters, and short- and long-term effects of victimization by disaster. I will also briefly examine differences across disasters that allow prediction of trauma or health consequences, including whether a disaster is caused by natural or human acts.

Space limitations do not permit a complete examination of victimization by disaster. Consequently, a number of variables that mediate disaster response will not be considered. Children, who are often affected by disaster, will not be discussed in detail, and sex differences in response, for which findings are inconsistent, will not be systematically considered either. Similarly, the role of adult age, predisposition to distress, and other demographic factors will not be discussed. Recognizing that these factors are important personal determinants of disaster response, I will emphasize psychological variables and factors related to individuals' responses and victimization and mood, behavior, and health outcomes. Other characteristics and levels of analysis that will not be covered here are not necessarily less important or meaningful but rather are not central to my focus here.

The Nature of Disaster

Disasters may be viewed and analyzed on several levels. On the one hand, they are events that vary with the medium in which they occur. Geophysical events, climatic or meteorological events, technological events, or biological events all may be distinguished one from another (e.g., earthquakes from drought, tornadoes from nuclear accidents or plague, and so on). On the other hand, disasters may also be political or economic events, influencing hierarchical organization and upsetting economic balances. As social events, they may cause social disruption, disorganization, and massive migration. As psychological events, they may produce trauma, fear, stress, and shock. The nature of disaster includes all of these levels of analysis, each interacting with the others to produce an event and its impact.

Because of this complexity, disasters are hard to define. There are essential characteristics, but the precise mix of these factors that make an event a disaster are hard to pin down. This is particularly frustrating because most of us know well what is a disaster and what is not. Most cases can clearly be called either disasters or not; the close calls or difficult distinctions are events where there are enough reasons to call something a disaster although it does not easily fit into one or another category.

For the most part, laypeople and scientists alike define disasters in terms of the peculiar nature of an event, the impact of the event, and the way in which victims respond. Earthquakes and tornadoes are almost automatically termed disasters, even though the destructiveness and scope of their impacts may vary tremendously. On the other hand, contamination of drinking water or release of radiation may not be as readily labeled as a disaster. If an event is destructive, it is often called a disaster, although events that cause no destruction may be disastrous as well. In addition, responses to disasters are as numerous as types of disaster events, ranging from shock and dazed disbelief to purposive and heroic activity.

The key to understanding disasters, including events and their impact, is to identify the conditions under which different responses occur. In this section of this chapter I discuss definitions, characteristics, and responses to disasters, to provide a basis for understanding psychological implications of disaster and predicting its short- and long-term consequences.

Defining Disaster

The concept of *disaster* includes many attributions or assumptions, almost all of which are negative. Defining it has proved difficult. Some people seemingly have equated it with its effects on individuals, including death, damage, loss, disruption, loss of control, and trauma. In addition, the nature of the event is often part of the picture—sudden, enormously powerful, and overwhelming events are often part of defining a disaster. Lastly, patterns of response to disaster are often included in concepts of disaster, including panic and dazed behavior of some victims, and social coalescence and heroic responses by other victims. However, the lack of preciseness of definitions of disaster is highlighted by the difficulty one might have in determining whether something is a disaster or not. How much damage is needed to make a storm a disaster? Is a hurricane necessarily a disaster, even if its impact is limited? Was the accident at Three Mile Island a disaster, even though little physical damage occurred?

Several approaches to these definitional problems have been taken.

Some researchers (e.g., McLuckie 1975) separate the disaster agent or event from the disaster itself, considering the former to be the physical event and the latter to be its impact. Emergency periods following an event and its immediate impact have been distinguished from the disaster events or impact. Greater emphasis appears to be on the effects of the disaster event, as reflected by the Federal Emergency Management Agency's (1984) definition of disaster:

> A major disaster is defined . . . as any hurricane, tornado, storm, flood, high water, wind-driven water, tidal wave, tsunami, earthquake, volcanic eruption, landslide, mudslide, snowstorm, drought, fire, explosion, or other catastrophe . . . which, in the determination of the President, causes damage of sufficient severity and magnitude to warrant major disaster assistance above and beyond . . . available resources of States, local governments, and private relief organizations in alleviating the damage, loss, hardship or suffering caused by a disaster. (p. 1)

In other words, a disaster is defined in terms of the damage it causes. Of course, this definition is constrained by its purpose; to regulate federal disaster assistance, the government must provide guidelines for granting aid rather than trying to distinguish and explain various aspects of these events. However, the emphasis on damage—the effects of the disaster—is not simply a matter of economics and the law; it reflects a pervasive social expectation or definition and emphasis on the immediate havoc associated with a disaster. What makes a disaster a disaster is the extent of damage done.

Perhaps the most obvious way to define a disaster is to equate it with particular events or physical agents. Hurricanes, fires, tornadoes, and the like are disasters that fall under such a scheme, equating disaster with their potential destructiveness and disruptions. Dynes (1970) called these events *disaster agents,* separating them from the effects of the event, such as social disruption, loss, or terror. Defining a disaster in terms of its agent, however, seems shortsighted; without considering the impact, such a definition becomes hard to defend. What characteristics of a potential event make it a disaster? What about a storm that ravages an area where nothing can be or is damaged? Clearly, something more is needed.

One solution is to consider the impact of an event, that is, if the event is sufficient to produce widespread destruction, disruption, or loss of life. Thus, a rainstorm can become a disaster if it causes flooding that, in turn, causes great destruction. Under normal conditions, however, it is simply a rainstorm. What criteria are to be used and how much destruction or death is necessary before something becomes a disaster? Though some models use benchmarks for such a determination, the complexity of assessing impact suggests that this will not be adequate. Is an event that causes great social disruption or individual fear and stress a disaster even if there is no visible damage? Barkun (1974) suggests that the answer is yes: "Disaster means damage—physical, social, and psychological" (p. 72).

If one considers impact alone—that is, whether there is damage of one sort or another—one runs the risk of including so many different events and situations that classification as a disaster loses some of its meaning. The nature of the agent must also be considered, but not exclusively. Thus, damage caused by any sudden, powerful event that is beyond the realm of everyday experience could be considered a disaster, although this would include rape, assault, and other individual stressors, as well as cataclysmic events that are clearly not what most people mean by disaster. To this definition, then, one might add the idea of scope; to be a disaster, a situation must involve a substantial proportion of the people in a community or area. Quarantelli (1985) has suggested that the degree of social disruption can be used to define disasters. Magnitude of impact is still the crucial parameter, but instead of focusing on loss of life or property, this approach considers effects on group and community functioning.

> Thus, if there is considerable destruction of material goods and/or a relatively large number of deaths or injuries, the event is viewed as a disaster. It is a disaster not because of the physical impact per se, but because of the assumed social consequences of the physical happenings. (p. 46)

This criterion adds teeth to previous definitions, because it includes only those events and impacts that are sufficient to produce social dysfunction whether or not physical damage occurs.

Quarantelli (1985) raises another interesting issue: What about events that cause little disruption but great disfigurement of the environment or those that engender social disorganization in the absence of any physical impact at all? For example, he points out that the major New Madrid earthquake of 1811–1812 had "massive physical effects on the topography of the region" (p. 47), but it is not often considered a disaster because few people lived in the region and relatively few were affected. Or, alternatively, what about an event that never materializes but causes social disorganization anyway? False rumors about a dam failure and impending flood produced social effects that were comparable to those associated with an actual dam break (Danzig, Thayer, and Galanter 1958; Golec 1980). These instances challenge formal definitions of disaster and suggest that, at some point, the search for specific and distinctive conceptualizations may cease to be useful.

Another approach to the definition of disasters is to consider disaster as a subordinate event, one of a type of events similar to Lazarus and Cohen's (1977) inclusion of disaster in their description of cataclysmic events. Disaster may also be viewed as a special case of crisis or collective stress situation (e.g., Barton 1970; Drabek and Haas 1970). In this mode, disaster is seen as an instance in which demands posed by a crisis situation exceed the resources, capabilities, and preparations for a response (Quarantelli 1985). This type of definition avoids anchoring a definition in any one or a combination of disaster characteristics; it matters little whether the event is sudden or occurs gradually, whether it is acute or chronic, or whether it causes loss or not, if it poses threats or demands beyond the individual's or group's ability to cope. These characteristics may affect the overall level of demand posed by a crisis, because sudden or long-term conditions may be more likely to overwhelm immediate resistance capabilities. By focusing on psychological, behavioral, and social responses, this conceptualization is more sensitive to varying perceptions of events and crises. Furthermore, because crises are consensual events, this concept eliminates events that are more open to debate or conflict, such as civil disturbances (Quarantelli 1985).

Lazarus and Cohen (1977) included disasters as one of several cataclysmic events—stressors characterized by great power, sudden onset, excessive demands on individual coping, and large scope (affecting many people). These events are generally outside the realm of normal, everyday experience, beyond the immediate control of victims, and considered to be as close to universally stressful as events generally can be. Also included in this class of stressors are humanmade catastrophes such as war, bombings, imprisonment, and relocation. Though not explicitly addressed in this definition, events such as the Three Mile Island accident would probably fall in this class because the scope, impact on local and worldwide communities, suddenness, unique nature, and lack of controllability are comparable with other cataclysmic events.

Cataclysmic events, then, are defined in terms of a number of characteristics; if an event exhibits enough of these characteristics, it may be considered cataclysmic, and expectations are affected accordingly. The effects of the event are only part of this conceptualization, because the nature of the event and its interpretation by potential victims are also crucial. Disasters share certain characteristics with these other events.

Characterization of disasters as stressful events has been a theme in several recent discussions of disaster (e.g., Baum and Davidson 1985; Warheit 1985). By viewing disasters in this context, one can use research and theory on stress to understand and predict the effects of disasters. The degree to which the characteristics of a disaster cause stress may be used as an index of impact or a predictor of mental health consequences, and the nature of the victimized population may be used as a mediator of stress that is produced in individuals. Thus, stress levels may increase if an event occurs suddenly, but if a community is prepared in advance, the stressful impact may be blunted. Similarly, stress levels may be higher when an event poses serious and immediate threats to life and property than when it does not, but if clear evacuation orders are issued and followed, this may not actually occur. The stressfulness of a disaster and, hence, its potential mental health effects are determined by an array of characteristics of the disaster event, the victimized population, and the individuals involved.

Disaster Characteristics

Much research has focused on identifying characteristics of the event or impact that predict mood and behavior change. In a paper relating disaster characteristics to trauma potential, Bolin (1985) listed several parameters that together define disaster impact. Some are related to the effects of the disaster event rather than the event itself: the degree to which victims are exposed to terror and horror is an important determinant of disaster impact. Terror is thought to be related to the proximity of victims to the "raw physical effects" of the disaster—the destruction of homes, collapse of buildings or bridges, or destruction of roads or fields by a flash flood. Horror, defined as witnessing death or dealing with dead or dying victims, is possible whenever death, injury, or disfigurement is involved.

Bolin (1985) discussed the duration of the event as a characteristic that also defines outcomes. He noted that the duration of the event impact must also be considered, and he suggested that longer duration of impact is associated with more severe consequences. Intensity must also be considered, as events of shorter duration are often more intense, and therefore may have major effects as well. The unexpectedness of a disaster event, a joint function of the nature of the event and the community's preparedness and prediction capabilities, reflects an interaction of event and situational characteristics. Similarly, the degree of the threat posed, affected by physical conditions and subjective risk assessments, may be seen as a product of enduring and more transient conditions. Generally speaking, the greater the degree to which these characteristics are present in a disaster, the greater the acute and chronic psychological effects.

Davidson and I (1985) presented a similar discussion of disaster characteristics, describing them in terms of potential for stress experience, independent of destruction and loss of life or property. Duration of the event or impact, the speed with which the event subsides and recovery can proceed, the extent of impact, and the predictability and controllability of the event and its impact are seen as contributing to stress and consequences of a disaster. Quarantelli (1985) also lists a number of characteristics of disasters that help to define them. They include the proportion of the involved population that is victimized, the duration of impact, suddenness, predictability, unfamiliarity, depth of involvement of the victimized population, and the likelihood of recurrence.

Warning is another characteristic of a disaster situation that appears to mediate its impact. Fritz and Marks (1954) suggested that a lack of warning can increase the impact of a disaster. However, being warned of an impending disaster does not ensure minimization of consequences. The effectiveness of the warning system, the preparedness of a community, and other factors intervene between the issuance and benefits of alerting news.

This was made clear in a study of response to warnings of a flood (Drabek and Stephenson 1971). The effectiveness of repeated warnings in getting people to evacuate was undermined by several factors. If families were separated at the time of warning, they tended to be more concerned with finding each other than with evacuation. In addition, unless a direct order to evacuate was heard, people sought confirmation of the danger and the need to leave. Some simply continued what they were doing, and overall there was a great deal of skepticism reported. Family and friends were important sources of confirmation or denial of the threat. Although the media actually notified the most people, it was the least effective in producing appropriate responses. Warnings from friends and relatives were far more effective. Similarly, response to hurricane warnings about several different hurricanes was affected by a number of variables; the source of the warning had less effect on response than did expectations of damage, confidence in weather forecasting, and site characteristics (Baker 1979).

Fritz and Marks (1954) also discussed two characteristics of a disaster situation that appeared to be associated with emotional disturbances. Consistent with other studies suggesting the primacy of concern for family members, Fritz and Marks suggested that separation of family members during a disaster engendered acute anxiety about each other's welfare. In addition, they found that horror, the trauma of witnessing death or exposure to the dead and badly injured, exacerbated emotional problems.

The analysis of disasters for trauma potential and their classification as stressful events, whether on an individual or collective basis, have identified a number of event and victim characteristics that may be associated with subsequent disruption and pathology. The extent of the horror or terror experienced appears to contribute to trauma, as do the suddenness, scope, and intensity of the event, the preparedness of the victims, the extent of warnings, and the familiarity of victims with the type of disaster event. Low points, when the worst has passed, appear to be important; if there is no clear low point, consequences may become chronic or may increase. Those characteristics that carry some psychological meaning appear to be more important than those with less experiential relevance; whether the event was a hurricane or a tornado appears to be less important in determining social and psychophysiological effects than are characteristics relating more directly to how individuals experience these events. Thus, Trainer and Bolin (1976) defined disasters almost exclusively in terms of psychologically relevant characteristics: disasters are abrupt, unanticipated events that produce severe disruption and a need for relocation.

Acute Response to Disasters

Research has produced varying findings with respect to effects of disasters on behavior and mental health. Some studies suggest that disasters result in profound disorganization and stress that may lead to continuing disturbance, whereas other studies suggest that psychological effects are acute and dissipate rapidly after the danger has passed. In such cases, chronic stress or psychiatric impairment is rare and may be limited to those victims with prior histories of psychological vulnerability or disturbance (e.g., Kardiner et al. 1945). At a larger community level, some studies have found that overall effects of disaster may be positive, because the acute response includes increased social cohesiveness within local groups and consequent social stability over the recovery period. Clearly, these findings are inconsistent and require explanation. Why do some studies find pervasive negative effects of victimization by disaster, whereas others find only benefits?

Warheit (1985) argued that the lack of clear conceptual frameworks to guide research is partly responsible for such findings. The events that are classified as disasters are very different, ranging from natural calamities associated with earthquakes and storms to humanmade events such as nuclear and toxic waste accidents, fires, and aircraft disasters. By attempting to group all of these events together without adequate understanding of the different demands and threats they pose, researchers have almost assured some degree of inconsistency.

Individual Response

The immediate response of individuals to natural disaster is often withdrawal, as if victims are overwhelmed and numbed by the calamity that has befallen them. The *disaster syndrome,* characterized by dazed behavior and psychic detachment, is frequently followed by shock, a sense of loss, anxiety, and in some cases, activity directed toward saving lives or restoring property to its former state. Tyhurst (1951) suggested that most victims show some stunned behavior but are not profoundly affected by the disaster, whereas 10 to 25 percent manifest "inappropriate" responses, including hysteria and paralyzing anxiety. Most victims appear to recover fairly quickly, though some may continue to wander about dazed and withdrawn. In a study of victims of a cyclone, Crawshaw (1963) reported that initial responses were characterized by shock, followed by denial, anger, and depression. Menninger (1952), reporting on response immediately after flooding in Topeka, Kansas, observed the inhabitants' disbelief (many did not leave their homes and subsequently required rescue), apathy, grief, and a desire to talk about the experience. The relief gained from talking about a disaster experience has been linked to affiliative tendencies (Hoyt and Raven 1973; Strumpfer 1970).

Fritz and Marks (1954) reviewed the effects of several disasters, including an airplane crash into a crowd of air show spectators, a series of explosions and fires, a coal mine explosion, three airplane crashes occurring within two months of one another in the same area, a tornado, and an earthquake. Based on interviews, studies of these events suggested that panic was rare and was caused primarily by an immediate threat coupled with the belief that escape was possible. However, response to the disasters was highly variable; about a third of the victims exhibited agitated but controlled behavior, less than 10 percent exhibited agitated behavior that was out of control, and a few showed signs of shock or of calm, unexcited behavior. Some victims were confused and disorganized, whereas others responded purposively. Some evidence of acute emotional and somatic responses was also reported.

Observations of responses to an earthquake in Managua suggested that early response may not be effective. Initial responses consisted of spontaneous efforts to assess effects and locate and rescue family, friends, and neighbors, but looting was widespread, and few attempts were made to limit secondary effects such as putting out fires, shutting down water mains, and so on (Kates et al. 1973). Groups that emerged were largely focused on local ties, and purposive responses aimed at regaining some semblance of normalcy were late in developing.

Several studies have shown that immediate response to disaster is not necessarily aimless or nonproductive. Bowman (1964) observed the behavior of mental patients after an earthquake near Anchorage, Alaska, on Good Friday, 1964. Contrary to Bowman's expectations, the patients' initial response was positive; wanting to help with problems that arose, the patients displayed "a stimulation of all the personnel, a feeling of unity, a desire to be helpful, and a degree of cooperation which I only wish it were possible to have at all times" (p. 314). Some felt trapped and isolated; others froze, were dazed, or ended up in a stupor, but no single response characterized the behavior among these patients after the earthquake.

Responses of Organizations

Disasters can disrupt organizations and communities as well as families and individuals, and, in some cases, the functions once performed by larger groups are supported by emergent small groups of victims. For example, one of the more serious problems in disasters is coordination of various organizations and relief efforts. Despite the need for centrality of coordination in successful disaster management, organizations are often hesitant to assume responsibility for overall coordination, and there is frequently an "atomization of the community into uncoordinated organizations and isolated islands of activity" (Loomis 1960:424). This atomization process and the lack of overall coordination apparently promote the emergence of cohesive local groups who must assume responsibility for those functions not being met by formal organizations. A lapse of authority also contributes to the development of these groups. Frequently, there is ambiguity regarding who has legitimate authority, and this is compounded by the tendency of leaders to avoid the assumption of responsibility early in a disaster (Loomis 1960).

Positive social response during or immediately after a disaster event also appears to be influenced by the needs of the community. When destruction is so vast that rescue teams and official relief efforts cannot cover all needs, locally based groups may emerge to fill the void. Thus, the demands created by the disaster may require some informal group response.

When these relief efforts are adequate, those groups not involved in direct rescue efforts may exhibit more negative reactions. For example, Weil and Dunsworth (1958), reporting on reactions to an explosion and partial collapse of a coal mine in Springhill, Nova Scotia, noted that while formal rescue efforts continued, the responses of local residents ranged from initial panic, grief, and anxiety to hope and euphoria when some trapped miners made their way to safety, and later changed to stress, grief, and fatigue as the rescue attempt was finally abandoned. The development of groups in the wake of disaster may support or facilitate coping, by allowing victims to respond in a meaningful way and compare their reactions with those of other victims, while they make sense of and adjust to the event.

The notion that disasters are often met not by panic or competition for scarce resources and looting but rather by rescue attempts, prosocial behavior, and group formation, runs counter to most people's general ideas of what happens during a disaster (Goltz 1985). Data from surveys of the public suggest that people believe that flight and incapacitating trauma are common (Wengner et al. 1975), and that most of the information they have about disasters comes from media coverage (Turner, et al. 1979; Wengner et al. 1975). It is tempting to attribute the more negative view of breakdown and chaos to media accounts, although recent data suggest that this may be inaccurate (Goltz 1985). Regardless, severe disorganization does not usually occur, although in some cases the prosocial responses discussed by Quarantelli and Dynes (1972) do not materialize.

Effects of Natural Disasters

There is a wide range of disaster effects, varying in level of impact as well as duration, intensity, and the like. Communities, organizations, families, and individuals are affected, and each set of effects occurs in the context of these other levels. Effects on individuals, for example, are affected and influence effects on families and communities. The focus here is on individual effects—changes in health and well-being—rather than on social and organizational sequelae. Although conclusions about mental health consequences of a disaster are difficult to draw because studies have used widely varying measures of effects, it is clear that the consequences are joint products of the overall impact of the disaster and premorbid individual vulnerability. In the context of emergent disaster groups, a sense of normalcy may quickly be reestablished and psychological disturbance minimized. In such cases, effects of the disaster would be modest and short-lived. For the purposes of this review, effects discussed here are divided into acute (lasting a year or so after the event) and chronic effects.

Acute Effects

Bennet (1970) reported on consequences of flooding due to heavy rainfall in Bristol, England. On the one hand, this event was seen as mild; "compared with earthquakes, tornadoes, and other natural disasters of fiercer climates, such flooding will seem trivial" (p. 454). However, some evidence of the flood's long-term effects was noted. Flood victims and other residents whose homes were not flooded were interviewed twice, the first time within two weeks of the flood and the second time, one year later. Approximately 33 percent of the flood victims reported development of psychological or physical symptoms, compared with less than 20 percent of the nonvictims. Rate of physician visits increased among flood victims relative to nonvictims, and hospital referrals more than doubled among victims after the flood. Mortality also increased among victims, but not in the rest of Bristol, and, in general, the health of victims was worse one year after the flood than was that of nonvictims. The increase in mortality was seen as being the result of exacerbated health problems that were present before the flood; "death can be *hastened* by the experience of having been flooded rather than somehow being caused by it" (p. 457).

A study of victims of flooding in Brisbane, Australia, also found evidence of mental health effects up to one year after the disaster (Abrahams et al. 1976). Though relatively few lives were lost, damage was extensive and more than 6,000 households were flooded. Comparison of 695 flood victims with 507 nonvictims indicated that the former were more likely to visit a physician during the year following the disaster. The number of psychological disturbances and reports of symptoms also increased among flood victims relative to the control group, although no differences in postdisaster mortality were found. Reporting on the same flood, Price (1978) indicated that 76 percent of the flood victims reported one or more psychiatric symptoms during the year after the disaster, whereas only 38 percent of the control subjects reported any symptoms.

Melick (1976) reported a three-year follow-up study of victims of flooding in Pennsylvania in the wake of Hurricane Agnes. Approximately 31 per cent of subjects who had not been flooded and 46 percent of those who had been flooded reported that someone in their immediate family had experienced distress as a result of the disaster, men expressing more distress than women. However, this distress did not appear to last long; only about one-third of those reporting distress indicated that it lasted 9 months or more, and the mean duration of postflood distress was 6 months. No differences were found between flooded and nonflooded groups for number, type, or duration of illnesses. Nearly half of the flood victims reported that they believed that the flood had affected their health, compared with only 6 percent of the nonvictim group.

Logue and Hansen (1980) compared 29 women from this same flooded area who later became hypertensive with 29 women from the same area who did not develop high blood pressure. Cases were matched on age- and weight-related variables and proved comparable on a range of social and personal characteristics. Retrospective reports of experience following the flood showed that women who became hypertensive reported greater perceived property loss, financial problems, alcohol use, and distress during recovery than did respondents who had not developed hypertension. Furthermore, hypertensive individuals were more likely to continue to be bothered by thoughts of the flood five years later and reported greater somatic distress and anxiety than did flood victims who had not become hypertensive. The data were interpreted as evidence of "a threefold risk of hypertension" (Logue and Hansen 1980:33) among flood victims who suffered substantial property loss (more than $30,000), although victims' experiences during the postflood recovery period were also associated with long-term health consequences. Other studies of the flooding in the wake of Hurricane Agnes suggest that, although victims were distressed initially, for the most part, they had adjusted to the disaster after a year or so (Logue, Hansen, and Struening 1979; Poulshock and Cohen 1975).

Further evidence of relatively mild mental health effects of a natural disaster is reported by Penick, Powell, and Sieck (1976). Studying 26 victims of a tornado that struck Joplin, Missouri (which killed 2, injured 87, and caused property damage for more than half of the residents), they found that the problems most likely to be reported concerned disruption of normal activities. Five months after the tornado, problems were substantially reduced; three-quarters of those interviewed reported no increase in strain and tension among adults in the household, and, although there was somewhat more reporting of psychiatric problems five months after the storm than there had been before it, the shift was small and involved few respondents. The authors interpreted their findings as indicating that victims of natural disasters "do not typically experience serious emotional problems which are incapacitating" (p. 67). Another study of a destructive tornado impact also suggested that changes in mental health occurred over the six months following the disaster, but that the effects were relatively mild (Taylor, Ross, and Quarantelli 1976).

A study of the consequences of evacuation during Cyclone Tracy, which devastated Darwin, Australia, on Christmas Day, 1974, provides limited evidence of lasting effects of disaster and disruption (Milne 1977). The storm destroyed more than half of the homes in Darwin, and about 50 people were killed. Interviews of residents who did not evacuate, residents who evacuated and later returned, and residents who left and did not return were conducted 7–10 months after the storm. Those who evacuated but did not return were most affected during the disaster event, whereas those who did not evacuate reported the least stress, injury, and loss during the storm. Nearly 33 percent of the women who left but did not return experienced postdisaster emotional disorders, compared with about 11 percent of those who stayed and 12 percent of those who evacuated and returned. Relatively few injuries or illnesses after the storm were reported by any subjects, and differences in the use of alcohol, cigarettes, and analgesics were small. Little evidence of increases in psychosomatic complaints after the storm were found, and those complaints that were discovered may have been related to relocation rather than to the disaster itself.

These findings were consistent with those of Parker (1977), who examined psychiatric cases after the same cyclone occurred. Immediately after the disaster, more than 50 percent of the subjects exhibited distress, although this dropped to 22 percent a little more than a year later.

Research on the effects of the Mount Saint Helens volcanic eruption in 1980 has suggested that this type of natural disaster can also have negative effects on affected area residents. Adams and Adams (1984) reported posteruption increases in services to the mentally ill, emergency room visits, arrests, and domestic violence, which suggested that the eruption and subsequent ashfall were stressful. Other studies also indicate that the incident was associated with stress, although this effect may have been short-lived (e.g., Leik et al. 1982; Murphy 1985). After a year, Shore, Tatum, and Vollmer (1986) found increased rates of anxiety, depression, and posttraumatic stress among the area residents most severely affected by the eruption and ashfall.

Chronic Effects

Chronic effects of natural disasters are not ordinarily seen; immediate reactions to most disasters are similar and short-lived, whereas long-term consequences are not as evident in most victims (e.g., Glass 1959; Goldsteen, Schorr, and Goldsteen 1985). In part, this is a result of a lack of studies directed toward assessing long-term effects, but the preceding review suggests that these effects are unusual. When they do occur, they have generally been attributed to the severity of disruption of individual and social functioning, to preexisting vulnerability and predisposition to psychological disturbance, and to coping and social assets (e.g., Barton 1969; Erikson 1976; Jacobs and Spilken 1971; Pearlin and Schooler 1978; Quarantelli and Dynes 1976).

One way of examining chronic effects of disasters is to determine the ways in which recovery of daily routine is facilitated and inhibited in the postdisaster period. Drabek and Key (1976) studied the changes in individuals' relationships with friends and relatives in the wake of a destructive tornado and found that changes were common in both directions. As if the strain associated with the disaster intensified preexisting tendencies, strong social ties became stronger and weak bonds became weaker. Trainer and Bolin (1976) have argued that long-term recovery is complex, depending on the ease of regaining one's home, employment, and stable daily activity (e.g., shopping, attending school, or visiting with friends).

In order to examine this, Trainer and Bolin interviewed survivors of the 1972 earthquake in Managua, Nicaragua. The quake destroyed a major portion of the city, including the central business area and several residential areas. Thousands of victims left the city, but many returned and were able to find shelter. Up to one-third of the 376 survivors who were interviewed 8 and 17 months after the earthquake reported less social activity than before, primarily as a result of the dispersion of people throughout the area and relatively poor transportation facilities. Leisure activity was also sharply curtailed in postdisaster Managua; 45 percent of the respondents at the 8-month point and 32 percent of the respondents at the 17-month point reported that they no longer engaged in preferred leisure activities, primarily because they lacked money to spend or because entertainment facilities had been destroyed in the earthquake. Shopping was drastically altered because most markets were destroyed, and, overall, more than half of the surviving residents were less satisfied with their life in Managua 17 months after the earthquake than before it.

Trainer and Bolin (1976) also studied survivors of a flash flood in Rapid City, South Dakota. This catastrophe left 238 dead and caused extensive damage. Some 1,200 families were homeless in the wake of the flood. Here, however, disruption of routine and recovery of daily activity were different; although a large number of the 125 survivors who were interviewed two years after the flood reported less social contact with neighbors, many said it was because of a lack of time. This also showed up in reported leisure activity; though a third or more reported that they no longer engaged in their preferred leisure activities, this was more often a result of a lack of time than anything else. When they had time, nearly three-quarters of the respondents indicated participation in leisure activity as they did before. Shopping and other routine activities were not affected over the long haul, and survivors of the Rapid City flood were less likely to be less satisfied with their lives than were survivors of the Managua earthquake.

In some cases, long-term social effects of disasters may be positive. Drabek et al. (1975) reported that three years after a destructive tornado struck Topeka, Kansas, there was still evidence of heightened group cohesion and positive responses. Victims reported fewer symptoms of emotional disturbance and comparable perceptions of health than did nonvictims. In another study of the Rapid City flood Hall and Landreth (1975) found mixed evidence of positive and negative effects. No changes in suicides, juvenile arrests, drunk driving arrests, accidents, infant deaths, illness rates, or prescriptions for tranquilizers were found. However, in the 17 months after the flood, the number of divorces and annulments increased, as did arrests for public intoxication. The authors concluded that "Rapid City did not experience a major mental health crisis after the flood . . . the community in general experienced the typical post-disaster utopian mood" (p. 60).

In summary, the issue of whether the long-term impact of disasters is positive or negative has not been resolved. The data do not suggest that natural disasters are usually associated with long-term mental or physical health problems, and Quarantelli and Dynes (1972) have argued that people behave heroically during a disaster, showing a stubborn determination to "beat the storm." Stricken communities show tendencies toward increased social cohesion during and after disasters (e.g., Barton 1970; Fritz 1961), and Drabek et al. (1975) found long-term benefits of this increased social cohesion. However, White and Haas (1975) have argued that research has not yielded a sufficiently broad, consistent conceptualization of disaster impact to allow a determination of these long-term effects. Frederick (1980) goes a step further, noting that

> based on a small number of research reports, for years it was thought that any mental or emotional effects of disaster were minimal. However, recent disasters have clearly indicated that this is not the case. The misperception principally has been due to inadequate, narrow research. (p. 71)

Consistent with this, Fredrick argued that because the expected panic had not occurred in most disasters, "all other psychological reactions were thought to be nonexistent" (p. 72).

Effects of Humanmade Disasters

In contrast to the research just reported, the consequences of humanmade disasters appear to be more persistent. They also appear to be heavily influenced by psychological factors. For example, Adler (1943) reported on acute effects of the nightclub fire at the Cocoanut Grove in Boston and also on follow-up observations of survivors nearly a year after the fire. Accidentally set, the fire killed 491 patrons of the club and was characterized by great terror and horror. More than half of the survivors developed psychiatric complications, including general nervousness, anxiety, guilt, nightmares, and fear. Of particular interest was the finding that of those who did not develop psychiatric problems, 75 percent had lost consciousness during the fire, most of them remaining unconscious for more than an hour. Among those who eventually exhibited psychological difficulties, only half lost consciousness, mostly for less than an hour. Unconsciousness, and therefore less exposure to the terror and horror during the fire, was associated with more positive psychiatric prognosis.

A variety of other disasters has been studied, though in many cases the number of survivors was so small that even by studying all of them, sample sizes were perilously low. Leopold and Dillon (1963), for example, reported on a four-year study of victims of a collision between two ships. They interviewed more than 80 percent of the survivors on the ship that was destroyed (34 men) and found evidence of fairly severe work-related problems and persistent psychiatric distress in more than three-quarters of the survivors. Panic did not occur, but mood disturbances increased over time, and psychosomatic disorders were reported. In addition, the majority of survivors went back to work in maritime activities, but several had to stop shortly after. Henderson and Bostock (1977) interviewed all seven male survivors of a shipwreck one to two years after it occurred and found that 71 percent developed some form of psychological disturbance. In a ten-year study of survivors of a coal mine cave-in, Ploeger (1972) also found substantial long-term effects among the ten men studied; nine exhibited changes in personality and experienced threatening memories, and six had developed phobic syndromes.

The Buffalo Creek Flood

One of the more carefully studied disasters was the Buffalo Creek flood in West Virginia. A slag dam gave way after extended rainfall and "unleashed thousands of tons of water and black mud on the Buffalo Creek Valley . . . [an] Appalachian tidal wave [that] destroyed everything in its path" (Titchener and Kapp 1976:295). The flood killed 125, left 4,000 people without homes, and wiped away all traces of the town of Saunders. A number of other communities were also destroyed. The dam and the company that owned it were seen as responsible for the disaster, and 654 survivors eventually filed suit against the company.

Titchener and Kapp (1976) interviewed these plaintiffs to assess the degree of psychological impairment attributable to the flood. Findings suggested substantial difficulty: anxiety, depression, and changes in character were evident in almost all of the survivors two years after the disaster. The plaintiffs reported feeling sluggish shortly after the flood, had difficulty controlling their emotions, and experienced anxiety, grief, and sleep disturbances. Over time, anxieties and fears were expressed as phobia, and 80 percent of the group exhibited traumatic neuroses.

In long-term follow-up interviews of residents of the valley two and five years after the flood, residents reported chronic symptoms of psychopathology and more severe disturbance than was found in normative studies of the assessment instrument (Gleser, Green, and Winget 1981). Furthermore, symptoms exhibited by flood victims were comparable with those of "highly distressed" psychiatric patients. Gleser, Green, and Winget (1981) also reported increases in the occurrence of ulcers among flood victims since the disaster and found evidence of a rise in diagnoses of hypertension as well. Before the flood less than 5 percent of the men were diagnosed as hypertensive, whereas a year or more after the flood nearly 15 percent were so diagnosed. Women showed a similar pattern; before the disaster, 13 percent were hypertensive, and after it, 28 percent were diagnosed as having hypertension. Because predisaster rates of illness were low, Gleser and her colleagues suggest that these changes could reflect adjustment to normative standards or that the relative lack of stress in the valley before the flood may have been a factor.

Other symptoms of chronic stress were also found: flood victims continued to experience sleeping problems two years after it had occurred, with 77 percent of the men and 87 percent of the women reporting some difficulty falling asleep (Gleser, Green, and Winget 1981). Flood victims also reported difficulty staying asleep, which was more often related to severity of disturbance, anxiety, and depression, and more frequent nightmares than would be expected based on surveys of other populations. Alcohol consumption and cigarette smoking increased primarily among those exhibiting the greatest distress, and the extent of victimization—victims' experiences during and after the flood—were related to symptoms of distress. Bereavement and the extent of initial flood impact experienced were associated with psychopathology, as were displacement and subsequent hardship. Children were also affected, but their degree of impairment was related to that of their parents. Families tended to exhibit similar effects, as spouses were also likely to respond comparably. Families were not necessarily comparable with regard to coping, however; men who were able to begin rebuilding or restoring their homes quickly showed better mental health than did men who could not, but among women, helping or recovery activities were not related to distress. After five years, some decrease in symptoms of psychopathology was observed (associated with settlement of the lawsuit among the men), but there was also evidence of persistent psychological distress among almost one-third of those interviewed.

Rangell (1976) described features of the Buffalo Creek flood that help to clarify its unusually persistent or severe effects. Many are related to its technological nature; though rain swelled the creek, it was a human-made dam that gave way and caused the great destructiveness. First, Rangell noted that the flood was not completely unexpected, as valley residents could see the dam and had expressed continuing concerns. "Another difference, which added the makings of a latent inner eruption . . . was that there were, in the minds of valley residents, people (the owners of the dam) who could and should have done something about the situation" (p. 31). Rangell observed that this may have been related to the persistence of numbness, apathy, and withdrawal in inhabitants of the valley two years after the flood.

The human context of the Buffalo Creek catastrophe was not the only contributing factor to chronic problems among victims. After disaster events pass and the destruction has ceased, people return to their homes and begin to rebuild. At Buffalo Creek, this was not possible; the valley had been so thoroughly transfigured by the flood that there was no home to return to for most survivors. Rangell (1976) argued that in such cases trauma does not recede with floodwaters, but rather continues and has cumulative consequences. Such a situation can result in severe blows to the social fabric holding a community together. Erikson (1976) discussed this loss of communality in the wake of the flood, suggesting that "it is, however, a form of shock—a gradual realization that the community no longer exists as a source of nurturance and a part of the self has disappeared" (p. 302).

Erikson clearly suggests that loss of social support and destruction of social networks can cause many problems associated with disasters such as the one at Buffalo Creek. When an individual is victimized, as in the case of an automobile accident, he or she does not lose support systems as well. When a larger segment of the community is affected, however, social support may be lost. At Buffalo Creek, most survivors

> remained in the general vicinity of their old homes, working in familiar mines, traveling along familiar roads, trading in familiar stores, attending familiar schools and sometimes worshiping in familiar churches. However, the people were scattered more or less at random throughout the vicinity—virtually stranded in the spots to which they had been washed by the flood. (Erikson (1976:303)

Preflood social networks, which had depended in part on physical proximity, were atomized by the disaster, inhibiting recovery and posing long-term adjustment barriers.

The Three Mile Island Reactor Accident

The accident at the Three Mile Island (TMI) nuclear power station has been extensively studied as well. Until recently it was an unprecedented event, and it has attracted a great deal of attention from researchers. Unfolding over the course of one week in the spring of 1979, the accident involved releases of unknown amounts of radiation, a reported partial meltdown of the reactor core, and, at various times, reports of possible explosions or radioactive emissions. It also created an information crisis; accounts of what was happening issued by responsible officials were often incomplete, incorrect, or contradictory, and the credibility of these officials suffered accordingly. Evacuation advisories were discussed and finally issued, and great media attention was focused on the event.

What actually occurred (i.e., pump malfunctions leading to exposure of the core, melting of fuel rods, release of radioactive emissions, spilling of radioactive water onto the reactor building floor) seems to have been less important than what nearby residents believed to be the course of events. Dohrenwend (1983) reported that how close people lived to the reactor affected distress during acute response to the accident, and if one had preschool children, distress was higher than if one did not. Similarly, distrust of authorities was high during acute response, but it persisted after symptoms of distress had dissipated.

The presence of stress and psychological disturbance has been the focus of several studies. Dohrenwend et al. (1979) found evidence of heightened demoralization during the month following the accident, but also reported that during the second month these effects declined rapidly. Houts et al. (1980) conducted telephone surveys about four and nine months after the accident, comparing residents living close to the plant with those living further away. Their results suggested that distress was associated with distance from the crippled reactor. Retrospective reports of levels of distress during the period immediately after the accident were higher than in either measurement period, and reported distress declined over the course of the study. After nine months, however, a subsample of 10–20 percent still exhibited symptoms of stress.

Bromet (1980) and her colleagues (Bromet et al. 1980) have conducted longer-term studies of TMI area residents, comparing plant workers at TMI and women in the community with preschool children with comparable groups working at an undamaged reactor site or living nearby. Early findings indicated that mothers of young children at TMI exhibited higher levels of distress than did their counterparts living near the undamaged plant and that these problems persisted throughout the first year after the accident (Bromet et al. 1980). Subsequent studies have indicated that these effects have persisted for more than three years (Dew, Bromet, and Schulberg in press).

A different approach to studying the effects of the TMI accident was taken by Mileti, Hartsough, and Madson (1982), who compared rates of stress-related behaviors such as alcohol sales, death rates, suicides, arrests, psychiatric admissions, and automobile accidents during the six months preceding and following the accident. These archival data indicated little change in crime, psychiatric admissions, and suicides but revealed small increases in automobile accidents and in alcohol sales after the accident. From these data, the authors concluded that stress following the accident was not severe. Houts and his associates also reported that utilization of medical care following the accident did not markedly increase (Houts et al. 1984). Incidence of spontaneous abortions after the accident was comparable with baseline rates more than a year after the accident, and estimation of health effects based on the amount of radiation released during the incident suggest minimal health consequences (Goldhaber, Staub, and Tokuhata 1983; Upton 1981).

Response during the accident and two-week emergency period was similar to that observed for natural disasters; panic did not occur and evacuation seems to have proceeded in a predictable fashion (Flynn 1981). Inhabitants experienced distress but overall chaos was not the case. Within three weeks after the accident, the community appeared to have regained a sense of normalcy, although disagreements about what had occurred and the dangers that had been posed continued (Flynn 1981). Thus, one might conclude that, though the accident may have caused substantial distress and disruption, response to it was not unusual and effects were largely short-lived. The data reported by Bromet and her associates (Bromet et al. 1980) provide the only suggestion that stress may have been more severe or persistent than these other accounts indicate.

Our research at TMI was initiated in 1980 to study the effects of the release of radioactive gases that had accumulated in the containment building around the reactor. Psychological, behavioral, and biochemical indexes of stress were measured in a randomly drawn sample of people living within 5 miles of the damaged reactor and were compared with responses of a control group drawn from an area more than 80 miles away. Data were collected just before, during, just after, and 6 weeks after the gases were vented into the atmosphere. Indicators in all of these stress measures were highest just before the release of the gas, as symptom reporting and levels of urinary norepinephrine and epinephrine declined as the venting proceeded (Gatchel, Schaeffer, and Baum 1985). Elevations prior to venting may have reflected an anticipatory stress response among TMI-area residents or may have reflected chronic levels of stress that were reduced by the successful venting procedure and removal of one threat still at the plant. This is suggested by the fact that TMI-area residents exhibited greater symptom reporting, poorer task performance, and higher levels of stress hormones in their urine than did controls at all or nearly all measurement periods.

Subsequent research has also indicated that these symptoms of stress have returned to pre-venting levels or in some cases exceeded them in the 6 or more years since the accident. Symptom reporting and urinary epinephrine and norepinephrine have remained at levels greater than those observed among control subjects, even when additional control groups of people living near undamaged nuclear and fossil-fuel power plants were considered (Baum, Gatchel, and Schaeffer 1983). Published data have shown that these symptoms of stress have persisted for at least 4 years, and preliminary data from recent measurements indicate that differences in stress levels were still significant 5 years after the accident (e.g., Davidson and Baum 1986). Furthermore, these stress levels have been associated with health-relevant variables such as complaints to physicians, blood pressure changes, and prescriptions received (Baum and Davidson, 1985).

These data suggest that stress has become chronic among residents of the TMI area. Vulnerability has been selective; not all area residents appear to have been affected in this manner. For example, coping and social support appear to have affected response to the TMI situation. Fleming et al. (1982) found that social support mediated stress symptoms that were exhibited by TMI-area residents 17 months after the accident. Those TMI subjects reporting higher levels of support reported less symptom distress than did those with less perceived social support. Control subjects did not show this relationship. However, Cleary and Houts (1984) reported that during the first 9 months after the accident, social support was not associated with stress. Number of friends was related, as were coping variables, to emotional regulation. Consistent with this, we found that direct, problem-focused coping aimed at "fixing" the situation was associated with greater distress than were coping actions that were oriented more toward making one feel better (Collins, Baum, and Singer 1983). Self-blame—taking responsibility for one's victimization—was also associated with fewer symptoms of chronic stress than was attributing blame to others (Baum, Fleming and Singer 1983).

Research on situations in which toxic chemicals have leaked or contaminated nearby ground, air, or water shows similar effects. Fleming (1985) found effects of the same type and magnitude as those observed at TMI among people living near a hazardous waste dump, and data suggest that TMI- and toxic waste-area residents exhibited comparable chronic symptoms of posttraumatic stress as well (Davidson, Fleming and Baum 1986). Other studies have also suggested that actual or perceived exposure to toxic chemicals as a result of leaking dump sites or application of dangerous chemicals is associated with persistent distress and disturbance (e.g., Gibbs 1986; Levine 1982). Schottenfeld and Cullen (1985) described a different instance of chronic response to exposure to toxic substances. Following real or imagined exposure to industrial toxins, symptoms of posttraumatic stress and somatic distress were observed: "Chronic exposure which initially may not be recognized as a discrete trauma or does not gain representation in clearly defined images or words may be preferentially recalled as reexperiencing of the bodily state associated with exposure" (p. 201).

Differences Between Natural and Humanmade Disasters

Throughout this chapter, I have maintained a distinction between natural and humanmade disasters. To some extent, such a distinction is based on the disaster event more than on its impact; although natural disasters are sometimes more powerful and destructive, both are typically disruptive and differences between them are primarily those of origin and psychologically relevant variables, such as predictability and opportunity for blame. For example, a flash flood causes comparable damage whether it is caused by a torrential rainstorm or by a dam failure. Clearly, the two events are different, but not necessarily in terms of direct impact. Instead, they vary along dimensions that define the ways in which the events are experienced.

In fact, one characteristic of humanmade disasters is often a lack of visible damage; compared with coastal damage from a hurricane or destruction from a substantial earthquake, many accidents caused by technological mishaps do little physical damage. There was less likelihood of the experience of loss, terror, and horror in the Love Canal or TMI situations than there is typically among victims of fierce storms or quakes. In many cases, these impact variables are not useful for predicting the response to or the lasting consequences of humanmade disaster. Such accidents reflect unpredictable events that result from loss of control over technological systems, and there are often parties or agencies to blame. As such they are different from those caused by natural forces. When humanmade events involve toxic substances, effects may be more prolonged and recovery inhibited further.

Several writers have discussed differences between disasters of natural and human origin. Some suggest that there is value in distinguishing between them, whereas others do not. The argument is not over whether they are different, but rather whether these differences translate into meaningful impact predictors—do they really matter in the determination of response to and effects of victimization? I will briefly consider some models that discuss possible distinctions between natural and technological catastrophe and then evaluate research findings to more carefully assess effects.

Warheit (1976) has argued that natural disasters and civil disturbances differ in several important ways. Although both types of events produce many sudden demands on individual and group functioning and disrupt normal behavior, the differences in origin, warning, scope, and duration may result in different degrees of dysfunction. Natural disasters are caused by nonsocial forces outside the regulatory control of the group or community, whereas civil disturbances are usually produced by social sources within the community. In addition, natural disasters do not serve human purposes, whereas civil disturbances often do. Warheit suggests that "natural disasters occur as purposeless, asocial events; civil disturbances can be viewed as instrumentally initiated to achieve certain social goals" (p. 132). Not all humanmade emergencies share this purposive quality, but riots, demonstrations, uprisings, war, economic decline, assassination, and the like may appear to be intentional at some level.

Warheit (1976) also believes that warning is important in distinguishing between these collective stress situations. Natural disasters often provide some warning, because storms can be tracked and various levels of alerts can be issued. However, civil disturbances are viewed as inherently unpredictable and are therefore associated with less warning. Warheit also noted differences in duration, suggesting that natural phenomena usually are briefer than is disruption associated with civil unrest. When events are brief, decisions can be made more quickly; when they are more drawn out, response cannot be as decisive. As Warheit notes, "Natural disasters create a social context marked by an initial overwhelming consensus regarding priorities and the allocation of resources" (p. 133).

Rogers and Nehnevajsa (1984) discussed natural disasters and technological crises as distinct events. Natural disasters are those involving natural forces, be they geological events that give little warning, such as earthquakes, landslides, and volcanoes, or disasters of the weather system, including hurricanes, cyclones, typhoons, blizzards, and so on. A number of differences may be drawn between these general classes of natural mishaps. The weather-induced crises are typically slower-onset events and provide more warning than those involving movement of the earth, and the ability to localize where the impact of weather will be greatest is better than with earthquakes or the like.

A third group of natural hazards is more like the first in that they are hard to predict and are characterized by more rapid onset—flash floods, avalanches, and fire storms are sudden crises set off by movement of water, snow, or fire on the earth's surface. In addition, these disaster events may be caused by humans, unlike the other classes of natural hazard. Floods are also events that fit this category, though they have considerably slower onset than do flash floods and may be predicted. Finally, long-term natural disasters heavily affected by climate patterns form a fourth group—drought, famine, crop failure. These slow-onset events, in the long run, may be more resistant to intervention than are the more sudden and powerful events.

Technological crises reflect failure in technological systems. These comprise four categories as well: those derived from large system failures (e.g., nuclear power plant accidents, blackouts, dam failures), structural failures (e.g., bridge or building collapse), low-level delayed-effect crises (e.g., pollution, energy shortages), and chemical hazards (e.g., oil spills, toxic fumes, leaking toxic waste). These classes of humanmade problems vary along several dimensions. Some are sudden and unpredictable, such as system and structural failures, whereas others are slower to develop and more easily predicted (e.g., pollution). Some crises affect relatively large numbers of people, as in system failures and low-level delayed crises, whereas others are more geographically concentrated, such as chemical accidents and structural failures.

These models of types of disasters reinforce the idea that differences between natural and technological disasters are, most importantly, differences related to psychological dimensions. Sheer physical impact is less important than are factors that affect victim response and perceptions of the event. Predictability, culpability, duration, and the opportunity for exposure to toxic substances are the primary distinctions that have been proposed, and these characteristics are most important in determining how victims perceive the disaster event and cope with its demands.

Characteristics of Catastrophes and Their Psychological Effects

We have suggested elsewhere that natural disaster and technological catastrophe should not automatically be included together as one class of stressor, but rather the capacity of each one for causing stress and long-term psychophysiological change should be compared and evaluated (Baum, Fleming, and Davidson 1983). We came to this conclusion as a result of findings from our continuing investigation of stress at TMI. Symptoms of stress, psychological disturbance, and physiological changes persisted long after we had expected them to disappear, and the reports of subjects suggested the presence of stressful conditions that had not been previously discussed. This led us to search the literature on disasters, and we found reports stating that substantial chronic effects are not often observed, but they seem more likely to occur after humanmade accidents than after natural calamities.

Earlier in this chapter, I reported evidence of chronic stress found among some TMI-area residents more than six years after the accident and discussed some of the sources of this lasting distress. Yet there was very little damage or property loss as a result of the accident, and although many area residents report continued concerns about past and future harm, experts have dismissed most claims of radiation release as unsupported. Why, then, has stress persisted among these residents? It may be related to continued controversy about the accident, the reopening of the plant, and other issues that have kept the situation in the public eye.

Yet we have also found chronic stress associated with living near a leaking toxic-waste dump that did not receive the same attention as did TMI. We came to believe that these types of disaster differ from natural disasters in ways that do not necessarily affect the intensity of distress but do support long-term problems and make cumulative effects of stress more likely. In our initial treatment of these differences, we focused primarily on the human versus natural origin distinction. Using several characteristics of disaster events, we attempted to draw psychologically relevant distinctions between natural and humanmade calamities (Baum, Fleming and Davidson 1983). These characteristics included suddenness, power, destruction, predictability, and the presence of a clear low point.

Natural Disasters

Natural disasters are more familiar events, occurring at seemingly greater frequency. They vary in duration from the quick but powerful impact of earthquakes and tornadoes to the long-term disruption of floods and episodes such as heat waves or drought. Such disasters do not all occur everywhere but rather each type tends to occur in only certain areas. Thus hurricanes do not affect people in the Midwest as much as they do along the Gulf of Mexico, whereas earthquakes do not traditionally occur in either locale. However, it is safe to say that there are few places where victimization by some natural force does not occur.

Natural disasters usually begin very quickly. Our ability to forecast events has made some more predictable, but onset of a natural disaster may be sudden. Hurricanes, floods, and tornadoes usually give warning of their approach, but the time gained by such warnings is often a matter of hours, and such storms may still be fairly sudden. Other types of natural disasters occur even more suddenly; earthquakes, for example, may come upon an area in a matter of seconds and are not usually preceded by a warning.

Natural disasters are also powerful. Lazarus and Cohen (1977) suggested that they are among the most universally threatening of stressors, with sufficient magnitude to cause death and great destruction. Not all people respond to these events as one would expect, but this does not appear to involve appraisal of threat so much as appraisal of appropriate coping options (Sims and Baumann 1974).

The enormous power of natural forces engenders substantial visible damage to property that often remains after the storm has passed. In such cases, damage provides tangible reminders of the events, causes disruption, and provides a focus for recovery efforts. As rebuilding is completed, a sense of closure on the episode may be attained and recovery may be enhanced.

As I have suggested, some forms of disaster have become more predictable as our ability to forecast meteorological and geophysical conditions has improved. Floods are often predicted days before they crest, although flash floods remain unpredictable (Drabek and Stephenson 1971; Gleser, Green, and Winget 1981). Tornadoes and hurricanes are also more predictable than they used to be, but only in a general way; forecasts and warnings are issued across entire counties for hours, but the exact point and time at which a tornado touches down usually cannot be predicted. This is also true of events such as earthquakes; locations where these events are likely to occur can be specified, but there is little basis to determine when such disasters will strike. People living along a fault know that an earthquake may occur, but knowing when a specific tremor will occur is rare.

The last characteristic of natural disaster reflects something we have chosen to call a low point (Baum, Fleming, and Davidson 1983). What we mean is a point at which the worst that is going to happen has already occurred; at the low point, "the worst is over." Although the destruction of homes and the loss of power and sanitation facilities will also create hardships, once a storm has passed or an earthquake has stopped rumbling, the worst is typically over, and people can turn their attention to rebuilding and recovery. The low point may be looked at in terms of a shift in appraisal from threat to loss, or as the point at which damage and disruption are greatest. After this point, people begin to feel better, the environment is restored, and everyday life gradually returns to normal.

Humanmade Disasters

Technological catastrophes are less familiar to most people than are natural disasters, partly because they have been less frequent. Like natural disasters, they include events that are powerful and sudden, including bridge collapses, dam failures, industrial accidents, and marine collisions. They are also precipitated by events that reflect breakdowns in technology in industries or locations where highly toxic substances are used or stored. Furthermore, these events are potentially widespread. One can argue that the proliferation of technology has made few places safe from breakdown or failure. Where technology exists, there also exists the possibility of loss of control over it.

The onset of technological catastrophes is sudden. There is little warning of a dam break or a bridge collapse, and the speed with which these events unfold often makes them difficult to avoid. As was the case at Buffalo Creek, those in the path of a flood following a dam break usually have little time to get to safety; for those on a bridge when it collapses, there is even less time to act.

Technological mishaps, like natural events, are powerful. The destruction and loss of life resulting from dam breaks are potentially as great as for natural disasters, and our present state of technological achievement has created the possibility of even greater devastation. Although the odds are small, the Nuclear Regulatory Commission has acknowledged the possibility of a nuclear accident that could claim 100,000 lives. Recent events at Chernobyl suggested, if not realized, the great potential for loss of life. Technology has allowed us to harness tremendous energy that, in the event of an accident, could cause destruction that matches or exceeds most natural disasters.

Technology is not supposed to break down. Although Perrow (1981) has argued that such accidents are inevitable, technological catastrophes are never supposed to happen. As a result, they are difficult to predict. Dams are not supposed to break, so one cannot generally predict when they will. Inspection and examination of a dam may suggest that it is weakening, but these warning signs may not be visible or may be overlooked. Parts of our technological system are expected to become obsolete, but they are not expected to fail before they are replaced. Accidents that endanger or threaten lives and property are not planned, and often there is inadequate knowledge of how to deal with an accident if one occurs. Prior to the incident at TMI, some experts believed that such an accident was nearly impossible, and most of us will not attempt to predict events that "cannot" happen.

Technological advances provide us with control over our environment; human evolution has been marked by increases in such control over the forces around us. However, when the system breaks down, control is lost. Presumably any predictive ability we have concerning technological disaster would be used to correct the situation; that is, if a prediction of a specific breakdown is possible, then something will be done to correct the problem before the accident occurs. Failures in the system reflect those problems that "slipped by" and are therefore unpredictable.

Some technological mishaps, such as factory explosions, train accidents, and mine accidents, have a well-defined low point. In these cases, coping with disaster may follow a course similar to that of natural disaster recovery. However, it appears that some of the most powerful technological disasters may also be those without a clear low point. For example, situations in which individuals believe that they have been exposed to toxic chemicals or radiation (e.g., Love Canal and TMI) involve long-term consequences connected with the development of disease many years after the initial exposure. Thus there may be considerable uncertainty as to the degree of damage that such technological catastrophes may have inflicted. For some technological disasters, there is no clear low point from which "things will gradually get better"; the worst may be over and done with, or it may yet surface. Thus it could be difficult for some persons to return to normal lives after the actual accident or catastrophe has ended.

Currently, we are studying other variables that affect response to victimization that are associated with natural and technological catastrophe in different ways. Duration of victimization, implicitly affected by the timing of the low point, may also be affected by variables such as the possibility of exposure to toxic substances. In addition, blame or attribution of responsibility for victimization appears more likely in the case of a humanmade catastrophe than in a natural disaster. Because duration of victimization appears to be an important factor in distress resulting from disaster, and because blame has been shown to affect response to victimization in other settings, these characteristics warrant closer examination.

Effects of Toxic Exposure

The presence of toxic substances in a disaster appears to generate more persistent distress, at least in some cases. Depending on what substance is involved, different degrees of chronic disruption may be expected; radiation, for example, is odorless, invisible, and feared. Experts argue about what levels of exposure are dangerous, and, partly because of the history of nuclear energy, possible exposure to radiation evokes strong emotional responses in many. Similarly, some toxic chemicals are feared and have effects that extend beyond acute exposure. Radiation and some toxic chemicals have effects that require a long time to develop. Thus, radiation may cause cancer and birth defects, but these effects may not be detectable for years or generations. In a sense, this pattern of influence extends the duration of victimization. Long after the TMI accident or the discovery of toxic chemical leaks at waste dump sites, concerns about possible future exposure to toxic substances are compounded by worry and concern about effects that have already been set in motion. The belief that one has been exposed to toxic substances may cause long-term uncertainty and stress, as well as pose a threat to one's health. The degree to which this stress will occur depends on the perceived consequences and time course of particular toxins; when effects are severe and delayed, stress may be more persistent.

Blame as a Reaction to Disaster

The notion of blame or attribution of responsibility is an important theme in the victimization literature and is reflected in studies of disaster as well. At one extreme, some have held that assignment of blame for a disaster is rare, and victimization is explained in other ways. Others have observed that disaster victims do attribute responsibility for disasters or victimization, ranging from scapegoating and attempts to assign blame to others to the tendency to assume personal responsibility for what has happened to them. Studies also vary in the degree to which they find consequences or correlates of different responses to victimization.

Scapegoating and blaming others for victimization by disaster appears to occur most often in the case of humanmade calamities, for obvious reasons. Studies have found evidence of attribution of blame for air pollution, fires, nuclear accidents, explosions, dam breaks and resulting floods, airplane crashes and toxic waste sites as well as after severe winter storms (e.g., Baum, Fleming, and Singer 1983; Bucher 1957; Drabek 1968; Erikson 1976; Levine 1982; Neal 1984; Neal and Perry 1980; Veltfort and Lee 1943). Blaming is more likely when someone has acted in ways that are perceived to isolate norms or community standards for his or her own benefit, most likely in the case of humanmade events (e.g., Neal and Perry 1980). Some have argued that blaming can occur only in the case of technological accidents if one considers the cause of the event, for obvious reasons (Turner and Killian 1972). However, under some conditions, particularly if responsibility for more than cause alone is considered, natural disasters may also be followed by scapegoating (Neal 1984).

In a study of the Cocoanut Grove fire, victims were found to blame others for the catastrophe (Veltfort and Lee 1943). Assignment of blame for what had happened was directed at public officials who were seen as having failed to pass laws and codes that would have resulted in fewer fatalities. Veltfort and Lee interpreted this external focus as unconscious, directed toward relieving emotionality and reducing fear, anger, guilt, and frustration. This focus was also viewed as an example of scapegoating, because victims disregarded more productive avenues of response, such as demands for better fire laws, in favor of blaming officials and clamoring for their punishment.

The pattern of assignment of blame following the fire is also of interest. The individual actually responsible for setting the club on fire (who struck a match while trying to change a light bulb) was not blamed by victims. Veltfort and Lee argued that this was a result of both his admission that he had been responsible and his own victimization. Instead, "more satisfying" scapegoats were chosen; victims would feel less guilt at seeing public officials punished, reflecting both a sensitivity to the vulnerability of the young man responsible for the fire and negative feelings for public officials in general.

Bucher (1957) recognized that few if any people attribute blame to themselves or others for natural disasters. In these cases, natural forces are seen as responsible for death, destruction, and disruption. According to Bucher, blaming other people for one's own victimization occurs only when conventional explanations are not sufficient to account for what has happened. In the case of attributing responsibility to others, two other conditions must be met: those who are blamed must be seen as having violated moral or community standards and as not being ready to take steps to rectify the situation to prevent similar ones. This latter variable, reflecting a concern with future safety, explains why people who are directly involved in a disaster (e.g., pilots of planes that have crashed) are rarely blamed. Idiosyncratic events or individuals who are seen as unique are poor targets for blame, as they provide little predictive power in explaining a theory of how or why an event occurred. In deciding who to blame, individuals create naive theories that are directed toward identifying more stable or global factors that might also predict future catastrophes. As a result, groups of people (e.g., authorities, public officials) who are seen as having the capability to prevent such disasters in the future are more likely to be held responsible.

Drabek and Quarantelli (1969) studied attribution of responsibility in a disaster at the Indiana State Fairgrounds in 1963. An explosion during a show in the coliseum killed 81 people, most of them immediately, and injured about 400 more. Here, conventional explanations for the disaster were inadequate, and the media coverage reflected a general search for the cause and responsibility for the explosion. Gas tanks that had been illegally stored in the coliseum were eventually identified as the cause, and officials of the company supplying the tanks, managers of the coliseum, and fire department officials were blamed for the catastrophe. Such response is consistent with Bucher's (1957) conditions (moral violation, impelling action to prevent similar occurrences). Drabek and Quarantelli go on to suggest that personal blame for disasters derives directly from institutional mandates. In legal systems such as the one in the United States, responsible individuals must be identified, and societal norms seem to place greater emphasis on identifying and punishing those who are responsible than on analyzing and preventing similar events. The public "trial" and punishment of people who were involved in a catastrophe like the Indiana Fairgrounds explosion provide a greater sense of rectification—that something is being done—than does more subtle legislative action or other activity directed precisely at rectification and prevention.

These data suggest that, following disasters, the public may feel a need to assign blame. When conventional explanations are not available, when moral conduct can be questioned, when feelings of fear or guilt require expression, and when there is a perceived need to force responsible officials to act to prevent future catastrophes, blaming other people is more likely. Furthermore, it can be argued that attributing blame to others may affect the likelihood of meaningful social change and effective prevention. However, these studies have not considered how attribution of responsibility affects coping with disaster, or how personal costs, may be related to how one allocates blame for victimization.

In general, attribution processes are directed toward explanation of events in ways that maintain a sense of order and provide some predictive power (Wortman 1976). The nature of attributions that people make are related to their perception of the environment, mediating the development of learned helplessness, emotion, and social interaction (e.g., Abramson, Seligman, and Teasdale 1978; Baum and Gatchel 1981; Schachter and Singer 1962; Wortman and Brehm 1975). How people compartmentalize responsibility for failure, how they view the role of other people in contributing to stressful social situations, and how they explain internal sensations, thoughts, and symptoms affects their response to events. This may be related to the need to believe in a just world or to the defensive use of external attributions, but the need to attribute responsibility for victimization also appears to be associated with perceived control. By blaming others for one's plight, victims may also yield a sense of control over the event and the likelihood of occurrence of similar ones. Assumption of responsibility for victimization, on the other hand, may allow victims to maintain perceived control over the events in question, and such assumption may reflect a purposeful attempt to maintain or create a sense of control over the environment.

Blame may reflect the outcome of several different processes that characterize victimization, as was suggested earlier. However, there is evidence of the control-enhancing or adjustment-facilitating effects of self-blame that are inconsistent with the common wisdom on the subject (Miller and Porter 1983). Internal attributions have been found to be both positively and negatively associated with helplessness and depressive symptoms (Abramson, Seligman, and Teasdale 1978; Baum, Fleming, and Singer 1983; Baum and Gatchel 1981), but self-blame for victimization has been associated with better postaccident coping (Bulman and Wortman 1977; Janoff-Bulman and Frieze 1983). The distinction between characterological and behavioral self-blame appears to be important, because the former may not bolster perceptions of control and enhance adaptive response (Janoff-Bulman 1979).

Attribution of responsibility for victimization in humanmade disasters may be related to the victims' desire to maintain control of their situation when it appears such control has been lost. Distinctions between technological and natural disasters are partly based on uncertainty and unpredictability. The predictability of technological disasters appears to be low, and they appear to generate greater uncertainty than do natural disasters. The nightmarish quality of some may be largely a result of uncertainty about the nature and extent of their effects. Because many effects take years to appear, technological disasters may pose long-term threats to victims' sense of control as well.

The situation at TMI is consistent with this reasoning. Research has shown that TMI-area residents report greater feelings of helplessness and less perceived control over their environment than do control subjects (Davidson, Baum, and Collins 1982). Data also suggest that many TMI-area residents are concerned and uncertain about what effects the accident had on them (Baum et al. 1981). Data suggest that some TMI-area residents seek to bolster their feelings of control by assigning blame for their problems to themselves (Baum, Fleming, and Singer 1983). Self-blame for the accident was rare but was more common when subjects were asked about the problems they experienced after the accident. Those area residents who reported that they assumed some responsibility for their situation exhibited stress levels that were comparable with control subjects' and substantially lower than TMI subjects who did not assume any responsibility for their problems. Assumption of responsibility was also positively related to perceived control.

Determinants of Chronic Consequences of Disasters

Although research has not systematically assessed the long-term effects of victimization by disaster nor resolved definitional problems regarding what distinguishes acute and chronic consequences and what constitutes an "effect," it is possible to draw some conclusions regarding natural and technological calamities and their long-term impact on mood and behavior. For example, Chamberlain (1980) reviewed a number of studies (many of humanmade disasters such as the Cocoanut Grove fire, the devastation at Hiroshima, and the Buffalo Creek flood) and concluded that physical and psychological trauma persists beyond the immediate disaster and postdisaster period. Chamberlain noted that there is evidence of long-term deterioration in health. Hargreaves (1980) suggested that when victims see a crisis or emergency as being caused by human action, the effects last longer. Similarly, Gleser, Green, and Winget (1981) proposed that the cause of a disaster, whether it was natural or humanmade, contributes to the scope and duration of disaster effects. Their observations of the humanmade flood at Buffalo Creek were similar to other studies, primarily those of other technological accidents.

All of this suggests that humanmade disasters, regardless of whether or not they generate effects of the same intensity as do natural ones, are more likely to engender chronic effects such as emotional disturbances or poor physical health. Response to the event and acute effects of disaster do not appear to differ greatly as a function of origin, but long-term effects do seem to vary along this dimension. In the case of Buffalo Creek, it was difficult to determine which of several factors were associated with distress; Gleser, Green, and Winget (1981) suggested that degree of threat, bereavement, prolongation of an intractable situation, loss of a sense of community, and displacement may also have been important. However, the conduct of a large lawsuit alone suggests extensive blaming of human "disaster agents," which may well have contributed to negative mental health effects.

Gleser and her colleagues (1981) also suggested that the proportion of victims who suffer psychological effects is often higher following humanmade disasters than it is following natural disasters. Of those interviewed eight days after the Cocoanut Grove fire by Cobb and Lindemann (1943), 44 percent exhibited evidence of emotional problems. Similarly, Adler (1943) found that more than half of the fire's victims suffered from psychiatric complications almost a year later. Leopold and Dillon (1963) reported that nearly all of the victims of a marine collision and explosion exhibited symptoms of posttraumatic stress several years after the accident, and Lidz (1946) found that all survivors of the Guadalcanal evacuation displayed long-term psychological symptoms related to the incident. These data are similar to those describing the long-term health of concentration camp survivors, nearly all of whom showed psychological problems, and the data are different from results from many studies of natural disasters.

Rates of disturbance from studies of floods, storms, and other natural disasters report lower impairment rates (e.g., Logue, Hansen, and Struening 1979; Milne 1977; Parker 1977; Poulshock and Cohen 1975). These differences may have been a result of the sampling procedures used in these studies or the method of assessing distress and may not reflect a greater extent or degree of disturbance among victims of humanmade disasters. However, a recent study that used comparable sampling and assessment procedures to compare victims of a flood with people living near a hazardous toxic waste dump as well as with a control group found differences in chronic effects of these disasters (e.g., Fleming and Baum 1986). Those living near the toxic waste site reported greater symptom distress and exhibited higher levels of sympathetic arousal than did either of the other groups almost a year after the announcement or discovery of toxic hazard.

Data suggest that technological catastrophes have more clear-cut effects than do natural disasters. In fact, in discussing their results, Gleser, Green, and Winget (1981) noted that Buffalo Creek appeared to have unprecedented effects, ones clearly different from those found for other floods. They point out that the closest approximations of the long-term effects measured at Buffalo Creek are found in the studies of nightclub fires and marine disasters. Thus, technological catastrophes appear to have effects that are similar to one another but different from those of natural disasters.

Relatively little research has been conducted on disasters involving toxic waste or radiation, but this will not be the case for long. Residents' experiences at Love Canal appear to have been stressful and should be expected to have chronic consequences for some victims, but available evidence is not conclusive about this (Levine 1982). Research at TMI that assessed several control groups and supplemented self-report data with behavioral and biochemical measures has indicated

TABLE 6.1
Summary of Characteristics of Natural and Humanmade Disasters

	DISASTERS	
Characteristics	*Natural*	*Humanmade*
Suddenness	Often sudden, some warning	May be sudden or drawn out
Powerful impact	Usually powerful	Usually powerful
Visible damage	Usually causes damage, loss	May not cause damage, loss
Predictability	Some predictability	Low predictability
Low point	Clear low point	Unclear low point
Perceptions of control	Uncontrollable, lack of control	Uncontrollable but potentially controllable; result of loss of control
Extent of effects	Usually limited to victims	Victims' and public's loss of confidence and credibility in perceived human agents
Persistence of effects	Up to a year, mostly acute	May be chronic, long-term uncertainty

that many residents continued to feel threatened by the plant for more than a year after the accident, and that a variety of stress symptoms has persisted for some residents as long as 17 months after the accident (Baum et al. 1983). The persistence of difficulties here is more easily explained than at Buffalo Creek, because some of the sources of danger remain at TMI. The dam that caused the flood at Buffalo Creek was not rebuilt, and the sources of threat there are no longer present. Still, the parallels between the findings for these kinds of catastrophes are striking.

Possible differences between natural and technological disasters are summarized in table 6.1. Although the two share some characteristics, they appear to be different in other ways. Both are relatively sudden and powerful, and although neither is very predictable, technological mishaps may be less so than natural disasters. Both may cause visible destruction and disfigurement of the environment, but technological catastrophes can leave an area intact, producing less visible threat. Furthermore, though it is not definitive, research suggests that humanmade catastrophes can have more chronic effects than do natural disasters.

Although one can argue that technological catastrophes are less predictable than are natural ones, it is fairly clear that both are relatively hard to predict and more or less uncontrollable. Despite the fact that neither type of event can be controlled, however, it is likely that perception of uncontrollability will be different for each. Natural forces are, by definition, uncontrollable. We can minimize damage and loss, but the occurrence of a storm, drought, or other natural event is uncontrollable. These events have never been controllable, and the fact that nothing could be done to prevent a particular instance merely serves to highlight or reinforce one's lack of control over it.

This is not always the case, however, as technological catastrophes reflect failure by systems that once were under control. Dams, nuclear reactors, and waste dumps are normally well-regulated parts of a technological network designed to be controlled by its human masters. When a breakdown occurs, there is a temporary loss of control over the system. In one sense, these mishaps may be more controllable than are natural disasters because there are often preventive actions that can be taken to avoid an accident or to minimize an impending catastrophe. In another sense, they are uncontrollable once they begin, and a loss of control, related to the failure to foresee and prevent the accident, may be salient. Not having control when one expects to have it appears to have different psychophysiological consequences than does not having control when one does not expect it (Baum and Gatchel 1981; Wortman and Brehm 1975).

The public's confidence in future controllability of technology is closely related to this. One dramatic instance—the TMI accident—of loss of control over nuclear technology greatly reduced many people's confidence in the safety and viability of nuclear power, despite the fact that control over the TMI reactor was regained before the core melted down. The effects of the Chernobyl accident are not yet known. It is possible that repeated technological breakdowns can erode confidence in our ability to manage and regulate other forms of technology.

Humanmade disasters may create dangers that pass quickly but that may also pose continuing threats. This is particularly true for catastrophes involving toxic substances. The possibility of illness resulting from exposure to toxic waste or radiation continues for many years, and toxic spills, leaks, or nuclear accidents require complex decontamination and clean-up procedures that may take years to accomplish. At TMI, radioactive gas remained trapped in the plant for more than a year before it was vented into the atmosphere, and large amounts of radioactive water remained on the site for more than six years after the accident. Delays in decontamination, the clean-up procedures themselves, and the presence of radioactive material remaining in the plant are all sources of continuing threats that may be responsible for chronic stress among area residents.

Summary and Implications

Disasters are events or impacts that cause substantial disruption of psychological, social, or physical functioning. They may be thought of as stressors, tending to be more intense, powerful, and universal than most threatening or demanding events. They affect relatively large numbers of people and pose heavy demands on coping. And they threaten property and life, whether directly, as in victimization by a natural disaster, explosion, or fire, or by virtue of long-term threat, as is generated by exposure to toxic substances. Particularly in the latter case, perceptions of the event and associated threats may be more important in determining chronic stress and mental health effects than is the actual threat or danger posed.

Response to disasters appears to be more orderly than many people expect. Evidence of panic in the face of a disaster is rare, and many studies suggest that initial response is purposive and prosocial. I have noted the emergence of cohesive social groups that last beyond the disaster period, and have argued that the long-term effects of disasters are typically positive. Some studies have observed shock, dazed behavior, and withdrawal, and a number have reported emotional distress and dysfunction following a disaster event. However, in most cases, these effects appear to be short-lived.

Some disasters appear to be associated with psychological effects that do not dissipate quickly but rather last for long periods of time. To some extent this is associated with the duration of sources of stress, but it also appears that chronic distress is most likely to be found following humanmade disasters. One explanation for this is that technological calamities are more likely to pose continuing threats, but this does not explain the persistence of problems following the Buffalo Creek flood. Rather, a combination of facts, including threats to perceived control, possible consequences, social disruption, and predictability and persistence of threats explain the differences between natural and technological disasters.

Interpretation of the disaster literature is made more difficult by the great variety of events studied and methods used. Data suggest that there is some generality of response across events, but differences in sampling procedures, design, measures, time frames, and focus have hindered meaningful conclusions about coping and consequences of disasters. From among the many levels of analysis and environmental impact, my colleagues and I have focused on psychological and psychophysiological aspects of victimization by disaster. Conclusions that we have drawn are tentative ones, awaiting systematic validation and analysis. Regardless of what is eventually learned, there are a number of implications for the psychological study of disaster.

Examination of differences between natural and technological cataclysms reveals some important modern realities. The built environment is continually expanding, and threats posed by modern technology to the natural ecosystem are well recognized. However, expansion of technology often outruns our society's ability to control it, and we have often failed to foresee the problems that the technology will create. Our current dilemmas regarding storage of toxic and radioactive wastes are cases in point. Examination of the unique effects of technology-based threats and hazards may be increasingly called for as more and more people are victimized.

By viewing humanmade disaster as different from others, psychologists may be better able to predict and treat the kinds of psychological and health consequences such events can have. Responding to a court order to consider psychological effects in its deliberations about restarting the undamaged reactor at TMI, the Nuclear Regulatory Commission in 1982 sponsored a gathering of experts on stress, disaster, and perception of hazard who were asked to make predictions about psychological health near TMI based on the "disaster literature." It soon became apparent that the predictions stemming from this research did not match the reality of the situation at TMI. Regardless of whether these discrepancies between theory and reality persist, it was clear at that time that policy decisions could not be based on the most extensive literature available. Earlier studies of natural disasters did not provide a good foundation for making decisions about TMI and will probably prove insufficient for understanding future technological mishaps.

At the outset of this chapter, I discussed the nature of disaster, focusing on questions about what constitutes a disaster. Was TMI a disaster? Was Love Canal a disaster? What is the key, the crucial factor that is required? The short-term effects of these calamities are consistent with those of events that are universally accepted as disasters; response to the TMI situation was not unlike response to storms or other natural hazards. Stress, fear, sleep disturbances, posttraumatic stress symptoms, anxiety, and depression on the negative side and social activism and more positive response in the other side have been observed. What was missing at TMI and Love Canal was the powerful surge, the destruction of property and immediate injury or loss of life, the terror and gruesome trauma, and bereavement (Hartsough and Savitsky 1984). The primary threat at TMI never materialized, but if it had—as it apparently did at Chernobyl—it would have produced casualties and attendant experiences for area residents. Instead, the terror and threat to life unfolded over several years, and many area residents are still waiting to see how they were affected.

This suggests that the TMI situation and other humanmade accidents involving toxic substances are disasters, whether or not the amount of toxic exposure involved can be proven to be dangerous to health. Individual perceptions, coping predilections, and other personal factors determine how events are appraised and experienced, and it is this subjective evaluation that appears most closely tied to the development of physical and mental health problems. There is argument about whether stress or "emotional injury" resulting from accidents like TMI are covered under current law or whether they should be considered in decisions regarding siting of potential hazards (Hartsough and Savitsky 1984). In the case of TMI, the Supreme Court decided it unwise or not mandated by law to consider psychological health in such planning. The chronicity of response to humanmade disasters and the role of stress in the etiology of illness suggests that the Justices were wrong. Future policy decisions and legal resolution of claims will require more systematic documentation of the issues that indicate that toxic events are disasters and that their effects may be substantial.

7

Stress, Coping, and the Meaning of Work

EDWIN A. LOCKE AND
M. SUSAN TAYLOR

> No I'm not disturbed any more. If I was just starting on this job, I probably would. But the older I get, I realize its a farce. You just used to it. It's a job. I get my paycheck—that's it. It's all political anyway.
>
> (As quoted in Terkel 1972:155).

> And working is my life. If you took that away from me, it would be worse than killing me. I've inherited the Yorkshire value of work from my father. Being idle wasn't what my father believed in.
>
> (Henry Moore, as quoted in Chandler 1982)

As these two quotations indicate, the meaning of work varies widely among individuals in our society. While each of us can observe this variation from personal experience, the research literature provides even stronger evidence of such differences. In one of the earliest studies on the meaning of work, Morse and Weiss (1955) examined a sample of 401 American males, and found that individuals in middle-class and farming occupations tended to emphasize the intrinsic interest and significance of their work, whereas those in lower-class occupations viewed work simply as an activity that kept them busy. Similarly, Near, Rice, and Hunt (1980) reviewed the literature on work and non-work domains and concluded that the importance of work varied by occupation; people in higher-skill jobs saw their work as more important than those in lower-skill jobs. Finally, Buchholz (1978) examined the work beliefs of over one thousand individuals, including employees, union leaders, and managers, and found individual differences according to age, education, and occupation. Young people displayed a stronger pro-work ethic than did older people, and those with graduate education expected more intrinsic outcomes (e.g., interest, challenge) from their work than those with less education.

These findings reflect considerable inter-individual variance in the meaning of work. By the meaning of work we mean the totality of values, including their importance that individuals seek and expect to derive from work. Values themselves are what individuals desire or consider to be good or beneficial. They have been defined as "that which one acts to gain and/or keep" (Rand 1964) and serve to govern individuals' emotional responses as well as to guide their choices and actions (Locke 1976). Values have been described as the motivational link between inborn needs and action (Locke and Henne 1986).

Although individuals generally begin work with a set of work values, we believe these values both affect and are affected by the experiences encountered in the workplace. These experiences are due partly to factors within individuals' control (e.g., effort, new learning) and partly to factors outside their control (e.g., economic conditions). Therefore, people may succeed in getting what they want from work or they may fail and experience conflict between what they desire and expect and what is experienced. This conflict may yield disappointment, frustration, or stress, causing individuals periodically to appraise and draw conclusions about their work experiences. As a result, they may change their actions, expectations, values or all of these. Depending on how individuals respond or cope after appraisal, work may come to hold more or less personal meaning.

. . .

Work Values and the Meaning of Work

Our review of the literature suggests that there are at least five different categories of values that people may seek to fulfill at work. These are similar but not identical to the categories developed by Rokeach (1960, 1973) for values in general and include: (1) material values (such as Rokeach's comfortable life, money, family security); (2) achievement-related values (Rokeach's sense of accomplishment, freedom, and wisdom; (3) a sense of purpose (Rokeach's inner harmony); (4) social relationships (Rokeach's true friendship and social recognition); and (5) enhancement or maintenance of the self-concept (Rokeach's self-respect).

For a relatively large segment of the population, work seems to be of value primarily because of its association with material outcomes, especially money. This meaning has been termed the economic function by Morse and Weiss (1955) and the instrumental function by Locke, Sirota, and Wolfson (1976). In an explanation of clerical workers' indifferent reactions to job enrichment, Locke, Sirota, and Wolfson (1976) offered the following observations about the relative importance of material and achievement related values:

> The workers' greatest concern was to get good ratings so that they could get promoted and get more pay. Many had given up more interesting jobs in order to take their present ones. They were quite willing, if not anxious, to have more interesting tasks but only on the condition that some practical benefit would result. (p. 710)

Those who work primarily to fulfill material values are not limited to lower-status occupation groups. Mortimer and Lorence (1979) surveyed a sample of 513 male college students at graduation and followed them up ten years later. The researchers found that the students who placed a high value on extrinsic (material) rewards later chose the highest paying jobs. However, to say that material outcomes are important to people is not to say that these are the only values people derive from work. For example, Yankelovich and Immerwahr (1983) found that only 31 percent of a national sample agreed with the statement that work was "purely a business transaction."

A second meaning of work concerns achievement-related values such as autonomy, success, challenge, growth, interest, variety, etc. This meaning was emphasized by the *Work in America Report* (1971) which proclaimed that all was not well with work in America because significant numbers of employed workers were locked into "dull, repetitive, seemingly meaningless tasks, offering little challenge or autonomy." (*Work in America* 1971:xx). Indeed, the assumed desirability of job characteristics such as autonomy, significance, variety, etc., forms the conceptual basis for much of the job enrichment literature (Aldag and Brief 1979; Griffin 1982; Hackman and Oldham 1976, 1980). Furthermore, like material values, the achievement ones also seem to affect subsequent job choice. In the study described earlier by Mortimer and Lorence (1979), those college students who valued achievement-related outcomes most highly in their senior year were found in jobs providing the highest levels of autonomy when resurveyed ten years later.

Research findings suggest that the achievement-related aspects of work are primary for only a small segment of society. For example, Morse and Weiss (1955) reported that only 5 percent of their sample listed "feelings of interest" and only 12 percent listed "the kind of work performed" as reasons for continuing to work. Furthermore, the work of Dalton and Thompson (1986) on the career stages of professionals seems to restrict the primacy of an achievement-focused work meaning to an even smaller subgroup, professionals working on individual tasks. The researchers noted:

> Why do most of the instances that we heard about concerning a deep interest in work involve unusual circumstances? Perhaps it is because in our society, a certain level of interest in one's work is expected among professionally trained individuals. But even if a certain level of interest is considered normal, we did not find that a deep and absorbing interest in one's work was a universal condition among professionals. . . .
> Interestingly, both White's examples of "deeply interested" individuals, and our own examples tended to be individuals performing individual tasks. (p. 226)

Work also may provide individuals with a sense of purpose. It may help them to keep active, to organize their activities and their lives on a daily basis, and to feel they are doing something significant. For example, Super (1986) noted that in our society being without a job symbolizes a loss of role, purpose, and meaning, and proposed that one major function of work was to provide a way of structuring time. Similarly, Sofer (1970) stated that work provides individuals with ways to structure the passage of time and to demonstrate their productive ability. Finally, 47 percent of Morse and Weiss' (1955) sample reported that they would continue to work even if economically secure because of positive reasons related to the purposeful aspect of work (e.g., keeps one occupied—32 percent, justifies one's existence—5 percent, keeps one healthy—10 percent). Another 37 percent listed negative reasons relevant to the structuring meaning (e.g., "feel lost"—14 percent, "feel useless"—2 percent, "feel bored"—4 percent, "not know what to do with one's time"—10 percent, "habit"—6 percent, "keep out of trouble"—1 percent).

A fourth meaning of work is based in social relationships that provide opportunities to interact with others, share information, attain visibility, and receive feedback and recognition for one's accomplishments. Super (1986) has identified social support and the prestige of others as primary meanings of work, while Sofer (1970) noted that having a work role provides opportunities simply to interact with others. Furthermore, a full 31 percent of the Morse and Weiss (1955) sample listed "the people known through or at work" as one of the things that would be missed if they stopped working. The importance of the social relationship meaning is further emphasized by the fact that a primary method of job analysis classifies jobs according to the level of interactions required with people (Fine and Wiley 1971).

A final meaning of work concerns its significance for the self-concept. In an extensive study of adult developmental stages conducted on a cross-section of American males, Levinson and his colleagues (1978) found one of the primary tasks of early adulthood is forming the "Dream," individuals' sense of self-in-the-adult-world that generally involved vocational accomplishments. Levinson et al. (1978) found that individuals' timely progression toward achievement of the Dream during early adulthood was highly related to their self-concept and life purpose.

> If the Dream remains unconnected to his life, it may simply die and with it his sense of aliveness and purpose. Those who betray the Dream in their twenties will have to deal later with the consequences. Those who build a life structure around the Dream in early adulthood have a better chance for personal fulfillment, though years of struggle may be required to maintain the commitment and work towards its realization. (p. 92)

Similarly, Markus (1986) has introduced the concept of possible selves which represents individuals' ideas of what they might become, would like to become, and are afraid of becoming. The possible self is believed to be a conceptual link between cognition and motivation that may provide means-ends patterns for new behavior, as well as additional meaning for current behavior. Markus (1986) has included occupational fields, or work, as one of the six proposed domains of the possible self.

The relationship of work to individuals' self-concept is also supported by other research. Morse and Weiss (1955) found that 9 percent of their sample indicated that "feelings of doing something important or worthwhile" and "feelings of self-respect" would be the things missed if they did not work. Bailyn (1977) classified a sample of recent MIT graduates into two categories—those who said that family needs were primary and those who said career success was most important. Ten to twenty years later, individuals who displayed a marked subordination of career to family interests tended to demonstrate low self-confidence, low interest in the nature of their work, and a lower probability of holding managerial positions. Finally, Evans and Bartolome (1980) interviewed a sample of 532 business managers and their wives from several different countries. Managers who had not yet reached their mid-forties reported that what happened at work had powerful effects on life at home, but there were few reports of spillover in the opposite direction. However, the researchers noted that after forty, managers' family life seemed to have a greater impact on their self-concept. Thus, there is considerable evidence that individuals' work experiences may be central to their self-concepts, at least in the case of males prior to age forty.

In summary, we have provided evidence that the value or meaning of work varies across individuals and have proposed that individuals may expect and desire to fulfill five different categories of values from their work—material values, achievement-related values, a sense of purpose, social relationships, and the enhancement or maintenance of the self-concept. The extent to which work is personally meaningful to people may change over time as individuals have successful or unsuccessful experiences and make changes in their actions, expectations, and values. Furthermore, previous research suggests a cyclical process whereby work values influence individuals' occupational choices and the experiences encountered in the chosen occupations may reinforce their original values (Brousseau 1978; Broussea and Prince 1981; Kohn and Schooler 1978, 1982; Mortimer and Lorence 1979). However, for most people the attainment of work-related values, even when earnestly sought after, is virtually never automatic. Attainment entails overcoming obstacles, setbacks, and challenges. Insofar as such situations are perceived as a threat, the individual will experience stress. How the individual copes with such stress may have profound implications for subsequent health and well-being.[1]

. . .

Coping and Job Values

The major types of threats to each of the five categories of job values discussed earlier are shown in figure 7.1. We shall use many examples, some taken from the first author's clinical practice and some taken from other sources, to illustrate various coping techniques.

Material Values

There are several ways in which material values can be associated with stress. One is that individuals may base their self-concept almost entirely on material outcomes, in particular, on the amount of money

FIGURE 7.1

Work Values and Meanings	*Threats (Potential Stress Initiators)*
1. Material Values	No raise No promotion Loss of job Loss of other values Loss of identity Poverty
2. Achievement-Related Values	Failure Job or career change Loss of control Boundary-spanning role Role conflict Role overload Time pressure Loss of interesting work
3. Sense of Purpose	Loss of job Career failure Career success
4. Social Relationships	Conflict, criticism Isolation, alienation Rejection
5. Self-Concept	All of the above Failure to pursue values Irrational standards Self-concept–work environment discrepancy

they earn. As a result, they attempt to relieve any self-doubt by compulsive attempts to make more and more money. Individuals' heavy reliance on money and material goods as a basis for their self-esteem can result in stress in two ways. First, they are easily devastated by the loss of material outcomes such as the failure to get an expected raise or promotion, or loss of a job. Such losses have negative consequences far beyond any practical threat, such that individuals feel they are worthless failures, regardless of whether they in any way caused the event to occur (e.g., they may have been laid off due to a merger or to poor economic conditions). The threat to their self-esteem may be so great that they take refuge in defense mechanisms (repression, withdrawal) or even substance abuse. They may be unwilling to accept other employment, or to remain in the same position (after being passed over for promotion) because their self-esteem will not permit any compromises in the area of material outcomes. Loss of job, of course, can have serious practical consequences, e.g., poverty, which can entail various physical threats.

A second way in which stress can result from individuals' over-reliance on material outcomes for their self-esteem is that other important values such as those pertaining to interest in one's job or to the meaning of one's family relationships become de-emphasized and even lost permanently. Thus, individuals may be shocked to find that the attainment of large quantities of material outcomes do not prove nearly as satisfying as expected because they were achieved at the expense of other important values. Consider the case of Professor A.

> Professor A moaned and groaned for years that Eastern University did not pay its professors enough and that he was losing potential earnings by staying there. Finally, he accepted an offer at Atlantic University at a substantial raise. However, two years later he tried (unsuccessfully) to get his old job back. Atlantic University did not have the same caliber of faculty or research focus as Eastern U. and he felt intellectually and professionally frustrated.

Korman (1980) and Maccoby (1976) have provided other examples of how individuals' overemphasis on material outcomes (career success) may cause them to ignore another important value, that of social relationships. As Maccoby (1976) put it:

> Careerism demands detachments. To succeed in school the child needs to detach himself from a crippling fear of failure. To sell himself, he detaches himself from feelings of shame and humiliation. To compete and win, he detaches himself from compassion for the losers. To devote himself to success at work, he detaches himself from family.

Korman (1980) has proposed that the sacrifice of social relationships (termed affiliative satisfactions) in order to achieve material outcomes is one of the greatest sources of personal and social alienation among today's managers. Unfortunately, individuals may erect strong defenses against the recognition of conflicts between the attainment of material outcomes and other values such as interesting work or social relationships so that the negative implications of these trade-offs go unrecognized for many years. By the time these conflicts are recognized, it may be much more difficult to attain them.

The value of material outcomes may also result in stress because individuals have failed to choose appropriate standards by which to judge themselves. They may strive solely to impress others with highly visible material outcomes. This case is exemplified by the response of Mr. B, when asked to describe a fantasy that would reflect what he really wanted in life.

> I see a big house with white columns sitting on a hill. I drive up to it in a Cadillac. My beautiful wife meets me at the door trailed by two large dogs and the kids. It is the most expensive house around. Everyone else is envious of me.

Individuals like Mr. B rely on others for their standards because they lack a set of personal values that would enable them to make their own choices. They are often threatened because they can never acquire enough. There is always someone with a bigger house, a more expensive car, a more attractive spouse, etc., relative to whom they feel inadequate. Further, these individuals often have difficulty establishing relationships with others because they have nothing unique to contribute to the relationship. Underneath the facade of confidence, there is no self; only a mirror of others' desires.

In each of the previous examples, effective coping with stress requires cognitive changes. These individuals must learn to disengage their self-esteem from the material outcomes they have acquired, develop their own unique set of values, and become more aware of other values that are just as important as material outcomes. Frequently, a significant setback, such as the failure to obtain an important promotion, loss of a job, or the loss of a meaningful personal relationship, is required before these individuals are willing to change. Furthermore, they may be quite defensive and require assistance in identifying the causes of the setback. Once the causes are identified, the individuals have to learn to act differently in similar situations, to acquire new skills, to develop better relationships with organizational superiors, to put more time into important personal relationships.

We do not wish to imply from the foregoing discussion that trying to make money and increase one's earning power is bad. It is not. Improving one's skills and abilities and progressing through a series of higher and more demanding jobs, tasks, and responsibilities which produce increasingly higher salaries is an important and legitimate source of pride and self-esteem. Such progress indicates the increasingly effective and productive use of one's mind. We strongly approve of people being proud of their earning power, but this is not the same as being obsessed with it and using it to relieve profound self-doubt.

Furthermore, being poor is itself a source of stress, not just because (for some) it is associated with failure (lack of skill, lack of motivation to work hard), but because it can pose many practical difficulties in living (e.g., problems in housing, transportation, nutrition, medical care, freedom to take vacations, etc.). Thus one way to eliminate some sources of stress is to make *more* money, not less. This requires a great deal of pro-active behavior, e.g., getting a good education, doing well in school, acquiring marketable skills, learning new things, working hard at one's job, looking for a better job, being willing to move and take risks, etc. Some people remain in poverty because of their failure to take such actions either out of laziness or fear of failure. Increasing one's earning power can be an indication of growth, and the failure to increase it an indication of intellectual and career stagnation (though there are exceptions to this association).

Thus one can feel stressed in the realm of material values for two broadly different reasons: because one (due to self-doubt) makes money too important and thus feels constantly threatened because it is never enough, or because one makes too little and is beset by practical difficulties and the recognition that one failed to grow.

Achievement-Related Values

The key threats to achievement-related values are the loss of feelings of competence (failure), of work that is interesting or challenging, or of personal control over one's work. In the case of threats due to failure, it is important for individuals to examine the standards they are using to judge their effectiveness, since these may be inappropriate. Individuals who strive to achieve such standards often experience extreme, albeit partially subconscious, conflict because they feel hopelessly tied to standards that they suspect may be impossible to achieve. In actuality, the standards may be totally arbitrary. Consider the case of Ms. C.

> Ms. C was contemplating suicide. When asked what the problem was, she said that she was a failure because she was unable to make any progress on the book she was writing. When asked how long she had studied the topic she was writing about, she responded that she had studied it for about two months and had read a couple of books on it. Ms. C was shocked to learn that the reason she could not write about the topic was that she knew hardly anything about it.

The standard that Ms. C was using to judge her performance was that of omniscience—a standard divorced from reality. She expected herself to master any new topic with a minimum amount of effort. When she could not meet this arbitrary and impossible standard, she judged herself a failure. Thus, effective coping in cases such as Ms. C's involves the development of more rational standards by which to judge success and failure. Such standards must reflect a realistic assessment of task difficulty vis-à-vis the individual's ability level.

On the other hand, if individuals' failure is judged on the basis of a rational standard, i.e., if the failure is real, then effective coping would lie in the realm of action. Such individuals must identify the causes of their failure and proceed to develop the needed skills or work habits. Sometimes this will require switching jobs or even careers to better match skills and interests with job requirements. At other times, they may need to discuss conflicting role requirements with superiors in order to increase the likelihood of success.

Threats to individuals' achievement values also may occur when there is a loss of personal control over their work and/or a loss of interest in what they are doing. For example, boundary-spanning roles that place individuals in a position between two conflicting groups may offer them little personal control with respect to the scheduling of job tasks or the results of those tasks. Job changes may bring about significant time pressures or work overload that cause similar decreases in personal control. Furthermore, as noted in the material outcomes section, individuals may trade away work that is inherently interesting in order to attain material outcomes such as the status of a managerial position or a higher salary.

Individuals who feel their choice of work activities is externally controlled may subsequently lose interest in performing the activities for their own sake (Deci 1975). Consider a Nobel laureate's description of what happened upon assuming his first faculty position as a physicist.

> At Cornell I'd work on preparing my courses, and I'd go over to the library a lot and read through the *Arabian Nights* and ogle the girls that would go by. But when it came time to do some research, I couldn't get to work. I was a little tired; I was not interested; I couldn't do research. . . . Then I had another thought: Physics disgusts me a little bit now, but I used to *enjoy* doing physics. Why did I enjoy it? I used to *play* with it. I used to do whatever I felt like doing —it didn't have to do with whether it was important for the development of nuclear physics, but whether it was interesting and amusing for me to play with. (Feynman 1985: 155, 157)

In cases where individuals' values for achievement-related outcomes are threatened by a lack of personal control over, or interest in, their work, effective coping generally involves both cognitive and behavioral methods. Such individuals often must consciously decide, as did Feynman, that they will not allow others to exert an unreasonable amount of control over their work and then respond behaviorally to reduce this control (e.g., negotiating with the organization to decrease time pressures, reducing workloads by delegating and utilizing time management techniques). Similarly, individuals often also must decide that the performance of interesting work is an important value worth the loss of some material outcomes. If their diminished interest in work is not caused by a loss of personal control but rather by the nature of the work itself, objective changes in job tasks may be required to restore this interest. Dalton and Thompson (1986) found that individual, rather than group, work was more likely to be intrinsically interesting. Further, Katz (1980) has argued that no matter how stimulating individuals' work is, periodic changes in job tasks are required in order for it to remain interesting and challenging.

Sense of Purpose

As noted earlier, work may have meaning for individuals because it gives them a sense of purpose, adding structure to their lives and the feeling of doing something meaningful. This sense of purpose can be threatened in a number of different ways. Much has been written on the demoralizing effect of job loss on the structure and sense of purpose that work provides (Cobb and Kasl 1977; Cohn 1978; Feather and Davenport 1981). However, it is not necessary for individuals to lose their jobs in order to feel such a threat. They may experience failure when changes in the goals or technology of the organization undermine the nature of their contribution. Consider the case of Professor D.

> Professor D says that she feels "like dirt" upon going home from work. She was tenured at the associate level in 1953 when Southern University was mainly a teaching-oriented university. She is a good teacher but has neither the interest nor skill to be a good researcher. Over the years Southern U. has gradually become a publish-or-perish institution. Professor D has found herself cut off intellectually from the younger faculty who talk mainly about their research. She feels penalized by the reward system since pay raises and promotions are based increasingly on publications. She has begun to see her contribution to the university, being a good teacher, as invalid and thus meaningless and has lost interest in her teaching as well as the day-to-day life of the university.

Professor D has several coping alternatives at this point. She probably will need to deal with the threat both cognitively and behaviorially. She might, for example, cognitively reappraise the situation, telling herself that different people have different values and that, while what she values is not extrinsically rewarded, it is still something that she thinks is important, loves, and finds pleasurable. The cognitive reappraisal might be bolstered by behaviors that emphasize teaching, such as putting in more time and effort, trying to attain some outside recognition by striving for teaching awards, etc. These might also include finding consulting activities to replace the income she will forfeit under the current university reward structure.

However, Professor D's reappraisal of her teaching contribution may not be convincing enough to keep her satisfied in the face of few extrinsic rewards. If not, she may cope behaviorally by moving to a work environment that values her teaching contribution more highly or by acquiring the research skills that would allow her to be rewarded in her current environment. The latter behavior also would require some additional cognitive change in her beliefs about the relative values of teaching and research. Finally, Professor D might attempt to cope with the threat by shifting the high value she places on her work to another arena (e.g., volunteer activities). If she is successful, Professor D would then need to make behavioral changes that focus on this arena.

People also may experience *self-induced* threats to the sense of purpose derived from their work. As noted earlier, when individuals become so obsessed with "career success" that they sacrifice the attainment of other valued outcomes such as family relationships or interesting work, work may come to hold little meaning (Korman 1980). At this point, effective coping often involves the decision to pursue these other values, e.g., building new personal relationships, changing careers, etc.

People also may lose their sense of purpose at work after *attaining* highly valued, long-term goals. The realization that one has achieved the "epitome" of success in one's chosen occupational area (e.g., an Olympic gold medal in swimming, going to the moon, etc.) may result in the feeling that further work is no longer meaningful because nothing can match what one has already achieved. In this situation, individuals may decrease the threat by assessing whether the goal itself was really the factor that gave their work meaning, or whether it simply was a surrogate for other attributes of the work such as high quality performance, creativity, etc. If the sense of purpose derived from work was based upon achievement of the particular goal, effective coping may consist of problem-solving activities undertaken to identify other occupational fields where individuals feel they can make a contribution. Conversely, if a sense of purpose was derived from other attributes of work that subsequently were overlooked, cognitive reappraisal may be effective in diminishing the threat to one's sense of purpose.

People may also still feel conflict after achieving a long range goal because they never wanted it in the first place. Consider Mr. E:

> Mr. E got out of the army and decided that what he really wanted was to be a lawyer. But various family members pointed out that this would be high-risk choice and that it would be a long time paying off. These comments plus his own self-doubts led him to take a secure job with the federal government instead. By most standards he has "succeeded" in this job. He has received several promotions, makes good money, and has job security. But the job means nothing at all to him; he experiences his work as unbearable drudgery. It is not what he really wanted to do, and never was.

Even at middle age, Mr. E could change if he had the courage to do so.

Social Relationships

Social relationships serve both an expressive and an instrumental function at work (Locke 1976). That is, individuals' interactions with their coworkers and customers often provide enjoyment in their own right as well as a mechanism for accomplishing cooperative aspects of their work.

People's value for social relationships at work may be threatened in several different ways. First, people may value the expressive aspect of these relationships so highly that job requirements involving even minor conflicts with others prove very threatening. Consider the case of Ms. F.

> Ms. F managed a small number of employees as part of her administrative duties. One of them was chronically late for work, rude to customers, and unproductive. It was F's job to confront this employee but she was too terrified to do so. "If she gets mad at me, I think I'll go to pieces," she confessed. Her self-esteem was quite low because she would not deal with situations involving confrontation in any sphere of her life.

Effective coping in Ms. F's case involved cognitive and behavioral methods. Through therapy she was able to change her beliefs about the importance of receiving constant approval from others and to rely more on her internal standards for correct and incorrect behavior. In addition, through the use of role play techniques she learned how to depersonalize disciplinary episodes and conflict situations at work so that she was more effective and comfortable when engaged in the less pleasant interpersonal demands of her job.

A second threat to individuals' interpersonal relationships at work occurs when they respond by totally ignoring other people. As Korman (1980) has noted, individuals may become so obsessed with career success that they experience personal alienation from others in the work environment. Korman (1980) proposed that the competitive, compulsive behavior believed to contribute to career success destroys the expressive aspect of work relationships and results in the loss of an important value for many individuals.

Effective coping in the case of personal alienation might involve getting individuals to reappraise the threat situation and explicitly acknowledge the trade-off in values that may result (preferably prior to accepting such jobs). Then, if such a trade-off is undesirable, they may also have to move to work environments that do not require such behaviors in order to be effective.

Another threat to people's value for social relationships at work may be caused by their poor social skills and pessimistic expectations of others. Consider the case of Mr. G.

> From the time he was two years old (his earliest memories), Mr. G concluded that people, including his parents, did not like him. Gradually he withdrew from people and as a result developed few social skills. Talking to him is an uncomfortable experience. He does not smile. He looks scared and nervous and yet on guard, ready to attack if he is attacked. At work people either ignore him or talk about him disparagingly behind his back. Being supervigilant, he often can hear them do this and feels strong anger towards them and a desire for revenge. He does not get along with the neighbors where he lives. He expects people not to like him and they usually don't.

The behavior and attitudes of individuals such as Mr. G frequently eliminate both the expressive and instrumental aspects of work relationships. Others do not even wish to be around him, much less to assist him in the accomplishment of job tasks. If Mr. G is unfortunate enough to become a manager, he will undoubtedly fail.

Effective coping in Mr. G's case might involve the examination of his beliefs about why others respond to him as they do and some changes in his value for others' feelings. The strengthening of major social skills (e.g., conversational skills, learning to smile and laugh, showing greater restraint in his personal attacks on others, etc.) also would be helpful. Finally, the use of problem-solving techniques to identify work environments where he would be more effective and feel less threatened would be important.

Self-Concept

Individuals' self-concept is essentially their view of themselves with respect to abilities, interests, knowledge, skills, and values, as well as their overall evaluation of themselves, i.e., their self-esteem. Of these, values are the most critical. Packer (1984) writes: "The key to personal identity is values. The more developed, integrated, and intensely held are a person's values, the stronger is his sense of identity" (p. 2). Thus, all of the threats mentioned in previous sections also constitute threats to the self-concept.

Work is an important arena for threats to the self-concept because the job offers a means to sustain life and key opportunities for individuals to develop and achieve the values that constitute the self-concept. The threat to the self-concept is especially acute among individuals who have a poorly developed set of work values. As noted previously, individuals who fail to develop their work values may rely solely on material values as a basis of self-evaluation (e.g., Mr. B). Thus they are threatened by situations involving the loss of, or failure to attain, material outcomes. Furthermore, they tend to overemphasize material outcomes such that they neglect to pursue other important, but initially unrecognized, values. The opposite may also be true. Individuals may undervalue material outcomes and the values that make them possible (e.g., the desire to better themselves) and thus suffer material as well as psychological impoverishment.

The failure to pursue values at work may have long-term negative implications for their mental health. As Kornhauser (1965) expressed it:

> The unsatisfactory mental health of working people consists in no small measure of their dwarfed desires and deadened initiative, reduction of their goals and restriction of their efforts to a point where life is relatively empty and only half meaningful. (p. 270) (Kornhauser arbitrarily attributes all such problems to the nature of the job and never to the workers themselves.)

Coping with such threats requires both thinking and acting; individuals need to identify and pursue important work-related values.

A second threat to the self-concept results from failures in the work arena. As noted earlier, these failures may occur because the standards individuals use to evaluate themselves (the basis of their self-esteem) are irrational; that is, impossibly difficult or based on attributes not under their control (e.g., Ms. C). In such cases effective coping involves changing the individuals' ways of thinking, i.e., they must realize that the standards are irrational and change them. In other cases, however, the self-concept is threatened by failures as determined by rational standards. In order to cope effectively with these threats, individuals generally must make behavioral changes that increase the probability of future success, e.g., develop new skills, work harder, etc.

A third source of threat results from a lack of congruence between individuals' self-concepts and the requirements of their work environment. Thus, individuals who view themselves as slow, methodical thinkers will feel threatened by work environments that require fast, intuitive decisions. Persons who view themselves as very family-oriented will be threatened by work environments that usurp family activities by requiring frequent overtime, relocations, and travel. Effective coping with such threats may sometimes be accomplished by preventative, cognitive methods whereby individuals predict the likelihood of such threats and choose environments where requirements are consistent with their self-concepts. However, as Professor D discovered, job requirements may change over time; thus, no one choice can guarantee permanent success. In instances of incongruence, effective coping will involve behavioral and cognitive methods that either bring the work environment into congruence with the self-concept (e.g., leave the organization to act or change organizational requirements) or the self-concept into congruence with the environment (e.g., change abilities, values, etc.).

Summary and Conclusion

A job or career allows the pursuit of many important values. It allows one to make money so as to earn a living. It can give one a sense of achievement or accomplishment as well as the pleasure of doing something one considers interesting. It gives one's life a sense of purpose. It allows one to develop meaningful social relationships. And it helps to define one's self-concept.

However, the actual achievement of these values is neither easy nor automatic. Inevitably, there will be obstacles in the way of value attainment. These obstacles may be self-imposed in that the value standards which one uses to judge oneself are irrational and arbitrary. Or they may be externally imposed by other people or nature. When one perceives these obstacles as a threat to one's physical well-being or self-esteem, stress is experienced. Stress is experienced emotionally as fear or anxiety.

When faced with stress, one has a choice between several alternatives. One can attempt to identify the actual causes of stress (inappropriate values and/or external blocks) and take mental and/or physical actions to remove them. One can ignore the causes and deal only with symptoms through defense mechanisms, palliation, or substance abuse. Worse yet, one can repress one's desires and stop pursuing many meaningful values in the realm of work. The result is that work loses meaning because important values can no longer be attained from it. If work loses meaning, life too can lose meaning, since a considerable part of one's life is spent at work. When this happens, one can feel burned out —and old. Whatever "Dream" or vision of the future one started with is gone. The feelings of youthful vigor, purpose, and meaning are lost.

NOTES

1. As the next two sections of Locke and Taylor's original article have been omitted here (because of overlap with other material in this anthology), the authors have written the following bridging note:

> In the next two sections of the paper, Locke and Taylor develop a model of stress and coping which is quite compatible with the models presented elsewhere in this volume. Stress is viewed as involving four elements: threat, felt need for action, uncertainty, and emotional response with anxiety or fear as the core emotions. Stress is defined as: *the emotional response, typically consisting of fear and/or anxiety and associated physical symptoms, resulting from: (1) the appraisal of an object, situation, outcome, idea, etc., as threatening to one's physical or psychological well-being or self-esteem; (2) the implicit belief that action needs to be taken to deal with the threat thus producing conflict; and (3) felt uncertainty regarding one's ability to successfully identify and carry out the requisite action.* (No distinction is made between primary and secondary appraisal.)
>
> Coping activities are classified into a four-celled (2×2) table: symptom-focused or cause-focused, and cognitive or behavioral. Social support, it is argued, can be involved in any one of the four cells, depending on the type of support provided. It is further argued that cause-focused coping is more successful in the long run than symptom-focused coping, whereas the relative efficacy of cognitive and behavioral coping depends on the circumstances. Successful coping is defined as: *the identification of the causal elements in the precipitating situation (both external and internal) followed by cognitive and/or physical actions aimed at modifying one or more of these causal elements so as to reduce or eliminate associated negative emotions and physical symptoms.* Successful coping leaves the individual free to enjoy positive emotions and to deal with situations objectively, unencumbered by cognitive distortions or fears which restrict action and the achievement of values.

The stress model is now applied to the categories of values discussed earlier. For Locke and Taylor's full discussion of stress and coping, *see* their original article (Locke and Taylor 1990).

8

Uplifts, Hassles, and Adaptational Outcomes in Early Adolescents

■

ALLEN D. KANNER
S. SHIRLEY FELDMAN
DANIEL A. WEINBERGER
MARTIN E. FORD

The role of positive experiences in facilitating psychological well-being and health has been a focus of controversy for many years. For example, the pioneering work of Holmes and Rahe (1967b) on major life events was based on the proposition that the amount of change induced by life events is critical to their impact, irrespective of whether the events are experienced as positive or negative. However, subsequent research has indicated that it is negative rather than positive life events that show substantial relationships with outcomes such as depression and psychosomatic symptoms (*see* Thoits 1983). Similarly, a long-standing

This research was supported by the Stanford Center for the Study of Families, Children and Youth. We gratefully acknowledge David Bergin and Jeffrey Munson for analyzing the data, and Thomas M. Gehring and Susan Nolen-Hoeksema for a critical reading of the manuscript.

debate in the study of emotions focuses on whether positive and negative affect are independent dimensions, and whether positive emotions can attenuate or buffer the adverse effects of negative emotions (*see* Diener 1984 for a recent review). The potentially buffering effects of social support on stress has also drawn a great deal of attention in recent years (Billings and Moos 1981; Cohen and Wills 1985; Reich and Zautra 1981).

The controversy surrounding the uncertain impact of positive experiences on personal functioning has recently re-emerged in the study of common, everyday pleasant and unpleasant events, termed daily uplifts and hassles (Kanner et al. 1981). Uplifts refer to "positive experiences such as the joy derived from manifestations of love, relief at hearing good news, the pleasure of a good night's rest, and so on" (Kanner et al. 1981:6), whereas hassles are "the irritating, frustrating, distressing demands that to some degree characterize everyday transactions with the environment" (Kanner et al. 1981:3). Uplifts and hassles are thought to be important for two reasons. First, over time these events may be cumulative and produce major effects on health and psychological functioning. Second, uplifts and hassles may symbolize larger ongoing issues and concerns. That is, they may be the daily manifestations of such stable features of life as social roles, personality traits, and psychodynamic conflicts and resolutions, and may function as the mechanism by which major life events come to have an effect on a day-to-day basis (Kanner 1981; Kanner et al. 1981; Lazarus 1984a). Indeed, studies of hassles have shown that common, daily stresses are associated with a wide range of adverse psychological and health outcomes for adults (Cox et al. 1984; DeLongis et al. 1982; Eckenrode 1984; Holahan, Holahan and Bells 1984; Meeks et al. 1985; Zarski 1984) and for children and adolescents (Bobo et al. 1986; Compas et al. 1987; Kanner, Harrison, and Wertlieb 1985).

In contrast to hassles, the results for uplifts have been equivocal or even counterintuitive (Kanner et al. 1981; Monroe 1983; Zarski 1984). There are three possible patterns with regard to uplifts. First, uplifts could show a negative association with undesirable outcomes such as depression, a result that would be consistent with theories emphasizing the buffering effects of positive experience (cf. Bradburn 1969). Alternatively, uplifts could show no relationship to undesirable outcomes, a finding that would support the notion that positive and negative events are independent of each other and associated with different domains of outcomes (Costa and McCrae 1980). Finally, uplifts and stressful outcomes could be positively correlated, as predicted by Holmes and Rahe (1967b). However, to date the results of research on uplifts do not readily support any of these patterns. Instead, they have shown a rather intriguing gender difference. For men, uplifts have been generally unrelated to negative outcomes (Kanner et al. 1981; Monroe 1983), a finding consistent with the second pattern described above. For women, however, uplifts have actually shown a positive relationship to undesirable outcomes. For example, a higher incidence of uplifts has been associated with an elevated level of depression (Kanner et al. 1981; Monroe 1983), a result that has also emerged for positive life events and depression in women (Matheny and Cupp 1983). These findings are consistent with the position taken by Holmes and Rahe (1967b).

Perhaps because of these confusing findings, researchers have often chosen to focus only on hassles when assessing everyday events in adults (e.g., Cox et al. 1984; Holahan, Holahan, and Bells 1984; Meeks et al. 1985; Weinberger, Hiner and Tierney 1987). A similar emphasis on hassles is emerging in the child and adolescent literature (cf. Bobo et al. 1986; Compas et al. 1987; Patterson 1983). As a result, at present it is not known how uplifts relate to adaptational outcomes prior to adulthood.

The trend towards ignoring uplifts is unfortunate for several reasons. First, in light of the large literature on the impact of positive emotions on outcomes such as depression and subjective well-being (Bradburn 1969; Diener 1984), it seems premature to conclude that uplifts have little impact on an individual's functioning. Second, it cannot be assumed that uplifts have the same impact in the lives of children and adolescents as they do in adults. That remains an empirical question. At this point, there is little understanding of developmental changes that may occur in the impact of uplifts on adaptational outcomes, or even of the relationship between uplifts and hassles prior to adulthood. Finally, the gender differences in uplifts suggests the need for more information about the processes by which uplifts are linked to adaptational outcomes. Such an understanding could greatly enrich general knowledge regarding gender differences.

The present study was designed to examine the nature and role of daily uplifts and hassles in the lives of early adolescents. First, theoretical and methodological issues involved in assessing positive and negative daily events are examined. Next, the uplifts and hassles of twelve-year-olds, who stand at the threshold of adolescence, are described. Then the relationship between adolescents' uplifts and hassles and a variety of adaptational outcomes are assessed, with special attention paid to the question of whether uplifts show any unique relationship to these criteria independent of hassles. Since girls and boys are frequently at different developmental stages in this age group, with girls often being pubertal and boys prepubertal, gender differences in uplifts and hassles are examined primarily within a developmental framework. Finally, the results of these analyses are linked to adult studies.

There are several substantive and methodological reasons for investigating uplifts and hassles in early adolescents. From a conceptual level, much of what has been said about positive and negative events in adults is also applicable to youngsters. For example, Lazarus, Kanner, and Folkman (1980) have proposed that positive experiences may play different roles at various points in the coping process. They note that positive episodes, such as recess or vacations, can function as "breathers" from stressful experiences during which time regrouping, resting, and incubation (as part of a creative problem-solving process) are possible. Uplifts can also act as "sustainers" of coping efforts, a function often played by compliments, good grades, or even paychecks. Finally, positive experiences can also serve as "restorers" after harm or loss, not only in terms of physical recovery but, for example, as part of reparation of self-esteem. Lazarus, Kanner, and Folkman (1980) also cite the importance of play in acquiring coping skills, even though playing is not a coping activity per se. In this regard the fun experienced during play can motivate children to increase their social and practical competence. Thus, as with adults, there are many reasons to expect daily uplifts to have a positive effect on the social, psychological, and physical functioning of children and adolescents.

Another reason for examining uplifts and hassles in adolescents is purely descriptive. At present there is little systematic knowledge regarding the daily pleasures and stresses of various age groups from childhood through adolescence, or how these events change over time. The present study begins to address this need by focusing on twelve-year-olds, who are in the midst of the developmental transition from childhood into adolescence. It is widely acknowledged that this transitional period is beginning at increasingly younger ages, and that these youngsters are facing issues such as peer group pressure and problems with alcohol, drugs, and dating that previously were not major areas of concern until adolescence was in full bloom. One might also speculate that sources of satisfaction and enjoyment may have similarly shifted so as to differ from previous generations. The assessment of uplifts and hassles in twelve-year-olds thus affords an opportunity to document current sources of pleasures and stress from the early adolescent's perspective.

From a methodological standpoint, stressful and pleasurable events in children's lives have been assessed primarily through the life events approach. Measures of children's life events often rely on parent or observer reports of events, although some utilize children's self-report (*see* Johnson 1986 for a recent review). The need for self-report measures for children is underscored by studies which indicate that children's own ratings of the stressfulness of events in their lives differ markedly from adult ratings of those same events (Colton 1985; Yamamoto and Felsenthal 1982). Since uplifts and hassles refer to commonplace, readily observable events that occurred in the recent past, they ought to be easier for children to report on than broader events that happened many months previously.

Cohen, Burt, and Bjork (1987), in a longitudinal study of self-reported positive and negative life events in seventh and eighth graders, present findings that are of particular relevance to the present research. They found that both positive and negative life events were significantly associated with depression, anxiety, and self-esteem in the expected direction, with the exception that positive events and anxiety were not significantly related. Since similar outcome variables are examined in the present study, it will be of interest to compare Cohen, Burt, and Bjork's (1987) life event's results with findings for uplifts and hassles.

Uplifts and Hassles in Children and Adolescents

To date, daily stress in children has been examined in only a handful of studies involving primarily adolescents. Hanson and Pichert (1986), for example, showed that everyday stress experienced by diabetic children was related to control of their blood sugar level. It is not clear, however, whether the items in their questionnaire are representative of stress in a normal population. Colton (1985) developed a measure of youngsters' stress that utilizes either items taken directly from the adult Hassles Scales (Kanner et al. 1981) or modifications of these items. Colton's scale (COPES) is a self-report measure that includes a mixture of both daily hassles and major life event items.

Recently three studies have focused directly on the problem of assessing daily stress in normal children. Bobo et al. (1986) developed the Adolescent Hassles Inventory by having a panel of child development experts make age-appropriate modifications of the adult Hassles Scale. They found that, for sixth graders, high hassle scores were associated with poorer self-reported satisfaction with peer relations, especially for boys. Compas et al. (1987) developed the Adolescent Perceived Events Scale, which includes both positive and negative major and everyday events. They reported that a high frequency of negative events was significantly associated with self-reported behavioral problems for younger adolescents and with both behavioral problems and psychological symptoms in older adolescents (Compas et al. 1985 cited in Compas et al. 1987). A parallel analysis for positive events was not presented. Finally, Kanner, Harrison, and Wertlieb (1985), using the two scales that serve as the basis for the present study, found that for nine- and eleven-year-olds hassles were negatively associated and uplifts positively associated with general self-worth. This pilot study, to our knowledge, is the only research available on the effects of uplifts on children or adolescents.

The current research expands upon earlier investigations of uplifts and hassles in early adolescents by examining a broad range of clinically and developmentally important variables. These variables include anxiety, depression, and distress, as well as self-restraint, perceived support from friends, social competence, and general self-worth. It also specifically attempts to further understanding of the daily lives of twelve-year-olds by examining their perceived uplifts as well as their hassles.

Method

Subjects

The sample consisted of 232 sixth graders (91 boys and 141 girls) from nine classrooms in two school districts in the San Francisco Bay area. The majority of the children were white (60 percent), but there were also substantial numbers of Asians (16 percent) and Hispanics (14 percent). Children came from families that were predominantly intact (62 percent), with 24 percent from single-parent families and 14 percent from blended families. Based on a subset of 108 children for whom there were family income data (provided by the mothers), the families were primarily middle class. The acceptance rate for participation in the study was 85 percent.

Procedure

In two one-hour sessions spaced one week apart, subjects were asked to complete a battery of questionnaires in their regular classroom setting.

Children's Hassles Scale (CHS). The CHS consists of a list of 25 hassles (*see* Appendix A) and is a modification of the 43 items used by Kanner, Harrison, and Wertlieb (1985). The items were generated from the responses of children and early adolescents (N = 60) to a semistructured interview about stress in their lives. The CHS covers the areas of family, school, friends, and play in children's lives. Youngsters were asked to check which hassles occurred in the last month and to rate whether they *didn't feel bad, felt sort of bad,* or *felt very bad* as a result. A *didn't happen* option was also included to prevent respondents from rating items that had not occurred in the last month.

Three summary scores were generated from the CHS: (1) *frequency* —a simple count of the number of hassles which occurred in the last month, yielded a score that could range from 0 to 25; (2) *frequency of bad hassles*—the number of hassles rated as either *sort of bad* or *very bad,* yielded a score that again could range from 0 to 25; and (3) *total intensity*—the sum of weights for items endorsed as occurring. Since weights ranged from 2 to 4, the total intensity had a possible range of 0 to 100.

Initially analyses were performed using all three scoring methods. Overall, the results were essentially the same for each of the three methods, with frequency appearing marginally less informative than the other two scores. Since *frequency of bad hassles* is the score closest to the original conception of hassles (i.e., events that are appraised as stressful; Kanner et al. 1981), unless otherwise indicated it is the score used in the subsequent analyses in this study.

Children's Uplifts Scale (CUS). The CUS consists of a list of 25 uplifts (*see* Appendix B) and is a modification of the 31-item preliminary version used by Kanner, Harrison, and Wertlieb (1985). The CUS covers the domains of family, peers, school, and punishment. Youngsters were asked to rate whether in the last month each event happened and felt *OK, sort of good,* or *very good,* or *did not happen.* Similar to the CHS, scores for *frequency, frequency of good uplifts,* and *total intensity* were generated, with similar results being obtained for each score. Therefore, as with the CHS, unless otherwise indicated, the *frequency of good uplifts* score was used in the analyses reported in this article.

In addition, the following instruments assessing adaptational outcomes were administered:

1. *Anxiety Scale.* The Spielberger Trait Anxiety Inventory for Children (Spielberger 1973) is a 20-item scale in which subjects indicate how often they have experienced a variety of anxiety reactions. Items include: "I worry about making mistakes," "I am secretly afraid," and "I notice my heart beats fast." Item scores ranging from 1 to 3 are summed to yield a total score which can range from 20 to 60. According to Spielberger (1973), the internal consistency of the inventory ranges

from .78 to .87, with a test-retest reliability over an eight-week period of .71.

2. *Depression Scale.* The Children's Depression Inventory (Kovacs 1980) is a 26-item questionnaire in which items are arranged in triplet sentences indicating absence of depression, moderate depression, or severe depression. For example, one item reads: "Nothing will ever work out for me," "I am not sure if things will work out for me," and "Things will work out for me OK." Each item is scored on a 0–2 scale, with item scores added to yield a total score with a range of 0–52. According to Kovacs (1980), the items form a single scale with an internal consistency of .87 and a test-retest reliability of .84.

3. *Distress Scale.* The Weinberger Adjustment Inventory, Short-Form (Weinberger et al. 1987) contains 12 items that pertain to distress. The total score is aggregated from items tapping anxiety (e.g., "I worry too much about things that aren't important"), depression (e.g., "I often feel sad or unhappy"), low self-esteem (e.g., "I'm not very sure of myself"), and low well-being (e.g., "I'm the kind of person who has a lot of fun"; item is reverse scored). Items are scored on 5-point scales and are summed to yield a total score which ranges from 12 to 60. Weinberger et al. (1987) report that the items have an internal consistency of .87 and a one-week test-retest reliability of .83.

4. *Restraint Scale.* The Weinberger Adjustment Inventory, Short-Form (Weinberger et al. 1987) also yields a restraint score based on 12 items. These items tap suppression of aggression (e.g., "I lose my temper and let people have it when I'm angry"; item is reverse scored), consideration of others (e.g., "Before I do something, I think about how it will affect the people around me"), impulse control (e.g., "I become 'wild and crazy' and do things people might not like"; item is reverse scored), and responsibility (e.g., "I will cheat on something if I know no one will find out"; item is reverse scored). Items are scored on 5-point scales and summed to yield a total score ranging from 12 to 60. The restraint items have an internal consistency of .84 and a one-week test-retest reliability of .88 (Weinberger et al. 1987).

5. *Friendship Support Scale.* The Friendship Support Scale consists of 21 items adapted from inventories by Frankel (1986) and Rubenstein and Rubin (1987). The scale includes both positive ($N = 9$) and negative items ($N = 12$) relating to emotional support provided by friends. Sample positive items include: "If I had a secret it would be safe with my friends," and "My friends help me get my mind off my problems." Sample negative items include: "My friends make fun of me," and "My friends decide to do things with other kids instead of with me." Items are rated on 5-point scales, with the negative items reverse scored. The

friendship support score can range from 21 to 105. The 21 items used in this study had an internal consistency of .93.

6. *Social Competence Scale.* The Perceived Social Competence Scale is a subscale of the Harter Perceived Competence Scale (Harter 1982). It consists of 7 items in which sentences are presented in pairs to youngsters, who first choose which sentence is a better description of themselves, and then choose how true (really true *versus* somewhat true) that statement is for them. The following is a sample item: (a) "Some kids find it hard to make friends" *versus* (b) "For other kids it's pretty easy." Items are scored on 4-point scales which are summed to give an overall (perceived) social competence score. Internal consistency of the scale ranges from .75 to .84, with test-retest stability over a nine-month interval reported to be .75 (Harter 1982).

7. *General Self-Worth Scale.* The General Self-Worth Scale, also a subscale of the Harter Perceived Competence Scale (Harter 1982), has 7 items similar in format to that described for the Social Competence Scale. A sample item is: (a) "Some kids are very sure of themselves" *versus* (b) "Other kids are not very sure of themselves." Internal consistency for this scale ranges from .73 to .82, with test-retest stability over nine months reported to be .70 (Harter 1982).

Results

The results are reported in four sections, with gender differences being presented throughout. First, the internal structure of the hassles and uplifts scales are examined. Then descriptive information is provided on the most frequent and potent hassles and uplifts. Next, correlations between hassles and uplifts and a variety of adaptational outcomes are examined. Finally, regression analyses are used to evaluate the unique contribution of uplifts, beyond hassles, to adaptational outcomes.

Internal Structure of the Scales

Factor Analysis. To assess whether hassle and uplift items load on separate factors, factor analyses were carried out on the combined pool of hassle and uplift items using principle component analyses with varimax rotation. The number of factors that could emerge was limited to two. This analysis was repeated three times: for the total sample, and separately for girls and for boys. In every instance all the hassle items loaded above .3 on one factor and all the uplift items on another. For the sample of girls one hassle and one uplift item loaded above .3

on both factors. Overall, the results demonstrate that hassles and uplifts are different dimensions of children's lives.

The internal consistency of both the bad hassles and good uplifts scores, assessed by Cronbach's alpha, was highly satisfactory (.87 for each scale). The relationship of hassles to uplifts was examined. Overall, bad hassles and good uplifts were positively but only modestly related ($r=.18$, $p<.01$). However, a substantial gender difference emerged. The correlation was highly significant for girls ($r=.33$, $p<.001$) but insignificant for boys ($r=-.04$, n.s.). Although the magnitude of these correlations is less than that found with adults (Kanner et al. 1981), the pattern of a stronger association for females than males is consistent with the adult literature.

The Uplifts and Hassles of Early Adolescents

Table 8.1 presents the percentage of subjects who report each item on the Hassles Scale as occurring (column 1), the percentage of the total sample who indicated that the hassle item made them feel bad (column 2), and the potency score of each item, that is the percentage of those children who, when the event happened, felt bad (column 3). Events on the Children's Hassles Scale occurred frequently, with each item being endorsed by 30 to 83 percent of the sample. This demonstrates that the items on the scale were relevant and appropriate for this age group. Seventeen of the 25 items occurred for more than half of the sample. On average, children indicated that 12 of the hassle items happened during the last month (range 0-25, SD=7.0). The most frequently occurring events were having to clean up their room (83 percent) and feeling bored (81 percent).

Despite the frequency with which the events on the Hassles Scale occurred in the lives of sixth graders, these events did not always make adolescents "feel bad." Only one of 25 events (being punished for doing something wrong) both occurred and was experienced as bad by more than half the sample. Moreover, several of the most frequently occurring events (e.g., having to clean room, comparing unfavorably to a peer) were not perceived as bad hassles by even one-third of the sample. In fact, there was only a moderate correlation between the percentage of youngsters endorsing an item and the percentage who were made to feel bad by that event ($r=0.47$, $p<.001$).

Also of interest was the potency of events, that is, the probability than an event would make adolescents feel bad given its occurrence. There were six events that made 75 percent or more of the sample feel bad when these events occurred. Three of these events concerned par-

TABLE 8.1
Percentage of Sample Endorsing Items on the Children's Hassles Scale

		PERCENTAGE		
Item Number	*Item Content*	*Occurrence*	*Feeling Bad*	*Potency*
2	You had to clean up your room	83	21	25
21	You felt bored and wished there was something interesting to do	81	48	59
24	Another kid could do something better than you could	75	30	41
8	You lost something	73	48	66
22	Your brothers and sisters bugged you	73	37	51
4	You got punished when you did something wrong	66	52	79
23	You didn't like the way you looked and wished you could be different (taller, stronger, better-looking)	66	45	69
15	You had to go to bed when you didn't feel like it	64	30	47
20	Your mother or father forgot to do something they said they would do	62	39	63
1	Kids at school teased you	61	31	51
9	Your mother or father got sick	59	47	80
12	Your schoolwork was too hard	59	31	53
17	You didn't know the answer when the teacher called on you	58	31	53
16	Your mother or father didn't have enough time to do something with you	57	39	68
7	Your mother or father wasn't home when you expected them	55	26	47
25	You didn't have enough privacy (a time and place to be alone) when you wanted it	54	35	66
3	You were punished for something you didn't do	50	44	88
14	You didn't do well at sports	45	25	56

Item Number	*Item Content*	PERCENTAGE *Occurrence*	*Feeling Bad*	*Potency*
11	Your teacher was mad at you because of your behavior	44	27	61
19	Your mother and father were fighting	43	35	81
18	When the kids were picking teams you were one of the last ones to be picked	39	24	62
5	Your pet died	36	32	89
10	Your mother or father was mad at you for getting a bad school report	35	28	80
13	You got into a fight with another kid	35	18	51
6	Your best friend didn't want to be your best friend anymore	30	24	64

ents (parent sick, parent mad about school report, and parents fighting), two concerned punishment (punished unfairly, punished for wrongdoing), and one was a miscellaneous item (pet died).

Uplift items were also analyzed in a similar manner, and the results appear in table 8.2. Events on the Children's Uplift Scale occurred very frequently, with 41 to 95 percent of sixth graders endorsing each item. Twenty-four of the 25 events occurred for more than half the sample. Subjects on average indicated that 17.5 (SD = 7.8) events on the Uplifts Scale occurred during the past month. Thus, early adolescents generally reported having more uplifts than hassles occurring in their lives ($t = 7.3$, $p < .001$).

In contrast to the data for hassles, when uplift events occurred their effect was generally affectively toned. Overall, 21 of 25 events made more than 50 percent of the early adolescents feel good (*see* column 2 in table 8.2). There was a very strong correlation between the percentage of the sample endorsing an item and the percentage who felt good as a result of that event ($r = 0.82$, $p < .001$). This correlation is markedly stronger than the comparable correlation for hassles ($z = 8.8$, $p < .001$). The most frequently occurring events that made youngsters feel good included getting a good mark at school (82 percent), having a good time with friends (82 percent), and having a school holiday (76 percent).

Potency scores were also calculated for uplift items (*see* column 3 of

TABLE 8.2
Percentage of Sample Endorsing Items on the Children's Uplifts Scale

Item Number	*Item Content*	PERCENTAGE *Occurrence*	*Feeling Good*	*Potency*
1	You got a good mark at school	95	82	87
10	You had a good time playing with your friends	93	82	89
6	Your teacher was pleased with you	89	69	81
7	You went out to eat	88	63	73
9	There was a school holiday	88	76	87
19	Your mother or father spent time with you	87	71	83
21	You got a phone call or a letter	87	53	62
22	You had fun joking with the kids at school	83	63	77
23	You learned something new	83	50	62
13	You got some new clothes	82	67	83
8	Your friends wanted you to be on their team	81	69	86
12	Your parents were pleased with a good grade that you got	80	68	86
14	You did something special with your mother or father	79	68	87
20	You made or fixed something by yourself	78	57	74
3	You won a game	77	63	83
2	You got a present you really wanted	76	72	96
18	You did well at sports	75	60	81
4	You found something you thought you had lost	73	59	82
5	You helped your brother or sister	71	44	63
25	You made a new friend	68	58	86
17	You played with your pet	64	48	76
24	Your mother or father agreed with you that something wasn't your fault	64	54	86
16	You were helped by your brother or sister	63	40	65
15	You had a good time at a party	60	52	88
11	You gave a talk at school that went well	41	30	75

table 8.2). Nineteen of the 25 items were classified as potent uplifts, that is, events which, when they happened, made 75 percent or more of the sample feel good. The most potent items (in descending order of potency) were: receiving a present (96 percent), having a good time with friends (89 percent), having a good time at a party (88 percent), getting a good mark at school (87 percent), having a school holiday (87 percent), and doing a special activity with parents (87 percent).

Gender Differences. In general, girls and boys did not differ in the number of hassles that they reported as occurring. At the item level, only two of the 25 items showed a gender difference; girls more often than boys reported not liking their looks ($\chi^2=9.5$, $p<.001$), whereas boys more often than girls reported that teachers were mad with them about their behavior ($\chi^2=5.3$, $p<.05$). Although hassles occurred equally often for boys and girls, they were experienced quite differently. Girls reported significantly more bad hassles than did boys ($Ms=9.6$ vs. 6.5 respectively, $t=4.3$, $p<.001$). This pattern held for 14 of the 25 hassle items, as shown in table 8.3, suggesting a general rather than a content-specific gender effect. Not surprisingly, gender differences were also found in the potency of 10 hassles. In all instances the events were more potent for girls than for boys, with the largest gender differences for the following items: parents fighting (93 vs. 64 percent for girls' and boys' potency scores respectively, $\chi^2=10.2$, $p<.001$); siblings bugged you (60 vs. 33 percent, $\chi^2=11.4$, $p<.001$); and not liking your looks (80 vs. 43 percent, $\chi^2=16.3$, $p<.001$). Additional significant gender differences (at $p<.05$) in potency scores emerged for the following events: kids teasing, losing something, parents sick, parents mad about school report, not knowing the answer when the teacher called on you, other kids were better at something, and not enough privacy. These items come from several different life domains, again suggesting a generalized gender difference in the impact of hassles on youngsters' affective experience. There were no gender differences in potency scores for uplifts.

Family Structure Differences. Adolescents from intact, blended, and single-parent families were compared on each hassle and uplift item on both the frequency with which each item occurred and their reaction to each event. Only the frequency of hassles differed for the three groups. Adolescents from intact families were less likely to have peer problems (teased by kids), χ^2 (2)$=7.1$, $p<.05$; lost best friend, χ^2 (2)$=10.0$, $p<.01$), feel incompetent at school (schoolwork too hard), χ^2 (2)$=6.5$, $p<.05$; not know answer when called upon in class, χ^2 (2)$=5.9$, $p<.05$) and feel that adults were upset with them (teacher mad about behavior),

TABLE 8.3
Gender Differences in Frequency of Bad Hassles

Item Number	*Item Content*	FREQUENCY (%) *Girls*	*Boys*	χ^2
1	Kids at school teased you	37	21	5.5**
2	You had to clean up your room	25	14	2.8+
6	Your best friend didn't want to be your best friend anymore	30	15	5.7**
8	You lost something	54	39	4.6*
12	Your schoolwork was too hard	37	23	4.0*
16	Your mother or father didn't have enough time to do something with you	45	30	3.9*
19	Your mother and father were fighting	42	26	4.6*
20	Your mother or father forgot to do something they said they would do	44	31	3.3*
22	Your brothers and sisters bugged you	45	25	7.9*
23	You didn't like the way you looked and wished you could be different (e.g., taller, stronger, better-looking)	59	23	25.1***
24	Another kid could do something better than you	37	18	8.0**
25	You didn't have enough privacy (a time and place to be alone) when you wanted it	42	24	6.7**

$+p<.10$; $^*p<.05$; $^{**}p<.01$; $^{***}p<.001$

χ^2 (2) = 7.2, $p<.05$; parents mad about school report, χ^2 (2) = 6.1, $p<0.5$). It is interesting that none of the items dealing with the availability of parents differentiated between youths from intact, blended, and single-parent families.

Ethnic Differences. There were scattered differences between white, Asian, and Hispanic adolescents. These findings are tentatively presented due to the small sample size and the number of analyses carried out. In terms of frequency of events, fewer Asian youths reported that they played with pets (χ^2 (2)=25.0, p<.001), that their parents agreed that something was not their fault (χ^2 (2)=8.7, p<.01), and that they were involved in fights (χ^2 (2)=6.4, p<.05). More Hispanic than other youths reported that parents were mad at them because of their school reports (χ^2 (2)=12.8, p<.001). Three items differentiated the ethnic groups in terms of reactions to uplift and hassle items. Hispanic youths were less likely to feel good when they got a present (χ^2 (2)=8.9, p<.05); Asian youths were less likely to feel good when they received a letter or phone call (χ^2 (2)=8.7, p<.05); and white youths were more likely to feel good when parents agreed that something was not their fault (χ^2 (2)=8.2, p<.05).

Relationship to Adaptational Outcomes

. . . In general, bad hassles were highly associated with negative outcomes (such as anxiety, depression, and distress) and moderately associated with the absence of positive outcomes (such as restraint, friendship support, general self-worth, and perceived social competence). Conversely, good uplifts were consistently linked to positive outcomes and negatively associated with depression and distress. The magnitude of correlations was generally higher for bad hassles (the absolute values of r ranging from .22 to .60, p<.001) than for good uplifts (the absolute values of r ranging from .03 to .38, p ranging from n.s. to <.001), with the strongest relationships appearing for anxiety, depression, and distress for bad hassles. Most noteworthy for good uplifts was the absence of a significant association with anxiety (r=.03, n.s.).

When examined separately by gender, the most striking deviation from the overall pattern was the stronger negative correlation between hassles and the positive adaptational outcomes for boys than girls. In fact, the magnitude of correlations for boys was greater than for girls on almost every outcome; a reversal of the pattern found for adults (Kanner et al. 1981). Correlations were all in the theoretically expected direction, with one exception; for girls there was a tendency for good uplifts and anxiety to be positively associated (r=.16, p<.05).

In light of the significant correlation between bad hassles and good uplifts for girls, analyses were conducted to explore the unique contribution of bad hassles and good uplifts to the adaptational outcomes. By use of partial correlations the possibility was addressed that the shared variance between good uplifts and bad hassles variance may actually

TABLE 8.4
Stepwise Multiple Regressions of Adaptational Outcomes, With Bad Hassles Entered First, Followed by Good Uplifts

Adaptational Outcomes	R	*Overall* R^2 *Bad Hassles*	R^2 *Good Uplifts*
Anxiety	.61***	.36***	.02*
Depression	.59***	.15***	.20***
Distress	.54***	.18***	.11***
Restraint	.31***	.05**	.04**
Friendship Support	.38***	.05**	.10***
Perceived Social Competence	.43***	.07***	.11***
General Self-Worth	.46***	.11***	.10***

*$p<.05$; **$p<.01$; ***$p<.001$

"muddle" or reduce the relationship between these factors and the outcome variables.

... The partial correlations between bad hassles and adaptational outcomes controlling for good uplifts ... show that the correlations were elevated for virtually all of the girls' outcomes, especially depression, friendship support, and social competence. ... The correlations between good uplifts and the same outcomes with frequency of bad hassles partialled out ... show consistent improvement in the strength of the girls' correlations between good uplifts and the outcome variables. Moreover, the previously observed counterintuitive trend toward a positive good uplifts/anxiety relationship for girls was no longer evident ($r = .03$, n.s.). Thus, it seems likely that shared good uplifts/bad hassles variance represents response bias that dilutes the findings for both scores.

The Unique Contribution of Uplifts

Another important question in this research is whether good uplifts can add significantly to the relationship between bad hassles and adaptational outcomes. That is, can good uplifts contribute "unique" variance beyond the effects of bad hassles? Although an affirmative answer to this question is suggested by the partial correlation analysis just presented, a stepwise regression analysis, in which the hassles variable is entered before the uplifts variable, provides a more direct answer to this question. As shown in table 8.4, for most of the adaptational outcomes good uplifts added significantly, and sometimes quite substantially, to the variance accounted for by bad hassles. However, for some adaptational outcomes the contribution of uplifts differed for boys and girls. For example, for girls, bad hassles accounted for approximately 7 percent of the variance in depression, whereas good uplifts contributed an additional 19 percent of the variance. For boys, bad hassles accounted for 37 percent of the variance in this variable, whereas uplifts added 15 percent unique variance.

Also noteworthy is the contrast in results for boys and girls vis-à-vis social competence. . . . Although the multiple *R* was .45 ($p<.001$) for each sex, for girls good uplifts accounted for 19 percent of the variance in social competence, whereas for boys it contributed an insignificant 1 percent of the variance beyond that of hassles.

Discussion

The present study addresses two major questions regarding the psychological correlates of daily uplifts and hassles. First, are uplifts and hassles associated with adaptational outcomes in early adolescents, as they evidently are in adults? Second, do uplifts contribute to adaptational outcomes independent of hassles, an intuitively attractive proposition that has yielded equivocal results for adults (Kanner et al. 1981; Monroe 1983)? The results of the present study provide strong evidence for an affirmative answer to both these questions, and raise further provocative issues regarding differences in the impact of uplifts and hassles as a function of age and gender.

In the present study, both uplifts and hassles were substantially associated with an array of adaptational outcomes. As expected, an increased frequency of hassles was associated with greater emotional distress and perceived interpersonal problems. Conversely, an increased frequency in uplifts was consistently associated with a diversity of indicators of emotional well-being and social adjustment. It needs to be borne in mind that the correlational nature of the data does not permit causal inferences. Nevertheless, in addition to providing an initial validation of the CHS and CUS, these findings provide the first reported instance for either adults or adolescents of a measure of daily uplifts showing substantial relationships to a range of adaptational outcomes in the anticipated directions.

A critical question in the *tandem* use of measures of uplifts and hassles in children is whether uplifts bear a relationship to adaptational outcomes that is independent of hassles. The results of this study clearly indicate that uplifts generally account for significant variance in social-emotional functioning above and beyond that attributable to hassles. In fact, for girls, uplifts were more closely associated with several adaptational outcomes than were hassles, even when shared hassles/uplifts variance was "credited" only to hassles.

. . .

Gender Differences

The gender differences found in this study are probably best understood when cast in a developmental framework and, when possible, comcomes. Three quite distinct correlational patterns were observed in the data. One pattern, that found for depression, was quite reasonable and straightforward. Specifically, both hassles and uplifts were correlated in the expected directions and showed independent associations with depression. These results support the notion that the *absence* of positive experiences adds to depression beyond the adverse effects due to the presence of negative experiences (Kanner, Kafry, and Pines 1978; Lewinsohn and Talkington 1979). The correlational results do not rule out the possibility that depression may also increase the perception of bad hassles and decrease the perception of good uplifts (*see* Cohen, Burt, and Bjork 1987).

A more puzzling pattern arose with anxiety for girls. The simple correlations revealed the expected positive association between hassles and anxiety. However, a higher frequency of uplifts was not associated with lower anxiety, but instead was modestly associated with higher anxiety. Moreover, in contrast to the pattern found with depression, uplifts did not show a relationship to anxiety that was independent of hassles. These different uplifts/hassles configurations for depression versus anxiety are especially noteworthy in light of recent suggestions that, at least in children, depression and anxiety are so closely related that they ought to be combined to form a broad-band construct referred to as "negative affectivity" (Wolfe et al. 1987). The results of this study caution us against moving in this direction. The findings are more consistent with a hierarchical view that subtypes of distress are highly inter-related but nonetheless distinct (Weinberger et al. 1987).

Finally, the results demonstrated yet another pattern, namely, that for girls, perceived social competence was more strongly associated with uplifts than with hassles, whereas for boys it was more strongly related to hassles than uplifts. This pattern runs contrary to recent claims that positive and negative experiences are primarily correlated only with other events of the same valence (Costa and McCrae 1980). Taken in conjunction with the other patterns just presented, it appears that both the particular outcomes being considered (e.g., depression, anxiety, social competence) and gender of the subject need to be taken into account in order to understand the respective contributions of positive and negative events. Stated somewhat differently, positive and negative experiences are not simply either "opposites" or "buffers" of each other, but instead are more complexly interwoven in the lives of early adolescents than previously imagined.

In attempting to understand patterns of positive and negative events in general, it is useful to compare the present findings with those of a recent study by Cohen, Burt, and Bjork (1987), who assessed positive and negative *life events* in a similar age group and with comparable outcome measures. They found that, as with hassles, negative life events were substantially associated with depression, anxiety, and self-esteem. Paralleling the findings for uplifts, positive life events were significantly related to depression and self-esteem, but not related to anxiety. In terms of future research, the life events measures generated by Cohen, Burt, and Bjork, along with the CUS and CHS, make it possible to compare directly the impact of daily events to major life events on the lives of early adolescents, as has been done for adults (cf. DeLongis et al. 1982; Kanner et al. 1981; Monroe 1983).

Another, more descriptive, approach to examining uplifts/hassles patterns is provided by comparing the most potent uplifts to the most potent hassles. Potent events were those events that made youngsters feel good or bad a high percentage of the time they occurred. In the present study, twelve-year-old children generally rated uplifts as more potent than hassles and reported a greater range of potency for hassles than uplifts. This may simply reflect the content of the items chosen for the scales or, consistent with other research, the fact that people tend to report more good than bad experiences (cf. Bradburn 1969). Within this context, the most potent hassles were with parents, whereas the most potent uplifts encompassed a number of areas, including both peers and parents. It seems that children of this age find the unavailability of parents to be particularly distressing. In contrast, significant pleasure can arise from several areas of life. It would not be surprising if, as these children continue through adolescence, peer relationships both surpass parental relationships as the most salient source of uplifts and come to rival parents as a primary source of hassles. In general, examining shifts over time in patterns of uplifts and hassles and their potency could provide a useful method for tracking developmental changes in stress and coping in children and adolescents.

Gender Differences

The gender differences found in this study are probably best understood when cast in a developmental framework and, when possible, compared to results of uplifts and hassles findings from the adult literature. One reason for this is that the twelve-year-old girls and boys were, in all likelihood, in different developmental stages. Twelve-year-old girls are typically in the early stages of adolescence, with its emerging focus on peer relationships, bodily changes, and autonomy needs. This is evidenced by girls' discontent with their appearance (our largest and strongest sex difference). Twelve-year-old boys, in contrast, are still by and large immersed in the developmental tasks of the so-called "latency" period, with its more "external" emphasis on rules, concepts of fairness, and mastery of the physical environment. Thus, a more complete assessment of sex differences for developmentally comparable groups to 12-year-olds may have to await the addition of data from 10-year-old girls and 14-year-old boys.

Several gender differences are worthy of note. First, although girls and boys reported the same number of hassles and uplifts, girls experienced the hassles as "bad" more often than boys. This is consistent with the widely held belief that girls experience and/or are willing to report more negative or vulnerable feelings than are boys. Developmentally it would be interesting to discover how early this difference first appears. Does this gender difference exist in childhood, or does it first emerge at puberty? If it is linked to puberty will pubertal boys also report being more troubled by everyday events than latency-aged boys?

Second, even though boys said they had fewer bad hassles than girls, the relationship between bad hassles and social-emotional adjustment was stronger for twelve-year-old boys than for girls, a result also reported by Bobo et al. (1986) for a more limited range of variables. Yet for adults, whether major or everyday events were assessed, the more powerful associations were reported for women (Billings and Moos 1981; Kanner et al. 1981; Matheny and Cupp 1983). It would seem that at some point between age 12 and adulthood a reversal occurs in the significance of positive and negative experiences for males and females. What these changes mean is far from clear, but before interpreting the adult pattern the developmental sequence that precedes it needs to be described. For example, Matheny and Cupp (1983) suggest that women somaticize more than men, and hence a stronger stress-illness relationship exists for them. Thus, for women, stress, psychological distress, and psychosomatic symptoms are all strongly interrelated. In the present study of early adolescents only stress and psychological distress were assessed. It would be interesting to include measures of psychosomatic symptoms in future studies to determine if a similar strong pattern of relationships among these three variables also exists for twelve-year-old boys.

Third, although a negative correlation between uplifts and anxiety emerged for boys, a weak positive association was found for girls. Is this a foreshadowing of the counterintuitive, but much stronger, positive association between *positive* events and a variety of undesirable outcomes found for adult women (Kanner et al. 1981; Matheny and Cupp 1983; Monroe 1983)? The present results suggest that positive experiences are at least mildly anxiety-producing for girls, and that whatever the cause, it increases in adulthood. One direction for future research is to chart the relationship between uplifts and undesirable outcomes for females and males at different phases of adolescence and into young adulthood.

In sum, this research links children's uplifts and hassles to several important areas of social-emotional functioning. It also provides the first evidence supporting the value of using uplifts to predict adaptational outcomes above and beyond hassles. The findings of the present study suggest that uplifts are not merely the inverse of hassles, but that the two operate together in complex ways that vary markedly as a function of the outcomes and the people being considered. Moreover, combined with the results of adult studies, there is the intriguing possibility that changes occur in the very meaning and impact of positive and negative events during the transition from childhood to adulthood.

APPENDIX A
Children's Hassles Scale

Here is a list of things that children sometimes feel bothered or upset about. We want to know if any of these things have happened to you *during the last month* and how you felt about them.

1. Kids at school teased you.
2. You had to clean up your room.
3. You were punished for something you didn't do.
4. You got punished when you did something wrong.
5. Your pet died.
6. Your best friend didn't want to be your best friend anymore.
7. Your mother or father wasn't home when you expected them.
8. You lost something.
9. Your mother or father got sick.
10. Your mother or father was mad at you for getting a bad school report.
11. Your teacher was mad at you because of your behavior.
12. Your schoolwork was too hard.
13. You got into a fight with another kid.
14. You didn't do well at sports.
15. You had to go to bed when you didn't feel like it.
16. Your mother or father didn't have enough time to do something with you.
17. You didn't know the answer when the teacher called on you.
18. When the kids were picking teams you were one of the last ones to be picked.
19. Your mother and father were fighting.
20. Your mother or father forgot to do something they said they would do.
21. You felt bored and wished there was something interesting to do.
22. Your brothers and sisters bugged you.
23. You didn't like the way you looked and wished you could be different (e.g., taller, stronger, better-looking).
24. Another kid could do something better than you could.
25. You didn't have enough privacy (a time and place to be alone) when you wanted it.

APPENDIX B
Children's Uplifts Scale

Here is a list of things children sometimes feel good about. We want to know if any of these things happened to you *during the last month* and how it made you feel.

1. You got a good mark at school.
2. You got a present you really wanted.
3. You won a game.
4. You found something you thought you'd lost.
5. You helped your brother or sister.
6. Your teacher was pleased with you.
7. You went out to eat.
8. Friends wanted you to be on their team.
9. There was a school holiday.
10. You had a good time playing with friends.
11. You gave a talk at school that went well.
12. Your parents were pleased with your grades.
13. You got some new clothes.
14. You did something special with your mom or dad.
15. You had a good time at a party.
16. You were helped by your brother or sister.
17. You played with your pet.
18. You did well at sports.
19. Your mother or father spent time with you.
20. You made or fixed something by yourself.
21. You got a phone call or a letter.
22. You had fun joking with the kids at school.
23. You learned something new.
24. You made a new friend.
25. Your parents agreed with you that something wasn't your fault.

III
The Concept of Coping

Part III marks a transition from an emphasis on the nature of stress to the ways in which people handle stress, i.e., coping. The first selection, written by Lazarus and Folkman (1984c), surveys orthodox approaches to coping. These traditional approaches to coping are based on two distinct literatures, one associated with animal experimentation and the other with psychoanalytic ego psychology. Lazarus and Folkman point out the limitations and defects of each of these approaches. For example, the animal model provides little information regarding cognitive forms of coping, while the ego psychology model often suggests that some forms of coping are better or more successful than others. To illustrate the latter point, defense mechanisms are regarded by traditional theorists as maladaptive and less desirable than other forms of "coping." As Lazarus and Folkman note, no strategy for handling stress should be considered inherently better or worse than any other. Judgments about the adaptiveness of a coping strategy should be made contextually. Lazarus and Folkman provide illustrations of when defenses, such as denial, may be appropriate and quite successful.[1]

In our next selection, Folkman and Lazarus (1990) consider the merits of breaking with traditional approaches to coping which emphasize static, structural elements (such as traits and styles) and of turning to the study of coping from a *process* vantage point.[2] To illustrate this newer approach to coping, Folkman and Lazarus explore the relationship between coping and emotion. They argue that coping is a mediator of emotion. Coping, in other words, affects emotional responses. Exactly how coping alters emotions is not clear but Folkman and Lazarus spell out several possibilities: 1) cognitive activity may influence the deployment of attention; 2) cognitive activity may alter the subjective meaning or significance of an encounter for well-being; or 3) actions may alter the actual person-environment relationship. Folkman and Lazarus emphasize the continually changing nature of coping and emotion, a fact that requires investigators to consider coping and emotion from a perspective which recognizes their temporal and unfolding complexion.

Cohen (1987) discusses several issues relevant to the measurement of coping, some of which were addressed by earlier articles. The unique contribution, however, of Cohen's paper is its listing of trait and episodic measures of coping. While the listing is not an exhaustive one, it does cover commonly used coping measures such as Folkman and Lazarus' (1980, 1988b) Ways of Coping Questionnaire, Byrne's (1961) Repression-Sensitization Scale, and Joffe and Naditch's (1977) Coping-Defense Scales. Each of the scales is discussed from the standpoint of its development and limitations.

Why do some people experience high degrees of stress (e.g., many stressful life events) without becoming ill? According to the work of some researchers, personality may have something to do with staying healthy.[3] For example, Kobasa (1979) found three personality factors that effectively buffered male management personnel from illness: a sense of *control* over what occurs in their lives, *commitment* to the various areas of their lives (especially a strong commitment to self, i.e., to one's values, goals, and priorities), and a view of change as a *challenge.* Together, these three characteristics (control, commitment, challenge) make up what Kobasa called the "hardy personality."

In our next selection, Maddi and Kobasa (1984a) discuss the hardy personality characteristics from the standpoint of how they develop. Maddi and Kobasa believe that one learns hardiness in a particular kind of family atmosphere.

> The social and physical environment changes frequently, and includes many moderately difficult tasks. Parents encourage their children to construe the changes as richness and support efforts to perform the tasks successfully. More generally, the parents are warm and enthusiastic enough toward the children that their interactions are usually pleasant, rewarding, and supportive of the child's individuality.(1984a:50)

To support their views, Maddi and Kobasa cite clinical examples as well as research studies involving animals and humans. Moreover, in other parts of their book, not included here, they provide advice on how to acquire hardiness as an adult if you did not learn it as a child and on how organizations can effectively cope with changes so as to minimize any risk to the health, morale, and effectiveness of their employees.

It remains to be seen whether Maddi and Kobasa's views are upheld in future research. The hardiness concept and its relationship to disease has generated hundreds of research studies to date. Despite the generally supportive findings, numerous investigations also have been critical (e.g., Allred and Smith 1989; Funk and Houston 1987; Hull, VanTreuren, and Virnelli 1987). If the concept is a reliable one, how hardiness buffers a highly stressed individual from illness and what hardy people actually do to cope with stress more effectively than others, need to be addressed adequately. (Maddi and Kobasa's suggestion that hardy individuals effectively resist illness because they use transformational coping rather than regressive coping is a controversial one.[4])

Our next selection, written by Belle (1987), tackles the frequently researched topic of social support. The vast literature on this topic has often been characterized by rather simplistic notions such that social support is always beneficial to health, or that the more one socializes, the better off one will be. Fortunately, many today recognize that the issues related to social support are complex and demand fairly sophisticated theories and research procedures. For example, it is now recognized that there are different types of social support and that social support may create problems for individuals and indeed serve as sources of stress in life.

Belle's paper explores gender differences in social support, a topic which has been relatively neglected in the coping field. Based upon her review of the literature, Belle concludes that

> women tend to (1) maintain more emotionally intimate relationships than do men, (2) mobilize more social supports in times of stress than do men while relying less heavily than men on the spouse as a source of social support, and (3) provide more frequent and more effective social support to others than do men. (1987:266)

The consequences of these findings are explored in terms of their positive and negative implications. For example, women's tendencies toward emotionally intimate relationships may induce them to take on the stresses of those with whom they are intimately close. Thus, the more frequent "giving" of social support may mean an increase in vulnerability for "getting" stress.[5]

The final selection in part III deals with a topic that has been at the forefront of popularity and controversy in the stress and coping domain —Type A behavior. This pattern of behavior is typically described as involving constant pressured interactions with the environment and a compelling sense of time urgency, aggressiveness, competitiveness, and generalized hostility (Friedman and Rosenman 1974). In a sense, this pattern is the Type A's mode of coping with internalized societal values of achievement and the work ethic. What makes the Type A behavior pattern so important is its presumed relationship with risk for coronary heart disease. Type As are twice as likely as Type Bs (people with a more relaxed, easygoing lifestyle) to have a heart attack (Haynes, Feinleib, and Eaker 1983; Haynes, Feinleib, and Kannel 1980; Rosenman et al. 1975). This relationship between the Type A behavior pattern and heart disease appears to hold up for males and perhaps females, though it may be strongest for white-collar, managerial-level males (O'Rourke et al. 1988).

Wright's (1988) article addresses several important issues pertaining to the Type A literature. First, Wright discusses the point that the *global* Type A pattern may not predict coronary heart disease as well as do some of its *components.* In other words, perhaps it is not everything about the Type A pattern that contributes to heart disease, but only key or essential ingredients. Debate about this has continued for some time. For example, some researchers (e.g., Spielberger, Krasner, and Solomon 1988; Williams 1989) argue that the *hostility/anger* component of the Type A pattern is the major culprit in the coronary-prone puzzle. Wright presents his argument for the importance of the *time-urgency/chronic-activation* component as well. Second, Wright explores factors in the development of the Type A behavior pattern and the value of various psychological theories for explaining this "personality type." Third, Wright reviews some of the possible physiological links between the Type A behavior pattern and coronary heart disease, such as the caustic effects of excessive levels of adrenalin and noradrenalin. Later sections of Wright's article address the concerns of researching, diagnosing, and treating Type A behavior,[6] along with some conclusions for the general public. All in all, Wright has provided an effective overview of a controversial and highly relevant field of study.

NOTES

1. *See* related comments in the introductory chapter earlier in this anthology.
2. Ibid.
3. *See* Taylor's (1990) article earlier in this anthology for a related discussion.
4. *Transformational* coping, according to Maddi and Kobasa, involves altering events so they are less stressful. This is done by interacting decisively with events, and by thinking about them optimistically. *Regressive* coping is less effective than transformational coping and involves thinking about events pessimistically and acting evasively to avoid contact with them (Maddi and Kobasa 1984b:28; cf. Lazarus and Folkman 1984b).
5. For more information on findings regarding gender differences in stress and coping, the reader should consult the volume from which Belle's article was selected, *Gender and Stress* (Barnett, Biener, and Baruch 1987).
6. *See* Roskies' (1987) article later in this anthology for further information pertinent to the modification of Type A behavior.

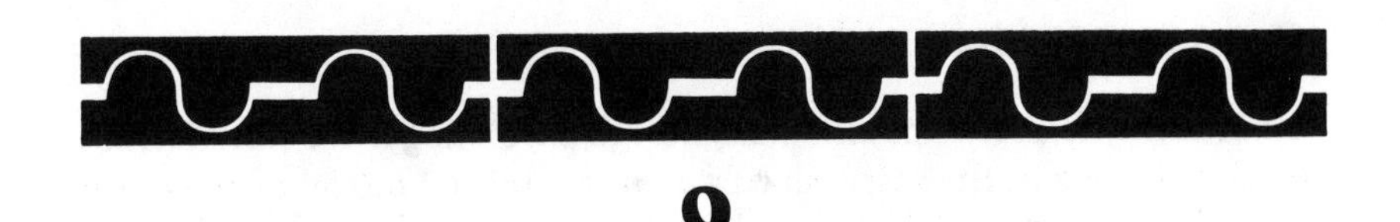

9

The Concept of Coping

■

RICHARD S. LAZARUS AND
SUSAN FOLKMAN

The concept of coping has been important in psychology for well over forty years. It provided an organizing theme in clinical description and evaluation in the 1940s and 1950s and is currently the focus of an array of psychotherapies and educational programs which have as their goal the development of coping skills. The subject of coping has also received widespread lay attention, as can be seen by scanning any magazine rack, best-seller list, or broadcast schedule. Indeed, coping is as much a colloquial term as a scientific one. Despite the rich history and current popularity associated with coping, however, there is little coherence in theory, research, and understanding. Even the most cursory inspection of readings selected from scholarly and lay publications reveals confusion as to what is meant by coping and how it functions in the process of adaptation.

Traditional Approaches

The concept of coping is found in two very different theoretical/research literatures, one derived form the tradition of animal experimentation, the other from psychoanalytic ego psychology. We have already discussed some of the research based on the animal model of stress and control. This approach is heavily influenced by Darwinian thought, according to which survival hinges on the animal discovering what is predictable and controllable in the environment in order to avoid, escape, or overcome noxious agents. The animal is dependent on its nervous system to make the necessary survival-related discrimination.

Within the animal model, coping is frequently defined as acts that control aversive environmental conditions, thereby lowering psychophysiological disturbance. N. E. Miller (1980) says, for example, that coping consists of the learned behavioral responses that are successful in lowering arousal by neutralizing a dangerous or noxious condition. Similarly, Ursin (1980) states that "the gradual development of a response decrement in the animal experiments as well as the human experiments is coping. The animal is learning to cope through the lowering of drive tension by positive reinforcement" (p. 264).

Some of the most interesting research on the psychophysiology of coping and cardiovascular responses has been done by Obrist (1981) and his colleagues, in particular their work on the concept of active, as contrasted to passive, coping. This research suggests strongly that active coping is an important mediator of sympathetically controlled cardiovascular changes.

It will come as no surprise that overall we consider the animal model of coping simplistic and lacking in the cognitive-emotional richness and complexity that is an integral part of human functioning. The central theme of the animal model, for example, is the unidimensional concept of drive or arousal, and research centers largely on avoidance and escape behavior. With this emphasis little can be learned about strategies that are so important in human affairs, such as cognitive coping and defense.

In the psychoanalytic ego psychology model, coping is defined as realistic and flexible thoughts and acts that solve problems and thereby reduce stress. The main difference between the treatment of coping in this model compared to the animal model is the focus on ways of perceiving and thinking about the person's relationship with the environment. Although behavior is not ignored, it is treated as less important than cognition.

Another difference between the models is that the psychoanalytic ego psychology approach differentiates among a number of processes that people use to handle person-environment relationships. For example, Menninger (1963), Haan (1969, 1977), and Vaillant (1977) each offer a hierarchy in which coping refers to the highest and most advanced or mature ego processes, followed by defenses, which refer to neurotic modes of adaptation, also hierarchically arranged, and finally, at the bottom, processes that Haan calls fragmentation or ego-failure and Menninger refers to as regressive or psychotic levels of ego functioning.

Menninger (1963), in one of the earliest formulations, identifies five orders of regulatory devices that are ranked according to the level of internal disorganization they indicate. At the top of this hierarchy are strategies for reducing tensions caused by stressful episodes in the course of ordinary living. These strategies are called coping devices, and include self-control, humor, crying, swearing, weeping, boasting, talking it out, thinking through, and working off energy. They are regarded as normal or, at worst, as idiosyncratic characteristics. If these strategies are used inappropriately or to an extreme, however, as when a person talks too much, laughs too easily, loses his or her temper frequently, or seems restless and erratic, they lose their status as coping devices and become symptoms indicating a degree of dyscontrol and threatened disequilibration. The greater the internal disorganization, the more primitive the regulatory devices become. For example, second-order devices include withdrawal by dissociation (narcolepsy, amnesia, depersonalization), withdrawal by displacement of aggression (e.g., aversion, prejudice, phobias, counterphobic attitudes), substitution of symbols and modalities for more frankly hostile discharge (e.g., compulsions, rituals), and substitution of the self or a part of the self as an object of displaced aggression (self-imposed restriction and abasement, self-intoxication or narcotization). Third-order devices are represented by episodic, explosive outbursts of aggressive energy, more or less disorganized, including assaultive violence, convulsions, and panic attacks. The fourth order represents increased disorganization, and the fifth order is total disintegration of the ego. In this system, coping devices are those that indicate minimal disruption and disorganization. Any device that indicates dyscontrol or disequilibration is by definition not a coping device.

Vaillant (1977) groups defenses in four levels progressing from psychotic mechanisms (e.g., denial of external reality, distortion, and delusional projection) through immature mechanisms (e.g., fantasy, projection, hypochondriasis, passive-aggressive behavior), neurotic mechanisms (e.g., intellectualization, repression, and reaction-formation), to the highest level, mature mechanisms (e.g., sublimation, altruism, suppression, anticipation, and humor).

Like Menninger (1963) and Vaillant (1977), Haan (1969, 1977) also uses a hierarchical system for classifying ego processes. She proposes a tripartite hierarchical arrangement—coping, defending, and fragmentation—and identifies the modes by the manner in which an underlying generic ego process is expressed. For example, the generic process, means-end symbolization, is expressed as logical analysis in coping, rationalization in defense, and confabulation in fragmentation. Sensitivity is expressed as empathy in coping, projection in defense, and delusion in fragmentation. The major criterion Haan uses to define processes in the coping mode is adherence to reality. If a person distorts "intersubjective" reality, he or she is not coping; "the person's accuracy is the hallmark of coping, whether or not he is actually situationally successful" (Haan 1977:164). The underlying presumptive value is that

> it is better to know one's intrasubjective and intersubjective situations accurately and to act in that framework, than it is to distort or negate one's appraisals and actions. The value is then one of accuracy in . . . interpersonal interchange, and to know that value is to match social and personal reality as it is defined by common, practical agreements about the nature of our mutual experiences.
>
> All the properties of coping . . . —choice of action, flexibility, and reality adherence—rest on the value of accuracy and can be deduced from it. (p. 80)

Coping Traits and Styles

The psychoanalytic ego psychology models that have dominated coping theory have also dominated coping measurement. The measurement purpose to which these models have been applied, however, has generally been limited to classifying people in order to make predictions about how they will cope with some or all types of stressful encounters. This application of the psychoanalytic ego psychology model results in viewing coping structurally as a style or trait rather than as a dynamic ego process. For example, a person may be classified as a conformist or conscientious, obsessive-compulsive, or as a suppressor, repressor, or sublimator (cf. Loevinger 1976; Shapiro 1965; Vaillant 1977).

A coping style differs from a trait primarily in degree, and usually refers to broad, pervasive, encompassing ways of relating to particular types of people such as the powerful or the powerless, the friendly or the hostile, the controlling or the permissive, or to particular types of situations such as ambiguous or clear, imminent or distant, temporary or chronic, evaluative or nonevaluative. Traits, which are regarded as properties of persons that dispose them to react in certain ways in given classes of situations, are usually narrower in scope. Examples of traits that have been identified with coping include repression-sensitization (e.g., Krohne and Rogner 1982; Shipley et al. 1978; Shipley, Butt, and Horwitz 1979), "anger-in" and "anger-out" (e.g., Funkenstein, King, and Drolette 1957; Harburg, Blakelock, and Roeper 1979), coping-avoiding (e.g., Goldstein 1959, 1973), or monitoring-blunting (e.g., S. Miller 1980). (For a comprehensive review of trait measures, *see* Moos 1974.)

Some of the richest descriptions of coping styles based on the ego psychology model can be found in case reports, as in the work of Vaillant (1977). Vaillant examined data on male college graduates that had been gathered over a 30-year period and then interviewed each subject. He put together his impressions with those of the investigators who had preceded him and evolved comprehensive descriptions of each subject. In addition, behaviors that occurred at time of crisis and conflict were interpreted by raters as to the defense mechanisms they suggested. Vaillant presents approximately half these subjects in case studies that are graphic and effective in conveying the styles with which these men managed their relationships with other people, troubling events, and the pursuit of commitments and goals. From these analyses he also distills what he calls the "adaptive style" that best characterizes the way these men manage their lives in general.

Unfortunately, descriptions of coping styles that are based on case analyses tend to be idiographic portraits rather than examples of common coping styles. As such, the utility of this approach is limited in that it does not facilitate interpersonal comparisons and group analysis. Furthermore, case studies used in research have the practical drawback of requiring enormous amounts of time and money for data gathering and analysis.

. . .

Cognitive Styles

The ego psychology model also spawned a body of theory and research on cognitive styles. Cognitive styles refer to automatic rather than effortful responses, and therefore we do not consider them as coping or coping styles. (We will discuss the issue of automatic versus effortful coping responses below.) Nevertheless, cognitive styles serve as control mechanisms and in their effect bear some resemblance to what is sometimes meant by coping style.

Cognitive Controls

Gardner et al. (1959) developed the concept of cognitive controls to describe the attributes of perceptual and memory apparatuses in the relatively conflict-free spheres of ego functioning. Cognitive controls are forms of cognitive styles that are assumed to be mediating variables accounting for individual consistency in attitudes and orientations. They are seen as directed, adaptive operations of ego structures that function to bring about an equilibrium between inner strivings and the demands of reality.

One cognitive control that has been identified as *leveling-sharpening,* which is relevant to individual consistencies between new stimuli and memories experienced previously. *Leveling* is the tendency to see things in terms of their sameness or similarity. *Sharpening* is a way of seeing things in terms of their differences. Other cognitive controls include: *focusing or scanning,* relevant to the extent of spontaneous attention deployment in a variety of situations; *equivalence range,* relevant to judgmental preferences concerning similarity and difference; *flexible and constricted control,* relevant to response in the face of perceived incongruity; and *tolerance for unrealistic experiences,* relevant to response in situations that defy or abrogate one's usual assumptions concerning external reality (Gardner et al. 1959).

Field Dependence-Independence

The global-analytic dimension developed by Witkin and his colleagues is a good example of another cognitive style with its roots in perception as well as in ego psychology (for a review *see* Witkin, Goodenough, and Oltman 1979). This work began with the examination of field-dependent and field-independent tendencies (cf. Witkin et al. 1962). A rod-and-frame apparatus is widely used to identify field-dependent and field-independent types. In this test, the subjects sit in a darkened room in sight of a movable luminous frame and rod. The frame is tilted by the experimenter and the subject is asked to bring the rod to a position perpendicular to the ground. A large tilt of the rod indicates an adherence to visual cues, whereas a vertical rod indicates independence of the visual field and reliance on bodily posture. The purpose of this test is to examine the extent to which subjects use the external visual field or the body itself as the main referent for locating the upright.

The manner of locating the upright was found to be related to relative ease of disembedding a figure from its field, and the latter was in turn found to be related to disembedding ability in intellectual activities. In later research and writing this dimension has been referred to as "psychological differentiation" (cf. Witkin, Goodenough, and Oltman 1979). The field-dependent/independent dimension was extended to describe structuring competence in both domains, called an articulated versus global field approach, and designated a cognitive style. Since 1962 an active program of research has confirmed the picture of self-consistency in cognitive functioning established in the earlier field-dependent/independent studies. In general, field-independent people are better able to restructure the components of a stimulus array than field-dependent people. The relevance of this dimension to stress and coping is shown in the study by Gaines, Smith, and Skolnick (1977). . . . Compared with undifferentiated subjects, differentiated or field-independent subjects reacted with greater increases in heart rate as the probability of hearing an uncomfortably loud noise increased. Heart rate change was viewed as a function of active preparation for the stressor, and psychological differentiation as a personality disposition that affects appraisal and coping.

Limitations and Defects of Traditional Approaches

A number of problems limit the usefulness of the traditional approaches to coping and the trait and style dimensions they have spawned. Some of these problems are not necessary consequences of existing theories, but arise from how theories have been expressed in operational measures of coping. We see four major issues: the treatment of coping as a structural trait or style; the failure to distinguish coping from automatized adaptive behavior; the confounding of coping with outcome; and the equation of coping with mastery.

The Treatment of Coping as Trait or Style

Traditional models of coping tend to emphasize traits or styles, that is, achieved ego-structures that, once created, presumably operate as stable dispositions to cope in this or that way over the life course. Even if such a static, structural perspective is not mandated by the theoretical formulation, in practice and research structural concepts take center stage, as in the trait-style concepts we discussed earlier in this chapter. We end up speaking of people who are repressors or vigilants, people who are field-dependent or -independent, people who are deniers, and so on.

If the assessment of coping traits really allowed us to predict what a person would actually do to cope in a specific stressful encounter, research would be a simple matter, since for all intents and purposes, traits could stand for process. If a person coped with threat by avoidance, whenever he or she felt threatened we would expect avoidance to occur. The assessment of coping traits, however, has had very modest predictive value with respect to actual coping processes.

The problem with traits as predictors is well illustrated by Cohen and Lazarus' (1973) research on coping with the threat of surgery. Surgical patients were interviewed in the hospital the evening before their operation and an assessment was made of how much they knew about their illness and its treatment and how much interest they had in learning more. This procedure assessed what the person thought and did in a specific threat context, as it was happening, something that trait measures do not provide. Patients varied from the extreme of avoidant coping, characterized by knowing little and not wanting to know, to the other extreme of vigilant coping in which they had much information and welcomed still more. Along with this direct assessment of coping with the threat of surgery, a standard trait measure with a similar theoretical rationale, the Byrne (1964) repression-sensitization scale, was also administered. No correlation was found between the trait measure and the process measure, and the process measure alone predicted the speed and ease of recovery from surgery: avoiders did better in this regard than vigilants. Most important to the issue being addressed here, the trait measure did not predict how people actually coped with the threat as it occurred.

Trait conceptualizations and measures of coping underestimate the complexity and variability of actual coping efforts. Most trait measures evaluate coping along a single dimension such as repression-sensitization (Byrne 1964; Welsh 1956) or coping-avoiding (Goldstein 1959, 1973). The unidimensional quality of most trait measures does not adequately reflect the multidimensional quality of coping processes used to deal with real-life situations. Naturalistic observation (e.g., Mechanic [1962] 1978b; Murphy 1974; Visotsky et al. 1961) indicates that coping is a complex amalgam of thoughts and behaviors. Moos and Tsu (1977), for example, point out that in coping with physical illness a patient must deal with many sources of stress, including pain and incapacitation, hospital environments, and the demands imposed by the professional staff and special treatment procedures. At the same time, the patient must preserve emotional balance, a satisfactory self-image, and good relationships with family and friends. These multiple tasks require an array of coping strategies whose complexity cannot be captured in a unidimensional measure.

We are of course not arguing that there are no stabilities in coping or that people do not have preferred modes of coping with the same or similar sources of psychological stress over time. Gorzynski et al. (1980), for example, located 30 patients who had been studied earlier by Katz et al. (1970) with respect to coping with the threat of breast biopsy. These patients were reevaluated using the same assessment techniques as earlier, including interview ratings of coping and cortisol secretion rates. Gorzynski et al. found that the "psychological defense patterns" were stable over time, remaining unchanged in 9 out of 10 subjects, and that hormonal secretions were also more or less stable, with a correlation across occasions of .64.

Other studies also suggest consistencies in coping (e.g., Kobasa 1979), although in most cases coping per se has not been assessed directly but has been inferred from some other variable. As Moskowitz (1982) has argued, improvements in the design and methodology of cross-situational studies of traits, using multiple references, situations, and observations, could well increase the evidence of cross-situational generality. Findings on this issue are clearly mixed, especially in children, and rather than argue for only a process-centered as opposed to a structural, trait-centered approach, we should recognize that there is both stability and change in coping, but that the research emphasis has been overwhelmingly on stable traits compared with coping as a process. Our message here is that in seeking to understand coping or its antecedent and consequent correlates there is no substitute for direct assessment of coping acts and how they change with the changing demands of the situations as these are appraised by the person. . . .

Coping Versus Automatized Adaptive Behavior

There is an important distinction that is not made in many traditional approaches to coping, namely, between automatized and effortful responses. The skills that humans need to get along must be learned through experience. One useful idea about human adaptation is that the more quickly people can apply these skills automatically, the more effectively and efficiently they can manage their relationships with the environment. We see an important difference between the early stages of skill acquisition, which require enormous effort and concentration, and the later stages, in which the skills become automatized.

For example, experienced drivers are not ordinarily conscious of using the clutch and brake, steering, stopping for traffic signals, and so on, nor is there much special effort involved. We do these things so automatically that we can think about a problem at work while engaging in all the complex acts needed to get us there. These acts are adaptive but they should not be called coping. If they were, coping would consist of almost everything we do. When there is a nonroutine occurrence, however, such as a road closed for repairs that requires a decision as to an alternative route, or a flat tire that needs changing, effort is required. In these circumstances coping *efforts* are clearly distinguishable from the automatic adaptive behaviors that occur in routine driving situations.

The distinction between coping and automatized responses is not always clear. When a situation is novel, responses are not likely to be automatic, but if that situation should be encountered again and again, it is likely that the responses will become increasingly automatized through learning. Consider the student driver's first hours behind the wheel of a car. He or she concentrates intensely on the operation of the car and its location in traffic, and probably wonders how other people manage to drive so easily (i.e., automatically). Gradually, the need for intense concentration wanes, and responses are made with less deliberation and effort. As the driver becomes experienced, the behaviors become automatized. At the beginning of this process coping is required; at the end the behaviors are no longer coping by our definition. The transition is gradual, and it would be difficult to say when the behaviors become automatized and can no longer be considered coping. That most people deal with many of the demands of daily living in ways that do not tax or exceed their resources is evidence that many coping responses become automatized as learning takes place. However, at one point most such demands do tax or exceed available resources and therefore require coping.

Murphy (1974), who also views coping as a process that involves effort, makes an additional distinction between coping and ready-made adaptational devices such as reflexes. She views ready-made, phylogenetically more primitive devices at one end of a continuum which has at its center coping efforts, and at its other end, complete and automatized mastery. Her concern with primitive responses evolves from her observations of infants and children, whose early responses to stressful situations depend primarily on instinctual, wired-in protective mechanisms. As the infant evolves into a more mature organism whose capacity for cognitive manipulations and symbolic reasoning becomes increasingly important for functioning, the role played by primitive mechanisms becomes less significant in relation to the role played by coping.

Similarly, we distinguish between cognitive style, which involves an automatized response, and coping, although the distinction is often difficult to pinpoint in real-life contexts. For example, in extreme circumstances such as the concentration camp, there is often a tunneling of vision or a restriction of perspective (*see* Frankl 1963). Rather than focusing on the meaning of imprisonment and the omnipresent threats to survival, attention may be focused on small segments of reality.

Friedman et al. (1963) report that for parents of leukemic children, long-range hopes for the child's well-being and happiness were gradually replaced, as the child moved closer to death, by the immediate, limited concern of a pain-free day. A similar reaction was observed in mothers of severely deformed thalidomide children, who insisted that they could continue to function only by forgetting the painful past, ignoring the uncertain future, and instead concentrating on living "day to day" (Roskies 1972). Mages and Mendelsohn (1979) observed that cancer patients "who felt overwhelmed by the multiple physical, emotional, and practical burdens of their illness often narrowed their interests to create a smaller and more manageable world" (p. 260).

When the tunneling of vision or restriction of perspective illustrated above is an automatic response, we would say it is due to the person's cognitive control mechanisms; when it is purposeful and requires effort, we would classify it as coping. The extent to which the above individuals reduced their focus automatically or purposefully could only be known by interviewing each subject about the situation.

Put differently, not all adaptive processes are coping. Coping is a subset of adaptational activities that involves effort and does not include everything that we do in relating to the environment. From this point of view, the cognitive styles we discussed above may be adaptive processes, but not coping. Klein and his colleagues (Gardner et al. 1959) have suggested, in fact, that cognitive styles emerge developmentally from the child's struggle to discharge drive or instinctual impulses safely and effectively in the face of environmental obstacles and dangers. They were originally defense mechanisms that later could be said to have become automatized. Piaget (1952) held a similar view of the development of intelligence as a product of the processes of assimilation and accommodation in transactions with the environment. It is the struggle to adapt that ultimately results in automatic styles of perceiving, thinking, and acting. Klein also noted that, alternatively, defenses could be the product of modes of thought that are characteristic of a given time of life. The direction of effect here remains one of the unsettled theoretical issues of cognitive and defensive development.

The Confounding of Coping with Outcome

In both the animal and psychoanalytic ego psychology models, coping is equated with adaptational success, which is also the popular meaning of the term. In the vernacular, to say a person coped with the demands of a particular situation suggests that the demands were successfully overcome; to say a person did not cope suggests ineffectiveness or inadequacy.

In the three psychoanalytic ego psychology models we described earlier, there is a hierarchy of coping and defense such that some processes are automatically considered superior to others. For Menninger the hierarchy represents the degree of disorganization or primitivization which, in turn, informs us about the severity of stress, a quite circular analysis. For Haan, coping reflects a strong and well-functioning ego, whereas defense is neurotic, and ego-failure or fragmentation represents the most disorganized functioning.

When efficacy is implied by coping and inefficacy by defense, there is an inevitable confounding between the process of coping and the outcome of coping. These conceptual systems are not appropriate to the investigation of the relationship between coping and outcome, and we must abandon the hierarchical assumption and manage to keep the study of process and outcome independent. In order to determine the effectiveness of coping and defense processes, one must be open-minded to the possibility that both can work well or badly in particular persons, contexts, or occasions.

The analytic and interpretive problems posed by hierarchies of coping and defense can be illustrated by the major study reported by Vaillant (1977), who defines coping as the adaptive application of defense mechanisms. Earlier we described this research on coping and defense in 94 men followed for many years in which each man was ranked according to the relative maturity and pathological import of his characteristic defenses. In this study it is not surprising that an association was found between level of defense and lifetime adjustment. The raters were given a lifestyle summary of each subject to assist them in assigning a defense level score to each behavior observed in times of conflict and crisis. Using information about a subject's overall functioning to help score a behavior as indicative of one or another level of defense creates a tautology; in effect, defense and outcome are totally confounded.

Kahn et al. (1964) also point out the importance of defining coping independently of outcome, adding that the study of coping behavior should include failures as well as successes:

> The concept of coping is defined by the behaviors subsumed under it, not by the success of those behaviors. It may even prove profitable to concentrate upon those behaviors which are intended to cope with stress but which fail to do so. The psychoanalytic study of defense mechanisms would have been seriously retarded had it confined itself to the observation of conspicuously successful defenses. It is often in situations of failure where the ramifications of a particular coping mechanism or defense can be seen most vividly. (p. 385)

Definitions of coping must include *efforts* to manage stressful demands, regardless of outcome. This means that no one strategy is considered inherently better than any other. The goodness (efficacy, appropriateness) of a strategy is determined only by its effects in a given encounter and its effects in the long term. This contrasts with the conceptualizations of coping in which predetermined criteria having to do with degree of disorganization or level of maturity are used to classify strategies on an evaluative dimension, based on ideas about pathology and health derived from the traditions of Freud and ego psychology. Heavy weight is given to the extent to which a strategy adheres to reality and indicates emotional equilibrium. We noted earlier that Haan's approach depends on assessing the accuracy of the person's intersubjective reality. This is difficult to ascertain. Much research in psychology (e.g., the New Look Movement in the 1950s) has been concerned with individual differences in intersubjective (objective) reality (*see* review by Erdelyi 1974), and few answers have emerged about how to define such a reality (*see also* Watzlawick, 1976). Without a technique to do so, studies of ego hierarchies are seriously handicapped.

Predetermined ideas as to the inherent quality of ego processes prejudice us against the possibilities of strategies ranked high in a hierarchy being maladaptive and low-ranked strategies being adaptive. Denial is a case in point; it is usually ranked toward the bottom of ego hierarchies as indicating disorganization, primitivization, or distortion of reality and is considered inherently maladaptive. This line of thinking can be seen in research stemming from Janis' (1958) observations on the "work of worrying" (*see also* Lindemann's [1944] concept of "grief work"). The central theme of this research is that people who use denial, or even avoidance, as a mode of coping with stressful encounters will experience greater emotional ease on the first occasion but will pay for that ease by continued vulnerability on subsequent occasions. On the other hand, people who vigilantly face a threat will be more distressed at the outset, but on subsequent occasions they will experience less distress because they will be better prepared to handle the demands.

In Janis' initial studies, patients who displayed little or no apprehension prior to surgery showed excessive distress postsurgically compared with those who displayed normal vigilance and anxiety. This finding suggested that because these patients put off thoughts about the expectable pain and indignity of the recovery period, they were unprepared to face its distressing realities. Later experimental studies by Goldstein (1973) supported the argument. However, subsequent work produced mixed findings. One can now speak of a box score of studies with contradictory results, some showing that those who deny or avoid threats are worse off than those who address them, and other studies in which denial is associated with positive outcomes.[1]

Denial or avoidance in the context of illness is considered ineffective because the person fails to engage in appropriate problem-focused coping (e.g., seeking medical attention or adhering to a medical regimen) that would decrease the actual danger or damage of illness. This drawback is different from that implied by psychoanalytically oriented conceptualizations. According to the latter, a person using denial to cope with a threat is vulnerable to disconfirmations by evidence to the contrary and is therefore forced to narrow his or her attention to only confirmatory experiences. Denial closes the mind to whatever *could* be threatening. People who defend themselves in this way must remain forever on guard, involved with "silent internal tasks" (Fenichel 1945), and may experience depleted energy or even depression. This psychoanalytic interpretation of the costs of denial is difficult to operationalize in research, and the issue remains unsettled as to whether or not denial operates in this manner.

A major methodological problem has to do with the meaning of denial, which is usually defined as the disavowal of reality. The first serious difficulty with this definition has to do with its breadth. Some actions that are considered to be behavioral exemplars of denial, such as not talking to others about an ailment or condition of life (e.g., in Hackett and Cassem's [1974] denial rating scale for post-coronary patients), are more akin to avoidance than the disavowal of reality (Dansak and Cordes 1978–1979). The patient who is reluctant to talk about a terminal illness such as advanced cancer, and who tries to keep it out of mind as much as possible, may readily acknowledge the reality of the illness and its attendant distress when asked directly. Other cognitive coping processes that have been classified as denial may be better regarded as efforts at positive thinking, or minimization, to use Lipowski's (1970–1971) term. These processes are capable of sustaining morale and constructive efforts to cope, and, again, do not disavow reality.

Breznitz (1983a) has identified seven different kinds of denial in an analysis that accords nicely with our concerns about the definition of denial and the diverse coping processes commonly included under its rubric. He distinguishes denial of information, threatening information, personal relevance, urgency, vulnerability-responsibility, affect, and affect relevance. These types of denial are arranged hierarchically, with the assumption that only when a higher form of denial fails does the individual proceed to the next one down. Thus, Breznitz offers a kind of stage model, with each level implying a progressively more severe challenge to coping. The use of any form of denial, moreover, implies helplessness to change the objective situation. For readers interested in the topic of denial, we recommend a book edited by Breznitz (1983b) which contains the above material as well as discussions of other aspects of the problem such as the relations between denial and hope, and denial and religion.

Aside from definitional problems, support can be found for both the costs and the benefits of denial and denial-like processes. What is needed, therefore, are principles that specify the conditions under which denial and denial-like forms of coping might have favorable or unfavorable outcomes. We offer the following as possibilities:

1. When there is nothing constructive that people can do to overcome a harm or threat, that is, when there is no direct action that is relevant, denial and denial-like processes contain the potential for alleviating distress without altering functioning or producing additional harm.

2. Denial and denial-like processes may be adaptive with respect to certain facets of the situation, but not the whole. Patients with diabetes can deny the seriousness of the situation as long as they also continue to give vigilant attention to diet, activity level, and insulin.

   The distinction made by Weisman (1972) between denial of fact and denial of implication is also relevant here. For example, it is probably more dangerous to deny that one *has* cancer than to deny that the diagnosis implies a death sentence. Denial of implication may be more akin to illusion, positive thinking, or hopefulness—which all of us experience and the capacity for which may be a valuable psychological resource—than to distortion of reality.

3. S. Miller (1980) points out that in situations that are subject to change, that is, from uncontrollable to controllable, the optimal strategy may be one that reduces arousal without completely impeding the processing of external threat-relevant information. However, in chronically uncontrollable (and unchangeable) situations, the strategy of choice may be one that effectively reduces both arousal and concommitant processing of information from the environment.

4. The timing of denial and denial-like forms of coping may be a major significance. Denial may be less damaging and more effective in the early stages of a crisis, such as sudden illness, incapacitation, or loss of a loved one, when the situation cannot yet be faced in its entirety, than in later stages. Hackett and Cassem (1975) and Hackett, Cassem, and Wishnie (1968), for example, observed both positive and negative effects of denial and avoidance depending on when their observations were made. During a heart attack these cognitive coping processes were damaging because they obstructed the effort to get medical help. After a heart attack, however, the same coping processes facilitated recovery and resulted in fewer deaths from subsequent attacks. Cohen and Lazarus (1983) reviewed other studies in which the same principle seemed to apply, that is, denial-like coping processes that proved helpful while the patient was still in the hospital seemed to have negative consequences when used after leaving the hospital.

We have used denial and denial-like processes to illustrate (1) no strategy should be labeled as inherently good or bad; (2) the context must be taken into account in judging coping; and (3) principles must be developed with which to judge whether a particular coping process fits with both personal and situational aspects of the transaction. This approach should be used not only for denial, but for virtually every form of coping.

Menninger (1963), Haan (1977), and Vaillant (1977) all acknowledge the importance of evaluating an ego process within the situational context. Vaillant states, "We cannot evaluate the choice of a defense without considering the circumstances that call it forth and how it affects relationships with other people" (pp. 85–86). Lipowski (1970–

1971), too, notes that the evaluation of denial must always include a consideration of what is denied, in what situation, and by whom. The hierarchic nature of these systems of ego processes, however, militates against such situational evaluations. A process ranked on the lower end of a hierarchy has an onus that is difficult to remove even when the strategy is effective, appropriate, and successful according to situational criteria. Denial is bad unless proved otherwise, and even then it is suspect.

. . .

The Equation of Coping with Mastery Over the Environment

There is an implicit corollary to those definitions of coping that consider certain strategies inherently better or more useful than others, namely, that the best coping is that which changes the person-environment relationship for the better. In keeping with deeply ingrained Western values regarding individualism and mastery, and the Darwinian impact on psychological thought, these definitions tend to venerate mastery over the environment as the coping ideal. Coping is viewed as tantamount to solving problems by acting effectively to obviate them.

The problem here is not that solving problems is undesirable, but that not all sources of stress in living are amenable to mastery, or even fit within a problem-solving framework. Examples include natural disasters, inevitable losses, aging and disease, and the ubiquitous conflicts which abnormal psychology and psychiatry have long addressed, all normal features of the human condition. Emphasizing problem solving and mastery devalues other functions of coping that are concerned with managing emotions and maintaining self-esteem and a positive outlook, especially in the face of irremediable situations. Coping processes that are used to tolerate such difficulties, or to minimize, accept, or ignore them, are just as important in the person's adaptational armamentarium as problem-solving strategies that aim to master the environment.

NOTES

1. A large number of studies discuss denial-like processes and their consequences. Below are some striking current examples in which there were negative or positive outcomes. Negative outcomes include: Andrew 1970; Auerbach 1973; Delong 1970; Hitchcock 1982; Katz et al. 1970; Lindemann 1944; Staudenmayer et al. 1979. Positive outcomes include: Bean et al. 1980; Cohen and Lazarus 1973; George et al. 1980; Hackette, Cassem, and Wishnie 1968; Ham-

burg and Adams 1967; Levine and Zigler 1975; Rosenstiel and Roth 1981; Stern, Pascale, and McLoone 1976. Additional articles in which denial was associated with mixed or inconclusive outcomes, or was merely discussed, include Beisser 1979; Billing et al. 1980; Knight et al. 1979; Sackheim in press; Spinetta and Maloney 1978; Yanagida, Streltzer, and Siemsen 1981. There is also the older research of Wolff et al. (1964) in which denial-like processes prior to the loss of an ill child to leukemia were associated with lowered adrenocortical hormonal output (stress responses). However, this was followed up by a later finding by Hofer et al. (1972) in which parents who had used denial-like processes for coping before the child's death showed higher physiological stress responses two years after the child's death compared with an opposite pattern for those who had confronted the tragedy without denial-like coping.

10

Coping and Emotion

■

SUSAN FOLKMAN AND
RICHARD S. LAZARUS

Historically, coping has been viewed as a response to emotion. Our purpose here is to evaluate this idea and offer a broader view based on cognitive and relational principles concerning the emotion process. We will explore the ways emotion and coping influence each other in what must ultimately be seen as a dynamic, mutually reciprocal relationship.

Traditional Approaches to Emotion and Coping

The emotion and coping relationship has been discussed in the context of two quite distinct systems of thought: the animal and ego psychology models. In the animal model emotion and coping are viewed from a Darwinian phylogenetic perspective (cf. Miller 1980; Ursin 1980) which emphasizes learned behaviors that contribute to survival in the face of life-threatening dangers. In the psychoanalytic ego psychology model coping is defined as cognitive processes, such as denial, repression, suppression, and intellectualization, as well as problem-solving behaviors that are invoked to reduce anxiety and other distressing emotion states (e.g., Menninger 1963; Vaillant 1977). The feature that is common to both the animal and ego psychology models is that coping is viewed as a response to emotion and as having the function of arousal or tension reduction.

Within the animal model, emotion, which is treated as drive, activation, or arousal, motivates behavioral responses that enable the animal to protect itself and/or vanquish its enemy. Two forms of emotion are emphasized: fear and anger. Fear motivates the behavioral response of avoidance or escape, and anger motivates confrontation or attack.

Emotion has another important survival-related function that is emphasized by ethologists: it communicates what an animal is feeling and hence allows another animal to know whether, for instance, a potential predator is about to attack. The expressive aspect of emotion can also communicate when it is safe to approach, as in mating rituals, or that help is needed, as when expressions of grief in baby monkeys generate sympathy and help in adult monkeys.

Other theorists have made additional suggestions about the adaptive functions of emotion. For example, based on Freud's ([1926] 1959) later treatment of anxiety, emotion has been viewed as a way of signaling intrapsychically the need for a protective behavioral or ego-defensive response. Mandler (1975) speaks of the interrupt function of emotion, which can be viewed as a way of rechanneling attention and action from an ongoing activity to a new, intrusive emergency. And Tomkins (1965) speaks of emotion as an amplifier that gives greater urgency to appraisals of threat or harm (or for that matter, challenge) and the adaptive response.

There has long been interest in the ways emotion can impair adaptation by interfering with cognitive functioning, as when anxiety interferes with performance (Krohne and Laux 1982; Spielberger 1966, 1972; van der Ploeg, Schwarzer, and Spielberger 1984). Two mechanisms of interference have been emphasized, a motivational one in which attention is redirected from a task at hand to a more pressing emergency (Easterbrook 1959; Schönpflug 1983), and a cognitive one in which anxiety-related thoughts impede functioning because they are irrelevant to or counterproductive for performance (Alpert and Haber 1960; Child and Waterhouse 1952, 1953; Sarason, Mandler, and Craighill 1952; *see also* Lazarus 1966 for an analysis).

There are several major differences between the animal and ego psychology models of coping. One is that the animal model focuses exclusively on behavioral responses, whereas the ego psychology model focuses more on thoughts (ego processes). A second difference is that the primary criterion of successful coping in the animal model is survival, whereas the ego psychology model includes criteria concerning the quality of the process, such as its adherence to reality and its flexibility (Haan 1977; Menninger 1963), as well as a large range of adaptive outcomes including psychological well-being, somatic health, and social functioning.

Two key difficulties inhere in the traditional animal and ego psychology models of coping and emotion. The first is incompleteness, which results from emphasizing emotional arousal or drive tension as the antecedent of coping. Coping is not merely a response to such tension; it is also strongly influenced by the appraised significance for well-being of what is happening, which is incorporated in the emotional arousal and affects the quality of the emotion, that is, whether it is anger, fear, guilt, disappointment, etc. Any model that fails to specify the nature of the cognitive activity in the emotion process is bound to be ambiguous and incomplete.

The second difficulty is that the relationship between emotion and coping is unidirectional and static. Undoubtedly emotion both facilitates and interferes with coping in the ways that the theorists mentioned above have noted. However, if what is happening is viewed over time, it will be seen that coping can also affect the emotional reaction. The effects of coping on emotion have not been emphasized in theory, nor even taken seriously, yet their importance in adaptational encounters seems to us to be equal to, if not greater than, the effects of emotion on coping. Therefore, our emphasis below will be on the flow from coping to emotion.

Cognitive and Relational Principles of Emotion and Coping

In this section we briefly present our definitions of emotion, coping, and cognitive appraisal, which is the centerpiece of our theory, and our process-oriented approach.

Definitions

Emotion

We have defined emotions as complex, organized psychophysiological reactions consisting of cognitive appraisals, action impulses, and patterned somatic reactions (Lazarus, Averill, and Opton 1970; Lazarus, Kanner, and Folkman 1980). The three components operate as a unit rather than as separate responses, and the patterning of the components reflects the emotion quality and intensity. Cognitive appraisal is an integral part of the emotion state. Anger, for example, usually includes an appraisal of a particular kind of harm or threat, and happiness includes an appraisal that a particular person-environment condition is beneficial. We have used the term action impulses rather than action to draw attention to the idea that the action of emotion can be inhibited as well as expressed. The mobilization that is often involved in action impulses is an important feature of the third component, the patterned somatic reaction, which refers to the physiological response profile that uniquely characterizes each emotion quality. (For a discussion of the debate about generalized arousal or specific response patterns *see* Lazarus and Folkman 1984b.)

Coping

Coping consists of cognitive and behavioral efforts to manage specific external and/or internal demands that are appraised as taxing or exceeding the resources of the person. These cognitive and behavioral efforts are constantly changing as a function of continuous appraisals and reappraisals of the person-environment relationship, which is also always changing. Some of the changes in relationship result, in part, from coping processes directed at altering the situation that is causing distress (problem-focused coping) and/or regulating distress (emotion-focused coping), from changes in the person that are a result of feedback about what has happened, and from changes in the environment that are independent of the person.

Note that this definition refers to two functions of coping: problem-focused and emotion-focused. Among the most striking and consistent findings that we and others have replicated (e.g., Baum, Fleming, and Singer 1983; Folkman and Lazarus 1980, 1985; Folkman et al. 1986a; McCrae 1982) is that people rely on both forms of coping, and their subvarieties, in managing the demands of stressful encounters. A full understanding of coping, therefore, requires that both functions be considered, as well as their subtypes.

Cognitive Appraisal

We speak of two forms of appraisal, primary and secondary. In primary appraisal the person asks "What do I have at stake in this encounter?" The answer to the question contributes to the emotion quality and intensity. For example, if self-esteem is at stake there is a potential for shame or anger as well as worry or fear, whereas if one's physical well-being is at stake, only worry and/or fear are likely to be dominant.

In secondary appraisal the concern of the person is "What can I do? What are my options for coping? And how will the environment respond to my actions?" The answer influences the kinds of coping strategies that will be used to manage the demands of the encounter. For example, problem-focused forms of coping are more likely to be used if the outcome of an encounter is appraised as amenable to change, whereas emotion-focused forms of coping are more likely if the outcome is appraised as unchangeable (Folkman and Lazarus 1980).

Appraisals of person-environment relationships are influenced by antecedent person characteristics such as pattern of motivation (e.g., values, commitments, and goals), beliefs about oneself and the world, and recognition of personal resources for coping such as financial means, social and problem-solving skills, and health and energy. Individual differences in these variables help explain why an encounter may be appraised as a threat by one person and as neutral or a challenge by another. For example, an entrance exam for medical school will be appraised as more relevant to well-being by a student who is deeply motivated to practice medicine than by a student who is not. And given a high level of motivation, the exam will be appraised as more threatening by students who question their ability than by those who are confident, regardless of the realities. Appraisal processes are also influenced by environmental variables such as the nature of the danger, its imminence, ambiguity and duration, and the existence and quality of social support resources to facilitate coping.

Emotion and Coping as Processes

To understand the relationship between emotion and coping it is essential to view them from the standpoint of process, which refers to the changing character of what the person thinks and does during the unfolding of specific person-environment encounters and across encounters. Structural approaches, in contrast, focus on recurrent cognitive, behavioral, and emotional patterns that express more or less stable features of the person's emotional life. A structural approach allows persons to be described as sad, angry, or cheerful (Ortony and Clore 1981), and assumes stable coping dispositions such as repression-sensitization (Byrne 1961), fatalism-flexibility (Wheaton 1983), or irrational cognitive assumptions that dispose the person to react in a characteristic way from occasion to occasion, as in the case of depression (Beck 1976; Ellis 1962; Ellis and Bernard 1985; *see also* Lazarus in press).

Although it is legitimate and useful to assess stable patterns of emotion and coping, they constitute only a part of the total picture. Clinical observation and empirical research (Epstein 1980; Folkman and Lazarus 1980, 1985; Folkman et al. 1986b; Menaghan 1982) make clear that emotion and coping are normally characterized by a high degree of variability among and within persons. Given the power of environmental conditions to shape reactions, this variability is functional and should not be a surprise. The evidence further suggests that existing measures of coping dispositions do not predict very well how people actually cope (Cohen and Lazarus 1973) in particular encounters.

Furthermore, coping is a multidimensional process. For example, in a series of recent studies (Folkman and Lazarus 1985; Folkman et al. 1986a; Folkman et al. 1987) we identified eight kinds of coping using the revised 67-item Ways of Coping Questionnaire, which lists a broad range of cognitive and behavioral strategies that people use to manage the demands of specific stressful encounters. Two kinds are primarily problem-focused in that they are directed at altering the troubled person-environment relationship. One of these is confrontive and interpersonal, and the second emphasizes planful problem-solving. Six additional kinds of coping are primarily emotion-focused in that they are directed at managing distress rather than altering the troubled person-environment relationship. These kinds of coping include distancing, escape-avoidance, accepting responsibility or blame, exercising self-control over the expression of feelings, seeking social support, and positive reappraisal. Factor analyses by other investigators who have used the Ways of Coping (e.g., Braukmann et al. 1981; Felton, Revenson, and Hinrichsen 1984; Vitaliano et al. 1985) have produced similar patterns.

Our designation of the eight kinds of coping as having primarily a problem-focused or emotion-focused function is provisional. The actual function of a given type of coping can be determined only in the context in which it is used. A strategy that is at first glance problem-focused, such as making a plan of action, can have an emotion-focused function, as when a person who is anxious about having too much to do realizes that the best way to reduce anxiety is to rank order the tasks and get to work on the first one on the list. Conversely, a strategy that is at first glance emotion-focused, such as taking a valium to reduce anxiety, can be problem-focused if the person uses it because he or she knows that in order to work, the anxiety must be reduced. Sometimes a particular strategy can serve both functions simultaneously as, when in the process of seeking advice, a person receives personal affirmation that reduces anxiety as well as task-related information that helps solve the problem.

Coping as a Mediator of Emotional States

We have posited that emotion and coping occur in a dynamic mutually reciprocal relationship. The behavioral flow begins with a transaction appraised as significant for the person's well-being, that is, as harmful, beneficial, threatening, or challenging. The appraisal influences coping, which in turn changes the person-environment relationship, and hence the emotional response. Viewed in this way, coping is a *mediator* of the emotional response. The process is summarized in figure 10.1.

Mediator variables are often confused with moderator variables. Moderators are antecedent conditions such as personality traits that interact with other conditions in producing an outcome. An example is the goal hierarchy that the person brings to the transaction. This hierarchy interacts with relevant environmental variable to produce an emotional reaction. A mediating variable, on the other hand, is generated in the encounter and it changes the original relationship between the antecedent and the outcome variable. Coping, for example, arises during the encounter and transforms the original emotion in some way. The difference between moderator and mediator variables is conceptually and methodologically important and is often misunderstood (cf. Frese 1986; Stone 1985; Zedeck 1971).

The mediating effects of coping on emotion have not been widely investigated. Many clinical interventions, however, are based on the premise that the quality of people's emotional lives can be improved by addressing deficiencies in coping skills. And the burgeoning interest in coping in the fields of behavioral medicine and health psychology is also based on the assumption that coping makes a difference in people's psychological and somatic well-being. Yet despite this apparently widely shared conviction relatively little research has been devoted to finding out in what ways given forms of coping affect emotional responses. Below we outline some of the possible pathways.

Pathways by Which Coping Affects Emotion

The key question is: How do the various forms of coping alter the person-environment relationship, either actually or phenomenologi-

FIGURE 10.1. Coping as a mediator of emotion.

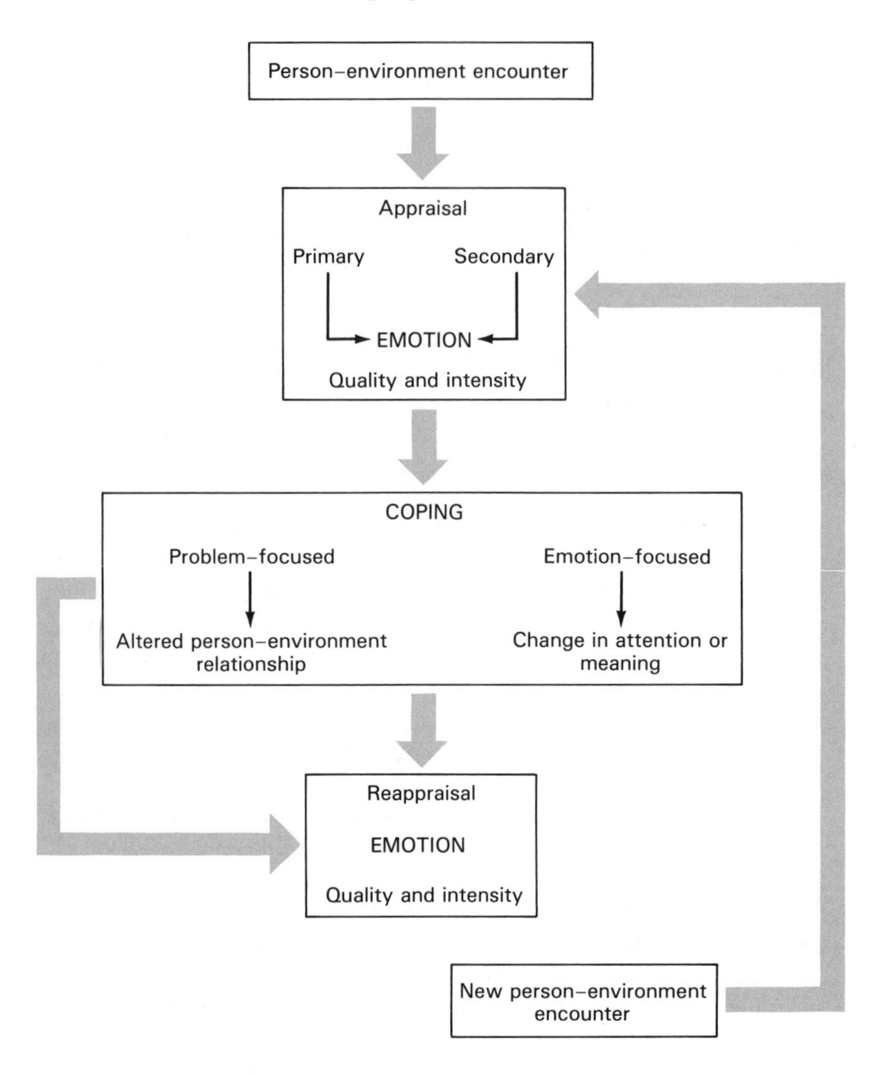

cally, and hence the emotional response? We consider three possibilities, namely, change that is brought about by: (1) cognitive activity that influences the deployment of attention; (2) cognitive activity that alters the subjective meaning or significance of the encounter for well-being;

and (3) actions that alter the actual terms of the person-environment relationship.

(1) Deployment of Attention

This refers to coping activity that diverts attention from the source of distress (avoidant strategies) or directs attention to it (vigilant strategies).

Coping by avoidance is one of the most common ways people deal with stress. For example, stress management programs often include jogging and relaxation. These are basically techniques for getting away from the source of stress. Vacations and hobbies also fall within this category when their purpose is to get away from a particular problem, setting, or condition. When such strategies are successful, they neutralize distress emotions, and some strategies, such as jogging, vacation, or hobbies, may have the added benefit of making the person feel physically better and thereby improve the emotional state. However, avoidant strategies can also be maladaptive if they draw the person's attention away from a problem that needs to be addressed.

Another group of avoidant strategies, which we have assessed in our research, seems to be less adaptive than those described above. We have labeled this group "escape-avoidance" on the factored Ways of Coping scale. It describes efforts to escape through wishful thinking (e.g., "wished that the situation would go away or somehow be over with"), eating, drinking, smoking, using drugs or medications, or sleeping. Although these strategies may provide a brief respite from distress, several studies have found that escape-avoidance is associated with symptoms of depression and anxiety (Coyne, Aldwin, and Lazarus 1981; Folkman et al. 1986b; Vitaliano et al. 1985) and with psychosomatic symptoms (Benner 1984). Because these studies are cross-sectional, it cannot be determined whether escape-avoidance causes psychological symptoms, or whether people who have such symptoms use escape-avoidance. Regardless of the direction of causality, certain forms of avoidant coping seem less likely than others to produce a beneficial effect, especially beyond the moment.

In contrast to avoidant coping, in which attention is diverted from the problem, vigilant coping strategies direct attention toward the problem in an effort to prevent or control it. The most complete description of vigilant coping is provided by Janis and Mann (1977) in their discussion of decision making under emergency conditions. In our research we assess two forms of coping that focus attention on the problem: information search, which includes strategies such as "I talked to someone to find out more about the situation," and planful problem-solving, which includes strategies such as "I made a plan of action and followed it" and "I came up with a couple of different solutions to the problem." These can alter the emotional response in two ways—by leading to plans of action that alter the terms of the person-environment relationship, which ultimately affects the emotional response; and by directly affecting the cognitive appraisals underlying the emotional response.

The mobilization that is involved in vigilance can increase the intensity of emotion. Vigilance that leads to information that things are worse than was previously thought, or that nothing can be done to make things better, can also intensify emotion. Finally, vigilance can increase distress in those situations where nothing can be done to alter the outcome of the situation; examples include perseverating with information search beyond the point where anything new is to be learned (cf. Breznitz 1971; Horowitz 1976) or with attempts at problem solving when there is no solution (cf. Collins, Baum, and Singer 1983).

On the other hand, vigilance can reduce distress by increasing understanding and a sense of control (cf. Averill 1973; Folkman 1984; Gal and Lazarus 1975; Rothbaum, Weisz, and Snyder 1982), even if nothing can be done to alter the outcome. For example, before the advent of antibiotics practitioners of medicine spent a major portion of their time trying to make diagnoses, even though a diagnosis would not mean that anything could be done for the patient. Yet, just having the diagnosis often brought emotional relief to the patient and the patient's family (cf. Thomas 1983). It may be that an ambiguous state of affairs is often more stressful than knowing even the most negative outcome. Further, the emotional response can change from negative to positive should the information search lead to a plan of action that increases the likelihood of bringing about a favorable outcome.

(2) Changing the Subjective Meaning or Significance of a Person-Environment Transaction

This type of effect is achieved through cognitive coping activity that ranges from denial-like strategies involving distortion of reality to strategies such as distancing or emphasizing the positive aspects of a situation, which depend on selective attention or interpretation.

We cannot undertake a discussion of the effects of denial on the emotional response here (see Lazarus 1983; Breznitz 1983a for a discussion of denial in the context of stress). However, we do want to point out that the extent to which denial and denial-like processes alter the quality and intensity of the emotional response depends in part on what is being denied.

Distancing describes efforts to detach oneself, such as "Didn't let it get to me—refused to think about it too much," and "Made light of the situation; refused to get too serious about it." In distancing, the person acknowledges the troubling problem but doesn't want to deal with its emotional significance. Distancing can be used to help people get through extremely stressful situations. For example, nurses in intensive care units use distancing to deal with the unrelenting life-threatening medical crises of their patients without falling apart emotionally (Hay and Oken 1972). We think of the use of humor in the operating room (e.g., "M*A*S*H") as another form of distancing.

Distancing should not interfere with successful problem solving; in fact, as the illustrations above suggest, it can actually enable problem solving in situations that are highly stressful. Distancing may also be adaptive in situations where nothing can be done, as when awaiting the outcome of a biopsy. For example, let us say parents are awaiting biopsy results on one of their children. Although there is nothing to do as far as the biopsy is concerned, the parents must tend to their other children's needs too. Successful distancing helps to keep the parents from being totally preoccupied about the biopsy and allows them to function in their parenting and other roles.

Also of interest are those cognitive coping strategies that involve selective attention that not only diminish the negative emotional response, but generate positive emotional responses as well. Such strategies include positive comparisons (e.g., Taylor, Wood, and Lichtman 1983), cognitive restructuring (e.g., Pearlin and Schooler 1978), comforting cognitions (Mechanic [1962] 1978b), and positive reappraisal (Folkman et al. 1986a). These strategies operate by influencing the appraisal process at two different phases of stressful encounters: the anticipatory phase and the outcome phase.

During the anticipatory phase of an encounter, cognitive coping strategies can transform a threat appraisal into a challenge through their effect on secondary appraisal. For example, an upcoming exam in which students have a major stake can be transformed from a threat into a challenge if they consider their coping resources (i.e., ability and time for study) as adequate to the task. It is important to note too that the appraisal of coping resources may itself rest on cognitive coping processes that support what may be an illusion—i.e., the person may be overestimating the available resources. To the extent that the illusion remains intact throughout the preparation period, the student's response is likely to include positive or challenge emotions, such as confidence, hopefulness, and perhaps eagerness, as well as negative emotions such as anxiety.

Another way cognitive coping can transform a threat into a challenge is through focusing on the possibilities for mastery or growth that inhere in a troubled person-environment relationship. Lipowski (1970–1971), for example, speaks of patients who view illness as a challenge, that is, "like any other life situation which imposes specific demands and tasks to be mastered and which is accomplished by any means available" (p. 98). There are also numerous anecdotal accounts of cancer patients who transform their appraisal of their fight for life from a threat to a challenge (cf. Moos 1977).

We have also investigated cognitive coping used to extract positive meaning from harm that has already occurred (Folkman and Lazarus 1988; Folkman et al. 1986a, 1986b). This form of cognitive coping, which we call positive reappraisal, comes into play at the outcome stage of an encounter. We assess it with items such as "I changed or grew as a person in a good way" and "I came out of the experience better than when I went in." Wortman and her colleagues (e.g., Bulman and Wortman 1977; Silver and Wortman 1980) point to the importance of this form of coping in coming to terms with the effects of severe life events. Positive reappraisal can generate benefit emotions such as pride and satisfaction, and perhaps reduce harm emotions such as anger and sadness.

The extent to which cognitive coping strategies work depends in part on how much distortion of reality is involved, and whether or not the cognitive construction is likely to be challenged by the environment, as when, for example, an illness that is denied or construed optimistically goes precipitously downhill. A major distortion of reality can be sustained longer if the person is well-defended. Presumably such persons are impervious to cues from within themselves or from the environment that contradict the cognitive construction. However, most people are not so well-defended that a major distortion of reality can be sustained in the face of continuing evidence to the contrary. Major distortions, such as the denial that a person has died or that one has lost the use of one's legs, are usually temporary, and often seen as a stage in bereavement or recovery from a trauma (Horowitz 1976).

The reduction of distress that is achieved through distancing or denial can be fragile in the face of an unexpected cue from the environment, which can redintegrate the full significance of the encounter. For example, a woman's efforts to put the pending results of a biopsy out of her mind can easily fail if she unexpectedly hears a report about cancer on her car radio, or in passing sees a friend who had a bout with cancer the previous year. Efforts at distancing or denial may also be undermined by cues from within the person in the form of fleeting cognitions or images, or what Horowitz (1976) calls intrusive thoughts. Thus, the effects of cognitive coping processes on the emotional response may only be temporary. If the person reinstitutes the coping strategy after an interruption, the pattern may appear cyclical, such that a period of calm is followed by a period of increased distress.

The palliative effects of strategies that involve selective attention are probably easier to sustain and less likely to be challenged by observers than strategies that involve a distortion of reality, especially if they appear to be boosting morale without interfering with functioning. Indeed, people are often coaxed into using positive reappraisal after a harm has occurred in order to help them diminish their distress and regain positive morale. People who are laid off from their jobs, for example, are told to look on the event as a challenge, as a chance to change directions, learn new skills, maybe even move to a different part of the country. In such cases, the environment is likely to collaborate with the person in sustaining this kind of cognitive construction.

(3) Changing the Actual Terms of the Person-Environment Relationship

This is brought about through what we call problem-focused coping, which involves cognitive problem-solving as well as direct action on the environment or on oneself. Our assessment procedures cover two forms of problem-focused coping. One is a confrontive, somewhat aggressive interpersonal form that includes strategies such as "stood my ground and fought for what I wanted" and "tried to get the person responsible to change his or her mind." The second describes rational and planful problem-solving techniques that we mentioned earlier (e.g., "I made a plan of action and followed it" and "I came up with a couple of different solutions to the problem").

Changes in the emotional response depend on a number of factors. One is the extent to which problem-focused forms of coping bring about a desired outcome. An ideal outcome would include a permanent resolution that is satisfactory to the person and to others. However, many real-life stressful encounters do not end quite so neatly. Sometimes resolutions are only partially satisfactory; sometimes there is no resolution at all; and sometimes even if there is a resolution there is little assurance that the situation will not happen again.

A second factor on which the quality of the outcome depends is the person's evaluation of his or her performance. An encounter outcome that is successful by most standards may still be appraised negatively by persons who are not easily satisfied, or who consider the way they conduct themselves or reacted emotionally to be unacceptable.

A third factor concerns the implications of the present encounter for the future. Even a successfully resolved encounter can have threatening implications, as when a student who receives a high grade on an exam experiences threat emotions because of the expectations that the present performance creates for future performances. The varying shades of successful and unsuccessful outcomes and the many dimensions on which outcomes are evaluated mean that the emotional response at the outcome phase of an encounter is likely to be a complex mixture of positive and negative emotions, which is, in fact, what we have found in our research (e.g., Folkman and Lazarus 1985, 1988).

An important consideration overall in understanding how problem-focused coping alters the person-environment relationship and hence affects the emotional response is the interpersonal aspect of coping. For example, the somewhat aggressive and hostile character of confrontive coping (as we assess it) is likely to generate negative emotions in the person who is being confronted, which in turn can lead to a downward spiral in the person-environment relationship. This pattern has been discussed in the context of depression by Coyne (1976), who pointed out that depressed people interact with others in a way that drives others away.

We found support for this idea in a study in which we compared people who were high and low in depressive symptoms (Folkman and Lazarus 1986). Those high in symptoms used significantly more confrontive coping and at the same time more self-controlling coping processes (efforts to keep one's feelings to oneself) than those low in symptoms. They also reported more anger and hostility during their encounters. The self-controlling coping may have been used to try to regulate the hostile impulses. Although our data did not provide information as to whether or not the depressed subjects' pattern of coping and emotion caused other people to disapprove or withdraw, the inference is plausible and consistent with theories of depression.

People who engage in rational, planful problem-solving, on the other hand, are less likely to communicate hostility than those who use confrontive coping. Instead, their demeanor is likely to be relatively calm and friendly, and may even invite others to provide support. This is, in fact, what we observed in a study of the relationship between coping and support received in stressful encounters (Dunkel-Schetter, Folkman, and Lazarus 1987). Planful problem-solving acted as a strong elicitor of all types of support (emotional, tangible, and informational).

Confrontive coping, in contrast, elicited primarily information rather than emotional support or tangible assistance.

The interpersonal effects of coping are not limited to problem-focused forms of coping. For example, the reduction of distress that is achieved through coping strategies such as distancing and escape-avoidance can simultaneously reduce the possibility of open communications with a spouse or close other at a time when such communications may be mutually beneficial. This could produce a secondary effect on the interpersonal relationship in that the spouse or close other might feel rejected or unappreciated and respond with sadness, frustration, or resentment.

Although in reviewing the three factors affecting the person-environment relationship noted above we have emphasized the effects of problem-focused coping on the emotional response, it is important to recognize that the quality of problem-focused coping, and hence its impact on the emotional response, also depends in part on the successful regulation of negative emotions, in effect, on emotion-focused coping. Too much emotional intensity could interfere with the cognitive functioning that is necessary for effective problem-focused coping (cf. Easterbrook 1959; Heckhausen 1982; Sarason 1975). A parent whose child has been injured, for example, knows that distress must be controlled in order to take the steps necessary to get the help the child needs. Also, unregulated emotional intensity might frighten off the preson on whom this individual depends for advice or information. Yet there is evidence that a modest degree of intensity has a motivating property that can facilitate problem-focused coping (Yerkes and Dodson 1908), an idea that emphasizes emotions as antecedents of coping, which we mentioned earlier.

Furthermore, whether negative emotions have a different impact on problem-focused coping than positive emotions have is addressed in a study by Goodhart (1986). Goodhart observed that positive thinking facilitated performance when the thoughts were relevant to the task and when subjects had positive expectations. However, in those situations where one or the other of these conditions was not met, negative thoughts led to better performance than positive thoughts did. Since positive thoughts produce positive emotions and negative thoughts negative emotions, Goodhart's study suggests that both types of emotions can facilitate problem-focused coping, depending on the context.

Research Support for the Impact of Coping on Emotion

Above we have suggested certain ways in which coping can mediate emotions during stressful encounters. Some of our recent research findings (Folkman and Lazarus 1988a) provide empirical support for such a process. We interviewed subjects monthly for five months about a recently experienced stressful encounter, asking them to describe the emotions they experienced at the beginning of the stressful encounter and, for those encounters that were concluded at the time of the interview, the emotions they experienced at the end of the encounter. Subjects also described the ways they coped with the demands of the encounter. This information allowed us to ask about the extent to which coping actively mediated the relationship between the emotions subjects reported at the beginning and at the end of each of their encounters.

The sample was composed of 75 married couples with at least one child living at home. The average age of the men was 41.4 years and the average age of the women was 39.6 years. The participants were Caucasian and Protestant or Catholic, and for the most part upper-middle-class (mean number of years of education was 15.5 years and the median family income was $45,000).

The measure of emotion used in this study is described elsewhere (Folkman and Lazarus 1986). Briefly, subjects rated on Likert scales the extent to which they experienced each of a number of emotions at the beginning and end of the stressful encounter. A factor analysis of these emotions suggested four scales: disgusted/angry; pleased/happy; worried/fearful; and confident/secure. Coping was measured with eight scales derived from factor analyses of the Ways of Coping. These scales, which were mentioned earlier, include confrontive coping, distancing, self-controlling, seeking social support, accepting responsibility, escape-avoidance, planful problem-solving, and positive reappraisal.

The extent to which coping mediated the emotional response was evaluated with four hierarchical regression analyses, one for each of the outcome emotion scales. All the concluded encounters were used in the analysis, which meant that each subject had multiple scores. To control for the intercorrelation due to dependent data, the means for each person on each of the variables in the analysis were entered on step 1. This allowed us to examine the contribution of the remaining variables to the variance around each person's mean. The score on the emotion scale derived from the beginning of the encounter was entered on step 2, and those on the coping scales were entered on step 3. In three of the four regression analyses, coping contributed significantly to the variance in outcome emotions over and above that contributed by the emotions at the beginning of the encounter. The exception was the worried/fearful scale. The regression analyses are summarized in table 10.1.

Because the data were all retrospective, we cannot make definitive causal statements. However, the results suggest that coping is indeed a significant mediator of the emotional response in actual stressful encounters. In the three regression analyses where the mediating effect of coping was significant, the same four coping strategies contributed significantly to the explained variance: planful problem-solving and positive reappraisal were significantly and positively associated with the variances of the pleased/happy scale and the confident/secure scale, whereas confrontive coping and distancing were significantly and negatively associated with these scales. The pattern of association was reversed for the angry/disgusted scale: planful problem-solving and positive reappraisal were negatively correlated, and distancing and confrontive coping were positively correlated.

It was fascinating to us that one pattern of problem- and emotion-focused coping (planful problem-solving and positive reappraisal) contributed to an improved emotional state, whereas a different pattern (confrontive coping and distancing) appeared to make the emotional state worse. The effects of planful problem-solving, positive reappraisal, and confrontive coping were consistent with the analysis presented earlier. However, the effects of distancing deviated from our theoretical expectations that it should help reduce distress. Distancing may have positive value as a mediator of emotion only for limited periods and only in certain kinds of encounters, as we noted above. To the extent that distancing does not work, not only might it fail to diminish distress, but it might even be associated with increases in distress because of interference with problem-solving, as when a woman with a breast lump denies its significance and fails to seek medical attention (Katz et al. 1970; Lazarus 1983). As we have stated elsewhere, it is important to determine the conditions under which distancing (as well as other forms of coping) works or does not work if we are to understand the role of coping in emotion and consider ways of influ[illegible]ally.

Coping Effectiveness and the Emotional Response

Elsewhere we have pointed out that a key factor in coping effectiveness is whether or not the choice of coping strategy fits the possibilities for

TABLE 10.1
Coping as Mediator of Emotions: Summary of Regression Analyses

Emotion Scale	R^2	*Adj.* R^2	R^2 *Chg.*	B^+
Worried/Fearful (N=443)				
Step 1: Scale means	.56	.55		
Step 2: Emotions at beginning of encounter	.58	.57	.02***	.18***
Step 3: Coping scales	.60	.58	.01 (ns)	
Disgusted/Angry (N=444)				
Step 1: Scale means	.44	.43		
Step 2: Emotions at beginning of encounter	.49	.48	.04***	.14***
Step 3: Coping scales	.58	.58	.09***	
Distancing				.17***
Planful problem-solving				−.20***
Confrontive coping				.27***
Positive reappraisal				−.24***
Confident/Secure (N=444)				
Step 1: Scale means	.58	.57		
Step 2: Emotions at beginning of encounter	.63	.62	.04***	.24***
Step 3: Coping scales	.68	.66	.05***	
Accept responsibility				−.08*
Confrontive coping				−.08*
Distancing				−.11**
Planful problem-solving				.14***
Positive reappraisal				.19***
Pleased/Happy (N=442)				
Step 1: Scale means	.46	.45		
Step 2: Emotions at beginning of encounter	.52	.51	.06***	.24***
Step 3: Coping scales	.61	.59	.08***	
Confrontive coping				−.22***
Distancing				−.11*
Planful problem-solving				.19***
Positive reappraisal				.25***

+ standardized beta coefficient.
*$p<.05$
**$p<.01$
***$p<.001$

coping in an encounter (Folkman 1984; Lazarus and Folkman 1984b). The major criterion has to do with the extent to which an outcome is within the person's control (cf. Bandura 1977a). If it is, problem-focused forms of coping that are intended to achieve the desired outcome are appropriate, and emotion-focused forms of coping that interfere with problem-focused coping are inappropriate. If, however, the desired outcome is not within the person's control, problem-focused forms of coping are inappropriate, and emotion-focused forms of coping that promote the reduction of distress are appropriate. In our view, coping strategies that have a poor fit with the actual conditions will ultimately have an adverse effect on the emotional response, regardless of any temporary benefits. Thus, problem-solving strategies that are applied to a situation in which no solution is possible are likely to generate frustration and anger, regardless of the quality of problem-solving activity.

The temporal ordering of coping strategies also influences coping effectiveness. For instance, often it is not clear at the outset whether or not an outcome is amenable to change. Clarification may depend on a certain amount of problem-focused coping, such as information search. If avoidant or denial-like processes are called into play prematurely, they can interfere with the information search, and thereby prevent a realistic appraisal of the options for coping. In such cases emotional relief in the short run is purchased at the expense of long-run, effective, problem-focused coping. On the other hand, as noted earlier, denial-like coping, distancing, and positive reappraisal are likely to be useful when they follow an information search that reveals that an outcome is not amenable to change. (For a full discussion of the costs and benefits of denial and denial-like strategies, *see* Lazarus 1983.)

Another interesting feature of coping effectiveness concerns the use of seemingly contradictory coping strategies within the same encounter. We noted one example earlier, namely, the use of self-controlling and confrontive coping within the same encounter. These two forms of coping are moderately correlated (Folkman et al. 1986a). One explanation is that self-control is used along with confrontive coping to moderate the latter's hostile component. Another explanation is that confrontive coping represents a failure of self-control. Although the presence of two forms of coping may at first appear to be contradictory, when they are viewed temporally as efforts to regulate an emotional state while trying to alter the troubled person-environment relationship, their functions appear complementary.

In general, the less effective a given strategy is, the more likely it is that a person will be forced to turn to a different strategy, which is another reason sometimes contradictory forms of coping may be used during the course of a single encounter. If distancing fails, for example, a person might try escape-avoidance. And if escape-avoidance fails, the person might seek social support or use confrontation. This hypothesis receives some support from studies that show that depressed people tend to use more coping strategies, regardless of type, than nondepressed people (e.g., Coyne, Aldwin, and Lazarus 1981; Folkman and Lazarus 1986). The sequence of coping activity in such cases can generate a volatile and complex emotional response.

Conclusion

Two principles need to be emphasized. The first is that every encounter, even the most simple, is usually complex and contains multiple facets and implications for well-being that either exist side by side or arise sequentially. This is why there can be more than one emotion in any encounter, and sometimes contradictory ones, as has been seen in younger children who can feel both happy and sad about what has transpired (Harris in press; Terwogt, Schene, and Harris 1985) and in students preparing for exams (Folkman and Lazarus 1985). To understand the emotion process, therefore, each emotion must be linked analytically to the cognitive appraisal that influences it.

The second principle concerns the temporal and unfolding quality of emotion and coping processes. Social scientists, especially those dealing with disaster, have long recognized that an encounter involving harm or benefit often has three or more stages: anticipation, confrontation, and postconfrontation. Coping in an anticipatory context offers an important opportunity to influence what happens at the point of confrontation by preventing or ameliorating a harm or facilitating a benefit. After confrontation, coping must be aimed at managing the consequences and their implications for the future. Emotions constantly shift throughout this process according to the changing status of the person-environment relationship. It is surprising that to date so little systematic attention has been given to the temporal aspects of the emotion process and to the place of coping within it.

Together, these two principles highlight the complex and dynamic nature of emotions and coping in social encounters and point the way for us to investigate empirically the precise mechanisms through which coping mediates the emotional response. Once their importance in emotion and adaptation is realized, static, cross-sectional research designs and theoretical models reminiscent of stimulus-response formulations of the recent past become unacceptable, and systems analyses of the emotion process and research designs that permit intraindividual analysis of the temporal flow of many person and environment variables become mandatory.

11

Measurement of Coping

■

FRANCES COHEN

Coping is increasingly implicated as an important factor influencing recovery from illness and surgery and mediating the relationship between stress and illness outcomes (Cohen 1979; Cohen and Lazarus 1979, 1983; Elliott and Eisdorfer 1982; Jenkins 1979). However, researchers wanting to measure coping often despair at the lack of consensus about how to measure it. The aim of this chapter is to review current measures of coping and to provide a framework within which they can be evaluated. To set the stage, a number of key issues concerning coping assessment are first discussed. For an introduction to other issues in the coping field *see* Lazarus and Folkman (1984b), Lazarus (1966), Coelho, Hamburg, and Adams (1974), and Cohen and Lazarus (1979, 1983).

Because of the vast array of studies purporting to measure coping, this chapter will not be exhaustive in its review. For other reviews of coping measures *see* Moos and Billings (1982), Haan (1982), and Moos (1974). This chapter will focus only on assessment of individual coping strategies measured from interviews or self-report questionnaires, thereby excluding coping ratings derived from case materials (e.g., Haan 1963, 1969, 1977; Vaillant 1976, 1977). It will for the most part include only coping measures that have been used in more than one study, thus eliminating the numerous unique coping measures utilized only once.

. . .

Measurement Issues

Coping measures differ in a number of important ways which will be outlined and discussed here. There are no simple answers as to which approaches are most fruitful. An investigator's choice of a coping measure will be guided by his or her theoretical assumptions and conceptual model as well as by the type of stress situation to be studied and the psychometric and predictive properties of the measure.

Dispositional (Trait) v. Episodic Approaches

Coping can be assessed either as a disposition, trait, or style, or as an episodic indicator (Averill and Opton 1968; Cohen and Lazarus 1973, 1979). Coping *dispositions* refer to tendencies of an individual to use a particular type of coping across a variety of stressful encounters. The person's tendency to use one or another coping mode is assessed by a questionnaire or projective measure and this test behavior is considered as an indicator of the type of coping behavior the individual would use in a stressful situation under study. For example, Andrew (1967, 1970) used a sentence-completion test to measure the tendency of a person to use "coping" (sensitizing) or "avoiding" strategies. Responses to these sentence stems were scored and used as a measure of whether subjects would be utilizing avoiding or coping strategies in response to a forthcoming surgical operation. The repression-sensitization scale developed by Byrne (1961, 1964) measures a similar dimension—the tendency to avoid or seek out threatening information—using true-false questions from the Minnesota Multiphasic Personality Inventory (MMPI).

Other investigators have measured coping processes or *episodic* coping, that is, the strategies individuals actually use in coping with a particular situation. Cohen and Lazarus (1973) interviewed patients preoperatively and rated whether they sought or avoided information about their illness and forthcoming operation. As another example, other researchers have interviewed parents during their child's terminal illness and evaluated the defenses those patients were using and the successfulness of those defenses (Wolff et al. 1964).

The dispositional approach has been criticized for assuming consistency in coping behavior (Cohen and Lazarus 1979). There is little evidence of consistency in mode of coping from one situation to another, and only weak or nonsignificant relationships have been found between measures of coping dispositions and actual coping behavior observed (Austin 1974; Cohen and Lazarus 1973; Hoffman 1970; Kaloupek, White, and Wong 1984). Thus coping dispositions do not seem to be predictive of how individuals actually cope in stressful situations.

Further, it appears incorrect to assume that individuals use the same coping strategies in dealing with all aspects of a particular situation. There is now considerable evidence that different modes of coping are used in dealing with different sub-areas of a stressful situation, and at different stages in a stressful encounter. For example, Cohen et al. (1986a) found that different coping modes were used in dealing with the pain of rheumatoid arthritis as compared to those used in dealing with the threats to self-esteem brought on by the disease. Different modes were used to deal with other specific stresses associated with arthritis such as mobility problems and difficulties with self-care (Cohen et al. in preparation). Further, several research studies have shown that there may be changes in individual coping modes during different periods of a stressful life situation (e.g. Folkman and Lazarus 1985; Hofer et al. 1972). Horowitz (1976) and Parkes (1972) describe how individuals oscillate between denial and intrusive modes in reaction to stressful life events such as bereavement. Mages and Mendelsohn (1979) outline different demands and strategies found in the various stages of cancer, arguing that such coping should be seen as a developmental process.

It thus seems clear that a dispositional measure of coping will not be able to characterize the array of coping strategies used in dealing with a complex stressful event. However, to the extent that dispositional coping measures tap general dimensions of personality, rather than tendencies to cope in a particular way, they may be meaningfully related to health-relevant outcomes and show good predictive validity.

Dimensions of Coping Tapped

The choice of a coping measure depends on whether or not it taps the dimensions the investigator thinks are important theoretically or the literature shows are empirically relevant. However, coping instruments vary widely in the dimensions they tap; there is no consensus about which dimensions are most useful, or the level of generality required. To illustrate the scope of the problem, table 11.1 presents a list of coping dimensions assessed by some commonly used instruments. Some

TABLE 11.1
Types of Coping Dimensions Assessed by Commonly Used Measures

I. Trait measures
  A. Unidimensional schemes
    1. Repression–Sensitization
      a. Byrne (1961) Repression–Sensitization Scale
      b. Epstein and Fenz (1967) modified Repression–Sensitization Scale
      c. Rorschach Index of Repressive Style (Gardner et al. 1959; Levine and Spivack 1964)
      d. Weinberger, Schwartz, and Davidson (1979) Repressive Style Index
    2. Goldstein (1959) Coping-Avoidance Sentence Completion Test (Andrew 1967, 1970)
  B. Multidimensional Schemes
    1. Defense Mechanism Inventory (Gleser and Ihilevich 1969)
      a. Turning Against Object
      b. Projection
      c. Principalization
      d. Turning Against Self
      e. Reversal
    2. Joffe and Naditch (1977) Coping-defense measure:
      a. coping cf. defense mechanism scale
      b. coping modes
        (1) objectivity
        (2) intellectuality
        (3) logical analysis
        (4) concentration
        (5) tolerance of ambiguity
        (6) empathy
        (7) regression in service of the ego
        (8) sublimation
        (9) substitution
        (10) suppression
      c. defense mechanisms
        (1) isolation
        (2) intellectualization
        (3) rationalization
        (4) denial
        (5) doubt
        (6) projection
        (7) regression
        (8) displacement
        (9) reaction formation
        (10) repression

TABLE 11.1 (*Continued*)

- d. categories of coping and defense
  - (1) controlled coping
  - (2) expressive coping
  - (3) structured defense
  - (4) primitive defense

II. Episodic measures
- A. Unidimensional schemes
  - 1. Cohen avoidance-vigilance interview (Cohen and Lazarus 1973)
  - 2. Hackett and Cassem (1974) Denial Scale (Shaw et al. 1985)
- B. Multidimensional schemes
  - 1. Folkman and Lazarus (1980) Ways of Coping of Questionnaire
    - a. Functions of coping
      - (1) emotion-focused
      - (2) problem-focused
    - b. Eight coping factors (Folkman et al. 1986a)
      - (1) confrontive coping
      - (2) distancing
      - (3) self-control
      - (4) seeking social support
      - (5) accepting responsibility
      - (6) escape/avoidance
      - (7) planful problem-solving
      - (8) positive reappraisal
  - 2. Billings and Moos (1984)
    - a. appraisal-focused (logical analysis)
    - b. problem-focused
      - (1) information-seeking
      - (2) problem-solving
    - c. emotion-focused
      - (1) affective regulation
      - (2) emotional discharge
  - 3. Cohen et al. (1986a) assessment of coping modes
    - a. direct actions
    - b. inhibition of action
    - c. information seeking
    - d. intrapsychic processes
    - e. turning to others for support

III. Cross-dimensional schemes
- A. Coping flexibility (Cohen et al. in preparation; Kemeny 1985)

measure only one dimension of coping, the most common being repression-sensitization or avoidance-vigilance, that is, one's tendency to be sensitized to or avoid threatening information. Other coping measures assess multiple dimensions such as the eight factors measured in Folkman and Lazarus' Ways of Coping. A few assessment techniques are cross-dimensional, combining coping assessments across several categories in order to provide a conceptually different measure, e.g. that of coping flexibility.

The variety of dimensions listed in table 11.1 is not exhaustive and is provided as background for understanding the number of different conceptualizations found in the literature. Moos and Billings (1982) have tried to incorporate a number of these dimensions into a conceptual scheme that emphasizes their similarity.

Situation-Specific Measures vs. Scales with Broad Applicability

Some coping scales aim for wide applicability (e.g., Folkman and Lazarus 1980; Billings and Moos 1981) while others are designed to measure coping in a particular context only (e.g., Weisman and Worden 1976–77). For example, the Ways of Coping (Lazarus and Folkman 1984b) can be used to assess coping in any stressful encounter since it contains general coping items (e.g. "stood my ground and fought for what I wanted"; "took it out on other people"; "I changed something about myself"). Use of this checklist yields general types of strategies but not the very specific coping responses that can be elicited in situation-specific structured coping interviews (e.g. "applied heat packs to alleviate my pain," "thought about others whose disease was so bad they had to stay in bed," "hid my cane in a closet before the interview so no one would know I needed it"; Cohen et al. 1986a). The situation-specific measures provide a richer portrait of how people cope and may be essential for understanding coping in situations of serious illness, where the specific strategies used vary depending on disease and treatment parameters. Some investigators have added items to the Ways of Coping in order to assess coping more accurately in a particular illness context (e.g. Nakell 1985). Others have dropped items, questioning their appropriateness (e.g. Bachrach and Zautra 1985). The choice of a scale thus depends on the type of situation studied, the level of generality desired, the researcher's goals, and whether consistency of coping across situations is a research question to be tested.

Interview vs. Self-Report Checklists

How can one best assess how an individual is coping in a particular situation? There are problems with just asking people how they are coping: each person may interpret the question differently, some do not know, others may forget, while others may try to present the best picture or be influenced by already knowing the outcome. Clinical evidence suggests that people may be more aware of the coping strategies they are struggling to use, or ones that are problematic, than they are of strategies they are successfully using or that have resolved the situation (Horowitz and Wilner 1980). People may also be unaware of particular strategies that they use (e.g., seeking social support) if the strategies dovetail with life routines (e.g., daily phone calls to friends).

Nevertheless, self-report can yield important information, and studies have shown significant relationships between self-reported coping and adaptational outcomes (Lazarus and Folkman 1984b). Shrauger and Osberg (1981) suggest that self-assessments of behaviors are at least as predictive of outcomes as are other assessment methods.

An alternative to self-report is a structured interview that asks questions about how people are dealing with a situation, and what they think and feel about it. The interview responses are not taken at face value; detailed criteria are used to evaluate what the person says and to make a clinical rating about how the person is actually coping. This approach has been used extensively by Cohen and her colleagues (e.g. Cohen 1975; Cohen and Lazarus 1973; Cohen et al 1986a; LaMontagne 1982; Shaw 1984; *see also* Hitchcock 1982) with good predictive validity and interrater reliability. Hackett and Cassem's (1974) Denial Interview is another example of this assessment approach (*see also* Shaw et al. 1985). However, interview methods are time-consuming and may not be feasible for some investigators.

Retrospective Assessments vs. Coping "As It Happens"

Similar problems plague retrospective accounts of coping as those described above for self-report checklists. If it is possible, the best solution is to assess coping "as it happens," that is, while the person is anticipating or confronting the stressor (e.g. Cohen and Lazarus 1973; Folkman and Lazarus 1985; Kaloupek, White, and Wong 1984; Stone and Neale 1984). If coping is assessed in regards to a past stressor, it may be most fruitful to examine quite recent stressors (Folkman et al. 1986a assessed coping with stressors that have occurred in the last week rather than stressors that took place during the previous month, as they had done in earlier studies).

Review of Trait Coping Measures

Repression-Sensitization

Interest in the dimension of repression-sensitization grew out of the perceptual defense literature in which it was shown that some people defended against threatening stimuli (i.e., had slower reaction time to emotional words than to neutral words), while others displayed perceptual vigilance (i.e., had faster response times to emotional words than to neutral ones). This type of dimension was also represented in psychodynamic writings as a dichotomy between the defensive processes of repression and isolation (Schafer 1954). Basically, the concept represents avoidant vs. vigilant/approach ways of dealing with threatening, anxiety-evoking cues. Numerous scales have been developed to measure the concept of repression-sensitization (Byrne 1961; Byrne, Barry and Nelson 1963; Epstein and Fenz 1967; Weinberger, Schwartz, and Davidson 1979), and the closely related concepts of repression-isolation (Gardner et al. 1959; Levine and Spivack 1964), avoidance-coping (Andrew 1970; Goldstein 1959), and denial-intellectualization (Lazarus and Alfert 1964).

Although the theoretical basis of these various dimensions appears to be similar, research reveals low or nonsignificant correlations among them (Cohen and Lazarus 1973; Levine and Spivack 1964; Silver 1970). Even similar scoring techniques (e.g., for rating repressive style from the Rorschach) showed correlations of only 0.54 with each other (Levine and Spivack 1964). The problem of low correlations between similarly named measures plagues the coping field in general, and no definitive studies have yet indicated which may be the best measure of the concept of repression-sensitization.

The most commonly used measure is the Byrne Repression-Sensitization (R-S) Scale, although it has come under considerable attack (e.g., Chabot 1973; Golin et al. 1967; Lazarus, Averill, and Opton 1974; Lefcourt 1966). The most serious problem has been the 0.9 correlation between the R-S Scale and the Taylor Manifest Anxiety Scale, leading many to conclude that the R-S Scale measures nothing but manifest anxiety. Lefcourt (1966) argues that it is a measure of attitudes toward emotional expression.

Bell and Byrne (1978) review evidence of the predictive validity of the R-S scale. They also argue that some of the high correlation between the Taylor Manifest Anxiety Scale and the R-S is due to overlapping items. However, the correlation between the scales after common items are omitted is still 0.76. Bell and Byrne conclude that the R-S scale is a useful measure of something and that research to date shows results that are consistent with the broad notion of what repression-sensitization should mean. They feel that the name generates productive research and "that a construct by any other name does not predict as sweetly" (p. 476).

Weinberger, Schwartz, and Davidson (1979) Repressive Style Measure

Weinberger and his colleagues developed a method for measuring repressive style that would differentiate those people who report no emotional distress in a stressful situation because they are experiencing low levels of anxiety ("low anxious") from those who are actually repressing anxious feelings ("true repressors"). Sensitizers report high levels of distress. They used both the Taylor Manifest Anxiety Scale (TMAS) (which correlated 0.9 with Byrne's R-S Scale) and the Marlowe-Crowne Social Desirability Scale (SD) to classify subjects. "True repressors" were viewed as those who would be low on the TMAS and high on SD, whereas the "low anxious" were thought to be those with low scores on both the TMAS and SD. Weinberger, Schwartz, and Davidson (1979) found significant differences between these two groups on self-report, physiological, and behavioral measures, with true repressors showing poorer performance on cognitive tasks and greater discrepancy between physiological reactions to stress and their report of emotional distress. These findings were recently replicated by Asendorpf and Scherer (1983). This scale has also shown good predictive validity in two studies with coronary heart disease patients (Shaw et al. 1985; Shaw et al. in press), and in a variety of other studies (Weinberger 1985).

However, the construct validity of this measure of repressive style has never been clearly established. Shaw (1985) did not find a relationship between this classification and scores on Hackett and Cassem's (1974) Denial Scale. Although the measure is intriguing and shows good predictive validity, it is not clear why "true repressors" would necessarily be high, and "low anxious" necessarily low, on the social desirability dimension. Further work is needed to establish what this scale is actually measuring. However, it is quite promising in its ability to predict discrepancies between psychological and physiological measures.

Defense Mechanism Inventory

The Defense Mechanism Inventory (DMI) was developed by Gleser and Ihilevich (1969) to measure defensive modes of ego functioning. It is a forced-choice test that measures the relative intensity of five major clusters of ego defense mechanisms: (1) turning against object (i.e., identification with the aggressor, regression, and displacement); (2) projection; (3) principalization (i.e., intellectualization, rationalization, and isolation of affect); (4) turning against self (i.e., masochism and autosadism); and (5) reversal (i.e., denial, undoing, reaction formation, repression, and negation).

The DMI presents ten short stories dealing with different conflict areas, and questions ask what the person would actually do in the situation and the thoughts, fantasies, and feelings the story evokes. Although there is some evidence for the predictive and construct validity of the instrument (Cooper and Kline 1982; Gleser and Sacks 1973; Walsh 1972), questions have been raised about its content validity and reliability (Juni 1982; Weissman, Ritter, and Gordon 1971). A multitrait-multimethod approach comparing the DMI to two other similarly named scales found a lack of convergent and discriminant validity (Vickers and Hervig 1981). Similar problems were found when the DMI was compared to the Blacky Defense Preference Inventory (Massong, Dickson, and Ritzler 1982). Further, a factor-analytic study concluded that three factors are measured by the DMI: turning attention outward, turning attention inward, and turning against self (Woodrow 1973). Juni and Masling (1980) suggest scoring the DMI on a single continuum, with one end representing defenses that facilitate the expression of aggression and the other end with defenses that inhibit acting out. Juni (1982) later reformulated this into a composite measure which includes only four of the subscales combined in the following way: turning against object + projection − principalization − reversal of affect. Inhibition and internalization of frustration are at one end of the scale and acting out and externalization of frustration at the other.

The scale has also been criticized because of its ipsative scoring which makes it difficult to interpret correlations between the DMI and other scales to determine construct validity (Cooper and Kline 1982).

Woodrow (1973) developed a version that uses a normative rating scale format.

Joffe and Naditch (1977) Coping-Defense Scales

Joffe and Naditch developed a paper-and-pencil measure of coping and defense using empirically derived scales. These were constructed by selecting California Psychological Inventory and MMPI items that predicted interviewer ratings of coping and defense ego mechanisms made according to the conceptual schema developed by Haan (1963, 1969, 1977). Haan's framework differentiates coping from defense processes on the basis of congruence with reality, rationality, flexibility of response, and other value-laden criteria. Joffe and Naditch derived three ways to score their scale: (1) summing coping and defense items separately; (2) scoring for controlled coping, expressive coping, structured defense, and primitive defense; and (3) scoring on each of the twenty ego mechanisms described by Haan (*see* table 11.1). However, not all of the twenty ego mechanisms could be measured accurately for both sexes. The Joffe and Naditch scale has been used in a few studies (Joffe and Bast 1978; Vickers, Conway, and Haight 1983; Vickers et al. 1981) with some evidence of predictive validity. However, a study that utilized a multitrait-multimethod approach to compare the Joffe and Naditch scale with the Defense Mechanism Inventory and Schutz's (1967) Coping Operations Preference Enquiry found poor convergent and discriminant validity (Vickers and Hervig 1981). These results are hard to evaluate since the validity of each of these scales is open to question.

Coping with Life Strains

Pearlin and Schooler (1978) used a survey questionnaire to measure the stresses of living that arise from four social roles—marriage partner, household economic manager, parent, and co-worker—and the types of coping strategies used in response. This is a trait measure of coping since it asks how people usually coped rather than how they actually coped in a specific encounter. They factor-analyzed the coping responses in each of the four areas (*see also* Fleishman 1984 for a similar factor analysis), producing six factors of marital coping (self-reliance vs. advice-seeking, controlled reflectiveness vs. emotional discharge, positive comparison, negotiation, self-assertion vs. passive forbearance, selective ignoring), five of parental coping (selective ignoring, non-punitiveness vs. reliance on discipline, self-reliance vs. advice-seeking, positive comparisons, exercise of potency vs. helpless resignation), four in the household economic area (devaluation of money, selective ignoring, positive comparisons, optimistic faith), and four concerning occupation (substitution of rewards, positive comparisons, optimistic action, and selective ignoring). Pearlin and Schooler evaluated the efficacy of these coping behaviors and found that coping modes varied among different sociodemographic groups. Those highly educated, affluent, and of the male sex made greater use of effective strategies. They also found coping to be most effective in dealing with problems of marriage and parenting, and least effective in the occupational arena.

Pearlin and Schooler's work has been influential in the coping field, both in its conceptualization of functions of coping, its focus on chronic life strains, and its provocative results. However, their measure is limited to the four stress areas outlined above. Further, because they focus on persistent life strains, that is, those that subjects were *not* able to resolve, the measure cannot be used to measure coping in response to acute stressful situations. It also probably excludes the types of coping responses that may be effective in altering stressful episodes.

Review of Episodic Coping Measures

Avoidance-Vigilance

Cohen and Lazarus (1973) developed a structured interview for assessing avoidance-vigilance in surgical patients, using a detailed set of criteria to judge the degree to which patients were using avoidant or vigilant coping strategies. The interview asks questions about the person's emotional state; knowledge about the illness, operation, and postoperative course; what other information the person wanted to know, and so on. Ratings are made on a 10-point scale. This interview has been used in other studies of surgical patients and a version for angioplasty patients has been developed (Shaw 1984). The interrater reliability of ratings has been high, averaging around 0.9 (Cohen 1975; Cohen and Lazarus 1973; LaMontagne 1982; Shaw 1984). Cohen and Lazarus (1973) found that this episodic coping measure was a better predictor of recovery from surgery outcomes than were two dispositional coping instruments (the Epstein and Fenz 1967 modified Repression-Sensitization scale; and the Andrew 1970 Sentence-Completion Test) measuring the same dimension.

Hackett and Cassem's Denial Scale

Hackett and Cassem (1974) developed an interview to assess denial in myocardial infarction patients. They define denial as a "multifaceted behavioral complex" (p. 95) and their interview taps indirect and direct manifestations of denial in present and past situations. Thus their measure is not truly an episodic measure, since it also evaluates past indicators of denial. The Hackett and Cassem measure has been criticized for lumping together a variety of "denial-like" coping mechanisms—such as minimization, avoidance, nonchalance, and delay in seeking treatment—thereby overextending the meaning of denial (Cohen and Lazarus 1979; Lazarus 1983). However, this measure is the most commonly used measure of denial in heart disease patients (e.g. Dimsdale and Hackett 1982; Soloff 1980; Stern, Pascale, and Ackerman 1977) and has been validated with clinician ratings (Froese et al. 1973).

The original Hackett and Cassem interview is semi-structured, which can lead to wide variability in the information collected. The scoring criteria are somewhat vague. Very little systematic work has been done assessing the reliability and validity of the scale. Recently Shaw et al. (1985) systematized the interview and rating criteria to make them less subject to individual variation. These authors developed a structured interview schedule and a detailed scoring manual that provided a more elaborate description of how situations would be coded. An independent rater scored a subsample of the interview tapes, and an interrater reliability of 0.82 was found. Shaw et al. (1985) found that denial was associated with less information gain from the cardiac rehabilitation program.

Despite the predictive validity of the scale, there still is question about what constructs the denial interview is assessing. For example, Shaw (1985) reports no significant associations between the denial rating and the Byrne R-S scale or the Weinberger, Schwartz, and Davidson (1979) index of repressive style. However, this may just reflect the lack of congruence usually found between trait and episodic measures of coping.

Ways of Coping

The Ways of Coping Questionnaire was originally developed as a checklist of 68 items that described a broad range of cognitive and behavioral strategies (Folkman and Lazarus 1980). It was intended for use as an episodic measure. Subjects responded in terms of a specified stressful situation, for example, a stressful situation that had happened over the last month, and checked off those strategies they had used to deal with it. Folkman and Lazarus revised the scale subsequently by deleting or rewording redundant or unclear items, adding items, and changing the response format to a 4-point Likert scale (Folkman et al 1986a; *see* Lazarus and Folkman 1984b for a copy of the revised 67-item version). In the revised version subjects indicate to what extent they used each of the strategies in dealing with the situation being described.

The Ways of Coping Questionnaire has been factor-analyzed using four different data sets, the latter two utilizing the revised Ways of Coping (Aldwin et al. 1980; Folkman and Lazarus 1985; Folkman et al 1986a; Vitaliano et al. 1985). Four different factor structures have been derived, each with somewhat different factors. The most recent factor analysis (Folkman et al 1986a) produced the following eight factors: (1) confrontive coping; (2) distancing; (3) self-control; (4) seeking social support; (5) accepting responsibility; (6) escape/avoidance; (7) planful problem-solving; and (8) positive appraisal. Five of these factors are similar to ones derived from the earlier factor analyses although each analysis contributed unique factors which may be influenced by the subject population (e.g., college students, cf. middle-aged adults) or the situation being studied (Folkman et al 1986a).

Modified versions of the Ways of Coping have been used in a number of different studies (e.g. Baum, Fleming, and Singer 1983; McCrae 1984; Nakell 1985; Parkes 1984). However, there is not yet any standard way to score this instrument. Some investigators use a large number of distinct mechanisms for analysis while others use only a few broad categories (e.g., emotion-focused vs. problem-focused).

Billings and Moos Coping Measures

Billings and Moos (1981) developed a 19-item checklist with a yes/no format to assess how people cope with a recent stressful event. The items were grouped into three coping method categories—active-cognitive, active-behavioral, and avoidance—as well as according to the emotion-focused vs. problem-focused distinction. Their classification of some of the coping items can be questioned (e.g., they consider "prepared for the worst" to be an avoidance strategy). Their results revealed that coping attenuated the relationship between negative life events and measures of personal functioning.

Billings and Moos (1984) revised their earlier coping procedure in a study of depressed patients. Respondents described their response to a recent stressful event by rating the frequency of use (on a 4-point scale) of 32 different possible coping responses. Using preliminary item analyses, they classified strategies into the conceptual categories they had described in earlier work (Moos and Billings 1982): (1) appraisal-focused coping (logical analysis); (2) problem-focused coping (information-seeking, problem-solving); and (3) emotion-focused coping (affective regulation, emotional discharge). This apparently reduced the scale to 28 items. Billings and Moos found these coping indices were significantly related to outcome measures of functioning. There was no evidence that coping had stress-attenuation or buffering effects.

It is hard to evaluate these measures since they have not been widely used. The coping dimensions they outline have influenced other researchers' classification of coping responses (e.g., Kaloupek, White, and Wong 1984).

Other Coping Measures

This review of coping measures has focused on measures used in more than one study. Space limitations prevent discussion of other coping measures that may nonetheless be of interest. For example, Miller and Mangan (1983) developed a trait measure to classify individuals as "blunters" or "monitors" (another attempt to measure a repression-sensitization strategy) based on their responses to four hypothetical situations. Stone and Neale (1984) present subjects with eight abstract coping categories and ask subjects to specify whether they did anything that fit those categories with respect to the daily problems of living they reported. The categories are: distraction, situation redefinition, direct action, catharsis, acceptance, social support, relaxation, and religion.

Review of Cross-Dimensional Coping Measures

Coping Flexibility

Recently there has been interest in developing new ways of categorizing coping that do not merely look at coping modes. It may not be important whether individuals utilize one coping strategy rather than another, but whether they can draw on very different ones adaptively depending on the requirements of the situation (Cohen et al. 1982). Unfortunately, we do not yet have a good way of assessing coping flexibility. Cohen and her colleagues (Cohen et al. in preparation; Kemeny 1985) assessed coping flexibility in studies of arthritis and herpes patients. In the study of arthritis patients, subjects' interview responses were coded in each of five stressor areas for the subject's use of five modes of coping (direct actions, inhibition of action, information-seeking, intrapsychic processes, and turning to others for support). Two coping flexibility measures were determined: the number of different coping modes used within a stress area (e.g., in dealing with mobility problems) and the number used across the five stress areas studied. However, the coping flexibility measure was significantly correlated with ratings of the stressfulness of each stress area and also with indicators of emotional distress. Thus, rather than being a measure of flexibility, the measure may indicate that in highly stressful situations more coping strategies may be required, or that individuals may use many methods because they cannot find a few that are effective.

Kemeny (1985) interviewed genital herpes patients monthly and assessed coping in response to two stressful situations of the previous month. Coping was rated on eleven different coping modes. Coping flexibility was measured by determining the number of different modes used across both situations. Kemeny also found coping flexibility scores associated with measures of life stress and anxiety. Further, her results showed that coping flexibility did not interact with stress in predicting recurrence rate or immunological change as had been originally hypothesized.

A more adequate measure of coping repertoire is needed. The number of strategies used does not really measure what is available. Further, although it may be good to have a large repertoire, the best idea may be to choose the most appropriate strategy for each situation. How to measure that may require looking both at the nature of the situation and the types of strategies used.

Conclusions

This chapter has discussed a number of issues relevant to the evaluation of coping, and has reviewed commonly used trait and episodic measures. The reader expecting a conclusion about the best scales will unfortunately be disappointed. Not enough is known about the construct validity of any of the coping measures reviewed. The distressing fact is that similarly named measures show low correlations with each other, and not enough validity information is available to suggest the best measure of each concept. Further, in terms of content validity, we do not know enough about what coping dimensions are most important to include nor what level of generality is required. Existing coping check-lists have been criticized for not including enough coping items, or for including too many that are irrelevant. More work is needed to evaluate the relative advantages and disadvantages of brief versus lengthy checklists.

The choice of a unidimensional or multidimensional scale is still a perplexing question. The unidimensional measures do not reflect the vast array of strategies people use in dealing with life stresors. And yet they have remained popular because they have good predictive validity and are intuitively appealing. Further, since there is no consensus about which dimensions to include in multidimensional scales, their use has not led to comparability in instruments which would make it possible to make comparative evaluations.

A considerable conceptual and empirical effort is needed to bring clarity to this area. Various conceptual frameworks have been suggested for classifying coping (e.g., Haan 1977; Lazarus and Folkman 1984b; Moos and Billings 1982; Pearlin and Schooler 1978) but no one can agree on which is best. Further, these different conceptual schemes have not been pitted against each other empirically to see which is the best predictor of outcome. Pitting similarly named coping scales against each other in predicting outcome would also be quite useful. For unidimensional traits such as repression-sensitization, episodic measures of coping seem to be better predictors than trait measures, but this type of question has never been examined with multidimensional instruments.

The choice of a coping instrument will depend on the type of situation to be studied, the researcher's goals and conceptual framework, the level of generality desired, and the degree to which it taps the dimensions of coping the investigator thinks are most important. If more investigators use more than one coping scale at a time, and evaluate their validity, we will be better able to judge in the future which measures are most useful.

12

The Development of Hardiness

SALVATORE R. MADDI AND
SUZANNE C. KOBASA

To determine how hardiness develops, we relied on our interviews of Illinois Bell executives, our clinical experience with psychotherapy clients, and research findings of other psychological studies. These various sources all point in the same direction: finding the conditions in early life that lead to the sense of commitment, control, and challenge—the marks of hardiness.

Parent-Child Interactions

Although children in earliest life have little conception about themselves and their world, they have needs and capabilities that push for expression. Children depend on others for such requirements as food, water, security, and love. Being idiosyncratic, the capabilities are more difficult to enumerate. One child may have capabilities for vigorous, frequent muscular actions and for social extroversion, whereas another may tend toward self-reflection, inactivity, and social introversion. A third child may be especially sensitive, empathic, and emotionally expressive. In any event, needs and capabilities jointly define the child's input to his or her interaction with parents.

To be sure, parents have needs and capabilities, too, and these get expressed in their interactions with their children. But parents have also lived long enough to have views about themselves, the world, and child rearing, which also influence how they interact. The quality of the interactions children have with their parents leads them, over time, to develop general viewpoints or dispositions toward themselves and their environments. Some of these dispositions help develop hardiness.

Supportive Early Interactions Build Commitment

How do some people come to experience their environment and themselves as interesting, worthwhile, and satisfying, whereas others find them dull, meaningless, and frustrating? This difference in sense of commitment to self and environment may well result from the overall degree to which the interactions they had with their parents were supportive (i.e., provided encouragement and acceptance). Children will attempt to satisfy their needs (such as for safety or love) and potentialities (such as mathematical or artistic ability) in many ways. When parents meet these efforts with approval, interest, and encouragement, the child feels supported and, on this basis, comes to view self and world as interesting and worthwhile. But if parents are generally hostile, disapproving, or neglectful toward expressions of needs and potentialities, the child comes to view self and world as empty and worthless. What is important in the development of commitment is the overall degree of parental support rather than any one or two interactions that are traumatic or wonderful.

There are many reasons why parents might be generally unsupportive of their children. Parents, for example, might be too wrapped up in their work lives away from the family or be continually resentful because they never wanted children in the first place. Another problem is that parents themselves may be so overwhelmed that they become neglectful and ungiving to others. Nor can it help if parents do not love each other. In contrast, parents who find family interaction fulfilling, who are managing to cope with their own lives, and who appreciate rather than resent their children, are much more likely to be supportive of them.

There is a particularly damaging (though subtle) way in which parents can be unsupportive and thereby undermine the child's sense of commitment to self and world. This occurs when parents impose on the child preconceived notions of what is acceptable and admirable despite the fact that the notions are at variance with the natural expressions of the child's capabilities. A female child who is naturally very physical may be regarded by her parents as unladylike and be supported only for signs of emotional sensitivity and imaginativeness. A naturally sensitive and imaginative male child may be considered unmanly and be supported only when he shows signs of physical prowess and aggression.

In this way, children may conform to parental expectations rather than express their capabilities vigorously. The result is a developing person who appears outwardly adjusted but carries around a nagging, restless sense that something important is missing, that life as currently lived is not enough. To avoid this sense of alienation in their offspring, parents need to support them not out of rigid preconceptions of what will be best for them but rather out of respect for the importance of the individuality that will result from natural expression of a child's capabilities and interests.

Early Environments Permitting Mastery Build Control

Why do some people believe that, and act as if, they can influence ongoing events, whereas others passively succumb to being the victims of circumstances? This difference in control may reflect the overall proportion of mastery, as opposed to failure experiences, in early life. As they grow older, children's developing physical and mental capabilities lead them to try to accomplish things. Their own needs and abilities define many competing goals for them to strive toward. When children succeed, they have a sense of mastery—and when they fail, a sense of failure. Arenas for mastery or failure include cleaning and dressing oneself, finding one's way outside the home, interacting with others, getting school work done accurately, riding a bicycle, and so forth.

As they develop, it is best for children when the tasks they encounter are just a bit more difficult than what they can easily perform. If the task is too easy, then succeeding at it will not bring a sense of accomplishment or mastery. Conversely, if the task is too hard, the child is likely to fail and feel powerless. What builds control is for the child's interaction with the environment to involve, predominantly, tasks that can be mastered because they are moderate in difficulty (McClelland 1958). If that is so, children will sense that they are able to influence things, and will learn a willingness to act on that sense. But if the largest proportion of the child's tasks are so hard as to provoke failure, powerlessness will be learned instead.

When children encounter too many hard tasks, it is often because parents are subtly competing with them. Out of resentment and an investment in exercising power over children, parents may actually impose tasks of such difficulty that failure is virtually assured. Then the child can be chastised for not having tried hard enough, thus providing what appears as a socially acceptable basis for punishment. If children encounter, instead, too many easy tasks, it usually means that parents are being overprotective. Although there is less resentment in this, it is actually just another way for parents to exercise power over their children. The assumption is that children are too weak and incapable to do anything on their own, so they need the parent's superior competence. However, parents who are genuinely interested in their children feeling and acting in an independently competent fashion make the effort to ensure that the child's tasks are generally of moderate difficulty.

Environmental Changes Construed as Richness Build Challenge

Why do some people expect life changes to be frequent and stimulating, whereas others expect stability and regard change as disruptive of security? This difference in a sense of challenge reflects the degree to which a person's early environment changed—and whether that change was regarded as richness or as chaos. An environment may have many large, obvious changes (e.g., many trips to foreign countries, many changes in residence and many different visitors to the home). But more subtle changes (e.g., varying tasks to perform around the home, interacting with parents and siblings who talk and act in differing ways because they are in a vigorous developmental process themselves, and having many hobbies) are perhaps even more important.

Neither obvious nor subtle changes are by themselves sufficient to build a sense of challenge. In fact, children may be overwhelmed by continual change unless they are helped to see it as richness rather than chaos. Parents must themselves see changes as interesting and developmentally valuable so they can communicate this to their children. In the communication, parents must encourage children to use their mental capabilities . . . to conceive of the challenges as signs of richness and possibility. In contrast, parents who themselves are disrupted by changes, and communicate this, are understandably unable to help their children learn to feel challenged rather than threatened.

The Atmosphere That Breeds Hardiness

Putting together the three themes outlined above gives a general sense of what family atmosphere breeds hardiness. The social and physical environment changes frequently, and includes many moderately difficult tasks. Parents encourage their children to construe the changes as richness and support efforts to perform the tasks successfully. More generally, the parents are warm and enthusiastic enough toward the children that their interactions are usually pleasant, rewarding, and supportive of the child's individuality.

In this atmosphere, youngsters are very likely to develop hardiness, taking it with them as they become older and leave their families. Having a general sense that the environment is satisfying, they examine it with curiosity and enthusiasm—with commitment, rather than alienation. Having confidence in their capability for mastery, they approach life's tasks and events as problems they can solve and as situations they can influence—with control, not powerlessness. Having a sense of the richness and possibilities of life, they approach changes as something of developmental value when properly understood—as challenge rather than threat.

Andy, Jim, Chuck, and Bill in Perspective

To make what we have been saying more vivid, let us look at the lives of four executives. Certainly, they are very different from each other on many bases besides hardiness. And certainly, it is difficult to generalize from only four cases. Yet some clear factors shine through.

In early life, Andy experienced more punishment than reward. His father was aggressive and punitive, while his mother was withdrawn and overwhelmed. Neither could have provided him with much warmth, admiration, and support, In addition, the competitive atmosphere created by his father did not seem to give Andy much opportunity to succeed at moderately difficult tasks. The tasks were too ambiguous, and father was a biased arbiter of success. Andy always felt that he had failed. So instead of learning commitment and control, Andy developed attitudes of alienation and powerlessness.

At first glance it might seem that Andy's family at least met the conditions for learning challenge. After all, they participated in many activities together, which would have made for at least a moderate level of change in Andy's day-to-day experiences. But a closer look at the circumstances gives a different picture. Andy's father apparently had a rather fixed notion of the right answer to the questions he posed. So instead of giving free rein to his imagination, Andy spent his time anxiously trying to guess what was in his father's mind. Andy learned a sense of threat rather than challenge in the face of an incomprehensible environment.

Jim, the other executive low in hardiness, also failed to experience a family atmosphere conducive to hardiness. There was some sort of reversal of fortune that Jim did not completely understand, a number of family deaths, including the father, and a mother who was strong in adversity but not very warm and giving. Very likely, interactions with the environment yielded more displeasure than reward. We don't know whether Jim encountered any moderately difficult tasks to perform, but it seems unlikely that his parents spent much time and effort regulating such matters. In Jim's confusion about what was going on and his sense of victimization by circumstances, we are seeing at an early age the sense of powerlessness he carries with him as an adult. His parents didn't construe the extreme and rapid changes that took place as being rich with developmental possibilities. More likely, father was withdrawing (overwhelmed?) from the children before he died. And mother's reaction to his death seems to have been a steely discipline and lack of emotion—a state inconsistent with encouraging her children to explore the richness of life. It seems understandable from all this that Jim did not learn much hardiness.

The early family lives of the two executives who are high in hardiness, Chuck and Bill, were very different from Andy's and Jim's. The parents of both men established a warm, cooperative, supportive environment for their children and themselves. The mothers were emotionally available even if they worked. The fathers were not necessarily at home a great deal, but when they were around they, too, were available to the children. Chuck and Bill's interactions within the family must have been largely pleasant and rewarding. It is not surprising that they developed a sense of commitment.

Both Chuck and Bill were also encouraged to perform tasks for themselves. In Chuck's case, this was necessary because his mother was taking in sewing. Necessity was less apparent in Bill's case. But both seem to have been provided with tasks that were difficult enough to stimulate development without ensuring failure. And both were encouraged in and rewarded for their efforts. In Bill's case, mother and father served as good models for the struggle to perform tasks well because both appreciated the craft involved in their own work and communicated this to him. For Chuck, father served as this kind of model more than mother; but at least there was one parent who communicated being influential at work. Thus, both executives had the prerequisites in early experience for developing a sense of control.

Chuck gave little information directly relevant to the development of challenge. There is no reason to believe that his early environment changed a lot and that he was encouraged to see this as richness rather than disruption. Perhaps the interview was simply not detailed enough on this point to provide information. But Bill gave lots of relevant descriptions. His parents had friends visit frequently, and they typically discussed in detail the issues of the day and of their interpersonal relationships. This kind of discussion was also very common within the family itself. The children were encouraged to reflect their experiences, to construe them in one way and then another, to explore their thoughts, feelings, and actions. Although the familiy did not travel much or have obvious upheavals, there must have been a lot of day-to-day change of a more subtle kind. And there was certainly an attempt to see this as richness and possibility.

The Irrelevance of Socioeconomic Background

Is the development of personality hardiness in early life restricted to economically and socially advantaged families? After all, there is all this talk about changing environments richly construed, and highly rewarding circumstances. It is all the more important, therefore, to realize that what we are talking about is atmosphere rather than background. *Atmosphere* is something established for children by their parents, and it bears little or no relationship to economic and social advantage or disadvantage. In fact, some wealthy and powerful parents neglect their children beyond all hope of their developing personality hardiness. In contrast, some parents who are relatively poor and socially marginal are nonetheless successful in constructing environments for their children that are developmentally beneficial. Parents can construct an atmosphere supportive of hardiness without having much money or social position, as long as they love and admire their children, believe in the importance of what they are doing, and are willing to spend the time that is necessary in such development.

From what we have just said, you can see that in our executives study, there was little or no relationship between personality hardiness

TABLE 12.1
Correlation of Personality Hardiness with Background Variables

	Age	*Education*	*Religious Practice*	*Ethnicity*	*Parents' Education*
Personality hardiness	.08	−.02	.13	.06	.09

Sources: Kobasa, Maddi, and Kahn 1982; Kobasa, Maddi, and Puccetti 1982.

and various estimates of background. Table 12.1 combines the results of several testing sessions. The numbers in the table are correlations, which can range from −1.00 through 0.00 to +1.00. The correlation values shown are very small, indicating that personality hardiness is essentially independent of the background factors studied.

So, in understanding the personality hardiness of our executives, it is unimportant how much education their parents had or, for that matter, how much their parents helped them to achieve. Since education is a typical measure of a family's socioeconomic status, this finding confirms our belief: economic and social advantage is relatively unimportant in the development of hardiness. The ethnicity variable measures the number of years between the family's emigration and the present. It appears from the results that the length of time the family has been American has no influence on hardiness. Nor could we find any relationship between hardiness and the particular nation from which the ancestors emigrated. The religious practice variable indicates the degree to which the family practiced whatever religion it recognized. Once again there is little relationship between religiosity and hardiness. We also checked to see whether hardiness occurs more frequently in one or another of the major religions and found nothing to report. Finally, hardiness is not a function of the executive's age at time of testing. All in all, the evidence indicates that, as expected, personality hardiness is not influenced by economic and social background.

Other Evidence

There is by now much research in the scientific literature that supports our statements. Interestingly, some of the most compelling demonstrations involve animals. This is not surprising because manipulating the early environments of humans is not only difficult but often unethical, and always illegal. So the human observations tend to involve naturally occurring situations, which, though relevant, lack the rigorous control of variables that is possible in planned experiments.

The Antecedents of Alienation and Commitment

Some time ago, Ribble (1944) and Spitz (1945, 1946) described the effects on children of growing up in a hospital or institutional setting. Usually, these children were in institutions because they were orphans or had been abandoned. However hard the hospital nursing staff tried, there were too few of them to provide anything near the attention, encouragement, love, and sheer stimulation that normal parents give. In these conditions (deprivation of pleasurable interaction with the social environment), children fail to develop vigorously. They are smaller in size and less physically vigorous than normal children, and are more susceptible to diseases. Especially relevant for us, they seemed unusually disrupted by change (stressful events) and preferred to be left alone in quiet circumstances (alienation from physical and social stimuli). However much these naturalistic observations have been criticized as lacking rigor, there always seem additional studies (e.g., Beres and Obers 1950) that make essentially the same points. This phenomenon of alienation has also been reported when young children are deprived of the company of their mothers in a situation where no mother substitute is available (Page 1971:414).

Researchers have found similar results in rigorous laboratory experiments on such primates as chimpanzees. Harlow (1958, 1959) conducted a series of studies in which infant primates were taken away from their natural mothers and reared alone in a cage with a terry-cloth mother substitute. The infant's physical needs were taken care of by the experimenters, and it could cling to the terry-cloth "mother" at will. Nonetheless, development was severely impeded. Particularly relevant is the finding that these primates, on reaching adulthood, tended to cringe in the back of the cage, often hiding their eyes and ears from even the moderate stimulation of the laboratory. When other primates were put into the cage, those that had the abnormal upbringing would have nothing to do with them. In this isolation from the social and physical environment, the experimental animals showed extreme alienation. They were also unable to deal with even the ordinary moment-to-moment changes of laboratory life.

Studies concerning the antecedents of commitment are more difficult to find. But there is a literature on the "gentling" of experimental animals that seems relevant (Thompson and Schaefer 1961). Typically, an experimental group of laboratory white rats will, from a very early age, be held, fondled, played with, hand-fed, stroked, and in other ways "loved" by the researcher. In contrast, the control-group rats will be reared in their cages, untouched by human hands, and fed through automatic devices. The point of such experiments is to see whether there are few differences between gentled and nongentled rats in subsequent performance. In general, gentled rats explore their environment more and therefore learn quicker. They also appear to be more able to adapt to stressful circumstances, as shown by less defecating, urinating, and freezing (i.e., becoming rigid) when changes occur. Such results definitely suggest that rats whose early experience is generally rewarding are subsequently more likely to show curiosity about and involvement with the environment. If even rats, with their relatively simple brains, can profit developmentally from rewarding early experiences, imagine how true this must be at the human level!

The Antecedents of Powerlessness and Control

Phares (1976) has summarized several pieces of research concerning how people develop the belief that they can influence or control events. These studies typically separate youngsters into those who have this belief and those who believe, instead, that they are passive victims of external forces. Then information is obtained from their mothers concerning how the youngsters were brought up. In general, the youngsters strong in a sense of control had mothers who expected them to be independent at an earlier age than youngsters who felt powerless. This is corroborated by similar research (McClelland [1951] 1976) showing that early independence training breeds an interest in and belief that one can achieve standards of excellence.

The kinds of tasks that mothers who breed a sense of control wanted their youngsters to achieve earlier than was wanted by other mothers included trying out new things, knowing the way around the city, and having interests and hobbies (McClelland [1951] 1976). Such tasks certainly seem like moderately rather than overly difficult ones for youngsters, but there is no definite evidence in these studies with which to be sure. Circumstantial evidence is available, however. Mothers whose early independence training leads their children to develop a sense of control do not seem to be expressing either neglect or punitiveness. They appear to apply standards in a flexible and reasonably permissive rather than harsh manner, and do not insist that their youngsters shoulder responsibility for chores around the home (McClelland [1951] 1976; Phares 1976). These mothers are lovingly encouraging their youngsters to try to master moderately difficult tasks in the way we theorized should build a sense of control.

There is some dramatic evidence at the subhuman level that is also consistent with our formulation. Seligman (1975) found that, when dogs are put in an experimental apparatus which will give them electric shocks they cannot escape from, the dogs develop what he calls "learned helplessness" (this amounts to powerlessness, in our terminology). What he means by learned helplessness is that, when the same dogs are subsequently put in a different experimental apparatus in which it is easy to avoid electric shock (usually by jumping over a low partition into an unshocked area), they will not learn to escape. Dogs put in this apparatus with no previous experience of inescapable shock have no trouble learning to jump over the partition. In an additional elaboration on this kind of study, Seligman (1975) demonstrated that, when dogs were shocked in an apparatus where they could learn how to escape, they have no trouble with subsequent apparatuses requiring different responses to escape.

From our point of view, the apparatus in which shock could not be escaped constituted a task that the dogs could not master through learning. That they never learned in subsequent apparatuses where escape was quite possible indicates that they had developed a sense of powerlessness rather than control. But when the initial task was not too difficult for mastery (escape from the shock was possible to learn), then they explored subsequent apparatuses and learned to escape shocks. These animals learned a sense of control rather than helplessness. Quite possibly, our formulation works even at the subhuman level.

The Antecedents of Threat and Challenge

The studies of Ribble (1944) and Spitz (1945, 1946) already mentioned are also relevant evidence for the development of a sense of threat. Children reared in institutions or otherwise deprived of mother's company (having to accept, instead, a relatively bland, unchanging, unstimulating environment) seem especially disrupted by subsequent changes. You will also recall that the same phenomenon is shown in chimpanzees reared with terry-cloth rather than flesh and blood mothers (Harlow 1958, 1959). All this definitely suggests that a rich and varied early stimulus environment leads to a later ability to assimilate changing events without debilitation.

At the human level, empirical evidence that a varied early environment encourages a sense of challenge is a bit difficult to find. There are studies, however, that demonstrate a substantial increase in the sort of problem-solving behavior useful on intelligence tests following exposure to a rich, varied, and stimulating environment (Thompson and Schaefer 1961). The children participating in such studies are not only exposed to a varied environment but are also supported and encouraged by teachers to interact with and construe the stimuli the children encounter. It seems reasonable to interpret improved performance on intelligence tests as indicating, in part, a greater sense of challenge. After all, in an intelligence test, you are asked unpredictable questions that have a right or wrong answer—sometimes you must even perform under time pressure. To do well, you must be able to take unexpected events in stride and find it interesting to struggle for understanding. This is, in a small way, reacting to changes as an occasion for development.

Once again, research on subhuman subjects contributes relevant evidence. Many studies have shown that various subhuman species (rats, dogs, monkeys) deprived of complex and varying stimulation in early life show behavioral deficits (slow learning, disruption by stressful events, inability to interact with others) in later life (Thompson and Schaefer 1961). Perhaps the most striking demonstration involves laboratory white rats that had been bred over generations for speed or slowness in learning a maze. This was accomplished by grouping the first generation into those who learned quickly and those who learned slowly. Then rats were interbred within these two groups. The same procedure of interbreeding maze-bright and maze-dull rats was continued for several generations. As a result, the difference in learning speed between these two groupings of rats increased with each generation.

Cooper and Zubek (1958) started by selecting from this pool a group of maze-bright and a group of maze-dull rats that were newly born. One half of each group was reared in a stimulus-rich environment (an open space with many moving and movable objects of different shapes and colors), and the other half of each group was reared in blander circumstances (plain laboratory cages). Then all rats were tested for speed of learning. In a dramatic demonstration of the effects of early environmental richness, these investigators reported that there was no longer any difference in learning speed between rats bred for maze-brightness and maze-dullness! Maze-dull rats profited from stimulus-rich rearing conditions as much as maze-bright rats were hindered by bland rearing conditions. In that speedy learning requires exploration of unfamiliar situations and an accompanying ability to weather the stress of changes, this study suggests (though it is not at the human level) the importance of richness in the early environment for a later sense of challenge.

Conclusions

It is family atmosphere rather than background that breeds personality hardiness. The desirable atmosphere involves a varied environment including many tasks of moderate difficulty. In addition, it involves parental warmth and support of youngsters' efforts to perform the tasks, express individuality, and construe the variation as richness and possibility. The resulting preponderance of rewarding experiences, mastery of tasks, and sense of development culminates in the commitment, control, and challenge that constitute hardiness.

Although we have looked at these issues in the earliest years, they are important throughout the life cycle. We might, for example, talk about the atmosphere that facilitates hardiness during the grammar and high school years, posing a number of questions about interactions with teachers and peers. Later, we might look at the extent to which hardiness is supported by professors and friends during college. Even further along in the life span, we may consider how commitment, control, and challenge are maintained and enriched (or diminished) through dealings with mentors, bosses, and co-workers. The developmental points raised in this chapter are applicable at many ages. . . .

13

Gender Differences in the Social Moderators of Stress

■

DEBORAH BELLE

Involvement in supportive human relationships has been hypothesized to protect stressed individuals against a variety of ills, from depression (Belle 1982a; Brown, Bhrolchain, and Harris 1975; Pearlin and Johnson 1977) to complications of pregnancy (Barrera and Balls 1983; Nuckolls, Cassel, and Kaplan 1972) to ill health following job loss (Gore 1978). Emotionally intimate, confiding relationships appear to be particularly powerful in some circumstances (Brown, Bhrolchain, and Harris 1975; Lowenthal and Haven 1968), while less intimate connections with acquaintances, workmates, and neighbors are often also associated with positive outcomes (Miller and Ingham 1976; Pearlin and Johnson 1977). Theorists have argued that members of our social networks can provide us with social support resources such as assistance in problem solving and reassurance of worth, and can support a "repertoire of satisfactory social identities" (Hirsch 1981:163) that are critical to our self-concept and self-esteem. Such resources, in turn, help to prevent demoralization in times of stress, increase our options when confronting change and loss, and often facilitate a more active style of problem solving (Antonucci and Depner 1982; Cobb 1976; Hirsch 1981).

Social networks can also have negative impacts on individuals, as several recent studies have demonstrated (Belle 1982a, 1982b; Cohler and Lieberman 1980; Eckenrode and Gore 1981; Fiore, Becker, and Coppel 1983; Fischer 1982; Kessler and McLeod 1984; Riley and Eckenrode 1986; Rook 1984; Wahler 1980). The theoretical links between the social network and stress reactions have been less fully developed than those between the social network and beneficial social support.

Research does suggest that networks can create or exacerbate psychological distress when network members convey disrespect or disapproval, betray confidences, or fail to fulfill expectations for aid (Belle 1982a; Fiore, Becker, and Coppel 1983; Wahler 1980), when network members place heavy demands on individuals to provide assistance and support (Cohler and Lieberman 1980; Stack 1974), and when the stressful life circumstances of network members produce a "contagion of stress" (Wilkins 1974) from sufferer to network member (Belle 1982a; Eckenrode and Gore 1981). As I have argued elsewhere, "one cannot receive support without also risking the costs of rejection, betrayal, burdensome dependence, and vicarious pain" (Belle 1982a:143). Studies that have separated the social network into stressful and supportive components have found evidence that the stressful components are actually more strongly related to mental health status than are the supportive ones (Belle 1982a; Fiore, Becker, and Coppel 1983; Rook 1984).

Furthermore, research suggests that the supportive aspects of social ties are more pronounced among those from subgroups favored with high levels of personal resources, such as incomes, education, and internal locus of control (Eckenrode 1983; Lefcourt, Martin, and Saleh 1984; Sandler and Lakey 1982), while the costs of social ties are greater among those with fewer such resources (Belle 1983; Riley and Eckenrode 1986). For instance, in a recent study of the impact of social ties on women with differing levels of material and psychological resources, Riley and Eckenrode found that maintaining a large support network was beneficial only for the women with higher levels of resources. Such networks actually appeared more harmful than helpful for low-resource women, who presumably had greater difficulty in responding to the needs of network members and who were more distressed by the stressful experiences of network members than were high-resource women.

While research on the social network as a stress moderator has proliferated in recent years, gender differences in this area have received little attention. This is surprising, since gender differences in interpersonal behavior and interpersonal relationships are evident throughout the life cycle, suggesting that men and women differ in the ways they participate in social relationships and in the resources they seek in such relationships. Throughout life, the norms for appropriate male behavior tend to promote self-reliance and inhibit emotional expressiveness, self-disclosure, and help-seeking (DePaulo 1982; Jourard 1971; Lowenthal and Haven 1968), while females are encouraged to value close relationships and even to define themselves in terms of the close relationships in which they participate (Chodorow 1974; Gilligan 1982; Miller 1976). Given such differences, it is likely that social moderators of stress function differently for males and females.

Existing research on social moderators of stress sheds little light on gender differences. Studies often investigate the impact of social support within a single sex group, usually in relation to a stressful situation which is entirely or disproportionately experienced by one sex or the other. Researchers often focus on women in their reproductive and family roles, for example, and on men in their roles as economic providers. Thus, we have studies of the importance of support for women who experience pregnancy and childbirth (Barrera 1981; Barrera and Balls 1983; Feiring and Taylor n.d.; Nuckolls, Cassel, and Kaplan 1972; Turner and Noh 1982) single parenthood (Colletta 1979; McLanahan, Wedemeyer, and Adelberg 1981; Stack 1974; Weinraub and Wolf 1983), battering (Butehorn 1985; Mitchell and Hodson 1986), widowhood (Bankoff 1983; Hirsch 1980), the myocardial infarction of the spouse (Finlayson 1976), or depression (Belle 1982a; Brown, Bhrolchain, and Harris 1975), and we have studies of men experiencing occupational stress (LaRocco, House and French 1980; LaRocco and Jones 1978) and job loss (Gore 1978). Several studies consider the importance of social support in enhancing women's maternal behavior (Abernethy 1973; Crnic et al. 1983; Crockenberg 1981; Feiring and Taylor n.d.; Longfellow et al. 1979; Wahler 1980; Weinraub and Wolf 1983), while no comparable research tradition has investigated men's behavior with their children in relation to the support resources these fathers receive.

Women appear to be overrepresented as subjects in social support studies, just as males are overrepresented in most stress research (Makosky 1980). For instance, in Benjamin Gottlieb's edited volume, *Social Networks and Social Support* (1981), three of the book's eleven chapters present new data on entirely female research populations (working-class mothers, pregnant adolescents, women experiencing marital disruption), while no chapters present data on solely male populations. Perhaps the very concept of social support is more compatible with cultural images of female psychological functioning.

Even when male and female responses to the same stressor (e.g., divorce) are investigated, the specific stress factors which might be moderated by social support may well differ for men and women. In the case of divorce, for instance, women are more likely than men to be faced with daunting child care responsibilities and extremely limited financial resources, while men are more likely than women to experience rootlessness and painful loss of day-to-day contact with their children (Brown and Fox 1979; Hetherington, Cox, and Cox 1978; Ross and Sawhill 1975).

Given the sparsity of existing research on gender differences in the social moderators of stress, this chapter reviews what is known about gender and (1) participation in social networks, (2) mobilization of social support in times of psychological distress, (3) response to network members who experience stress reactions, and (4) the positive and negative implications of involvement in social networks. The review is limited almost entirely to research from Western industrialized societies and to studies completed in the last twenty years. Within these constraints, this chapter highlights several findings which suggest that there are gender differences in the ways males and females relate to their social networks in times of stress, and argues that further research to elucidate these gender differences would also help to unravel some of the central theoretical confusions within the social support-social network research tradition.

Participation in Social Networks

Some researchers have characterized male participation in social networks across the life cycle as more "extensive" but less "intensive" than that of females. There is ample evidence that males tend to participate in more activity-focused relationships than do females, while females at all ages maintain more emotionally intimate relationships than do males.

Several studies have reported a tendency for boys to play in groups of three or more, which allows for more elaborated games and team sports, and for girls to prefer dyadic interaction, with its opportunities for emotional intimacy (Lever 1976; Tietjen 1982; Waldrop and Halverson 1975). Bryant (1985) found that school-aged boys knew and interacted with more adults than did girls, and tended to interact with more peers as well. Tietjen (1982) reported that boys had a larger circle of friends than did girls. Bryant (1985) also found, however, that girls were more likely than boys to engage in intimate talks with peers and tended to have more such talks with adults—and even with pets! During adolescence, girls have been found to report more intimacy in friendship than do boys (Hunter and Youniss 1982; Kon and Losenkov 1978) and to disclose more about themselves than do boys (Dimond and Munz 1967; Rivenbark 1971).

There is some evidence that men have more acquaintances than do women, while women have more friends than do men. Booth (1972) and Miller and Ingham (1976) found that adult men had larger networks (including close friends and acquaintances) than women, while Weiss and Lowenthal (1975) discovered that the women in their sample had more friends than did the men. However, Caldwell and Peplau (1982) found no differences between male and female unmarried college students in the numbers of friends named.

The relative size of men's and women's networks seems to be strongly affected by many factors. Fischer (1982) found, for instance, that having children restricted the social involvements of mothers more than those of fathers. Mothers more than fathers differed from childless adults in having fewer friends and associates, fewer social activities, less reliable social supports, and more localized networks. Age and ill health, however, restricted the size of men's networks more than those of women. Social class and employment status have also been shown to affect differentially the size of men's and women's networks (Booth 1972, Depner and Ingersoll 1982; Lowenthal and Haven 1968).

While the relative size of men's and women's networks varies with many factors, women's greater investment in close, confiding relationships seems to endure throughout life. In their cross-cultural research, Whiting and Whiting (1975) found that girls seek more help from others in early childhood and offer more help and support to others in the preadolescent years than do boys. Candy, Troll, and Levy (1981), in an exploration of friendship among women from age 14 to 80, were struck by the consistency with which disclosing private feelings and offering emotional and instrumental support were named as functions of women's friendships. Booth and Hess (1974) found that women's interactions were more dyadic and intimate and that women seemed to have more close personal relationships than did men. In middle age and old age, women are more likely than men to have close relationships (Depner and Ingersoll 1982) and confidants (Lowenthal and Haven 1968).

While women's relationships tend to emphasize emotional intimacy, men's friendships tend to center around shared activities and experiences, such as sports (Caldwell and Peplau 1982; Weiss and Lowenthal 1975), repeating the gender differences observed in childhood.

Mobilization of Support in Times of Stress

Throughout the life cycle, females show a greater propensity to mobilize social supports in times of stress. Females are more likely than males to seek out such support, to receive such support, and to be pleased with the support they receive. In childhood, girls are more likely than boys to seek help when facing problems (Nelson-LeGall, Gumerman, and Scott-Jones 1983) and are more likely to confide their experiences to at least one other person than are boys (Belle and Longfellow 1984). In a study of 8- to 15-year-old children whose parents had divorced, Wolchik, Sandler, and Braver (1984) found that girls reported more family members who provided emotional support and positive feedback and more individuals from outside the family who provided advice, goods and services, and supportive feedback than did boys. Girls also felt more positively than did boys about the individuals who provided this support.

Among adolescents, girls name more informal sources of support, such as friends and other adults, than do boys (Cauce, Felner, and Primavera 1982) and are more likely to turn to their peers for support than are boys (Burke and Weir 1978). Among college students, females report more available helpers, receive more support, and rate other people more helpful in dealing with problematic events than do males (Cohen et al. 1984).

Women facing stress have been found to seek out more sources of both formal and informal support than do men. Women experiencing divorce are more likely to turn to at least one other person for help, to turn to multiple categories of helpers, to participate in Parents Without Partners (a mutual support group), and to utilize professional counseling (Brown and Fox 1979; Chiriboga et al. 1979). Divorced women are also more likely than divorced men to turn to their own children, friends, and doctors for support (Chiriboga et al. 1979).

These patterns were also found in a general study of help-seeking (Veroff, Douvan, and Kulka 1981; Veroff, Kulka, and Douvan 1981). Women were more likely than men to utilize both formal and informal sources of help, more likely than men to turn to more than one friend or family member in times of crisis, and more likely to turn to friends and to children in times of unhappiness.

What is most striking about men's mobilization of support is that it is so heavily focused on one support provider—the wife. Among an elderly population sample, wives were the most frequently mentioned confidants of men, while women were about twice as likely as men to mention a child or other relative and more likely to name a friend as a confidant (Lowenthal and Haven 1968). Veroff, Douvan, and Kulka (1981) found that married men were more likely than married women to turn solely to their spouses in times of stress. Even following divorce, men were significantly more likely than women to report that in the ideal situation the most helpful person to them would be their spouse (Chiriboga et al. 1979).

Not only do men and women tend to differ in their utilization of potential support figures in times of stress, there is also suggestive evidence for gender differences in the particular support resources sought by men and women. Brown and Fox (1979) reported that among divorcing men and women who had sought counseling, men were more likely than women to report that counseling improved their communication skills, while women were more likely than men to say they found emotional support from the counseling. In a projective study with college students, only women envisioned a troubled person who confided in a friend as gaining relief from stress, enhanced insight, or strength through sharing her worry with the friend (Mark and Alper 1985). Men, on the other hand, typically depicted the friend giving advice or the two friends working on a solution to the problem together. However, "none of the men imagined any kind of self-enhancement, growth, strengthening, or relief as a result of confiding" (p. 86).

The disposition to utilize support resources in times of difficulty has been linked to psychological femininity as assessed by Bem's measure of gender-role orientation (Vaux, Burda, and Stewart in press). McMullen and Gross (1983), who conducted a major review of gender differences in help-seeking, concluded that "our culture has included help-seeking among the behaviors that are designated as more appropriate for females than males" (p. 251). Men may regard help-seeking as a threat to their competence or independence, while women may view help-seeking as a means of creating or sustaining interpersonal relationships, and thus a desirable experience in its own right (DePaulo 1982).

Men may also refrain from help-seeking because of explicit social sanctions against such behavior, particularly in the workplace. Weiss (1985) found in an interview study of upper-income men in administrative and business-related occupations that the occupational setting seemed to prohibit or punish the display of emotions other than anger. "Failing to maintain the proper facade of self-assurance could be penalized in the world of work" (p. 57). For the men Weiss studied, this prohibition often seemed to extend beyond the workplace into the home, so that men concealed their "weaker" emotions from their wives and even from themselves.

McMullen and Gross (1983) have also argued that because help-seeking has been considered a feminine activity, and because the male role is more highly valued in our culture, there has probably been "a general cultural devaluation of this activity and the person who seeks help" (p. 252). As men and women increasingly move away from such traditional sex role norms, we may well see a lessening of the stigma against seeking help in times of stress and more appropriate help-seeking by both men and women (McMullen and Gross 1983).

Response to Network Members Who Experience Stress

> Women's place in man's life cycle has been that of nurturer, caretaker, and helpmate, the weaver of those networks of relationships on which she in turn relies. (Gilligan 1982:17)

Just as females are more frequent utilizers of social support, they appear to be utilized more often than males as *providers* of social support when others are under stress. Fischer (1982) found that while men and women tended to name persons of their own gender for most support, women were named disproportionately as counselors and companions by both men and women. In their family roles as wives, mothers, and "kin keepers," and in their community roles as neighbors and friends, women provide considerable social support to others. What has sometimes been called women's "expressive function" (Parsons and Bales 1955) can also be viewed as the provision of social support to others (Vanfossen 1981).

Within marriage, husbands more than wives report being understood and affirmed by their spouses (Campbell, Converse, and Rodgers 1976; Vanfossen 1981), and husbands have generally been found to confide in their wives more frequently than wives do in their husbands (Lowenthal and Haven 1968; Warren 1975). However, in one study of male professionals and their wives, Burke, Weir, and Harrison (1976) discovered that wives disclosed problems to their spouses more often than husbands did to their wives. In a study of upper-income married men, Weiss (1985) found that, while husbands typically told their wives little of the events of the workday, men did communicate their feelings about their work through their moods and through the "leakage" of information, such as overheard telephone conversations. Thus wives could often guess the issues which were preoccupying their husbands, while at the same time they were discouraged from talking about them. Whatever the extent or nature of their confiding behavior, husbands are much more likely than wives to rely solely on the spouse as confidant, as discussed above (Veroff, Douvan, and Kulka 1981).

While adult gender roles are changing to some extent, mothers still retain more responsibility for the care of children than do fathers, and are still named more frequently as confidants by children (Belle and Longfellow 1984) and adolescents (Rivenbark 1971). Hunter and Youniss (1982) found that mothers exceeded both fathers and friends as sources of intimacy and nurturance to children at the fourth-grade level, and studies have shown that mothers are major sources of advice, guidance, and intimacy to their adolescent children as well (Kandel and Leser 1972; Kon and Losenkov 1978). Even when children are themselves adult, mothers may be more knowledgeable about and more emotionally involved in children's problems than are fathers (Loewenstein 1984).

A striking piece of evidence for the importance of females as support providers comes from a study of 7- and 10-year-old children who were asked to name the ten individuals who were most important to them (Bryant 1985). Each child in the study had a sibling who was two to three years older than the interviewed child. Not only were more older sisters (95 percent) than older brothers (73 percent) named among the children's "top ten," but these older sisters were represented more frequently on "top ten" lists than any other figures, including mothers and fathers. However, Furman and Buhrmester's recent study of fifth- and sixth-grade children (1985) did not confirm the salience of the older sister as support figure. In their study both older and same-sex siblings were named as particularly important support figures. Instrumental aid was actually seen as coming more frequently from brothers than sisters.

Studies of black families, white working-class families, white ethnic families, and low-income families emphasize the importance of the instrumental assistance and emotional support shared among female kin, friends and neighbors, particularly around child rearing (Belle 1982a; Cohler and Lieberman 1980; McAdoo 1980; Stack 1974; Young and Willmott 1957). The importance of such female networks in ensuring day-to-day survival and maintaining family solidarity has been noted by many.

There is also evidence that females tend to be more supportive friends than are males. Wheeler, Reis, and Nezlek (1983) found that among both male and female college seniors, loneliness was negatively related to the amount of time spent with females, while time spent with males did not appear to buffer loneliness. Only when the "meaningfulness" of interactions with males was taken into consideration did contact with males appear to stave off loneliness. In an ingenious role-play study of friendships (Caldwell and Peplau 1982), women who role-played a friend calling to congratulate another on a recent success made more supportive statements than did men. They were more likely than men to say they were happy for the successful person, were more likely to express enthusiasm for the friend's success, and were more likely to ask about the friend's own feelings than were men role-playing the same conversation. Perhaps, however, this study's criteria for supportiveness simply reflect a feminine style of support provision. It would be interesting to know whether other, more indirect statements, such as humor, irony, or mock criticism actually served to convey support between male role-players.

In addition to the support women provide informally to their husbands, children, other relatives, neighbors, and friends, many women are professionally involved in the provision of support to those under stress. Many predominantly female occupations, such as teaching, nursing, and social work, require empathic attention to the needs of others and the ability to provide emotional support to those in distress. While a full discussion of women's professional involvement in providing social support is beyond the scope of this chapter, it should be noted that many women "already gave at the office" when they come home to provide support to members of their informal social networks.

What accounts for the tendency of both males and females to turn to females disproportionately in times of stress and for women to offer support to so many others? Wheeler, Reis and Nezlek (1983) have argued that women are simply more effective as social partners than are men. Men, in contrast, tend to lack training in supportiveness skills (Bernard 1971), so that their attempts at providing social support are not as effective as those of women. Whiting and Whiting (1975) have shown that across diverse cultures infants tend to elicit nurturant behavior from those in contact with them, and that girls consistently spend more time than boys close to home and in the company of mothers and infants. Girls thus have more ample opportunities than do boys to practice nurturant behaviors and to come to feel comfortable and adept in a nurturing role.

Miller (1976) has argued that women's socialization and especially their subordinate status, which requires attention to others, better prepares them "to first recognize others' needs and then to believe strongly that others' needs can be served" so much so that women organize their lives around the principle of nurturing others and promoting their growth. This is consistent with Gilligan's argument (1982) that women's moral sense tends to presume responsibility for the well-being of others.

Bernard (1971) has argued that the supportive or "stroking" function (first outlined in work by R. F. Bales on emotional-expressive behavior in groups) in which one shows solidarity, raises the status of others, gives help, rewards, agrees, concurs, complies, understands, and passively accepts, is the quintessential female function. "No matter what job a woman is doing or what role she is performing, high or low, the supportive function is assumed to be part of it. Indeed, the behaviors that constitute stroking . . . add up to a description of the ideal-typical woman wherever she is found" (p. 90). Women are simply expected to engage in "stroking" and are punished if they do not do so. "Men do not expect support from men; they are nonplussed when it is not forthcoming from women" (p. 94).

Positive and Negative Implications of Involvement in Social Networks

The research reviewed earlier in this chapter certainly gives rise to the expectation that the moderating effects of social networks and supports may function differently for men and women. As indicated, women tend to (1) maintain more emotionally intimate relationships than do men, (2) mobilize more social supports in times of stress than do men while relying less heavily than men on the spouse as a source of social support, and (3) provide more frequent and more effective social support to others than do men. The remainder of this chapter considers some possible consequences of such gender differences in social networks and social supports.

Women Maintain More Emotionally Intimate Relationships Than Do Men

Two lines of research evidence suggest that important consequences flow from the differential investment by men and women in close, confiding, and intimate relationships. One line suggests that the preferred patterns of network involvement may actually be differentially beneficial to males and females over the life course. In her study of social support in middle childhood, Bryant (1985) found that boys appeared to derive benefits from the extensive, casual involvements they typically preferred, rather than from intensive, intimate involvements, while the reverse was true for girls. Specifically, casual involvement with many adults was positively linked to social perspective-taking skill, internal locus of control, and empathy for boys, while such involvements were negatively related to social perspective-taking skill and internal locus of control among girls. Intimate involvements with adults predicted positive socioemotional development for girls, but not for boys. Similarly, Waldrop and Halverson (1975) found that social maturity and facility with peers had very different correlates for boys and girls. Boys who were more socially at ease, spent more hours with peers, and were judged to find peers more important to them differed from boys with less social facility chiefly in the *numbers* of friendships they had. Girls who were more socially at ease, spent more hours with peers, and were judged to find peers more important to them differed from other girls chiefly in the *intensity* and *intimacy* of the friendships they had. Interestingly, peer sociability at age 2½ tended to predict these very different patterns of social involvement at age 7½ for boys and girls. While these longitudinal results are striking, they do not prove that boys and girls find different types of social involvements inherently beneficial. The findings may also be interpreted as suggesting that socially adept boys and girls are more successful than their less accomplished peers in determining the kind of social relationships that are considered socially appropriate for their gender.

Among adults, Miller and Ingham (1976) reported that for women, having a good confidant and having a sizeable array of acquaintances were both associated with positive outcomes, while for men, only the acquaintanceship measure was associated with well-being. The authors note, however, that this gender difference may have resulted from the small sample size for men. Additional evidence about the relative importance to men and to women of casual versus intimate relationships would add to our understanding of this issue.

A very different line of research suggests that women's propensity for intimate social involvements may predispose women to the "contagion of stress" that is felt when troubling life events afflict those to whom they are emotionally close. Dohrenwend (1976) found, for instance, that when men and women were asked to list recent events that had occurred to themselves, family members, and other people important to them, a higher proportion of the events women reported had happened to family members or friends rather than to the respondents themselves. Eckenrode and Gore (1981) reported that women whose relatives and friends experienced stressful life events such as burglaries and illnesses found these events stressful to themselves, and reflected this vicarious stress in their own poor health. Kessler and McLeod (1984) argue that this sensitivity to the undesirable life events of others actually accounts for women's greater vulnerability to stressful life events in comparison to men. Wethington, McLeod, and Kessler (1987) were able to show that while men are distressed by events that happen to their children and spouses, women are distressed not only by these events but by events which occur to other members of the social network. Thus, it is women's greater "range of caring" that seems to expose them to additional vicarious stress.

Women Mobilize More Varied Social Supports in Times of Stress Than Do Men

Research on bereavement provides the most impressive evidence that men's and women's differential investment in social support figures has consequences for their well-being. In particular, a man's heavy investment in his wife as confidant and support figure may account for the higher mortality rates of widowers versus widows in the months and years following bereavement. In one large-scale prospective study which matched widowed adults to married persons on race, sex, year of birth, and place of residence, mortality rates for widowed women were virtually no different from those for married women, while male mortality rates were significantly higher for widowers than for married men (Helsing and Szklo 1981). Similarly, Berkman and Syme (1979) found in a nine-year follow-up study of almost 7,000 adults that marriage was much more protective for men than for women, even after mortality statistics were adjusted for self-reported physical health status at the time of the initial survey, for socioeconomic status, health practices such as smoking, alcoholic beverage consumption, obesity and physical activity, and a cumulative index of health practices. Stroebe and Stroebe (1983) concluded from their literature review on sex differences in the health risks of the widowed that men are more vulnerable to mental and physical health sequelae, and that the most adequate explanation for the greater vulnerability of men focuses on their lack of alternate support figures following the death of the spouse.

While men appear particulary vulnerable when they lose a spouse to death, other research suggests that differences in the actual supportiveness of the spouse when alive may be more important to women than to men. Husaini et al. (1982) studied the stress-buffering properties of social support among rural married men and women and found that various aspects of the marital relationship (marital satisfaction, spouse satisfaction, spouse as confidant) were more powerfully associated with mental health status among women than among men.

Why should the mere presence of a wife be beneficial, while only the supportiveness of a husband is protective? Such a finding is reminiscent of previously discussed research on gender differences in the supportiveness of friends. Loneliness among college students was negatively related to the amount of time spent with females but only with the reported "meaningfulness" of time spent with males. Such findings are open to different interpretations but may reflect a ceiling effect: the average wife (or female friend) may provide such a high level of support that further increments in supportiveness make little difference to health and mental health outcomes. It may also be that since the role of wife is so central to a woman's social status and self-concept, a nonsupportive spouse is particularly devastating to a woman's well-being.

To complicate matters further, Vanfossen (1981) has shown that the mental health impact of spouse support varies for men and women depending on what facets of marital support are considered, and also depending on the employment status of the wife. Specifically, emotional intimacy and affirmation from spouses are crucial to the emotional well-being of married men and nonemployed wives, while equity in the marital relationship and affirmation from the spouse are particularly important to employed wives.

When we turn from the marital relationship to other network ties, there is evidence that men and women may be differentially protected by their involvements. In their prospective study of mortality, Berkman and Syme (1979) found that overall the protective effects of social contacts were stronger for women than for men. While, as discussed earlier, marriage was much more protective for men, it was women who benefited more from contact with friends and relatives and from involvement in formal and informal groups. Holahan and Moos (1981) reported that the quality of family relationships was associated with well-being for women but not for men, while the quality of work relationships was more strongly related to well-being for men than for women.

Women Provide More Frequent and More Effective Social Support to Others Than Do Men

Several authors have pointed to women's heightened vulnerability to stress resulting from women's propensity to take care of needy and stressed network members. Fischer (1982) found that women, especially mothers of young children, were much more likely than others to report too many demands from members of their households.

> In general women and parents, especially parents of infants and toddlers, were most likely to feel pressed by their households, but the combination of being a woman and being a parent was especially deadly. . . . The general point is clear: children demand and women respond to those demands, as well as to the demands of others. (p. 136)

Similarly, Cohler and Lieberman (1980) discovered that among first- and second-generation adult members of three European ethnic groups, the women who were more involved with relatives and friends experienced *more* psychological distress than their less involved peers, while network involvement among the men was either unrelated to mental health or showed small positive associations with morale. Cohler and Lieberman note that, particularly within the ethnic communities they studied, women are socialized from childhood to care for others. Such socialization may then contribute to the contagion of stress women experience from the disasters and disappointments of others. In addition to the vicarious pain they feel, women may also find themselves burdened with new tasks and obligations to aid the suffering individual. The close contact experienced in such kin-keeping may then keep the sufferer's pain vivid to the person who aids him or her.

Women's specialization as support providers and men's relative neglect of this activity may also have consequences for cross-sex friendships and for romantic and marital relationships. In a male-female relationship, the female may experience a "support gap" (Belle 1982b) when she receives less support from a significant male figure than she provides to him. If the flow of supportive provisions is highly unequal, and if the woman is heavily involved in providing support to children, needy friends, or relatives while receiving little support in return, the result may well be demoralization and depression.

This review has suggested that there are pervasive gender differences in the ways men and women construct their networks and utilize them in times of stress, and that these differences have consequences for men's and women's well-being. Many challenges remain, however, before a full understanding of these issues is achieved.

One topic which has not yet received the attention it deserves is the question of what supportive provisions men and women (and boys and girls) actually desire in their interpersonal encounters, and how these different provisions then relate to the outcomes of the supportive experience. If men receiving counseling during their marital breakups believe they have found help with communications skills, while women point to the emotional support they received, perhaps the single term "support" is too *global* to capture the diverse provisions men and women perceive and receive in other situations as well. Studies have shown that boys and girls tend to prefer different styles of personal networks, but little research has addressed the specific provisions that boys and girls find in their preferred types of networks or the ways in which boys and girls come to value the specific experiences they can find in such networks.

While most network studies emphasize the benefits to be gained by network involvement, a new line of research is demonstrating that the costs of network ties may, if anything, be greater than the benefits. Studies have also shown, as noted earlier, that the costs and benefits of networks are not distributed randomly among the population, but tend to vary with gender and with access to personal resources (which also tends to vary with gender).

In addition to the gender differences in network involvements that have been discussed thus far, it is important to note the impact of society-wide inequalities in access to crucial resources as these affect men's and women's utilization of support resources. A growing body of research has shown, ironically, that those most in need of supportive provisions from their social networks are those least likely to receive them, while they are also most likely to experience the costs of network involvement (Belle 1983; Eckenrode 1983; Lefcourt, Martin, and Saleh 1984; Riley and Eckenrode 1986; Sandler and Lakey 1982). In American society at large, women are more likely than men to fall into the ranks of the impoverished, to hold relatively powerless positions in the workplace, and to lack the independent resources that can give bargaining advantages within marriage. Research to date has not examined the importance of access to such material and psychological resources along with gender in predicting the impact of network involvements.

An examination of gender differences in the social moderators of stress has exposed complexities and confusions in our current theoretical models of social support which associate social ties with exclusively positive outcomes. Close attention to women's experience has suggested several plausible mechanisms by which networks may exacerbate or may relieve stress. If such mechanisms are valid, then they should apply as well to men whose networks and style of network involvement match those more typically associated with women. Men, for instance, who experience strong emotional identification with the sorrows of others and men who feel strong community or personal imperatives to care for distressed and needy network members should be more susceptible than men without such patterns to the contagion of psychological distress and its vicarious pain. Men who maintain intimate emotional ties with persons other than the spouse should be more resilient following bereavement than men who confide only in their wives. Pursuing the leads that have been discovered could lead to clarification and enrichment of our ideas about the social moderators of stress for both men and women.

14

The Type A Behavior Pattern and Coronary Artery Disease

Quest for the Active Ingredients and the Elusive Mechanism

■

LOGAN WRIGHT

I would like to begin by offering a word of explanation about the types of information that comprise this report. Basically, I rely on three sources: first, personal and (in the Titchenerian sense) introspective observations (that is, a personal statement); second, a state-of-the-art-literature review; and third, some ideas based on my own research. To further explain the personal source, let me confide that in May of 1983 I was discovered to have a significant blockage in a major coronary artery. This came as a great surprise because of what had appeared to my physician and others to be an excellent state of cardiovascular health. Almost a decade of annual physicals had shown good blood pressure readings and serum cholesterol levels well below 200. There was also ample evidence for an active, as opposed to sedentary, life style. And, of some significance, which will be clarified later, I possessed *none* of the traditional risk factors, such as family history or smoking. Though I had not experienced a heart attack, I nonetheless was required to undergo bypass surgery.

Though my previous professional experience had been primarily with children, I had been a pediatric *health* psychologist, and I had regularly attended the annual multidisciplinary retreat meeting of the approximately 100 members of the Academy of Behavioral Medicine Research. Thus, the concept of the Type A behavior pattern (TABP) was not strange to me. However, I had never placed great stock in its pathogenic potential. And, in spite of what I now recognize as a Guinness-record-sized blind spot, I had never viewed myself as a card-carrying Type A personality. Bypass surgery, however, has a way of getting one's attention. Thus, an undeniable health crisis became the first step in a new research journey.

Introspection and Hypothesis Generation

Even if I had not been personally involved, I think I might have been intrigued by the occurrence of coronary heart disease (CHD) in a person like myself who was free of any of the traditional risk factors. However, one of my first discoveries was that the traditional (non-TABP) risk factors explained only 50 percent of the variance in CHD (Jenkins 1971, 1976). Second, I found that the National Institutes of Health's Review Panel on Coronary Prone Behavior and Coronary Heart Disease (1981) had concluded that

> the available body of scientific evidence demonstrates that Type A Behavior . . . is associated with an increased risk of clinically apparent CHD in employed middle-aged U.S. Citizens. This increased risk is greater than that imposed by age, elevated levels of systolic blood pressure, serum cholesterol, and smoking (p. 1200)

However, my personal picture remained unclear because a comparison of my functioning with the standard TABP failed to produce total goodness of fit.

As described by its originators (Rosenman et al. 1964), the TABP refers to a competitive, multiphasic, achievement-oriented person who possesses a sense of time urgency and impatience and who is both easily aroused and hostile or angry. Quite early I realized that some Type A traits existed in individuals who, though advanced in years, had not manifested CHD and that not all TABP traits existed in individuals with TABP-related heart disease. I was particularly impressed by the absence of CHD in some people who possessed a high degree of job involvement and in many apparently hostile individuals.

All of this seemed related to the large number of false positives identified by traditional TAPB diagnostic measures such as the Jenkins Activity Scale (JAS; Jenkins, Zyzanski and Rosenman 1971) and the Structured Interview (SI; Rosenman 1978). It suggested that the false-positives problem might be caused by a subset of Type A traits that are the ones actually responsible for coronary-prone risk. These particularly deadly components were first called "major facets" and "core elements" by Matthews (1982) and were later labeled "active ingredients" by Watkins (1986). As stated by Dembroski and Williams (in press), "Only certain aspects of the multidimensional TABP are 'toxic' . . . assessment of the global TABP will provide a measure which contains a considerable amount of 'noise' in addition to the coronary-prone 'signal.' "

At this point let me pause to provide what I feel is a necessary apologetic for the use of subjective methods such as introspection. For a combination psychotherapist and Type A patient like myself, introspection provided the opportunity for an extraordinary $N = 1$ case study. The observations were not for an hour or two per week, but for 16–18 hours every day. Seldom did a single five-minute period pass without some internal experience that was related to the Type A issue. In exploring the TABP, such introspections were more enlightening than they would have been in a search involving disorders that fall within traditional nosological categories—for example, depression. The reason for this is that we have a pretty good idea of what depression is, but for now, we are still trying to figure out (at least as to *self*-perception) exactly what constitutes the TABP. Because I possessed no non-Type-A risk factors, I seemed to represent a case of both strong and *unadulterated* Type A tendencies. The fact that this Type-A-like phenomenon was apparently the only factor responsible for my own CHD seemed to make the introspections even more worthwhile, especially during the early hypothesis-generating phase of the research. However, in going public with my own health problems, as well as some of the personality traits that accompany them, I hope this "true confessions" material will fall somewhere to the *Psychological Bulletin* side of center and not toward the *National Enquirer* end of the continuum.

In any event, if certain so-called active ingredients, or subcomponents, of the TABP are what is really responsible for coronary-prone risk, one would expect them to correlate more highly with CHD than does the global Type A pattern itself. Theoretically, the remaining (non-coronary-prone) aspects of the TABP could be composed of ingredients ranging from "non-CHD-related" to "healthy" (the latter is suggested by Hansson et al. 1983; Matthews et al. 1980). *These* would be expected to add more error than predictive validity to efforts designed to link the global TABP to CHD, and they also presumably bear major responsibility for the false-positives problem.

Active Ingredients of the Type A Behavior Pattern

Convinced that it made more sense to worry about active ingredients than the global Type A pattern itself, I, along with a small group of research colleagues from the University of Oklahoma, began spending every Wednesday on the coronary care unit of a large hospital. There we were exposed to several dozen new CHD patients each week. As we attempted to take a fresh look at what did and did not characterize Type A individuals, I was struck by the role played by one particular Type A substrate that seemed to explain more variance than global measures of the TABP or any of its other components. It consisted of a cluster involving time urgency, chronic activation, and multiphasia. The term *time urgency* refers to concern not over large amounts of time (e.g., "My life is short"), but more often over a few seconds (e.g., changing lanes to make up a car length or two; peeping out of the corner of one's eye at the yellow light in order to be ready when red changes to green). The term *chronic activation* refers to a tendency to stay active or keyed up for most of the day, every day. The term *multiphasic* refers to a tendency both to have many irons in the fire and to do more than one thing at a time (e.g., reading while watching TV, eating, or going to the bathroom).

Redford Williams and his colleagues (Dembroski and Williams in press; Williams 1984; Williams et al. 1980) have eloquently defended the conclusion that the "hostility/anger dimension is the 'major' if not the 'only' coronary-prone element" (Dembroski and Williams in press). However, the data from which they draw their conclusion come almost exclusively from self-report psychometric devices. And it is clear that what the JAS as well as the SI measure is primarily a Type-A/anger factor (Matthews et al. 1977). But because William's opinion differed from the one I had reached from clinical observations, I was convinced that either there are at least two active ingredients (anger *and* time urgency) or that possibly these are separate manifestations of a single phenomenon.

To pursue the latter possibility, let me point out that a fine line could exist between an aggressive approach to *tasks* (i.e., time urgency and chronic activation) and an aggressive interpersonal approach. Take, as an example, the case of a somewhat well-known public figure, John McEnroe. Some students of the sport of tennis feel that much of McEnroe's talent lies in the intensity he mobilizes in order to pursue an important game. At some levels, it must become difficult (possibly more so for certain individuals, such as McEnroe) to separate task-oriented aggression from interpersonal aggression. One function may not be easily inhibited while the other is pursued with abandon. A contrasting style, in which task-directed aggression did *not* seem to trigger interpersonal aggression, might be illustrated by the legendary Muhammad Ali, who always seemed to be having fun: "floating like a butterfly" while he was "stinging like a bee."

Second, the link between time urgency and anger can be further solidified if we realize that the human body's neuroendocrine response to what we perceive as two separate emotions is essentially the same. It is, in fact, the "fight or flight response" consisting of increased catecholamine (adrenalin and noradrenalin) output, liberated blood sugar, increased heart rate (HR), and increased blood flow to the large muscles. Thus, our subjective experience of two separate emotions may be purely *attributional* in nature.

Yet a third commonality can be demonstrated between hostility and task-oriented time urgency. Note the following physical-appearance characteristics that Type A individuals are described as having: (1) a frequent straining type of facial grimace, even during minimal exertion; (2) dramatic or overly forceful movements while conducting minimal tasks such as opening and closing drawers or bottles and while inserting or extracting their contents (e.g., some wives of Type A men report that they cannot get caps off toothpaste tubes because their husbands close them so tightly); (3) overly forceful speech style, both in volume and content; (4) rapid eating; (5) hyperalertness; (6) short response latencies; (7) frequent, breathy sighs; (8) repetitive (or fidgety) movements of the feet, fingers, or jaw; (9) an intense look with frequently inhibited smile or laugh; (10) a kind of wide-eyed look or protruding cornea (most of these are taken from Friedman, Hall, and Harris 1984).

The protruding cornea is a response that has been known for some time to be related to excess adrenalin in the bloodstream. The facial grimace usually accompanies what should entail minimal physical exertion, such as putting on a pair of socks. Likewise, the breathy sighs inevitably follow activation or arousal when one cannot react with an extensive physical response (and therefore is not actually short of breath). It is as though the preexertion response (the adrenalin/activation response) and the postexertion response (a deep breath) are present, but without the intended intervening response for which the Type A person is mobilized. This leaves the Type A responder in a kind of "suspended suspense," with a resulting emotional and hormonal surplus. The sigh is simply a symptom of these residua. These tendencies, along with the forceful speech, hyperalertness, rapid eating, short response latency, and fidgety movements described above, are interpreted by some (e.g., Friedman and Ulmer 1984) as overt manifestations of underlying anger. However, if we reexamine these tendencies carefully, might they not just as easily be manifestations of task-related activation, or at least of a tendency to overly mobilize the body's physical resources in response to minimal physical tasks?

A fourth way that we may be able to link anger and time urgency is by examining the possibility that much anger is *secondary* to time urgency. If one is a card-carrying, Type A person, then one may be not only time-urgent but more like a religious fanatic. In the early biblical sense, Type A individuals are idol worshippers, and the idol is time. This, in turn, "sets them up" to be perturbed or otherwise angry. For example, it is disconcerting when that which we worship is not reverenced (i.e., is "blown off") by others. Even worse are situations in which others' infidel-like insensitivity to time impacts us more directly: they are late and thus delay us. They drive too slowly and will not let us pass. They are the ones responsible for slow-moving lines (e.g., the proverbial person at the supermarket who has both coupons to cash in and a check to write). As one of my Type A patients said, "I think there may be an express line into heaven, and I'm trying to keep it to eight sins or less!" (Personally, I'm worried that St. Peter may be Type B and that I will become impatient and blow the whole thing.) In any event, because we are time worshippers, we become angry at anything or anyone who wastes our "precious" time.

The comment of one patient serves as an appropriate postscript to how anger may be secondary to time urgency and chronic activation: "You'd be angry too if you had to work as hard as I do to achieve." Thus, Type-A-related anger can be linked to time urgency either because our physiologic responses to the two emotions are similar or because much anger is *caused by* time urgency or its precursor, a driven need to achieve.

Once our small research group had developed a firm hypothesis that time-urgency/chronic-activation was a legitimate candidate for active-ingredient status, the stage was set for Phase 2 of our research, in which we asked not only "What are the active Type A ingredients?" but also the following: (1) How do "active" TABP ingredients develop ontogenetically? (2) What psychological theories possess the greatest potential for explaining these ingredients? (3) What mechanism(s) underlie the relationship between active ingredients and CHD? (4) What kinds of studies are best suited to test hypotheses concerning active TABP ingredients? and (5) What diagnostic and therapeutic advances should we be striving to achieve?

Ontogeny of the Type A Behavior Pattern

Two major questions surface early concerning the ontogeny of the TABP: What key experiences play the critical role in the development of Type A tendencies? Is the development of these Type A tendencies a continuous, linear progression from childhood to adulthood, or is it more discontinuous?

Because our patients had already convinced us that time urgency was an important active ingredient, it is not surprising that the critical experiences we identified from our clinical observations were related to time urgency. The following are samples of the kinds of early experiences we noted in our anamnesis-oriented, clinical interviews with CHD patients who possessed strong Type A tendencies: (1) high, and possibly insatiable, need for achievement, which tended not to surface until late adolescence or early adulthood and which was based on the patient's linking of achievement to self-esteem (there also seemed to be an assumption that achievement resulted from competitive, rather than personally gratifying, activities); (2) early (no later than adolescence) success, which seemed to breed a greater than usual sense of hope that striving efforts would eventually pay off; and (3) early exposure to timed and/or competitive activities such as sports and working by the job rather than by the hour (e.g., throwing papers, mowing yards, roofing houses—such jobs allowed individuals to earn the same amount of money in less time, and thus to have more time for other, possibly also achievement-oriented, activities; they thus seemed to provide a blueprint for a time-urgent set in response to achievement challenges.)

Thus, our answer to the question of what constitute the critical experiences in the development of the TABP is a triad involving (1) a high need to achieve (meaning *competitive* success), (2) early success and therefore reinforcement for striving efforts; and (3) exposure to timed activities that provide a personal blueprint for achieving more by more efficient use of time and by chronic activation.

These so-called "key" developmental experiences seemed relevant only in cases where self-esteem was lacking. The low self-esteem could apparently stem from a variety of sources ranging from poor parenting techniques to more "act of God" circumstances, such as death, divorce, handicap, and ordinal position.

The three key factors seem best viewed as *predisposing* in nature. The other necessary part of the ontogenetic formula appeared to be the decision to remedy low self-esteem via achievement, which, in turn, appeared to result in a somewhat multiphasic ("shotgun-like") effort to achieve as much as possible in multiple (as many as possible) areas. This decision provided the most common *precipitating* factor and often followed a significant failure or setback that was experienced against the backdrop of earlier successes. Following such experiences of failure, the fledgling Type A subject would heap upon his or her self an unceasing series of achievement-related demands. Quite soon, this created a set of "never being caught up." (If by chance the subjects *were* caught up, it was time to strategize about future achievement efforts.) If one is never caught up, then one never has a moment to waste—hence the syndrome of time urgency plus the feeling of being "uncomfortable if not doing something all the time." The latter is (as often stated by Type A patients) an *unconscious* set of "If I never caught up, and I find myself not doing something, I *should* be doing something."

The above scenario provides what (from our clinical experience with time-urgent patients) appear to be the key developmental factors, both precipitating and predisposing, in the ontogeny of the TABP. Regarding the question of whether or not Type A tendencies develop in a linear fashion, Matthews (Matthews and Jennings 1984; Matthews and Volkin 1981) has assumed that they do. She cited both behavioral and physiologic similarities between Type A children and Type A adults. She suggested that the fatty acid lesions of the coronary arteries that are responsible for CHD may have their genesis in the first decade of life, rather than in the second decade, where their existence is well documented.

The work of Steinberger (1986), however, fails to support Matthews' assumption. Using data collected as a part of the New York Longitudinal Study, Steinberger found Type A tendencies to be positively correlated with psychological adjustment in children, unrelated to adjustment in adolescents, and negatively correlated with adjustment in adults. These conclusions conform better to our own clinical observations, which suggest that Type A behavior begins in adolescence or early adulthood as a compensation for essentially non-Type-A phenomena that have existed earlier.

Psychological Theories and the Type A Behavior Pattern

Let us now move to our second question: What psychological theories possess the greatest potential for explaining the TABP? To make optimal progress in any area of psychological research, the issues must be related to theory. This can be achieved by resolution of the topic (in our case, the TABP) with existing psychological theories, or new theories may have to be developed to provide the most testable hypotheses. At this point, I would like to flag what I believe to be a critical discrimination. It is that the best theory for explaining the TABP may very well change depending on whether one is dealing with (1) overt behavior (the global TABP itself), (2) psychological constructs (the active ingredients), or (3) an underlying physiological mechanism that may be involved. To my knowledge, no authors to date have made this distinction when discussing Type-A-related theory. Having made this point and proceeding on the assumption that explaining something via an observable physiological mechanism is more reductionistic (and therefore better) than relying on even the best-anchored psychological construct, I now offer my nominations for the most promising theoretical explanations for various aspects of the Type A gestalt.

Most Type A research has focused on the *overt* TABP. Recent efforts at applying psychological theory to this area have proposed rather complex and sophisticated behavioral models. One example is a cognitive/social learning theory system that relies heavily on social modeling (Bandura 1971) and familial/cultural reinforcers. For a detailed account of this approach, I recommend Price (1982:37–39).

Traditional psychological theories may hold greater promise if we are able to conceptualize the TABP as a manifestation of a psychological disorder that falls within traditional nosological categories. It is possible that the TABP may be just another example of a familiar disorder (such as obsessive-compulsive neurosis). Perhaps because the label "Type A" does not sound like something from the *Diagnostic and Statistical Manual of Mental Disorders* (American Psychiatric Association 1980), we have been distracted from understanding the true nature of this construct.

It would be ironic if labeling proved to be a problem for the study of Type A behavior. That rather nondescript term actually came about as a result of efforts by Rosenman and by M. Friedman to avoid confusion by avoiding labels that might possess *surplus* meaning. However, such action may have served to prejudice us in another direction—that is, toward believing that the TABP represents a previously unidentified disorder, rather than simply a previously unspecified form of an existing disorder.

The term *workaholic,* which is sometimes applied to Type A individuals, betrays what may be a true aspect of the TABP, that it is just another manifestation of obsessive-compulsive neurosis. If this is so, we can better understand the TABP simply by taking our pick of the existing theories capable of explaining obsessive-compulsive disorders. These include such familiar approaches as psychoanalysis, Guthrie's (1959) contiguity theory, Hebb's (1949) neuropsychological theory, and possibly others such as Allport's (1937) functional autonomy theory and Rogers' (1951) self-concept theory.

Psychoanalysis regards obsessive-compulsive symptoms as an anxiety-managing defense, which "succeeds" by virtue of its ability to prevent painful (to the ego) material from rising out of the unconscious into consciousness. Type A individuals presumably saturate their experience with work-like activity so that few unrelated thoughts or feelings have any hope of achieving conscious awareness. Other traditional psychoanalytic concepts are relied on to explain the nature of the threatening thoughts and feelings as well as how the repressive/suppressive style for dealing with them may have come about.

My own clinical experience, prior to doing Type-A-related work, long ago impressed me with the potential of certain *non*psychoanalytic theories to explain both the genesis, and the remediation, of obsessive-compulsive behavior. That experience involved an array of typical obsessive disorders as well as problems such as stuttering, tics, fetishes, kleptomania, exhibitionism, nymphomania, and tracheotomy addiction. Clinical exposure to these problems has convinced me that simply making a response may have more to do with increasing the probability that the response will reoccur in the future than it does with whether the response is reinforced. (This refers to the developmental or etiologic phase of the problem. During the treatment phase, *not* making a response seems to affect the probability that a response will *not* be made in the future more than does whether the response is punished or simply not reinforced.)

If simply making a response is more critical than reinforcement, then Hebb's (1949) neuropsychological theory, Guthrie's (1959) continguity theory, and Allport's (1937) functional autonomy theory should hold some promise for explaining obsessive-compulsive acts. Because of page constraints, it is not possible to provide a detailed account of how each of these theories would explain the TABP or of the empirical evidence that supports them. Suffice it to say that each theory speaks to how "habits" are made and broken. I prefer Hebb's approach to that of Guthrie and Allport because it offers a more specific, neurophysiologic-like (though nonetheless psychological) construct.

Rogers' self-concept theory is also not without potential for explaining obsessive-compulsive tendencies, especially the TAPB. The basic premise of Rogerian theory is that an individual acts in a manner consistent with his or her self-concept. The self-concept is derived from so called "evaluational interactions" with others, especially significant others such as parents. Rogers (1951) also stated that the most basic drive is "to actualize, maintain, and enhance the self" (p. 487). Thus, all that is necessary to explain the TABP is a set of circumstances in which individuals come to think of themselves in terms such as "efficient" (especially time-efficient), "high achiever," "tough," "go-getter," "multifaceted," and so forth. Their feelings about self need not be preceded by feelings of low worth or feelings that self-esteem is contingent on achievement. In cases where they are, however, the TABP would be viewed as a compensatory response combining at least one positive characteristic (confidence) and one negative one (low self-esteem requiring some form of compensation). But Rogerian theory is also capable of explaining the TABP in the *absence* of negatives, that is, Type A behavior without compensation as its basis. Because previously cited authors (such as Hansson et al. 1983; Matthews et al. 1980) have suggested that certain aspects of the TABP are adaptive, it is comforting that at least one theory allows for the existence of TABP-like functioning in which the deviation from the psychological norm is in a positive rather than a negative direction.

Underlying Mechanisms Relating Type A Behavior and CHD

Having discussed the role of psychological theory in explaining the etiology of the overt TABP, let us now consider the relationship of psychological theory to possible underlying physiologic mechanisms that may link the Type A pattern to CHD. There are basically two theories on how Type A tendencies may corrupt the coronary arteries. One is the *mechanical* theory of Eliot and Buell (1983). It suggests that in some individuals, stress (presumably including Type A, self-induced, stress) causes vasoconstriction in peripheral areas of the body and, at the same time, accelerates heart rate. Thus, these individuals are attempting to transfer more and more blood through vessels that are shrinking. The metaphoric analogy proposed by Eliot and Buell is that of a car with the brakes on and the accelerator pushed to the floor. Presumably this produces "wear and tear" on the coronary arteries, which in turn produces the atherosclerotic lesions responsible for most CHD. Individuals possessing this vasoconstriction tendency are called "hot reactors."

An alternative mechanism for explaining the TABP's impact on coronary arteries is a (hormone-related) *chemical* theory suggested by authors such as Haft (1974), Wright (1984), Dembroski and Williams (in press), and others. Whereas chronically high blood pressure has been established as a bona fide risk factor, the "hot reactor" trait has never been empirically linked to CHD. Hormones, such as adrenalin and noradrenalin, have, however, been so linked. They are known to induce myocardial lesions (Haft 1974; Herd 1978; Marx and Kolata 1978; Raab, Chaplin, and Bajusz 1969). What now confronts us is to show how a psychological theory can explain a catecholamine response. To do this, classical conditioning seems to be a logical place to begin. (Note: Although one may exist, I have yet to read an article devoted to the classical conditioning paradigm as a means of explaining the TABP.)

To apply a classical conditioning paradigm, one need only assume that the unconditioned stimulus (UCS) is an "emergency" cue that sets off the unconditioned response (UCR, e.g., spillage of adrenalin, noradrenalin, and possibly other hormones). The conditioned stimulus (CS) is any set of cues associated with the emergency-like UCSs. In the case of the TABP, this association is most likely accomplished via stimulus generalization rather than simultaneous presentation. Because the central nervous system interprets both perceived and real threat similarly, all that is required for stimulus generalization to occur is a genuine "do-or-die" attitude toward work or other achievement-related stimuli. Examples include "publish or perish" and "If I don't keep on succeeding, my mother and/or my wife will reject me."

But why would Type-A-related hormones be caustic or abrasive to the walls of the coronary arteries when there is no evidence that the fight-or-flight response is caustic under normal circumstances? Some adrenalin-producing responses, such as jogging, are, in fact, deemed beneficial by cardiovascular experts. The answer may be twofold. First, it may have something to do with whether the *activation* (and consequent discharge of adrenalin or other hormones) is infrequent or *chronic* (i.e., from the moment of arising in the morning until retiring at night, seven days per week). Second, it may be possible that adrenalin discharged under the conditions for which it was intended (e.g., running, fighting) is metabolized differently from adrenalin discharged when no extensive, large-muscle response is possible. In the latter case, one is left in the kind of "suspended suspense" referred to earlier, which may leave hormones to be metabolized differently and thus more free to exact a harmful toll on the very thin endothelial walls of the coronary arteries.

The above explanation also provides a possible rationale for why (as suggested by Dembroski et al. 1985; Glass et al. 1983; Spielberger et al. 1983; Spielberger et al. 1985) anger-in may be more "coronaryogenic" than overtly expressed anger. In the latter case, the organism should experience less "suspended suspense," which possibly alters the metabolism of potentially harmful hormones. Also, jogging may be healthy because it either exhausts or mellows one in such a way that total hormone discharge is reduced for an extended period of time (e.g., the remainder of the day).

The difference in how hormones are metabolized during large-muscle versus smaller- or no-muscle activity may also provide a key for understanding why white-collar, and not blue-collar, workers develop Type-A-related CHD (*see* Matthews 1982). When activated, blue-collar workers are more likely to respond with large-muscle activity (*heavy* work), which is more akin to what the fight-or-flight response was developed for in the first place. As such, large-muscle activity may elicit a healthier set of metabolic circumstances for managing potentially toxic hormones.

In thinking about the psychological theories that best explain fight-or-flight-like responses, we are forced to consider emerging psychobiologic theory. If the tendency toward elevated hormone levels that concerns us is the result of overly frequent fight-or-flight responses, then we may be dealing with a response tendency that is DNA-transmitted. The major question is, Why are the fight-or-flight responses of some individuals so easily evoked by work-related stimuli? Are these individuals congenitally predisposed to the TABP because of overly vigorous endocrine glands? Why not!

To date, it has been assumed that the locus of inherited vulnerability for CHD resides in the walls of the coronary arteries or possibly in the cholesterol-related mechanism. But if (as Adler 1917 suggested) there is such a thing as "organ inferiority," then there may also be such a thing as "organ superiority" in the form of an overly powerful hormone-producing apparatus. The archetype/collective-unconscious component of Carl Jung's theory is another way of viewing DNA-transmitted, endocrine-based "instincts" that could explain ethnic and cultural, as well as individual, differences in TABP tendencies. Presumably, this could include a tendency for fight-or-flight responses to be unleashed in response to work-related stimuli.

I have one final (and somewhat syllogistic) thought on how the hormonal aspects of the fight-or-flight response might become a habit: When chemical substances are involved, we commonly refer to habit as an "addiction." Adrenalin and other hormones are chemical substances. Is it possible that some Type A individuals are actually *hooked on their own hormones?* If one can become dependent on stimulants such as caffeine and nicotine, which produce a physiologic reaction similar to that produced by adrenalin, then could one not become addicted to adrenalin itself? Why do Type A individuals have to be doing something all of the time? (Because they are *uncomfortable when idle!*) Why are they discomforted, as some report, when dropping off to sleep or first beginning to wake up? Could this not be a withdrawal reaction? Perhaps this is why Type A individuals tend to "get going" as soon as their feet hit the floor in the mornings. For them getting up may be like others' coffee or cigarettes, that is, a way of starting the adrenalin flowing and thus ridding themselves of withdrawal-based discomfort.

Appropriate Research Stategies

And now for our third question, What kinds of data-based research do our theoretical ruminations suggest? This section deals with the kinds of studies that, given my circumstances, I have found the most compelling.

At this stage in the zeitgeist, we obviously need to force an experimental showdown between the two hypothetical constructs; that is, between time urgency and chronic, *task*-oriented activation on the one hand, and anger and *interpersonally* oriented aggression on the other. This can be approached in two ways. One is a kind of experimental shootout at the OK Corral, based on the assumption that our town (the TABP) is not big enough for both of them. It assumes that one, *but not both,* ingredients may be the "true" active ingredient. The second possibility involves and OK Corral more in the sense of "I'm OK, you're OK." It assumes that *both* ingredients may play a role, either simultaneously or independently. In any event, some partialing out of active TABP ingredients (be they anger, time urgency, and/or others) seems most in order at this stage.

For my colleagues and me, this suggested at least four potentially productive research strategies: (1) studies of TABP *components* (ingredients) and their *concomitants* (so as to provide a clearer picture of the TABP and its active ingredients); (2) development of *new instruments* to measure separate components (presumably active ingredients) of the TABP; (3) *prediction* research, designed to associate active ingredients with CHD; and (4) *mechanism*-related research, designed to explain the physiologic process that links TABP ingredients to CHD.

Components and Concomitants

Strategy 1 (components and concomitants) seeks to clarify the active-ingredients picture via factor analytic or other correlation-type studies. It also seeks to identify certain Type A concomitants that, although not a part of the traditional TABP, are correlated with it and may possess CHD-related risks of their own.

The concept of control is an example of one such concomitant. On the one hand, certain forms of control (i.e., locus of control, Rotter 1966; desirability of control, Burger and Cooper 1979) are generally regarded as adaptive. On the other hand, clinical observations suggest that Type A individuals tend to be inappropriately controlling of others, particularly in work, family, and other social situations. That is, they seem to take upon themselves more than their share of decision-making responsibility for the group. The term *nonmutuality* seems most descriptive of this tendency. In one of our early studies (Bussman et al. 1987) the relationship of the TABP to the three types of control listed above was investigated using non-CHD patients. The results indicated no relationship between Type A and either locus of control or desirability of control. Results did indicate the maladaptive form of social control ("nonmutuality") to be a concomitant of the TABP and, potentially at least, an active ingredient in the development of CHD. This CHD risk possibility for certain forms of control is supported by the previous finding of Weiss, Stone, and Harrell (1972) and of Contrada et al. (1982) that demonstrated increased adrenalin and noradrenalin output in both rats and humans in association with *attempts* to control complex environmental events.

A subsequent study using CHD patients (Wright 1987) tested the relationship of the control variables cited above to CHD. We wanted to see if results obtained with a sample that presumably contained a large ratio of false positives (college professors without documented CHD used in the first study) would be different from those obtained with a group presumably containing a large ratio of true positives (middle-aged CHD patients). The results of the second study were essentially identical to those of the first: there was no relationship between Type A and adaptive forms of control, but there was a significant relationship between the TABP and a maladaptive form of social control (i.e., nonmutuality). In all of our studies, this latter variable was measured by the Way of Life (WOL) scale developed by Wright (1985). It is currently being refined psychometrically and is available from the author upon request.

Because both of the two studies cited above relied on a self-report measure (the JAS) to assess the TABP, the possibility was left open that some form of social desirability might explain the results. Are individuals who are willing to admit that they are socially manipulative more willing to admit to being Type A? To further clarify this possibility, it seemed wise to assess the relationship between nonmutuality, or inappropriate social control, using both the JAS and the SI to assess Type A tendencies. This project is currently under way.

A second example of the component/concomitant type of research strategy involves our efforts to compare several variables (rather than just Type A and control measures, as was done in the three studies mentioned so far). If measures of several variables suspected of being active TABP ingredients are administered to a single sample, then factor-analytic treatment of the resulting data should contribute to a progressively clearer picture of exactly which variables collapse into a single construct and which ones constitute separate constructs. Most factor-analytic studies of the TABP have employed only TABP measures, that is, the JAS or the SI. As mentioned earlier, these tend to yield a single factor consisting of Type-A/anger. We felt that the Type A picture might be clarified if we factor-analyzed data from the JAS and the SI along with *other measures of possible Type A components,* such as the Spielberger state/trait measures (Spielberger et al. 1979) and other measures of anger and control. This resulted in the initiation of a three-phase study.

In Study 1, several measures were compared. These included self-report measures of negative affect (anger and anxiety), positive achievement striving (state and trait creativity), adaptive control (locus of control and desirability of control), and maladaptive control (inappropriate social control, or nonmutuality) along with the TABP measure (the JAS divided into its four subscales of Type A, Speed and Impatience, Job Involvement, and Hard Driving Ambitions). Subjects were a group of male college professors. The factor analysis yielded two factors. One was a rather familiar-looking, negative factor consisting of Type A (sans JAS Subscale 3, Job Involvement) trait anger and trait anxiety. The second was a rather positive-appearing factor consisting of JAS Subscale 3 (Job Involvement) and both state and trait curiosity. These data were interpreted as supporting the ideas that the TABP (1) is a multifaceted construct and (2) as suggested by authors such as Hansson et al. (1983) and Matthews (1982), contains both positive and negative ingredients.

In Study 2, when these same measures were administered to a group of hospitalized CHD patients, essentially identical results were obtained. It is worth noting that Study 2, the same factor structure resulted when the CHD patients completed the psychometric measures a second time, reporting how they would have answered if they had taken the test prior to the discovery of their CHD. Even more striking is the fact that in a third variation of Study 2, the same factor structure was also obtained when spouses rated the CHD patients on the psychometric measures.

In a third phase of our efforts to factor-analyze the TABP and related measures (Study 3), we are currently comparing these same variables but with structured interview data as well as data from self-report measures. Here we hypothesize that the same factor structure will *not* be replicated but rather that separate self-report and clinical observation (SI) factors will emerge that are not highly correlated. If obtained, such results would support the existence of a social desirability or denial factor that operates when self-report measures of Type A components are used.

Development of New Instruments

Next let me illustrate some of the studies involving our second research strategy, scale development. Very early it became necessary to develop a new scale (the WOL) in order to study a potential TABP concomitant of interest to us. However, a lack of adequate instruments is not limited to suspected concomitants of TABP. It is a problem that haunts our efforts to investigate even time-honored ingredients such as anger and time urgency.

The availability of measures is least problematic in the area of anger. A number of reasonably good psychometric devices for measuring anger were developed prior to the flourishing of TABP-related research. These include such instruments as the Cook and Medley (1954) H_o scale of the Minnesota Multiphasic Personality Inventory and the state/trait measures of anger developed by Spielbeger et al. (1979). Spielberger et al. (1985) have more recently developed a measure of anger-in. However, no psychometric measures of time urgency or chronic activation have ever been developed. If we are to have meaningful research on these active ingredients of the TABP, then we must have tests for assessing them that are robust and (because of the social desirability and denial phenomena mentioned earlier), it is to be hoped, bias-proof. Unfortunately, both the JAS and the SI contain only a small number (JAS = 20; SI = 12) of time-urgency items. An even smaller number of chronic-activation items exists (JAS = 9; SI = 2).

To address this problem, we first considered the possibility of using *nonpsychometric* measures. Colson and Wright (1986) reviewed the existing psychological literature in an attempt to publish a catalog (an annotated bibliography with evaluative comments) of nonpsychometric measures of time urgency. Five such measures were identified: (1) appointment arrival time; (2) project deadline behavior; (3) observations of driving and traffic behavior; (4) temporal judgment; and (5) reaction-time measures.

Next, our small research group at the University of Oklahoma addressed the issue of *psychometric* measures. At present, there are no existing scales (outside of the small number of items contained in the JAS and the SI) for measuring time urgency or chronic activation. Consequently, a study by McCurdy and Wright (1986) produced a 106-item scale for time urgency and a 27-item scale for assessing chronic activation. Refinement studies of these instruments (i.e., of their reliability, validity, and factor-analytic structure) are currently under way. Copies of the tests themselves are available from the author upon request.

As mentioned earlier, the problems of social desirability and denial of Type A tendencies may be formidable. There seems to exist an incredible willingness among many Type B individuals to tell (with apparent sincerity) about their strong Type A tendencies. And correspondingly, there is a great willingness on the part of many Type A individuals to deny their TABP behavior. Thus, any psychometric instrument that purports to measure Type A phenomena might benefit from some form of bias control.

Our first effort at controlling the distortion tendencies of Type A individuals was the development of forced-choice, bias-resistant scales for measuring time urgency and chronic activation. Our method was the same as that initially developed by Wherry and Fryer (1949). A pool of items made up of valid correlates of a given criterion (in the first study, time urgency) was developed. Social desirability was ascertained for these items as well as for a group of items possessing *no* validity for assessing time urgency. We did this by asking a large group of Type A men to provide two ratings for all of the above items on a 1–6 Likert-type scale. One rating was for how willing they would be to make a given statement about themselves (the *stated* social desirability index of the item). The second rating was for how true the item was for them (defacto, or actuarial, social desirability). Items possessing equal stated and actuarial desirability but different validities were paired to compose forced-choice items. Thus the respondent was forced to identify himself as either time-urgent or not, but presumably without social desirability or denial entering into the choice.

The above scale and a similar one for assessing chronic activation are currently under development and should be available in the future. Also under way is a project to develop a similar bias-proof measure of the Type A global construct using Jenkins-like items paired with non-valid items of equal stated and actuarial desirability. This scale will also be made available in the future.

A third aspect of our scale development strategy involves the creation of new structured interview techniques. Structured interview methods have clearly proven to be the best for assessing TABP phenomena (Matthews 1982). However, when we raise issues relating to time urgency, habitual activation, and hostility, the traditional (Rosenman 1978) SI fails to provide a very robust (in terms of number of items) device. In fact, it has only 12 items that lend themselves to inferences about time urgency, 2 of which bear on chronic activation, 4 on anger-out, and 5 on anger-on.

To address this problem, Wright and Schmidt-Walker (1986) developed a supplement to the SI designed to aid in assessing time urgency, activation, anger-out, and anger-in. This device was tested in a pilot study with approximately 100 subjects, approximately 65 of whom had documented CHD. Three of the initial 24 supplemental items were discarded on the basis of their limited ability to add anything to SI ratings. Final selection of items was based on the agreement of two interviewers that the additional items contributed significantly to the assessment of either time urgency, chronic activation, anger-out, or anger-in. A copy of this SI supplement is also available from the author upon request.

Prediction Research

Having summarized the work of the University of Oklahoma group relying on both component- and instrument-related strategies, I will now attempt to summarize our efforts aimed at prediction. The obvious issue, of course, is which active ingredient may be able to predict CHD better than global TABP measures. If active-ingredient measures should prove to be the better predictors, this would presumably be because they contain less error associated with the inactive, or possibly even healthy, ingredients.

Ideally, prediction research of this type would involve prospective, longitudinal studies. Unfortunately, however, the logistical and time demands of such studies exceed the capability of our research group. Such efforts are generally limited to more ambitious projects such as the Framingham or Western Collaborative Studies. We were left with our more modest efforts.

In the absence of longitudinal capability, traditional CHD research has attempted to link a predictor to CHD by assaying the frequency of a particular characteristic (such as high blood pressure) in patients with CHD compared to patients without CHD. The Rosenman et al. (1975) study represents a typical example of this approach.

Assuming that certain TABP ingredients have the capability to cause CHD in the absence of other risk factors, we might anticipate a strong presence of certain TABP-like ingredients in CHD patients *without* the traditional factors of smoking, family history, and so forth. This rationale is supported by another aspect of the Rosenman et al. (1975) study, indicating that the coronary-prone impact of the TABP is *not* associated with the traditional physiologic risk factors.

We have attempted to test for the possibility of two classes of CHD patients, one possessing the traditional risk factors and one without these factors. To do this, 40 men between the ages of 40 and 55 who were patients on the coronary care unit of a large southwestern medical center were administered self-report, spouse-report, and structured-interview measures for the global TABP. They were also administered self-report, spouse-report, and structured-interview measures for the suspected active ingredients of time urgency, chronic activation, anger-out, and anger-in. Each of the above measures was correlated with each of seven established CHD risk factors: family history, smoking, history of high serum cholesterol, history of high blood pressure, sedentary lifestyle, adequacy of diet, and inadequacy of weight control. In addition, each TABP active-ingredient measure was correlated with a global risk score obtained by weighting and summing the traditional risk scores according to a method suggested by Rosenman et al. (1975). Finally, all of these data were intercorrelated and factor-analyzed.

The results obtained were interesting. They suggest what appear to be at least five separate routes to coronary artery disease: (1) inherited (family-history-related) risk; (2) self-imposed (but non-Type-A) risk (i.e., smoking, poor diet and exercise styles) (3) anger-in; (4) anger-out in combination with time urgency and chronic activation; and (5) the traditional Rosenman and Friedman TABP. Also, there appeared to be a possible sixth route, consisting of an interaction between hypoactivity-based obesity and anger-in.

For coronary risk based on Type-A-like factors, anger-in proved to be the key ingredient. In fact, the two strongest Type-A-like factors were (1) controlled anger and denial and (2) consciously controlled anger-in (this trait is found in individuals who know what they are doing, but who either feel it is inappropriate to express anger or who just cannot do it). The third strongest factor was anger-out in combination with time urgency and chronic activation.

The fourth strongest Type-A-like risk factor was the standard Rosenman and Friedman TABP. Thus, factor-analytically, two kinds of active ingredients (anger-in and time-urgency/anger-out) were differentiated from the global TABP. Both appeared to be more highly correlated (than the global TABP) with CHD, independent of traditional risk factors such as smoking, family history, and so forth.

Contrary to my earlier discourse on the similarity of anger and time urgency, anger-in and time urgency tended to separate into two distinct factors. Also, to our surprise (because we had been clinically impressed with the role of time urgency), anger-in appeared to be the more potent ingredient. However, more in line with our earlier expectation, anger-out did collapse into the same factor as time urgency and chronic activation.

From these data, it appears that the traditional Rosenman and Friedman TABP was a conglomerate of at least two ingredients (anger-in vs. time-urgency/chronic-activation) that possess no essential relationship to one another. Anger-in appears to be the more common and possibly the more powerful initiator of CHD. This would explain how we obtained separate factors for (1) anger-in, (2) anger-out/time-urgency/chronic-activation, and (3) the traditional TABP. It is only in cases where factors 1 and 2 (which are essentially unrelated) happen to appear together that one obtains factor 3 (the traditional TABP).

For the purpose of predicting CHD, it became clear that there are at least three separate ways of measuring Type-A-like phenomena. These include the self-reports and structured interviews previously relied on and, in addition, ratings by spouses. In the case of our strongest Type-A-like predictor (controlled anger and denial), only spouse ratings (and not self-reports or even structured interviews) were able to pick up this trait complex. Spouse ratings also proved to be the best method for measuring anger-out. The SI proved superior for measuring the traditional TABP and for measuring anger-in. Both structured interviews and spouse reports were equally effective in measuring the active ingredients of time urgency and chronic activation. Self-reports were effective in the assessment of only one factor, which consisted of conscious anger, time urgency, and chronic activation.

Mechanism-Related Research

Shifting from psychometrically based prediction research, the modest physiologic differences between Type A and Type B individuals obtained in laboratory settings (Jennings and Choi 1981; Lovallo and Pishkin 1980a; Scherwitz, Berton and Leventhal 1978) underscore the need for in vivo physiological studies. Our assumption is that the artificial laboratory setting serves to elicit forms of self-control from Type A individuals that are less likely to operate in vivo (especially in work-related situations). Actually, I doubt that research on underlying physiologic mechanisms related to the TABP (the final area of our research on which I will report) can ever be maximally productive in laboratory settings.

To date, our efforts to study possible physiological mechanisms related to the TABP have involved one pilot study designed to explore a heart rate-(HR) and blood pressure-(BP) related (mechanical) mechanism. We assessed, in vivo, HR and BP patterns of Type A individuals with and without documented CHD and of Type B individuals with and without CHD. Four subjects for each of the four groups were identified using both the SI and JAS. The assumption was that although all subjects might be expected to have elevated HR and BP at certain times (e.g., after running up a flight of steps), Type A subjects might manifest the same dramatic elevations while doing simple, work-related tasks such as opening mail, talking on the phone, or directing a secretary.

A Space Labs Model ICR-BP 5200 ambulatory BP and HR device was used. It provided BP and HR readings every five minutes over a 24-hour period. Three separate 24-hour periods were monitored for each subject —two working days and one weekend day. Subjects provided tape-recorded verbal descriptions indicating the type of activity in which they were engaged at a given time. This allowed HR and BP to be related to the type of physical, mental, and emotional activity that was occurring simultaneously. Obtained results indicated no statistically significant differences between any of the groups on HR or BP. Neither were differences found between groups in the amount of heavy physical activity or light physical activity, the degree or frequency of emotional arousal, or the amount of mental, task-related activity.

Two additional mechanism-related investigations are currently in the preparation phase. Both are in vivo efforts to relate hormone output to the TABP and thus to test for the existence of a so-called chemical mechanism.

In our next study, we will attempt to determine differences between Type A and Type B individuals, with and without documented CHD, on in vivo output of four hormones. According to Williams et al. (1982), adrenalin, noradrenalin, cortisol, and/or testosterone might be expected to have such effects. The hypothesis is that measures of these hormones obtained in vivo will more clearly separate Type A individuals with CHD from the other three groups (Type B individuals with and without CHD and Type A individuals without CHD). These relationships will be compared to the degree of association with CHD for (1) measures of the TABP and (2) TABP ingredients, as well as (3) hormone output in laboratory settings. Our hypothesis is that in vivo hormone output will better differentiate Type A individuals with CHD from all Type B persons and from other Type A persons without CHD than will psychometric measures of the TABP, its active ingredients, or hormone measures obtained in more artificial laboratory settings.

Diagnostic and Therapeutic Research Goals

And now for our final question: "What diagnostic and therapeutic procedures should we be trying to develop?" What I will say is speculative, but I cannot resist.

It is to be hoped that TABP research will soon produce better measures of active ingredients and (possibly through that) will soon identify the physiologic mechanism(s) involved in linking the TABP to CHD. Hormones may be identified as the offending agents. Or other functions such as HR, BP, and/or vasoconstriction may be found to play the major role. In any event, we should be able to develop a technology for measuring the offending mechanism directly and, it is hoped, as it is occurring. Technologic breakthroughs with other disorders are encouraging and hold promise for dealing with TABP-related CHD. Take diabetes, for example. We now have the ability to provide diabetic patients with more or less permanent indwelling catheters for obtaining blood. We also now have sensors that can provide ongoing measures of the level of sugar in the bloodstream (Wallis 1983). This litmus-paper-like test is capable of providing information around the clock. When insulin levels become dangerously low, corrective steps are taken.

Should hormones such as adrenalin prove to be the offending agent in TABP-related CHD, then individuals identified by nonevasive measures (such as psychometric and/or interview measures of the active TABP ingredients) could receive similar catheters in order to provide a clear picture of their hormone output. This would be for diagnostic purposes and would be approached in a manner similar to the way in which arteriograms are obtained on individuals who produce suggestive stress test (i.e., treadmill) results.

Likewise, for treatment purposes, individuals with dangerously elevated hormone levels could also be fitted with a catheter. Then, when the as-yet-to-be-developed sensor indicated that excess hormones were being produced, the patient could interrupt this unhealthy chain of events by treating himself or herself with the most effective forms of hormone-biofeedback-aided intervention. These could include medication, relaxation techniques, or cognitive methods, such as meditation. Once perfected, these diagnostic and therapeutic techniques could be applied early, probably with late adolescents and young adults. In so doing, TABP-related CHD could be prevented.

I sincerely believe we are on the threshold of a breakthrough in TABP/CHD research. This only serves to accelerate the already growing excitement and promise associated with the field of clinical health psychology.

Conclusions for the Layperson

In concluding, I would like to step back from the esoteric aspects of the TABP and present a summary glimpse of that construct with laypersons' interests in mind. What do we know about Type A individuals, and what can be done about their problem?

No one has yet reported a method for identifying TABP subjects and altering those tendencies in a manner that reduces the probability of CHD. Thoresen and his associates (Friedman, Thoresen, and Gill 1981) have reported a method of intervention that has been associated with a lower reoccurrence rate for heart attacks. However, prior to the occurrence of heart attack and/or bypass surgery, Type A individuals are notorious for denying their TABP tendencies and for refusing to alter this aspect of their lifestyles.

Over the past four years, I have dealt with several hundred Type A individuals in an inpatient hospital classroom setting. These subjects are dramatically different from pre-CHD Type A subjects in both their awareness of and interest in their Type A tendencies. The behavioral prescriptions that can be offered them or other interested parties fall into three categories. However, no empirical data, beyond clinical observation, support the merits of any of these approaches. Nonetheless, I will list and describe them briefly.

The first approach is ongoing self-monitoring—developing acute introspective skills that alert one if one is drifting into hyperactivation. When this happens, subjects employ the techniques that best deactivate them, such as deep breathing, thought stopping, and so forth.

Next is the Friedman and Ulmer (1984) approach. The obsessive-complusive, Type A tendency is turned against itself in a manner similar to the way in which alcoholics are encouraged by AA to obsess about *not* drinking (i.e., worrying incessantly about whether there is rum in the cake icing). Type A persons are encouraged to worry about such things as getting into the *longest* line at the supermarket or making sure a meal lasts at least a certain, lengthy amount of time.

The third type of approach is change of venue. This approach involves an acknowledgment by Type A individuals that they cannot control themselves when exposed to work-related stimuli. Therefore, they retire or change to another (often manual or agricultural) occupation that holds no prospect (and therefore no pressure) for advancement.

Because any of the self-corrective measures described above probably exceed the ambition of most people, I will close by simply leaving a thought, which if kept in mind might do some good. It is intended not only for those who are Type A-inclined but also for the benefit of others who serve as parents, teachers, counselors, and friends. The thought is that although much Type A functioning may be productive, one *must* still learn to glide.

One can drive a car at the speed limit either relaxed or "wired." An equal number of Type A and Type B individuals achieve fame. The difference is that Type B persons tend to do one thing well, whereas Type A persons are multiphasic. Job involvement does not appear to be an active, coronary-prone ingredient.

It would be nice if we were able to keep "the baby" (drive, ambition) without the "bath water" (hyperactivation and the resulting CHD). Unfortunately, most suggestions to which developing Americans are exposed involve admonitions that, if followed, would lead us to either retain or discard both. What is needed are new and more sophisticated values and mores, as well as better means of communicating these to offspring, students, and clients, that discriminate between achievement gained efficiently and achievement requiring overactivation and possibly CHD. What is needed are ways of training ourselves and others to maintain diligence with pacing—that is, to run the race of life like a marathon and not a series of 100-yard dashes.

IV

Coping With the Stress of Living and Dying

Readings in part IV center on coping with issues related to life stresses and death. Determinants of coping, such as cultural, situational, and personality factors, are discussed as they affect individuals handling threatening circumstances.

In our first selection in part IV, Anthony (1988) discusses responses to overwhelming stress in children.[1] While many traditional personality theories have taken a developmental perspective and clinicians have frequently noted psychological disorders in children—as reflected in DSM-IIIR (American Psychiatric Association 1987)—children have often been excluded as subjects in stress and coping research. Many reasons account for this omission, including the tendency of society to protect or buffer perhaps its most vulnerable persons from the prying, though well intentioned, researcher.

Anthony addresses several important issues. For example, do stressful experiences during childhood serve to strengthen or inoculate children against future adulthood stressors, or do they weaken children, making them more susceptible to future harm? In what ways do parents and other adults help or hinder the child's response to stressful circumstances? Anxious parents may communicate their anxiety to the child, with a resulting contagion effect. How do children's reactions to stressful experiences differ from those of adults? Because of differing views of the world, and differing coping abilities, children and adults often do react differently to stressors. As noted by Davison and Neale in their discussion of post-traúmatic stress disorder (PTSD),

> DSM-IIIR alerts us to the fact that children can suffer from PTSD, but they may show it differently from adults. Sleep disorders with nightmares about monsters are common as are general behavioral changes, as when a previously garrulous and sociable youngster becomes very quiet and withdrawn and loses interest in normal play activities or school. Conversely, a previously quiet child may begin to act aggressively. Some children develop the idea that they will not become adults. In addition, the child may lose already acquired developmental skills such as toilet habits or even language skills. Most importantly, young children have much more difficulty talking about their upset and concern than do adults; this feature is especially important to remember in cases of possible physical or sexual abuse by adults. (1990:157–58).

Pearlin's (1980) article describes a fascinating bit of research and theory focusing on psychological distress among adults and how it relates to "life strains." Life strains refer to types of circumstances that have the capacity to elicit emotional distress. Pearlin mentions three such life strains: slow-to-change problems of daily life (e.g., conflict); scheduled events in the life cycle (e.g., getting married); and nonscheduled events (e.g., being fired or laid off). How adults cope with these life strains in their occupations and families is discussed at length. Throughout his article, Pearlin emphasizes the importance of society in eliciting distress as well as in helping people to cope with it. For example, social status affects the availability of informal and formal helping agents—that is, of social supports—as well as the nature of the social and economic hardships one might face. As Pearlin (1980:176) states: "Social organization is both a wellspring of many life strains and, paradoxically, of the resources capable of moderating the negative effects of the strains."[2]

Mechanic ([1962] 1978b) argues that there are basically two components of adaptation, one dealing directly with the situation ("coping"), and another dealing with one's feelings about the situation ("defense"). The amount of stress one experiences is therefore dependent upon the effectiveness of, and available means for, coping and defense.[3] In a classic naturalistic investigation of graduate students studying for a major examination, Mechanic carefully observed and interviewed students and their families for three months prior to and one month following the exam. The brief selection included here emphasizes "defensive" modes (such as joking and humor) used by students anticipating their examinations. Mechanic found that older and very anxious students found little about their plight to joke about and among all students joking tended to occur most frequently at certain points in time (e.g., just prior to the examination week). Moreover, as the exams became imminent, the nature of the jokes changed from that of tension-release (i.e., poking fun at the study material) to "avoidance-banter" (i.e., humor which permitted avoidance of the anxiety-provoking material); as time was running out, the switch to the latter type of joking was "adaptive" in that it protected students from being confronted with new and potentially stressful ideas. Mechanic's study is one of the more thorough and wide-ranging naturalistic studies of stress and coping, and the reader may want to examine his book, *Students Under Stress,* in its entirety.

The remaining articles in part IV deal primarily with coping with one's own impending death or the death of another. Many philosophers and psychological theorists have speculated that even when people are not facing imminent death, our inevitable mortality is a source of continual psychological stress, which we deal with by avoidance or denial and, perhaps, efforts to remain a vital force in the world even after our deaths. In any case, the threat of imminent death, as in life-threatening or terminal illness, is a major source of stress to both the person facing it and those whose lives are deeply affected by it, such as spouses, friends, and family.

Few would argue that acquired immune deficiency syndrome (AIDS) is perhaps the most critical communicable public health problem of the 1980s and 1990s. Weitz (1989) discusses how uncertainty affects persons with AIDS or those at risk, and how these individuals cope with their uncertainty. The person's uncertainties may range from whether AIDS will develop to whether, once it does, he or she will be able to die with dignity. Throughout her article, Weitz emphasizes the importance of gaining a sense of control in coping with the stress associated with AIDS.[4]

Weitz's study primarily involved interviews with gay and bisexual men with AIDS or AIDS-related complex (ARC). All of the interviewees were residents of Arizona, an area with relatively few AIDS cases. Consequently, Weitz's study may not pertain directly to those with AIDS living in more populated, and relatively more liberal, areas such as New York or California.[5] For example, the rather large amount of *self*-blame expressed by Weitz's sample (such as, that they developed AIDS because of punishment for sin) might not be as prevalent in other, more politically powerful gay communities. Such views by Weitz's subjects may well reflect the predominant views of their surrounding communities. Only further research will be able to address adequately these, and related, concerns. All in all, Weitz research represents one of the few efforts to study those with AIDS from a phenomenological perspective.[6]

Schulz and Schlarb (1987–88) believe that the study of dying individuals has been largely neglected by stress researchers and deserves more attention. In their article, Schulz and Schlarb critically examine available research on the dying patient. For example, they discuss the well-known work of Kübler-Ross and conclude that the sequential stages of dying she hypothesizes do not always occur as suggested.

> Probably the best conclusion we can draw from this research as a whole is that dying evokes a variety of predominantly negative emotions such as fear, anger, sadness, and depression, and that these emotions occur in no particular order. In addition, the data suggest that there is a continuity of affective style from the nonterminal to the terminal phase. The overall proportion of positive or negative affect displayed by the terminal patient is closely related to the emotional style of the individual before becoming terminally ill. (1987–88:303)

The overall point of the Schulz and Schlarb article, however, is that learning more about how people handle the dying process will provide not only practical information, but also the opportunity to develop more enriching theories of coping—a point consistent with Weitz' study.

Coping with irrevocable loss is the topic of our next selection. Wortman and Silver (1989) argue that some of our beliefs about how one should respond to loss are myths, inaccurate beliefs that actually may increase the distress experienced by mourners. For example, beliefs such that healthy grieving should include a period of intense depression shortly after the death of a loved one followed by a period of "working through" the loss after a "reasonable" period of time, lead often to the conclusion that something is wrong with the person who displays a very different pattern of mourning. Wortman and Silver believe that professionals often intervene unnecessarily in some cases of "abnormal" mourning. While some individuals may require professional attention following irrevocable loss, identifying pathological responses needs to be done with the recognition that there are many normal patterns of mourning that do not fit with traditional theories or expectations. The lack of distress, for example, immediately following loss does not necessarily lead to a "delayed grief" reaction. In fact, Wortman and Silver find evidence that individuals who have a relatively mild initial reaction to loss often remain less distressed than those with the greatest initial upset. This is surprising because Wortman and Silver's views conflict with those of towering figures in the clinical field, such as Bowlby, Freud, and Lindemann—controversy is most certain to continue in this arena.

NOTES

1. Baum (1987) deals with similar material in relation to adults; *see* chapter 6 in this anthology.

2. *See also* Coehlo, Hamburg, and Adams (1974) for further discussions of the importance of social organization in stress and coping.

3. *See* the earlier article in this anthology by Lazarus and Folkman (1984c) for a comparable point of view.

4. Weitz's emphasis on the importance of coping to gain a sense of control is compatible with other articles in this volume, e.g., *see* Maddi and Kobasa (1984a).

5. Between July 1988 and June 1989 there had been 182 reported cases of AIDS in Phoenix, Arizona (an incidence rate of 8.5 per 100,000). During the same period of time, 5,546 cases of AIDS were reported in New York City (an incidence rate of 64.5 per 100,000) (*World Almanac and Book of Facts 1990,* New York: Pharos Books, 1989, p. 170).

6. For discussions of the possible role of *stress* as a co-factor in the development of AIDS, *see* Bridge, Mirsky, and Goodwin (1988) and Livingston (1988).

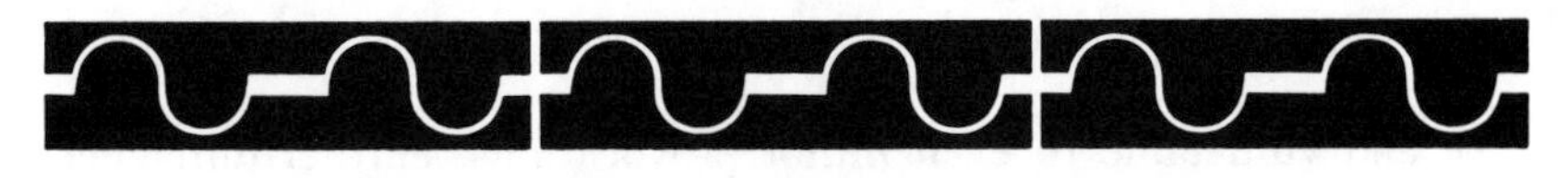

15

The Response to Overwhelming Stress in Children: Some Introductory Comments

E. JAMES ANTHONY

The domain of stress is full of pitfalls for the clinical inquirer, but its very ambiguities have attracted a good deal of attention from both clinicians and investigators. States of stress follow, according to some still largely unknown etiological transmissions, in the aftermath of traumatic experiences, natural or manmade disasters, parental mismanagement or abusiveness, overwhelming environments, intrapsychic conflicts, and biological upheavals among a whole array of unsettling internal and external impingements. It appears to constitute the final common pathway for all of these actual or potential threats, and once established, it can generate, immediately or eventually, stress or stress-related disorders. In western-type industrialized societies where patterns of living are complex and demanding, stress is encountered everywhere and at all stages of the life cycle, so that it has come to be regarded as inherent in the human condition. However, it varies in degree of severity from one set of circumstances to another and is not evenly distributed throughout the population; some individuals and families have more than their fair share of significant stresses. At the same time, response to stress may also vary, with some individuals reacting resiliently and masterfully, while others appear unduly sensitive and vulnerable to even minor provocations. Further differences result from the amount of buffering and support provided by families and the social milieu.

Another factor tied to the idiosyncratic nature of apperception may be also related to the degree of sensitivity that makes the response to stress even more unpredictable. This subjective appraisal by the individual of the stress confronting him is the "black box" (or at least one of several black boxes) in the chain of events that follows exposure to a disturbing event and befuddles attempts to carry out clean-cut research.

To understand the child's response to overwhelming stress, several theoretical constructs have been put forward.

1. A model of self-induced pathology has been developed according to which individuals are prone to a helpless or hopeless response as part of a giving up or given up complex operating in the presence of environmental pathogens or constitutional vulnerabilities (Schmale 1972).
2. A second model, bearing on individual differences in vulnerability to stress-induced conditions, has been related the general expectation of individuals that disturbing events entering their lives are controllable from the inside or the outside along an internal-external dimension (Rotter 1966). The internal locus of control expectancy has been equated with competence, coping ability, and relative invulnerability to stress (Campbell, Converse, and Rodgers 1976).
3. A third model has been derived from laboratory research on physiological and psychological responses to stressful stimuli. The thesis stemming from it postulated that individuals differ in vulnerability to the degree that they suppress awareness of threatening stimuli or, contrariwise, are hyperalert to them. Studies of response styles of threatening illnesses suggest that repression may lead to a better recovery (Cohen and Lazarus 1973). The mechanism involved in this is denial (or as Freud would term it, "disavowal"), and it constitutes an unconscious defense against overwhelming *external* stimuli and a refusal to recognize the reality of a traumatic perception (Goldberger 1983). This is probably an element in all outer-directed defenses, such as projection, displacement, and so on, and is viewed psychodynamically as a primitive process at work in the prestage of defense. The "turning away from reality" may be adaptive or maladaptive from the viewpoint of safety. Some

deniers may give a history of risk-taking or recklessness pursued with a sense of invulnerability, and so-called field-dependent individuals respond to threatening situations by narrowing their perception, as if they were wearing blinders (Sandman 1972).

4. Since children are often exposed to dangerous conditions in the company of adults, a comprehensive model must also include the presence of social supports such as the family, formal helping agencies, friendship networks, and so on (Caplan 1976). The result of studies to date indicate that a full understanding of individual differences in response to stressful events cannot be achieved without examining the interpersonal context.

As in most stress research, the developmental point of view is not included in this model making. This represents a significant deficit. Two crucial questions immediately arise and need to be answered, if the important time dimension is brought in: Does the experience of early stress affect the adjustment in later years? and, Do certain negative experiences in early life tend to increase immunity in later stressful events? The latter involves what is usually referred to as the "inoculation effect."

Another important consideration implicates the activities of the individuals working toward their own readjustment through the use of coping strategies. Janis (1958) has discussed the "work of worrying" that made it possible for individuals to anticipate realistically and work through stressful events, and Lindemann (1944) spoke of the "work of grieving" that allowed for a successful negotiation of the bereavement crisis with emancipation from the emotional bondage to the deceased and the formation of new relationships.

The reactions of children to high degrees of stress are varied and range from the mild and transient to an acute evolving psychopathology at the core of which is an overwhelming experience of anxiety. As the acute psychopathology unfolds in the more stress-sensitive child, certain reactions may appear that eventually cluster together to present different facets of a post-traumatic stress disorder. As the child grows older, the clusters grow larger and more complex. The total response passes through a recognizable series of stages as the traumatic experience is gradually worked through and the pressure of reexperiencing diminishes in conjunction with the intrusive imagery. Whether originating in violence, bereavement, uprooting, natural or manmade disaster, or conditions of war, the presenting clinical pictures have a great deal in common, although there are some distinctive aspects that relate to particular stresses. For example, all the clinical syndromes include a tendency for the victims to reexperience the stressful event, to detach themselves from the environment, to be apprehensive about further exposure, and to show exaggerations of attachment behavior, especially toward family members (Bowlby 1973). However, each predicament also has its own salient features. For instance, in the uprooting and dislocation syndrome with its "defamiliarization," one finds feelings of alienation, the projection of persecutory anxieties onto the new environment coupled with homesickness for the old. In the bereavement syndrome, feelings of loss predominate, manifested by grief reactions with the familiar sequence of protest, despair, and detachment (Bowlby 1973). Death anxiety and survivor guilt are very much to the forefront in the disaster syndrome linked to intense feelings of insecurity and vulnerability and extinction imagery.

In all these syndromes, prior to the emergence of a well-defined psychopathology, there are periods of confusion, disorientation, and disorganization, degrees of "psychic" numbness, and a pervasive sense of meaninglessness, hopelessness, and helplessness, all of which are magnified in the case of the solitary victim.

The Biology of Stress

Selye (1946), the pioneer in this field, viewed stress as a nonspecific response to any demand for change which therefore acted as a universal stressor. In laboratory animals, the consistent and almost stereotyped responses to unpleasant stimuli were linked to increased hormonal levels in the pituitary-adrenocortical axis with macroscopic and microscopic pathological changes in the gastric mucosa, lymphoid tissue, and adrenal cortex. The responses appeared in three phases: the alarm phase during which defenses were mobilized and the sympathetic and pituitary-adrenocortical systems were triggered into action; the stage of resistance during which these adaptive defenses were maintained; and a stage of exhaustion in which the defenses were overcome and death ensured. This tripartite response was termed the "general adaptation syndrome" and could be distinguished in all varieties of serious stress. Further work has incriminated new hormones, such as prolactin, melatonin, and endorphins, that could be measured more accurately. In more recent years, certain psychosocial stressors, such as bereavement, have shown impaired immune system responses.

Currently, attention is being focused on central nervous system structures and mechanisms that initiate or transmit the stress signal.

Some preliminary evidence has suggested that both the heart rhythm and its force of contraction are regulated by the same centers in the frontal cortex of the brain that control the sensory perception during acute fear. From an evolutionary or teleologic viewpoint, the stimulation of the sympathetic nervous system, under the aegis of the cortical authority and the resultant outpouring of the epinephrine were essential to the life-preserving "fight or flight" reactions of primitive man, but the nature of stress for the individual today is different. It is only occasionally and unexpectedly that one is confronted with overwhelming, life-threatening exposures; one's problem is with the annoying stress and strain of everyday life, such as getting stuck in traffic jams, coping with financial difficulties, and so on. The problem is that the body still continues to respond in the archaic fashion, making the release of epinephrine not only inappropriate, but actually harmful. The stress disorders that we see clinically today could thus be labeled "diseases of civilization."

The reactions of stress-resistant individuals (children or adults) do appear to be different from those of stress-sensitive ones. When exposed to the same major threat, the stress-resistant respond to the challenge in a controlled way without being overwhelmed by it. Recent research (Ekman, Levenson, and Friesen 1983) has challenged the conventional concept that automatic responses to positive and negative emotions are the same. It is possible to differentiate between such emotional states psychophysiologically.

It would seem, therefore, that while stress is a very complex phenomenon, many of its disastrous consequences are mediated by the release of neurohumoral chemicals, related to epinephrine and various small brain peptides either as a response to external stimuli or as unappreciated results of self-induced secretion. This can have profound effects on immune competency.

Some Overlooked Victims of Overwhelming Stress

Throughout the centuries, populations have been exposed to cataclysmic disasters and meticulous records have been maintained on property destruction, injury, and death, especially where litigation was involved. Until recently, material damage received most of the attention and the psychosocial effects were scarcely observed. Within the past few decades, however, certain overlooked victims have been recognized and investigated, such as children that were witnesses or participants who until now had remained almost unnoticed amid the prevailing confusion of the aftermath; survivors who left the scene and wanted most to forget about it; families who had to cope with loss and bereavement, often with little or no help; communities where the "tissues of social life" and the "prevailing sense of commonality" had been damaged by the collective trauma (Erikson 1976); and finally, the rescuers and researchers from the outside who were drawn into the raw horror of catastrophe and rapidly became profoundly involved with it. With each study, it began to look as if the specific mode of stress was of less importance than the overwhelming anxiety that gripped victims, onlookers, families, rescue workers, clinicians, and investigators. Degrees of post-traumatic stress disorder could afflict any one of these groups, depending on relative vulnerabilities. Davidson (1979) called attention to the difficulties encountered by rescue personnel following air crashes. The rescuers were faced with extremely difficult tasks for which they were hardly prepared and many of them complained of nightmares, insomnia, gastrointestinal ailments, and general anxiety. Their recoil from scenes of carnage was similar to what was observed in survivors.

Everyone within the orbit of disaster appears to suffer mainly from the psychological stress of remembering and for varying periods after a devastating experience, even distantly related stimuli can evoke an instant replay of the imagery of impaction.

Focus on the Child Victim and Witness

Here, we are taking a closer look at children, whose reactions in the aftermath of trauma we know less about than with adult victims.

In 1953, a tornado struck a town in Mississippi, affecting a particular movie theater in which children were attending a program. The parents were questioned later and revealed that approximately one-third of the children showed some alterations in behavior: clinging to parents, inability to sleep alone, hypersensitivity to noise, or a striking tendency to avoid situations associated with the tornado. Boys were more affected than girls, older children more than younger ones, those nearer the impact zone more than those further away, and those who were injured or whose family members were injured more than those who came through unscathed. The children's reactions were closely reflected in the manner in which the parents had responded. The latter often clung to the children "as if they were talismen," and families were often found huddling together (Bloch, Silber, and Perry 1956). A similar increase in attachment behavior following disasters was described by Wolfenstein (1957) with family members seeking one another out and struggling to remain together.

A major breakthrough in our understanding of children's responses to overwhelming stresses occurred when 234 children were interviewed and evaluated in-depth following the Buffalo Creek flood (Newman 1976). Most of them were found to be significantly impaired emotionally by the experience, manifesting an increased vulnerability to further stresses, a modified sense of reality, a good deal of extinction imagery and curious changes in their apperception of the destructive environment, viewing it as cradling and life-sustaining rather than threatening and lethal. An intriguing finding was the increase in creative activity in some children following the traumatic experience, which generally took the form of attempting to meld their reactions and observations into a meaningful whole. The clinical symptoms, as with other post-traumatic stress disorders, included troubling and intrusive imagery, terrifying nightmares and sleepwalking, increased nervous tension, withdrawal and depression, enuresis, hypochondriasis, failing grades at school, and, from seven years onward, evidence of personality changes.

Four years later, in 1976, 26 children aged 5 to 14, along with their school bus driver from Chowchilla, California, were kidnapped by masked men on the way to an outing. They spent the next 11 hours being driven around in two blackened vans and the subsequent 16 hours buried alive in a stifling, moving van, sunken in the dry riverbed of an abandoned rock quarry with nothing to eat or drink and no toilet facilities. Terr (1979) reviewed the reactions of the children 5 to 13 months after the incident, then reevaluated them four years later. Among the long-term effects she found on follow-up were recurrent dreams of the child's own death, pessimism about the future and fear of further trauma, repetitive, monotonous, and compulsive play that maintained the level of chronic anxiety, and personality changes (Terr 1981). Terr later set up a control study of 25 so-called normal schoolchildren in two towns similar to Chowchilla. Among these randomly chosen children, she found 10 extremely frightened ones and 5 who had probably been traumatized, suggesting that traumatic events and their psychological aftermaths were far more common than might have been expected. Another common finding among the Chowchilla children was their "discovery" of "omens," the little magical acts or incidents that warned of impending disaster and could only be ignored at the individual's own risk. According to Terr, experience of overwhelming anxiety is not a potentially toughening experience, but rather poses a significant and persistent burden on the child's personality development.

Garmezy (1982b) has adopted a more optimistic stance and speaks admiringly of stress-resistant children whose resilience stems from such factors as inherent biological dispositions, satisfactory early development within a reasonably good environment and sustaining relationships with parents, families, and other supportive figures. These children come through a stressful experience surprisingly well, and even with enhancement of capacities.

The question of which view is right may depend on the intensity and depth of the investigation and the length of time that it is pursued. Benedek (1985) considers that a number of factors may be responsible for discounting the long-term effects of child victims of disasters: clinicians and clinical investigators who do not deal with children find it hard to credit the view that a single traumatic event can have such a lasting influence, particularly when such conclusions are based on naturalistic observations of play; second, that professional adults and adults in general tend to deny that children can apprehend disturbing events in complex ways that can become chronic; and third, those who study children "macroscopically" and globally may tend to overlook the microscopic psychological consequences.

Currently, it is difficult to side with one or the other side of this argument. A good deal depends on mitigating or aggravating circumstances such as the availability of help, the presence or absence of parents, the stability of the family and the solidarity of the community. Even the parent is hard to evaluate as a single, unique protective shield. For instance, children who were subjected to heavy bombing during the air raids on London in World War II were described as being relatively free from anxiety in the company of their parents (Freud and Burlingham 1944), but on the other hand, parentless children, who had experienced severe physical and emotional stresses through periods in concentration camps followed by the loss of family and uprootness, did not display signs of stress disorder because they had developed a corporate life of their own. Nevertheless, this did not prevent the development of later maladjustment (Freud and Dann 1951). The absence of parents may leave the child relatively unbuffered and prone to shock, but the presence of panic-stricken parents can conduce to acute and even unmanageable anxiety in the child. Such paradoxical reactions may not make psychological sense on surface examination. Sensitive research instruments are clearly needed to plumb the underlying feelings of the child which are not accessible to direct observation or to paper-and-pencil techniques.

Pynoos and Eth (1986) have developed an interview format for assessing coping and defense capacities. Whether it is better to let the child forget or provoke him or her to remember is still a moot point. In some cases it is true that if one allows nature to take its course, the disturbance may reverberate for a while and then gradually subside. Yet, investigators are finding in follow-up studies that the buried anxieties can persist and contribute to chronic changes in personality. It could also be argued that reexperiencing the trauma in a therapeutic setting, with support and understanding at hand, is a different order of experience from a direct confrontation with horrendous reality.

In an interesting review, Benedek (1985) called attention to certain "countertransferences" in those evaluating the enormity of a disaster. They may either insist that the immaturity of the child's mental apparatus cannot appreciate the enormity of the situation or that the use of play as a research method cannot be taken seriously by the scientifically minded. Behind such reactions, there is an unwillingness to take the child seriously and to credit the complexity of his or her feelings and concerns. At the other extreme, the countertransferences can involve an overidentification with the child as a helpless victim of poor planning, deficient safeguards, unhelpful environments, and the sheer, blind maliciousness of nature or fate, any of which can invoke raging responses that are not helpful to the child. It is by no means easy under such circumstances to remain sympathetic, empathetic, and objective.

Some Underlying Mechanisms Involved in the Response to Overwhelming Stress

Some stimulant situations, such as abrupt changes of location, darkness, aloneness, and separation are not intrinsically dangerous, and often turn out not to have been dangerous at all except to the mind of the individual. Ethological work has suggested that humans, like animals, are genetically programmed to respond to a wide variety of circumstances with anxiety and apprehension, and then resort to certain safety measures. Such alarm signals appear to be transmitted almost contagiously in groups, most strikingly from parent to child. The safety precautions in the human child involve an intensification of normal attachment behavior, the use of transitional objects or activities, and the search for cover and support. These timeless alerting mechanisms can become grossly exaggerated and deviant when danger becomes disaster and normal flight or fight turns into panic and chaos. There would thus seem to be a primitive groundwork for disaster behavior that should be kept in mind when examining survivors.

The subjective aspects of the setting must also be considered since children especially tend to personalize their environment and to imbue it with elements drawn from their attributes, possessions, competences, and caretakers. Aspects of this "personal environment" have been studied with regard to traffic accidents (Backett and Johnston 1959) where it was found that injured children, when compared to a noninjured control group, were deemed to be significantly unwanted and unloved by mothers who were excessively preoccupied with themselves. When dislocations follow disastrous events, as with earthquakes, floods, and war, the familiar "home range" (as ethologists refer to it) with its sustaining network of relationships, sets the survivor at risk. The stimulus properties of a new setting have to be learned before the individual accords them equal status to those operating in his home range. In moments of danger or following disaster, the individual or group may retreat to the home range as a "haven of safety" (Harlow and Harlow 1965). Once familiarization has been established in the new location, there tends to be an intensification of "psychological conservatism," which reduces undue excitation (Titchener and Kapp 1976).

The psychological "righting" mechanism that restores equilibrium has been ascribed to a specialized ego function responsible for generating a sense of safety and a freedom from apprehension under normal circumstances (Sandler 1960). The child gradually develops his own code of safety, but until this is dependable, his security is buttressed by the adult caretakers. In the aftermath of disaster, there is a striking diminution in this sense of safety, increased feelings of vulnerability, and a heightening of attachment behavior.

Rangell (1976) has postulated that this regressive clinging following extreme trauma is based on an interference with what he termed "an attachment to ground," the psychological prerequisite for maintaining poise. This is clearly demonstrated by earthquakes and storms at sea when the physical base no longer proves reliable and a primitive anxiety connected with the possible annihilation of the self takes over. During ontogenic development, the relationship to the ground beneath extends first to the space around and subsequently to people, institutions, and cultures. When ground attachment is lost, survivors who eventually reach solid ground immediately construct a social "envelope" within the unfamiliar space which replaces the stimulus barrier that has been damaged (Erikson 1976).

Conclusions

These tenuous notions, obtained from relatively unsystematic studies, are the first findings in a very difficult field of inquiry where rigorous research may be deemed cold-blooded and the outpourings of high anxiety tend to smudge the scientific perspective. Every disaster has its affective epicenter from which waves of uncontrollable feeling flow, inundating even those who work peripherally. This represents one major problem for research. Another difficulty relates to the *post hoc* nature of disaster investigations that precludes predisaster assessments of the population involved, except in those rare instances when evaluations have been made for a different purpose before disaster strikes. It is possible that such important research preparations may be undertaken in areas at high risk for potential disasters—the East Coast which experiences hurricanes, the Midwest, tornadoes, and the West Coast's earthquakes—not to mention certain areas which regularly expect floods or the leak of toxic wastes.

The purpose of this chapter, however, is to call much needed attention to child victims exposed to overwhelming anxieties from natural or manmade predicaments since they have been so curiously passed over in the catastrophes that have punctuated the course of history. The reason for this may not be entirely due to unintentional oversight; it is not easy for investigators to reach the child victim since the agencies that buffer him in the disaster continue to interpose themselves during the aftermath.

There are so many unanswered questions still to be researched. As yet we do not know why or when a particular stress ceases to be a stimulation and becomes a calamity; we do not know to what extent stress sensitivity or resilience is inherent in the child's make-up or whether he learns to deal helpfully or helplessly with stress or derives his robustness or vulnerability from the parental models; and we do not know whether a hard life steels the child, as suggested by Manfred Bleuler (1978) or sensitizes him to adversity. Surely we need more objective measures than are available at the present time, as well as dependable tests of internal stress. We also need reliable methods for evaluating and quantifying the network of social supports.

Since competence and creative coping have been mentioned in several studies, their role in mitigating the impact of stress also needs to be carefully considered. It is only through long-term studies in disaster-prone settings that answers to these questions and others become possible including the remote effects of the so-called death imprint (Lifton 1976).

It is evident from the work to date that the reactions to overwhelming predicaments are closely related to the interacting biological, psychological, and social processes. The hiatuses in our knowledge are still large and numerous, but the gaps are gradually closing as workers from different areas come together and pool their findings. Child psychiatrists bring their special expertise to this field, culled from a developmental understanding of the child and the capacity to elicit feelings and fantasies through various modalities of play and unobtrusive inquiry. Echoing Winnicott (1958) that "there is no such thing as a baby," the child psychiatrist may equally affirm that in states of overwhelming anxiety, there is no such thing as a child; there is only a child in his family. Newman (1976) underscores this when she reported the reaction of an eight-year-old girl from the Buffalo Creek disaster to the deserted bird fable: What does a little baby bird, who can only fly a little, do if a strong wind blows the family nest from the tree, scattering the mother and father and baby bird? The child's response was as follows:

> The mother makes another nest, with twigs, on a stronger branch. The little bird grows up to have a family or, maybe the mommy bird might get sick or die, or a cat might eat her up. Or, the little bird might get sick or poisoned. It might mistake weedkiller for seed. That *could* happen. Oh well, the little bird probably got old and then died.

Here we can detect the characteristic oscillations between fantasy and reality, optimism and pessimism and the different poles of ambivalence. However, before the little girl gave her response, she first wanted to know whether the bird family, after the strong wind had disrupted their nest, were "all close together or far apart?" It was a most perceptive question and pinpointed the central predicament of children following a disaster.

16

Life Strains and Psychological Distress Among Adults

■

LEONARD I. PEARLIN

In recent years my colleagues and I have sought to draw out the complex linkages between the social circumstances of adults and the emotional distress they experience. Although this work is far from being either definitive or complete, it has brought into view a number of general features of the adult portion of life. For example, we see adulthood as a period in which newness is more commonplace than stability. Adulthood is not a quiescent stretch interspersed with occasional change; it is a time in which change is continuous, interspersed with occasional quiescent interludes.

It has become similarly apparent from our work that adults are responsive to life circumstances and to fluctuations in these circumstances. This means, as Bernice Neugarten (1969) has observed, that adulthood is much more than that part of life in which people simply act out feelings and dispositions acquired from childhood experience. Thus, a satisfactory explanation of levels of emotional distress among adults cannot rely only on personality characteristics formed early in life, but must also take into account current experience and ongoing change. Furthermore, the results of our work indicate that no single phase of adulthood seems to have a monopoly on change. There may be distinctive constellations of problems that are especially likely to converge at particular periods, such as the transitions of middle age (Levinson 1977), but people have to confront severe challenges at other times of their lives as well.

Although much of our analysis has emphasized variations in psychological distress, we recognize that there are many ways in which lives can take on new directions. Values, beliefs, ideologies, interactional patterns, interests, and activities—indeed, the entire range of dispositions and behaviors—are subject to modification as one moves across the life span. However, these kinds of changes, which may give the appearance of being removed from and unrelated to distress, often find expression in anxiety and depression, for such feelings represent the emotional summation of important circumstances in the lives of people. In addition, of course, distress is important in its own right. It is an unpleasant condition that can come to dominate our awareness and from which we actively seek relief. Thus emotional distress both signals important life changes that are under way and, at the same time, constitutes a state against which people are likely to launch a barrage of coping responses. In either case, psychological distress is a central element in life changes, though certainly not the sole element.

The search for conditions affecting the emotional states of people necessarily leads to the larger society and its organization. Inevitably, the study of adult development entails more than the study of adults: it must also seek to identify those elements of social structure that are intertwined with and give direction to the lives of people. There are at least three ways in which societies and their organization are implicated in the emotional development of their members. First, they may be the source of the forces that have the capacity to adversely (and beneficially, too) affect the well-being of people. Even stressful situations that appear to stem from the confluence of chance conditions, as in marital conflict, are often traceable to fundamental social arrangements (Pearlin 1975b). But the most convincing indication of the contributory role of basic social organization is that many stress-provoking circumstances are unequally distributed among people having different social positions and statuses (Pearlin and Lieberman 1979). The different life strains among the rich and the poor, for example, or among men and women, or among the married and unmarried provide a clue that strains do not result from the chance experience of individuals but that they derive from the locations of people within the broader societal organization. Thus, in studying adult development in general and psychological distress in particular, a foremost task is to determine the difference in vulnerability to stressful circumstances of different groups within the society.

Second, while exposure to stressful circumstances varies with the social characteristics of people, it is also true that identical circumstances may have very different effects on individuals within a group if they occur in different social contexts. For example, retirement may result in chronic depression for the person who is separated from the sole source of activities he loved, but may be the source of elation for another to whom retirement is an escape from dreaded labor. Giving birth can be a blessed event for the mother having her first child, or an event leading to depression for the mother who already has several young children (Pearlin 1975a). There are many events and circumstances, then, that do not by themselves move people along a particular course of emotional change or development; instead, the consequences of these circumstances are given meaning by the context or situation in which people are embedded at the time.

A third general mode of social influence on adult development is represented in the coping resources people possess. Some of these resources are represented by the informal and formal helping agents to whom one can look for aid. Because the availability of these resources varies for different social groups, people do not necessarily have equal access to important social supports. There are also psychological resources that one draws upon from within oneself, and the distribution of these, too, may follow lines of social demarcation. For example, among the psychological coping resources of adults, self-esteem and mastery are most effective (Pearlin and Schooler 1978), and the likelihood of having these important elements of personality increases with one's position in the socioeconomic system (Rosenberg and Pearlin 1978). Status within the broader society, therefore, helps to determine access to crucial coping resources. And these are indeed resources to be prized, for they are instrumental in helping people withstand some of the deleterious effects of severe social and economic hardships.

Thus, societies have a dominant part in influencing individual change and adaptation by being the source of challenges and hardships, by providing the contexts that give meaning to and determine the consequences of these hardships, and by allocating resources—both social and psychological—that help people fend off the harmful emotional distress that may otherwise result. Social organization is both a wellspring of many life strains and, paradoxically, of the resources capable of moderating the negative effects of the strains. I point out these different contributions for two reasons. First, I wish to underscore that adult development does not go on apart from surrounding social circumstances, as though it simply involves the acting out of a preexisting scenario. Second, in calling attention to the different modes of social contributions to adult development, I seek to emphasize that development should not be construed as a single course universally followed by all people. It would perhaps fit reality better if we were to assume that there are many developmental patterns, each shaped and channeled by the confluence of the social characteristics of adults, their standing in the social order, the problematic experiences to which they must adapt, the social contexts and situations in which they are embedded, and the coping resources with which they are equipped. Simply knowing that most adults get married, have children, enter occupational life, and retire does not come close to providing us the information we need to examine properly the processes of adult development.

In our own work we are far from having evaluated all of these considerations as they relate to psychological distress, but we do have information that cuts across some of the issues. For much of this information I shall rely largely on research in which I and several collaborators have been engaged in recent years. For this reason, it would be useful to provide some of the background and perspectives of our work.

The aim of this research, which began several years ago, was to explore the relationships between persistent hardships threaded through daily life and psychological distress. We first conducted unstructured exploratory interviews with about 100 people, asking them to discuss the problems they faced as workers, breadwinners, wives and husbands, fathers and mothers. From these discussions several recurring themes concerning the problems people face in their occupational and family life were identified. Through a series of pre-tests these themes were gradually transformed into standardized questions that, in 1972, were asked in scheduled interviews with a sample of 2,300 people between the ages of eighteen and sixty-five representative of the adult population of the Chicago urban area. The detailed and lengthy enumeration of the problems about which people were queried and the batteries of questions used to measure them are partially reproduced in Pearlin and Schooler (1978). Here I shall provide only a general description.

With regard to the occupational arena, first of all, we assessed the presence and intensity of a range of problems, such as the noxiousness of the work setting (the existence of dirt, dust, noise, or danger); estrangement from and conflicts with both fellow workers and authorities; and various work pressures and overloads. Next, information was gathered indicative of three types of marital problems and conflicts: the lack of reciprocity, or inequalities in give and take between husbands and wives; the failure of one's spouse to fulfill a variety of role expectations, such as affection, sexual partnership, and provider-homemaker duties; and, third, the lack of recognition and acceptance by one's spouse of one's own "real," quintessential self. Finally, in the parental area, the problems about which we inquired concerned children's violations of parents' standards of general conduct; deviations from long-range parental aspirations and goals; failure to accept parental definitions of morality; and lack of consideration or respect for parents. Much of the inquiry, then, sought to evaluate the extent to which the lives of individuals are invaded by a host of conflicts and hardships arising from work and economic life, marriage and child rearing—indeed, from labor and love.

In addition to measures of these relatively persistent role problems, information was gathered regarding a large array of devices people employ to cope with the problems. As in the case of the role problems, coping behavior was first identified in the early, unstructured interviews; questions were then systematically developed and standardized for use in the sample survey. Still another body of questions was intended to provide measures of various manifestations of psychological distress. For this purpose we employed scales that had been developed from presenting symptoms of patients diagnosed as suffering from such emotional ailments as anxiety and depression (Derogatis et al. 1971; Lipman et al. 1969).

Overall, then, the range of information gathered by the research conducted in 1972 has made it possible to examine a network of connections between the social characteristics of people, the persistent problems that pervade their daily experiences in major social roles, their patterns of coping with such experiences, and the psychological outcomes that emerge from the confluence of these factors.

During 1976 we returned to Chicago and reinterviewed a subsample of our respondents.[1] We repeated virtually all of the questions about role problems, coping responses, and symptomatologies of emotional distress, thus providing the opportunity to assess changes that may have occurred in these domains between 1972 and 1976. However, in concentrating on persistent role problems, the initial survey omitted from consideration other key sources of psychological distress. In particular, it did not include the many crucial life events that have the potentiality for arousing psychological disturbance. While the persistent role problems are likely to surface so insidiously that their onset may be difficult to recognize, life is liberally sprinkled, too, with events that have discrete temporal origins, are difficult to ignore, and require acclerated adjustments. The follow-up survey was designed to capture these events.

A good deal of attention has been given in recent years to life events and their effects (Myers et al. 1972; Paykel, Prusoff, and Uhlenhuth 1971), much of it based on the Social Readjustment Rating Scale developed by Holmes and Rahe (1967b). Considerable criticism has been leveled at this scale on methodological grounds (Brown 1974; Rabkin and Struening 1976), but the conceptual deficiencies of the instrument are equally outstanding. On the positive side, the scale does succeed in identifying a number of apparently potent events. Unfortunately, it does not differentiate among events in ways that permit the reconstruction of an individual's experience as he traverses time and space. Instead, it treats important life events as haphazard and interchangeable occurrences, thus obscuring the variations in patterns of events among people with different social status, the anchoring of these patterns in different social roles, and the emergence of events at different stages of adult life. It was our goal to distinguish among events in a manner that goes beyond the simple compilation of undifferentiated occurrences.

Pivotal to our efforts in this direction is the distinction between scheduled and nonscheduled events.[2] Scheduled events involve those transitions into and out of roles and statuses that are normally experienced in the course of the life cycle. Because they are so closely tied to the life cycle, they usually have a high predictability. We refer to them as scheduled events in order to underscore the regularity of their unfolding in the lives of people. Thus, whereas the enduring role problems entail the chronic frustrations, conflicts, and hardships people encounter within existing roles and statuses, transitional events focus on the scheduled yielding and acquiring of those roles and statuses attendant upon life-cycle changes.

Our follow-up interview inquired into a number of such events within each role area. In occupation we considered the following to represent events of this type: entry into the labor market; withdrawal from occupation in order to have and care for a family; and retirement because of age. Being newly married and experiencing "timely" widowhood are the two transitional events in the marital area. The parental role is somewhat unique because, strictly speaking, one can only acquire the role of parent but not lose it. However, we do treat as scheduled events a number of critical junctures which serve as benchmarks in the child's progress toward eventual independence. These include such transitions as the child's entry into school, completion of school, departure from the parental household, and marriage of the adult child. At each of these steps the parental role, although it is retained, undergoes some transformation.

The second type of event about which we inquired in our follow-up survey involves crises, eruptive circumstances, and other unexpected occurrences that are not the consequence of life-cycle transitions—the nonscheduled events. Although events of this order may be widespread, people typically do not count on them occurring within their own lives. Such exigencies may be no less common than problems woven into the fabric of day-to-day roles or those that emerge in the course of scheduled transitions, but they are ordinarily not among the occurrences that people expect to experience personally. Events of this type in the occupational arena are being fired, laid off, or demoted, having to give up work because of illness, and—more desirable—being promoted and leaving one job for a better one. Divorce, separation, and the illness or premature death of a spouse are events within marriage that, while widespread, do not have the scheduled regularity of transitional events. And finally, the illness or death of a child represents such events in the parental arena.

Underlying our research, then, are a few simple perspectives. We hold, first, that adult emotional development does not represent the gradual surfacing of conditions that happen to reside within individuals. Instead, we see it as a continuing process of adjustment to external circumstances, many of them rooted in the organization of the larger society and therefore distributed unequally across the population. We have identified three types of circumstances that have the capacity to arouse emotional distress; we refer to these collectively as life strains. This category includes the dogged, slow-to-change problems of daily life; the highly predictable, scheduled regular events that are attached to the life cycle; and the less expected and often (though not always) undesirable eruptive events. Because many of these vicissitudes are anchored to major social roles, they vary in space as people move among their multiple roles, as well as through time as the roles they occupy undergo change. The configuration of life strains may differ from one stage of adulthood to another, but the process of adjustment and change goes on through the entirety of life.

Although these are the guiding considerations and perspectives of our research into psychological distress among adults, we have only begun to discern the outlines of the vast web of interrelationships among the issues. In the following pages I shall describe some of our empirical findings, looking first at the periods of life when different life strains are likely to surface, the effects of the strains on psychological distress, and then how people cope with them.

Age Distribution and the Emotional Impact of Life Strains

Many of the life strains we have delineated for study have previously been shown to occur unequally across important groups in the society (Pearlin and Lieberman 1979). The distribution of the strains among people of different age levels is especially germane to developmental concerns. There is no simple way to summarize this distribution, for the persistent problems, the scheduled transitional events, and the nonscheduled events each have somewhat distinctive associations with age. Furthermore, the strains rooted in the world of work are related to age in a different fashion than are the strains involving the more expressive worlds of marriage and parenthood. Thus, the relationships of life strains to age vary both with the type of strain and with the role from which the strains arise. The data are somewhat complex, therefore, but it is this very complexity and richness, so often overlooked in research into psychological well-being, that we seek to capture in conceptually distinguishing different types of circumstances and events as they present themselves within major social roles.

Within the occupational arena we find that the younger the worker is, the more likely it is that he will be exposed to most of the strains included in our study. With regard to the relatively persistent problems, for example, younger workers are somewhat more apt than older workers to feel job pressures and overloads and to have depersonalizing and separating experiences with fellow workers and authorities. Even more powerful associations with age are found for those strains represented by scheduled life events. Thus, people leaving the work force to have or to care for families are usually young (and almost always women). It is typically the younger, too, who are either entering or re-entering the job market. The only predictable transition more commonly found among older than younger workers is, of course, retirement from work for reasons of age. Finally, the nonscheduled events, such as being fired, laid off, or demoted are almost exclusively the experiences of younger workers, as are promotion and movement between jobs. The only nonscheduled event occurring with disproportionate frequency among older people is retirement from work because of ill health. Overall, there is a very clear picture of younger workers more often having to confront the changes associated with the establishment, interruption, or advancement of career, of being vulnerable to occupational insecurities and disruptions, and of facing the more continuing and persistent problems of work. These findings suggest that the world of labor may become gentler with age.

Some of this picture changes when we examine marital strains, for these are somewhat more evenly distributed across the age span. As in occupation, the relatively persistent problems of marriage tend to be found among the younger wives and husbands. Thus, it is the younger married men and women who are particularly likely to see their spouses as failing to fulfill ordinary role expectations; they are also less likely to feel accepted by their spouses in a fashion that supports the valued elements of their self-image. The two scheduled transitions, being newly married and being widowed, are divided between extreme age groups, the first being predominantly an experience of the younger and the latter, of course, of the older. There is a similar age split involving, on the one hand, divorce and separation and, on the other, illness and disability, the former, expectedly, being mainly an experience of younger people and the latter of older people. In the parental area, we find that the persistent problems of child rearing are primarily confronted by younger parents. However, the transitional events occur across a wide age range, for they closely follow life-cycle developments. Thus, it is younger people who are becoming parents and seeing their children off to school and then through adolescence. But it is the older parents who see the departure of children from the household and into marriage.

An overview of the age distribution of the life strains described above reveals several patterns. Young adults simultaneously face the formidable tasks of having to establish themselves in their occupations, having to accommodate to marital relations that probably are not yet crystallized, and having to take responsibility for young children who of necessity are heavily dependent on them. Thus, chronic hardships and conflicts that can be found within these major social roles are much more likely to invade the lives of young adults, and to have been reconciled or left behind by the older adults. Some of the more undesirable nonscheduled events are also more common at younger ages, particularly those involving the loss of jobs and the termination of marriage by divorce and separation. By contrast, a number of the scheduled transitions are events experienced later in life, especially such life-cycle transitions as retirement, the loss of a spouse because of death, or the departure from the household of the last child.

Younger people, then, have more life strains to contend with, but they are frequently of a sort that dissipate with time. The strains faced by older people, although perhaps fewer in number, are more irreversible in their character. These differences make it difficult to judge on which group the greatest demands for adjustment fall. There is one matter of which we can be quite certain, however: as the adult part of the life span unfolds, people are exposed to a continuous, although shifting, flow of circumstances that challenge their adjustive capacities and have the potential for creating intense psychological distress. The study of adults, therefore, is to a large extent the study of conditions of work and of expressive relations as these engage people at different segments of the adult period of life, setting the stage for further psychological development.

Let us turn from the age distribution of the various life strains to a consideration of their emotional impact. The problems and vicissitudes that people encounter are not equal in their potential to arouse distress. On the contrary, we have observed considerable difference among them in this regard (Pearlin and Lieberman 1979). In the world of work, for example, it is the nonscheduled loss of job or job status that is most likely to result in anxiety and depression, emotional states that we have combined into a composite measure of distress. Thus those who have been fired or laid off in the four-year period between 1972 and 1976 are considerably more apt than those whose occupational life has been stable to experience distress. The coefficient of association for this relationship (gamma) is .31. Being demoted produces an even closer relationship (gamma = .41), and having to give up work because of poor physical health is most closely associated of all (gamma = .74). Somewhat surprising, retirement from work because of age has no appreciable consequence for emotional distress, but giving up work in order to have or care for a family does have fairly substantial consequences for distress (gamma = .30). Promotion and changes in place of employment, despite their being apparently desired events, still have significant positive (although quite modest) relationships (.14 and .22, respectively). Finally, each of the more persistent problems of work (with the exception of working in noise, dirt, or other noxious environmental conditions) has distressful effects, the most notable among them being problems with fellow workers and authorities (gamma = .32). It is noteworthy that those circumstances and events in the work world that are most emotionally painful are also those most likely to impinge on younger people.

Marital strains are somewhat different from those in occupation, for in this domain it is the more durable strains encountered in everyday marital relations that exert the greatest impact, not the scheduled or nonscheduled events. Thus the coefficient of association for the relationship of distress to divorce and separation is .23, and that of distress to widowhood, .31. By contrast, perceived failure of spouses to fulfill role expectations, to exercise reciprocities in the relationship, and to recognize and accept their partners as they want to be seen have coefficients of association with distress of .40, .34, and .40, respectively. Where marriage is concerned, therefore, it is evidently psychologically less disturbing to have the relationship terminated than to live out the relationship under conditions of frustration and conflict. New marriages have some special interest in this context. From one perspective they represent a transition to a new role whose importance persumably makes it capable of producing distress. Yet, from another perspective, being newly married means that the more chronic strains may not have had the opportunity to appear or become crystallized, thus minimizing psychological distress. The latter effect apparently prevails, for being newly wed has no statistically discernible deleterious psychological effects.

From the very few cases in our sample where the death of a child has occurred, it is evident that for parents to outlive a child is probably the most severe hardship that people can endure. On the other hand, there are a number of more common events of parenthood linked to the life cycle which, although often viewed as emotionally difficult, are not at all inimical to well-being. I refer to such events as the child's entrance into school, or completion of school, or of his departure from the parental home. Indeed, the marriage of a last child is to a notable extent negatively associated with emotional distress (gamma = −.21). The surge of well-being associated with seeing one's children married and out of the house may result not only from contemplating the delights of the empty nest but also from knowing that a succeeding generation is in the process of creating its own nests. Perhaps the caring for and commitment to succeeding generations, what Erik Erikson refers to as generativity ([1950] 1963), extends beyond one's children to embrace one's grandchildren as well. Whatever the reason, the confrontation by parents of the daily problems of child care and training is considerably more distressful than those transitional events signaling the growing independence of children and their final departure from the household.

These, then, are some of the principal relationships between life strains and psychological distress. But regardless of how well we succeed in identifying pivotal events and persistent problems in the various role sectors of adulthood, our ability to predict their emotional consequences will be limited if we do not also take into consideration how people cope with them.

Coping

It is fair to state that interest in coping far exceeds our knowledge about it. Because it has been approached from a variety of perspectives by scholars representing a variety of disciplines, the growth of our understanding of coping has not been cumulative. Our work differs from that of most others in that it emphasizes those elements of coping that are learned from and shared with the groups to which one belongs, ignoring the more idiosyncratic individual coping styles. But despite differences in their perspectives, all students of coping are in agreement, at least implicitly, that people are not merely passive targets of problems that arise in their lives, but that they actively respond to them in an effort to avoid being harmed by them. Largely because of these responses, emotional distress cannot be explained solely in terms of impinging life strains, for the manner in which people cope mediates the psychological consequences of the strains.

Although much remains to be discovered, a great deal has already been learned about coping from the 1972 data (Pearlin and Schooler 1978), more than can be presented in detail here. I shall confine myself to discussing the connections between the coping dispositions of individuals and the value system of the surrounding society. To understand these connections, it must be recognized that the most common mode of response to life strains is the employment of a large inventory of perceptual and cognitive devices enabling one to view one's problems as relatively innocuous. Essentially this entails defining a situation or problem in a manner that reduces its threat and consequently minimizes its stressful impact. This type of coping does not eradicate the problem itself; it controls and shapes the meaning that the problem has for the individual so that its stressful effects are buffered.

The control of meaning typically relies heavily on the selective use of socially valued goals and activities. Many illustrations can serve to explicate this statement. If a man is exposed to intense strain in his work, he may avoid distress by relegating work to a marginal place in his life, committing himself instead, for example, to being a good husband or father. Thus, adults not infrequently will move those roles in which there is painful experience to the periphery of importance, making more central those that are comparatively free of hardship. In rearranging their priorities, people temper stress by demeaning the importance of areas in which failure and conflict are occurring. This selective commitment to different areas of life is possible, first, because there is a temporal and spatial segregation of important roles, and, second, because societies offer a veritable smorgasbord of values to their members. It is the plethora of equally acceptable desiderata, each congenial to society's ideals, that makes it a simple matter to substitute one commitment for another. One doesn't *have* to be a dedicated worker; he will still be conforming to the cherished values of the society if he chooses instead to be a devoted father. And this option may save him a great deal of pain.

The rearrangement of priorities may take place within roles as well as between roles. A woman reports, for example, that when her husband drinks to excess, which is frequently, he becomes abusive toward her. When asked how she deals with this problem, she replies that she pays no attention to it, for in the things that really matter—being a steady worker and a good earner—he is a prince. One can predict what she would prize if he were an inadequate breadwinner but a considerate husband. And if the situation were reversed so that she did esteem her husband for his kindness and ignored his failure as a breadwinner, she would be no less adhering to social values.

The selective use of valued goals and activities to mold the meaning of circumstances is an easily available coping tool, commonly used and quite efficacious. But whereas this strategy functions to limit the intensity of emotional distress, other devices function more as strategies for enduring distress. The coping strategies of this type help people live with and manage distress without being overwhelmed by it. There are many devices that potentially serve this function, such as immersing oneself in television viewing (Pearlin 1959) or drinking for the relief of anxiety (Pearlin and Radabaugh 1976). Here, however, I shall focus on those distress management techniques that make use of widespread beliefs and precepts. Many of these find expression in commonly used and easily recognized adages that represent prescriptions for surviving stress. Some, for example, seem to promote a passive forebearance in the face of adversity with a promise of better things to come: "things always work out for the best," "time heals all wounds," and so on. Others urge that we "look on the positive side," or that we "count our blessings." Sometimes it is the problems of others that make us aware of our blessings. This is powerfully illustrated in Betty Rollin's account of her intense effort to adjust to her mastectomy. She relates that some weeks after her surgery a friend called and recited a litany of domestic problems. Rollin became involved in her friend's travails and describes how, following the telephone conversation, "it occurred to me that I was doing something I hadn't done for a long time. I was worrying about someone else. At last, I thought" (1976:188). Other people's miseries can lighten our own.

Other beliefs indicate that our suffering is an inherent part of the design of life, perhaps even a manifestation of higher purpose. Commonly used exhortations to "take the bad with the good," or that "it is meant to be" suggest that people attempt to cope with hardships by seeing them as preordained, part of a divine plan. This theme is poignantly expressed by miners' wives in interviews that are being conducted as part of an investigation into the ways people cope with this perilous occupation.[3] One woman whose husband was killed in a mine accident, for example, tells us that when she is depressed and asking herself why her husband died, she tells herself: "You know God doesn't make mistakes, you know that, so why are you acting like an idiot." She states: "Talking out loud to myself . . . does help." Societies, then, offer a potpourri of beliefs, and their selective use enables people not only to survive distress but to make a moral virtue of it. As might be guessed, coping at this level is more commonly found among older than younger adults.

There is a possibility that changes in adults' lives resulting from scheduled role transitions and those stemming from nonscheduled crises bring forth different coping modes. We have little empirical information to go on at this time, but there is reason to believe that the different types of life strains evoke coping efforts particularly suited to their nature. Thus the salient feature of role transitions is the predictability of their emergence; scheduled changes can be anticipated far in advance of their actual occurrence. We know about retirement before we receive our gold watches; we know something about marriage before the wedding ceremony. Because such role transitions are built into the life cycle, we begin learning about some of the changes they entail far ahead of the events themselves. Our adjustments to the conditions imposed by the loss and gain of roles thus depend to some extent on how accurately or with what distortions we foresee what we will later encounter. Effective coping with role transitions, therefore, would seem to depend on the role rehearsals that we conduct in our imaginations, the selection and use of role models, and other techniques that enable us to estimate how well present dispositions will fit with future demands. Where there is a perceived lack of congeniality between the present and the future, we engage in anticipatory adjustments. The success or failure of coping with transitions is very likely predetermined by the authenticity of the preparatory learning and the anticipatory adjustments people begin to make prior to the actual change.

Neither the selective use of values and beliefs to control meaning or to control distress itself—the responses I described earlier—nor the anticipatory role rehearsals used to contend with scheduled transitions would appear to be well-suited to coping with more sudden and eruptive life changes. Events of this sort lack the persistence needed for the crystallization of perceptual and cognitive adjustments; and because they also lack the predictability of the scheduled transitions, anticipatory preparation for the event is more difficult. How, then, do adults cope with eruptive conditions? It is in dealing with events having a crisis quality, perhaps, that people are most likely to engage in help-seeking behavior. The nature of the particular crisis, of course, has a great deal to do with what help people want and from whom they may seek it. To deal with some kinds of nonscheduled events, people, without necessarily being aware of it, may seek only subtle emotional support within an informal network of friends or family; for other problems they may turn to experts in the hope of receiving from them information or prescriptions for ameliorative actions. In any event, it is likely that seeking help, as in the case of other coping modes, is selectively invoked by adults in dealing with different kinds of exigencies and crises.

The adult portion of the life span, then, is peppered with socially generated life strains that differ with regard to their persistence and predictability. Many life strains may have their roots in the fundamental arrangements of society; but societies are at the same time also the source of many efficacious devices people use to withstand the full impact of the strains. Indeed, as varied as the life strains are, the ways of responding to them are richer yet. One learns from his experiences, from his membership groups, and from his culture a vast array of acceptable modes of anticipating, appraising, and meeting challenge. If these modes fail him, either because of their inherent lack of coping efficacy or because the challenging circumstances are not amenable to individual coping efforts, then he becomes vulnerable to psychic distress. But if one copes effectively, as people typically appear to do, then life strains may even have a positive contribution to one's development through the adult portion of the life span. Although much is still conjectural, we can be quite certain that to understand the well-being of adults, we need to observe the unfolding of the circumstances and events they experience, the meaning of the experience for them, and their attempts to avoid being harmed by it.

I have to this point deliberately omitted certain complexities so as to delineate more clearly the main currents of our work. One of these omissions concerns the reciprocity between the circumstances and events of life and psychological distress. Although I have talked of distress solely as following from life strains, there is a distinct possibility that distress, in addition to being an effect of life strains, is also an antecedent of strains. Even with the availability of longitudinal data such as ours, a great deal of care and rigor is required before the causal ordering of important social and psychological phenomena can be established. However, certain of our data, especially the discrete events that occurred in the lives of respondents in the four-year period between interviews, give some ready indication of what is causing what. By their very nature particular events can be considered as relatively impervious to influence by preexisting psychological dispositions. Being widowed may be taken as a suitable case in point. The coefficient of association (gamma) between the 1972 psychological distress level and subsequent widowhood is .19, but the coefficient between widowhood and the later, 1976 identical measure of distress is .32. It is remotely possible that preexisting distress could contribute to the demise of a spouse, but it is clearer, both because of the nature of the event and the magnitude of the associations, that the spouse's death is an antecedent condition for distress. Virtually all of the preliminary examinations made along these lines, including those of events that are less clearly susceptible to influence from prior distress, indicate a similar asymmetry of influence. Psychological distress, although it may very well contribute to future events, is more likely to result from conditions of life than to give shape to these conditions. However, it is clear that new methodologies are needed in order to reconstruct with confidence the processes by which social forces and events affect people, and by which people may come to affect the forces and events that play upon their lives.

Under special conditions, some events may lose their scheduled or nonscheduled distinctiveness; that is, many of the events that are ordinarily highly predictable may, in a given set of circumstances, lose their predictability. Consider a woman who, after years of trying to have children, becomes pregnant at the age of forty. Not only is she outside the remarkably clear timing norms for this kind of event (Neugarten, Moore, and Lowe 1965), but she may also feel that she is at some special risk. Consequently, an event easily anticipated and prepared for under usual circumstances can, under unusual circumstances of timing and meaning, become cloaked in uncertainty and doubt. Correspondingly, other events that are usually considered as eruptive crises may acquire the features of highly regular occurrences. Thus, a miner's wife relates that she anticipates that after ten years of work her husband will become ill with black lung disease. She is not merely engaging in gloomy guesswork in making this prediction, for this is what happened to her father and two uncles. A limiting illness at the age of about forty is, in these circumstances, a predictive event tied to a patterned occupational career. Where the meaning and nature of events are altered by special conditions, the effects of these events and the coping responses they evoke will probably also be altered.

Underlying many of the relationships that I have talked about is a question that merits consideration if we are better to understand adult development and change: what is it about events that creates anxiety and depression? One possible answer might hold that it is the undesirability of many events that explains their exacerbation of psychological distress. This does not stand up, however, for even events that are patently desirable, such as being promoted, are nonetheless still associated with distress. Another explanation might emphasize the loss entailed by certain events, that being separated from something that was once part of ourselves leads to emotional disturbances. This argument may have some merit, for several of the events most powerfully related to distress do involve the loss of role or status. Nevertheless, there are some losses—for example, those represented in the departure of children from the home or in retirement—that do not have deleterious effects. And if loss is painful, it could be reasoned that gain should be beneficial. But this is not the case, for there are some acquisitions, such as entering into a new occupation, that are capable of generating distress. A third explanation would assert that events impose an alteration in a delicate balance within us. Disequilibrium among our inner psychic forces, in turn, is an inherently intolerable condition that produces tension and other symptoms of distress that are likely to persist until a new equilibrium is established. This explanation, however, fails to explain the low level of distress following some quite dramatic changes, such as retirement or the emptying of the nest.

There is yet another possible explanation, one that we tested empirically. Events may not affect adults because they are unwanted, or invoke loss, or because they throw the organism out of delicate psychic balance. Instead, events promote emotional distress when they adversely alter the more durable conditions of life with which people have to contend. The effects of events, we suggest, are channeled through the structured circumstances that people have to grapple with over time. Considerable support for this interpretation emerged from the analysis of our data. Thus, in looking at certain events involving role loss, such as retirement, divorce, or widowhood, the loss itself matters far less to psychological well-being than the quality of experience one has in being newly retired, divorced, or widowed. For example, if retirees who are free of economic hardships and who enjoy ties to social networks are compared with those who have limited economic resources and are relatively isolated, it is only the latter who are found to possess the symptoms of distress. The same is true for those who are newly single, whether because of the death of a spouse or divorce: when the durable conditions of singlehood are benign, the yielding of the marital role does not arouse distress. Where newly single persons experience hardships, on the other hand, they are very likely to suffer intense distress. The injurious psychological effects of events entailing the movement from one role to another, therefore, appear to depend not on the loss or transition per se but almost entirely on conditions people live with at the end of their role passage. Change by itself does not affect emotional well-being; change that leads to hardships in basic, enduring economic and social conditions of life, on the other hand, does. Even those transitions brought about voluntarily may result in pain when they lead to negative conditions that are beyond one's ameliorative control.

In mulling over what we have learned from observing the distressful effects of life strains, we have addressed a question that is a fundamental concern of this book: Do problems in labor and in love intrude upon each other? More concretely, can one confront hardships in one's occupation without these eventually leading to strife in one's family relations; can one suffer frustration and conflict as a husband or wife, father or mother, without experiencing increased strains as a worker? On the one hand, people are whole, and it is difficult to think of important experiences occurring in one part of life without influencing the other parts. But on the other hand, there is a structural separation of social roles that enables people to segregate painful experiences arising in one role from the experiences arising within other roles. Our efforts to find the answers to this question are hardly final, but from evidence at hand it appears that disruptions of labor and love are indeed somewhat independent. Thus the intensity of strain a person experiences in his occupation bears relatively little relationship to those he experiences as a spouse or parent. To an appreciable extent adults apparently do contain strains and stresses in time and space; and this, in turn, says a great deal about the organization of coping behavior.

NOTES

1. This time in collaboration with Morton A. Lieberman of the Committee on Human Development at the University of Chicago.

2. I am grateful to Neil Smelser for suggesting these conceptual labels.

3. These are currently being conducted in collaboration with Nancy Datan and Carol Giesen of the Department of Psychology at West Virginia University.

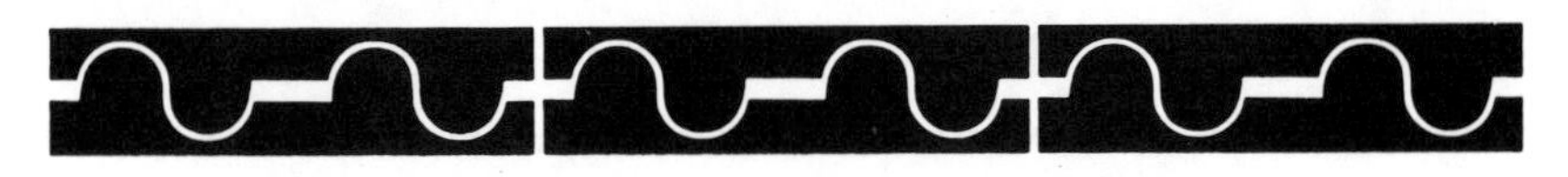

17

Some Modes of Adaptation: Defense

■

DAVID MECHANIC

As we see it, a person's behavior represents a more or less consistent pattern of response—what we call his *personality.* He attempts to maintain cognitive integration by controlling the information that enters the cognitive system and by making it congruent with his views and needs (Festinger 1957).

Organizing his behavior around attitudes of the self and the relations of the self to the external world, he deals not only with objective situations, but also with perceived subjective threats. The information that enters the cognitive system may be relevant or irrelevant, important or unimportant to the task at hand or to the attitudes the person holds about himself in relation to the task. In instances where relevant information does enter the system, the individual either may integrate it into his cognitive orientation or attempt to reject it. In doing this he seeks various kinds of support from others in the communication structure of which he is a part and from cues which he finds in his environment.

The system of defenses described by the classical psychoanalytic theorists attempts to indicate *what* occurs, but tells us little that is clear as to *how* this occurs. Thus, whereas the descriptions of behavior

TABLE 17.1
Perceived Importance of Defending Against Stress by Students and Faculty

Items	*Percent of Students Responding Very or Fairly Important (N-22)*	*Percent of Faculty Responding Very or Fairly Important (N-21)*
Ability to remain relaxed	68	29
Ability to work under pressure	100	76

—repression, denial, projection, intellectualization, and so on—sensitize us to these happenings, the conditions under which these distortions occur and how they develop remain unclear.

A step in the direction of solving this problem has been provided by some interesting studies by David Hamburg and his associates (Hamburg, Hamburg, and deGoza 1953). Studying the adaptive processes of badly burned soldiers, they observed that many of the adaptive processes were social—that these processes involved communication as well as cognition, and that cognitive defenses were associated with environmental cues. These insightful papers suggested that perhaps we might learn a good deal more if we would attempt to understand the social and social-psychological contexts within which defense occurs.

The Need for Defense

The students under study most definitely saw stress as a major factor in the challenge of passing the examinations. Many of them believed that if they could defend adequately and maintain their anxiety at some comfortable level, they would be adequate in their performance. Both students and faculty were asked to indicate the importance of the ability to remain relaxed and the ability to work under pressure for students taking preliminary examinations. The difference in perception of stress as a factor was quite considerable when viewed through the eyes of students and faculty in table 17.1.

Since students do find that preparation is a major factor in reducing anxiety, tasks that keep them from working on examination preparation were likely to raise their anxiety level. We expected, therefore,

TABLE 17.2
Rated Importance of the Ability to Put Aside Everything for Studies by Students and Faculty

	Percent Responding Very or Fairly Important
Students (N-22)	91
Faculty (N-21)	38

that students would think it more important than faculty to put aside everything for their studies in order to pass the examinations. And, as analysis of table 17.2 shows, they did just this.

Comforting Cognitions and Favorable Social Comparison

The most consistently observed defense device used by the students under study was that of seeking comforting information from the environment that was consistent with the attitudes and hopes the student held about the examinations. Often these comforting cognitions were made on the basis of comparing oneself favorably with others, or by finding cues in the environment that made the person more confident about his situation. A number of these comforting cognitions have already been pointed to in preceding chapters. For example: "most students who had failed preliminary examinations in the past had had difficult personalities"; "the faculty expects less from this year's group as compared with earlier ones because most of the people in the present group have been here for only two years."

This is not to say that what is necessarily comforting for one student is comforting for all. But in general the persons who most often verbalized these attitudes were those for whom they were most comforting as measured by other criteria. For example, as we have pointed out, the attitude concerning the faculty expecting less of second-year students was developed and communicated by second-year students. It is true that one or two of the older students also accepted this idea, but these students had little to lose by its acceptance. In addition, the fact that a belief may be accurate does not invalidate it as a defense; on the contrary, accurate beliefs are valuable as defenses because they do have

TABLE 17.3
Students' Reported Use of Comforting Cognitions

	PERCENT OF STUDENTS	
Comforting Cognitions	*Who Report Using This Cognition Very or Fairly Often*	*Who Report Using These Cognitions With any Frequency*
I'm as bright and knowledgeable as other students who have passed these examinations	64	91
I've handled test situations in the past—there's no good reason why not now	59	86
I am doing all I can to prepare—the rest is not up to me	50	86
I wouldn't have gotten this far unless I knew something	50	86
I'm well liked in this department	45	77
I've already demonstrated my competence on past work, they will pass me	26	77
You can't fail these examinations unless you really mess up	23	73
They wouldn't fail me—they've already decided I'm going to pass	18	30
This is a test of stress; I can deal with that	14	59
If I'm not cut out for the field, it's best that I know it now	14	55

environmental support. Thus, while the inaccurate defenses may be more striking to the observer, they are probably more likely to lead to later problems of adaptation. The student who can draw satisfaction from the fact that he is competent and that others think him competent is in a better position than the student who holds this as an illusion.

A number of comforting thoughts, verbalized in early interviews with the students, were included in the questionnaire administered to students. They were asked to indicate how often they had felt, thought, said, or done each of a number of things (*see* table 17.3).

The assurance that occurred most frequently resulted from favorable social comparison—a student compared himself with other students who had taken examinations in prior years and passed, and told himself that he was as knowledgeable or more so than the student with whom he was comparing himself. Others *drew on past experience,* and, by reassuring themselves of their competence in the past, they felt more competent in the present: "I wouldn't have gotten this far unless I knew something," "I've handled situations in the past," and other such similar statements. Still others saw themselves as well liked, and almost all of the students believed to some extent that if you were liked, your chances of having a good outcome on the examinations were better. Others sought to externalize responsibility: "If I am doing all I can, what's the use of worrying?" Let us take some examples from the interviews to illustrate how the student verbalized these comforting comparisons and cognitions.

> I think I'll pass because I think that if decisions have been made previously, that I'm one who will pass rather than fail. . . . So I'll really have to botch up writtens to get them to alter their opinion of me. . . . I evaluate the people on the faculty as being reasonable people . . . who should make reasonable demands for performance on writtens which I should be able to meet.

> [I was saying] that we are pretty scared of the questions that were asked on the old examinations and yet we haven't seen the answers that people have given to these questions to see what they were like; to see the quality of the answers—the answers which were acceptable in terms of passage. Perhaps, if we were able to see some of the answers that have been acceptable, we would feel a little better. I don't feel that we are significantly more defective than other people who have passed these . . . or that we worked any less. From this standpoint, it would seem that our chances of passing are just as good as those who passed.

> I was afraid that reading so few books wouldn't be enough. Then I found out that other people were reading these and felt secure with them. Now I feel better.

> It seems that people pass [the examinations] pretty easily.

> I have a much better memory than most people.

> [I tell] myself how clever I am. . . . I usually have done better. I think it contributes to my normal state of well-being.

> Considering the people who passed previously, I think my chances are at least even.

Hundreds of such statements came up in the interviews with students. The examples took many forms, and enumerating them would be unnecessary for our argument. What is important to recognize is that these beliefs arose in the interaction process; they were exchanged back and forth among students, and many were held commonly and were consensually validated.

This is not to suggest that all social comparisons are favorable. As we indicated earlier, social comparison often aroused anxiety. It is through social comparison processes that the individual attempts to ascertain both his strengths and his weaknesses, and to evaluate what soft spots need plugging. The student who fails to take part in this type of social comparison can lose considerable information about the examinations and possible modes of preparation, although as a result he may be able to keep his anxiety at a lower level. This was especially true of two, low-anxiety, isolated students who were not comparing themselves to others, and who had little idea how much others were studying. Both of these students studied considerably less than the rest of the group, and both performed at a level below the expectations of faculty. One of these two students had communicated and compared himself so little with others, that he had no idea that other students were aiming to pass at the Ph.D. level. All along, he prepared casually, feeling that he would be satisfied attaining an M.A. pass. After the examinations the student became considerably agitated about his performance, knowing that had he set his expectations higher he might have performed better and closer to the expectations others had of him. The reactions of these two low-anxiety persons were somewhat similar to the reactions that Grinker and Spiegel (1945:128) observed among some soldiers: "One sometimes sees men who err in the opposite direction and fail to interpret danger when they should. As a consequence, they are protected against developing subjective anxiety. . . . The defect in discrimination gives them the appearance of being unrealistic and slap-happy, illustrating the maxim that fools walk where angels fear to tread."

It is thus the process of social comparison that allows the student to pace himself. For example, one student decided a few weeks prior to examinations to postpone them until the following fall. Notice how social comparison was a prime influence in this decision.

> I think, to a great degree, interacting with people like you who keep asking me what I am doing and other people who are doing things, sort of hearing that certain people are reading this, that, and the other, has kind of gotten me to the point of feeling that I'm not preparing for them like other people are. I really don't have a chance to. Maybe

it would be best that I didn't take them at all rather than take them and not do so well. . . . I talked to a couple of people, [student *X*] and [student *Y*], in Central Building, and I've heard some from my office partner who knows [students *A*, *B*, and *C*] who are taking them and he related some of the things that they are doing. I feel, myself, that I would like to do some of these things . . . I don't have the time this semester. . . . So these sorts of things have gotten me to think that I'm not preparing too well. And I think that it would be best that I don't take them at all.

Joking and Humor

Joking as a useful form of defense has been given considerable attention by philosophers, psychologists, and humorists, but only in recent years have its social functions been noted to any significant degree. In recent studies by Coser (1959), Fox (1959), and Hamburg and associates (Hamburg, Hamburg, and deGoza 1953) on the hospital ward, some of the social functions of joking under stress have been pointed out.

Four weeks prior to examinations students were asked to indicate how much they joked about examinations. Every student indicated that he had joked to some extent.

The older students who were more anxious and more upset about examinations seemed to find it more difficult to find humor in the examination situation.

Since joking is an interpersonal event and may serve as an avoidance device in interaction, we would expect that joking about examinations would be more likely to arise among the second-year students, who are more centrally located in the communication structure, than among those more isolated. Table 17.6 confirms this.

It appears that joking occurred primarily among those who were

TABLE 17.4
The Extent of Student Joking About Examinations

Extent of Joking	*Percent of Students (N-22)*
Joked a great deal	23
Joked some	54
Joked not very much	23
Joked none	—

TABLE 17.5
Student Status and Joking

	PERCENT OF STUDENTS WHO JOKED		
	A Great Deal	*Some*	*Not Very Much*
Older students (N-8)	—	62	38
Second-year students (N-14)	36	50	14

high-moderate and moderate-anxiety types. Students who were very anxious, with some exceptions, did not see the examinations as humorous as did some of the moderate-anxiety students. This was true especially of the older students who felt that they had suffered considerably in going through the process; yet it did appear that humor was an important mode of anxiety reduction. Also it seemed that joking occurred most frequently at certain points in time. For example, it seemed to increase in intensity just prior to the week of examinations, and the form that it took also seemed to change. Well before examinations, joking consisted mainly of poking fun at the material—a form of tension release. As examinations approached, however, tension-release humor still was present, but avoidance banter seemed to increase in significant quantity. A possible explanation for the change in the kind of joking forms was that as the examinations approached, time pressures increased and students became aware that time for future coping effort was limited. Therefore, a useful defense would allow for avoidance of serious discussion about examinations and avoidance of the

TABLE 17.6
Joking Among Second-Year Students and Centrality in the Comunication Structure *

	PERCENT OF STUDENTS WHO JOKED		
Degree of Centrality	*A Great Deal*	*Some*	*Not Very Much*
Three or more communication links (N-6)	67	33	—
Less than three communication links (N-8)	12	63	25

* This relationship did not hold among older students. Having three or more communication links was atypical of older students.

kinds of anxiety stimuli that were discussed in an earlier chapter. For example, a few days prior to examinations, it would be of little use for a student to discover that five important textbooks had been read by others while he had spent his time on less significant details. Joking as an avoidance technique allowed for keeping further information that might have been disruptive out of one's frame of reference.

Before going on to describe and give some examples of the kinds of humor that developed, the reader should be warned that he might not find student humor terribly humorous. Humor is highly situational, and often specific to those sharing a common frame of reference. Regardless of how the jokes appear to the reader, they were in fact funny from the student's perspective.

Joking as a Form of Tension Release

Joking is a useful device to reduce tensions resulting from uncertainty. One of the more common problems for students in dealing with examinations is the uncertainty they feel as to which questions or areas will appear on examinations and the sampling used in choosing these questions. Students feel that it is conceivable that one can know an area well yet encounter an examination where he cannot answer the questions. Put in another way, students believe that an element of chance is operating, that the student may be lucky or unlucky in the questions he encounters. In the student story that follows, the uncertainty in the examination process was made to appear ludicrous.

> I heard a cute story the other day about the manner in which certain people go around assigning questions for the examinations. . . . He grabs down a great big book and goes thumbing through it and happens to pick up one little area, one little section in the bottom of the page in the middle of the volume. And he says: "Hmmmm, this strikes my fancy. I've never seen this before. I think I'll put this on the examinations and see what they could tell me about this."

One of the situations found most amusing by the students concerned a discussion about a possible question on examinations. As the reader will remember, most of the students felt that if you do not know the answer to a question, you still should attempt to write something. The situation described below deals with a discussion of this strategy.

> When I walked into the Monday class, everyone was joking around . . . [student *D*] was telling us his point of view of what he would do

> if he didn't know a question. . . . He would give another answer to it. . . . The other fellows said, "Okay, we'll test you out. What is the [Spencer] hypothesis?" or some obscure thing I never heard of. And so [student *D*] sort of laughed and said, "Well, I never heard of that but I'm sure getting familiar with the [Zipp] effect."
>
> [Later student *D*] came in and said, "Okay, I found out what [Spencer] is." And [student *A*], who doesn't take our other course, said "WHAT???" And everybody said, "You better be sure you know that, that's very important." And someone said it was such and such and such. And somebody else turned around and said, "What is its presents status?" and everybody laughed.

Here again, the question, "What is its present status?" was experienced by the group as a humorous remark. This is probably due to the fact that many of the questions on doctoral examinations ask students to discuss the development and present status of various concepts. In a sense the group was having a good laugh over the examinations and, to some extent, over the stereotyped forms the questions sometimes take.

Another source of humor was the obscure items that students often pick up in their reading for examinations, that they then go around and jokingly ask other students about. In a sense this represents a take-off on the anxiety-arousing effect students have on one another, and also is sometimes used as a device to hide one's own anxiety about examinations. Below are some examples:

> Generally we joke about things that don't mean too much . . . and obscure things. [Student *F*] said something like, did I know that the average visual acuity of an eight-year-old elephant was the same as a female horse?
>
> He came across a little bit about Meyer, the photosensitive crab. So this seemed like a particular bit of nonsensical information which he passed all over the department. "You got to know about Meyer." It has kind of been the joke of the week.

One of the students who participated a great deal in joking described what he perceived to be the function of joking about examinations.

> All of this doesn't mean anything. It's not going to be useful in preparing for the writtens . . . but I think it's a tension-reducing mechanism. It keeps you from getting too serious about them, in a sense, letting the thing get the better of you, which I'm sure has happened to some people in the past, and I'm sure it has had an adverse effect.

Students also made seemingly silly comments to one another, or thought of funny comments they might make. Apparently this made the whole process seem a little more unreal, a little less serious.

> I was thinking about walking in on the first examination and yelling, "Hey, I thought this was going to be multiple choice."

"Sick" Humor

This type of humor is represented by jokes about failing. Usually these jokes involve saying, "I'm going to fail, ha, ha, ha," or "We'll fail and then we can go out and kill ourselves." By attaching an absurdity to the situation, the student seemed to make the real situation and the threat it presented more remote and more impossible.

Another kind of "sick" humor pertained to what the student should do should he fail. Once again the same function was apparent. By making the possibilities absurd, failure seemed more remote.

> [Student *C*] said, "Next year at this time, I'll be getting ready to get out of this place, and I'll be looking for a job." And I said, "Yeah, next year at this time I might be selling shoes." Someone else said, "Yeah, if it weren't for these writtens."
>
> We got into a discussion, you know, how I always wanted to sell shoes. . . . A lot of talk is this sort of humorous thing about it.

Whether the jokes were concerned with selling shoes or picking cotton, their intent was the same: to debunk the seriousness of the possible outcomes. This could take various forms; for example, one student usually referred to the examinations as the "spring quizzes."

Joking as an Avoidance Device

Joking is one of the most effective methods for avoiding a serious discussion. Certainly anyone who has ever tried to have a serious discussion with a person who insists on being jovial will realize how effective humor may be as an avoidance device. It allows an individual to fend others off in a friendly but effective fashion, and it makes them keep their distance. It also can be used as a form of attack on others, and should they object, one always can have the recourse to "I was only joking." It is this ambiguous function of joking that allows one to attempt attack and avoidance without making himself too vulnerable to being charged with his offense. One student explained how joking might be utilized in this fashion:

> When [student *X*] comes in, he wants to talk seriously about the examinations. But I don't want to talk seriously about them because I feel that I'm not going to pass and that isn't very funny. Another thing is that I don't want to tell him that I don't think I'm going to pass. . . . [Student *X*], he's pretty serious and I tease him. He comes in and asks, "What are you studying for statistics?" And I spend the next five minutes reeling off all this nonsense (laughs), and he's getting more and more anxious. He just bothers most people more because he is serious. He's pretty anxious really. . . . Everybody is just real childish and real silly. It's easier to be funny than to be serious.

The joking playfulness one can observe here combined teasing, hostility, and anxiety avoidance. One student, for example, related how he became very anxious after he had found a question he could not answer on an old examination. After asking another student if he knew the answer, he reported that the other student also became anxious, and, feeling that he had done his duty, he went to bed. Another student, from the viewpoint of the recipient of the comunication, related a somewhat similar situation:

> When I try to study in the office, somebody will come up to me and say, "What are you studying? What are you studying?" When I tell them, they say, "Oh, you don't want to study that. What do you want to study that for?" And they'll go on. It makes me angry. They're doing it because they feel threatened sort of . . . Everyone wants to be sure that nobody knows anything more than they do . . . So instead you tease.

One student who generated considerable anxiety, and who a number of students were avoiding, was sometimes heavily sanctioned by names. This was done to discourage his serious attitude toward examinations, which made the other students anxious.

Students also did a considerable bit of clowning.

> [Student *B*] was on a jag a couple of weeks ago. Every time someone walked into the room, he asked them, "Why are you so hostile to me?" . . . It's just easier to keep laughing. It doesn't bother you as much to joke about it.

This kind of joking, especially among one of the cliques, continued until writtens began, and then to some extent seemingly subsided. At any rate, there was an apparent decrease in the hostile jabbing that had taken place just before the examinations. Once examinations started, however, students became more genuinely friendly to one another and supported one another more than they had at any prior period. It would appear that once the examinations had begun, and some of the tension was reduced, the competitive jockeying was no longer necessary. The clearly defined threat now was not other students but the examinations themselves. And the group seemed to unite against this threat.

. . .

A Dynamic View of Feelings and Behavior as Examinations Approach

As the examinations approached and as student anxiety increased, various changes occurred in behavior. Joking increased, and, while students still sought social support and talked a great deal about examinations, they began specifically to avoid certain people who aroused their anxiety. Stomach aches, asthma, and a general feeling of weariness became common complaints, and other psychosomatic symptoms appeared. The use of tranquilizers and sleeping pills became more frequent.

For those who had started studying intensively at an early date, exhaustion crept in and they lost their desire and motivation to study.

> I just don't seem to be picking up things. you know, like I'll look over stuff and I just don't seem to get it. It's very depressing to spend time and not feel it's doing any good. . . . I just wish they would get them over with. It's just bugging me. . . . I'm getting tired of sitting at that desk. I have all sorts of psychosomatic complaints. My back hurts and so forth. . . . I wish they were over. They're so awful. . . . I was about ready to turn myself into [the psychiatric ward] but now I'm taking antidepressant pills.

A number of other students also complained of an inability to concentrate on their studies:

> My minute-to-minute motivation seems to have gone down. When I started, I was a real eager beaver but now it seems, the last week or so, I've had a little trouble. If I have a half hour off, I'll sit in the social room rather than study for that half hour.

> Lately I've been feeling depressed. I don't feel that I know anything. I just feel so mentally defective, like what I have done goes into one ear and out the other. . . . Instead of putting in a last-ditch effort, I can't. I'm just sort of tired of the whole business. I'm tired of studying. I'm tired of school. I'm just tired.

While the student feels saturated with study, he still is acutely aware of the short time available for further preparation. Thus he is torn between the feeling that he must study and his inability to concentrate and study effectively, which leads to considerable anxiety, self-doubt, and disgust. As anxiety reaches a high level, students come to agreements not to discuss examinations, but as the saliency of examinations is too great these agreements are rarely maintained. Also, the excessive concern about examinations is reflected in dreams about them. Unreality is another common feeling, the "this isn't happening to me" effect.

As examinations approach, the most common feeling is one of unpreparedness and impending disaster, although these reports of impending doom usually are disqualified in some way. The student, for example, will predict doom and then declare that he must be pretty stupid to say something as silly as that. Listed below are some of the indications students gave that failure was imminent.

> I feel now, rather unrealistically, I think, that I can't remember any names. I can't remember this. I can't remember that. I feel unprepared for this.
>
> I spoke to [student *C*] . . . about how depressed we were. . . . The main thing he hopes is that they'll let him take them again. He keeps saying this over and over because he's now in one of these stages which I think we all go through, where you just feel that there's no possibility of passing and that you are a failure.
>
> I kept having the feeling like I'm going to fail and that I don't know anything.

When the examinations are nearly upon the student, anxiety is very high, even for those rated as low-anxiety persons, although students do fluctuate between confidence and anxiety. Since studying is difficult, the student questions his motivation, interest, and ability in the field. He reassures himself that he does not care how well he does—that all he really wants out of the process is the Ph.D. degree. Even four weeks prior to examinations 82 percent of the students reported that they had said to themselves, "All I really want from this process is the Ph.D. degree." They attempted to defend against their feelings by behaving in a silly, manic way, and avoidance joking became very prevalent. Expectation levels were set lower and lower, and many of the students jokingly talked about what they were going to do after they failed or how they were going to prepare for examinations the next time they took them. It appears that for the student supreme confidence at this point was considered not only presumptuous, but sacrilegious. Under these conditions the group became very cohesive and individuals became supportive of one another and exclusive of younger students in the department. . . .

18

Uncertainty and the Lives of Persons with AIDS

■

ROSE WEITZ

Uncertainty exists whenever people lack a cognitive framework for understanding their situations and thus feel that they cannot predict the outcomes of their behaviors. At least as far back as Malinowski ([1926] 1948), researchers have recognized that few people tolerate uncertainty well; therefore most people seek ways to reduce it or, if that is not possible, to cope with it. Researchers have identified means of dealing with uncertainty as disparate as developing magical rituals (Felson and Gmelch 1979) and gathering scientific information about the consequences of various possible actions (Janis and Mann 1977). Most recently, scholarly interest in uncertainty has produced a vast literature on how persons perceive and respond to the risks of natural and technological disasters (e.g., Douglas and Wildavsky 1982; National Research Council 1982; Slovic, Fischhoff, and Lichtenstein 1977).

Medical sociologists have long recognized that uncertainty is a criti-

This research was made possible by a grant from the Arizona Disease Control Research Commission and by a small grant from the Arizona State University College of Liberal Arts and Sciences. The comments of Peter Conrad, Rochelle Kern, Karolynn Siegel, and the anonymous reviewers were much appreciated, as was the research assistance of Kathleen Abbott, Melissa Bolyard, and Shirley Philp.

cal issue for chronically and terminally ill persons (Conrad 1987:7–9; Glaser and Strauss 1968) and a major source of stress in their lives (Mishel 1984; Mishel et al. 1984; Molleman et al. 1984). To cope with this uncertainty, such persons, like others in stressful situations, can use two basic strategies: vigilance and avoidance.

In vigilance, persons attempt to reduce uncertainty by seeking knowledge and acting on that knowledge. For example, ill persons whose physicians prove unable to diagnose their problems can research possible diagnoses themselves (Schneider and Conrad 1983; Stewart and Sullivan 1982). Once their illnesses are identified, they can reduce uncertainty about why disease has struck them and about what they can expect in the future by searching for similarities between their cases and those of fellow sufferers (Comaroff and Maguire 1981; Cowie 1976; Roth 1963; Schneider and Conrad 1983; Wiener 1975).

In avoidance, people cope with uncertainty by protecting themselves against unpleasant knowledge. For example, many ill persons deal with uncertainty about the meaning of their initial symptoms by attributing those symptoms to less serious ailments or to preexisting illnesses and by avoiding any contact with physicians (Cowie 1976; Schneider and Conrad 1983). Even after they seek medical care, they may prefer not to know their diagnoses or prognoses and may ignore persons who propose pessimistic definitions of their situations (Comaroff and Maguire 1981; McIntosh 1976).

Although these two strategies may appear antithetical, they are linked in fact by a common goal: the construction of normative frameworks that enable individuals to explain their situations to themselves. These frameworks give people the sense that they understand what has happened and will happen to them. By making the world seem predictable, these frameworks help individuals to choose (albeit sometimes from among limited options) how they will live their lives. Thus even when normative frameworks are factually inaccurate and when the resulting actions seem short-sighted or self-destructive, I would hypothesize that these frameworks reduce the stresses of uncertainty, for they enable people to feel that they are at least minimally in control of their lives. In this chapter I suggest that in the final analysis, it is this sense of control which enables people to tolerate uncertainty.

AIDS and Uncertainty

This chapter describes how uncertainty affects persons with AIDS (or PWAs, as they call themselves), and how they cope with that uncertainty. Few published research studies have analyzed the experiences of PWAs; none has looked specifically at the issue of uncertainty. Instead the social science literature on AIDS consists largely of quantitative studies regarding why people do or do not change their sexual behavior to protect themselves against infection (reviewed in Becker and Joseph 1988).

Because most medical authorities believe that AIDS eventually kills all its victims, it may seem that uncertainty is not an issue for PWAs. As this chapter will show, however, uncertainty affects PWAs in several ways.[1] Even before health problems appear, persons who are at risk for AIDS must wonder whether they will develop the disease. Once symptoms become evident, PWAs are uncertain how to interpret and respond to those symptoms. After they receive their diagnoses, PWAs must question why this calamity has befallen them. Because AIDS causes unpredictable flare-ups and remissions, PWAs face uncertainty each morning about how ill they will be that day. As their illness progresses, they also experience anxiety about whether they will be able to live with dignity even though they are ill, about whether AIDS eventually will kill them. Finally, those who conclude that death is inevitable must wonder whether they will be allowed to die with dignity.[2] This chapter will describe how PWAs seek control over these uncertainties and how their illness impairs their ability to do so.

Methods and Sample

Between July 1986 and March 1987, I interviewed 25 Arizona residents who had either AIDS or AIDS-related complex (ARC).[3] Four to six months after the initial interviews, I reinterviewed 13 respondents. (Two respondents declined to participate in the follow-up interviews, two moved without leaving addresses, and eight died or suffered brain damage in the interim). Two of the 25 respondents were heterosexual women who had used intravenous drugs. The rest were men, all of whom described themselves as gay or bisexual (although none mentioned any recent relationships with women). Three of these men also had used drugs. The data presented in this paper come from the 23 initial and 11 follow-up interviews with gay and bisexual men, except where noted otherwise.

At the time I began the study, the Arizona Department of Health Services had confirmed 110 reports of AIDS cases. State officials believed that approximately 40 of these persons were still living, as well as an unknown number of persons with ARC. Because AIDS is still rare in Arizona, the situation of PWAs there is very different from that in places like New York or California, where most of the previous research on PWAs has taken place. Research conducted in Arizona can help us to understand what it is like to have AIDS in an area which lacks a politically powerful gay community and in which AIDS is just beginning to have an impact. Therefore this study can help us to predict what the lives of PWAs will be like in the future, as the disease spreads from the current centers of infection to more conservative and more typical areas of the country.

Most respondents learned of this study through letters mailed to them by the Arizona AIDS Project (N = 15) or the Tucson AIDS Project (N = 4), two nonprofit groups that offer emotional and financial support to PWAs. To increase sample size and diversity I posted signs in gay bars, placed announcements in gay newspapers and in the mainstream press, and announced the study in AIDS political action groups. I also asked several physicians and AIDS support group counselors to inform their clients of the study. Finally, I asked my respondents to give my name to any other PWAs they knew. No names were given to me by any source; instead, PWAs were invited to contact me if they wanted to participate.

The sample is comparable to the state population in regard to religion and is comparable to the population of reported Arizona AIDS cases in regard to sex, geographical location (overwhelmingly urban), and mode of transmission (Arizona Department of Health Services 1987). Because participation in the interviews required both mental competence and some physical stamina, the sample undoubtedly underrepresents the more seriously ill PWAs. It also underrepresents persons with Kaposi's sarcoma (8 percent of the sample but 21 percent of reported cases), perhaps because these individuals did not want a stranger to see their disfigurement. In addition, the sample underrepresents nonwhites (0 percent of the sample but 13 percent of reported cases), who typically are less well integrated into the AIDS support networks and therefore were less likely to have heard of the study. Finally, the sample overrepresents persons in their thirties (60 percent of the sample but 42 percent of reported cases) and underrepresents older persons. Unfortunately, there is no way of knowing how well the state's statistics on reported AIDS cases reflect the actual distribution of AIDS cases.

The data for this chapter were obtained through semistructured interviews. I entered each interview with a preset list of questions, but also probed any new topics that arose during the interview. Initial interviews ranged from two to five hours in length and averaged about three hours; follow-up interviews were considerably shorter. All interviews were audiotaped and transcribed, and took place at respondents' homes unless they preferred another location (usually my home). I attempted to ask all questions and to respond to all answers in an unbiased and nonjudgmental manner, whether my respondent was describing sadomasochistic homosexual behavior or fundamentalist Christian theology. I believe that I was successful in that no respondents acted hostilely, broke off the interviews (except from physical exhaustion), or suggested in any other way that they felt uncomfortable in discussing these issues with me.

Following the suggestions of Glaser and Strauss (1967), I analyzed the data using categories that I developed from the respondents' descriptions of their situations. After each interview I revised the interview schedule to focus it more closely on these emerging themes. When the themes were collapsed and reorganized, they formed the structure of this chapter.

Findings

Uncertainty affects PWAs at many levels. From the time when they realize that they are at risk, they must question whether they will contact AIDS. Once they start to have symptoms, they must wonder what those symptoms signify. And once they are diagnosed, they must question why they have contracted AIDS and whether they will be able to function tomorrow, to live with dignity, to "beat" AIDS, or to die with dignity. The following sections show how these uncertainties affect PWAs and how they cope with their situations.

"Will I get AIDS?"

Fear of contracting AIDS permeates the lives of many gay and bisexual men. Finding this uncertainty too much to endure, several respondents dealt with their fear by assuming that they were infected long before they were diagnosed. The rest, however, had lived through long months of anxiety about whether they would become ill; although they could change their behavior to protect themselves against future infection, they could not stop the disease's development if they were infected already.

Unable truly to control their health prospects, these men coped with uncertainty about whether they would contract AIDS by finding ways at least to *feel* that they were in control of their lives. They did so by developing theories that explained why they were not really at risk, despite their behaviors. Typically these theories suggested that AIDS attacks only physically weak, "promiscuous" persons, who choose their partners unwisely. The theories also emphasized that AIDS occurs only elsewhere. One Phoenix resident explained that he and his friends had not followed safe sex guidelines because they had convinced themselves that "there's only nine people in Arizona that have it and four of them are dead and two of them live in Tucson. So what are your chances? Even though we knew about it and we knew how awful it was, it was like, no, that's something that happens someplace else, not in Phoenix."

As more cases of AIDS appeared, however, these theories provided less comfort (especially for the nine respondents who had seen friends or lovers die). As a result, most found themselves alternately denying and brooding on the risks they had taken. Emotionally they were unable to accept the fact that they might die from a dread disease; yet intellectually they could not reject the possibility. One man shifted in a matter of moments from describing how his fear of contacting AIDS had kept him awake nights to describing how he "thought it would never happen to me."

Beginning in mid-1985, Arizonans could eliminate some uncertainty by having their blood tested to learn whether they had been exposed to the AIDS virus. The test could reduce uncertainty significantly for those who tested negative. For those who tested positive, however, the test merely replaced one form of uncertainty with another because it could not show whether they would develop AIDS. Moreover, a positive test result could increase stigma and anxiety significantly (Beeson, Zones, and Nye 1986; Moulton 1985). As a result, all but two of the men decided that they would feel more in control of their destinies if they refused to obtain such potentially ambiguous knowledge. As one said, "I figured if I was tested and tested positive, I'd worry myself into coming down with it, . . . so I decided against it. . . . If I came down with it, I came down with it, and I'd have to worry about it then."

"What Do My Symptoms Mean?"

People who have been infected with AIDS may remain asymptomatic, and therefore ignorant that they are infected, for several years. Once symptoms start to appear, however, these individuals must decide what the symptoms mean and how or whether they should react.

Because symptoms generally build gradually, PWAs at first can accommodate to the difficulties they cause. As a result, like persons who develop other chronic illnesses (Bury 1982:170; Cowie 1976:88; Schneider and Conrad 1983; Stewart and Sullivan 1982), they may explain their symptoms initially using preexisting cognitive frameworks which minimize the symptoms' importance. Several men blamed their night sweats and exhaustion on the Arizona heat. Others confused the symptoms of AIDS with the side effects of drug use; both can cause weight loss, sweating, and diarrhea. Although these theories eventually proved wrong, in the interim they allowed the men to feel that they understood their situations and thus helped them to reduce stress.

Although in some cases the men minimized their symptoms out of ignorance, in other cases they appeared to have chosen consciously or unconsciously to downplay their symptoms because they preferred uncertainty to the certainty of the AIDS diagnosis. One individual explained that he did not go to a physician despite a variety of symptoms because "I didn't want to find out I had AIDS. Even though I kind of figured I did, I didn't want to know. I wanted to live a normal life for as long as I could." By avoiding the physicians he was able to assert control over his emotional well-being despite his lack of control over his physical well-being.

Those who minimize their symptoms for whatever reason may defer seeing a physician for some time. As the disease progresses, however, they find eventually that they can neither control their bodies nor maintain their everyday living patterns. Once they reach this point, PWAs can no longer maintain their cognitive frameworks and are motivated to seek diagnosis and treatment.

As they discover soon, however, seeing a physician does not necessarily end their uncertainty. Many physicians simply lack the knowledge needed to diagnose AIDS (Lewis, Freeman, and Corey 1987). Others may not consider diagnoses of AIDS unless they know that their clients are at risk, even if their clients' symptoms fit the classic patterns for AIDS. Yet clients may not disclose that they are at risk for fear of the social consequences.

Even if physicians have the intellectual knowledge to diagnose AIDS, they may lack the emotional ability to do so. Several respondents complained that physicians neither tested them for AIDS nor diagnosed them with AIDS, even though the respondents had multiple, classic symptoms, stated that they were gay, and requested AIDS testing. One man described how his physician refused several requests for AIDS testing, even though the physician knew that he was gay and that something was wrong with his immune system:

> I was concerned. The symptoms were there, and I was not getting any better, not feeling any better, still getting weaker and weaker, losing more weight, and I kept mentioning all these things and I said, "Look, I've been reading more articles about AIDS." And he said, "Oh, people are just panic-stricken. You don't have AIDS. I'm not doing a test on you."

Stories like this suggest that even in obvious cases some physicians consciously or unconsciously avoid diagnosing AIDS.

For all these reasons, then, PWAs may not receive accurate diagnoses until several months after they seek care. Initially, some of my respondents accepted or even welcomed the alternative diagnoses that their physicians proposed. When symptoms continued, however, these men found themselves in what Stewart and Sullivan (1982:1402) described (with regard to multiple sclerosis) as "an ambiguous and uncertain limbo," in which they suffered anxiety about the meaning of their symptoms and could not function normally, but lacked social support for adopting the sick role (cf. Bury 1982:172; Schneider and Conrad 1983; Stewart and Sullivan 1982; Waddell 1982). Consequently they could not maintain these positions indefinitely. To cope with this situation, some respondents went from doctor to doctor to obtain a diagnosis. Others researched their symptoms, diagnosed themselves, and then pressed their physicians to test them for AIDS. Only then did their uncertainty about the nature of their illnesses end.

"Why Have I Become Ill?"

A diagnosis of AIDS ends individuals' uncertainty about what is wrong with them, but it raises new questions about why this terrible thing has happened to them. Only by answering these questions can PWAs make their illness comprehensible.

Despite the price exacted by AIDS, two of my subjects developed positive explanations for their illnesses. One, a fundamentalist Christian, felt that God had given him AIDS to enable him to share his religious faith with others. He had accepted several invitations to speak about having AIDS at schools and churches, and had used these opportunities to share his belief "that you can be a homosexual and still go to heaven." Another, whose disastrous choice of lovers had left him suicidal on several occasions, considered his diagnosis literally an "answer to a prayer." He believed that God had given him AIDS as a way of providing the extra incentive he needed to avoid any further romantic entanglements.

The rest, however, had no such comforting explanations. Their search for meaning was painful, set as it was in the context of popular belief that AIDS is punishment for sin.

At least on the surface, the majority rejected the idea that AIDS was divine punishment. Instead they argued that AIDS results from the same biological forces that caused other illnesses. Consequently they dismissed the idea that they or anyone else deserved AIDS. As one man said:

> Nobody deserves it. I have friends that say, "Well, hey, if we weren't gay, we wouldn't get this disease." That's bullshit. I mean, I don't want to hear that from anybody. Because no germ has mercy on anybody, no matter who they are—gay, straight, babies, adults.

Yet other statements by some of these men suggested that at a less conscious level they did feel that they were to blame for their illnesses (cf. Moulton 1985). One man denied that he deserved AIDS but suggested later than AIDS might have been God's way of punishing him for being gay or "for not being a good person. . . . I should have helped people more, or not have yelled at somebody, or been better to my dad even though we have never gotten along. . . . Maybe if I had tried to get along better with him, maybe this wouldn't be happening."

Others maintained that they did not deserve AIDS, but used language which suggested considerable ambivalence. Several attributed their illness not to their "nonmonogamy" or "multiple sexual partners" but rather to their "promiscuity." One man said he contracted AIDS "probably because I was a royal whore for about four years." Their use of such morally loaded terms suggests that they were not describing their behavior objectively but were condemning it on moral grounds. Thus it seems that they believed emotionally, if not intellectually, that they deserved punishment, although perhaps less severe punishment than AIDS.

Still other respondents had no doubts that they deserved AIDS. Some felt that they deserved AIDS simply because of their lack of forethought in engaging in high-risk behaviors. One man stated, "I knew better. I mean, it's like, you deserve it. You knew what was going on and yet you slipped and this is the consequence." Others stated explicitly that they deserved AIDS as punishment for their immoral activities. Among these men a diagnosis of AIDS seemed to unleash preexisting guilt about being gay or bisexual (or, in one case, about using drugs). Such guilt seemed particularly prevalent among the nine respondents from fundamentalist Christian or Mormon families; more than half of these men expressed regret about being gay and two-thirds believed at least partially that they deserved AIDS. One fundamentalist Christian who had engaged in homosexual behavior for several years said, "I reaped what I sowed: I sowed sin, I reaped death. I believe, biblically, I received AIDS as a result of my sexual sin practices."

Regardless of how an individual explained why he developed AIDS, simply having an explanation made it easier to tolerate having the illness. For this reason the persons who showed the most distress were those who believed that others deserved to get AIDS but that they themselves did not. Consequently they raged at the unfairness of their situation. As one respondent stated:

> I get real angry. I don't know how to explain why I got it and somebody else didn't because I don't consider myself that I was that promiscuous. When I go out I see other guys out in the bars and they're hopping around, two and three guys a night basically, and it's like why aren't they getting it? Why is it me?

Similarly, some persons who believed that they were born gay considered it unfair that their innate orientation put them at risk for AIDS. Therefore they had to cope not only with the physical trauma of illness but also with the emotional trauma of losing their faith that this is a just world.

"Will I be Able to Function Tomorrow?"

Like many chronic illnesses, AIDS causes unpredictable flare-ups and remissions. As a result, PWAs can never know from one day to the next how sick they will be. As one man said:

> Probably the hardest thing is not knowing when you're well what's going to happen tomorrow because when you're well all you're thinking about is, "What am I going to get? What's the next infection I'm going to have to put up with?" Of course, when you're sick it's like, "Well, I hope they can make me well. I wonder if they can or not."

Because PWAs can become incapacitated without warning, they expose themselves to possible disappointment whenever they make long- or even short-range plans. One man said that he feared going "for a little trip tomorrow even though I am capable of doing that, but I may have diarrhea and who wants to be driving down the highway with shit in your pants?" He and others like him accepted that they had lost control over their physical health. As one man said, "AIDS has become my life. I live for AIDS. I don't live for me anymore, I live for AIDS. I'm at its beck and call and I'll do what it tells me when it tells me." Therefore they chose to avoid making plans as a way to protect themselves against disappointment (cf. Charmaz 1983). By acknowledging their lack of control over their physical health they could assert control over their emotional health.

This strategy was not without cost, however; although it protected PWAs against disappointment, it increased their frustration. As one man explained, "I may have a day where I feel great, where I have plenty of energy and everything is fine, and then you have nothing going, you're just sitting there in the house rotting. So that is really frustrating." Consequently PWAs must walk a tightrope—making the plans they need in order to lead a meaningful life without setting themselves up for disappointment when those plans collapse. For this reason several respondents compared themselves to recovering alcoholics, who must learn to live "one day at a time."

"Will I be Able to Live with Dignity?"

AIDS takes it toll on the human body in many ways, some of which leave individuals with little dignity during either their living or their dying. Consequently PWAs face tremendous uncertainty about the nature of their remaining days.

Fear of death is minimal compared to fear of what their lives may become. In the words of a man who had already suffered one agonizingly debilitating episode, "Death doesn't bother me. Being ill as I was terrifies me." In particular, PWAs fear that they will be among the 70 percent who suffer neurological impairment or the 10 percent who become disfigured by the lesions of Kaposi's sarcoma. They especially fear esoteric illnesses whose effects they cannot predict. As one respondent said:

> I'm not [as] afraid of getting infections from people as I am from inanimate objects, like fruits and moldy tile. . . . I know what a cold is like. . . . [It's] something I have experienced. I've never experienced a mold infection.

PWAs have little control over whether they will develop such infections. To cope with the uncertainty that this lack of control creates, some PWAs try to develop a realistic picture of what they can expect in the future. To learn about the consequences and treatments of various infections (as well as to obtain emotional support), PWAs may attend support groups offered by community organizations. Others research their illnesses on their own, in some cases developing extensive libraries on AIDS. The knowledge that they gain allows them to feel that they can respond appropriately if some problem should arise, and thus that they can exert some control over their situations.

Other PWAs cope with anxiety about what their lives will be like by attempting to maintain unrealistic images of their futures. One man had not joined an AIDS support group because he did not "want to see what other people [with AIDS] look like." This sentiment was especially common among the healthier respondents, who feared that gaining knowledge would lead to depression and that choosing to maintain ignorance was therefore the more sensible approach.

"Will I be Able to 'Beat' AIDS?"

All PWAs must grapple with questions about the likelihood of an early death. These questions seem least answerable to those who initially receive diagnoses of ARC. Faced with conflicting, probabilistic estimates of when and whether they will contract AIDS, persons with ARC experience enormous stress. In the words of one respondent whose diagnosis changed from ARC to AIDS between the initial and the follow-up interviews:

> The worst feeling was when I was ARC, waiting for a bomb to explode. Not knowing when or if ever it would do it. There was always that tentative (sic) in my life that it may or may not—beware! Now that the diagnosis has come in, it's like "Okay. I can relax now. The worst is over."

Even persons diagnosed with AIDS, however, may continue to wonder whether God or medicine will cure them. To cope with this uncertainty and to gain a sense of control over their lives, they search for and adopt any courses of action that might preserve or improve their health. A few respondents relied primarily on prayer. The rest ate more balanced meals, took vitamins, limited their use of caffeine, tobacco, and illegal drugs, and exercised, if possible. They tried to limit their exposure to germs by (for example) avoiding animals and swimming pools and by scanning public buses for passengers who looked unhealthy before choosing a seat. They also sought any treatments, including the experimental, the illegal, or the toxic, which might increase their chances for survival.

Faced with the prospects of an early death, some PWAs are willing to go to extraordinary lengths to obtain promising treatments. The drug most in demand by my respondents was zidovudine (formerly called azidothymidine or AZT). Zidovudine is now available by prescription (although it costs about $12,000 per year). During most of the study period, however, PWAs could obtain zidovudine legally only if they were among the few chosen to participate in pharmaceutical experiments. The rest had to rely on various subterfuges. Some convinced their physicians to diagnose them inaccurately so they would meet the experimenters' criteria. Others received zidovudine from physicians who continued to collect pills from the researchers for clients who had died. Still others obtained unused pills from friends who were research subjects. These friends gave away pills that the experimenters had instructed them to destroy when they had forgotten to take their pills on schedule or had skipped them because of unpleasant side effects. Friends also could obtain an extra set of pills to give away by registering as research subjects under two names with two physicians.

Finally, PWAs also tried to increase their chances for survival and their sense of control over their lives by maintaining a positive attitude. As one man explained, "The main killer with having AIDS is that mental psyche, because your mind controls your body. . . . There are so many people that can't get past that 'I'm sick and going to die.' And therefore, they don't even start—they die." He and others like him simply refused to believe that they would die or to make plans for their deaths. One man said that he had not written a will because of "that whole will to live bit. Once I get that done, that means one less thing I have to do. As long as I don't have it done, it seems like, well, I can't die yet." He went on to explain his belief in the importance of

> being active about this disease, whether it involves drinking a certain kind of tea or standing on your head twice a day or doing something, something that gives the patient a feeling of control over his own life that if you do these things, this might help you a little bit. . . . It's a sense of being in control, of being actively involved in your own health, which in itself produces health.

"Will I be Able to Die with Dignity?"

Despite the lengths to which PWAs will go to survive, their greatest fear is not death but being kept alive against their will and beyond the point of meaningful life. As one respondent said, "I'm not afraid to die. I can truthfully say I'm not. I'm a Christian, I'm saved, and I'm going to heaven. It's getting from here to there that worries me. That's the rough spot."

To alleviate uncertainty and to maintain a sense of control over the nature of their dying, several respondents had made plans to commit suicide if that seemed to be warranted. As one man explained, "If I'm going to die, I would rather it be my business. I guess it's a lack of control. I want to reassert as much control as I can." Others had decided to let the disease take its natural course. They had signed living wills to prohibit physicians from keeping them alive by extraordinary means and had decided to stop taking their medications as soon as life no longer seemed worthwhile. One man had thrown away all his medications without informing his physician. As he explained, "I don't want to die, but I don't have a choice. I have to—period. I mean, no question. So if I have to die, why not tackle the chore and get it over with?"

Learning to Live with AIDS

By the time of the follow-up interviews (four to six months after the initial interviews), AIDS had become far more comprehensible to my respondents. They now had cognitive frameworks that enabled them to understand the changes in their bodies. One man said:

> I remember, a little over a year ago when I was first told what I had, it was very frightening. . . . You didn't know what the future held. A lot of that has been, at least, resolved. I don't worry about it so much, as I did in that respect. It's still not something I want, but I guess you learn to live with it a little better. Then, when you get a case of pneumonia, you know what it is and you don't really think anything of it, other than the fact that "Well, we know what's caused this."

Not only had uncertainty been reduced; it also had become an accepted part of life. Stress had decreased because the men had learned both to assert control over some aspects of their lives and to accept that they could not control other aspects. One man, comparing his feelings at the initial and the follow-up interviews, said, "All I think I've done is adjust to it. I'm not so afraid. I guess I have realized that there's nothing that I can do about it."

Although more respondents still hoped for a cure, their frenetic search had abated. As one respondent said:

> At first, I got on the bandwagon of vitamins and getting nutrition and proper meals and eating my spinach and everything. One day I finally said, "What for?" It's not going to save me. I don't know of anybody that has not died from AIDS just because they ate spinach."

Those who accepted that death was inevitable now focused on living for the present—doing whatever they could do to give pleasure to themselves and their loved ones. By doing so they could feel that they controlled their present circumstances at least partially, even if they could not control their futures.

Discussion

Previous studies showed that uncertainty is a central concern for all seriously ill persons. This study suggests that uncertainty and its ramifications may have an even greater impact on PWAs than on those who suffer from most other illnesses, for several reasons. First, PWAs are more likely than most to know before diagnosis that they are at risk. As a result they suffer difficulties that other ill persons do not experience, because uncertainty and anxiety often sap their emotional energy and physical resources months or even years before they become ill.

Second, PWAs are more likely to feel guilt about the behaviors that led to their becoming ill. Thus, when faced with uncertainty about why they became ill, they are more likely to conclude that it was a deserved punishment. Moreover, PWAs are far more likely to find that their friends, families, and the general public also believe that PWAs cause and deserve their own illness. As a result, these others often reinforce the guilt that PWAs feel.

Third, PWAs are more likely to face difficulties in obtaining an accurate diagnosis. Like other illnesses, AIDS can be difficult to diagnose because it is rare and causes multiple symptoms. These problems are exacerbated because physicians often deliberately (although sometimes unconsciously) avoid questions or actions that would lead to diagnosis.

Fourth, PWAs face greater uncertainty than other ill persons in predicting how their illness will affect their lives; AIDS causes more extensive and less predictable physical and mental damage than most other illnesses.

Fifth, because AIDS is such a new disease, PWAs are more likely to lack answers to their questions about treatment and prognosis. Moreover, because physicians' knowledge about AIDS is developing rapidly and changing constantly, PWAs often are reluctant to trust the answers they do receive.

Uncertainty can be even more troublesome for PWAs who (unlike those described in this chapter) are not gay men. Such PWAs face additional problems in obtaining diagnoses because they may not know that they are at risk. Some women, for example, do not know that their male partners are bisexual. Some bisexual men (as well as many heterosexuals, including those who use drugs) may believe that only gays are at risk. Moreover, their physicians may be less alert for and knowledgeable about AIDS than the physicians of gay men, who often specialize in gay health care.

After diagnosis, PWAs who are not gay and who cannot argue that God-given biological needs forced them to put themselves at risk for AIDS may experience more guilt and more loss of self-esteem than gay men. (In fact, all three gay drug users in the sample exhibited more guilt about their drug use than about their sexuality.) Nongay PWAs (especially women) also experience more difficulty in predicting their futures because so many studies have examined only how AIDS affects the health of gay men. Moreover, they are far less likely to have networks of fellow sufferers to whom they can turn for advice and information. Some live on the margins of society and lack either access to or knowledge of community resources. Others either are unwilling to accept help from groups dominated by gay men because of their own homophobia or are unable to obtain help because their problems are too different from those of gay men. Finally, other PWAs may suffer greater uncertainty than gay men about whether they might transmit AIDS to others. Many gay men function in social circles where everyone is presumed to be at risk, but other PWAs may be overwhelmed by the belief that they are the sole potential source of infection for their loved ones.

Yet despite all the difficulties faced by PWAs because of uncertainty, they are not completely helpless. As this chapter has described, they find ways to reduce or (if necessary) to live with uncertainty.

These data on how PWAs cope with uncertainty have significant implications for the study of uncertainty in general: they highlight the role of control in making uncertainty tolerable. Previous research on uncertainty hinted that loss of control might make uncertainty stressful; studies on helplessness demonstrated that loss of control causes stress and depression (Lazarus 1966; Peterson and Seligman 1984). This study specifies further the links among uncertainty, loss of control, and stress. As this chapter has shown, individuals can cope with uncertainty by developing normative frameworks that make their situations comprehensible. These frameworks, combined with other tactics (such as deciding not to make plans, in the case of PWAs), help individuals to gain control or at least the sense of control over their lives. Thus in some situations they enable people to reduce uncertainty. In other situations, where uncertainty is either unavoidable or preferable to certainty, such frameworks enable people to reduce the stresses of living with uncertainty.

Policy Implications

According to Janis (1983), people can handle stressful situations most effectively if they feel that they are in control of their lives. To achieve this goal he proposes "stress inoculation," in which people (1) are given information about what to expect, which is realistic but which still allows them to maintain optimism; (2) are encouraged to identify possible actions that can help them to survive and to find internal and external resources that would allow them to take those actions; and (3) are helped to develop their own plan for responding to their situation.

The results of this study support Janis' model; they, too, suggest that the key to coping with the uncertainty of having AIDS is achieving a sense of control. Thus if we are to improve PWAs' lives, doctors, counselors, relatives, and others who care for or about PWAs must learn both how uncertainty affects PWAs and how they can help PWAs to feel that they are in control. Paradoxically, in some cases this process will mean learning to recognize when PWAs would prefer to maintain uncertainty rather than to learn the truth about their situation. As Janis suggests, knowledge is counterproductive if it makes persons feel that their situations are hopeless. In most cases, however, help will entail involving PWAs in their own care—making sure that they understand what is happening to them and believe that decisions (including decisions about when to terminate care) are left to them. In addition, caregivers must learn to go beyond simply providing information; they also must learn to help PWAs identify their internal and external resources and decide on their own plan of action—even if the resulting steps seem useless or even harmful (cf. Cohen and Lazarus 1983). Health care workers need to understand that both trust and therapeutic effectiveness will suffer unless they learn to convince PWAs that they can discuss safely and honestly any nonmedically approved actions they are taking.

Finally, those who care for or about PWAs must recognize that PWAs have a strong need to find a logical explanation for their illness. Physicians, counselors, and AIDS activists must learn that although talking in terms of "risk behaviors" can be useful in discussing the possibility of AIDS with persons not yet infected, it can reinforce guilt feelings among those who have AIDS and thus can increase their emotional difficulties. Family members and friends, as well as health care workers, must learn to ascertain whether PWAs are blaming themselves and to intervene in such instances, or at least to refer them for counseling. In sum, those who work with PWAs need to learn how psychosocial factors affect PWAs and to develop ways of responding to PWAs' emotional as well as physical problems.

NOTES

1. Although uncertainty about contagion is a major cause of social rejection, this chapter does not address how uncertainty affects PWAs' social relationships. I have chosen to address that subject in a separate paper both because of its complexity and because stigma rather than uncertainty seems to be the more crucial factor affecting PWAs' social lives.

2. These various aspects of uncertainty need not be sequential. For example, individuals may question whether they will be well enough to work tomorrow even before they obtain names for their illnesses.

3. For this analysis I combined persons with AIDS and persons with ARC because I could not separate the two categories adequately. Some individuals said that they had ARC when they clearly had AIDS, some said that they had AIDS when they seemed to have ARC, and some vacillated in their statements about which disease they had. Since these interviews were conducted, the Centers for Disease Control have broadened their definition of AIDS to include most cases considered previously as ARC.

19

Two Decades of Research on Dying: What Do We Know About the Patient?

RICHARD SCHULZ AND
JANET SCHLARB

We have available to us large quantities of data regarding demographic aspects of death, such as age, sex, causes, and location of death, but we know very little about the circumstances surrounding death. We have little direct information about the length of illness prior to death, the magnitude of patients' disabilities, the physical pain and psychological distress experienced by the patient, coping strategies used, the amount of care received or needed, or even basic information regarding the number of patients who are aware of their terminality before dying.

Although the volume of published material on the topic of dying has increased dramatically in the last decade, the quantity of useful new data available to us suggests that the study of dying has not yet been accepted into the mainstream of the scientific community. For example, even though research on stress and coping has become a central focus among researchers in a variety of disciplines such as psychology, psychiatry, and sociology, the topic of dying is rarely treated in this

Preparation of this chapter was in part supported by grants from the National Institute of Aging (AGO5444) and the National Institute of Mental Health (MH41887).

context. Perhaps researchers implicitly make the assumption that if an individual is going to die anyway, then issues such as coping are irrelevant. One of the goals of this chapter is to convince the reader that the systematic study of dying is an important endeavor that deserves the attention of sophisticated researchers in many disciplines.

This chapter is concerned with terminal patients and the nature of their experiences during the time before death. Our discussion is divided into four parts. First, we examine the magnitude of the problem by identifying the number of individuals each year who must confront their own death. Second, we discuss the emotional response of dying patients to their impending death. The third section deals with interventions for the dying patient, and the fourth identifies areas for future research.

Magnitude of the Problem

In 1983, for the first time in our history, more than two million people died in the United States, and it is estimated that more than 80 percent of these deaths occurred with at least several weeks' warning (Myers 1985; Osterweis, Solomon, and Green 1984; U.S. Department of Health, Education, and Welfare 1978). It is widely known that heart disease, cancer, and stroke are the major causes of death, accounting for almost 70 percent of all deaths, and that these diseases are associated with an aging population (Matarazzo 1984). Given the projected exponential growth of the number of older persons world-wide and the similarity across countries in the causes of adult mortality, it seems reasonable to conclude that a majority of the world's adult population will have to cope with the prospect of their own imminent death (*Demographic Yearbook* 1984; Myers 1985).

In order to generate some estimates of the number of persons who are aware of their terminality, we will focus on U.S. data and use, for the moment, a definition of terminal illness adopted by the Department of Health and Human Services. An individual must be terminally ill in order to be eligible for hospice coverage of the Medicare program. Terminal illness in this context is defined as certification by a physician that the individual has a life expectancy of six months or less. It seems reasonable to us that the number of individuals who die each year while enrolled in a hospice program represents the lower limit of the number who must confront their own death, although it is certainly possible that some hospice enrollees are not aware of their terminality (Greer, Mor, and Kastenbaum in press). According to the National

Hospice Organization, 100,000 individuals were enrolled in hospice programs in 1984. To this number we should add those individuals who are eligible but are not referred, or choose not to participate, and those who are ineligible for reasons such as age, or type of disease.

Since most deaths among adults are the result of some chronic physical illness, it is rare for people to die completely unexpectedly. Although comparable U.S. data are not available, Cartwright, Hockey, and Anderson (1973) found that all but 22 percent of their randomly selected sample of 785 British respondents received hospital or institutional care in the last twelve months before dying. This suggests that a large number of terminal patients have the potential to know of their condition, but this does not tell us whether they actually do know. In the same study, retrospective data collected from individuals who knew the deceased indicated that 49 percent of the dying persons knew of their condition (the illness) and 37 percent of its probable outcome (death). Another 17 and 20 percent fell into the "half knew/uncertain" category with respect to condition and outcome, respectively. These data suggest an upper limit of approximately 60 percent as the proportion of the terminally ill who actually know they are going to die. Of those individuals who did know, 44 percent knew the outcome three months or more before they died; 38 percent knew the outcome less than three months but more than a week; and 18 percent knew the outcome less than a week.

Because of the substantial differences in the health care delivery systems between the United States and Britain we must be cautious in generalizing from the British data. However, combining the British data with the hospice data, it is safe to conclude that in the United States somewhere between 100,000 and 1.2 million people each year become aware of and must cope with their impending death, and almost half of these individuals must live with this knowledge for a minimum of three months.

Given the significance of this problem, it is remarkable that there exists so little generalizable factual information about dying persons and their experiences before death, especially in light of the relatively large literature focused on the relatives of the dying patient (Kosten, Jacobs, and Kasl 1984; Osterweis, Solomon, and Green 1984). For some reason, the dying person has been left out. The data that do exist are either methodologically flawed, limited in scope, or are based on small and nonrepresentative samples. With few exceptions (e.g., Cartwright, Hockey, and Anderson 1973; Greer, Mor, and Kastenbaum in press), studies of the final days, weeks, or months of a person's life suffer from at least one or several of these problems.

The Stress of Dying

Since most adult deaths in the United States and throughout the world are caused by a physical illness, the dying individual has to contend with at least one, and often two types of stressors. All terminal patients have to cope with the physical, psychological, and social stressors associated with an often chronic, progressively disabling physical illness. The subset of patients who become aware of their impending death must additionally cope with the psychological stress resulting from this knowledge. For health professionals as well as researchers it would be valuable to be able to discriminate among these types of stressors and their associated patient outcomes.

The work of Elizabeth Kübler-Ross (1969) on the stages of dying undoubtedly is the most widely known work on the psychological trajectory of dying patients, although it has been criticized by Schulz and Aderman (1974) and others (Kastenbaum 1977; Shneidman 1973) for its ambiguity, sampling, investigator bias, and the confounding of physical symptoms with psychological responses. An earlier study by Hinton (1963) is broader in scope but limited in sample size. Hinton assessed mood, physical distress, level of consciousness, and awareness of dying in approximately 70 dying patients at weekly intervals. His analysis of the data yielded reports of high levels of physical stress and impaired consciousness among 55 percent of his sample, and high levels of depression among approximately half of the patients.

Achte and Vauhkonen (1973) compared a group of terminal cancer patients with a group of nonterminal controls who also had cancer. The higher frequency of depression in the terminal group was the biggest difference between the two groups, although anxiety and tension were also more frequent among terminal patients. These findings are generally consistent with those reported by Hinton and Kübler-Ross. However, Achte and Vauhkonen also identified a subgroup of patients whose illness terminated quickly. These aggressive patients most closely resembled Kübler-Ross' patients in the denial and anger stages. Apparently their deaths occurred before they had passed through the remaining Kübler-Ross stages.

The controversy surrounding the Kübler-Ross stages of dying was still alive in 1987. Antonoff and Spilka (1984–85) carried out a study in which they examined the patterning of facial emotional expressions in terminally ill patients who were either in the early, middle, or late stages of their illness. Observers rated the facial expressions of terminal patients during an interview to assess levels of fear, anger, sadness, and happiness. Contrary to the Kübler-Ross stages, sadness increased from the early to the late phase of illness, and no systematic patterns were found for anger and happiness. Fear was highest in the early period, as predicted.

In another recent study, Baugher et al. (1985) examined the responses of 1,100 patients, ranging in age from 20 to 91, who were terminally ill with cancer. Both cross-sectional and longitudinal data were collected so as to assess whether or not the process of social disengagement occurs as one approaches the last weeks and days of life. Four areas that are indicative of disengagement were examined: (1) social concerns; (2) self-concern; (3) focus on "the beyond"; and (4) mood state. In general, the results of the study were nonsupportive of disengagement, regardless of awareness or lack of awareness of the terminal condition. The authors were careful to note several possible confounding factors, though, including the following: (1) only patients terminally ill with cancer were studied; (2) the largest majority of the patients did not lack a primary care person; and (3) for over half of the patients, the primary care person responded for the terminally ill individual.

A very different approach to the study of the last days of life was undertaken by Weisman and Kastenbaum (Kastenbaum and Weisman 1972; Weisman and Kastenbaum 1968). Using a procedure called the psychological autopsy, these authors attempted to reconstruct the final phases in the life of a patient. Their procedure involved interdisciplinary conferences in which information about a recently deceased patient was presented and discussed with the aim of studying the psychosocial context in which the death occurred. After reviewing 80 cases in one sample and 35 in another, they concluded that patients entering the terminal period could be separated into two groups on the basis of their responses to impending death. One group seemed to be aware of and to accept impending death. Most of these patients withdrew from daily activities and remained inactive until the end. The other group was also aware of the imminent death but vigorously engaged in daily life activities and even initiated new activities and interpersonal relationships. Death for these individuals came as an interruption in daily living.

Probably the best conclusion we can draw from this research as a whole is that dying evokes a variety of predominantly negative emotions such as fear, anger, sadness, and depression, and that these emotions occur in no particular order. In addition, the data suggest that there is a continuity of affective style from the nonterminal to the terminal phase. The overall proportion of positive or negative affect displayed by the terminal patient is closely related to the emotional style of the individual before becoming terminally ill.

Dying Children

Terminally ill children have been the subject of numerous studies over the past two decades. The primary focus of this research has been on the distress and anxiety that dying children experience. The earliest works in this area reported that fatally ill children under the age of ten do not experience or express death anxiety, and concluded from this that such children lack an awareness of what they are experiencing (Knudson and Natterson 1960; Morrissey 1965; Natterson and Knudson 1960; Richmond and Waisman 1955). The more recent studies, though, report that terminally ill children under the age of ten are, in fact, aware of their prognoses and do experience anxiety (Spinetta 1972; Spinetta, Rigler, and Karon 1973; Waechter 1968, 1971). According to Waechter (1971), the prognosis is communicated to the child by the change in affect among those around him and through subtle nonverbal cues. Thus, even without ever being explicitly told about his impending death, the child becomes aware of his prognosis. In a similar vein, Spinetta, Rigler, and Karon suggest that the anxiety experienced by the child may not be overtly expressed:

> Even though the concern of the six- to ten-year-old child may not take the form of overt expression about death, the more subtle fears and anxieties are nonetheless real, painful, and very much related to the seriousness of the illness. (1973:844)

According to Lewis, Horton, and Armstrong (1981–82), the method of assessing distress in ill children has a great impact on the results. In their study of 19 fatally and chronically ill children, seven different commonly used measurement methods were used to assess seven areas of personality functioning. The results indicated that the method of assessment contributes significantly to the outcome. They conclude that a longitudinal, qualitative psychodynamic methodology may be the most appropriate method for assessing the distress of fatally ill children.

The value and importance of a longitudinal, qualitative methodology for the study of dying children has been recognized by Bluebond-Langner (1978), who maintains that fatally ill children gain an awareness of their prognoses through a long and difficult information acquisition process. Approaching her study from a symbolic interactionist perspective, Bluebond-Langner's major emphasis is on the negotiation processes that occur between child and parents, and between child and medical staff. Death is viewed by the author as a sociocultural phenomenon, a perspective that enables her to explain how children become aware of their situation and why they may choose to conceal this awareness from their loved ones.

Personal Accounts of Dying

Another important source of information about dying are the many personal accounts of dying written either by individuals who were themselves dying (e.g., Alsop 1973; Jaffe 1976), or friends and relatives of terminal patients (e.g., Jaffe and Jaffe 1976; Kavenaugh 1974; Margaret 1977). Stewart Alsop's book, *Stay of Execution,* is representative of this genre. He describes in detail the process of becoming aware of his terminality—the numerous trips to the hospital and the terrified waiting for results—the emotional responses to his condition such as anger and depression, and the heightened sense of appreciation for his family and the mundane aspects of life. As a group, these descriptions of specific individuals coping with dying are revealing, insightful, and engaging. And although these accounts have been influential in shaping therapeutic interventions for the dying, it is important to keep in mind that the persons described in these books are a very select group of individuals. They are highly educated, and have opted to cope with their dying by thinking about it and discussing it openly with others.

Hospice Dying

Studies describing and assessing the effectiveness of hospice care also provide data concerning the last days of life of terminally ill people. In one recent large-scale study of 1,745 participants, researchers asked terminal patients what they considered to be important two to eight weeks prior to their deaths. During this difficult time, supportive friends were most often mentioned as a source of strength, followed by religion and being needed by someone else. When these patients were asked what they wanted during the last three days of their lives, the most common responses were having certain people present, being physically able to do things, and feeling at peace. The results also indicated that patients tended to vacillate between such contrary feelings as calm and frightened or content and hopeless, rather than remaining consistently depressed (Greer and Mor 1983).

The cautionary note concerning personal accounts of dying applies to hospice participants as well. They are a select group of terminal patients. They are generally white, in their mid-sixties, with some form of cancer, and they typically have a spouse caregiver available to support them (Bass, Garland, and Otto 1985–86).

Emotional Response and Duration of Survival

How we respond psychologically and behaviorally to a physical illness may affect both the intensity and duration of symptoms associated with the illness. Given the wide range of emotional responses exhibited by terminal patients, several researchers have asked the question, does patient response to the illness affect the duration of survival? Unfortunately, the data do not provide a simple answer to this question. For example, Greer, Morris, and Pettingale (1979) found that women suffering from breast cancer who responded with stoic acceptance or expressed feelings of helplessness and hopelessness were likely to die sooner than women who expressed either denial or a fighting spirit. Holden (1978) also found that patients who were more despairing and had few social contacts died sooner than individuals who expressed more anger toward their disease and their doctors. However, contrary to the findings of Greer, Morris, and Pettingale, Holden found that those who died more quickly tended to use denial and repression as coping mechanisms.

The results of Holden were partially replicated by Derogatis, Abeloff, and Melisaratos (1979). In their study of women dying of breast cancer, those who survived the longest were judged to show significantly poorer adjustment to their illnesses and to have poorer attitudes toward their physicians. However, the long-term survivors also reported higher levels of anxiety, dysphoric mood, and alienation than short-term survivors. To further add to the confusion, a recent study showed no relationship between survival time and psychosocial factors such as hopelessness/helplessness, life satisfaction, and social ties (Cassileth et al. 1985).

In sum, there is little disagreement about the importance of psychosocial variables such as social support as determinants of longevity in general, but the verdict is still out on the role of individual emotional responsiveness and coping styles as determinants of survival time among terminal patients. Moreover, one might take issue with the desirability of survival time as an appropriate outcome measure for individuals who are terminally ill.

Interventions for the Dying

Except for rare instances, knowledge of one's impending death elicits strong emotional reactions, including fear and anxiety, despair, depression, and anger and hostility (Hinton 1979). Recognition of this fact has resulted in a number of intervention programs and a large literature on how to help the dying patient. Discussions of the needs of the dying patient and how to meet them are central features of virtually every death and dying book published in the last decade. In the typical book, the needs and fears of the dying patient are listed, followed by descriptions of how family, health care professionals, and clergy should interact with the patient to facilitate a "good" or appropriate death. These recommendations are usually based on equal measures of common sense and compassion, and typically fall into two generic categories: interventions designed to control pain and physical discomfort, and interventions to ease the psychological discomfort of being terminally ill. The latter category usually includes interventions designed to preserve dignity and self-worth, and to provide love and affection (Schulz 1978). It would be difficult to argue against the broadly stated goals of any intervention program for the terminally ill; however, operationalizing these objectives is a challenging task that raises several difficult issues.

The problem of controlling pain is treated elsewhere, . . . but it is worth noting here that pain control is perhaps more manageable a problem because we can at least identify the options available for achieving this goal. The methods available to us for easing psychological discomfort, for preserving dignity, and for providing love are more difficult to articulate. For example, are we preserving the patient's dignity when we reinforce his or her denial of a terminal illness? Or conversely, does a dignified death require that we facilitate the patient's acceptance of terminal status? One can also imagine situations where easing the patient's psychological discomfort creates a great deal of discomfort for individuals close to him or her, which over time may distress the patient.

Some of the data reported earlier suggest that how we respond emotionally to a terminal illness may affect the duration of survival. Persons who express anger, anxiety, or a dysphoric mood may live longer than individuals who are more despairing and accepting of their status.

What are the implications of such findings for the design of intervention programs? Although we would normally consider anxiety and dysphoric mood to be signs of psychological discomfort requiring treatment, should they be viewed this way in this context? Answers to some of these questions can be found by examining some of the intervention programs currently available.

The Hospice Approach

In 1978 the International Work Group on Death, Dying and Bereavement disseminated a document identifying the assumptions and underlying standards for terminal care (Kastenbaum 1975a, 1975b; Rando 1984), and in 1981 the National Hospice Organization outlined standards and principles of hospice care (Rando 1984).

These documents articulate the philosophy and approach used by hospices throughout the United States to provide care to approximately 100,000 persons each year. The primary goal of hospice care is to help terminally ill patients continue their lives with as little disruption as possible. An interdisciplinary team consisting of a physician, nurse, social worker, and counselor strives to keep the patient alert, involved with family and friends, and as free from pain as possible. The team spends considerable time talking with and listening to patients, comforting and reassuring them, holding hands, and generally providing a warm emotional atmosphere. Both the family and the patient play an active role in making decisions about the care received.

Does hospice care help? This question can be answered at many levels. We can examine what it does for the family, how it affects health care utilization patterns and costs (Birnbaum and Kidder 1984; Greer et al. 1986), or how well it relieves symptoms of pain in the patient. Our focus here is on the patient, and the primary issue for us concerns how hospice care affects the socio-emotional life of the patient, but we touch on some of these other questions as well.

The National Hospice Study was designed to provide answers to all of these questions by comparing outcomes for a matched group of hospice and non-hospice terminal patients and their families. This quasi-experimental study involved terminal cancer patients from 40 hospices and 14 conventional oncological care settings. Periodic interviews with the terminal patients and their primary care persons were conducted in an effort to determine if their experiences were significantly different due to care setting (i.e., hospital-based hospices, home-based hospices, and conventional care settings). The primary results were as follows (Greer and Mor 1986; Greer et al. 1986; Morris et al. 1986);

1. Patients receiving hospice care underwent less aggressive intervention therapy and diagnostic testing.
2. The patients' qualify of life (i.e., "performance status, global quality of life, pain and symptoms, satisfaction with care, and social involvement" [Greer and Mor 1986:6]) was not significantly different due to care setting, except that in the hospital-based hospice setting pain and symptom control may have been better and patient satisfaction with care tended to be higher.
3. There were no significant differences in the following family outcomes due to care setting: secondary morbidity, hospitalization rates, medication for nervousness, or alcohol consumption.
4. Families of patients in home-care hospices were more satisfied with site of death (which was more likely to be the home) than were families of patients in conventional care settings, but they also experienced higher levels of stress, social disruption, and bereavement-related psychosocial distress.
5. Home-based hospice costs were less than those of hospital-based hospice care, which were roughly equivalent to the costs of conventional care.

The findings of the National Hospice Study were not dissimilar to those of the randomized controlled trial of hospice care conducted by Kane and colleagues at a Veterans Administration hospital in Los Angeles (Kane et al. 1985a, 1985b; Kane et al. 1984; Wales et al. 1983). This study is especially noteworthy because of its randomized controlled design, but the researchers carefully qualify the generalizability of their findings since only one hospice program was studied. Their results indicate that there were no significant differences between hospice patients and control patients (those randomly assigned to receive conventional care) regarding pain, symptoms, activities of daily living, or affect. Additionally, hospice care was found to be at least as expensive as conventional care. And as in the National Hospice Study, patients were more satisfied with their care in the hospice setting than were those in the conventional care setting.

Still other studies (Hinton 1979; Parkes 1979a) have indicated other positive effects attributable to hospice care. For example, Hinton found that hospice participants report lower levels of depression when compared to individuals receiving conventional care. And the work of Parkes and others indicates that the family of a terminal patient is more prepared for the death and better able to deal with bereavement when the terminal patient has been involved in hospice care (Cameron and Parkes 1983; Godkin, Krant, and Doster 1983–84; Parkes 1979b, 1980, 1985; Parkes and Parkes 1984). Typical comments by such family members reflect that they feel more in control of the situation and are glad to be actively involved in the care of their loved ones.

On another level, the hospice movement, in all of its various forms, has been most useful in creating an awareness (both inside and outside of the medical community) of the importance of care as well as cure: once a patient's condition has been deemed to be terminal, every effort should be made to make his or her remaining time as comfortable and satisfying as possible. The maturation of the "hospice ideology" has helped to establish this as a genuinely important goal, and it is now being addressed by hospice and conventional care practitioners alike (Bass 1985). We maintain that the primary value of hospice care is that it provides the patient and family with another choice; the fact that large numbers of individuals have opted for this alternative suggests that it is a choice worth having. (*See* Mor, Wachtel, and Kidder 1985 for factors that affect the patient's choice of hospital vs. home-care hospice programs.)

Psychotherapeutic Approaches

Given the unique dilemma of the terminal patient, it is not surprising that the intervention strategies available to the patient range from the mundane to the controversial. Practitioners have used conventional methods such as group therapy (Parsell and Tagliareni 1974); behavior therapy including the rational-emotive approach (Ellis 1981; Sobel 1981); weekly case conferences with the dying patient (Hertzberg 1972); logotherapy (Zuehlke 1975); and self-help groups (Kalish 1981b); somewhat less conventional approaches such as "friendship contracts" (Feigenberg 1980); and controversial methods such as the imaging techniques of Carl Simonton (Simonton, Matthews-Simonton, and Creighton 1978) and LSD therapy (Grof and Halifax 1977; Pahnke 1969).

Unfortunately, data concerning the efficacy of these varied approaches tell us little about how, why, or even whether a particular method works. Hertzberg (1972) found that weekly case conferences increased sensitivity of ward personnel to the emotional concerns of the patients and their families. Parsell and Tagliareni (1974) reported positive feedback from their patients who participated in their group therapy sessions. In a study in which patients were randomly assigned to either logotherapy or a control group, Zuehlke concludes that patients, as a result of the psychotherapy sessions, "were able to lower their efforts to deny their concerns about dying and to participate more openly in exploring the true nature and extent of their feelings" (1975:15). While it may be argued that all of these interventions benefited the patient in one way or another, none of these studies present strong evidence that would warrant such a conclusion. It is not clear to us, for example, why an increase in death anxiety should be construed as a positive therapeutic outcome.

Another option for the dying and their families is provided by the local chapters of two national organizations, Centers for Attitudinal Healing and Make Today Count (Kalish 1981b). These groups hold regular meetings for individuals (and their families) suffering from a life-threatening disease. Their goal is to provide a context where members can benefit from the social, emotional, and informational support that derives from interacting with others facing similar problems. There exist no formal evaluations of these programs, but the fact that they exist is a "kind of de facto positive evaluation of their value" (Kalish 1981b:542).

A more conventional therapeutic approach to working with the dying patient was described by Loma Feigenberg (1980) as forming friendship contracts with dying patients. The essential kernel of this approach is the formation of a contract with the dying patient. The contract guarantees to the patient that the therapist will not communicate with either nursing staff or relatives of the patient: in other words, that the relationship between therapist and patient is an exclusive one. Presumably this facilitates open communication, making it easier for dying patients to bring up topics that are important for them emotionally. Feigenberg believes that this approach helped the dying persons, but does not provide any data to substantiate this.

Simonton and his colleagues have proposed a health treatment program for terminal patients that is designed to keep them alive rather than have them come to terms with their dying (Simonton, Matthews-Simonton, and Creighton 1978). According to this approach, the patients must first take responsibility for having caused their cancer before they can affect its removal. The patient is encouraged to develop a visual image of the site of the cancer and then to visualize healthy cells attacking and destroying the cancerous cells. Used in conjunction with relaxation techniques and appropriate traditional medical interventions, Simonton claims that 63 of 159 patients treated were alive an average of two years after treatment began, even though their predicted life expectancy was only one year. Like much of the research on interventions with the dying, these studies suffer from a number of methodological problems, including the absence of control groups, random assignment procedures, and blind assessments. Research on the therapeutic effects of LSD on terminal cancer patients suffers from similar methodological problems. In one study of 50 cancer patients given LSD, 18 improved greatly on indicators of physical and emotional stress, and 18 improved moderately; only four persons showed any detrimental effects (Kalish 1981a). However, there was no control group, raters may have been biased because they were aware of what was going on, and patients were also receiving psychotherapy.

Advocates of "rational suicide" offer a very extreme form of dealing with terminality (Mannes 1973; Siegel and Tuckel 1984–85). They suggest that individuals suffering from painful terminal illness might wish to terminate their physical distress by committing suicide. Such an act would be considered rational when the mental processes of the individual leading to the decision to commit suicide are unimpaired by psychological illness or severe emotional distress, and the motivational basis for the decision is understandable to the majority of the members of the individual's community or social group. Although these criteria appear well-reasoned in the abstract, they are probably impossible to meet in practice. Nevertheless, several researchers claim that suicide in response to physical illness is a fact of life, particularly among physical ill old persons (Farberow et al. 1971; Miller 1979).

Evaluating Interventions

One of the common themes of our discussion concerns the difficulty of evaluating interventions for terminal patients. Even if methodologically rigorous studies were designed for each of the intervention strategies described above, we would still be faced with the dilemma of specifying appropriate outcome measures. Outcomes which under non-life-threatening circumstances are clearly desirable, such as the reduction of anxiety or the elimination of negative affect, paradoxically can be viewed as detrimental to the terminal patient. Decreasing anxiety and depression may shorten the patient's life, but we don't know how desirable is a trade-off between more time and less negative affect.

One way of approaching the problem of specifying appropriate outcome measures is to ask the question: what are the needs of the dying patient, or as Kalish puts it, how can we best enable the dying person to live the "end of life as much as possible the way the individual wishes" (1981a:177–78)? Another way of saying this is: how can we best facilitate informed choices that optimize satisfaction of the patient's needs for pain control, self-esteem, and love and affection (Schulz 1978)? Inherent in this need hierarchy are the outcome measures appropriate for intervention studies of the dying. We have available a large literature on how to assess subjective pain (Karoly 1985; Turk and Rennert 1981), and self-esteem (Rosenberg and Kaplan 1982). The measurement of love and affection may require some ingenuity, but even this construct can be operationalized relatively easily with self-report and behavioral measures. Perhaps the most important measure that needs to be added to this list is one that assesses the patient's views regarding the availability of choices and options. According to this perspective, an intervention program would be deemed successful to the extent that it enhances a patient's feelings of choice, perceived control, and self-efficacy. The rationale for this argument comes from a large literature demonstrating that human beings exposed to a large variety of stressors cope better to the extent they have control (Rodin 1985; Rodin, Timko, and Harris 1985; Schulz and Decker 1985; Schulz and Hanusa 1980; Schulz, Tompkins, and Rau 1987) and possess high levels of self-efficacy—the belief that one can personally produce and regulate important outcomes for oneself (Bandura 1982).

Conclusion and Future Research

This chapter has focused primarily on the dying patient. We have tried to identify the number of people in the United States that must confront their impending death, describe how individuals cope with this knowledge, and discuss the range of intervention options available to the dying patient. Although significant strides have been made in enlarging the data base for each of these areas, the available data are often limited and methodologically flawed. The remainder of this chapter identifies some of the major unresolved questions and some strategies for seeking answers to them.

Much of the existing literature on terminal patients is based on relatively young individuals (e.g., under 60 years of age) dying of cancer, but most people in the United States die at a relatively old age after a prolonged period of physical decline and chronic disabilities. It would be useful to know what percent of the population becomes aware of their terminality and how this awareness evolves over time. As individuals age and their health problems increase, does the prospect of death have little significance to them, or does it arouse the intense emotional reactions described in the existing literature? In brief, we need data on normative dying, and its variations as determined by demographic variables such as age, religion, ethnic and cultural background, education, and financial status.

Dying is a physical, technical event, but also one that is heavily laden with socio-emotional aspects. A good description of the circumstances surrounding death must include an adequate assessment of both aspects of the dying process, and their interaction. For those individuals who do not die because of suicide, homicide, or accident, the most important questions concern the types of symptoms experienced before death, their intensity and duration, and the restrictions experienced prior to dying. With respect to socio-emotional aspects of dying, our past efforts have been focused too exclusively on the emotional responses of the dying patient. It may prove to be more fruitful to step back and ask what factors determine the socio-emotional life of a dying patient. For example, it would be useful to know:

1. the extent to which the individual patient's beliefs, lifestyle, and preferences are identified and taken into account in planning his or her care;
2. the amount of assistance and training given to the patients in order to involve them in their care, and to maximize feelings of control and participation in decision making regarding care;
3. the openness of communication between the patient, family, and health care staff, if desired by the patient, regarding prognosis and expected progress of the disease;
4. the amount and character of interaction between staff and patients and family and patients;
5. the degree to which patients and families are able to interact with the desired frequency and privacy; and
6. the amount of social support provided to the patient by families and friends.

Answers to these specific questions would not only provide a rich descriptive data base about the circumstances surrounding death, but they would also help us design and evaluate appropriate intervention programs.

How should such data be collected? The study by Cartwright, Hockey, and Anderson (1973) described earlier provides a good example of how to pursue answers to some of these questions, and is being replicated in part by the National Institute on Aging (NIA). In its study of the last days of life, the NIA is focusing on all the resident decedents age 65 and older in one of the health service areas of Connecticut (Brock 1983). A sample of 1,500 death certificates will be drawn, and the relatives, friends, and health care providers of each decedent will be asked to provide information about the events and conditions prior to death, and medical, demographic, and socio-emotional information about the decedent. Although the data will be based on retrospective accounts of survivors, this study is an important first step in generating broad population-based information about dying. It will be important to follow up this study with similar studies that focus in greater detail on specific aspects of the circumstances surrounding death.

It is even more important, however, that we study the process of dying prospectively. The National Hospice Study shows that this can be done, and it teaches us as well that it may be more useful to focus our research efforts on discrete aspects of dying such as the amount of pain or depression it engenders rather than struggling to define a good or dignified death in a global sense. Future prospective studies should expand the population base to include individuals who die in long-term care facilities (Fisher, Nadon, and Shedletsky 1983).

Similarly, it may be useful to recognize that conventional care and hospice care are not as disparate as they once were. Both types of care take a variety of forms and offer numerous services and programs to the terminal patient and his or her family. Here again then, we suggest that future research concern itself less with contrasting hospice care with conventional care, and concentrate more on identifying the specific desired outcomes of care for terminal patients and their families.

Finally, it is worth noting that studying dying affords valuable opportunities in developing theories about coping with stress. For example, readers familiar with the stress literature know that one of the most frequently used instruments in research on stress is the Holmes and Rahe Life Events Scale (Holmes and Rahe 1967b). According to this instrument, the death of someone close to us such as a spouse or a child is one of the most stressful experiences one can encounter. This event is given 100 points, and is followed by a variety of less stressful events such as physical illness, being arrested, having to move, etc. Although this scale does not claim to include all of the stressful events human beings might experience, it is curious that one of the most stressful events we can imagine—our own impending death—does not appear on the scale. Stress researchers have developed a rich array of theories, research instruments, and methodologies that could be used in research with terminal patients. We believe that bringing dying into the mainstream of stress research would substantially and quickly improve the data base on dying and enrich the theoretical literature on stress.

20

The Myths of Coping with Loss

■

CAMILLE B. WORTMAN AND
ROXANE COHEN SILVER

In this article, we focus on how people cope with loss events that involve permanent change and cannot be altered or undone. It is our belief that such experiences provide an excellent arena in which to study basic processes of stress and coping. In the health and medical areas, many specific losses might be considered irrevocable: the permanent loss of bodily function, the loss of particular body parts, the loss of cognitive capacity, the death of a loved one, or one's own terminal illness. In an attempt to advance theoretical development in this rich and complex area, this article updates an earlier review we completed on reactions to undesirable life events (Silver and Wortman 1980). Because the most rigorous empirical studies have been in the areas of physical disability and bereavement, we shall focus on these two areas in this chapter.

The order of authorship was arbitrary.

Research and preparation of this article were supported by U.S. Public Health Service Grant MCJ-260470 and by National Institute on Aging Program Project Grant A605561 to Camille B. Wortman and Roxane Cohen Silver.

For a more detailed discussion of these issues, the reader is referred to Wortman and Silver (1987).

When a person experiences an irrevocable loss, such as the death of a loved one or permanent paralysis, how will he or she react? We maintain that people hold strong assumptions about how others should respond to such losses. As we have discussed in more detail elsewhere (Silver and Wortman 1980; Wortman and Silver 1987), such assumptions are derived in part from the theories of loss offered by prominent writers in the area, and in part from clinical lore about coping with loss and our cultural understanding of the experience. As detailed below, individuals who encounter a loss are expected to go through a period of intense distress; failure to experience such distress is thought to be indicative of a problem. Moreover, it is assumed that successful adjustment to loss requires that individuals "work through" or deal with their feelings of grief rather than "denying" or "repressing" them. Within a relatively brief period of time, however, people are expected to resolve their loss and recover their earlier level of functioning.

Because it is generally assumed that the coping process unfolds in a particular way, others may evaluate or judge those who do not conform to these expectations as reacting abnormally or inappropriately. For example, because they believe that people should recover relatively soon after the loss, outsiders might react judgmentally to continuing signs of distress (cf. Silver and Wortman 1980; Tait and Silver 1989). In fact, if laypersons hold unrealistically narrow views of what constitutes a normal grief response, they may have difficulty offering the appropriate forms of assistance to friends and family members who are trying to cope with loss. Moreover, because they too may hold assumptions about how one should react when a loss is experienced, individuals who have encountered loss may harshly evaluate their own responses and may believe them to indicate underlying problems or pathology (Silver and Wortman 1980).

Because assumptions about the grieving process are likely to have a pervasive impact on how reactions to loss are evaluated, we feel it is important to identify those assumptions that are most prevalent in our culture and to consider systematically the available research data in support of each one. We have identified five assumptions that we believe to be very prevalent in the grief literature. In the following sections, the validity of each assumption is evaluated against the available research data. While much of the early work in this area suffered from serious methodological shortcomings (e.g., reliance on subjective impressions of unstructured interview data, unstandardized measurements, and biased samples, etc.; *see* Silver and Wortman 1980 for a review), recent research in the bereavement and physical disability areas has improved on the deficiencies of previous literature. In the following discussion, we review only what we believe to be the best empirical work available to test the assumptions we have identified. Except where indicated, all of this work has used standardized outcome measures and structured interviews of relatively large, unbiased samples and followed them over time. In the concluding sections of this article, we explore the implications of the available data for theory, research, and intervention following loss, and consider why such myths about coping with loss may have been perpetuated despite the absence of validating data.

Distress or Depression Is Inevitable

It is widely assumed in our culture that when a major loss is experienced, the normal way to react is with intense distress or depression. The most prevalent theories in the area of grief and loss, such as the classic psychodynamic models (e.g., Freud [1917] 1957) and Bowlby's (1980) attachment model, are based on the assumption that at some point, individuals will confront the reality of their loss and go through a period of intense distress or depression. In the recent authoritative report on bereavement published by the Institute of Medicine, it was stated that there is a "near-universal occurrence of intense emotional distress following bereavement, with features similar in nature and intensity to those of clinical depression" (Osterweis, Solomon, and Green 1984:18). Similarly, depression has been the foremost reaction reported and discussed in the literature on spinal cord injury (Bracken and Shepard 1980; Deegan 1977; Gunther 1971; Knorr and Bull 1970).

As empirical evidence has begun to accumulate, however, it is clear that the assumption of intense universal distress following a major loss such as bereavement or spinal cord injury may be unwarranted. It is true that in the bereavement literature, some studies have reported that feelings of sadness or depressed mood are fairly common. For example, Glick, Weiss, and Parkes (1974) have noted that 88 percent of the widows they studied experienced depressed mood (*see also* Clayton, Halikas, and Maurice 1971). However, in those investigations that have included a more systematic and rigorous assessment of depression or distress, it is clear that such a reaction is by no means universal. In one study, Clayton, Halikas, and Maurice (1972) interviewed widows within 30 days of losing their spouse. Using strict diagnostic criteria to assess depression, they found that only a minority of respondents (35 percent) could be classified as definitely or probably depressed. Similarly, Vachon et al. (1982) found that 1 month after the loss, 30 percent of the widows they studied scored below 5 on the General Health Questionnaire (GHQ)—a score considered insufficient to warrant further psychiatric assessment. In their sample of primarily Mormon elderly bereaved individuals, Lund, Caserta, and Dimond (1986) reported that only 14.6 percent of the men and 19.2 percent of the women they studied at 3 weeks postloss evidenced "at least mild" depression on the Zung Depression Scale. In fact, only 12.5 to 20 percent of this sample reported scores exceeding the cutoff score delineated as indicating depression at any of six different assessment points from 3–4 weeks to 2 years postloss.

Examination of empirical data in the spinal cord injury literature reveals a similar pattern. For example, Howell et al. (1981) conducted a careful assessment of 22 patients who had been injured approximately 1 month, and followed them for an average of 9 weeks. Each patient was interviewed utilizing the Schedule of Affective Disorders and Schizophrenia and completed the Beck Depression Inventory weekly. Only a minority of patients (22.7 percent) experienced a depressive disorder following injury that met Research Diagnostic Criteria (*see also* Fullerton et al. 1981). Similarly, Lawson (1976) studied spinal-cord-injured patients 5 days a week for the entire length of their rehabilitation stay. Despite a multimethod assessment of depression (self-report, professional ratings, and psychoendocrine and behavioral measures), there was no clear period of at least a week in which measures were consistently in the depressive range for any patient (*see also* Malec and Neimeyer 1983). Thus, the few systematic investigations that are available have failed to demonstrate the inevitability of depression following loss.

Distress Is Necessary, and Failure to Experience Distress Is Indicative of Pathology

The clinical literature is clear in suggesting that those who fail to respond to loss with intense distress are reacting abnormally (e.g., Deutsch 1937; Marris 1958). Bowlby has identified "prolonged absence of conscious grieving" (1980:138) as one of two types of disordered mourning. In the previously mentioned Institute of Medicine report, "absent grief" was classified as one of two forms of "pathologic" mourning (Osterweis, Solomon, and Green 1984:65). This report emphasized that it is commonly assumed, particularly by clinicians, "that the absence of grieving phenomena following bereavement represents some form of personality pathology" (p. 18). Although the authors noted that there is little empirical evidence in support of this assumption, they concluded nonetheless that "professional help may be warranted for persons who show no evidence of having begun grieving" (p. 65). The assumption that distress or depression is a necessary part of the grieving process is also quite prevalent in the literature on spinal cord injury (e.g., Karney 1976; Kerr and Thompson 1972; Nemiah 1957; *see* Trieschmann 1978, 1980 for reviews). In fact, authors have maintained that depression is therapeutic because it signals that the person is beginning to confront the realities of his or her situation (e.g., Cook 1976; Dinardo 1971; Nemiah 1957).

The belief that distress should occur is so powerful that it also leads to negative attributions toward those who do not show evidence of it. One such attribution is that the person is denying the loss. As Siller (1969) has maintained regarding the disabled,

> occasionally a newly disabled person does not seem to be particularly depressed, and this should be a matter of concern. . . . A person should be depressed because something significant has happened, and not to respond as such is denial. Such obvious denial is rare except in the case of a retarded person or in the very young. (p. 292)

A second attribution is that the person is emotionally too weak to initiate the grieving process. Drawing from clinical experience with patients undergoing psychiatric treatment, Deutsch (1937) maintained that grief-related affect was sometimes omitted among individuals who were not emotionally strong enough to begin grieving. A third attribution is that individuals who fail to grieve are simply unable to become attached to others. For example, Raphael (1983) suggested that among those who do not show signs of grief, the preexisting relationship may have been "purely narcissistic with little recognition of the real person who was lost" (pp. 205–6).

If, in fact, depression is necessary following loss, those people who experience a period of depression should adapt more successfully than those who do not become depressed. However, this view has not been substantiated empirically. In contrast, several studies have found that those who are most distressed shortly following loss are among those likely to be most distressed 1 to 2 years later. For example, Vachon et al. (1982) found that among 162 widows, an elevated score 1 month postloss on the GHQ, a measure of distress and social functioning, was the most powerful predictor of high distress 24 months later. Similarly, Lund et al. (1985–1986) found that the best predictor of long-term coping difficulties among elderly widows and widowers was the presence of strong negative emotional responses to the loss (such as expressing a desire to die and crying) during the early bereavement period (*see also* Bornstein et al. 1973; Parkes and Weiss 1983 for similar findings).[1] Comparable results have been obtained by investigators studying spinal cord injury. In a cross-sectional study of 53 male spinal-cord-injured patients, Dinardo (1971) assessed depressed mood by self-report and professional assessments. Results indicated that the absence of depression was associated with higher self-concepts and with staff ratings of successful adjustment to the disability, leading the author to conclude that "those individuals who react to spinal cord injury with depression are less well adjusted at any given point in their rehabilitation than the individuals who do not react with depression" (p. 52) (*see* Lawson 1976 and Malec and Neimeyer 1983 for comparable findings).

An important component of the view that depression is necessary is that if individuals fail to experience distress shortly after the loss, symptoms of distress will erupt at a later point. Marris (1958) has commented that "much later, in response to a less important or trivial loss, the death of a more distant relative, a pet—the bereaved person is overwhelmed by intense grief" (p. 27) (*see also* Bowlby 1980; Rando 1984). It is also widely believed that the failure to grieve will result in subsequent health problems. The Institute of Medicine report (Osterweis, Solomon, and Green 1984) reviewed the work of several clinicians who suggested that those who fail to grieve outwardly may manifest their depression through a variety of physical symptoms or somatic complaints.

Despite its prevalence, available evidence provides little support for the assumption that those who fail to experience distress shortly after loss will have difficulties later. In the previously mentioned study of bereavement by Clayton et al. (*see* Bornstein et al. 1973), interviews were conducted with 109 widows and widowers at 1 month, 4 months, and 13 months postloss. As noted earlier, only 35 percent of these respondents were classified as either definitely or probably depressed at the 1-month interview. However, only 3 of the remaining 71 respondents had become depressed by the 4-month interview. Moreover, only 1 subject evidenced depression for the first time at 13 months postloss, leading the investigators to conclude that "delayed" grief is relatively rare. Similar findings were obtained in a longitudinal study of 99 widows conducted by Vachon et al. (1982). Thirty-two of these women were classified as "low distress" by virtue of their scores on the GHQ 1 month postloss, and 94 percent continued to evidence "low distress" when interviewed 2 years later. In fact, only 2 women in the study who had low distress scores at 1 month had high distress scores at the 2-year interview.

A very similar pattern of findings was obtained in our recent longitudinal study of 124 patients who had lost an infant to Sudden Infant Death Syndrome (SIDS; Silver and Wortman 1988; Wortman and Silver 1987, in press). Parents were classified as exhibiting low or high distress at the initial interview 3 weeks postloss on the basis of their scores on the depression subscale of the Symptom Check List-90 (SCL-90; Derogatis 1977). As in the previously described research, most respondents in this study who showed low distress at 3 weeks also showed low distress 18 months later. Only a small percentage of the sample moved from low to high distress over the period of study. Those parents who were evidencing low distress shortly after their baby's death were no more likely than parents who reported high distress to indicate that the pregnancy had been unplanned or difficult to accept; nor did they differ in their evaluation of their babies as having been beautiful, intelligent, and happy while alive. Thus, these data fail to support the notion that absence of distress may be due to insufficient attachment to the lost loved one.[2]

In summary, the bulk of research to date provides little support for the widely held view that those who fail to exhibit early distress will show subsequent difficulties. The data clearly suggest that "absent grief" is not necessarily problematic, and, at least as it is assesssed in the studies conducted to date, "delayed grief" is far less common than clinical lore would suggest.

The Importance of "Working Through" the Loss

It is widely assumed that a period of depression will occur once the person confronts the reality of his or her loss. Then, it is commonly believed, the person must "work through" or process what has happened in order to recover successfully (*see* Brown and Stoudemire 1983; Doyle 1980). Implicit in this assumption is the notion that individuals need to focus on and "process" what has happened and that attempts to deny the implications of the loss, or block feelings or thoughts about it, will ultimately be unproductive (cf. Bowlby 1980; Parkes and Weiss 1983). Marris (1958) maintained that "if the bereaved cannot work through this process of grieving they may suffer lasting emotional damage" (p. 29). Rando (1984) concurred with this assessment, stating that "for the griever who has not attended to his grief, the pain is as acute and fresh ten years later as it was the day after" (p. 114).

On the basis of statements such as these, it might be expected that those who show evidence of "working through" their loss in the weeks or months following it will be more successful in resolving the loss than those who do not. However, the limited evidence that is available suggests that this may not be the case. Although they did not assess "working through" the loss specifically, Parkes and Weiss (1983) conducted a comprehensive study of bereavement that provided data of possible relevance to this concept. Respondents were rated by coders on the degree to which they evidenced yearning or pining for the deceased 3 weeks after their loss. Subjects were divided into a "High Yearning" group, composed of those respondents who appeared to yearn or pine constantly, frequently, or whenever inactive, and a "Low Yearning" group, who yearned never, seldom, or only when reminded of the loss. In fact, high initial yearning was found to be predictive of poor mental and physical health outcomes at 13 months postloss. As Parkes and Weiss (1983) expressed it, "We might suppose that people who avoid or repress grief are the most likely to become disturbed a year later, yet this is not the case" (p. 47). Interestingly, high initial yearning was associated with poor outcome even at the final interview conducted 2 to 4 years after the loss.

In our previously described study of parents who suffered a SIDS loss (Silver and Wortman 1988; Wortman and Silver 1987), we also examined the impact of early evidence of "working through" the loss on subsequent adjustment. "Working through" was operationalized as active attempts by the parent to make sense of and process the death, including searching for an answer for why the baby had died, thinking of ways the death could have been avoided, and being preoccupied with thoughts about the loss. Results indicated that the more parents were "working through" the death at the 3-week interview, the more distressed they were, as measured by the SCL-90 18 months later. In addition, those subjects who showed the least evidence of emotional resolution 18 months after the death of their infant (measured by distress in thinking and talking about the baby, feeling bitterness about the loss, and being upset by reminders of the baby) were those most likely to be processing the loss shortly after the death.

To date, there is relatively little empirical evidence relevant to the issue of "working through." If behaviors such as yearning for the deceased or being preoccupied with thoughts about the loss are conceptualized as "working through," however, the available research challenges the assumption that the absence of this process is necessarily maladaptive. Like early evidence of intense distress, early signs of intense efforts to "work through" the loss may portend subsequent difficulties.

The Expectation of Recovery

It is generally assumed that although a person who experiences an irrevocable loss will go through a phase of intense distress, this will not last indefinitely. In fact, after a relatively brief period of time, the person is expected to achieve a state of recovery and return to normal role functioning (cf. Silver and Wortman 1980). Almost every stage model of coping with loss postulates a final stage of adaptation, which may be called recovery (Klinger 1975, 1977), acceptance (Kübler-Ross 1969), or reorganization (Bowlby 1980). "Chronic grief" or failure to recover is identified as a major type of "pathological" mourning in virtually every major treatise on the bereavement process (e.g., Bowlby 1980; Osterweis, Solomon, and Green 1984; Raphael 1983). Similarly, failure to accept the loss of one's abilities is felt to impede motivation and rehabilitation of the spinal-cord-injured patient (e.g., Heijn and Granger 1974).

None of the theories postulate precisely how much time should elapse before recovery from an irrevocable loss. In the bereavement literature, notions about the length of the recovery process have been shifting over the last four decades. Early studies of bereavement suggested that its psychological impact was relatively transient. In fact, in his study of people who lost a loved one in Boston's Cocoanut Grove nightclub disaster, Lindemann (1944) painted an optimistic picture of the recovery process, noting that with appropriate psychiatric intervention, it was ordinarily possible to settle an uncomplicated grief reaction in 4 to 6 weeks. However, recent research evidence suggests that it may take considerably longer to recover from the loss of a loved one, especially when the loss is sudden and traumatic (*see* Silverman and Wortman 1980; Tait and Silver 1989 for reviews). In the previously discussed studies by Vachon and her associates, 38 percent of the widows studied were experiencing a high level of distress after 1 year, and 26 percent were still classified as exhibiting high distress at the end of 2 years (Vachon et al. 1982a; Vachon et al. 1982b). In the longitudinal study of widows and widowers conducted by Parkes and Weiss (1983), more than 40 percent of the sample was rated by trained interviewers as showing moderate to severe anxiety 2 to 4 years after the loss. Feelings of depression, as well as problems in functioning, were also quite common at the 2- to 4-year interview, particularly if the loss was sudden. Zisook and Shuchter (1986) had widows and widowers complete interviews and questionnaires at 11 points in time, ranging from 3–4 weeks after their loss to 4 years later. Even at 4 years postloss, at least 20 percent of the bereaved assessed their own adjustment as "fair or poor," while only 44 percent assessed it as excellent (*see* Lund et al. 1985–1986 for comparable findings).

A study by Elizur and Kaffman (1982, 1983), which examined behavior changes over a 3½-year period among normal kibbutz children whose fathers had been killed in war, found negative consequences in response to the deaths. While none of these children evidenced unusual psychopathology prior to their loss, they were subsequently found to be at risk for a variety of problems. Almost 50 percent showed emotional disturbance in each phase of the study—6, 18, and 42 months postloss. More than two-thirds of the bereaved children reacted with severe psychological problems and impairment in diverse areas of functioning. Similar findings were obtained in a study by Lehman, Wortman, and Williams (1987), which focused explicitly on the long-term effects of the sudden, unexpected loss of a spouse or child in a motor vehicle accident 4 to 7 years earlier. Interviews were conducted with bereaved respondents, who were matched with a control group of nonbereaved individuals on sex, age, income, education, and number and ages of children. Significant differences between bereaved and control respondents were found on several indicators of functioning, including depression and other psychiatric symptoms, social functioning, divorce, psychological well-being, and mortality.

Taken together, the aforementioned evidence suggests that prevailing notions of recovery deserve reconsideration. There is growing evidence that a substantial minority of individuals continues to exhibit distress for a much longer period of time than would commonly be assumed.

Reaching a State of Resolution

It is widely assumed that over time, as a result of "working through" their loss, individuals will achieve a state of resolution regarding what has happened. One important type of resolution involves accepting the loss intellectually. Parkes and Weiss (1983) argued that people must come up with a rationale for the loss; they must be able to understand what has happened and make sense of it (*see also* Moos and Schaefer 1986). Similarly, Craig (1977), in her writings on the loss of a child, maintained that an essential part of grief work is to resolve the meaninglessness of the crisis (*see also* Marris 1958; Miles and Crandall 1983). A second type of resolution involves accepting the loss emotionally. Emotional acceptance is thought to be reached when the person no longer feels the need to avoid reminders of the loss in order to function. The lost person can be recalled, and reminders can be confronted without intense emotional pain (Parkes and Weiss 1983). It is generally expected that much of the grief work engaged in by those who have endured loss, such as reviewing the events of the death or the course of the illness or accident, will aid in resolution.

Although few studies have focused on the issue of resolution, the limited data that are available suggest that a state of resolution may not always be achieved (e.g., Silver, Boon, and Stones 1983). In the study by Parkes and Weiss (1983), 61 percent of the respondents who had suddenly lost their spouse, and 29 percent of those who had forewarning, were still asking why the event had happened 2 to 4 years later. More than 40 percent of those who had suddenly lost a spouse, and 15 percent of those with forewarning, continued to agree with the statement "It's not real; I feel that I'll wake up and it won't be true." Similar data were obtained in our aforementioned study of coping with the loss of an infant to SIDS. At all three of the time points we studied (3 weeks, 3 months, and 18 months postloss), the vast majority of respondents were unable to find any meaning in their baby's death and were unable to answer the question "Why me?" or "Why my baby?" (Wortman and Silver 1987). A particularly intriguing feature of our data is that we found little evidence that resolution is achieved over time. In contrast, the number of parents who were unable to find meaning in their babies' deaths increased significantly between the first and second interviews.

The aforementioned study of the long-term impact of losing a loved one in a motor vehicle accident (Lehman, Wortman, and Williams 1987) also found that even after 4 to 7 years, most respondents had not achieved a state of resolution. In this investigation, almost half of the sample had reviewed events leading up to the accident in the month prior to the interview. A majority of the respondents were unable to find any meaning in the loss, had had thoughts that the death was unfair, and had had painful memories of their spouse or child during the past month.

In the spinal cord literature, there is a dearth of longitudinal studies following individuals for very long after their injury. Nonetheless, there is limited evidence suggesting that it may take individuals longer to resolve their loss than is commonly assumed. In a cross-sectional study of patients disabled up to 38 years earlier, Shadish, Hickman, and Arrick (1981) reported that many of them still thought about the things they could not do since their injury and "really missed" these things almost weekly.

Considered together, these data provide convergent evidence that, contrary to popular belief, individuals are not always able to achieve resolution regarding their loss and to come up with an explanation for the experience that is satisfying to them. Particularly when the event is sudden, a majority of individuals appear to have great difficulty in coming to terms with what has happened.

Implications for Theory, Research, and Intervention

Theories of grief and mourning, as well as clinical lore, maintain that virtually all individuals who experience an important loss should go through the grief process, beginning with a phase of intense distress and followed by ultimate recovery over time as the person comes to terms with the loss (Donovon and Girton 1984; Jette 1983; Osterweis, Solomon, and Green 1984). Alternate patterns are usually labeled as pathological or deviant (Brown and Stoudemire 1983; Osterweis, Solomon, and Green 1984; Simons 1985). Our analysis suggests that, in contrast to this view, there are at least three common patterns of adaptation to loss. Some individuals indeed seem to go through the expected pattern, moving from high to low distress over time. But others appear not to show intense distress, either immediately after the loss or at subsequent intervals. Still others seem to continue in a state of high distress for much longer than would be expected.

Traditional theories of grief and loss are able to account for those who move from high to low distress and resolve their grief over time. But these theories offer little explanation of why some people might consistently respond with less distress than expected and others might fail to recover or resolve their loss over time. In this section we consider the theoretical, research, and clinical implications of each of these groups in turn.

Failure to Become Depressed

Because of the assumption that early distress is inevitable, limited research has carefully examined the range of emotions that may occur in the first few weeks or months after a loss. Are there some individuals who show very little, if any, feelings of distress (Silver and Wortman 1988), or do virtually all people experience some feelings of sadness (Wright 1983)? Can people show other indications of mourning, such as preoccupation with the loss or pining for it, without becoming depressed? Are those individuals who show little distress also likely to show few signs of positive emotion (Deutsch 1937)? Among those who show very little distress, is this best understood as a "shock" or "denial" reaction, or is it a sign of coping strength and resilience? Research that assesses respondents frequently in the early period following loss (e.g., Lawson 1975) would help to address these questions.

Although failure to become distressed following loss is typically viewed as indicative of a problem, we have little evidence to suggest that those who initially show minimal distress following loss are likely to become significantly depressed at a later point. In subsequent studies, it will be important to look closely at people who show low initial levels of distress. Are such people more vulnerable to subsequent minor losses, as some theorists would lead us to expect? Are they more likely to develop somatic symptoms or physical health problems (Brown and Stoudemire 1983) or problems in other areas of their lives, such as at work or in their interpersonal relationships? The data we have reviewed above provide suggestive evidence that low initial distress may not signal pathology. However, more systematic data are needed before we can dismiss the firmly entrenched view that "absent grief" is a cause for concern. In collecting such data, it will be important to go beyond the self-report methodology that is used almost exclusively in current research on reactions to loss. Individuals who indicate that they are not distressed immediately after a loss may also be unwilling to admit subsequent problems in other areas of their lives. Supplementing self-reports of symptomatology with more objective indicators of problems, such as measures of behavioral physiological functioning (e.g., from physical health records or from observational ratings made by members of the individual's work and social networks), are important directions for subsequent work in this area.

If results obtained from further studies are consistent with the results reviewed herein, we must acknowledge the possibility that a sizable minority of people may come through the bereavement process relatively unscathed. As psychologist Norman Garmezy has indicated, "our mental health practitioners and researchers are predisposed by interest, investment, and training in seeing deviance, psychopathology, and weakness wherever they look" (Garmezy 1982a:xvii). By assuming latent pathology among those who fail to show intense distress following a loss, attention appears to have been deflected away from identifying strengths (e.g., high self-esteem; Lund et al. 1985–1986) or coping resources (e.g., premorbid coping styles or adequate social support systems; *see* Kessler, Price, and Wortman 1985) that may protect these people from distress. The data also suggest that some people may have something in place beforehand—perhaps a religious or philosophical orientation or outlook on life—that enables them to cope with their experience almost immediately (Silver and Wortman 1988). Clearly, future research is necessary to examine the role that such resources may play in protecting people from the deleterious effects of loss.

The implications of our analysis for treatment and intervention are straightforward. Rather than recognizing the absence of grief as a sign of possible strengths of the individual (Gans 1981), the expectation that individuals must go through a period of distress may lead health care providers to provoke such a reaction, even if it is not warranted. For example, regarding spinal cord injury, Nemiah (1957) has written, "It is often necessary to confront the patient gently but firmly with the reality of his situation, and to force him into a period of depression while he works out his acceptance of his loss" (p. 146). When dealing with the bereaved, physicians have been reminded to encourage patients to express their distress, and to bring "latent anger and guilt to a conscious level of awareness" (Brown and Stoudemire 1983:382). In a manual for grief counselors, Doyle (1980) has discouraged the use of tranquilizers or antidepressants by the bereaved during the early stages of grief, since grief "needs to be felt in all its ramifications" (p. 15) (*see also* Rando 1984).

Failure to Resolve or Recover From the Loss

Because it is widely believed that individuals will recover from a loss within a year or so, only a handful of studies have focused on the issue of long-term recovery. Yet, as noted above, there appears to be considerable variability in the length of time it may take to recover from a loss, and some people do not seem to recover despite the passage of many years. This has led to increasing interest in identifying mediating factors that may promote or impede psychosocial recovery (Kessler, Price, and Wortman 1985; Silver and Wortman 1980). Recent research has, in fact, identified factors that may enhance the likelihood that individuals will react to loss with intense and prolonged distress. These include the nature of the relationship with the deceased, circumstances surrounding the loss, the presence of concomitant stressors, and the availability of social support (*see* Wortman and Silver 1987 for an extended discussion).

In our judgment, an unfortunate consequence of the pervasive belief in recovery from loss is that attention has been deflected away from examining the possible mechanisms through which loss may produce subsequent and continued mental or physical health problems. A number of different mechanisms have been suggested in the literature (Jacobs and Douglas 1979; Klerman and Izen 1977; Osterweis, Solomon, and Green 1984; Stroebe and Stroebe 1983). For example, grieving appears to involve changes to the respiratory, autonomic, cardiovascular, and endocrine systems (*see* Osterweis, Solomon, and Green 1984 for a review). In fact, the Institute of Medicine report on bereavement concluded that "preliminary data now available make it clear that traumatic loss experiences may have a long-term impact on the body's immune system" (Osterweis, Solomon, and Green 1984:170). Such changes may result in increased susceptibility to illness and infections, as well as long-term health problems, both of which may also have deleterious psychological effects. Loss may also result in changes in health maintenance behavior, such as eating regular meals and exercise. Moreover, loss of a loved one often removes a major source of social support, and this may account for the pathogenic effects of bereavement. Finally, experiencing an irrevocable loss such as bereavement or spinal cord injury might alter the individual's view of the world (e.g., Lilliston 1985; Parkes and Weiss 1983). Indeed, in their study of the long-term effects of losing a loved one in a motor vehicle accident, Lehman, Wortman, and Williams (1987) found that many of the respondents had come to see the world as a hostile place where things can be taken away in a moment. Such an altered world view is likely to be associated with depression, passivity, and impaired motivation to engage in subsequent coping efforts. Clearly, evidence concerning the precise mechanisms through which loss leads to long-term difficulties is essential not only for theoretical advancement, but also to guide intervention efforts in the area of grief and loss.

The expectation that individuals will recover from irrevocable loss within a limited period of time may unfortunately lead health care providers to react negatively to those who fail to recover. In fact, those who do not recover within the prescribed time limits have been derogated in the literature (e.g., Falek and Britton 1974). And although it has been acknowledged that the progression to adjustment may be unsteady, health care professionals are nonetheless often reminded to encourage movement forward. As Stewart (1977–1978) has written, "To be blunt, a pat on the back and a kick in the pants are often necessary" (p. 341).

Conclusion

As reviewed above, assumptions about the process of coping with loss fail to be supported and in some cases are contradicted by available empirical work on the topic. Why might such erroneous beliefs continue in the absence of validating data collected in methodologically rigorous research and in the presence of data indicating extreme variability in responses to loss? As Silver and Wortman (1980) discussed, even if they are not supported by data, widespread assumptions about the coping process may be particularly resistant to disconfirming evidence. Social psychological research has demonstrated repeatedly that "people tend to seek out, recall, and interpret evidence in a manner that sustains beliefs" (Nisbett and Ross 1980:192). Thus, the interpretation of data tends to be strongly biased by the expectations researchers, clinicians, and laypersons may hold (Nisbett and Ross 1980; *see also* Goldiamond 1975; Wright 1983), and these errors in information processing lead people's implicit theories to be "almost impervious to data" (Nisbett and Ross 1980:169).

As noted earlier, the assumption that distress is inevitable shortly after a loss has resulted in its absence being treated as pathological, even if there is no objective reason to assume this to be true. Studies that fail to find problems resulting from the absence of grief may be dismissed for not looking long enough, not looking closely enough, or not asking the correct questions (Volkan 1966). Such insistence on distress following loss has been labeled the "requirement of mourning" (Dembo, Leviton, and Wright 1956; Wright 1983). This hypothesis describes the need of outsiders to "insist that the person they consider unfortunate is suffering (even when that person seems not to be suffering) or devaluate the unfortunate person because he or she ought to suffer" (Dembo, Leviton, and Wright 1956:21). This requirement of mourning may explain why health care professionals tend to assume the presence of significantly more distress following loss than individuals report experiencing themselves (Baluk and O'Neill 1980; Gans 1981; Klas 1970; Mason and Muhlenkamp 1976; Schoenberg et al. 1969; Taylor 1967; Wikler, Wasow, and Hatfield 1981).

A series of complementary processes might explain the perpetuation of the assumption that the presence of long-term distress is "abnormal." Silver and Wortman (1980) argued that outsiders may minimize the length of time a loss will affect an individual who encounters it because they may be unaware that, in addition to the loss itself, the individual must also contend with the simultaneous destruction of future hopes and plans that were vitiated by the loss. Outsiders may also be unaware of the possible alterations in views of the world that may occur as a result of a loss (Silver and Wortman 1980). The fact that individuals who have experienced loss are often implored to control their expressions of grief and to stop "dwelling on their problems" (Glick, Weiss, and Parkes 1974; Maddison and Walker 1967) suggests that outsiders also believe that the distressed could behave more appropriately if they wished. In fact, as Wright (1983) maintained, society frowns upon open displays of distress and has a "requirement of cheerfulness" that in fact contradicts its simultaneous "requirement of mourning." It is likely that this subtle yet sometimes explicit message discourages the person who has encountered loss from expressing distress to others at all. Over time this process may become even more intensified. Perhaps so as to maintain harmonious social relations and not to be perceived as abnormal, the individual may continue to hide the true degree of his or her distress from members of the social network (Tait and Silver 1989). Thus, the stigma that is associated with persistent difficulties following loss may result in self-presentational strategies that are in line with societal expectations, resulting in a discrepancy between public expressions and private experience of ongoing distress (Tait and Silver 1989). The very act of concealing common aspects of the loss experience is likely to perpetuate the misconception that grief is time limited for all but the few whose reactions are deemed pathological.

In summary, we maintain that a complex mixture of biased input and interpretation of data by outsiders, their own personal needs, as well as limited opportunity for open communication between parties, has led to a perpetuation of unrealistic assumptions about the normal process of coping with loss. In addition, unrealistic assumptions held by health care professionals and the social network may also unnecessarily exacerbate feelings of distress among those who encounter loss, and lead to a self-perception that their own responses are inappropriate and abnormal under the circumstances.

Of course, the ability to identify pathological responses to loss would enable health care professionals to target those individuals who may be in need of professional assistance (Bracken and Shepard 1980; Falek and Britton 1974; Silver and Wortman 1980). Perhaps this goal has overridden acceptance of alternatives to the current views regarding adjustment to loss. As Zisook and Shuchter (1986) have indicated, at the present time "there is no prescription for how to grieve properly for a lost spouse, and no research-validated guideposts for what is normal vs. deviant mourning. . . . We are *just beginning* to realize the full range of what may be considered 'normal' grieving" (p. 288, italics added). Recognition of this variability is crucial in order that those who experience loss are treated nonjudgmentally and with the respect, sensitivity, and compassion they deserve.

NOTES

1. Of course, this does not necessarily imply that it is detrimental to go through a period of depression following loss. Undoubtedly, some of the people who are most depressed after the loss may be those who have enduring psychological difficulties that were present prior to the loss. In the research that has been conducted to date, it is not possible to discriminate between those respondents who became depressed primarily as a result of their loss and those who had a lifelong history of psychological disturbance. Only prospective designs, which assess such confounding variables prior to the loss, can help to shed light on this issue. Because most loss events are relatively infrequent, prospective studies are prohibitively costly and thus have rarely been attempted.

2. The only evidence for delayed grief that we have been able to uncover comes from a study by Parkes and Weiss (1983). These investigators found that widows who reported having had marriages characterized by high conflict displayed little or no emotional distress in the weeks following their loss. However, at the thirteen-month and two- to four-year follow-up interviews, these widows were evidencing greater difficulties than those women whose marriages were characterized by low conflict.

V
Stress Management

Psychologists, physicians, and other professional workers have offered scores of suggestions and techniques for managing stress more efficiently. While empirical validation of effectiveness is lacking in many instances, the popularity of stress management strategies continues to soar. Selections in part V are offered as some examples of currently popular stress management techniques and guidelines, as well as of contemporary criticism and controversy in this area. We present these techniques and guidelines without implying anything about their effectiveness—they are, however, examples currently being regarded as serious and sensible approaches to managing stress. (A more complete accounting of stress management procedures may be found in Davis, Eshelman, and McKay 1988; Girdano, Everly, and Dusek 1990; Greenberg 1990.)

Roskies (1987) traces the roots of stress management and distinguishes it from other approaches to helping people in distress.[1] Essentially, Roskies argues that stress management is based on the view that problems develop when the person uses inappropriate or ineffectual attempts to cope with a perceived imbalance between demands and resources. Unlike traditional forms of psychotherapy, stress management does not assume that stress-related problems are the result of intrapsychic conflicts, psychopathology, or intractable emotional distress. It attempts to teach new coping skills so that the person can manage his or her environment more effectively or with less distress. Cognitive behavior therapy is favored by Roskies because of its emphasis on improving the person's competency in handling significant aspects of the surrounding world through the teaching of coping skills.

Cox's (1990) article offers the application of stress management techniques to sport psychology, a field of study which relates the principles of psychology to the athlete—to enhance athletic performance and promote human enrichment. One of the more interesting aspects of Cox's material has to do with his emphasis on the importance of applying the various techniques on an individual basis, rather than indiscriminately to all team members. For example, depending on initial levels of arousal, some athletes will benefit from efforts to reduce arousal, while others will benefit from efforts to "psych them up."[2] Team coaches need to tailor intervention strategies carefully to individual players.

Some of the techniques Cox discusses are oriented primarily around the reduction of tension and anxiety through the elicitation of the "relaxation response," a series of physiological changes that oppose the activity of the sympathetic nervous system. Other techniques are primarily cognitive strategies used to help the athlete mentally prepare for competition and/or reduce the debilitating effects of stress on performance. Still other techniques are actually combinations of the above techniques, packaged or tailored to meet the needs of individual athletes. Finally, Cox discusses intervention strategies which are useful for increasing an athlete's arousal and activation levels in situations where motivation for performing may be inappropriately low.

Drug and alcohol abuse, smoking, compulsive overeating, and other habits are sometimes adopted as ways of coping with stress. There is great ferment about how to deal with drugs and alcohol in our society. Because such habits are often dangerous to health, illegal, and so on, people will at times decide to "kick the habit." When done with the help of professionals, the statistics regarding quitting are not particularly encouraging—leading some to conclude that addictions are almost impossible to overcome. In our next selection, Peele (1983) provides an optimistic picture of the effectiveness of *self-help* in many cases of addiction. He argues that reliance on professionals and an emphasis on addiction are detrimental to success because they foster dependency on another (namely, on the therapist) and a sense of not being responsible for one's own behavior. Peele takes issue with the usual explanation of addictions—that they are entirely biologically based. He believes addictions—which should be called dependencies—are caused partly at least by the individual's social situation, attitudes, and expectations. The stages of self-cure, according to Peele, include:

accumulated unhappiness about the addiction, a moment of truth, changing patterns and identity, and dealing with relapses.

Peele's article was written for a popular magazine and thus while it makes reference to research studies, details are sketchy. Moreover, his views are certain to alienate those professionals who see addictions as "disease." As but one example of the controversy generated by Peele's position, consider the traditional warning given to recovered alcoholics by groups such as Alcoholics Anonymous. The warning is that a recovered alcoholic must never have another drink, lest he or she will once again become hooked by uncontrollable drinking. But, as Peele suggests, the addict who successfully modifies his or her life can control occasional lapses, just as people who quit smoking and who diet have to learn also to deal with lapses. Regarding the alcoholic in particular, preliminary studies do suggest that controlled drinking is a possibility (e.g., Marlatt 1985; Marlatt, Demming, and Reid 1973; Sobell and Sobell 1976, 1978). Though these and related studies are controversial (e.g., Marlatt 1983), they nevertheless do highlight Peele's stance and provide some support for it. All in all, Peele's article raises some extremely important issues and concerns regarding the management of what are often self-destructive coping behaviors.

Stress management in the workplace is the focus of our last selection. Pelletier and Lutz (1988) review studies of stress management programs in the workplace and conclude that the usual pre-packaged training and stress management seminars offered to the business community do not provide an effective format for learning to manage stress. They suggest that successful programs should, among other things, be geared to symptomatic and high-risk individuals, employ traditional, problem-focused, brief psychotherapy, and include program evaluation.[3]

One of the criticisms of stress management programs in the workplace is that they essentially "blame the victim" for experienced stress, overlooking the many possible occupational stressors present in the work environment. As noted by Schore

> The dominant approach to stress reduction developed from a focus on executive and managerial stress. This approach, however, does not adequately take into account the conditions of clerical, service, and blue-collar workers, nor has it developed remedies that are as useful to these workers. It is an approach that remains focused on treating the individual and reducing the effects of stress that are felt by that individual. While it utilizes some valid and important techniques that can reduce the physiological symptoms of some stress reactions, it generally does not look beyond the individual to identify the sources

> of stress. It emphasizes a good person-environment fit, but the person is expected to do the fitting. Sophisticated tests are being developed so that corporations can presort what kinds of personality types will fit into existing job categories. There is no comparable attempt to change the jobs to fit the needs of the existing human beings. While we believe that individuals can be helped to find relief from the effects of stress, any attempt to reduce stress must act to reduce or mitigate the stressors in the environment. (1984:297–98)

Or as Pelletier and Lutz caution, "Whether group or individual approaches are employed, it is also essential to modify hazardous working conditions to avoid the paradox of 'healthy people in unhealthy places' " (1988:12).

NOTES

1. In tracing the roots of stress management, Roskies summarizes some of the historical and theoretical materials covered elsewhere in this anthology (*see* Folkman and Lazarus 1990; Selye 1982; Singer and Davidson 1986). We have left Roskies' description intact because of its usefulness to this section of the book and its clarity.

It should be noted that Roskies' discussion was originally presented in the context of describing stress management procedures for treating Type A behavior. Her discussion, however, is a general one and applies to other stress-related problems as well.

2. Much of what Cox discusses is based in part on classic work in learning psychology such as the inverted-U concept of Yerkes and Dodson (1908).

3. Compare Pelletier and Lutz' views of stress management with those of Roskies.

21

Stress Management: A New Approach to Treatment

ETHEL ROSKIES

A recent cartoon strip by Jules Feiffer neatly summarizes the current fad of stress treatments: a rather bedraggled young woman declares that she once had anxiety, but now she has stress. Therefore, she goes to a weekly stress lab where she stress raps, takes stress tests and stress exercises, follows a stress diet and pops stress vitamins, goes out with stress mates, and plays stress games. She even has stress sex. As she triumphantly concludes: "Anxiety was so isolated; thank God for stress."

Like all good cartoons this one caricatures reality, but also reflects it. Stress has become the fashionable disease of our time, and treatment of stress is a popular and profitable activity (*see* Roskies 1983). Moreover, this is an activity in which everyone can participate, since there are no evident restrictions on types of therapists, treatments, or clients. Even if one excludes the obviously fraudulent and bizarre, the list of treatments currently being packaged under the stress management label is wide; massage, exercise, nutrition, progressive relaxation, meditation, biofeedback, social skill training, and stress inoculation training are only a few of the better known ones. The clientele to whom these assorted treatments are being addressed is equally diverse, including top military brass (Gill et al. 1985), corporate workers (Murphy 1984), the elderly (De Berry and Einstein 1981), teachers (Forman 1982), and even the physically handicapped (Garrison 1978). In fact, the most distinctive characteristic of stress management as a treatment is its universality; there is no one for whom treatment is apparently unneeded or inappropriate.

It is tempting to dismiss this confusing diversity of treatments and clienteles as just another therapeutic fad, a successor to previous fads such as T groups, soon to be succeeded itself by the next fashionable disease and its accompanying treatments. Nevertheless, in spite of the hyperbole surrounding it, stress management is also a novel and fruitful way of treating human distress. However, contrary to popular views, stress management is not a specific treatment technique applied to a specific illness labeled "stress." Rather, stress management is best conceptualized as a general treatment approach to a broad category of adaptational and health problems. The theoretical basis for this treatment approach lies both in conceptions of health and illness provided by stress theorists, and in the self-management therapies developed by the cognitive behavioral practitioners (Roskies and Lazarus 1980). This chapter traces the twin theoretical roots of stress management and defines the characteristics that distinguish it from other psychotherapeutic approaches.

Conceptions of Stress Problems

A fundamental prerequisite of any rational intervention is an understanding of the condition being treated: what are stress problems, and who are the people likely to be affected by them? Unfortunately, in spite of its widespread usage, there is no single, precise definition of the term *stress* or, consequently, of *stress problems.* In fact, to try to understand the concept of stress via the writings of stress theorists and researchers is analogous to the old story of a group of blind men seeking to learn about an elephant by feeling different parts of its body. The man who felt the trunk and declared that the elephant was a long tube was partially right, as was he who felt the flank and declared the elephant to be a rough wall. In each case, however, the reality reported was colored by the specific and limited perspective from which the phenomenon was viewed. Similarly, most stress theorists agree that the elephant (i.e., stress) does exist; they might even go so far as to concur that the term describes a disturbance of homeostasis, an interruption in the smooth flow of habit that forces the individual to engage in active efforts to regain the old equilibrium or to attain a new one.

How this disturbance is defined and studied, however—stimulus versus response, universal versus individual reactions, physiological versus psychological and social levels—depends on the particular perspective of the specific researcher.

Stress as a Physiological Response

Selye is popularly considered to be the father of modern stress theory, the man, in fact, who both gave the field its name and provided one of the first systematic descriptions of stress responses (Selye [1956] 1976b). As defined by Selye, stress was an orchestrated sequence of hormonal and tissue changes observed in response to any form of noxious stimulus. The stress response occurred when the insult was neither extreme enough to kill the organism immediately nor mild enough to be easily overcome. The physiological changes observed reflected the struggle to overcome this disturbance in equilibrium or, as we would now phrase it, to cope with it. Extreme cold, various toxins, and a physical blow would each produce different specific physiological effects, but in addition there would be the constant or "nonspecific" physiological markers of the struggle to resist the noxious agents.

The genius of Selye's work lies in the recognition that ultimately the effects of struggle against the invader might be more harmful to the organism than the direct effects of the noxious agent itself. Should the resistance phase be prolonged unduly, the animal might even die from sheer exhaustion. Thus, the emphasis in Selye's work is not on the stressor per se, but on the toll exacted by the efforts to cope with it. Disease is no longer defined solely in terms of external agents, but is also considered to be a product of the organism's finite resources and energy in adapting to its environment. This conceptualization and description of the role of the organism, or in epidemiological terms the *host,* marks an important shift in our understanding of the etiology of disease.

Selye's general adaptation syndrome—complete with diagrams depicting the three stages of alarm, defense, and exhaustion—constitutes an obligatory part of most stress management manuals and is commonly used to "explain" stress. But Selye's theory alone cannot provide an adequate blueprint for clinical diagnosis or treatment of stress disorders, because the stress phenomena with which he dealt are very different from those of interest to the clinician. Selye's empirical work was largely based on the study of the *typical, physiological reactions* produced in animals by *physical stressors,* such as cold and toxins. As clinicians, our primary interest is in people, of course, but also in *individual, idiosyncratic behavioral and emotional reactions to psychological threats and challenges.* The general adaptation syndrome may provide an accurate depiction of most rats' sequence of physiological reactions to a toxin, but it does not help us understand why one college student copes with the anticipation of an exam by devising a study schedule, and a second collapses in helpless panic.

In spite of its limitations for clinical purposes, the physiological work of Selye and his successors remains important for the clinician because it provides the needed link between behavior and biology. If excessive environmental demands or inadequate coping resources are believed to have physical illness as a possible outcome, then biological pathways must be found to explain how one could lead to the other.

. . .

However, if we as clinicians are to appeal to physiological stress theories as scientific support for our treatments, then it behooves us to keep abreast of developments in this complex and fast-moving area. For even on the physiological level itself, the stress reactions described by Selye present only part of the picture. By focusing on the sympathetic-adrenomedullary system, instead of the pituitary–adrenocortical system, Cannon ([1939] 1963) described a rather different sequence of physiological reactions, the well-known "fight or flight" syndrome. Subsequently, technical advances in hormonal analysis have made it possible to go beyond these two systems and study a broad spectrum of hormones and endocrine systems, including the pituitary–gonadal, growth hormone, and insulin systems (Mason 1975c; Ursin, Baude, and Levine 1978). Based on this research, it appears that there is no single "stress hormone," neither corticosteroid nor catecholamine, but that all endocrine systems are responsive to psychological stress. Furthermore, recent work in the new field of psychoimmunology suggests that the immune system, too, is responsive to psychological demands (Ader 1980). Thus, even the physiological response to stress cannot be described solely in terms of the general adaptation syndrome or the fight-and-flight response but, instead, must be viewed as a complex and interrelated patterning of autonomic, hormonal, and immune systems.

Stress as an External Stimulus

When most people speak of being under stress, they are usually referring to external demands impinging on them, such as pressure at work or illness of a family member. The study of stress as a stimulus coincides with the popular view, focusing as it does on the triggers that provoke emotional, behavioral, and physiological reactions. For clinical purposes, it would be desirable to have a ranking of stress triggers, either in terms of types of problem engendered (child beating vs. heart disease) or even in terms of severity of consequences (major vs. minor). No such global rankings exist; instead, once again, there is a variety of classification systems, each providing somewhat different indications concerning outcome.

In the Institute of Medicine report *Stress and Human Health* (Elliott and Eisdorfer 1982), stressors are classified according to duration: (1) acute, time-limited stressors, such as a job interview or a visit to the dentist; (2) stressor sequences, or series of events that occur over an extended period of time as the result of an initiating stress trigger, such as the multiple residential, financial, job, parental, and social changes that can follow a divorce; (3) chronic intermittent stressors, such as periodic arguments with a spouse or a weekly project meeting; and (4) chronic stressors, such as permanent disabilities and marital strife, which may or may not be initiated by a discrete event and which persist continuously over a long time. Presumably, longer-lasting stressors would have more serious consequences than acute, time-limited ones, although studies on chronic illness and physical handicap (Davis 1963; Goffman 1963) suggest that habituation may attenuate the impact of at least some chronic stressors. Thus, duration in itself is not an adequate criterion for predicting the impact of a given stressor.

A second taxonomy of stress triggers is based on the quality of the event, rather than its duration. Lazarus and Cohen (1977) speak of three types of stress triggers: major changes, often cataclysmic and affecting large numbers of persons (e.g., war, earthquake, financial depression); major changes affecting one or a few persons (e.g., bereavement, divorce); and daily hassles. Most of the research literature has focused on major changes, both collective and individual, with the assumption that the most serious adaptational and health consequences are likely to flow from events such as war and bereavement. However, the vast majority of individuals who complain of suffering from stress have not experienced initiating stress triggers of the catastrophic type. Instead, as they describe job and family stresses, there is a multitude of apparently trivial episodes: running out of coffee and an early morning argument about who was supposed to buy it, disagreement about this weekend's plans, an important letter left untyped, a feeling of anxiety concerning the report one is preparing, worrying about the monthly bills, the stubbornness of a colleague in refusing to see one's point of view, the malevolence of a computer that goes down when we most need it, and so on ad infinitum. Moreover, instead of representing sharp divergences from normal routine, many of these minor challenges and threats occur repeatedly and frequently.

Until recently, stress researchers paid little attention to this third category of stress trigger, perhaps because these daily hassles are so universal. However, a number of recent empirical studies by Lazarus and his colleagues (DeLongis et al. 1982; Kanner et al. 1981) have provided data suggesting that these daily hassles, perhaps because of their frequency, may be even more important for adaptation and health than the better recognized major catastrophes and changes. This shift in conceptualization of stress triggers, from major catastrophe to minor irritant, has important clinical consequences in that it helps us understand why even "normal" people living in "normal" circumstances may complain of stress. What it cannot do, of course, is explain the differential effect: if presumably everybody experiences daily hassles, why do some people suffer more than others?

A third way of classifying stressors is by quantity, rather than by quality or duration. The life events approach, exemplified by Holmes and Rahe (1967b), put forth the view that the negative consequences of stress for health resulted more from the *accumulation of stressors* requiring adjustment, rather than from the damage wrought by any single one. Thus, positive as well as negative changes, if too many occur in too short a period, can tax the adaptive capacity of the organism and lead to increased susceptibility to psychological and physical illness. This theoretical approach had the unusual advantage of being accompanied by a measuring instrument, the Social Readjustment Rating Scale (SRRS), that made it possible to classify individuals in terms of their exposure to change and consequent vulnerability to illness. In fact, this scale has been used to successfully predict both psychological distress and physical illness in a variety of populations (Holmes and Masuda 1974; Rahe 1975; Thoits 1983). Unfortunately, this measure of illness vulnerability is not as simple and clear-cut as it initially appears. In addition to conceptual and methodological concerns about what specifically is being measured and how, there is the practical consideration that the amount of variance explained is low, usually not more than 4–10 percent (Rabkin and Struening 1976; Thoits 1983). Thus, while SRRS has become another staple of stress management manuals and popular articles about stress, there is little scientific basis for using it to predict illness vulnerability in the *individual.*

For the clinician, the wide number and diversity of stress triggers is eventually self-defeating. If the list of stressors includes acute as well as chronic events, daily hassles as well as major catastrophes, positive as well s negative changes, then presumably all of us are stressed. But not all of us show the same severity or type of negative effects. There is a difference between the individual who survives a concentration camp with surprisingly few signs of pathology (Antonovsky et al. 1971) and the one who breaks down under stressors that appear relatively minor, at least to others. There is also a difference between the individual whose inability to handle stress leads to a heart attack and the one whose stress problem takes the form of addictive drinking. Once again, we are confronted with the problem of individual differences in stress perception and response.

The Vulnerable Organism

One way of overcoming the inability of either the response or the stimulus definition to account for individual variations in stress perception and reaction is to focus directly on differences in individual susceptibility. In this way the stimulus-response (S-R) paradigm is transformed into a stimulus-organism-response (S-O-R) one. For instance, Schmale (1972) hypothesized that individuals who have unresolved infantile conflicts concerning separation and loss are likely to react to analogous situations in adulthood with feelings of helplessness and hopelessness, thereby increasing their vulnerability to illness. Similarly, categorization of persons according to coping styles, such as repression-sensitization (Byrne 1964; Welsh 1956) or coping–avoiding (Goldstein 1959, 1973), presumably should increase our ability to predict which stimuli are likely to be perceived as stressful, as well as the nature of the stress response.

Unfortunately, this type of effort to incorporate the organism within stimulus–response theories of stress has proven unsatisfactory, because it is both limited and static. Classifications based on a single static trait are usually not complete or dynamic enough to take account of the complexity and variability of actual coping efforts in a specific stress situation. Thus, for patients anticipating surgery, Cohen and Lazarus (1973) found no correlation between their global classification as vigilants versus avoiders on the Byrne (1964) scale and the way that the patients actually coped with the specific threat of surgery. Moreover, even if one could accurately categorize coping style in a particular context, such reactions do not remain immutably fixed in time but are subject to change. For instance, in the classic longitudinal study of parental reactions to fatal illness in a child, Friedman et al. (1963) found that parental reactions were not rigidly fixed, but varied according to changes in the external situation and the changing meanings that parents attributed to these events. In short, just as the study of stimuli and responses in isolation is insufficient to understand stress processes and outcomes, so focus on individual typology or pathology is equally insufficient. Personality traits and past experiences may indicate predispositions, but it would indeed indicate an extreme of pathology for an individual to be totally immune to the influence of external events, or even to feedback from the consequences of his or her own responses during the course of a stress episode itself.

Psychological Stress as Cognitive Appraisal

Since no definition of stress has succeeded in capturing the nature of this complex phenomenon, or even in satisfying the majority of stress researchers (Elliott and Eisdorfer 1982), some researchers have suggested that the term *stress* be abandoned completely. Lazarus (1966), on the other hand, believes that the term should be retained, but that it should be clearly understood that *stress* does not refer to a specific variable but is a general organizing concept for understanding a wide range of phenomena of great importance in human and animal adaptation. Stress is not the domain of a single discipline but is an interdisciplinary field that encompasses both the activities of the anthropologist investigating stress in an entire culture and the biochemist concerned with variations in a single hormone. Furthermore, although social stress may be linked to psychological stress and to physiological stress, phenomena at each of these three levels of analysis are sufficiently independent that one cannot be reduced to another. Therefore, to avoid the confusion resulting from the multiple meanings attached to the same term, it is incumbent on each stress researcher to define the level of analysis that he or she is using (Lazarus and Folkman 1984b).

As a psychologist, Lazarus is clearly interested in stress at the level of the individual person; the specific perspective he uses is that of a thinking, feeling person continuously appraising his or her relationship with the surrounding environment. Stress is the result of a judgment that a disturbance has occurred in the person–environment relationship: The individual perceives challenge/threat/harm, judges that his or her resources may not be sufficient to manage the disruption, and considers the outcome important to his or her well-being. Thus, stress is localized neither in the environmental trigger nor in the physiological response, but in the individual's conscious appraisal of disturbance.

Without this appraisal, there is no psychological stress, regardless of the degree of actual danger to the organism (Lazarus 1966; Lazarus, Averill, and Opton 1970; Lazarus and Folkman 1984b; Lazarus and Launier 1978). For instance, rapid technological change may make many types of jobs obsolete, but a specific worker will not experience this social upheaval as psychological stress until he or she becomes aware of a threat to personal well-being. Conversely, individuals may experience acute psychological stress even when the threat or challenge appears minimal to the observer; one has only to remember the social embarrassments of adolescence to be convinced of this fact.

The individual's judgment that a stressful situation exists, whether it appears reasonable or unreasonable to the observer, initiates a complex process. Immediately, there is an effort to reduce the feelings of disturbance, by seeking to change either the situation, the person's reactions to it, or both. This coping effort and its consequences will itself change the person's appraisal of the situation, which, in turn, will alter the subsequent response, and so on. Thus, stress is not a fixed person–environment relationship but an evolving process, involving multiple appraisals and reappraisals.

Lazarus' theory of stress can also be viewed as a theory of coping, for the individual's continuous appraisal of coping resources and strategies is as fundamental to the process as the appraisal of challenge/threat/harm itself. What is initially judged to be stressful depends not only on the taxing qualities of the environment as appraised but also, and equally as important, on the appraised strength and suitability of the available resources to meet these demands. For example, the same traffic that produces strong emotional and physical reactions in the beginning driver may hardly be noticed by the experienced and confident one. Furthermore, during the course of the stress episode itself, the person is continuously making judgments about how well his or her coping efforts are succeeding, and these appraisals will affect, in turn, the initial evaluation of the stressor. For instance, the beginning driver may see the traffic as less threatening or more threatening depending on his or her perceived success in handling it. Finally, after the dust of battle has settled, it is the individual's evaluation of the way he or she handled the situation, as much as the results themselves, that will determine whether the person emerges feeling strengthened or diminished.

In contrast to previous stress models, Lazarus' is less concerned with isolating common characteristics of stressed people or stressful situations than with exploring the range of behavior manifested by specific individuals in specific situations. Many elements contribute to the individual's stress appraisal (e.g., perception of external environment, perception of coping resources, pattern of commitments, values and beliefs that increase or decrease vulnerability to specific types of threats or challenges, etc.); therefore, we can expect not only that individuals will vary in their appraisal of stressors, but also that the same individual will make quite different appraisals of the same stress trigger at different times or in different contexts.

Coping, too, is viewed as context-bound, an effort to manage a particular stressor, rather than as a universal manner of handling all stressors. Thus, the individual who handles a work conflict regarding division of responsibility as an exercise in negotiation and problem solving may react with anger and denial to a spouse's apparently similar request for reconsideration of household responsibilities. Furthermore, coping strategies not only vary from situation to situation, but they also change during the course of the specific stress episode itself. Even for an acute time-limited stressor, such as an examination, the person may seek to manage the situation by intensive studying and active search for social support before the exam, but may rely more on emotional detachment and wishful thinking during the period of waiting for the results (Folkman and Lazarus 1985).

Lazarus' stress model obviously differs from those previously described in a number of important respects. For clinical purposes, however, the most important difference is the predominant role assigned to the individual in the perception and management of disturbance. Rather than being the passive victim of environmental forces, or his or her own body, the individual is seen as a thinking, feeling being actively monitoring his or her relationship with the surrounding environment and seeking to maintain or improve it. Furthermore, because both the person and the environment are changeable, the individual is not necessarily the victim of his or her past but can change cognitions and behavior from one stress episode to another, and even within a single stress episode. This, of course, is very close to the clinician's view of the world, with its double emphasis on both the power and the perfectibility of the individual. It is not surprising, therefore, that this theoretical model of stress and coping has proved particularly attractive to clinicians seeking to develop a conceptualization of stress problems that could be treated by psychological means. . . .

Differentiating Clinically Treatable Stress Problems from Stress in General

In spite of the many differences between them, the various stress models that have been described are linked by a common belief: challenges and/or threats that tax or exceed the individual's capacity to handle them can have important consequences for physical and mental well-being. This view of malfunctioning as a demand–resource imbalance is heuristically powerful for it enables us to group a wide variety of apparently disparate phenomena within a single conceptual framework. However, it also makes it essential to distinguish from the large universe of possible stress problems those that legitimately lie within the province of the clinician. In some cases the distinction is obvious: both the angry father who beats his crying child and the South African black who hits out at the arresting policeman may be suffering from an insufficiency of resources to meet the demands of the situation, but the first clearly qualifies as a clinical stress problem, while it would be ridiculous to view or attempt to treat the second in those terms. In other cases, however, the lines are less clear-cut or more controversial. For instance, the high alcoholism rate observed in a specific group of workers can be seen either as a deficiency of individual coping abilities requiring clinical treatment (the probable management view) or as a deficiency in working conditions requiring environmental restructuring (the probable union view).

From the clinician's point of view, *the most important criterion for diagnosing a given complaint as a clinical stress problem is the judgment that it is amenable to improvement by changing the way the person perceives and manages his or her transactions with the immediate environment.* Essentially, the diagnosis of a clinical stress problem has less to do with the etiology or severity of the problem itself than with the prediction of its responsiveness to the teaching of coping skills. Thus, we treat the nausea of the cancer patient undergoing chemotherapy by stress inoculation training, not because we consider his or her lack of coping resources to be the root of the problem, but because this is the most effective way we currently have of reducing the distress. Similarly, we may choose to treat the unhappy employee rather than the employing organization, not because of attributions concerning the source of the problem, but because the individual is more motivated for change than is the corporate structure.

The distinction between problems best treated via improving the individual's coping skills—versus those best handled via political action, improvement in drug treatment, or other means—is a judgment, and it will obviously be influenced by the specific values and beliefs of the person or persons making the judgment. Sometimes the diagnosis of a deficiency in coping skills will already have been made by the client himself or herself even before approaching the therapist, as in the case of the panic-stricken college freshman seeking help in coping with the stress of an oncoming examination. At other times, however, as in the case of the chronic-pain patient, it may take all the skill of the therapist to convince a potential client to focus on coping abilities, rather than to continue the search for the magical remedy that will eliminate the pain itself. But unless therapist and client can agree on a conceptualization of the problem that involves learning new coping skills, or using existing ones more effectively, there is no basis for clinical stress treatment. This development of a conceptual consensus constitutes a major challenge for therapists seeking to work with healthy Type As or similar populations.

The Teaching of Coping Skills

All psychotherapies seek to help the person feel more comfortable, both within his or her own skin and in relations with others. The distinguishing characteristic of the cognitive behavioral approach to therapy,[1] however, is that it approaches this goal via improving the person's *competency in managing important aspects of the environment.* The basic assumption here is that the individual's well-being depends in large measure upon the relationship with the external world; to feel good about oneself, the person must be able to manage environmental demands in a manner satisfactory to himself or herself and significant others. Effective management, in turn, depends both on possessing the necessary cognitive and behavioral skills to confront a given stressor, and on being able to mobilize these skills whenever necessary. Because of this emphasis on actually teaching coping skills, in contrast to viewing improved ability to handle environmental demands as a natural consequence of the resolution of internal conflict, there are important differences between cognitive behavioral and other therapies in defining the goals and methods of treatment, as well as the nature of the therapist–client relationship.

The Goals of Treatment

The criterion of successful treatment for the cognitive-behavior therapist is not necessarily the person's ability to change a troublesome situation, or even to eliminate all painful feelings concerning it. Rather, cognitive-behavior therapy defines success in terms of the individual's ability to function adequately *in spite of some distress.* Thus, the ideal model is not the exam-anxious student who takes the exam without experiencing any anxiety whatsoever, but the one who can control anxiety, and even harness it to improve performance. Similarly, the aim of treatment is not to eradicate completely the food binger's yearnings for chocolate cake, but to enable him or her to manage thoughts and behavior so as to reduce the likelihood of succumbing. In short, the successfully treated individual is not "cured" of the presenting problem but is able to cope with it better via improved self-management.

Underlying this focus on effective self-management is the assumption that environmental challenges and threats are an integral and inevitable part of human existence. Even successful treatment is unlikely to prevent the appearance of new problems, and perhaps not even the reappearance of the old one. But the person who has overcome a difficulty in managing one situation should be able to face the next inevitable hurdle both with additional coping skills and with increased confidence in his or her ability to use them (Bandura 1977a, 1977b). Or, to put it in simpler terms, functional coping is that which permits the individual to emerge from a given stress episode in better shape to cope again another day.

While all cognitive-behavioral therapy is designed to increase coping skills, for most stress problems there is no single outcome that can be used as the a priori definition of competent coping. In fact, many stress problems have a range of possible "good" outcomes: the college student can handle exam panic by increasing his ability to manage anxiety, or by lowering his goals of the grade desired, or, alternatively, by learning how to withdraw with honor from a too difficult course; the overweight person can change eating and exercise habits or, alternatively, change her image of what constitutes ideal weight. Which choice will be made in these or similar situations is a question not only of health and illness, or right and wrong, but also of the values and beliefs of both therapist and client. Sometimes, the outcome toward which coping is directed is implicitly agreed to by therapist and client even before their initial encounter, as in the therapist who advertises a weight loss group, or the client who consults for help in overcoming a flying phobia. In other cases, however, specification of the desired outcome may constitute an essential part of the treatment process itself, as in the case of the client with marital problems hesitating between "learning to live with it" and ending this relationship and seeking a better one.

The Methods of Treatment

The teaching of coping skills borrows from both educational and psychotherapeutic methods. The influence of educational methods is evident in the step-by-step process used to teach a given skill, such as relaxation or problem solving; as in the learning of any complex skill, the task is divided into graded steps, with the individual repeatedly practicing a given step in a variety of contexts until it is integrated within his or her repertoire. The influence of psychotherapeutic methods is evident in the attention paid to the affective component of learning, for example, motivation for and fears concerning change, resistance to a given technique or goal, relationship with the teacher/therapist, handling of successful and unsuccessful practices, expectations concerning extent and rate of change, attributions concerning sources of change, and so on.

Meichenbaum (1985) provides a prototype for cognitive-behavioral treatment methods with his division of the treatment process into three main phases: conceptualization of the problem and goals of treatment; skill acquisition and rehearsal phase; application and follow through. Although I define the content of the latter two stages somewhat differently than he does, this division is useful for describing the treatment process.

The first phase is one of mutual education of therapist and client. The therapist will engage the client in a data-gathering process, concerning both the characteristics of the presenting problem (e.g., nature, severity, generality from one situation to another, consequences, reasons for seeking change) and the manner in which the potential client is currently attempting to handle it. At the same time, the therapist is providing information about the process of treatment itself. A number of the assumptions and methods of the cognitive-behavioral treatment approach will become apparent in this stage: the importance of person-environment relationships; the active role of the individual in shaping these relationships; the focus on current interactions instead of seeking initial causes; the emphasis on specific behaviors and thoughts in particular situations, rather than fixed, global personality traits. Should therapist and client reach an agreement concerning how the presenting problem is to be conceptualized, the outcome or outcomes considered desirable, and the methods of seeking these outcomes, then therapist and client will have a viable treatment contract and a basis for proceeding further. However, this stage is not simply a preparation for the real work of therapy; on the contrary, often the most significant change occurring in treatment will be a new way of looking at an old problem.

The second phase in treatment is the actual acquisition and rehearsal of specific coping skills. This is probably the most controversial part of the treatment process, since much of the scientific as well as the popular literature has been devoted to fierce battles over the relative merits of specific treatment techniques. For instance, Meichenbaum has termed relaxation to be the aspirin of cognitive-behavioral therapy, but the number of "brands" under which this useful "drug" is packaged appears endless (classic Jacobsonian progressive muscular relaxation, modified progressive muscular relaxation, the relaxation response, meditation, autogenic training, multiple forms of biofeedback, etc.), and the wars waged by the devotees of a particular variant bear an uneasy resemblance to the brand wars of television commercials. However, as Meichenbaum (1985:53–54) points out, while component analysis studies of stress inoculation training have indicated that the skills acquisition phase is critical for treatment outcome, currently at least, there are no research-based guidelines for which techniques to use with each type of patient, nor in what order. Instead, each therapist now constructs his or her own treatment package or packages.

The range of possible techniques is wide. Lazarus and Launier (1978) have divided coping techniques into two general categories: instrumental (problem-focused) and palliative (focused on regulating emotional distress). Included under instrumental coping are such techniques as information gathering, problem solving, communication and social skills training, time management, mobilizing supports, and direct efforts to change the environment or to remove oneself from it. The palliative techniques include denial, diverting attention, searching for meaning, emotional distancing, expressing affect, cognitive relabeling, and relaxation training. Which ones a therapist actually chooses should ideally be a decision based on the therapist's assessment of client needs; in practice, it is also likely to be based on the range of techniques with which a particular therapist is familiar and feels comfortable.

Current practice would encourage the use of multiple techniques on the grounds that "having a particular weapon in one's arsenal is less important than having a variety of weapons" (Pearlin and Schooler 1978). Thus, individuals who complain of shyness in social situations might be helped by direct training in communication and social skills, but also by learning to regulate their physical and emotional reactions via relaxation and cognitive relabeling of stressful social situations. For individuals facing a stressful situation that can neither be avoided or altered (e.g., victimization, serious illness), the primary emphasis might be on regulation of emotional distress, but even here instrumental techniques, such as problem solving and mobilizing support, can be included. The major danger with multimodal therapies is that the client will be overwhelmed by an indigestible smorgasbord of techniques; it is important both to limit the number of techniques used and to develop a rationale explaining how each contributes to the goals of treatment.

The actual learning of techniques may involve a number of steps of graded difficulty. For instance, relaxation training can proceed from a 20-minute practice exercise following live instructions, to the same exercise using taped instructions, to a shorter version of the same exercise also with taped instructions, to self-instruction relaxation exercises, to the use of self-instructed relaxation when feeling tense, and so on. As in any skill training, simple description or demonstration does not in itself lead to learning the skill; for true skill acquisition, the person must also engage in repeated practices with corrective feedback on successes and failures. Depending on the skill to be learned, and the stage of learning, practice sessions can take place both within the confines of the therapist's office and in the natural environment. To enable the client and therapist to monitor in vivo practices, the client is often asked to keep a record of the event for discussion in the subsequent session.

While some of the coping techniques taught are new to the client, often it will become apparent during this stage of therapy that the client already possesses the necessary skills but is not using them appropriately. For instance, the shy teenager who consults because of inability to converse with members of the opposite sex may know, from avid reading of advice-to-the-lovelorn columns, exactly what to say to open a conversation at a party, but be too anxious to implement this knowledge at the social gathering itself. Here the focus of therapy will change from the teaching of social skills to the management of inhibiting anxiety. Similarly, the business person who complains of lack of communication with a spouse may have considerable theoretical knowledge of communication skills, gained in multiple seminars and workshops, but may have never considered these skills relevant to the management of marital difficulties. The task here may be more one of reconceptualizing the marital problem than of learning a new skill.

The third stage in treatment marks a shift in emphasis from techniques to situations. Rather than practicing a single coping skill or coping formula, the person will concentrate instead on applying his or her coping skills to meet the needs of different situations. This involves both the ability to combine skills when necessary and sufficient flexibility to vary coping strategies according to the needs of the specific situation. Thus, the typical coping stratagem for handling the irritation produced by a tardy employee might involve the combination of three skills: relaxation, cognitive relabeling to reduce the supervisor's level of arousal, and communications skills to transmit the supervisor's wish for increased promptness to the employee. Depending on the specific circumstances, however, the most appropriate coping strategy might range from overlooking the tardiness completely to outright firing of the employee. A second characteristic of this application phase is the client's growing independence from the therapist in providing his or her own corrective feedback and reinforcement. Ideally, this stage should also include some preparation for self-management after the end of treatment, particularly anticipation of possible relapses and development of methods for handling them.

Like all models, this one is only a prototype, and actual practice is likely to see some variation in the sequence and content of stages. For instance, the sequence described here is based on an individual therapist–client relationship, where the therapist has maximum flexibility regarding length, content, and pacing of treatment phases. However, much of cognitive-behavior therapy, at least that which is reported in the literature, employs a group format, thereby imposing a priori structures on form and content of treatment. For example, when socially inhibited individuals are treated in a group, the therapist will usually decide in advance on the conceptualization of the problem, the general manner in which it is to be treated, and the length of treatment. Here clinical skill is demonstrated via the ability to select appropriate clients and to adapt to individual needs within the confines of the group structure.

The Therapist–Client Relationship

Behavior therapy has traditionally been technique-oriented, ignoring the affective relationship between therapist and client. In recent years, however, there has been a rapprochement with psychodynamic psychotherapy in recognizing that the therapeutic relationship is fundamental in mediating behavioral change. As described by Waterhouse and Strupp (1984), the therapist's ability to build rapport and to establish a collaborative working relationship early in therapy is an important predictor of treatment outcome. Nevertheless, even though cognitive-behavioral therapists may agree with therapists of other persuasions on the importance of the therapeutic alliance, there are some differences in the way this alliance is defined.

The teaching of coping skills is an educational as well as a psychotherapeutic enterprise, and, reflecting this dual orientation, the therapist in cognitive-behavior therapy is also a teacher. In fact, in his recent book on stress inoculation training, Meichenbaum (1985) consistently refers to the therapist as a *trainer.* Thus, rather than serving as a shadowy focus for transference wishes, the therapist plays the active role of coach, explaining, demonstrating, and encouraging. Furthermore, the teacher does not present himself or herself as someone who is immune to the problems manifested by the client, or even as someone who has mastered them completely. Instead, the model presented by the teacher is of someone who must also struggle with some of the same problems confronting the client—all individuals, regardless of their specific life situation, experience pressures and anxieties in some form or other—but who is able to cope with them without feeling overwhelmed or engaging in destructive behaviors. To further strengthen the model of the teacher as a fellow coper, *selected* self-disclosure of the therapist's own coping problems is a useful therapeutic technique.

In this teacher–student relationship, the client is not a passive recipient but an active collaborator. The ultimate goal of therapy is to make clients better problem solvers in handling future stressful events as they arise, and to fulfill this aim the client must learn enough of the therapist's "magic" to be able to use it himself or herself. Thus, from the outset of treatment the therapist seeks to make the therapeutic process as transparent and comprehensible as possible. If a client is asked to gather observations on the frequency of certain behaviors, or asked to practice certain skills at home, he or she must understand not only what to do but also how this self-monitoring and skill rehearsal will contribute to the desired outcome. Similarly, as the treatment progresses, the client should become increasingly familiar with the general process of behavior change, from the initial clarification of the problem to post-treatment handling of relapses.

Cognitive-behavior therapy emphasizes the role of the therapist as teacher, but good teaching involves far more than proficiency in the techniques to be taught, or even a warm, accepting manner. Instead, the distinguishing characteristic of the skilled professional, in cognitive-behavior therapy as in other forms of psychotherapy, is the ability to adapt general principles and techniques to the specific needs of individual clients. Most clients who seek help present not a single, well-circumscribed complaint, but a constellation of person–environment difficulties. It is part of the skill of the teacher to select those that are most amenable to change, and to choose the coping skills most likely to change them. Even more important is the therapist's ability to arouse and sustain the client's wish for improvement, in spite of the difficulties inherent in changing any established behavior pattern. In fact, because many of the dysfunctional coping patterns brought to the therapist have been overlearned over years, the skill of the therapist may lie more in mobilizing and sustaining the wish for change, rather than in teaching specific coping skills.

In sustaining client motivation, the therapist's sensitivity to language is particularly crucial. Words, or the lack of them, are the manner in which an individual expresses his or her manner of looking at the world. The good therapist listens carefully to the client's language and presents his or her own comments in a manner that facilitates assimilation to the client's existing schemata. The ultimate aim of therapy is to produce change, the the competent therapist reduces the fear of the unfamiliar by couching new thoughts in familiar language.

The Range of Problems Treated

Up to now we have been discussing the teaching of coping skills as a form of psychotherapy. This treatment is offered to clients who, in sociological terminology, have accepted or been thrust into the sick role; the distinguishing characteristic of these individuals is that they or others have identified dysfunctional emotional states and/or behaviors (e.g., abusing children, excessive drinking, frequent headaches, anxiety attacks, performance anxieties, etc.) resulting from their inability to manage important aspects of the environment, and the aim of treatment is to reduce or eliminate the problem emotional states and behaviors. The range of problems treated under this heading is broad; in a recent summary of published studies, Meichenbaum (1985) identifies at least 20 distinct coping problems to which stress inoculation training or closely related stress management procedures have been applied, ranging from adolescents with anger-control problems to adults experiencing dental fear and pain.

However, stress management can also be used to prevent pathology in individuals who are currently well but who are considered to be "at risk." The usual reason for labeling a person "at risk" is exposure to stressful environmental circumstances that are likely to disrupt the individual's habitual way of looking at and dealing with the world. Rape victims, cardiac patients awaiting open heart surgery, and elementary school children making the transition to high school could all be grouped in this category. The aim here would be to reduce emotional distress, and head off deterioration in functioning, by increasing participants' awareness of potential stress reactions and by teaching them coping skills appropriate to the situation they are confronting. A second use of "at risk" stress management programs is directed to individuals in occupations considered particularly stressful, such as nurses, teachers, and police officers.

Stress management for healthy Type As also constitutes treatment of an "at risk" population, albeit of a different kind. Here it is not environmental factors per se that place the individual under strain, but rather his or her way of reacting to the environment. Nevertheless, the healthy Type A is classified as being at risk, rather than sick, because, until or unless he or she develops clinical heart disease, neither the individual nor society is likely to view this coping pattern as dysfunctional.

For the clinician, treatment of individuals in this "at risk" category poses some difficult challenges. These individuals do fulfill two of the essential requirements of treatment: they need help, and they appear likely to benefit from the type of help offered by stress management training. However, in order to be truly helpful, the clinician must be able to treat them in a manner befitting their nonpatient status. A working policeman, whose functioning and well-being can be improved by training in handling some of the stresses inherent in the job, is very different from a client with acknowledged symptoms, and it would be counterproductive to expect him to assume the sick role as a condition of treatment. Similar, though perhaps less obvious, is the distinction between the healthy Type A and the one who has already suffered a heart attack. The first may be at increased risk for coronary illness, but he or she is not yet sick, and to be acceptable and relevant to the healthy Type A, stress management programs destined for this population must acknowledge the difference.

Conclusions

Stress theory and research have provided novel ways for conceptualizing a broad range of human adaptational problems in terms of demand–resource imbalance and a wealth of data concerning the negative consequences of inappropriate or ineffectual attempts to redress this imbalance. Stress management, the effort to prevent or alleviate stress-related problems, is based on this theoretical viewpoint and, consequently, differs from conventional psychotherapeutic approaches by emphasizing person–environment interactions in preference to intrapersonal conflicts: the goal of treatment is to improve, via the teaching of coping skills, the person's ability to manage his or her environment. Other novel features of this treatment approach are the goal of improved coping instead of total cure, the combination of educational and psychotherapeutic methods, and the collaborative therapist–client relationship.

Like stress theory itself, however, stress management has suffered from the confusion engendered by the use of the same label for quite different treatment programs directed to different clienteles. Both stress as a socially acceptable problem and stress management as a fashionable treatment can be considered victims of their own popularity, in that the rubrics are now applied as if they were self-explanatory when, in fact, they mean different things to different people. In fact, there is no all-purpose stress management program that will serve as a universal panacea for all stress ills. Instead, deciding that a given stress problem might be profitably treated by stress management techniques is only the first step in program development. It must be followed by a detailed appraisal of client needs, delineation of specific treatment goals, and selection of appropriate treatment methods. . . .

NOTES

1. The number of therapists identifying themselves as cognitive behaviorists is growing rapidly, and it is impossible to name them all. Some of the major contributors to the development of this treatment approach are Beck (1976), Goldfried (1977, 1979), Mahoney (1980), Meichenbaum (1977, 1985), and, of course, their predecessor, Ellis (1962).

22

Intervention Strategies

■

RICHARD H. COX

. . . Ryan was an extremely gifted multiple-sport athlete who experienced difficulty in dealing with anxiety while competing in track events. Specifically, he would become so anxious prior to sprinting and hurdling events that he literally could not run efficiently. During practices, Ryan experienced little or no tension and anxiety. During three years of high school track he had never lost a race during practice with teammates.

It was clear that Ryan was going to be a track "drop out" if some sort of intervention wasn't provided. Ryan's father talked to a professor of sport psychology at the local college to find out if there was something psychological that could be done to help Ryan. After three weeks of studying Ryan's anxiety response to competition, the sport psychologist concluded that an individualized intervention program could be developed to help him. The program that was recommended was one very similar to the stress inoculation training (SIT) program that is described later on in this chapter. In this program, Ryan learned what caused his anxiety and learned how to cope with anxiety when it occurred. Ryan's success at reversing the damaging events of anxiety did not occur overnight. However, during his senior year he made up for many of his earlier failures by setting a state record in the 220-yard sprint.

. . .

The purpose of this chapter is to identify strategies to help athletes to intervene and alter their existing levels of arousal or anxiety. Perhaps one of the most famous examples of this occurred before the first heavyweight boxing match between Muhammad Ali and Ken Norton in 1973. Norton hired a professional hypnotist to help him with his self-confidence and anxiety. He won the match in a stunning upset, effectively calling attention to hypnosis as an intervention strategy.

Other famous athletes who have used intervention strategies such as imagery and relaxation include Dwight Stones in the high jump, Jack Nicklaus in golf, and Chris Evert in tennis. For the 1984 National Collegiate Athletic Association basketball championships, two teams employed professional sport psychologists to help their athletes with their concentration and relaxation. The psychologists were Dan Smith at the University of Illinois and Robert Rotella of the University of Virginia. Virginia went to the final four, and Illinois reached the final eight. Neither team was expected to do this well.

In this chapter, we will use the term *intervention* to refer to various cognitive and physiological strategies for altering existing levels of anxiety, arousal, and self-confidence. Other authors have chosen to use the term *stress management* to refer to much the same thing (Zaichkowsky and Sime 1982). The important thing to remember is that certain strategies are available to the athlete to change the existing level of arousal and tension in the body. The term *tension* will be used to mean much the same thing as anxiety. Tension specifically refers to the tightness that we feel in certain muscle groups as a result of excessive worry and frustration.

Another term that has been used interchangeably with *intervention* is *ergogenic* or *ergogenic aid*. An ergogenic aid is any sort of technique or substance, beyond actual training regimens, that is employed to improve performance (Williams 1983). In the case of sport psychology, these ergogenic aids are referred to as *psychological ergogenic aids*. Some of the ergogenic or intervention techniques that will be introduced in this chapter include relaxation, autogenic training, hypnosis, imagery, and goal setting.

Numerous books, monographs, and articles have been published that deal with various authors' perceptions of how intervention programs can be approached by and developed for the athlete (e.g., Gauron 1984;

FIGURE 22.1 The effects of a pep talk on the activation levels of four different athletes.

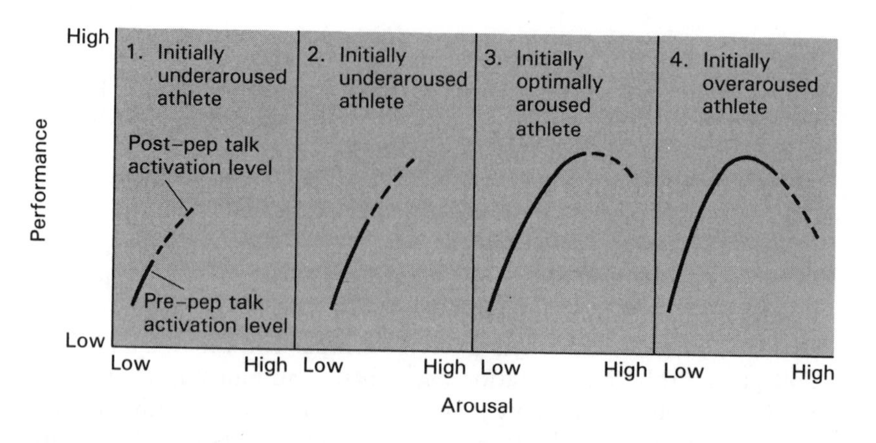

Harris and Harris 1984; Martens 1987; Nideffer 1985; Orlick 1986). In addition, various sport psychologists have reported on the application and development of specific intervention regimens. For example, Hellstedt (1987a) described a psychological-skills training program that was developed for students enrolled in an alpine ski academy. Skills taught included anxiety control, imagery, relaxation, and goal setting. In a similar vein, Mahoney, Gabriel, and Perkins (1987) describe the development of a Psychological Skills Inventory for Sports (PSIS). The PSIS ascertains an athlete's knowledge relative to mental preparation skills. The authors reported that the PSIS effectively discriminates between high- and low-skill athletes.

Coaches have been looking to the sport psychologist to help learn how to maintain optimal levels of arousal in athletes. This is a most promising development, since many coaches have improperly prepared their athletes for competition. The typical approach has been to "psych up" the athlete through various kinds of pep talks and activation techniques. There is, of course, a proper time to get athletes excited and aroused, but often these techniques are applied at the wrong time. It is commonplace, for example, to see high school volleyball coaches leading their players in cheering and psyching-up sessions immediately before a match. Generally, these athletes have only an intermediate level of skill, and the extra arousal serves only to induce unforced errors. This problem is illustrated in figure 22.1. Each athlete in this figure begins with a different initial level of arousal. Increasing arousal affects each athlete differently. In most cases, intervention procedures

1. *Principle* Group activation strategies such as pep talks may help some athletes reach an optimal level of arousal but may cause others to become overaroused.

   Application Indiscriminate use of activation procedures to psych up athletic teams should be avoided. Instead, help each athlete to find his or her own optimal arousal level.

are best applied on an individual basis; each athlete should be treated differently. Some will need a pep talk, but others may need an entirely different form of intervention.

As can be observed in figure 22.1, using a pep talk to increase the arousal level of four different athletes has interesting ramifications. Only in situations 1 and 2 did the pep talk have the desired effect. In situation 3, the athlete was already at an optimal level of activation and it was destroyed by the coach's pep talk. In situation 4, the athlete was overactivated to begin with; the intervention was totally inappropriate. How many coaches overactivate their athletes by their pregame locker room pep talks?

This chapter contains four major sections. The first deals with relaxation procedures designed to lower and control physiological arousal, anxiety, and muscular tension. The second identifies three different cognitive strategies designed to alter and improve an athlete's competitive-readiness level. In section three, various relaxation and cognitive intervention strategies are combined and discussed in terms of "packaged" or formal intervention and stress-management programs. Finally, in section four, various strategies used by coaches and athletes to get psyched for competition are discussed.

Relaxation Procedures

> I think a lot of it has do with me pressing. It's in my head. I'm trying harder, and the harder I try, the worse it goes. I've just got to try and relax. But the more I miss, the harder it is to relax, so it's just a vicious circle.
>
> Jeff Jaeger, Place Kicker, Cleveland Browns, 1987

While some athletes may suffer from low levels of arousal, the more difficult problems occur with athletes who experience excessively high levels of anxiety and tension. For these athletes, any strategy calculated

2. *Principle* An important part of any relaxation procedure is to focus attention on a mental device.

   Application Two mental devices are highly recommended for the athlete. The first is to take a deep breath and exhale slowly, and the second is the use of a mantra or key word or phrase. Athletes can focus on the key phrase and slow air release as they relax.

to heighten arousal can only cause greater anxiety and tension. Typically, what happens is an initial increase in anxiety leads to a decrease in performance. This decrease in performance itself results in even greater anxiety, resulting in the so-called *anxiety-stress spiral.* There is only one way out of this spiral, and that is to reverse the process by reducing the anxiety and tension. *Relaxation procedures* can effectively reduce tension and anxiety associated with sport. In this section, we will discuss some of them.

Four popular relaxation procedures can be adequately categorized under the broad heading of relaxation. These are (1) progressive relaxation, (2) autogenic training, (3) transcendental meditation, and (4) biofeedback. Each procedure is unique in its own way, but they all yield essentially the same physiological result. That is, they all result in the *relaxation response.* The relaxation response consists of physiological changes that are opposite the so-called fight-or-flight response of the sympathetic nervous system. Specifically, procedures such as progressive relaxation, autogenic training, and transcendental meditation result in decreases in oxygen consumption, heart rate, respiration, and skeletal muscle activity while they increase skin resistance and alpha brain waves . . .

Benson, Beary, and Carol (1974) explained that four different factors are necessary for eliciting the relaxation response. Each of these factors is present to some degree in the specific relaxation techniques that we will discuss. These four elements or factors are (1) a *mental device,* (2) a passive attitude, (3) decreased muscle tonus, and (4) a quiet environment. The mental device is generally some sort of word, phrase, object, or process used to shift attention inwardly. We will now turn to a brief discussion of the specific relaxation procedures.

Progressive Relaxation

Modern progressive relaxation techniques are all variations of those outlined by Edmond Jacobson (1929, 1976). Jacobson began his work with progressive relaxation in the early part of the twentieth century. It was Jacobson's basic thesis that it is impossible to be nervous or tense in any part of the body where the muscles are completely relaxed. In addition, Jacobson believed that nervousness and tenseness of involuntary muscles and organs could be reduced if the associated skeletal muscles were relaxed.

Jacobson's *progressive relaxation* procedure requires that subjects lie on their backs, with their arms to the side. Occasionally a comfortable chair and a sitting posture is recommended. In either case, the room should be fairly quiet and arms and legs should not be crossed; this is to avoid unnecessary stimulation. While the goal of any progressive relaxation program is to relax the entire body in a matter of minutes, it is essential that in the beginning the subject practice the technique for at least one hour every day. Once the relaxation procedure is well learned, the relaxation response can be achieved in a few minutes.

Jacobson's method calls for the subject to tense a muscle before relaxing it. The tensing helps the subject to recognize the difference between tension and relaxation. Once the subject can do this, he or she should be able to relax a limb completely without tensing it first. Jacobson warns that only the first few minutes of any relaxation session should be devoted to muscle tensing. The rest of the time should be devoted to gaining complete relaxation. For a muscle to be considered relaxed, it must be completely absent of any contractions and must be limp and motionless.

Jacobson's full progressive relaxation procedure involves systematically tensing and relaxing specific muscle groups in a predetermined order. Relaxation begins with the muscles of the left arm and proceeds to the right arm, left and right legs, abdomen, back, chest, and shoulder muscles, and concludes with the neck and face muscles. The full training procedure lasts many months. In the beginning stages, an entire session should be devoted to the total relaxation of a single muscle group. While it probably is unrealistic to expect an athlete to devote this much time to learning to relax, Jacobson's point is well taken. A well-developed relaxation training program requires a great deal of practice in the beginning. It is unrealistic to expect an athlete to elicit the relaxation response at will after only one or two fifteen-minute practice sessions. However, after several months of practice and training, it should be possible to evoke the relaxation response in a matter of seconds (Nideffer 1981).

The ultimate goal of any relaxation training program is to evoke the relaxation response to counter stress in a specific situation. For example, a professional golfer does not have thirty minutes to relax prior

3. *Principle* Learning how to relax the muscles of the body is a foundation skill for all stress management and intervention strategies.

   Application As a first step in learning how to control anxiety and stress the athlete must become proficient at relaxing the mind and the body.

---

to a fifteen-thousand-dollar putt. The golfer must be able to accomplish this while waiting to putt. This ability takes many hours of practice to master.

Most of the progressive relaxation research has verified the relaxation response. An athlete who learns to evoke the relaxation response through progressive relaxation procedures can reduce state anxiety, physiological arousal, and muscular tension. However, this says nothing directly about improving athletic performance. Based on the inverted-U theory, we can expect an athlete whose arousal level is initially too high to perform better after evoking the relaxation response. However, this is difficult to demonstrate scientifically. If the relaxation response brings arousal below the optimal level, we may actually observe a decrement in performance. Consequently, most research on performance and progressive relaxation has been case studies. Nideffer and Deckner (1970) reported one such study, in which a shot-putter's performance improved significantly after the athlete was taught how to relax. Winter (1982) has claimed that sprinters at San Jose State have broken thirty-seven world records by learning how to relax. However, researchers such as Bennett and Stothart (1980) and Weinberg, Seabourne, and Jackson (1981) have failed to observe a performance effect using relaxation procedures alone. More recently Griffiths et al. (1985) observed both anxiety reduction and performance facilitation as a result of relaxation and mental-rehearsal strategies. Divers in the experimental group enjoyed a reduction in state anxiety and an increased ability to perform a standard SCUBA "bail-out" procedure as a result of stress management training.

Autogenic Training

In many ways, *autogenic training* is very similar to Jacobson's progressive relaxation training. However, greater emphasis is placed upon how various limbs and parts of the body feel (e.g., arm feels heavy and warm) rather than how relaxed they are. According to Ulett and Peterson (1965), self-hypnosis plays an important role in autogenic training.

Autogenic training procedures were developed by Johannes H. Schultz, a German physician (Schultz and Luthe 1959).

Autogenic training as outlined by Schultz and Luthe is composed of six psychophysiologic exercises. Each exercise must be practiced until the desired results are obtained, and only then may the subject move on to the next exercise. After about four months of training, the individual should be able to complete all six steps in a matter of minutes. The end result is the relaxation response and its accompanying changes in various physiological parameters.

Vanek and Cratty (1970) have reported the widespread use of autogenic training by athletes in Europe. The technique is practiced on willing athletes using a wide range of variations. To use the technique successfully, athletes must be intelligent, extremely attentive, and reasonably open to suggestion. Once the technique is thoroughly mastered, it is applied in stressful situations to help reduce tension and anxiety. Vanek and Cratty outline the following basic steps: (1) athlete is placed in a comfortable position (usually on his or her back); (2) athlete is taught to breathe deeply and to concentrate on his or her own breathing; (3) athlete tenses and relaxes all of the muscles in the body several times; (4) athlete concentrates on relaxing specific parts of the body and experiencing feelings of heaviness in each limb; (5) athlete experiences feeling of warmth in limbs and abdomen and coolness of the forehead; and (6) athlete repeats to him- or herself statements such as, "I feel quite relaxed." An example of autogenic training being practiced with frogmen is provided by Spigolon and Annalisa (1985).

Various authors have outlined autogenic training and relaxation programs that can be adopted by the athlete (Harris and Harris 1984; Nideffer 1985; Orlick 1986). In addition, numerous relaxation and autogenic training cassette tapes can be commercially purchased or developed (Rotella, Malone and Ojala 1985). In table 22.1 I have outlined a series of statements that can be used for teaching athletes to relax. In this list, I freely intertwine statements and principles that may be considered integral parts of progressive relaxation, autogenic training, or both.

Transcendental meditation

Transcendental Meditation (TM) is a meditation procedure with religious and mystical overtones. Transcendental meditation, along with Zen and Hatha Yoga, had their origins in India more than four thousand years ago. The procedure uses devices such as concentration on breath-

TABLE 22.1
Suggested Statements That May Be Included in an Autogenic Training Presentation

1. Find a comfortable position where you can sit or lie down.
2. Do not cross your arms or legs; try to get comfortable.
3. Close your eyes and put away thoughts of the outside world.
4. I want you to concentrate on your breathing as you inhale and exhale.
5. "Inhale," "exhale," "inhale," "exhale," "inhale," "exhale."
6. Each time you exhale I want you to *feel* the tension being expelled from your body.
7. "Inhale," "exhale," "inhale," "exhale," "inhale," "exhale."
8. You are beginning to feel very relaxed and very calm.
9. Now, as you continue your breathing, I want you to systematically tighten and then relax all of the muscles in your body.
10. Let's first start with your left leg. Tense the muscles of your left leg and left foot. Now, totally relax the muscles in that leg.
11. As you relax the muscles of your left leg, notice how heavy and warm your foot feels.
12. Continue on your own to tense and relax all of the muscles in your body. Start with your lower extemities and move upward.
13. "Tense and relax," "tense and relax," "tense and relax, . . ."
14. At this time your muscles feel very relaxed. Your arms and legs feel heavy.
15. Your hands and feet feel warm and your forehead feels very cool.
16. Let's return now to concentrating on your breathing.
17. "Inhale," "exhale," "inhale," "exhale," "inhale," "exhale."
18. You feel very relaxed and calm.
19. Each time you exhale you are expelling anxiety and tension from your body.
20. Think to yourself, "I feel quite relaxed and quite calm."

ing, visualization, relaxation of muscles, and the repetition of the *mantra* to gain the desired effect. The mantra is a simple sound selected by the instructor as a mental concentration device. On such sound, "om or ahhom," has been a popular one (Nideffer 1976). The modern founder of the transcendental meditation movement was Maharishi Mahesh Yogi of India.

In practice, the subject sits in a comfortable position with eyes closed. The subject concentrates on deep breathing while at the same time repeating the mantra silently. Reportedly, the sound of the mantra soon disappears as the mind experiences subtler levels of thought and finally arrives at the source of the thought. While most Oriental approaches teach a sitting meditation position, both Zen and transcendental meditation emphasize that standing or sitting are acceptable (Layman 1980).

From a physiological point of view, the practice of meditation results in the relaxation response (Wallace and Benson 1972). In fact, when stripped of its religious and mystical overtones, transcendental meditation is essentially identical to the four elements identified by Benson, Beary, and Carol (1974) for eliciting the relaxation response.

While it is clear that transcendental meditation can reduce anxiety and tension by evoking the relaxation response, it is not clear whether its practice has a facilitative effect on athletic performance. Again, while it seems clear that a reduction in arousal and muscle tension should help the anxiety-prone athlete, this is very difficult to verify. The evidence is typically anecdotal or based on single case study reports (Layman 1980). However, since 1976 several scientific investigations have related transcendental meditation with motor performance. Reddy, Bai, and Rao (1976) randomly assigned subjects to control and experimental TM training conditions for six weeks. At the end of the training period, the subjects were tested on various motor tasks. Results showed a significant difference in improvement for the TM group on the fifty-meter dash, an agility test, standing broad jump, reaction time, and coordination. Reliable differences were not noted between the two groups on a strength test and the shot put. The investigators concluded that transcendental meditation helps the athlete develop a broad range of qualities essential to motor performance: agility, speed, endurance, fast reactions, and mind-body coordination.

While the research by Reddy, Bai, and Rao (1976) suggests that transcendental meditation has a facilitative effect upon *gross motor skills*—skills that require large muscle involvement—research by Williams and associates (Williams 1978; Williams and Herbert 1976; Williams, Lodge and Reddish 1977; Williams and Vickerman 1976) showed no such effect for *fine motor skills,* those that require delicate muscle control. Subjects trained in transendental meditation techniques did not demonstrate superior learning or performance on fine motor tasks compared to control subjects. Williams (1978) concluded that certain physiological effects attributed to the practice of transcendental meditation, such as lowered anxiety and arousal, are not manifested in terms of learning and performance of a novel perceptual fine motor skill such as mirror tracing or rotary pursuit.

4. *Principle* Teaching athletes how to elicit the relaxation response will help them avoid or curtail the anxiety-stress spiral.

   Application Athletes should be taught to relax in a matter of seconds using progressive relaxation, autogenic training, or transcendental meditation.

Biofeedback

It has been proven that humans can voluntarily control functions of the autonomic nervous system. Research on animals by DiCara (1970) and on humans by Benson, Beary, and Carol (1974) has verified this. *Biofeedback* is a relatively modern technique that is based upon this principle.

Biofeedback training uses instruments to help people control responses of the autonomic nervous system. For example, a subject monitors an auditory signal of his or her own heart rate and experiments with different thoughts, feelings, and sensations to slow the heart rate. Once the subject learns to recognize the feelings associated with the reduction of heart rate, the instrument is removed, and the subject tries to control the heart rate without it. This is the goal of the biofeedback therapist. People suffering from chronic anxiety or illnesses caused by anxiety can often benefit from biofeedback training, because when they learn to reduce functions of the sympathetic nervous system, they are indirectly learning to reduce anxiety and tension (Brown 1977; Danskin and Crow 1981). Biofeedback is essentially the same as progressive relaxation, autogenic training, and meditation. Using the latter three techniques, the subject relaxes, which lowers arousal and decreases the activity of the sympathetic nervous system. With biofeedback, the subject begins by lowering certain physiological measures with the help of an instrument. This decreases arousal and increases relaxation.

Instrumentation

Theoretically, biofeedback can be very useful to athletes who suffer from excessive anxiety and arousal. If athletes could be trained to control their physiological responses in the laboratory, they should be able to transfer this ability onto the athletic field. The main drawback to biofeedback in athletics is expense. The cost of purchasing a machine for measuring heart rate, EEG, EMG, or GSR changes is out of reach for the average school's athletic budget. However, not all biofeedback measurement techniques are expensive, and many are still in the experimental stages. Some of the basic measurement techniques used in biofeedback training will be listed (Danskin and Crow 1981; Schwartz 1987).

Skin Temperature. The most commonly used and least expensive form of biofeedback is skin temperature. When an athlete becomes highly aroused, additional blood is pumped to the vital organs. Part of this additional blood supply comes from the peripheral blood vessels, leaving the hands feeling cold and clammy. Thus, the effect of stress is to decrease the skin temperature of the extremities. Subjects can monitor skin temperature to discover what kinds of responses, thoughts, and autogenic phrases are most effective in increasing it. Typically, subjects are trained to use progressive relaxation techniques and autogenic phrases to assist them in the biofeedback process. Although sophisticated instruments are available, a simple and inexpensive cardboard-backed thermometer can be used to monitor skin temperature. For use, the cardboard is cut off just above the bulb and the thermometer is taped to the finger. . . .

Electromyography. Another very popular biofeedback technique employs the use of an electromyographic feedback instrument (EMG). Electrodes are attached to a particular group of muscles in the forearm or forehead, and the subject tries to reduce muscular tension by using auditory or visual cues of muscle electrical activity. Auditory cues typically come through earphones in the form of clicks. Visual cues come through a meter that the subject watches.

Electroencephalogram. A third major instrument used for biofeedback is the electroencephalogram (EEG). Use of the EEG is commonly called brainwave training. Tiny electrical impulses from billions of brain cells can be detected by electrodes placed on the scalp and connected to an EEG. Four basic types of brain waves are associated with EEG recordings. Beta waves predominate during periods of excitement and of high arousal. Alpha waves predominate when the subject relaxes and puts his or her mind in "neutral." It is the alpha waves that the subject tries to produce. The other two types are theta waves, which predominate during drowsiness, and delta waves, which are associated with deep sleep (Fisher 1976).

Other Methods. While skin temperature, EMG, and EEG are the most common methods used in biofeedback training, several others are used to a lesser degree. These are the galvanic skin response (GSR), heart rate, and blood pressure. Some other methods of biofeedback training techniques are still in the experimental stages. One of these is the use of a stethoscope to monitor heart rate. Others include monitoring respiration rate, vapor pressure from the skin, stomach acidity, sphincter constriction, and blood chemistry.

Biofeedback and Performance

In a laboratory setting, the athlete learns to control the autonomic nervous system. The feelings and experiences associated with learning how to reduce sympathetic nervous system responses in the laboratory are then transferred to the athletic environment. In some cases biofeedback may be practiced in the athletic environment. For example, Costa, Bonaccorsi, and Scrimali (1984) reported the use of biofeedback training with team handball athletes to reduce precompetitive anxiety.

As observed by Wenz and Strong (1980), the difference between success and failure of two equally matched athletes often depends on an individual's ability to cope with the perceived stress of competition. Biofeedback provides a way for athletes to determine their levels of physiological arousal and to learn how to make conscious changes calculated to reduce anxiety and improve performance. A number of scientific investigations have been conducted to determine the effect of biofeedback on athletic performance. The following three studies are representative of the research conducted in this area.

DeWitt (1980) reported two studies in which biofeedback significantly enhanced performance. In the first, six football players received twelve weeks of biofeedback, relaxation, and mental rehearsal training in two one-hour sessions per week. The results showed a significant reduction in muscle tension (EMG), and the coaching staff felt that four of the six improved in football-playing ability. In the second study, twelve basketball players were assigned to either a control or biofeedback treatment condition. The results showed that biofeedback subjects significantly reduced heart rate and EMG levels as a result of training. Also, post-test performance ratings of biofeedback subjects were superior to those of the control subjects. The author concluded that biofeedback training reduces anxiety and arousal and facilitates athletic performance. . . .

French (1978) tested thirty college males on the stabilometer test of balancing and recorded their EMG scores. The subjects were then assigned into three matched groups according to their performance scores. Experimental groups 1 and 2 received a combination of relaxation,

5. *Principle* Biofeedback is an effective and powerful tool for reducing the debilitating effects of anxiety and stress.

   Application If an athlete can't control anxiety and stress using progressive relaxation, autogenic training, or meditation, then biofeedback training should be tried. To get started with feedback training, it may be necessary to identify a professional therapist. Equipment necessary for biofeedback training may not be readily available to the athlete or coach.

autogenic, and biofeedback training prior to a post-test on the stabilometer. During the post-test, only experimental group 1 received auditory EMG feedback. All groups received a post-test on the stabilometer while EMGs were being monitored. The results revealed that biofeedback training effectively reduced EMG recordings, but that stabilometer scores were unaffected.

Daniels and Landers (1981) compared a group of shooters receiving verbal instructions with an experimental group receiving biofeedback training. The results showed that the subjects who received biofeedback training significantly improved shooting accuracy and pattern consistency while showing greater control over the autonomic pattern. This research demonstrated that shooting performance can be improved using biofeedback.

In summary, it seems clear that the relaxation procedures introduced in this section effectively reduce anxiety and arousal. Theoretically, this should help the athlete to reduce anxiety and tension during competition. However, the indiscriminate use of these procedures does not guarantee better athletic performance. Just as pep talks can overarouse an athlete, relaxation can underarouse an athlete if improperly applied.

Cognitive Strategies

Cognitive strategies are psychological procedures used by athletes to mentally prepare themselves for competition (Ravizza and Rotella 1982). In that they are used to alter the existing anxiety, frustration, confidence, and arousal levels of the athlete, they are also classified as intervention strategies. The cognitive strategies discussed in this section may be used to reduce the debilitating effects of anxiety and stress upon athletic performance. However, many of these procedures can also be used either to elevate or to reduce arousal levels. A case in point would be imagery. Depending on the kinds of images that are attended to, the athlete could be either aroused or relaxed. For example, imagining yourself sitting on a California beach is much different than imagining a scene of aggression in professional hockey. The cognitive strategy of goal setting is primarily used to motivate athletes by directing their attention to specific aims and objectives. Three of the most common cognitive intervention strategies are discussed in this section (imagery, hypnosis, and goal setting).

Imagery

Game six of the 1987 baseball World Series provided an excellent example of the use of imagery by a professional athlete. During game six, Don Baylor, the Minnesota Twins' designated hitter, faced pitcher John Tudor of the St. Louis Cardinals. It was the bottom of the fifth inning; St. Louis was leading 5 to 3; and there were no outs and one man on second base. Baylor had last faced Tudor in 1983 when he was with the Yankees and Tudor was with the Red Sox. Preparing to face Tudor in this classic match-up of game six, Baylor recalls, "I reminisced about the last time he pitched me then. Let's just say I was somewhat more ready for him than he was for me" (Wulf 1987). History records that Baylor took Tudor's first pitch deep into the left-field stands for a two-run homer.

Block (1981) identified human *imagery,* the use of visualization to imagine situations, as one of the most important topics in cognitive science. Two general theories have evolved. The first states that when we imagine a scene in our mind's eye, we are scanning an actual image that has somehow formed in our brain. This is not to say that a brain surgeon could find actual physical pictures lodged in our brains, but that the images are as real to us as an image taken from the retina of the eye. This position is held by the so-called pictorialists. The second position is that of the descriptionist. The descriptionist argues that there is no such thing as a mental image. That is, when we imagine a physical scene in our mind's eye, we are not really seeing an internal image, but the graphic and detailed nature of our language makes it seem so. Our thoughts, as it were, actually manufacture an image so clear that we think we are seeing one (Block 1981).

Regardless of which view one takes, the images we see are vivid enough, and therefore it makes little difference whether they are pictorial by nature or descriptively represented in our minds. Some experimental findings about imagery are (1) mental images can be scanned, (2) small mental images are hard to see, (3) when images are expanded, they eventually overflow, (4) and images overflow from a roughly elliptical shape (Kosslyn et al. 1981).

Consistent with Block's (1981) notion of the nature of imagery, Fisher (1986) clarifies that imagery is the language of the brain. In a real sense, the brain really can't tell the difference between an actual physical event and the vivid visualization of the same event. For this reason, imagery can be used by the brain to provide repetition, elaboration, intensification, and preservation of important athletic sequences and skills.

Smith (1987) identified five basic principles of the application of imagery to sport. These five principles are (1) imagery skills can be developed, (2) the athlete must have a positive attitude relative to the effectiveness of imagery, (3) imagery is most effective when used by skilled athletes, (4) knowing how to relax is a necessary precursor to the effective use of imagery, and (5) there are two kinds of imagery, internal and external. Using the principles outlined by Smith (1987), Fenker and Lambiotte (1987) reported a case study in which a performance enhancement program, based on the development of imagery skills, was implemented for a major college football team. The program used imagery training techniques to help the team achieve its best record in twenty years. The mere fact that a major football program was willing to adopt an imagery performance enhancement program is evidence that imagery is being taken seriously by coaches and athletes.

Internal and External Imagery

Sport psychologists have identified two methods of sport performance imagery: *internal* and *external* imagery (Mahoney and Avener 1977). *Internal imagery* is considered to be primarily kinesthetic in nature. That is, athletes pretend to be within their own bodies while performing. Athletes feel themselves performing, and can see the object of attention, but cannot see their own bodies. *External imagery* is considered to be primarily visual in nature. That is, athletes pretend to watch themselves perform from outside. The research by Mahoney and Avener (1977) seemed to indicate that the first-person or internal type of imagery was superior. Their conclusions were based on elite gymnasts who claimed a reliance upon internal imagery as opposed to a group of less successful gymnasts who relied upon external imagery. One explanation for the supposed superiority of kinesthetic (internal) imagery is that it actually results in subliminal muscle activity in the muscles associated with the imagined actions. This concept was first demonstrated by Jacobson (1931) and was verified by Hale in 1982. Hale

6. *Principle* Two kinds of imagery are available to the athlete.

   Application Internal imagery allows athletes to kinesthetically experience the correct execution of a skill, while external imagery allows them to see themselves performing the skill. Athletes should develop skill in both internal and external imagery.

showed that weight lifters who used an internal imagery style experienced greater biceps muscle activity than those who used an external style. Likewise, Harris and Robinson (1986) demonstrated that internal imagery elicited greater EMG activity in the deltoid muscle group than external imagery during a lateral arm-raising task. They further demonstrated that advanced karate students not only used internal imagery to a greater degree than beginning karate students, but that the internal imagery generated greater EMG activity.

These findings provide evidence that a physiological difference exists between the two types of imagery. Internal imagery generates greater muscle EMG activity than does visual imagery. Whether or not internal imagery is actually better than external imagery in terms of facilitating physical performance is still open to debate. The Harris and Robinson (1986) findings suggest that internal imagery may be superior, since higher-skilled karate athletes favored its use. However, Epstein (1980) reported research showing that neither method is superior in terms of dart-throwing performance. In fact, the research is uncertain on this point (Rotella et al. 1980). Because of this, it would seem reasonable to assume that some type of guided combination of the two styles would be most beneficial. Certainly the athlete can benefit from both visual and kinesthetic image rehearsal.

Effectiveness of Imagery in Sport

Current interest in imagery makes one wonder why this has all occurred so recently. The fact is that interest in the topic has always been strong, but it was previously known as mental practice, not imagery or visualization. The current findings regarding imagery are consistent with earlier published information. Representative of some of this research are selected studies by Clark (1960) and Corbin (1967a, 1967b). Clark compared the effect of mental practice with that of physical practice in the learning of the Pacific Coast one-hand foul shot. He placed 144 high school boys into physical and mental practice groups on the basis of varsity, junior varsity, or novice experience. All subjects were given a twenty-five-shot pretest before and a twenty-five-shot

7. *Principle* The more skillful and experienced an athlete is, the more he or she will be able to benefit from the use of imagery.

   Application To avoid discouraging young athletes from the use of imagery, make sure that he or she is familiar enough with the activity to know the difference between a good or bad performance. An athlete must know both what the skill looks like and how it feels in order to effectively use imagery.

---

post-test after fourteen days of practice (thirty shots per day). Results showed that mental practice was almost as effective as physical practice for the junior varsity and varsity groups, but physical practice was far superior to mental practice for the beginners. Corbin (1967a, 1967b) observed similar results using a wand-juggling task. From the results of these studies, it seems clear that for mental practice or imagery to facilitate performance, a certain amount of skill is necessary. In other words, a coach or teacher should not expect imagery training to be effective with athletes who are unskilled in their sports. The more skillful they are, the more useful mental rehearsal techniques will be for them. In support of this position, Landers, Boutcher, and Wang (1986) observed that skilled archers use imagery to a significantly greater extent than lesser-skilled archers.

Imagery or mental practice is most effective for activities that require some thought—those that have a large cognitive component (Ryan and Simons 1981). For example, a balancing task would have a small cognitive component, while a finger maze would have a large cognitive component. In terms of sport, one should expect better results using imagery for tennis than for a rope-pulling contest.

As a general rule, the use of mental practice and imagery to enhance performance is supported by the literature. In a meta-analysis (summary analysis) conducted by Feltz and Landers (1983), a review of over one hundred studies revealed that mental practice is better than no practice at all. Price and Meacci (1985) demonstrated that relaxation and imagery is as effective as physical practice in improving putting in golf. However, it is important to note that negative outcome imagery is more powerful in causing a decrement in performance than positive outcome imagery is for facilitating athletic performance (Woolfolk et al. 1985.) This is why it is so important that the athlete master the techniques of *thought stopping* and *centering*. . . . The more competent an athlete is in mastering imagery skills, the more effective its application (Kohl, Roenker and Turner 1985).

Developing Imagery Skills

As with relaxation training, imagery abilities can be improved with practice. Hickman (1979:120–21) listed thirteen steps to effective training in mental imagery and rehearsal. These are summarized in the following six steps:

1. Find a quiet place where you won't be disturbed, assume a comfortable position, and relax completely.
2. Practice imagery by visualizing a circle that fills the visual field. Make the circle turn a deep blue. Repeat the process several times, imagining a different color each time. Allow the images to disappear. Relax and observe the spontaneous imagery that arises.
3. Create the image of a simple three-dimensional glass. Fill it with a colorful liquid, add ice cubes and a straw. Write a descriptive caption underneath.
4. Select a variety of scenes and develop them with rich detail. Include sport-related images such as a swimming pool, tennis court, and a beautiful golf course. Practice visualizing people, including strangers, in each of these scenes.
5. Imagine yourself in a sport setting of keen interest to you. Visualize and feel yourself successfully participating in the scene. Relax and enjoy your success.
6. End the session by breathing deeply, opening your eyes, and adjusting to the external environment.

The potential of imagery as an effective cognitive strategy is enormous. An athlete can physically practice shooting basketball free throws for years, and yet never feel comfortable or confident doing the same thing in a game situation. Generally, practice conditions do not match the anxiety and fear associated with the real-life situation. In an effective mental imagery session, athletes can imagine themselves successfully making basket after basket in pressure-packed game situations.

Stress management strategies using imagery have proven effective in improving athletic performance. Perhaps the strongest evidence comes from Suinn's (1972) visual-motor behavior rehearsal program (VMBR). This program will be discussed in greater detail later in this chapter. A body of supporting literature that speaks well of the use of imagery to improve athletic performance is continuing to emerge (Kolonay 1977).

8. *Principle* Imagery allows the anxiety-prone athlete to practice relaxation skills in a stressful situation.

   Application Since actual practice situations are rarely as stressful as competition, the athlete should use imagery to create numerous anxiety-provoking situations.

If there is a shortcoming to research involving imagery, it is in terms of determining whether or not an athlete is using it. For example, how can you be sure that an athlete who is supposed to be practicing visual imagery really is? And how can you be sure that control subjects are not using the technique? These and other methodological problems present challenges to the researcher.

Hypnosis

Of all the intervention strategies, hypnosis is the least understood. Yet a close analysis reveals that in many important ways hypnosis (especially self-hypnosis) is identical to relaxation training and transcendental meditation. This is especially true during the induction phase of hypnosis. Once an individual is hypnotized and is asked to perform some act (waking hypnosis), then certain physiological differences may emerge. For example, if while hypnotized, the subject is asked to imagine that a raging tiger is approaching, you can expect that the person's heart rate and respiration rate will go up, not down. Yet . . . hypnosis yields the same type of relaxation response as do the other intervention strategies. This is because suggestions of deep relaxation were given to the subjects. This pattern also emerges before hypnotic suggestions are given.

A case study in which hypnosis was used to help an amateur boxer was documented by Heyman (1987). In this chronology, a single-case experimental design was presented in which hypnosis was systematically used as an intervention strategy. The athlete was described as suffering a performance decrement due to anxiety caused by crowd noise. As a result of the controlled and professionally applied use of hypnosis, the athlete was able to show some improvement. While there may be some potential risks associated with the indiscriminate use of hypnosis by an untrained therapist (Morgan and Brown 1983), most concerns about hypnosis are unfounded. It is probably fair to say that hypnosis is clouded by more myths and misconceptions than any other form of psychological intervention (Clarke and Jackson 1983).

The following discussion should demystify hypnosis to some degree and explain its relationship to sport performance. The subject is divided into four subsections. They are (1) defining hypnosis, (2) obtaining the hypnotic trance, (3) self-hypnosis, and (4) the effect of hypnosis on athletic performance.

Hypnosis Defined

Ulett and Peterson (1965) define *hypnosis* as the uncritical acceptance of a suggestion. This is a definition that almost all psychologists can agree upon, since it does little to explain what causes hypnosis or how it differs from the waking state. Four events occur when a subject is hypnotized. First, the subject elicits the relaxation response and becomes drowsy and lethargic. Second, the subject manifests responsiveness to suggestions. Third, the subject reports changes in body awareness and feeling. Finally, the subject knows that he or she is hypnotized (Barber, Spanos, and Chaves 1974).

There are at least two theoretical explanations for the phenomenon of hypnotism (Barber, Spanos, and Chaves 1974). The first represents the hypnotic trance viewpoint, while the second represents the cognitive-behavioral viewpoint. The traditional or hypnotic trance viewpoint is that the hypnotized subject is in an altered state or hypnotic trance. The cognitive-behavioral viewpoint rejects the notion of a trance and simply bases the hypnotic phenomenon on the personality of the subject. That is, subjects carry out hypnotic behaviors because they have positive attitudes, motivations, and expectations that lead to a willingness to think and imagine with the themes suggested by the hypnotist. Since only about 16 percent of subjects who go through the hypnotic induction procedure can reach a deep trance (Edmonston 1981), the cognitive-behavioral viewpoint is certainly plausible.

From the hypnotic trance viewpoint, the trance has also been referred to as a state of cortical inhibition (Orne 1959). The cortical inhibition viewpoint is supported by the work of Watzlawick (1978). According to this explanation, hypnosis appeals directly to the functioning of the nondominant cerebral hemisphere. The process of hypnosis inhibits the functions of the dominant hemisphere (thinking, logic, language, details) and allows the nondominant hemispheric functions (whole movements, whole ideas, pictures rather than words, music rather than ideas) to take over (Pressman 1980).

A third explanation for the phenomenon of hypnosis was proposed by Orne (1959). According to Orne, a simple increase in suggestibility results from the hypnotic induction procedure. The weakness of this explanation is that it does not say how or why the subject becomes more responsive to suggestions. This is undoubtedly why Barber, Spanos, and Chaves (1974) did not include it. Consequently, we can agree that hypnosis is a state of uncritical acceptance of suggestions, but we are torn between two divergent explanations of how this is brought about.

The acceptance of Barber's cognitive-behavioral viewpoint certainly would tend to demystify hypnosis. However, by itself it may be too simplistic an explanation. Regardless of which position one takes, the end result is the same: a subject is extremely responsive to suggestions when he or she was not as responsive during the waking state.

Achieving the Hypnotic Trance

Five phases are associated with inducing the *hypnotic trance* in a subject. They are preparation of the subject, the induction process, the hypnotic phase, waking up, and the posthypnotic phase.

When subjects are prepared for hypnotism, they must be relieved of any fears and apprehensions they have about hypnotism. Some myths may need to be exposed. For example, subjects may be under the impression that they will lose control, that they will be unaware of surroundings or will lose consciousness. They must have complete trust in the hypnotist and must want to be hypnotized. They also must be told that they will remain in control at all times and will be able to come out of the hypnotic trance if they want to.

It is during the *hypnotic induction* phase that the hypnotist actually hypnotizes the subject. There are many induction techniques. The best ones are associated with relaxation, attentional focus, and imagery. In fact, the steps involved in eliciting the relaxation response using these techniques are essentially identical to those in hypnosis. The only difference is that the word hypnosis is never used in eliciting the relaxation response. It should also be pointed out that in terms of physiological responses, hypnotic induction is identical to the relaxation responses associated with progressive relaxation, transcendental meditation, and autogenic training. Coleman (1976) verified this in a study in which he compared the physiological responses associated with hypnotic induction and relaxation procedures.

Generally, induction procedures are fairly standard. They are typically comprised of a series of suggestions aimed at eliciting the subject's cooperation and directing his or her attention to thoughts and feelings about being relaxed and peaceful. The selection of an induction technique is generally based on the hypnotist's comfort with it or because he or she believes the subject's attentional style or personality is compatible with it. Some of the more common techniques involve fixation on an object, monotonous suggestions ("you feel sleepy"), and imagery. Regardless of which technique is used, the effect is the same. The subject becomes very lethargic, experiences the relaxation response, and becomes very susceptible to suggestions. The hypnotist can use a number of techniques to make the subject become more responsive to hypnotism. Most of these are associated with relaxing the subject and gaining his or her confidence. Others include using the word *hypnotism* to define the situation and the manner in which suggestions are given. For example, a good time to suggest to the subject that he or she is becoming tired is when the hypnotist observes that the subjects' eyelids are drooping. The hypnotist must also avoid making suggestions that the subject may fail.

Once the hypnotic state has been induced, the subject is in *neutral hypnosis.* In this state, physiological responses are identical to those of the relaxation response. The hypnotized subject is generally asked to respond either in imagination or physically to suggestions of the hypnotist. Typically, these suggestions are alerting and arousing, and bring about the "alert" trance, or *waking hypnosis* (Edmonston 1981). If subjects are asked to carry out suggestions while in a trance, they are doing so in the state of waking hypnosis. Subjects may, of course, be given suggestions of deep relaxation while in the hypnotic state. This will result in the relaxation response. . . . Generally, subjects will be given suggestions to carry out after they are awake. These are referred to as *posthypnotic suggestions.* Ken Norton was given posthypnotic suggestions for his fight with Muhammad Ali.

The fourth phase of hypnosis is coming out of the trance. Actually, a hypnotized subject can come out of the trance anytime. The only reason subjects do not come out on their own is because they don't want to. The relationship between the hypnotist and the subject can be a very pleasant one. When the hypnotist wishes to bring a subject out of a trance, he or she does so simply by suggesting that the subject wake up on a given signal. For example, the hypnotist might say, "Okay, when I count to three you will wake up." Occasionally a subject will resist coming out of the trance. If this happens, the subject is taken back into a deep trance and asked why he or she doesn't want to come out. After a few minutes of discussion and another suggestion to wake up, the subject will generally do so.

Suggestions given to subjects during hypnosis are often designed to influence them during the posthypnotic phase, or after they have come out of the hypnotic trance. Posthypnotic suggestions given to athletes

9. *Principle* A trained psychologist should be present if heterohypnosis is used as a cognitive strategy.

   Application The hypnotized person is very susceptible to suggestions. For this reason, failure to employ a professional may do more harm than good.

---

should focus on the way they should feel in certain competitive situations. For example, a baseball player may be told that "when you get into the batter's box, you will find that you feel relaxed and confident." Specific suggestions such as "you'll be able to get a hit almost every time," should be avoided, since failure will tend to undermine the effectiveness of the suggestions (Nideffer, 1976).

Autohypnosis

There are two kinds of hypnosis. The first kind is *heterohypnosis,* and the second is called *autohypnosis,* or self-hypnosis. Our discussion up to this point has dealt primarily with heterohypnosis, that which is induced by another person, usually a trained hypnotist or psychologist. Heterohypnosis should only be practiced by trained professionals. Even though an attempt has been made in this text to demystify hypnosis, this does not mean that potential dangers do not exist. Heterohypnosis is based upon a rather delicate rapport between the hypnotist and the subject. Consequently, if heterohypnosis is to be practiced on athletes, it should be done so by a competent psychologist (Morgan and Brown 1983).

Autohypnosis is not based on a relationship with another individual. Yet all of the effects that can be achieved through heterohypnosis can be achieved through autohypnosis. It should also be emphasized that in one sense, all hypnosis is self-hypnosis, since people cannot be hypnotized unless they want to be. Furthermore, hypnosis is a natural state of consciousness that we slip into and out of dozens of times a day (Pulos 1979).

As explained by Ulett and Peterson (1965), there are two kinds of autohypnosis. The first is self-induced, and the second is induced as a posthypnotic suggestion following heterohypnosis. The latter method is easier to achieve. In this method, subjects are told during hypnosis that they will be able to hypnotize themselves anytime they wish simply by following some relaxation and attentional focus induction procedures. Because they have already been hypnotized, they know how it feels and they enjoy the feeling. Therefore, it is much easier for

10. *Principle* Self-hypnosis or autohypnosis is just as effective as heterohypnosis, and does not place the athlete in a situation of dependence.

    Application If hypnosis skills are taught, autohypnosis is preferred to heterohypnosis. Autohypnosis is very similar to autogenic training and is safe.

---

them to hypnotize themselves. With each repetition of self-hypnosis, it becomes easier and easier to achieve. What will initially be relaxation will later become effective hypnosis as subjects learn to narrow their field of attention.

The phases involved in autohypnosis are identical to those outlined for hypnosis generally. If a coach or teacher wishes to employ autohypnosis as an intervention strategy for reducing anxiety and improving concentration and imagery, he or she should go over these steps with the athlete. First, the athlete must be completely comfortable regarding the use of hypnosis. The athlete should begin with the reminder (suggestion) that he or she is in complete control and can disengage from the hypnotic trance at any time. The induction procedures are the same as for heterohypnosis. Some common strategies for induction are to sit in an easy chair and stare at a spot on the wall, imagine a blank screen, or look into a mirror.

Posthypnotic suggestions given during autohypnosis should always be couched in positive terms, stressing what is to be accomplished rather than dwelling on negative things to be eliminated. For example, the athlete may wish to concentrate on being more positive when he or she prepares to receive a tennis serve from a tough opponent. A suggestion such as "I will feel relaxed and agile," would be better than "I'm going to hit a winner." The second suggestion contains the seeds of defeat, since you can't always hit a winner. Suggestions such as "I won't feel nervous," are negative because they only call attention to the problem. The athlete should have specific suggestions already in mind before the hypnotic phase begins. In some cases, the athlete could have the suggestions written on a card (perhaps by the coach) to read during the hypnotic trance.

Hypnosis and Athletic Performance

Since 1933, several important reviews have been published on the relationship between hypnosis and motor performance. These reviews have centered primarily on the literature comparing hypnosis and mus-

11. *Principle* Giving negative suggestions to a hypnotized athlete will likely result in a performance decrement.

    Application If an athlete under hypnosis is told that she will be successful, that may or may not happen. However, the athlete who is told under hypnosis that he or she will fail probably will. Negative suggestions must be completely avoided when working with athletes.

---

cular strength and endurance. None of these early reviews (Gorton 1949; Hull 1933; Johnson 1961; Weitzenhoffer 1963) resulted in clear-cut conclusions about the effectiveness of hypnosis in facilitating motor performance. All of the reviews identified research design problems and lack of standardization procedures as factors that led to the inconsistent results. However, Johnson (1961) made several important conclusions. These are very important and remain valid.

1. The deeper the hypnotic trance, the more likely it is that suggestions will work.
2. General arousal techniques are more useful in enhancing muscular strength and endurance than hypnotic suggestions.
3. Negative suggestions invariably work to the detriment of the performer.
4. Hypnosis can help a successful athlete, but it can't make a good performer out of a poor one.
5. Hypnotizing athletes may do more harm than good.

Probably the most important review conducted to date on this subject was done by Morgan (1972). Morgan reviewed the literature in two phases. First, he took a second look at the research already reviewed prior to 1963, and second, he reviewed the literature from 1963 to 1971. His review included the literature about muscular strength and endurance as well as the rather scanty research dealing with athletic performance. Morgan's conclusions for both types of tasks were remarkably similar to Johnson's (1961). He indicated that positive suggestions were effective in facilitating performance regardless of whether or not the athlete was hypnotized, and that negative suggestions almost always caused a decrement in performance.

Since Morgan's review was published, several investigations have been conducted on the relationship between hypnosis and athletic performance. We will consider three of them. As we shall see, the results of these three studies are generally consistent with the conclusions drawn by Johnson (1961) and Morgan (1972).

Ulrich (1973) conducted a study to determine the effect of hypnotic and nonhypnotic suggestions on archery performance. Using archery students (forty-three males and nine females), he assigned each student to one of four treatment conditions. First of all, the subjects were tested on their susceptibility to hypnosis and categorized as high or low on this variable. The highly susceptible subjects were matched in terms of archery skill and assigned to either a hypnotism-plus-positive-suggestions group or to a positive-suggestions-only group. Likewise, the less susceptible subjects were matched according to skill and assigned to either a positive-suggestions-only group or a control group receiving neither suggestions nor hypnotism. Statistically, the groups were compared on shooting performance from distances of 15, 20, and 25 yards. The results revealed no reliable differences among the groups. The researcher concluded that identical suggestions given in the normal waking state appeared to be as effective as the same suggestions given in the hypnotic state.

Baer (1980) studied the effect of time-slowing hypnotic suggestions on volleying in a video tennis game. Fourteen female subjects were screened for hypnotic suggestibility, but only three of them were retained for being high in suggestibility. After establishing both a waking and a hypnotic baseline for length of volleys, subjects were given alternating suggestions for ball slowing and quickness of response. Results revealed that the initial suggestions for ball slowing did not result in improved volleys, but in subsequent presentations, longer volleys were made. The author concluded that highly suggestible subjects could improve volleying performance as a result of hypnotic suggestions.

Ito (1979) further investigated the relative effect of suggestibility upon motor performance. Ito studied the effects of hypnosis and motivational suggestions on muscular strength. In this experiment, thirty male subjects performed a hand dynamometer strength task under four different conditions. The four conditions were performance in the waking state, motivating instructions in the waking state, hypnosis alone, and performance in the hypnotic state with motivating instructions. The results showed that the subjects who received motivating instructions did the best, regardless of whether they were hypnotized or not. At this point, Ito categorized his thirty subjects as being high, medium, or low on hypnotic suggestibility. With this further manipulation, it was discovered that the highly suggestible subjects who were both hypnotized and who received motivating instructions had the highest strength scores ($p = .05$). We can conclude that the question of susceptibility to hypnosis was the critical factor in research involving hypnosis.

The reviews by Johnson (1961) and Morgan (1972) explain quite well the relationship between hypnosis and motor performance. Little has been reported since 1972 that would alter Morgan's conclusions. In a more recent work, Morgan and Brown (1983) reiterate many of the conclusions derived from the early review but with greater emphasis on the need for a psychotherapist when dealing with heterohypnosis. Finally, the question of susceptability to hypnosis as mentioned by Ito (1979) seems to be a viable issue, and perhaps future research involving hypnosis should pay particular attention to this variable.

Goal Setting

While the notion of goal setting to enhance achievement is not new, its specific application to athletic performance has become an important cognitive strategy in recent years. A study by Dmitrova (1970) involving sprinting, and a more recent study by Wankel and McEwan (1976) involving a 450-meter run, verifies the utility of goal-setting procedures in sport. In the study by Wankel and McEwan, eighty-four high school boys were evenly divided into three treatment conditions based upon a pretest on the 450-meter run. Subjects in the control group were given knowledge of results (KR) of their first run and told to do their best on the post-test. Subjects in a private goal-setting condition were also given KR for their first run and asked to set private goals for their second run. Finally, those in the public goal condition met as a group and were asked to write down their goals on a piece of paper for the second run. They were informed that their goals would be posted for everyone to see. The results of the second run revealed significant differences favoring the public goal-setting group over the other two.

This study confirms our expectation that goal setting is an effective psychological strategy for improving performance. Research also shows that the nature of the goals being set is very important (Gould 1983). Several factors make goal setting more effective. First, in order to obtain a long-term goal, such as becoming a varsity basketball player, an athlete must meet several short-term goals along the way. . . . The best way to reach the top step is to take each step one at a time.

A second important characteristic of effective goal setting is to set hard but realistic goals. A goal that is not realistic and cannot be reached may discourage the athlete. For example, setting a goal to run one hundred meters in less than nine seconds is certainly unrealistic.

12. *Principle* Athletes who practice good goal-setting skills are more successful than those who do not.

    Application Goal-setting skills should be an integral part of an athlete's psychological skill development. Good goal-setting skills do not come naturally; they must be taught.

On the other hand, if you can run the mile in six minutes and you set a season goal to run it in five minutes, this is a hard goal, but certainly realistic.

Another important characteristic of good goal setting is to set specific behavioral goals that can be measured. We can easily determine if we are meeting our behavioral goals. For example, if a basketball player's goal is simply to become a good shooter, how does one determine when this goal has been met? It cannot be determined. On the other hand, if this player's goal is to hit eight out of ten 15-foot jump shots, the accomplishment of this goal can easily be determined.

A fourth important characteristic of goal setting is to outline a specific strategy or plan for meeting the goal. Many goals are not reached simply because there is no systematic plan for achieving them. For example, exactly how does one achieve the goal of becoming an 85 percent free-threw shooter? If left to chance, it will probably never happen. The coach and athlete together must devise a plan for achieving this goal. The athlete may have to stay after practice every day and shoot an extra one hundred baskets. Other strategies such as increasing wrist and arm strength may also be considered.

Finally, a good goal-setting program requires constant monitoring and evaluation by player and coach. A day should not go by without the athlete considering goals and evaluating progress. It may be that a particular goal cannot be achieved. In this case the athlete should redefine that goal in a more realistic manner. However, in most cases the regular evaluation of progress will help athletes see improvements that will provide them additional motivation to achieve their goals.

The foundation for research associated with goal setting to enhance human performance comes from Edwin Locke. The basic premise of Locke's theory is that conscious intentions in the form of goals regulate subsequent actions and behaviors (Locke 1968). More specifically, the setting of realistic but difficult goals will result in greater performance than no goals, easy goals, or "do your best" goals. Prior to turning his attention to goal setting in sport, Locke reported that of 110 studies reported between 1969 and 1980, 99 of them showed positive or partially positive effects favoring goal setting in industrial and related environmental settings (Locke et al. 1981).

In testing the utility of employing goal-setting strategies in sport, researchers initially had difficulty in demonstrating the superiority of goal setting over a "do your best" strategy (Weinberg, Bruya, and Jackson 1985). However, researchers quickly recognized that the inability to demonstrate the superiority of the goal-setting strategy was due to the researchers, failure to control variables such as competition and social evaluation (critical evaluation by peers and others) that are prevalent in sport (Hall and Byrne 1988). When problems associated with field experiments (as opposed to laboratory experiments) were taken into consideration, researchers were able to demonstrate the importance of goal setting in the obtaining of athletic success (Hall, Weinberg, and Jackson 1987; Weinberg et al. 1988).

That athletes and coaches currently employ goal-setting strategies in sport is quite obvious. Coaches are very fond of stating that their goal for a team is to make the playoffs or to win a certain number of games in a particular season. What is not so obvious is that the goal-setting strategies employed by coaches and athletes are often very general and unmeasurable. In applying his theory of goal setting to sport, Locke has suggested eleven specific principles that the coach or athlete can use to refine goal-setting strategies (Locke and Latham 1985). These eleven principles are based on previous research. . . .[1]

Package Intervention Programs

Numerous stress management and cognitive intervention programs may be identified for reducing competitive anxiety and increasing athletic performance. Using karate as the athletic medium, Seabourne et al. (1985) demonstrated that individualized and packaged intervention programs are more effective than a nonindividualized program in which participants select their own strategies. Athletes benefit most from intervention strategies when designed to fit their needs or presented in a systematic and organized fashion. Merely informing an athlete about various cognitive strategies is not particularly effective.

In this section I will describe four intervention programs that have received attention from psychologists, sport psychologists, and researchers. However, there are several other programs that are quite similar and should be briefly mentioned. Included among these are Suinn's (1983) seven steps to peak performance; Kirschenbaum et al.'s (1984) criticism inoculation training; Murphy and Woolfolk's (1987) cognitive-behavioral stress reduction program; and Llewellyn and Blucker's (1982) mental self-improvement program. All of these programs, including those to follow, are based on many of the relaxation and cognitive strategies outlined previously in this chapter.

Visual-Motor Behavior Rehearsal

Visual-Motor Behavior Rehearsal (VMBR) was developed by Suinn (1972) as an adaptation of Wolpe's (1958) desensitization procedures for humans. The process of desensitization was used to help patients to overcome phobias. For example, a patient fearing heights would be desensitized to this phobia through a series of systematic approximations to the fearful stimuli. Although Suinn used VMBR to treat people with depressions, he was especially interested in applying the techniques to athletes. His particular method of training consisted of (1) relaxing the athlete's body by means of a brief version of Jacobson's (1929) progressive relaxation techniques, (2) practicing imagery related to the demands of the athlete's sport, and (3) using imagery to practice a specific skill in a lifelike stressful environment (Suinn 1976, 1980).

Basically, VMBR combines relaxation and imagery into one procedure. It also requires the athlete to mentally practice a specific skill under simulated game conditions. Theoretically, this would be better than actual practice, since the practice environment rarely resembles a game situation. Coaches and teachers typically go to great lengths to minimize distractions to their athletes during practice sessions. VMBR teaches the athlete to use relaxation and imagery techniques to create lifelike situations. Going through these stressful experiences mentally should make it easier to deal with the stress of actual competition. Suinn generally recommends the use of internal kinesthetic imagery for VMBR training, but suggests that in addition the athlete should use external imagery to identify performance errors.

In testing the VMBR program, Suinn experimented with alpine skiers (Suinn 1972); Olympic Nordic and biathlon athletes (Suinn 1976); and a long-distance kicker in American football (Titley 1980). While the results of these anecdotal reports were impressive in terms of perceived results, they were admittedly lacking in scientific controls.

Because of the need for statistical evidence for the theory, Kolonay (1977) conducted a scientific investigation of VMBR. The results of this study provided evidence in favor of VMBR. Kolonay used four groups of male college basketball players. Each group was assigned to a different treatment condition: a VMBR group, a relaxation-only group, an imagery-only group, and a control group. Before and after the six-week training period, each player's free-throw shooting percentage was recorded. Improvement in free-throw shooting was essentially used as the dependent variable. Kolonay's results showed a significant improvement in free-throw shooting percentage for the VMBR group.

The Kolonay study represented the first scientific investigation to study visual-motor behavioral rehearsal as a technique to improve athletic performance. However, the study had weaknesses that tended to throw some doubt on the conclusions. Recognizing the limitations of the Kolonay research, several other investigators studied VMBR. Noel (1980) researched the effect of VMBR training on the tennis-serving performance of high- and low-ability players. While a significant difference was not noted between the VMBR and control groups on serving accuracy, an interaction between skill level and stress management suggested that the performance of high-ability VMBR subjects improved with mental imagery, while the low-ability VMBR group performed worse. This finding is consistent with the basic mental practice research findings reported earlier by Clark (1960). Specifically, skilled performers use mental imagery and rehearsal better than do unskilled performers.

Weinberg, Seabourne, and Jackson (1981) replicated the Kolonay study with an effort at improving the statistical analysis and better defining the dependent variable. Subjects in this study were college-age males enrolled in a karate club. They were matched according to skill and assigned to one of four treatment conditions. As with the Kolonay study, the four treatments were VMBR training, relaxation training, imagery training, and a control group. In terms of anxiety, the results of the study showed that all subjects reduced their trait anxiety scores and that the VMBR and relaxation subjects had lower A-state scores at the end of the six-week training session than did the control or imagery training subjects. In terms of performance scores, the results were broken down into three categories—skill, combinations, and sparring. The results showed no reliable differences among the treatments in terms of skill and combinations. However, in terms of sparring scores, the VMBR group performed significantly better than the other three groups.

Seabourne, Weinberg, and Jackson (1982) did another study using karate students as subjects. Subjects were eighteen male and twenty-six female college-age students enrolled in one of two karate classes. Each class met twice a week for sixteen weeks. One class was randomly assigned to a VMBR training condition (in-class and at-home practice), while the other class served as a placebo control group studying the tradition and art of karate. The dependent variables used in the research were trait anxiety, state anxiety, and karate performance (skill, combinations, and sparring). The results of the research showed that both groups decreased their trait anxiety scores. The VMBR group also showed a significant reduction in state anxiety compared to the placebo group, and the VMBR group performed significantly better in all aspects of karate performance than the control group.

The effectiveness of VMBR with karate performers was further verified by a follow-up study by Seabourne, Weinberg, and Jackson (1984). In this investigation, VMBR was observed to effectively reduce state anxiety and improve karate performance over time.

Hall and Erffmeyer (1983) introduced a modeling strategy to enhance the effectiveness of VMBR. They reasoned that a performance effect was not observed in studies in which subjects had not mastered the VMBR technique. Highly skilled female basketball players were randomly assigned to one of two treatment conditions. Treatment 1 used traditional imagry and relaxation techniques, while treatment 2 featured a film of expert performers shooting free throws. After watching the film, treatment 2 subjects imagined themselves executing a perfect free throw. The results showed that the addition of the model enhanced the effectiveness of the VMBR procedure, since treatment 2 (with model) resulted in higher post-test shooting percentages than treatment 1.

In summary, it appears that VMBR training is extremely effective in reducing an athlete's trait and state anxiety levels. This is certainly important in terms of stress management. The potential for VMBR training to improve athletic performance is very good, but its effectiveness depends on the type of task, skill level of the performer, and the athlete's ability to relax and use imagery. The study by Hall and Erffmeyer (1983) highlights the importance of skill level in the use of imagery and the additional effectiveness of VMBR if a skilled model is used. Highly skilled athletes are more effective in using VMBR training and mental practice to enhance performance than are the unskilled.

Stress Inoculation/Management Training

In addition to VMBR, two other stress management training programs will now be addressed. The first is called *stress inoculation training* and was developed by Meichenbaum (1977). The second was developed by R. E. Smith (1980) and is called the *cognitive-affective stress management training* program. The key element associated with stress inoculation training is the progressive exposure of the athlete to situa-

13. *Principle* VMBR is an effective intervention program that incorporates principles derived from relaxation training and imagery to reduce anxiety, focus attention, and enhance performance.

    Application An athlete who suffers from the debilitating effects of anxiety as well as nonaffected athletes can benefit from visual motor behavior rehearsal.

---

tions of greater and greater stress. The key element of stress management training is that, through imagery, the athlete experiences feelings identical to those experienced during competition.

According to Long (1980), *stress inoculation training (SIT)* involves four phases. In phase 1, the trainer talks with the athlete about the athlete's stress responses. During this phase, the athlete learns to identify and express feelings and fears. The athlete is also educated in lay terms about stress and the effect it can have upon athletic performance and psychological well-being. In phase 2, the athlete learns how to relax and use self-regulation skills. This is done in small groups, using a problem-solving approach, with members of the group helping each other find solutions. Stressful experiences are described in detail, and potential hazards identified. In phase 3, the athlete learns specific coping self-statements designed to be used in stressful situations. For example, in preparation for a wrestling match, the athlete may learn to say, "I'm okay, just relax. Take a deep breath, let it out slow. Slow things down, I'm in control here, and I'm in top condition." In the important final phase, the trainer guides the athlete through a series of progressively more threatening situations. As the athlete learns to cope and confront a relatively mild situation, he or she is immediately exposed to a situation of greater stress. In each situation, the athlete practices relaxation and coping statements. The threatening situations are presented through imagery, films, role playing, and real-life situations. For example, if the fear of competition is stressful, the athlete is allowed to experience competition in small gradations. The first grade may be a friendly game of "horse" in basketball. As soon as the athlete is able to cope with a low level of stress, the situation is changed, and a more stressful situation is presented. In this way, the athlete becomes inoculated to progressively increasing levels of stress. Eventually, the athlete's fear of competition is minimized to the degree that he or she can cope with it.

Smith's (1980) cognitive-affective *stress management training (SMT)* program is quite similar to Suinn's (1972) anxiety-management training program, the precursor to VMBR. SMT is also quite similar to the first three phases of SIT. The fundamental difference between SMT and SIT is in the final phase. Basically, the SMT program involves three phases. In phase 1, the athlete learns to conceptualize the stress experience. This phase is educational in nature, as the athlete learns to understand the stress response and what causes it. This typically entails a discussion between the trainer and the athlete. Phase 2 of the SMT program involves the development of psychological skills for coping with stress. The athlete learns progressive relaxation techniques with particular emphasis on deep breathing to facilitate relaxation. The final phase requires the athlete to practice stress coping skills in stressful situations. As with SIT, stress is induced through imagery, films, electric shock, and real-life situations. Regardless of the type of situation, it is critical that the athlete actually experience the affect associated with stress, which distinguishes SIT from SMT. In SMT the feelings experienced in the actual stress situation are induced. In this way, the athlete learns how to cope with the stress of actual competition, even if it is only being visualized.

These two stress management programs were tested in a study by Ziegler, Klinzing, and Williamson (1982). The purpose of the study was to determine the effects the two stress management programs have on the heart rate and oxygen consumption of cross-country runners. Subjects in the treatment groups met with an experimenter twice a week for five-and-a-half weeks for stress management training. Results of a twenty-minute postsubmaximal run indicated significant differences in cardiorespiratory efficiency between the stress management training groups and a control group. Reliable differences were not noted between the SMT and SIT programs.

Reports by Boutcher and Rotella (1987) and Mace and Carroll (1985) provide additional support for the effectiveness of SIT. In the report by Boutcher and Rotella (1987), SIT was incorporated into the final phase of a four-phase psychological skills education program. In the study reported by Mace and Carroll (1985), SIT was effectively used to reduce anxiety levels of subjects involved in repelling from the roof of a 70-foot building.

Psychological Skills Education Program

The Psychological Skills Education Program (PSEP) was developed by Boutcher and Rotella (1987) for athletes who perform closed skills such as weight lifting (clean-and-jerk) or a closed skill such as free-throw shooting in a sport that is primarily open skill in nature (basketball).

Open-skill sports such as basketball and football are classified as such because they are open to the environment. An opponent cannot interfere with an athlete's attempt at a clean-and-jerk in weight lifting, but an opponent can alter or interfere with a pass, dribble, or jump shot in basketball because they are open to the environment. The program was conceived as a four-phase program in which various intervention strategies are applied in the final phase.

In phase one, the *sport analysis* phase, the sport psychologist does a thorough analysis of the characteristics of the closed skill that is involved. If the athlete is trying to improve his or her golf swing, the sport psychologist must become familiar with the important biomechanical elements of the golf swing as well as physiological and psychological requirements. The important point is that the sport psychologist should not prematurely attribute all problems to a psychological cause.

In phase two, the *individual assessment* phase, the psychological strengths and weaknesses of the athlete must be determined from a psychological perspective. It is at this point that various psychological inventories should be administered and interpreted. Appropriate inventories might include the Sport Competition Anxiety Test (SCAT), the Profile of Mood States (POMS), and Cattell's 16 Personality Factor Questionnaire. If after interpreting the selected inventories it is concluded that the athlete demonstrates abnormal clinical symptoms, he or she should be referred to the appropriate professional sources.

In phase three, the *conceptualization/motivation* phase, the sport psychologist discusses with the athlete the kind of commitment that is needed in order to change inappropriate behaviors. It is during this phase that the athlete must come to grips with his or her own desire to excel. Whether or not an athlete has the desire to develop effective psychological skills must be determined prior to entering into phase four.

In phase four, the *development of mental skills* phase, the athlete learns specific intervention techniques that can influence anxiety and performance. These mental skills include relaxation, imagery, and thought stopping. In learning various intervention strategies the athlete is taken through three training stages. In the first stage, the athlete practices and learns a psychological skill such as imagery in a general environmental setting. In stage two, the athlete applies the psychological skill to a situation-specific visualized setting. Finally, in stage three, the athlete develops appropriately designed performance routines. These performance routines are similar to the ritualistic steps that many professional baseball players go through in the batter's box. All good

14. *Principle* Package intervention programs that are individualized for the athlete are more effective than nonstructured and nonindividualized approaches.

    Application Select an intervention program that the athlete feels comfortable with. Apply the principles and practices of the program in an organized and systematic fashion.

athletes have well-developed preperformance routines they go through in preparation for skill execution. The rather precise routine that a professional golfer goes through each time he or she addresses a golf ball is another example. These performance routines are important to the athlete to help him or her direct attention to appropriate stimuli.

Psyching-Up Strategies

Generally speaking, *psyching-up* strategies are techniques designed to increase an athlete's arousal and activation level. While overanxiety and overarousal may be a major stumbling block for the *anxiety-prone* athlete, too little activation can also be a problem. This is especially so for highly skilled athletes who must defeat a relatively weak team in order to play a better team in a tournament. Underarousal causes the downfall of talented teams every year in the National Collegiate Athletic Association basketball tournament. Invariably, one or two highly seeded teams will be beaten by weaker teams simply because they were not ready for them.

Many of the cognitive strategies already discussed in this chapter can be used to heighten arousal as well as lower it. For example, both imagery and self-hypnosis can be used to stimulate an athlete to greater levels of arousal and motivation, simply by selecting or suggesting stimuli that promote the activation of the sympathetic nervous system. It is also interesting that when a group of athletes are asked to "get psyched," they report using all kinds of different cognitive strategies not normally associated with activation. For example, in a study by Caudill, Weinberg, and Jackson (1983) using track athletes, 25 percent reported using relaxation/distraction procedures to psych up. These are cognitive strategies normally reserved for reducing activation. Other psych-up strategies reported by these subjects were preparatory arousal (7 percent), imagery (16 percent), self-efficacy statements (25 percent), and attentional focus procedures (16 percent).

It is important that athletes learn to prepare for competition using the strategy best for them. This may involve using one strategy to control anxiety and another to get psyched up. However, for a team rather than an individual, a different strategy may need to be used. For example, if a coach determines that his team is not taking an opponent seriously, he or she must do something to get the players prepared. The coach runs the risk of overactivating a few anxiety-prone members of the squad, but this is usually better than running the risk of an uninspired effort from the whole team. And if the coach identifies the players with very high trait anxiety profiles, he or she can work with them individually.

Oxendine (1970) indicated that an above-average level of arousal is essential for optimal performance in gross motor activities involving strength, endurance, and speed. We would expect psyching-up strategies to facilitate strength and muscular endurance activities. The research supports this conclusion. Shelton and Mahoney (1978) demonstrated that psyching up facilitated performance on a static strength task (hand dynamometer). In a similar study, the effects of psyching up on three different motor tasks were investigated by Weinberg, Gould, and Jackson (1980). The three tasks were dynamic balancing, dynamic leg strength, and an arm movement task for speed. For each task, the subjects were encouraged to select their own cognitive psyching-up strategy. Only in the case of leg strength was a significant effect observed between control and experimental subjects. Gould, Weinberg, and Jackson (1980) conducted another investigation in which they concluded that in the first experiment, preparatory arousal and imagery were the best psyching-up techniques for enhancing leg strength, and in the second experiment, only preparatory arousal was effective in enhancing leg strength. In a study involving hypnosis (Ikai and Steinhaus 1961), it was discovered that subjects' static elbow flexion strength was enhanced on trials in which subjects either shouted or performed immediately after a gunshot. Caudill, Weinberg, and Jackson (1983) reported that psych-up procedures used by sprinters enhanced performance. Most recently, Wilkes and Summers (1984), using an isokinetic exercise system, and Weinberg and Jackson (1985), using selected muscular endurance tasks (sit-ups, push-ups, pull-ups), confirmed that mental preparation strategies effectively increase muscular strength and endurance when used to psych up the athlete.

It seems clear that heightened arousal can facilitate performance on strength, speed, and muscular endurance activities. It would also follow that heightened arousal would help any athlete whose precompetitive arousal level was below optimal. The key, regardless of the activity, is the inverted-U. If the athlete is either overaroused or optimally aroused for a particular activity, then psych-up procedures are inappropriate. However, if the athlete is underaroused, then psych-up procedures are called for.

Coaches can use a number of specific strategies to psych up their athletes (Voelz 1982). If these strategies are properly planned and not overused, they can help get a team fired up for competition.

Goal Setting

Goal setting was discussed in some detail in a previous section as a cognitive strategy. Goal setting is also an extremely effective tool for psyching up an athlete or a team. Athletes rarely need to be psyched up for high-visibility games such as city or state rivalries. However, how does an athlete get excited about playing a team that his or her team has defeated ten times in a row? How does a professional baseball player get psyched up to play the last twenty games of a season when the team is fifteen games behind in the standings? These and situations like these present a tremendous challenge to athletes, coaches, and managers. The solution lies in effective goal setting.

In preparing a top-ten–rated basketball team with twenty-five wins and two losses to play an unranked team in the NCAA playoffs, the coach must do something to keep his or her team from overlooking a potential "giant killer." One useful strategy is to help each member of the team to set personal performance goals for the game. The star rebounder might be challenged to accept the personal goal of getting thirteen "bounds" in the game. Similarly, the guards might be challenged to keep their turnovers below three between them. With each member of the team working to achieve realistic but difficult goals, it is likely that the team as a whole will perform well.

Pep Talks

A pep talk by the coach or a respected member of the team is the most effective method now used to increase the activation level of athletes. But like any verbal communication, it can be either effective or ineffective. Perhaps the most important element of the pep talk is an emphasis on the ingredient that is lacking in the team. If the team is obviously taking an opponent lightly, it must be impressed upon them that on a given night, any team can be a "giant killer." Some of the elements of an effective pep talk may include personal challenges, stories, poems, silence, reasoning, and voice inflections.

Bulletin Boards

In many ways the visual messages on a bulletin board are identical to a pep talk, but they are visually rather than verbally conveyed. Poster board displays should be placed where team members cannot miss them. Such places as locker room dressing areas and confined training areas are ideal. The bulletin board should always convey positive motivating thoughts and ideas. Catchy phrases such as "when the going gets tough, the tough get going" can be effective. Athletes remember these simple phrases and will repeat them later when they need reinforcement. Other messages on the display board might include personal challenges to members of the team. . . . This poster could reflect either great performances for the season or challenge performances for the next match.

Challenging or inflammatory statements by opposing teammates or coaches should also appear on the bulletin board. If an opponent is quoted as saying that he or she will dominate a certain player, this should be posted for all to see. It will give the team something to get excited about.

Publicity and News Coverage

The school newspaper and other advertisements can be very helpful in generating a team spirit. If the members of the team sense that the student body is behind them, they will work harder to get prepared. Ads can be placed in the newspaper by the coach to call attention to an important game or contest. These same ads can be used to recruit new players for the team. For many teams, publicity comes easy, but for others it does not. It may be necessary to cultivate a close relationship with the media and school sports reporters. Invite them to games and send them positive information about players and upcoming contests.

Fan Support

Those who enjoy sport for its recreational value do not need people watching in order to enjoy the game. However, if you practice ten to fifteen hours a week and have a twenty-game schedule, it doesn't hurt to have fan support. Fans tell the athletes that what they are doing is important to someone other than themselves. A full season of daily basketball, football, or tennis can burn out many players. Those responsible for promoting the team must do all they can to get people to support the team by coming to watch them.

Self-Activation

Often, lethargic activity on the part of an athlete can be reversed through the application of mental strategies to increase activation. Over the years I have observed Jimmy Connors psych up in a tennis match by slapping himself on the thigh and by using positive self-statements. Research has clearly shown that specific attempts to "get psyched" using various internal cognitive strategies are effective in enhancing strength and muscular-endurance activities (Weinberg and Jackson 1985).

Coach, Athlete, and Parent Interaction

The interaction among an athlete's parents, the athlete, and the coach is an often overlooked source of motivation for an athlete (Hellstedt 1987b). Coaches are often wary about the overinvolved and demanding parent. However, often just the opposite is true and parents are excluded from active involvement in motivating a young athlete. Parents provide tremendous support for an athlete's involvement that sometimes goes completely unnoticed. Parents provide transportation for games and practices, and sacrifice vacations and leisure time to watch their son or daughter perform. When called on, they are observed serving as scorekeepers, water "boys," bus drivers, and sometimes as assistant coaches. What a tremendous source of support and motivation a parent can be when properly nurtured!

Precompetition Workout

In the mid-sixties when the Japanese were dominating the international volleyball scene, I observed an interesting phenomenon. Prior to an international men's match between the United States and Japan, the Japanese team came out two hours early and went through a full work-

15. *Principle* Athletes are sometimes underaroused, and psych-up strategies are necessary in these situations.

    Application Goal setting, pep talks, bulletin boards, news coverage, fan support, parental involvement, and self-activation measures are all effective for getting athletes psyched up for competition. However, these techniques should not be overused or indiscriminately applied.

---

out. This was no warm-up as typically observed prior to competition, but a full-blown practice session to exhaustion. The Japanese team went on to defeat the U.S.A. in three relatively easy games. I have often wondered if this was an effective strategy that would have proven effective against the powerful U.S.A. men's team of the 1984 and 1988 Olympics.

Husak and Hemenway (1986) were apparently thinking along similar lines when they tested the effects of competition-day practice on activation and performance of collegiate swimmers. In this investigation, members of a collegiate swimming team engaged in brisk workouts four to six hours prior to competition. The results did not yield a significant performance effect, but they did show a reduction in feelings of tension and anxiety on the part of the precompetition workout group. Because tension and anxiety could easily hamper performance in swimming competition, precompetition workouts could be an effective tool for preparing an athlete for competition. Precompetition workouts that enhance and increase activation are apparently effective in reducing precompetitive anxiety.

Summary

Intervention strategies can help athletes find and maintain the optimum level of arousal for high performance. Relaxation techniques reduce anxiety and tension by eliciting the relaxation response. The relaxation response counters the effects of the sympathetic nervous system. Progressive relaxation, autogenic training, transcendental meditation, and biofeedback all elicit the relaxation response.

Cognitive strategies can help athletes improve their psychological skills and improve athletic performance. These cognitive skills are used in conjunction with relaxation techniques to bring about the desired result. Cognitive strategies discussed in this chapter included imagery, hypnosis, and goal setting. Internal imagery provides athletes with a kinesthetic feel for the skill, while external imagery allows them to see themselves perform. If heterohypnosis is used, a trained psychologist should be present. Autohypnosis may be practiced by the athlete without supervision. Both kinds of hypnosis are equally effective in reducing anxiety and in enhancing performance.

Four different kinds of packaged intervention programs were discussed. These programs, VMBR, SMT, SIT, and the Psychological Skills Education Program, all employ combinations of the relaxation and cognitive strategies discussed earlier. Intervention programs are extremely effective in controlling stress and in many cases enhance athletic performance. Individualized intervention and stress management programs are more effective than nonindividualized programs.

Techniques proven effective in psyching up the athlete were also discussed. The use of goal setting, pep talks, bulletin boards, news coverage, fan support, self-activation, parent involvement, and precompetition workouts were identified as being effective strategies for increasing the activation level of athletes.

NOTES

1. Editors' Note: Some of Locke and Latham's (1985) principles of goal setting include: (1) specific goals are more effective than vague or general ones; (2) difficult or challenging goals produce better performance than moderate or easy goals; and (3) goal setting (a) forces the athlete to focus attention on relevant activities, (b) regulates the expenditure of effort, (c) enhances persistence, (d) promotes the development of new strategies, and (e) only works if there is timely feedback showing progress.

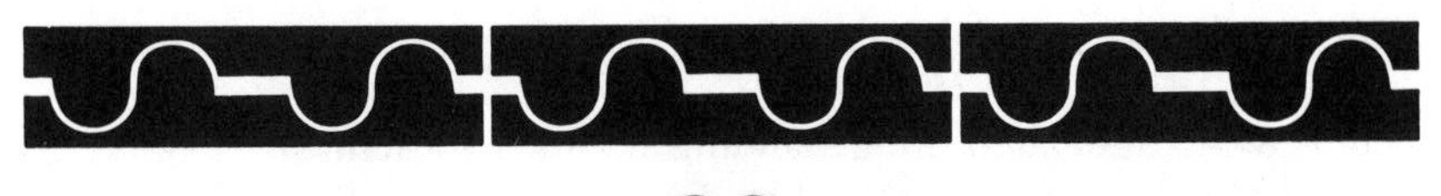

23

Out of the Habit Trap

■

STANTON PEELE

A man who had been drunk every night for many years arrived home late, bombed once again. The next morning his mother, with whom he was living, found him staring at himself in the mirror. He turned to her and announced: "I'm giving up drinking and, while I'm at it, smoking." Then he placed a pack of cigarettes and a bottle of beer on the mantelpiece. "What's that for?" his mother asked. He said: "That's so I'll know where to find a smoke or drink if I want one. Then I can just kill myself instead." He has touched neither cigarettes nor booze for nearly ten years.

A union official, noting that the price of cigarettes had risen yet again, put the extra nickel in the vending machine. A coworker laughed at him: "You'll pay whatever they ask." The smoker thought: "God, he's right; the tobacco company has me where it wants me." Then and there, he quit his three-pack-a-day habit forever.

Talk-show host Merv Griffin watched a comedian imitating him—as a fat man. The comic had stuffed himself with padding and Griffin could not bear the caricature. He put himself on a diet and exercise program, and soon showed off his new, thin self to his audience.

Stories like these seldom make the newspapers; for that matter, people who quit their long-standing habits by themselves often go unrecognized by scientific studies. Instead, we hear dire stories about people who can't seem to quit, and gloomy statistics on relapse rates. Among people in therapy to lose weight, stop smoking, kick a drug or drink addiction, as few as 5 percent actually make it.

But here's the irony and the help: self-cure can work, and depending on someone else to cure you usually does not.

This is the case of addictions like cigarette smoking and alcoholism, as well as for some more complex habits. Obesity, for example, may involve compulsive overeating—an addiction to food that some thin people also struggle with for years. But genetics and a lifetime of inactivity and bad eating habits also play a role. Whatever the cause, though, losing weight takes a major change in lifestyle—and the people who do it best are those who do it on their own.

Therapists tend to fail their clients by undermining self-reliance; they encourage people to rely upon others for cure, and to give up responsibility for their own behavior. But because therapy works so rarely, many researchers have come to view addictions as almost impossible to beat. And that mistake makes habits harder to break.

Many have begun to think of addiction as an exclusively biological process—one that cannot be overcome by psychological effort or will power. In this view, alcoholics have a "disease," a "genetic susceptibility" to liquor. Obese people have a preordained weight level. Smokers are hooked on nicotine, and their bodies cannot tolerate a depletion of the drug.

All of these theories stem from the grandfather addiction of them all, heroin. Everyone knows the image: the suffering heroin addict, inexorably bound to a physiological dependence. The penalty for withdrawal is intolerable agony, so the addict increases the doses until death. Remember *The Man with the Golden Arm?*

For more than ten years, I have been conducting interviews with all sorts of addicts and reviewing the research on all kinds of addiction. Addiction, I've found, may be affected by biological factors, but they are not enough to explain it. True, addiction is caused partly by the pharmacological action of the drug (if it's a drug addiction), but also by the person's social situation, attitudes and expectations. Even people who are constitutionally sensitive to a substance can control their use of it, if they believe that they can.

There is now good evidence for these heretical assertions. The most compelling statistics come from the success of people who cure themselves without therapy:

> University of Kentucky sociologist John O'Donnell, analyzing a national survey of drug use among men in their twenties, found that only 31 percent of the men who had ever used heroin had touched the drug in the previous year.
>
> Similarly, when American soldiers who had used heroin in Vietnam returned home after the war, over 90 percent of them gave the drug up without difficulty. Addiction experts predicted an epidemic of heroin abuse by the vets, but it never materialized. Washington University psychologist Lee Robins found that even among men who had truly been addicted in Vietnam, only 14 percent became dependent on narcotics in the U.S.
>
> Harvard psychiatrist George Vaillant found that more than half of the one-time alcohol abusers in a group of several hundred men had ceased problem drinking (the men had been interviewed over a period of 40 years).
>
> Social psychologist Stanley Schachter at Columbia University, interviewing members of two different communities, discovered that about half of those who had once been obese or hooked on cigarettes had lost weight or quit smoking. The formerly overweight people said they had lost an average of 35 pounds and kept it off for an average of 11 years.

Some of these statistics, admittedly, are open to question. When you're asking people to talk about how they've changed over the past several years, they may paint an excessively rosy picture of their ability to improve themselves. But even if the percentages are inflated, the evidence is still good that people can change for the better, far more than they have been given credit for.

Often, people simply outgrow their bad habits. Sociologist Charles Winick of City College of New York has examined the lives of drug addicts. Many, in Winick's words, "mature out" as they get older. Long-term studies of alcoholics and smokers show the same pattern. Some people even outgrow their teenage cravings for Twinkies and sugar "fixes."

Why Biology Is Not Destiny

There's other intriguing evidence that hammers away at the theory of the "biological trap" of addiction. For example, most addicts, of all kinds, regularly overcome withdrawal pangs. As Harvard psychiatrist Norman Zinberg and his associates discovered, heroin addicts often cut down or quit their heroin use on their own. Alcoholics often don't need to "dry out" in a hospital, but frequently just go on the wagon with no particular anguish. Practically every cigarette smoker stops at some point—for anywhere from a few days to years. (Orthodox Jews quit weekly for the Sabbath.)

It is actually long *after* the phase of "withdrawal pangs" that most addicts slide back into their habits. When they do backslide, it is not because of a physiological craving as much as it's stress at work or home, or social pressures ("Come on Mort, join us . . . one for the road").

It's also a myth that a single experience of a drug can catch you chemically (hence the "first fix is free" strategy of drug dealers). Most people have to learn to become addicted. As Zinberg found, hospital patients given strong doses of narcotics every day for ten days or more —doses higher than those street addicts take—virtually always leave the hospital without even a twinge of craving for the drug.

For an addiction to develop, the pharmacological effects of a drug have to produce an experience that a person with certain needs, in a certain situation, will welcome. When the need is great enough, people can become "addicted" to almost anything. Addicts may switch not only from one chemical substance to another, but from a chemical to a social "high." Vaillant reports that former alcoholics often shift to new dependencies—candy, prayer, compulsive work, hobbies, gambling.

Addiction also depends largely on people's beliefs about what a substance will do to them. Psychologist Alan Marlatt at the University of Washington found that alcoholics will behave drunkenly when they only *think* they are drinking liquor—but when they're actually drinking tonic and lime juice. He also found the reverse: when alcoholics drink alcohol, but believe it's tonic and lime juice, they don't behave drunkenly.

Despite such evidence, the search has continued, unsuccessfully, for a single physiological factor that might be the underlying cause of all addictions. The prime candidates have been endorphins, morphinelike substances found to occur naturally in the body. Some pharmacologists speculated that people are susceptible to drug addiction if their bodies don't produce a normal level of endorphins. Maybe all addictive involvements elevate your endorphin levels, the theory went.

When it turned out that people could even become addicted to serious jogging, biochemical studies of runners were also done. Sure enough, jogging was found to boost endorphin levels. But endorphins failed to explain the difference between those who stop running when they're injured or it's inconvenient and those who behave like true addicts.

One very lean man, who insisted on running hard every day regardless of inclement weather, family obligations, or his own injuries, explained his addiction to me this way: "I feel great every day I run; but I'm afraid I'll balloon back up to 200 pounds the moment I quit." His desire to run was more than chemical; he saw running as a magical talisman against returning to his former self.

The best explanation of addiction takes both mind and body into account. The effects of a substance can't be isolated from the context of human experience. Thinking of addiction solely as a "disease" or a "chemical dependency" ignores the power of the mind in generating the need for the drug—and in breaking that need.

The cycle of addiction begins as a response to a stressful problem (getting drunk to avoid dealing with a bad job, running to get away from a bad marriage) or as an attempt to produce certain feelings (as Harvard psychologist David McClelland and his coworkers showed, many men feel a sense of power while drunk).

These feelings, in turn, lead into a cycle that makes the addiction harder to escape. For example, a man who abuses his family when he is drunk may feel disgusted with himself when he sobers up—so he gets drunk again to boost his self-esteem. Soon the addictive experience feeds on itself. It becomes central to the person's life, and it becomes a trap.

The Steps to Self-Cure

How does anyone manage to kick a habit after years of living with it? To find out, San Francisco sociologists Dan Waldorf and Patrick Biernacki interviewed heroin addicts who quit on their own, and sociologist Barry Tuchfeld at Texas Christian University talked with some 50 alcoholics who recovered without therapy or AA. And in conducting our own field research with addicts of all types, my associate Archie Brodsky and I have outlined the critical steps in self-cure.

The key word is *self:* taking charge of your own problem. Some psychologists call this self-mastery; others, self-efficacy; others, the belief in free will. It translates into three components necessary for change: an urge to quit, the belief that you *can* quit and the realization that *you* must quit—no one can do it for you. Once you have quit, the rewards of living without the addiction must be great enough to keep you free of it.

The stages of successful self-cure are remarkably similar, regardless of the addiction:

1. *Accumulated unhappiness about the addiction.* Before a change can take place, unhappiness with the addiction has to build to a point where it can't be denied or rationalized away. This phase of the process of self-cure, to use Vaillant's analogy, is like the incubation of a chick. Just because the chick hatches, rather abruptly at that, doesn't mean it happened spontaneously. A lot of changes go on first beneath the outer shell.

   To break an addiction, you must believe the rewards you'll get (from not smoking, from exercising and losing weight, from cutting down on or giving up alcohol or drugs) will surpass what you got from the habit. Heroin addicts who "mature out" typically explain to interviewers that a life of hustling, prison, and the underworld was no longer worth it.

2. *A moment of truth.* An alcoholic pregnant woman told Tuchfeld: "I was drinking beer one morning and felt the baby quiver. I poured the rest of the beer out and I said, 'God forgive me, I'll never drink another drop.' " Another woman who had quit (and resumed) smoking several times found herself sorting through the butts in an ashtray late one night, desperate for a smoke: "I saw a snapshot of myself in my mind's eye," she told me, "and I was disgusted." She has not been a smoker for fifteen years now.

   Most ex-addicts can pinpoint a moment at which they "hatched" from the addiction and left it behind. It is impossible to distinguish the real moment of truth from the addict's previous vows to quit, except in retrospect. But it is just as foolish to disregard these reports altogether. Because they are part of such a high percentage of successful cures, they seem to have an important meaning to the ex-addict.

   Epiphanies that work can be brought on by dramatic, catastrophic events: an alcoholic becomes falling-down-drunk in front of someone he admires, or a cigarette smoker watches a friend die of lung cancer. But most moments of truth seem to be inspired by trivial remarks or chance occurrences. Either way, they work because they crystallize the discrepancy between the addict's self-image and the reality.

3. *Changing patterns.* People successful at self-cure usually make active changes in their environment—they may move away from a drug culture, become more involved in work, make new friends. But some people break a habit without changing their usual patterns. The man whose story began this article—the heavy drinker and smoker—was a musician who continued to spend nearly all his nights in bars. He wrapped himself in a new identity—"I'm a nondrinking, nonsmoking musician"—that protected him from his familiar vices.

4. *Changing the identity of addict.* Once former addicts gain more from their new lives than from the old ways—feeling better, getting along with people better, working better, having more fun—the lure of the addiction pales. One long-time heroin addict quoted in the book *High on Life* quit the drug in his thirties, went to school and got a good job. Later, during a hospital stay, he was given an unlimited prescription for Percodan, a synthetic narcotic. He marveled at how he had no desire to continue the drugs when his pain stopped: "I had a different relationship with people, with work, with the things that had become important to me. I would have had to work at relapsing."

5. *Dealing with relapses.* One of the problems with biological theories of addiction is the image of imminent relapse it creates for the addict—the idea that one slip is a return to permanent addiction. Many of Schachter's ex-smokers admit having a puff at a party. Half of those ex-addicts who had been in Vietnam did try heroin at home, Lee Robins found, but few returned to a full-fledged addiction. The addict who has successfully modified his or her life catches the slip, and controls it.

The steps out of addiction, therefore, are: to find a superior alternative to the habit you want to break; find people who can help you puncture your complacent defenses; change whatever you need to in your life to accommodate your new, healthier habits; celebrate your new, nonaddicted image whenever you can.

The common feature in all these steps is *your* action, *your* beliefs. Self-curers often use many of the same techniques for breaking out of an addiction that formal treatment programs do. But motivated people who have arrived at these techniques on their own are more successful than those in therapy.

Why should this be? One possibility, of course, is that the people who go for professional help are the hard cases—those who have tried to change on their own and found it impossible. People may try to quit smoking a dozen times, or lose and regain a few hundred pounds, before deciding they need help. Therapy often represents only one attempt at cure, whereas people usually come to grips with a problem over a period of years.

But I also think that therapy itself may inadvertently impede cure, by lowering the addict's sense of self-mastery and self-control. In turning to therapy, addicts unwittingly acknowledge that they are powerless to break the addiction. Thus medical supervision of drug withdrawal, for example, can actually inflate the difficulty of doing something that drug addicts accomplish repeatedly on their own.

Therapy can be especially demoralizing when it's based on the notion that addiction stems from an unchangeable biological weakness. Such a philosophy can make quitting even more difficult. Sociologist Charles Winick observed two decades ago that adolescents who failed to mature out of heroin addiction were those who "decide they are 'hooked,' make no effort to abandon addiction and give in to what they regard as inevitable."

We now see why that discovery applies to the general problem of breaking self-destructive habits. Only death and taxes, it now appears, are truly inevitable. Everything else is negotiable—and open for improvement.

24

Healthy People—Healthy Business: A Critical Review of Stress Management Programs in the Workplace

■

KENNETH R. PELLETIER AND
ROBERT LUTZ

Background

Stress is widely recognized by health professionals, public-policy makers, and corporate medical planners as a significant health factor. It is estimated that 60–90 percent of visits to health care professionals are for stress-related disorders (Cummings and VandenBos 1981; Elite 1986). Both basic and clinical experimental research have determined stress to be a major factor in a wide range of conditions including hypertension, cardiovascular disease, gastrointestinal disorders, tension and vascular headaches, low-back pain, and decreased immunological functioning with its implications for susceptibility to disorders ranging from colds and flus to cancer and AIDS (Pelletier 1977; Pelletier and Herzing in press). Stress has been demonstrated to also affect health-related

Research for this chapter was supported by a grant from the State of California Department of Mental Health, Southwestern Bell Foundation, and the San Francisco Foundation.

behaviors such as cigarette smoking, alcohol use, work productivity, and absenteeism rates (McLeroy et al. 1984; Seamonds 1983). Furthermore, stress has long been implicated in the development of mental disorders and decreased life satisfaction (Pelletier 1977, 1984, 1986). Estimates of the impact of stress disorders in financial terms to business are that $150 billion are lost annually in industrial costs due to decreased productivity, absenteeism, and disability. With national health care exceeding one billion dollars daily, it is apparent why the Surgeon General's 1979 report, "Healthy People," identified stress as a major priority in the formation of a national prevention strategy through 1990.

Worksite Stress Management Programs

There are obvious and compelling reasons for the business community to take a more active role in promoting employee health. Of the $511 billion 1987 budget for medical care, private corporations control approximately 40–43 percent of that total through the medical plans they purchase. Future trends are likely to increase that percentage to as much as 70 percent or higher due to the aging of the workforce, cost shifting from government to the private sector, unfunded retirement plan liabilities, extended long-term care, expanded mandatory benefits, and new medical technologies. Medical care costs and benefits are currently about a third of the average person's salary and are continuing to rise at a rate that is two to three times greater than the overall inflation index. Cardiovascular disease alone was estimated in 1963 to account for 12 percent of work days lost, and represented an economic loss of $4 billion (Felton and Cole 1963). AT&T recently estimated their medical expenses for a single employee suffering a heart attack at about $60,000. Data collected in the 1970s (Bonica 1980) demonstrated chronic back disorders to cost $12 billion annually in lost work days and another $4 billion in medical costs. Recurrent headaches resulted in a $6.2 billion loss in work days and another $1.2 billion in health costs. In 1982, work accidents cost $31.4 billion and resulted in over 12,000 deaths (Jones and Dosedel 1986).

Stress has been directly linked to each of the above medical disorders, and inferentially with a host of others. Cost increases related to stress also include reduced productivity, absenteeism, job dissatisfaction, terminations, and litigation for stress disabilities (Brodsky 1984). Reports from the Bureau of National Affairs (1984) indicate that about 50 percent of worker absenteeism was avoidable through appropriate attention to the physical and emotional needs of employees. Given these cost incentives, and the literature demonstrating decreased health costs associated with mental health care, it is not surprising that many companies have been motivated to try on-site stress management programs.

Although the focus of this chapter is upon objective assessment of health and cost outcome, there are numerous worksite stress management programs which are justified by the sponsoring corporation based solely on indirect benefits. In these instances, the direct benefits of health and/or cost efficacy are simply not deemed to be important. Among the reported indirect benefits are enhanced employee morale, improved corporate image, ability to attract and retain key personnel, consistency of a corporate product with the image of a healthy company, and as a perk for key executives. These are legitimate reasons in their own right, but in a decade of increasing competition, mergers, takeovers, and the ubiquitous "bottom line," it is more likely than not that such good intentions may initiate a program but not sustain it. Overall, the trend is toward objective evaluations of both health and cost efficacy in all aspects of health promotion including workplace stress management programs.

Three questions arise constantly with regard to stress management programs in the workplace: (1) what types of interventions have been used; (2) where are the objective studies demonstrating efficacy; and (3) are such interventions cost-effective? Numerous national surveys have indicated that stress management programs and their outcomes are the foremost concern of employees, employers, researchers, and science writers (Wang 1987). One survey of 164 corporate health programs indicated that stress management programs are cited four times more frequently as a priority for development than the next closest category which is the behavioral management of coronary heart disease (Pelletier 1984). This observation was later confirmed in a survey sponsored by the U.S. Office of Disease Prevention and Health Promotion (Windom, McGinnus, and Fielding 1987). Clearly, stress management programs and their health and cost efficacy is a major area of corporate and academic concern.

To address this complex area, it is essential to provide a context. Since it is not the intent of this chapter to review the general area of stress management interventions, it is necessary to point out that there is unequivocal, clinical experimental evidence for a wide range of interventions that can successfully alleviate stress-related disabilities. Among the multiplicity of interventions are meditation (Shapiro and Walsh 1984), clinical biofeedback (Shapiro et al. 1979/80), autogenic training (Luthe 1965), Jacobson's progressive relaxation (Bernstein and Borkovec

1973), hypnosis (Kroger 1963), the relaxation response (Benson 1979), and visualization therapies (Borysenko 1987). Despite the impressive and growing evidence of clinical efficacy, the three questions noted earlier regarding the transfer of such intervention into the workplace remain largely unanswered. One of the many reasons why this is a critical issue is that corporate health promotion programs frequently adopt stress management programs based upon the claims of ubiquitous vendors that their prepackaged interventions have proven efficacy. Given this claim, it is essential to point out that these unfounded claims are based solely upon clinical experimental data derived outside the workplace and there is no evidence at the present time that prepackaged stress management programs are effectively transferred into the work environment.

Finally, there are two other contextual issues to be considered. Stakes are very high in developing lifestyle interventions to prevent chronic disease and disability. The Carter Center report "Closing the Gap" (Carter Center of Emory University 1985) indicated that given our present medical knowledge and capabilities, approximately two thirds of all deaths in this country are premature, and further, that about two thirds of all years of life lost before age 65 are preventable. These are astounding statements especially given the fact that prevention-related research is allocated less than 5 percent of overall health funding in the United States. Translated into economic terms, the projected medical budget for 1987 is estimated to exceed half a trillion dollars ($511 billion), or 11.4 percent of the gross national product.

It seems intuitively imperative that far greater expenditures could be productively allocated to developing clinical experimental protocols for behavioral medicine interventions to alleviate premature morbidity and mortality. Furthermore, determining the areas for the greatest efficacy is certainly no mystery. Writing in the *Journal of the American Medical Association,* Assistant Secretary of the U.S. Department of Health and Human Services William H. Foege (1985) has stated,

> The scientific basis for the influence of lifestyle choices on health continues to grow; lifestyles are changing and it is probable that these changes are already reducing the toll of diseases. In the coming decades, the most important determinants of health and longevity will be the personal choices made by each individual. This is both frightening for those who wish to avoid such responsibility and exciting for those who desire some control over their own destiny.

Finally, the overall field of health promotion programs in the workplace, of which stress management would be only one aspect, has not been adequately evaluated by rigorous design and appropriate data analysis (Elias and Murphy 1986). Given the lack of such analytic work, it is therefore not surprising that stress management per se has not been adequately evaluated. To date there are only nine studies of sufficient precision which evaluate comprehensive health promotion programs and present evidence of efficacy. These precious few studies are in obvious sharp contrast to the overly zealous claims by vendors of health promotion programs and stress management interventions in particular. Among the rigorous studies of overall health promotion programs to date are those from AT&T (Spilman et al. 1986), Prudential Insurance (Bowne et al. 1984), Canada Life and North American Life (Shephard et al. 1982), Tenneco (Baun, Bernacki, and Tsai 1986), Blue Cross and Blue Shield of Indiana (Gibbs et al. 1985), Blue Cross of California (Lorig et al. 1985), Control Data Corporation (Jose and Anderson 1986), and two studies from Johnson & Johnson demonstrating the health efficacy of a systems approach (Blair et al. 1984) and overall positive impact of the program in comparative worksites (Bly, Jones, and Richardson 1986). Eight of the nine studies demonstrated clear efficacy in improving health, with one exercise program (Baun, Bernacki, and Tsai 1986) evidencing equivocal results. Cost reduction is evident in three (Blair et al. 1984; Bly, Jones, and Richardson 1986; Gibbs et al. 1985) out of the nine, although the most recent Johnson & Johnson study has been challenged on both methodological grounds and on cost efficacy since program costs were not included in the final analysis.

Most significantly for this chapter is that only the 1984 Johnson & Johnson study reported a positive objective outcome of improved stress management by employees, and none of the nine studies isolated and assessed the specific impact of the stress management component of the respective programs. In any consideration of the nature, health outcome, and cost efficacy of workplace stress management programs, it is essential to bear in mind this context as well as these limitations in the data.

Although the focus of this review is upon workplace stress management programs, it is necessary to briefly cite the non-workplace research since it is more extensive and has a direct bearing on questions of the relative efficacy of worksite programs.

Clinical Stress Management Programs

Clearly, the magnitude of stress-related disorders in terms of their cost to society, as well as in human suffering is enormous. The tragedy, or promise, depending on your perspective, is that many stress-related health problems are preventable. The data base supporting the reversibility of rising stress-related health care costs comes largely from studies by health maintenance organizations (HMOs) and third-party carriers (TPCs). These studies primarily addressed the impact of brief outpatient psychotherapy in medical settings. Although brief psychotherapy may seem a large step away from the typical stress-management program offered in worksites, it is exactly this difference in formatting (and resulting outcomes) that warrants close examination. This is particularly true since these objectively efficacious studies are often cited to support implementing prepackaged worksite stress management programs.

An early review article by Jones and Vischi (1979) analyzed 13 studies focusing on the relationship between mental health services and medical care utilization. Reductions in medical utilization of 5–85 percent were reported in 12 of the 13 studies. One study which reported an increase rather than a decrease in medical use stemmed from data collected in a new neighborhood health center where medical needs were previously underserved and could thus be expected to rise greatly with the new services offered. In a later paper, Mumford, Schlesinger, and Glass (1982) reviewed 13 studies evaluating the effects of psychological intervention on recovery from surgery and heart coronary occurrences. Virtually all of the studies used very brief, psychotherapy-oriented interventions, yet were able to reduce hospitalization time by an average of two days for experimental patients versus control groups.

An earlier study by Jameson, Shuman, and Young (1978) examined the effects of fee-for-service outpatient psychiatric care on overall costs of third-party coverage. One hundred thirty-six Blue Cross claims records of persons using mental health services were examined over a 48-month period. Of these, 83 percent had 15 or less psychological contact services. Analysis of their pre- versus post-psychotherapy claims showed that their overall cost in claims for medical/surgical utilization dropped by more than 50 percent following psychotherapy. In a similar but more recent study, Schlesinger et al. (1983) examined medical costs of patients covered by Blue Cross/Blue Shield who were diagnosed with chronic diseases, and compared those who subsequently received mental health services with those who did not. Persons receiving psychological services had medical charges significantly lower than the comparison group. They conclude that mental health services combined with medical services can both improve the quality of care and lower provider costs.

Health maintenance organizations theoretically share with the business world a direct fiscal incentive to keep members healthy in order to contain overall medical costs. Despite this apparent incentive, HMOs have tended to function nearly identically to fee-for-service providers in terms of having a disease treatment approach rather than a "health maintenance" or prevention orientation. Factors such as self-selection by younger and healthier patients and possible underutilization of diagnostic and invasive procedures may be responsible for perceived HMO cost-effectiveness. With these caveats in mind, it is useful to examine the recent experience of the Kaiser-Permanente Health Plan which is the forerunner of the modern HMO. Reporting on the twenty-year experience of Kaiser in assessing psychotherapy and medical utilization, Cummings and VandenBos (1981) note that the 60–90 percent of stress-related medical costs are more than offset by appropriate psychological interventions. Based on this major study, they state,

> The findings indicated that: (a) persons in emotional distress were significantly higher users of both inpatient (hospitalization) and outpatient medical facilities as compared to the health plan average; (b) there were significant declines in medical utilization by those emotionally distressed individuals who received psychotherapy, as compared to the control group of matched patients; (c) these declines remained constant during the five years following the termination of psychotherapy; (d) the most significant declines occurred in the second year after the initial interview, and those patients receiving one session only or brief psychotherapy (two to eight sessions) did not require additional psychotherapy to maintain the lower level of medical utilization for five years.

These conclusions are further bolstered by more recent data from a pilot project in Hawaii demonstrating a 37 percent decrease in medical use following brief psychotherapy (Cummings 1985). In sum, data for the efficacy of brief psychotherapy to address stress-related symptoms and medical care costs is quite well established. However, the questions of whether or not such approaches and outcomes are transferable to the corporate world must remain unanswered at present.

Efficacy of Worksite Stress Programs

To date, the best *methodological* critique of workplace stress management programs is that of McLeroy et al. (1984), who critiqued the methodological adequacy of 19 worksite stress management programs. Among the studies reviewed were those located in public and private institutions serving both blue collar and white collar workers. Sixteen of the 19 studies used volunteer subjects as opposed to selecting subjects on the basis of diagnosed stress symptoms or "at risk" status as in the psychotherapy/medical care utilization studies previously described. The majority of worksite studies used individual sessions of training in stress management, although very few individualized such training. Standardized interventions were the rule. Relaxation and/or meditation training was provided in 80 percent of the programs, and half of these studies used this as the sole stress management technique. Other studies combined some form of relaxation training with either biofeedback or cognitive restructuring techniques. Virtually all programs provided participants with information about the nature and importance of stress along with the stress management training. Stress *reduction* methods such as assertiveness training or increasing employees' actual work options were employed in only three of the 19 studies. Approximately two thirds of the studies provided stress management training on a once-a-week basis for four to eight weeks. Only eight of the 19 studies reported any follow-up data whatsoever. These generally noted some deterioration in treatment effects which appeared partly related to lack of carry-over and/or long-term compliance with the stress management exercises.

Perhaps because of the methodological focus taken in the review by McLeroy and colleagues (1984), the many instances of negative findings on dependent measures for stress reduction were not well elucidated. Although most worksite studies that were reviewed reported some positive effects, overall they were inconsistent and not very compelling. Only four of the 19 studies directly measured cost-affected dependent variables. Manuso (1983) reported two studies measuring changes in use of health services. Seamonds (1982) and Jackson (1983) reviewed company records to assess absenteeism. Of these studies, Manuso and Seamonds were the only three studies of the 19 reviewed by McLeroy to select subjects on the basis of stress symptoms or "at risk" status. Of the 15 remaining studies, ten indicated at least one objectively measured physiological dependent variable. Five studies measured blood pressure, four measured EMG and/or peripheral temperature circulatory changes, and one included urine lab values. None related the physiological outcome data to subsequent medical care use. Thirteen of the 19 studies included various paper and pencil tests to measure variables such as job satisfaction, coping effectiveness, stress level, anxiety, depression, and somatic complaints. Ten of the 19 studies employed experimental designs with random assignment of subjects to experimental and control conditions.

The most consistently reported findings appear to be in reducing subjective feelings of emotional distress such as anxiety, although even in that case, the results are certainly not highly consistent. Reductions in somatic complaints (other than blood pressure) are inconsistent across studies, and those studies obtaining reductions tend to observe significant regression in follow-up data. This is in sharp contrast to the HMO studies cited earlier which show increasing treatment gains over time. Job satisfaction indices show the most inconsistency with one study actually reporting increased job dissatisfaction after stress management training (Murphy 1983). This latter finding is almost certainly linked to the fact that virtually all programs educate participants as to the sources and effects of stress, yet almost none attempt to actually reduce work stressors. Increasing worker sensitivity to job stress and then not offering any work modification options is clearly not an advisable strategy to increase job satisfaction for most employees.

Differences Between Worksite and Clinical Programs

HMO and TPC studies demonstrating cost-effectiveness for stress reduction rely on three factors: (1) effective identification of symptomatic persons; (2) thorough evaluation of identified persons by health professionals who then make recommendations and/or referrals; and (3) reliance on appropriate, brief, symptom-oriented interventions when indicated, most often in the form of brief psychotherapy.

Brief psychotherapy itself shares many commonalities with *one-on-one* stress management therapies, and may be synonymous in many instances. One-on-one stress management may more commonly involve the learning of at least one specific relaxation and/or cognitive stress management skill. On the other hand, brief psychotherapy may more clearly devote the importance of the therapeutic relationship and attention to broader individual differences and needs. However, both one-on-one stress management therapy and brief psychotherapy involve a focused, time-limited and stress-alleviating orientation to defined problems. It would seem that the combination of brief psycho-

FIGURE 24.1. Average outcome effect size in improving recovery to surgery and heart attack.

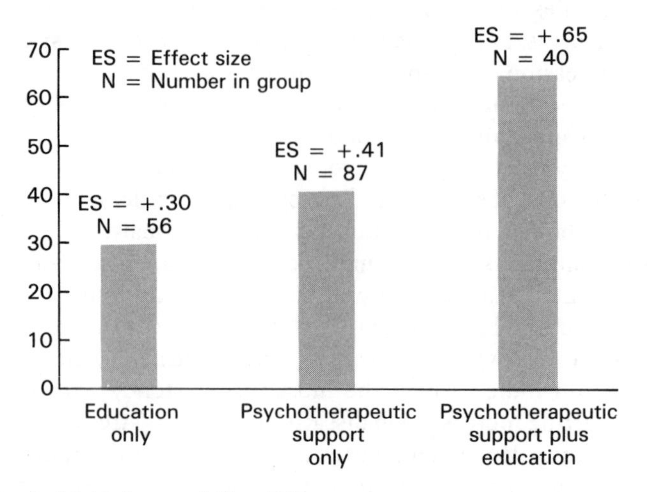

Source: Mumford, Schlesinger, and Glass 1982

therapy and stress management skills would provide an optimal approach to stress-related disorders. Relevant to this assertion, Mumford, Schlesinger, and Glass (1982) noted that although both educational and psychotherapeutic interventions were effective by themselves in improving the recovery of patients following surgery and heart attacks, they were still more effective when used in combination. Figure 24.1 shows these summary data.

In sharp contrast to brief psychotherapy, most worksite stress management programs offer employee volunteers a predetermined, nonindividualized stress management package. There is a huge discrepancy in the outcome data generated in most prepackaged worksite stress management programs with the previously described brief psychotherapy data generated by HMOs and TPCs. Further, this discrepancy appears to reflect a systematic difference in the *manner* in which stress management interventions are conducted.

Misleading Assumptions

Common use of relatively simplistic stress management training modules in worksites is likely a reflection of their marketability due to their apparent low cost and purported efficacy. Unfortunately, this approach seems to reflect a misinterpretation of what works in lowering stress and stress-related medical costs. Relaxation and biofeedback training used in clinical practice have been shown to decrease stress/tension-related somatic symptoms, and also to significantly reduce excessive or inappropriate medical utilization (Manuso 1983). Clearly, these interventions do have certain "generic" components. Therefore, it is not unreasonable to assume that these techniques could be transplanted from their clinical context, developed into a standardized but flexible program format, and applied as a generic intervention for stress disorders. However, this appears to be an erroneous assumption. While the development of such programs may be theoretically possible and a plethora of vendors make claims based on this false assumption, it is evident that empirically effective prepackaged stress management programs do *not* exist at the present time, so "caveat emptor."

Manuso's (1983) study of a workplace stress management program provides a good illustration. It is one of the most frequently cited studies in the literature, and one of the few worksite stress intervention studies to date to report a dollars-and-cents cost-benefit index. It is also commonly oversimplified in reviews to suggest direct support for prepackaged programs. Murphy (1982) describes Manuso's study in support of the efficacy of biofeedback:

> Several recent studies indicate that biofeedback training can be effective in worksite stress management training programs. Biofeedback training has been employed along with breathing exercises and muscle relaxation in an emotional health program at the Equitable Life Assurance Society to help 30 employees cope with chronic anxiety and recurring headaches. Training sessions were held three times per week over a five-week period. Participants were able to reduce muscle tension levels by 50 percent after training and variability of response by 600 percent. At follow-up three months later, participants reported fewer visits to the health center, decreases in stress symptoms, increases in work satisfaction, and decreases in symptom interference with work. Cost/benefits analysis indicated an impressive 1:5.5 ratio for the training program.

Simplifying the Manuso study still more, the review by McLeroy et al. (1984) describes Manuso's intervention simply as "a five-week program of biofeedback and muscle relaxation."

In actuality, Manuso's study is quite unlike prepackaged worksite stress programs. Because it is so different in format and outcome, it warrants further consideration. Manuso (1983) reports a four-stage intervention. First, employees with a long history of a stress-related disorder were identified and referred for evaluation. He notes that they were then screened medically, neurologically, and psychologically to assure their suitability. Employees also had to show their motivation and complete home record keeping. Second, baseline measurements were obtained over a two-week period involving biofeedback readings and daily self-monitoring logs. In the treatment phase, individuals were scheduled for two to three training sessions per week over five weeks and were helped to wean themselves from reliance on instrumental-aided autoregulation. They also were given a number of home exercises to increase treatment generalizability. Finally, follow-up provided once or twice a year included baseline reassessments and advice to maximize treatment effects. To describe this clinical screening and intervention trial as simply biofeedback greatly obscures what was done, and lends itself to the misperception that simple interventions can produce dramatic and cost-effective results. Manuso's 1983 study is one of only three studies reviewed by McLeroy et al. (1984) which reported positive, cost-relevant outcome measures. Most significantly, both of the other studies, a companion study by Manuso (1983) on Type A versus Type B employees, and a study showing decreased absenteeism following individual counseling (Seamonds 1982), also used thorough evaluation and identification of symptomatic or high-risk subjects.

A recent study lends further support to the greater efficacy of individualized programs with targeted participants over more common prepackaged stress training in the workplace. Reporting in the *American Journal of Health Promotion,* Steffy et al. (1986) reported on organizational stress management to reduce employee accidents and consequent costs. Their approach was applied in three settings including a medium-sized hospital, a trucking company, and a small hospital. The authors identified five general components to their overall interventions: (1) increasing the awareness of senior management to stress in their organization and its relationship to insurance losses; (2) feedback to management on their assessment regarding the sources and levels of stress as a function of location, department, job shift, and demographics; (3) identification of high-risk groups/units, along with personal consultations to correct underlying problems; (4) establishing an employee assistance program to provide ongoing psychological services to employees and their families for work- and non-work-related problems; and (5) various health programs typically including stress management training and educational inducements toward exercise, healthy lifestyle management, and avoiding stress-related back injuries.

All three intervention sites in the Steffy et al. (1986) study showed significantly reduced accident claims and costs. Combined hospital accident-related losses went from an average of $24,199 per month in the two years pre-intervention to $2,577 per month in the 11 months post-intervention. One hospital reduced the number of claims from 3.1 per month to 0.6 and the average monthly cost from $7,329 to $324. Cost of the program relative to the retrieved losses was not reported. In general, when such ratios are analyzed, the costs for stress management interventions are more than offset by the savings in disability costs and lost productivity.

Conclusions

Stress management seminars and prepackaged training which generally involves some form of relaxation skill carry a relatively low fee and are logistically easy to implement within most work settings. However, such simple interventions should not be expected to significantly alter stress-related costs of medical care or productivity. It may be worthwhile to consider the few common elements which the most efficacious programs share before considering a fundamentally different and more effective model. Based on the methodological critique of McLeroy et al. (1984), a position paper prepared for the Washington Business Group on Health (Jaffe, Scott, and Orioli 1986), and two previous critical reviews (Pelletier 1986; Pelletier, Lutz, and Klehr 1987), several elements appear in common and may serve as the basis for the development and evaluation of future, prepackaged programs which may actually be of demonstrable benefit. Among these aspects are: (1) complete programs take place once per week for four to eight weeks; (2) sessions are usually 45 minutes in length; (3) an ideal number of participants range from 12 to 15; (4) peer-led programs appear to be equally effective or ineffective as professionally-led interventions; (5) all programs taught participants one or more stress management techniques such as abdominal breathing and/or assertiveness training; (6) since none of the studies indicated continued practice at three to six months, programs should include homework, generalization skills, and periodic follow-up; (7) evaluation to determine a program's efficacy; and (8) ideally, the workplace environment needs to correct its inherently stressful nature to avoid their frequent "blame the victim" orientation. Although these characteristics are approximations in the absence of hard data, they do provide an initial set of criteria by which more effective programs may be developed and evaluated. Below are outlined the key components common to successful (health- and cost-effective) stress management programs applied in worksites and HMOs alike:

Identification of symptomatic and high-risk individuals.

Thorough evaluation by qualified health professionals to assess both the medical and psychological status and needs of high-risk individuals.

Appropriate referral or treatment of motivated individuals. Applied treatments not to be limited to work stressors or a strict definition of stress management.

Treatments are symptom-oriented and provided by professionals skilled with brief intervention protocols.

Appropriate follow-up is provided to assure treatment maintenance and generalization.

Evaluations are conducted to determine health and/or cost efficacy.

Based on the above analysis, the Steffy et al. study (1986) provides a *potential* model for effective stress reduction/health promotion in the workplace. Their program includes many of the key program components cited in this literature review, but orients them more specifically toward the workplace. Thus, identification of high-risk organizational units are emphasized in addition to individuals. Problems are also addressed through systems-level organizational changes, as well as individually oriented treatments and referrals. Unfortunately, these authors have not yet reported the effects of their program on reducing medical care utilization, absenteeism, or toward increasing productivity. Further research needs to address these questions, as well as whether such systems-level intervention additions provide significantly more benefits over individually oriented programs so as to remain cost-effective.

Finally, the magnitude of the problem of potentially preventing two thirds of all morbidity and mortality before age 65 and the reallocation of $511 billion is simply overwhelming. Consensus indicates that lifestyle interventions such as effective stress management programs are the cornerstone of such efforts. However, it is critical to underscore that the resolution of such a colossal undertaking is dependent upon the effective coordination of the three basic elements of a true health care system: (1) quality, cost-effective medical care; (2) cost containment and utilization review procedures to guard against over- or underutilization; and (3) quality, cost-effective health promotion and behavioral medicine programs. At the present time, there are a few promising instances of addressing these three elements in HMO and corporate settings. One example is an innovative medical plan termed "CustomCare" at Southwestern Bell Corporation in St. Louis which contains all three elements and is the subject of a coordinated research effort by Southwestern Bell, Prudential Insurance, and Johnson & Johnson Health Management Incorporated (Fielding 1987). This evaluation is scheduled for completion in 1990.

There is an ongoing program initiated in 1984 at the University of California School of Medicine in San Francisco involving faculty from the Department of Medicine and representatives from 14 major corporations including AT&T, Apple Computer, Bank of America, Levi-Strauss, Lockheed, Hewlett Packard, Southwestern Bell Corporation, and Wells Fargo Bank (Pelletier, Klehr, and McPhee 1987). In essence the project is designed to develop and evaluate an array of innovative medical, cost-containment, and health promotion programs on an objective basis. Additionally, a program development project for the State of California Department of Mental Health (Pelletier, Lutz, and Klehr 1987) has as its main objective to develop and evaluate a stand-alone self-care stress management program which will be made available to residents of the state of California and eventually to residents of other states as well. This program will consist of print materials and audiotapes aimed for intermediate- to low-literacy populations. It may be possible to modify this program for use within the workplace but this would require rigorous development and evaluation. Finally, since there is no evidence that a freestanding, self-care stress program is efficacious per se, the program will be clearly tied to eliciting self-referrals to state and private mental health care providers. This is in recognition that stress management is a complex problem requiring a system resolution, not a simplistic panacea.

In these instances, stress management programs continue to be the number one priority cited by both employers and employees. Unfortunately, the commonly used prepackaged stress management programs do not appear to be either health- or cost-effective at the present time based on objective assessments. Obviously, one cannot show positive health care outcomes as easily if your target audience is neither symptomatic nor at high risk, since they already have low health care costs. Here, as noted earlier, employers and employees may have reasons for desiring stress management other than health-cost incentives.

At present, the best health- and cost-efficacy data indicate that stress management is most effective with an identified high-risk or symptomatic employee population utilizing traditional, problem-focused, brief psychotherapy. Whether group or individual approaches are employed, it is also essential to modify hazardous working conditions to avoid the paradox of "healthy people in unhealthy places" (Pelletier 1985). Finally, the one unequivocal conclusion of this critical review is that program evaluation is as essential as program development. Through the collaborative research efforts of corporations and universities, the pressing but unresolved issues of today should yield a plethora of insights tomorrow.

REFERENCES

Abernethy, V. 1973. Social network and response to the maternal role. *International Journal of Sociology of the Family* 3:86–92.

Abrahams, M. J., J. Price, F. A. Whitlock, and G. Williams. 1976. The Brisbane floods, January 1974: Their impact on health. *Medical Journal of Australia* 2:936–39.

Abramson, L. Y., M. E. P. Seligman, and J. Teasdale. 1978. Learned helplessness in humans: Critique and reformulation. *Journal of Abnormal Psychology* 87:49–74.

Achte, K. A., and M. L. Vauhkonen. 1971. Cancer and the psyche. *Omega* 2:46–56.

Adams, P. R., and G. R. Adams. 1984. Mount St. Helens's ashfall: Evidence for a disaster stress reaction. *American Psychologist* 39:252–60.

Ader, R. 1980. Psychosomatic and psychoimmunological research: Presidential address. *Psychosomatic Medicine* 42:307–21.

Ader, R. 1981, ed. *Psychoneuroimmunology.* New York: Academic.

Adler, A. 1917. *Study of Organ Inferiority and Its Physical Compensation: A Contribution to Clinical Medicine.* New York: Nervous and Mental Disease Publication Co.

Adler, A. 1943. Neuropsychiatric complications in victims of Boston's Cocoanut Grove disaster. *Journal of the American Medical Association* 17:1098–1101.

Affleck, G., H. Tennen, C. Pfeiffer, and J. Fifield. 1987. Appraisals of control and predictability in adapting to a chronic disease. *Journal of Personality and Social Psychology* 53:273–79.

Aldag, R. J., and A. P. Brief. 1979. *Task Design and Employee Motivation.* Glenview, Ill.: Scott, Foresman.

Aldwin, C., S. Folkman, C. Schaefer, J. C. Coyne, and R. S. Lazarus. 1980. Ways of Coping: A process measure. Paper presented at meetings of the American Psychological Association, Montreal, September.

Alexander, F. 1950. *Psychosomatic Medicine.* New York: Norton.

Allee, W. C. 1951. *Cooperation Among Animals.* New York: Henry Schuman.

Allen, M. T., K. A. Lawler, V. P. Mitchell, K. A. Matthews, C. J. Rakaczky, and W. Jamison. 1987. Type A behavior pattern, parental history of hypertension, and cardiovascular reactivity in college males. *Health Psychology* 6:113–30.

Allport, G. W. 1937. *Personality: A Psychological Interpretation.* New York: Holt.

Allred, K. D., and T. W. Smith. 1989. The hardy personality: Cognitive and physiological responses to evaluative threat. *Journal of Personality and Social Psychology* 56:257–66.

Alpert, R., and R. N. Haber. 1960. Anxiety in academic achievement situations. *Journal of Abnormal and Social Psychology* 61:207–15.

Alsop, S. 1973. *Stay of Execution: A Sort of Memoir.* New York: Lippincott.

American Heart Association. 1984a. *Exercise and Your Heart.* Dallas, Tex.: American Heart Association.

American Heart Association. 1984b. *Nutritional Counseling for Cardiovascular Health.* Dallas, Tex.: American Heart Association.

American Heart Association. 1988. *Cigarette Smoking and Cardiovascular Disease: Special Report for the Public.* Dallas, Tex.: American Heart Association.

American Psychiatric Association. 1980, 1987. *Diagnostic and Statistical Manual of Mental Disorders.* Washington, D.C.: American Psychiatric Association.

Andrew, J. M. 1967. Coping styles, stress-relevant learning, and recovery from surgery. Ph.D. dissertation, University of California, Los Angeles.

Andrew, J. M. 1970. Recovery from surgery, with and without preparatory instruction, for three coping styles. *Journal of Personality and Social Psychology* 15:223–26.

Anthony, E. J. 1988. The response to overwhelming stress in children: Some introductory comments. In E. J. Anthony and C. Chiland, eds., *The Child in His Family: Perilous Development: Child Raising and Identity Formation Under Stress,* 8:3–16. New York: Wiley.

Antonoff, S. R., and B. Spilka. 1984–85. Patterning of facial expressions among terminal cancer patients. *Omega* 15:101–8.

Antonovsky, A., B. Maoz, N. Dowty, and H. Wijsenbeek. 1971. Twenty-five years later. *Social Psychiatry* 6:186–93.

Antonucci, T., and C. Depner. 1982. Social support and informal helping relationships. In T. Wills, ed., *Basic Processes in Helping Relationships.* New York: Academic Press.

Appley, M. H. 1967. Invited commentary. In M. H. Appley and R. Trumbull, eds., *Psychological Stress: Issues in Research,* pp. 169–72. New York: Appleton-Century-Crofts.

Appley, M. H., and R. Trumbull, eds. 1986. *Dynamics of Stress: Physiological, Psychological, and Social Perspectives.* New York: Plenum Press.

Arizona Department of Health Services. 1987. Definitive and presumptive AIDS cases in Arizona and AIDS Related Complex (ARC): Surveillance report for Arizona. February 2.

Asendorpf, J. B., and K. R. Scherer. 1983. The discrepant repressor: Differentiation between low anxiety, high anxiety, and represson of anxiety by autonomic-facial-verbal patterns of behavior. *Journal of Personality and Social Psychology* 45:1334–46.

Ashley, F., Jr., and W. Kannel. 1974. Relation of weight change to changes in atherogenic traits: The Framingham Study. *Journal of Chronic Diseases* 27:103–14.

Asterita, M. F. 1985. *The Physiology of Stress.* New York: Human Sciences Press.

Auerbach, S. M. 1973. Trait-state anxiety and adjustment to surgery. *Journal of Consulting and Clinical Psychology* 40:264–71.

Austin, S. H. 1974. Coping and psychological stress in pregnancy, labor, and delivery, with "natural childbirth" and "medicated" patients. Ph.D. dissertation, University of California, Berkeley.

Averill, J. R. 1973. Personal control over aversive stimuli and its relationship to stress. *Psychological Bulletin* 80:286–303.

Averill, J. R., and E. M. Opton, Jr. 1968. Psychophysiological assessment: Rationale and problems. In P. McReynolds, ed., *Advances in Psychological Assessment,* 1:265–88. Palo Alto, Calif.: Science and Behavior Books.

Averill, J. R., and M. Rosenn. 1972. Vigilant and nonvigilant coping strategies and psychophysiological stress reactions during the anticipation of electric shock. *Journal of Personality and Social Psychology* 23:128–41.

Bachrach, K. M., and A. J. Zautra. 1985. Coping with a community stressor: The threat of a hazardous waste facility. *Journal of Health and Social Behavior* 26:127–41.

Backett, E. M., and A. M. Johnston. 1959. Social patterns of road accidents to children: Some characteristics of vulnerable children. *British Medical Journal* 1:409.

Baer, L. 1980. Effect of a time-slowing suggestion on performance accuracy on a perceptual motor task. *Perceptual and Motor Skills* 51:167–76.

Bailyn, L. 1977. Involvement and accommodation in technical careers: An inquiry into the relation to work at mid-career. In J. V. Maanen, ed., *Organizational Careers: Some New Perspectives.* New York: Wiley.

Baker, E. 1979. Predicting responses to hurricane warnings: A reanalysis of data from four studies. *Mass Emergencies* 4:9–24.

Baluk, U., and P. O'Neill. 1980. Health professionals' perceptions of the psychological consequences of abortion. *American Journal of Community Psychology* 8:67–75.

Bandura, A. 1971. *Psychological Modeling: Conflicting Theories.* Chicago: Aldine-Atherton.

Bandura, A. 1977a. Self-efficacy: Toward a unifying theory of psychological change. *Psychological Review* 84:191–215.

Bandura, A. 1977b. *Social Learning Theory.* Englewood Cliffs, N.J.: Prentice-Hall.

Bandura, A. 1982. Self-efficacy mechanism in human agency. *American Psychologist* 37:122–47.

Bandura, A. 1986. *Social Foundations of Thought and Action: A Social Cognitive Theory.* Englewood Cliffs, N.J.: Prentice-Hall.

Bankoff, E. A. 1983. Social support and adaptation to widowhood. *Journal of Marriage and the Family* 45:827–39.

Barber, T. X., N. P. Spanos, and J. F. Chaves. 1974. *Hypnosis, Imagination, and Human Potentialities.* New York: Pergamon Press.

Barkun, M. 1974. *Disaster and the Millennium.* New Haven, Conn.: Yale University Press.

Barnett, S. A. 1960. Social behaviour among tame rats and among wild-white hybrids. *Proceedings of the Zoological Society of London* 134:611–21.

Barnett, S. A. 1963. *The Rat: A Study in Behaviour.* Chicago: Aldine.

Barnett, S. A. 1964. Social stress. In J. D. Carthy and C. L. Duddington, eds., *Viewpoints in Biology,* 3:170–218. London: Butterworths.

Baron, R., and J. Rodin. 1978. Personal control as a mediator of crowding. In A. Baum, J. E. Singer, and S. Valins, eds., *Advances in Environmental Psychology: Vol. 1. The Urban Environment,* pp. 145–92. Hillsdale, N.J.: Erlbaum.

Barrera, M. 1981. Social support in the adjustment of pregnant adolescents: Assessment issues. In B. H. Gottlieb, ed., *Social Networks and Social Support.* Beverly Hills, Calif.: Sage.

Barrera, M., and P. Balls. 1983. Assessing social support as a prevention resource: An illustrative study. *Prevention in Human Services* 2:59–74.

Barrow, J. H., Jr. 1955. Social behavior in fresh-water fish and its effect on resistance to trypanosomes. *Proceedings of the National Academy of Science* 41:676–79.

Barton, A. H. 1969. *Communities in Disaster.* Garden City, N.Y.: Doubleday.

Barton, A. H. 1970. *Communities in Disaster: A Sociological Analysis of Collective Stress Situations.* Garden City, N.Y.: Anchor-Doubleday.

Bass, D. M. 1985. The hospice ideology and success of hospice care. *Research on Aging* 7:307–27.

Bass, D. M., T. N. Garland, and M. E. Otto. 1985–86. Characteristics of hospice patients. *Omega* 16:51–68.

Baugher, R. J., C. Burger, R. A. Smith, and K. A. Wallston. 1985. A comparison of terminally ill persons at various time periods to death. Paper prepared in conjunction with the National Hospice Study, Vanderbilt University, Nashville, Tenn.

Baum, A. 1987. Toxins, technology, and natural disasters. In G. R. VandenBos and B. K. Bryant, eds., *Cataclysms, Crises, and Catastrophes: Psychology in Action,* pp. 5–53. Washington, D.C.: American Psychological Association.

Baum, A., and L. M. Davidson. 1985. A suggested framework for studying factors that contribute to trauma in disaster. In B. J. Sowder, ed., *Disasters and Mental Health: Selected Contemporary Perspectives,* pp. 29–40. Rockville, Md.: U. S. Department of Health and Human Services.

Baum, A., R. Fleming, and L. Davidson. 1983. Natural disaster and technological catastrophe. *Environment and Behavior* 15:333–54.

Baum, A., R. Fleming, and J. E. Singer. 1983. Coping with victimization by technological disaster. *Journal of Social Issues* 39:117–38.

Baum, A., and R. J. Gatchel. 1981. Cognitive determinants of reaction to uncontrollable events: Development of reactance and learned helplessness. *Journal of Personality and Social Psychology* 40:1078–89.

Baum, A., R. J. Gatchel, R. Fleming, and C. R. Lake. 1981. *Chronic and Acute Stress Associated with the Three Mile Island Accident and Decontamination: Preliminary Findings of a Longitudinal Study.* Washington, D.C.: U.S. Nuclear Regulatory Commission.

Baum, A., R. J. Gatchel, and M. A. Schaeffer. 1983. Emotional, behavioral, and physiological effects of chronic stress at Three Mile Island. *Journal of Consulting and Clinical Psychology* 51:565–72.

Baum, A., N. E. Grunberg, and J. E. Singer. 1982. The use of psychological and neuroendocrinological measurements in the study of stress. *Health Psychology* 1:217–36.

Baum, A., M. A. Schaeffer, C. R. Lake, R. Fleming, and D. L. Collins. 1986. Psychological and endocrinological correlates of chronic stress at Three Mile Island. In R. Williams, ed., *Perspectives on Behavioral Medicine,* pp. 201–17. New York: Academic Press.

Baum, A., J. E. Singer, and C. S. Baum. 1981. Stress and the environment. *Journal of Social Issues* 37:4–35.

Baum, A., and S. Valins. 1977. *Architecture and Social Behavior: Psychological Studies in Social Density.* Hillsdale, N.J.: Erlbaum.

Baumann, L. J., and H. Leventhal. 1985. I can tell when my blood pressure is up, can't I? *Health Psychology* 4:203–18.

Baun, W., E. Bernacki, and S. Tsai. 1986. A preliminary investigation: Effect of a corporate fitness program on absenteeism and health care costs. *Journal of Occupational Medicine* 28:18–22.

Bean, G., S. Cooper, R. Alpert, and D. Kipnis. 1980. Coping mechanisms of cancer patients: A study of 33 patients receiving chemotherapy. *Cancer Journal for Clinicians* 30:257–59.

Beck, A. T. 1976. *Cognitive Therapy and the Emotional Disorders.* New York: International Universities Press.

Becker, M. H., and J. G. Joseph. 1988. AIDS and behavioral change to reduce risk: A review. *American Journal of Public Health* 78:394–410.

Beecher, H. K. 1955. The powerful placebo. *Journal of the American Medical Association* 159:1602–6.

Beeson, D., J. S. Zones, and J. Nye. 1986. The social consequences of AIDS antibody testing: Coping with stigma. Paper presented at the annual meeting of the Society for the Study of Social Problems, New York.

Beisser, A. R. 1979. Denial and affirmation in illness and health. *American Journal of Psychiatry* 136:1026–30.

Bell, P. A., and D. Byrne. 1978. Repression-sensitization. In H. London and J. E. Exner, eds., *Dimensions of Personality,* pp. 449–85. New York: Wiley.

Belle, D. 1982a. Social ties and social support. In D. Belle, ed., *Lives in Stress: Women and Depression.* Beverly Hills, Calif.: Sage.

Belle, D. 1982b. The stress of caring: Women as providers of social support. In L. Goldberger and S. Breznitz, eds., *Handbook of Stress: Theoretical and Clinical Aspects.* New York: Free Press.

Belle, D. 1983. The impact of poverty on social networks and supports. *Marriage and Family Review* 5:89–103.

Belle, D. 1987. Gender differences in the social moderators of stress. In R. C. Barnett, L. Biener, and G. K. Baruch, eds., *Gender and Stress,* pp. 257–77. New York: Free Press.

Belle, D., and C. Longfellow. 1984. Turning to others: Children's use of confidants. Paper presented at the annual meeting of the American Psychological Association, Toronto.

Benedek, E. 1985. Children and disaster: Emerging issues. *Psychiatric Annals* 15:168–72.

Benner, P. 1984. *Stress and Satisfaction on the Job: Work Meanings and Coping of Mid-Career Men.* New York: Praeger.

Bennet, G. 1970. Bristol floods 1968. Controlled survey of effects on health of local community disaster. *British Medical Journal* 3:454–58.

Bennett, B. K., and C. M. Stothart. 1980. The effects of a relaxation-based cognitive technique on sport performances. In P. Klavora and K. A. W. Wipper, eds., *Psychological and Sociological Factors and Sport.* Toronto: University of Toronto Press.

Benoit, J., I. Assenmacher, and E. Brard. 1955. Evolution testiculaire du canard domestique maintenu à l'obscurité totale pendant une longue durée. *Comptes-Rendus Academie des Sciences* (Paris) 241:251–53.

Benoit, J., I. Assenmacher, and E. Brard. 1956. Etude de l'évolution testiculaire du canard domestique soumis très jeune à un éclairement artificiel permanent pendant deux anx. *Comptes-Rendus Academie des Sciences* (Paris) 242:3113–15.

Benson, H. 1979. *The Mind/Body Effect.* New York: Simon and Schuster.

Benson, H., J. F. Beary, and M. P.Carol. 1974. The relaxation response. *Psychiatry* 37:37–46.

Beres, D., and S. J. Obers. 1950. The effects of extreme deprivation in infancy on psychic structure in adolescence. In R. S. Eissler, A. Freud, H. Hartmann, and E. Kris, eds., *Psychoanalytic Study of the Child,* 5:212–35. New York: International Universities Press.

Berkman, L. F., and S. L. Syme. 1979. Social networks, host resistance, and mortality: A nine-year follow-up study of Alameda County residents. *American Journal of Epidemiology* 109:186–204.

Bernard, C. 1879. *Leçons sur les phénomènes de la vie commune aux animaux et aux végétaux.* Vol. 2. Paris: Baillière.

Bernard, J. 1971. *Women and the Public Interest.* Chicago: Aldine.

Bernardis, L., and F. Skelton. 1963. Effect of crowding on hypertension and growth in rats bearing regenerating adrenals; *and* Effect of gentling on development of adrenal regeneration hypertension in immature female rats. *Proceedings of the Society for Experimental Biology and Medicine* 113:952–57.

Bernstein, D. A., and T. A. Borkovec. 1973. *Progressive Relaxation Training.* Champaign, Ill.: Research Press.

Billing, E., B. Lindell, M. Sederholm, and T. Theorell. 1980. Denial, anxiety and depression following myocardial infraction. *Psychosomatics* 21:639–45.

Billings, A. G., and R. Moos. 1981. The role of coping responses and social resources in attenuating the stress of life events. *Journal of Behavioral Medicine* 4:139–57.

Billings, A. G., and R. H. Moos. 1982. Family environments and adaptation: A clinically applicable typology. *American Journal of Family Therapy* 10:26–38.

Billings, A. G., and R. H. Moos. 1984. Coping, stress, and social resources among adults with unipolar depression. *Journal of Personality and Social Psychology* 46:877–91.

Birnbaum, H. G., and D. Kidder. 1984. What does hospice cost? *American Journal of Public Health* 74:689–97.

Birnbaum, R. M. 1964. Autonomic reaction to threat and confrontation conditions of psychological stress. Ph.D. dissertation, University of California. Berkeley.

Blair, S., T. Collingwood, R. Reynolds et al. 1984. Health promotion for education: Impact on health behaviors, satisfaction, and general well-being. *American Journal of Public Health* 74:147–49.

Blake, K. 1976. Vitamin C: The case looks stronger, but. . . . *Pastimes* (Airshuttle edition, Eastern Airlines), March.

Blanchard, E. B., G. C. McCoy, D. Wittrock, A. Musso, R. J. Gerardi, and L. Pangburn. 1988. A controlled comparison of thermal biofeedback and relaxation training in the treatment of essential hypertension: II. Effects on cardiovascular reactivity. *Health Psychology* 7:19–33.

Bleuler, M. 1978. *The Schizophrenic Disorders.* New Haven, Conn.: Yale University Press.

Bloch, D. A., E. Silber, and S. E. Perry. 1956. Some factors in the emotional reaction of children to disaster. *American Journal of Psychiatry* 113:416–22.

Block, J. 1982. Assimilation, accommodation, and the dynamics of personality development. *Child Development* 53:281–95.

Block, N., ed. 1981. *Imagery.* Cambridge, Mass.: MIT Press.

Bluebond-Langner, M. 1978. *The Private Worlds of Dying Children.* Princeton, N.J.: Princeton University Press.

Bly, J., R. Jones, and J. Richardson. 1986. Impact of worksite health promotion on health care costs and utilization: Evaluation of Johnson & Johnson's Live for Life program. *Journal of the American Medical Association* 256:3235–40.

Bobo, J. K., L. D. Gilchrist, J. F. Elmer, W. H. Snow, and S. P. Schinke. 1986. Hassles, role strain, and peer relations in young adolescents. *Journal of Early Adolescence* 6:339–52.

Bolin, R. 1985. Disaster characteristics and psychosocial impacts. In B. J. Sowder, ed., *Disasters and Mental Health: Selected Contemporary Perspectives,* pp. 3–28. Rockville, Md.: U.S. Department of Health and Human Services.

Bonica, J. 1980. Pain research therapy: Past and current status and future needs. In L. Ng and J. Bonica, eds., *Pain, Discomfort and Humanitarian Care.* Amsterdam: Elsevier.

Booth, A. 1972. Sex and social participation. *American Sociological Review* 37:183–93.

Booth, A., and E. Hess. 1974. Cross-sex friendship. *Journal of Marriage and the Family* 36:38–47.

Bornstein, P. E., P. J. Clayton, J. A. Halikas, W. L. Maurice, and E. Robins. 1973. The depression of widowhood after thirteen months. *British Journal of Psychiatry* 122:561–66.

Borysenko, J. 1987. *Minding the Body, Mending the Mind.* Reading, Mass.: Addison-Wesley.

Botvin, G. J., and A. Eng. 1982. The efficacy of a multicomponent approach to the prevention of cigarette smoking. *Preventive Medicine* 11:199–211.

Boutcher, S. H., and R. J. Rotella. 1987. A psychological skills education program for closed-skill performance enhancement. *The Sport Psychologist* 1:127–37.

Bowlby, J. 1973. *Attachment and Loss: Separation Anxiety and Anger.* New York: Basic Books.

Bowlby, J. 1980. *Loss: Sadness and Depression (Attachment and Loss, Vol. 3).* New York: Basic Books.

Bowman, U. 1964. Alaska earthquake. *American Journal of Psychology* 121:313–17.

Bowne, D., M. Russell, J. Morgan, S. Optenberg, and A. Clarke. 1984. Reduced disability and health care costs in an industrial fitness program. *Journal of Occupational Medicine* 26:809–16.

Bracken, M. B., and M. J. Shepard. 1980. Coping and adaptation following acute spinal cord injury: A theoretical analysis. *Paraplegia* 18:74–85.

Bradburn, N. M. 1969. *The Structure of Well-Being.* Chicago: Aldine.

Braukmann, W., S. H. Filipp, A. Angleitner, and E. Olbrich. 1981. Problem-solving and coping with critical life-events—A life-span developmental study. Paper presented at First European Meeting on Cognitive-Behavioral Therapy, Kisboa, Portugal, September 1981.

Breznitz, S. 1971. A study of worrying. *British Journal of Social and Clinical Psychology* 10:271–79.

Breznitz, S., ed. 1983a. *The Denial of Stress.* New York: International Universities Press.

Breznitz, S. 1983b. The seven kinds of denial. In S. Breznitz, ed., *The Denial of Stress.* New York: International Universities Press.

Breznitz, S. 1984. *Cry Wolf: The Psychology of False Alarms.* Hillsdale, N.J.: Erlbaum.

Bridge, T. P., A. F. Mirsky, and F. K. Goodwin, eds. 1988. *Psychological, Neuropsychiatric, and Substance Abuse Aspects of AIDS.* New York: Raven Press.

Brock, D. B. 1983. Design of a survey of the last days of life. Social Statistics Section *Proceedings of the American Statistical Association*, pp. 326–30. Washington, D.C.: American Statistical Association.

Brodsky, C. 1984. Long-term work stress. *Psychosomatics* 25:361–68.

Bromet, E. 1980. *Three Mile Island: Mental Health Findings.* Pittsburgh, Pa.: Western Psychiatric Institute and Clinic and the University of Pittsburgh.

Bromet, E., D. Parkinson, A. Schulberg, L. Dunn, and P. C. Gondek. 1980. *Three Mile Island: Mental Health Findings.* Pittsburgh, Pa.: Western Psychiatric Institute and Clinic.

Bronson, F. H., and B. E. Eleftheriou. 1965a. Adrenal response to fighting in mice: Separation of physical and psychological causes. *Science* 147:627–28.

Bronson, F. H., and B. E. Eleftheriou. 1965b. Relative effects of fighting on bound and unbound corticosterone in mice. *Proceedings of the Society for Experimental Biology and Medicine* 118:146–49.

Brousseau, K. R. 1978. Personality and job experience. *Organizational Behavior and Human Performance* 22:235–52.

Brousseau, K. R., and J. B. Prince. 1981. Job person dynamics: An extension of longitudinal research. *Journal of Applied Psychology* 66:59–62.

Brown, B. A. 1977. *Stress and the Art of Biofeedback.* New York: Harper & Row.

Brown, C. C., ed. 1967. *Methods in Psychophysiology.* Baltimore: Williams and Wilkins.

Brown, G., M. Bhrolchain, and T. Harris. 1975. Social class and psychiatric disturbance among women in an urban population. *Sociology* 9:225–54.

Brown, G. W. 1974. Meaning, measurement, and stress of life events. In B. S. Dohrenwend and B. P. Dohrenwend, eds., *Stressful Life Events: Their Nature and Effects.* New York: Wiley.

Brown, J. T., and G. A. Stoudemire. 1983. Normal and pathological grief. *Journal of the American Medical Association* 250:378–82.

Brown, P., and H. Fox. 1979. Sex differences in divorce. In E. Gomberg and V. Franks, eds., *Gender and Disordered Behavior: Sex Differences in Psychopathology.* New York: Brunner/Mazel.

Brownell, K. D., G. A. Marlatt, E. Lichtenstein, and G. T. Wilson. 1986. Understanding and preventing relapse. *American Psychologist* 41:765–82.

Bryant, B. 1985. The neighborhood walk: Sources of support in middle childhood. *Monographs of the Society for Research in Child Development* 50 (3, Serial No. 210).

Bucher, R. 1957. Blame and hostility in disaster. *American Journal of Sociology* 62:467–75.

Buchholz, R. A. 1978. An empirical study of contemporary beliefs about work in American society. *Journal of Applied Psychology* 63:219–27.

Bulman, R. J., and C. B. Wortman. 1977. Attributions of blame and coping in the "real world": Severe accident victims react to their lot. *Journal of Personality and Social Psychology* 35:351–63.

Bureau of National Affairs. 1984. Personnel policies forum survey. 132:3–11.

Burger, J. M. 1989. Negative reactions to increases in perceived personal control. *Journal of Personality and Social Psychology* 56:246–56.

Burger, J. M., and H. M. Cooper. 1979. The desirability of control. *Motivation and Emotion* 3:381–93.

Burish, T. G., and L. A. Bradley. 1983. *Coping with Chronic Disease: Research and Applications.* New York: Academic Press.

Burish, T. G., and J. N. Lyles. 1979. Effectiveness of relaxation training in reducing the aversiveness of chemotherapy in the treatment of cancer. *Journal of Behavior Therapy and Experimental Psychology* 10:357–61.

Burke, R. J., and T. Weir. 1987. Sex differences in adolescent life stress, social support, and well-being. *Journal of Psychology* 98:277–88.

Burke, R. J., T. Weir, and D. Harrison. 1976. Disclosure of problems and tensions experienced by marital partners. *Psychological Reports* 38:531–42.

Bury, M. 1982. Chronic illness as biographical disruption. *Sociology of Health and Illness* 4:167–82.

Bussman, K., A. Friedman, K. S. Walker, P. Heston, and L. Wright. 1987. Type A Behavior Pattern and Measures of Control. Manuscript.

Butehorn, L. 1985. Effects of the social network on the battered woman's decision to stay in or leave the battering relationship. Ph.D. dissertation, Boston University.

Byrne, D. 1961. The repression-sensitization scale: Rationale, reliability, and validity. *Journal of Personality* 29:334–49.

Byrne, D. 1964. Repression-sensitization as a dimension of personality. In B. A. Maher, ed., *Progress in Experimental Personality Research,* 1:169–220. New York: Academic Press.

Byrne, D., J. Barry, and D. Nelson. 1963. Relation of the revised repression-sensitization scale to measures of self-description. *Psychological Reports* 13:323–34.

Caldwell, M. A., and L. A. Peplau. 1982. Sex differences in same-sex friendship. *Sex Roles* 8:721–32.

Calhoun, J. B. 1949. A method for self-control of population growth among mammals living in the wild. *Science* 109:333–35.

Calhoun, J. B. 1962. Population density and social pathology. *Scientific American* 206:139–48.

Cameron, J., and C. M. Parkes. 1983. Terminal care: Evaluation of effects of surviving family of care before and after bereavement. *Postgraduate Medical Journal* 59:73–78.

Campbell, A., P. E. Converse, and W. L. Rodgers. 1976. *The Quality of American Life.* New York: Russell Sage Foundation.

Candy, S. G., L. W. Troll, and S. G. Levy. 1981. A developmental exploration of friendship functions in women. *Psychology of Women Quarterly* 5:456–72.

Cannon, W. B. [1929] 1953. *Bodily Changes in Pain, Hunger, Fear, and Rage.* Boston: C. T. Branford.

Cannon, W. B. [1939] 1963. *The Wisdom of the Body.* New York: Norton.

Caplan, G. 1976. The family as a support system. In G. Caplan and M. Kallilea, eds., *Support Systems and Mutual Help: Multidisciplinary Explorations,* pp. 19–36. New York: Grune & Stratton.

Caplan, R. D., S. Cobb, and J. R. French. 1975. Job demands and worker health. *Journal of Applied Psychology* 60:211–19.

Carpenter, C. R. 1958. Territoriality: A review of concepts and problems. In A. Roe and G. G. Simpson, eds., *Behavior and Evolution,* pp. 224–50. New Haven, Conn.: Yale University Press.

Carter Center of Emory University. 1985. *Closing the Gap: National Health Policy Consultant.* Atlanta, Ga.: Emory University.

Cartwright, A., L. Hockey, and J. L. Anderson. 1973. *Life Before Death.* London: Routledge & Kegan Paul.

Carver, C. S., M. F. Scheier, and J. K. Weintraub. 1989. Assessing coping strategies: A theoretically based approach. *Journal of Personality and Social Psychology* 56:267–83.

Caspi, A., N. Bolger, and J. Eckenrode. 1987. Linking person and context in the daily stress process. *Journal of Personality and Social Psychology* 52:184–95.

Cassel, J. 1976. The contribution of social environment to host resistance. *American Journal of Epidemiology* 104:107–23.

Cassileth, B. R., E. J. Lusk, D. S. Miller, L. L. Brown, and C. Miller. 1985. Psychological correlates of survival in advanced malignant disease. *New England Journal of Medicine* 312:1551–55.

Cauce, A. M., R. D. Felner, and J. Primavera. 1982. Social support in high-risk adolescents: Structural components and adaptive impact. *American Journal of Community Psychology* 10:417–28.

Caudill, D., R. Weinberg, and A. Jackson, 1983. Psyching-up and track athletes: A preliminary investigation. *Journal of Sport Psychology* 5:231–35.

Chabot, J. A. 1973. Repression-sensitization: A critique of some neglected variables in the literature. *Psychological Bulletin* 80:122–29.

Chamberlain, B. C. 1980. Mayo seminars in psychiatry: The psychological aftermath of disaster. *Journal of Clinical Psychiatry* 4:238–44.

Charlesworth, E. A., and R. G. Nathan. 1984. *Stress Management: A Comprehensive Guide to Wellness.* New York: Ballantine.

Charmaz, K. 1983. Loss of self: A fundamental form of suffering in the chronically ill. *Sociology of Health and Illness* 5:168–95.

Chesney, M. A., and R. H. Rosenman. 1980. Strategies for modifying Type A behavior. *Consultant* 20:216–22.

Child, I. L., and I. K. Waterhouse. 1952. Frustration and the quality of performance: I. A critique of the Baker, Dembo and Lewin experiment. *Psychological Review* 59:351–62.

Child, I. L., and I. K. Waterhouse. 1953. Frustration and the quality of performance: II. A theoretical statement. *Psychological Review* 60:127–39.

Chiriboga, D. A., A. Coho, J. A. Stein, and J. Roberts. 1979. Divorce, stress and social supports: A study in help-seeking behavior. *Journal of Divorce* 3:121–35.

Chitty, D. 1958. Self-regulation of numbers through changes in viability. *Cold Spring Harbor Symposium of Quantitative Biology* 22:277–80.

Chodorow, N. 1974. Family structure and feminine personality. In M. Rosaldo and L. Lamphere, eds., *Women, Culture, and Society.* Stanford, Calif.: Stanford University Press.

Christian, J. J., and D. E. Davis. 1956. The relationship between adrenal weight and population status of urban Norway rats. *Journal of Mammalogy* 37:475–86.

Christian, J. J., V. Flyger, and E. E. Davis. 1960. Factors in mass mortality of a herd of Sika deer *(Cervus nippon). Chesapeake Science* 1:79–95.

Christian, J. J., and H. O. Williamson. 1958. Effect of crowding on experimental granuloma formation in mice. *Proceedings of the Society for Experimental Biology and Medicine* 99:385–87.

Cinciripini, P. M. 1986a. Cognitive stress and cardiovascular reactivity. I. Relationship to hypertension. *American Heart Journal* 112:1044–50.

Cinciripini, P. M. 1986b. Cognitive stress and cardiovascular reactivity. II. Relationship to atherosclerosis, arrhythmias, and cognitive control. *American Heart Journal* 112:1051–65.

Clark, L. V. 1960. Effect of mental practice on the development of a certain motor skill. *Research Quarterly* 31:560–69.

Clarke, J. C., and J. A. Jackson. 1983. *Hypnosis and Behavior Therapy: The Treatment of Anxiety and Phobias.* New York: Springer.

Clayton, P. J., J. A. Halikas, and W. L. Maurice. 1971. The bereavement of the widowed. *Diseases of the Nervous System* 32:597–604.

Clayton, P. J., J. A. Halikas, and W. L. Maurice. 1972. The depression of widowhood. *British Journal of Psychiatry* 120:71–78.

Cleary, P. D., and P. S. Houts 1984 (Spring). The psychological impact of the Three Mile Island incident. *Journal of Human Stress* 28–34.

Cobb, S. 1976. Social support as a moderator of life stress. *Psychosomatic Medicine* 38:300–14.

Cobb, S., and S. V. Kasl. 1977. *Termination: The Consequences of Job Loss.* Cincinnati, Ohio: U. S. Department of Health, Education and Welfare.

Cobb, S., and E. Lindemann. 1943. Neuropsychiatric observations after the Cocoanut Grove Fire. *Annals of Surgery* 117:814–24.

Coelho, G. B., D. A. Hamburg, and J. E. Adams, eds. 1974. *Coping and Adaptation.* New York: Basic Books.

Cofer, C. N., and M. H. Appley. 1964. *Motivation: Theory and Research.* New York: Wiley.

Cohen, F. 1975. Psychological preparation, coping, and recovery from surgery. Ph.D. dissertation, University of California, Berkeley.

Cohen, F. 1979. Personality, stress, and the development of physical illness. In G. C. Stone, F. Cohen, N. E. Adler, and Associates, eds., *Health Psychology —A Handbook: Theories, Applications, and Challenges of a Psychological Approach to the Health Care System,* pp. 77–111. San Francisco: Jossey-Bass.

Cohen, F. 1981. Stress and bodily illness. *Psychiatric Clinics of North America* 4:269–86.

Cohen, F. 1987. Measurement of Coping. In S. V. Kasl and C. L. Cooper, eds., *Stress and Health: Issues in Research Methodology*, pp. 283–305. Chichester, Great Britain: John Wiley & Sons.

Cohen, F., M. Horowitz, R. S. Lazarus, R. Moos, L. N. Robins, R. Rose, and M. Rutter. 1982. Panel report on psychosocial assets and modifiers of stress. In G. R. Elliott and C. Eisdorfer, eds., *Stress and Human Health*, pp. 147–88. New York: Springer.

Cohen, F., and R. S. Lazarus. 1973. Active coping processes, coping dispositions, and recovery from surgery. *Psychosomatic Medicine* 35:375–89.

Cohen, F., and R. S. Lazarus. 1979. Coping with the stresses of illness. In G. C. Stone, F. Cohen, N. E. Adler, and Associates, eds., *Health Psychology—A Handbook: Theories, Applications, and Challenges of a Psychological Approach to the Health Care System*, pp. 217–54. San Francisco: Jossey-Bass.

Cohen, F., and R. S. Lazarus. 1983. Coping and adaptation and health and illness. In D. Mechanic, ed., *Handbook of Health, Health Care, and the Health Professions*, pp. 608–35. New York: Free Press.

Cohen, F., L. B. Reese, G. A. Kaplan, and R. E. Riggio. 1986a. Coping with the stresses of arthritis. In R. W. Moskowitz and M. R. Haug, eds., *Arthritis and the Elderly*, pp. 47–56. New York: Springer.

Cohen, F., R. E. Riggio, L. B. Reese, and G. A. Kaplan. In preparation. Coping modes of elderly rheumatoid arthritis patients.

Cohen, L. H., C. E. Burt, and J. P. Bjork. 1987. Life stress and adjustment: Effects of life events experienced by young adolescents and their parents. *Developmental Psychology* 23:583–92.

Cohen, L. H., J. McGowan, S. Fooskas, and S. Rose. 1984. Positive life events and social support and the relationship between life stress and psychological disorder. *American Journal of Community Psychology* 12:567–87.

Cohen, S. 1988. Psychosocial models of the role of social support in the etiology of physical disease. *Health Psychology* 7:269–97.

Cohen, S., G. W. Evans, D. S. Krantz, D. Stokols, and S. Kelly. 1981. Psychological, motivational, and cognitive effects of aircraft noise on children: Moving from the laboratory to the field. *American Psychologist* 35:231–43.

Cohen, S., G. W. Evans, D. Stokols, and D. S. Krantz. 1986b. *Behavior, Health, and Environmental Stress*. New York: Plenum.

Cohen, S., and G. McKay. 1984. Social support, stress and the buffering hypothesis: A theoretical analysis. In A. Baum, J. E. Singer, and S. E. Taylor, eds., *Handbook of Psychology and Health: Vol. 4. Social Psychological Aspects of Health*, pp. 253–67. Hillsdale, N.J.: Erlbaum.

Cohen, S., and T. A. Wills. 1985. Stress, social support, and the buffering hypothesis. *Psychological Bulletin* 98:310–57.

Cohler, B. M., and M. A. Lieberman. 1980. Social relations and mental health: Middle-aged and older men and women from three European ethnic groups. *Research on Aging* 2:445–69.

Cohn, R. M. 1978. The effect of employment status change on self-attitudes. *Social Psychology* 41:81–93.

Coleman, J. C., J. N. Butcher, and R. C. Carson. 1984. *Abnormal Psychology and Modern Life.* 7th ed. Glenview, Ill.: Scott, Foresman.

Coleman, T. R. 1976. A comparative study of certain behavioral, physiological, and phenomenological effects of hypnotic induction and two progressive relaxation procedures. Ph.D. dissertation, Brigham Young University, Provo, Utah.

Colletta, N. 1979. Support systems after divorce: Incidence and impact. *Journal of Marriage and the Family* 41:837–46.

Collins, D. L., A. Baum, and J. E. Singer. 1983. Coping with chronic stress at Three Mile Island: Psychological and biochemical evidence. *Health Psychology* 2:149–66.

Collins, R. L., S. E. Taylor, and L. A. Skokan. 1989. A better world or a shattered vision? Positive and negative assumptions about the world following victimization. Manuscript.

Colson, S., and L. Wright. 1986. Catalogue of Nonpsychometric Measures for Time Urgency. Manuscript.

Colton, J. A. 1985. Childhood stress: Perceptions of children and professionals. *Journal of Psychopathology and Behavioral Assessment* 7:155–73.

Comaroff, J., and P. Maguire. 1981. Ambiguity and the search for meaning: Childhood leukemia in the modern clinical context. *Social Science and Medicine* 15B:115–23.

Compas, B. E., G. E. Davis, C. J. Forsythe, and B. M. Wagner. 1987. Assessment of major and daily stressful events during adolescence: The Adolescent Perceived Events Scale. *Journal of Consulting and Clinical Psychology* 55:534–41.

Conrad, P. 1987. The experience of illness: Recent and new directions. *Research in the Sociology of Health Care* 6:1–31.

Contrada, R. J., D. C. Glass, L. R. Krakoff, D. S. Krantz, K. Kehoe, W. Isecke, C. Collins, and E. Elting. 1982. Effects of control over aversive stimulation and Type A behavior on cardiovascular and plasma catecholamine responses. *Psychophysiology* 19:408–19.

Cook, D. W. 1976. Psychological aspects of spinal cord injury. *Rehabilitation Counseling Bulletin* 19:535–43.

Cook, W., and D. Medley. 1954. Proposal hostility and pharasaic-virtue scales for the MMPI. *Journal of Applied Psychology* 238:414–18.

Cooper, C., and P. Kline. 1982. A validation of the Defense Mechanism Inventory. *British Journal of Medicine and Psychology* 55:209–14.

Cooper, R. M., and J. P. Zubek. 1958. Effects of enriched and restricted early environments on the learning ability of bright and dull rats. *Canadian Journal of Psychology* 12:159–64.

Corbin, C. B. 1967a. Effects of mental practice on skill development after controlled practice. *Research Quarterly* 38:534–38.

Corbin, C. B. 1967b. The effects of covert practice on the development of a complex motor skill. *Journal of General Psychology* 76:143–50.

Coser, R. L. 1959. Some social functions of laugher. *Human Relations* 12:171–82.

Costa, A., M. Bonaccorsi, and T. Scrimali. 1984. Biofeedback and control of anxiety preceding athletic competition. *International Journal of Sport Psychology* 15:98–109.

Costa, P. T., Jr., and R. R. McCrae. 1980. Influence of extraversion and neuroticism on subjective well-being: Happy and unhappy people. *Journal of Personality and Social Psychology* 38:668–78.

Cousins, N. 1976. Anatomy of an illness (As perceived by the patient). *New England Journal of Medicine* 295:1458–63.

Cousins, N. 1983. *The Healing Heart: Antidote to Panic and Helplessness.* New York: Norton.

Cousins, N. 1989. *Head First: The Biology of Hope.* New York: E. P. Dutton.

Cowie, B. 1976. The cardiac patient's perception of his heart attack. *Social Science and Medicine* 10:87–96.

Cox, D. J., A. G. Taylor, G. Nowacek, P. Holley-Wilcox, and S. L. Pohl. 1984. The relationship between psychological stress and insulin-dependent diabetic blood glucose control: Preliminary investigations. *Health Psychology* 3:63–75.

Cox, R. H. 1990. Intervention strategies. In R. H. Cox, *Sport Psychology: Concepts and Applications,* pp. 143–89. 2d ed. Dubuque, Ia.: Wm. C. Brown.

Coyne, J. C. 1976. Depression and the response of others. *Journal of Abnormal Psychology* 85:186–93.

Coyne, J. C., C. Aldwin, and R. S. Lazarus. 1981. Depression and coping in stressful episodes. *Journal of Abnormal Psychology* 90:439–47.

Coyne, J. C., C. B. Wortman, and D. R. Lehman. 1988. The other side of support: Emotional overinvolvement and miscarried helping. In B. Gottlieb, ed., *Marshalling Social Support,* pp. 305–30. Newbury Park, Calif.: Sage Publications.

Craig, Y. 1977. The bereavement of parents and their search for meaning. *British Journal of Social Work* 7:41–54.

Crawshaw, R. 1963. Reactions to a disaster. *Archives of General Psychology* 9:157–62.

Crnic, K. A., M. T. Greenberg, A. S. Ragozin, N. M. Robinson, and R. B. Basham. 1983. Effects of stress and social support on mothers and premature and full-term infants. *Child Development* 54:209–17.

Crockenberg, S. B. 1981. Infant irritability, mother responsiveness, and social support influences on the security of infant-mother attachment. *Child Development* 52:857–65.

Croog, S. H., D. S. Shapiro, and S. Levine. 1971. Denial among male heart patients: An empirical study. *Psychosomatic Medicine* 33:385–97.

Cummings, K. M., S. L. Emont, C. Jaen, and R. Sciandra. 1988. Format and quitting instructions as factors influencing the impact of a self-administered quit smoking program. *Health Education Quarterly* 15:199–216.

Cummings, N. 1985. Saving health care dollars through psychological service: Preliminary data from pilot project. Manuscript.

Cummings, N., and G. VandenBos. 1981. The twenty year Kaiser-Permanente experience with psychotherapy and medical utilization. *Health Policy Quarterly* 1(2).

Curry-Lindahl, K. 1963. New theory on a fabled exodus. *Natural History* 122:46–53.

Dalton, G. W., and P. H. Thompson. 1986. *Novations, Strategies for Career Management.* Glenview, Ill.: Scott, Foresman.

D'Amato, M. E., and W. E. Gumenik. 1960. Some effects of immediate versus randomly delayed shock on an instrumental response and cognitive processes. *Journal of Abnormal and Social Psychology* 60:64–67.

Daniels, F. S., and D. M. Landers. 1981. Biofeedback and shooting performance: A test of disregulation and systems theory. *Journal of Sport Psychology* 3:271–82.

Dansak, D. A., and R. S. Cordes. 1978–1979. Cancer: Denial or suppression. *International Journal of Psychiatry in Medicine* 9:257–62.

Danskin, D. G., and M. A. Crow. 1981. *Biofeedback: An Introduction and Guide.* Palo Alto, Calif.: Mayfield.

Danzig, E. R., P. W. Thayer, and L. R. Galanter. 1958. *The Effects of a Threatening Rumor on a Disaster-Stricken Community.* Washington, D.C.: National Academy of Sciences, National Research Council.

Davidson, A. 1979. Aftershocks of a jet crash. *Human Behavior* 8:8.

Davidson, L. M., and A. Baum. 1986. Chronic stress and posttraumatic stress disorders. *Journal of Consulting and Clinical Psychology* 54:303–8.

Davidson, L. M., A. Baum, and D. L. Collins. 1982. Stress and control-related problems at Three Mile Island. *Journal of Applied Social Psychology* 12:349–59.

Davidson, L. M., I. Fleming, and A. Baum. 1986. Post-traumatic stress as a function of chronic stress and toxic exposures. In C. Figley, ed., *Trauma and Its Wake,* pp. 55–77. New York: Brunner Mazel.

Davis, D. E., and C. P. Read. 1958. Effect of behavior on development of resistance in trichinosis. *Proceedings of the Society for Experimental Biology and Medicine* 99:269–72.

Davis, F. 1963. *Progress Through Polio.* Indianapolis: Bobbs-Merrill.

Davis, M., E. R. Eshelman, and M. McKay. 1988. *The Relaxation and Stress Reduction Workbook.* 3d ed. Oakland, Calif.: New Harbinger.

Davison, G. C., and J. M. Neale. 1990. *Abnormal Psychology.* 5th ed. New York: Wiley.

De Berry, S., and A. Einstein. 1981. The effect of progressive muscle relaxation on stress related symptoms in a geriatric population. *Psychosomatic Medicine* 43:87–88 (Abstract).

Deci, E. 1975. *Intrinsic Motivation.* New York: Plenum.

Deegan, M. J. 1977. Depression and physical rehabilitation. *Journal of Sociology and Social Welfare* 4:945–54.

Deevey, E. S. 1960. The hare and the haruspex: A cautionary tale. *American Scientist* 48:415–29.

Delong, D. R. 1970. Individual differences in patterns of anxiety arousal, stress-relevant information and recovery from surgery. Ph.D. dissertation, University of California, Los Angeles.

DeLongis, A., J. C. Coyne, G. Dakof, S. Folkman, and R. S. Lazarus. 1982. Relationship of daily hassles, uplifts, and major life events to health status. *Health Psychology* 1:119–36.

Dembo, T., G. L. Leviton, and B. A. Wright. 1956. Adjustment to misfortune: A problem of social-psychological rehabilitation. *Artificial Limbs* 3:4–62.

Dembroski, T. M., and P. T. Costa, Jr. 1987. Coronary-prone behavior: Components of the Type A pattern and hostility. *Journal of Personality* 55:211–35.

Dembroski, T. M., J. M. MacDougall, R. B. Williams, T. L. Haney, and J. A. Blumenthal. 1985. Components of Type A, hostility, and anger-in: Relationship to angroginphic findings. *Psychosomatic Medicine* 47:219–33.

Dembroski, T. M., and R. B. Williams. In press. Definition and assessment of coronary-prone behavior. In N. Schneiderman, P. Kaufmann, and S. M. Weiss, eds., *Handbook of Research Methods in Cardiovascular Behavioral Medicine.* New York: Plenum.

Demographic Yearbook. 1984. New York: United Nations Publications.

DePaulo, B. 1982. Social-psychological processes in informal help seeking. In T. A. Wills, ed., *Basic Processes in Helping Relationships.* New York: Academic Press.

Depner, C., and B. Ingersoll. 1982. Employment status and social support: The experience of the mature woman. In M. Szinovacz, ed., *Women's Retirement: Policy Implications of Recent Research.* Beverly Hills, Calif.: Sage Yearbooks in Women's Policy Studies, vol. 6.

Derogatis, L. R. 1977. *SCL-90: Administration, Scoring and Procedures Manual-1.* Baltimore, Md.: Johns Hopkins University School of Medicine.

Derogatis, L. R., M. D. Abeloff, and N. Melisaratos. 1979. Psychological coping mechanisms and survival time in metastatic breast cancer. *Journal of the American Medical Association* 242:1504–8.

Derogatis, L. R., R. S. Lipman, L. Covi, and K. Rickles. 1971. Neurotic symptom dimensions. *Archives of General Psychiatry* 24:454–64.

Deutsch, H. 1937. Absence of grief. *Psychoanalytic Quarterly* 6:12–22.

Dew, M. A., E. J. Bromet, and H. C. Schulberg. In press. A comparative analysis of two community stressors: Long-term mental health effects. *Journal of Applied Social Psychology.*

DeWitt, D. J. 1980. Cognitive and biofeedback training for stress reduction with university athletes. *Journal of Sport Psychology* 2:288–94.

Diamond, E. L. 1982. The role of anger and hostility in essential hypertension and coronary heart disease. *Psychological Bulletin* 92:410–33.

DiCara, L. V. 1970. Learning in the autonomic nervous system. *Scientific American* 222:30–39.

Diener, E. 1984. Subjective well-being. *Psychological Bulletin* 95:542–75.

Diener, E., and R. A. Emmons. 1985. The independence of positive and negative affect. *Journal of Personality and Social Psychology* 47:1105–17.

Dimond, R. E., and D. C. Munz. 1967. Ordinal position of birth and self-disclosure in high school students. *Psychological Reports* 21:829–33.

Dimsdale, J. E., and T. P. Hackett. 1982. Effect of denial on cardiac health and psychological assessment. *American Journal of Psychiatry* 139:1477–80.

Dinardo, Q. 1971. Psychological adjustment to spinal cord injury. Ph.D. dissertation, University of Houston, Houston, Texas.

Ditto, W. B. 1982. Daily activities of college students and the construct validity of the Jenkins Activity Survey. *Psychosomatic Medicine* 44:537–43.

Dmitrova, S. 1970. Dependence of voluntary effort upon the magnitude of the goal and the way it is set in sportsmen. *International Journal of Sport Psychology* 1:29–33.

Dohrenwend, B. P. 1983. Psychological implications of nuclear accidents: The case of Three Mile Island. *Bulletin of the New York Academy of Medicine* 59:1060–76.

Dohrenwend, B. P., B. S. Dohrenwend, S. V. Kasl, and G. J. Warheit. 1979. Report of the Task Group on Behavioral Effects to the President's Commission on the Accident at Three Mile Island. Washington, D.C.

Dohrenwend, B. P., and E. P. Shrout. 1985. "Hassles" in the conceptualization of life stress variables. *American Psychologist* 40:780–85.

Dohrenwend, B. S. 1976. Anticipation and control of stressful life events: An exploratory analysis. Paper presented to the annual meeting of the Eastern Psychological Association, New York City.

Dohrenwend, B. S., and B. P. Dohrenwend, eds. 1974. *Stressful Life Events: Their Nature and Effects.* New York: Wiley.

Dohrenwend, B. S., and B. P. Dohrenwend. 1978. Some issues in research on stressful life events. *Journal of Nervous and Mental Disease* 166:7–15.

Dohrenwend, B. S., B. P. Dohrenwend, M. Dodson, and P. E. Shrout. 1984. Symptoms, hassles, social supports, and life events: Problem of confounded measures. *Journal of Abnormal Psychology* 93:222–30.

Donovon, M. I., and S. E. Girton. 1984. *Cancer Care Nursing.* Norwalk, Conn.: Appleton-Century-Crofts.

Douglas, M., and A. Wildavsky. 1982. *Risk and Culture.* Berkeley: University of California Press.

Doyle, P. 1980. *Grief Counseling and Sudden Death: A Manual and Guide.* Springfield, Ill.: Charles C. Thomas.

Drabek, T. E. 1968. *Disaster in Aisle 13: A Case Study of the Coliseum Explosion at the Indiana State Fairgrounds, October 31, 1963.* Columbus: Disaster Research Center, Ohio State University.

Drabek, T. E. 1970. Methodology of studying disasters: Past patterns and future possibilities. *American Behavioral Scientist* 13:331–43.

Drabek, T. E., and J. E. Haas. 1970. Community disaster and system stress: A sociological perspective. In J. McGrath, ed., *Social and Psychological Factors in Stress,* pp. 264–86. New York: Holt, Rinehart, & Winston.

Drabek, T. E., and W. H. Key. 1976. Impact of disaster on primary group linkages. *Mass Emergencies* 1:89–105.

Drabek, T. E., W. H. Key, P. E. Erickson, and J. L. Crowe. 1975. The impact of disaster on kin relationships. *Journal of Marriage and the Family* 37:481–94.

Drabek, T. E., and E. L. Quarantelli. 1969. Blame in disaster: Another look, another viewpoint. In D. Dean, ed., *Dynamic Social Psychology*, pp. 604–15. New York: Random House.

Drabek, T. E., and J. J. Stephenson. 1971. When disaster strikes. *Journal of Applied Social Psychology* 1:187–203.

Dubos, R. 1965. *Man Adapting.* New Haven, Conn.: Yale University Press.

Dudley, D. L., J. W. Verhey, M. Masuda, C. J. Martin, and T. H. Holmes. 1969. Long-term adjustment, prognosis, and death in irreversible diffuse obstructive pulmonary syndromes. *Psychosomatic Medicine* 31:310–25.

Dunbar, F. 1943. *Psychosomatic Diagnosis.* New York: Hoeber.

Dunkel-Schetter, C., S. Folkman, and R. S. Lazarus. 1987. Correlates of social support receipt. *Journal of Personality and Social Psychology* 53:71–80.

Dynes, R. R. 1970. *Organized Behavior in Disaster.* Lexington, Mass.: Heath Lexington.

Easterbrook, J. A. 1959. The effect of emotion on cue utilization and the organization of behavior. *Psychological Review* 66:183–201.

Eastman, M. 1971. *The Enjoyment of Laughter.* Johnson reprint of 1937 edition. New York: Simon and Schuster.

Eckenrode, J. 1983. The mobilization of social supports: Some individual constraints. *American Journal of Community Psychology* 11:509–28.

Eckenrode, J. 1984. Impact of chronic and acute stressors on daily reports of mood. *Journal of Personality and Social Psychology* 46:907–18.

Eckenrode, J., and S. Gore. 1981. Stressful events and social support: The significance of context. In B. Gottlieb, ed., *Social Networks and Social Support.* Beverly Hills, Calif.: Sage.

Edmonston, W. E., Jr. 1981. *Hypnosis and Relaxation: Modern Verification of an Old Equation.* New York: Wiley.

Ekman, P., R. W. Levenson, and W. V. Friesen. 1983. Autonomic nervous system activity distinguishes among emotions. *Science* 221:1208–10.

Elias, W., and R. Murphy. 1986. The case for health promotion programs containing health care costs: A review of the literature. *American Journal of Occupational Therapy* 40:759–63.

Eliot, R. S., and J. C. Buell. 1983. The role of the central nervous system in sudden cardiac death. In T. M. Dembroski, T. Schmidt, and G. Blunchen, eds., *Biobehavioral Bases of Coronary-Prone Behavior.* New York: Karger.

Elite, A. 1986. Stress management program: RFP background paper. Internal paper, California Department of Mental Health, July 25.

Elizur, E., and M. Kaffman. 1982. Children's bereavement reactions following death of the father: II. *Journal of the American Academy of Child Psychiatry* 21:474–80.

Elizur, E., and M. Kaffman. 1983. Factors influencing the severity of childhood bereavement reactions. *American Journal of Orthopsychiatry* 53:668–76.

Elliott, G. R., and C. Eisdorfer, eds. 1982. *Stress and Human Health.* New York: Springer.

Elliott, R. 1965. Reaction time and heart rate as functions of magnitude of incentive and probability of success. *Journal of Personality and Social Psychology* 2:604–9.

Ellis, A. 1962. *Reason and Emotion in Psychotherapy.* New York: Lyle Stuart.

Ellis, A. 1981. The Rational-emotive therapy approach to thanatology. In H. J. Sobel, ed., *Behavior Therapy in Terminal Care.* Cambridge, Mass.: Ballinger.

Ellis, A., and M. E. Bernard. 1985. What is rational-emotive therapy (RET)? In A. Ellis and M. E. Bernard, eds., *Clinical Applications of Rational-Emotive Therapy.* New York: Plenum.

Ellis, P. E., and J. B. Free. 1964. Social organization of animal communities. *Nature* 201:861–63.

Elton, C. S. 1958. *The Ecology of Invasions by Animals and Plants.* New York: Wiley.

Engel, G. L. 1977. The need for a new medical model: A challenge for biomedicine. *Science* 196:126–29.

Epstein, M. L. 1980. The relationship of imagery and mental rehearsal to performance of a motor task. *Journal of Sport Psychology* 2:211–20.

Epstein, S. 1967. Toward a unified theory of anxiety. In B. A. Maher, ed., *Progress in Experimental Personality Research,* 4:1–89. New York: Academic Press.

Epstein, S. 1980. The stability of behavior: II. Implications for psychological research. *American Psychologist* 35:790–806.

Epstein, S., and W. D. Fenz. 1967. The detection of areas of emotional stress through variations in perceptual threshold and physiological arousal. *Journal of Experimental Research in Personality* 2:191–99.

Erdelyi, M. H. 1974. A new look at the new look: Perceptual defence and vigilance. *Psychological Review* 81:1–25.

Erikson, E. H. [1950] 1963. *Childhood and Society.* New York: Norton.

Erikson, K. 1976. Loss of communality at Buffalo Creek. *American Journal of Psychiatry* 133:302–5.

Etkin, W. 1964. *Social Behavior and Organization Among Vertebrates.* Chicago: University of Chicago Press.

Evans, P. A., and F. Bartolome. 1980. The relationship between professional life & private life. In C. B. Derr, ed., *Work, Family and the Career.* New York: Praeger.

Evans, R. I. 1988. Health promotion—science or ideology? *Health Psychology* 7:203–19.

Evans, R. I., R. M. Rozelle, M. B. Mittlemark, W. B. Hansen, A. L. Bane, and J. Havis. 1978. Deterring the onset of smoking in children: Knowledge of immediate physiological effects and coping with peer pressure, media pressure, and parent modeling. *Journal of Applied Social Psychology* 8:126–35.

Eysenck, H. J. 1984. Lung cancer and the stress-personality inventory. In C. L. Cooper, ed., *Psychosocial Stress and Cancer.* Chichester, England: Wiley.

Falek, A., and S. Britton. 1974. Phases in coping: The hypothesis and its implications. *Social Biology* 21:1–7.

Farberow, N. L., et al. 1971. An eight-year survey of hospital suicides. *Life-Threatening Behavior* 1:184–202.

Feather, N. T., and P. R. Davenport. 1981. Unemployment and expressive affect:

A motivational and attributional analysis. *Journal of Personality and Social Psychology* 41:422–36.

Federal Emergency Management Agency. 1984. *Program Guide, Disaster Assistance Programs.* Washington, D.C.: U. S. Government Printing Office.

Feigenberg, L. 1980. *Terminal Care: Friendship Contracts with Dying Patients.* New York: Brunner/Mazel.

Feiring, C., and J. Taylor. (n.d.). The influence of the infant and secondary parent on maternal behavior. Toward a social systems view of infant attachment. Manuscript, University of Pittsburgh.

Feist, J., and L. Brannon. 1988. *Health Psychology: An Introduction to Behavior and Health.* Belmont, Calif.: Wadsworth.

Felson, R. B., and G. Gmelch. 1979. Uncertainty and the use of magic. *Current Anthropology* 20:587–89.

Felton, B. J., T. A. Revenson, and G. A. Hinrichsen. 1984. Coping and adjustment in chronically ill adults. *Social Science and Medicine* 18:889–98.

Felton, J., and R. Cole. 1963. The high cost of heart disease. *Circulation* 27:957–62.

Feltz, D. L., and D. M. Landers. 1983. The effects of mental practice on motor skill learning and performance: A meta-analysis. *Journal of Sport Psychology* 5:25–57.

Fenichel, O. 1945. *The Psychoanalytic Theory of Neurosis.* New York: Norton.

Fenker, R. M., and J. G. Lambiotte. 1987. A performance enhancement program for a college football team: One incredible season. *Sport Psychologist* 1:224–36.

Festinger, L. 1957. *A Theory of Cognitive Dissonance.* Evanston, Ill.: Row, Peterson.

Feynman, R. P. 1985. *Surely You're Joking, Mr. Feynman.* Toronto: Doubleday.

Field, T. M., P. M. McCabe, and N. Schneiderman, eds. 1988. *Stress and Coping Across Development.* Hillsdale, N.J.: Erlbaum.

Fielding, J. 1987. Personal communication.

Fine, S. A., and W. A. Wiley. 1971. *An Introduction to Functional Job Analysis: A Scaling of Selected Tasks from the Social Welfare Field.* Kalamazoo, Mich.: W. E. Upjohn Institute of Employment Research.

Finlayson, A. 1976. Social networks as coping resources: Lay help and consultation patterns used by women in husbands' post infarction career. *Social Science and Medicine* 10:97–103.

Fiore, J., J. Becker, and D. B. Coppel. 1983. Social network interactions: A buffer or a stress? *American Journal of Community Psychology* 11:423–39.

Fischer, C. 1982. *To Dwell Among Friends: Personal Networks in Town and City.* Chicago: University of Chicago Press.

Fisher, A. C. 1976. *Psychology of Sport.* Palo Alto, Calif.: Mayfield.

Fisher, A. C. 1986. Imagery from a sport psychology perspective. Paper presented at the meeting of the American Alliance for Health, Physical Education, Recreation and Dance, Cincinnati, Ohio, April.

Fisher, R. H., G. W. Nadon, and R. Shedletsky. 1983. Management of the dying elderly patient. *Journal of the American Geriatrics Society* 31:563–64.

Fleishman, J. A. 1984. Personality characteristics and coping patterns. *Journal of Health and Social Behavior* 25:229–44.

Fleming, I., and A. Baum. 1986. Comparisons of stress persistence between victims of a toxic waste site and victims of a flood. Manuscript.

Fleming, I., A. Baum, L. M. Davidson, E. Rectanus, and S. McArdle. 1987. Chronic stress as a factor in physiologic reactivity to challenge. *Health Psychology* 6:221–37.

Fleming, I. C. 1985. The stress reducing functions of specific types of social support for victims of a technological catastrophe. Ph.D. dissertation, University of Maryland, College Park.

Fleming, R., A. Baum, M. M. Gisriel, and R. J. Gatchel. 1982. Mediating influences of social support on stress at Three Mile Island. *Journal of Human Stress* 8:14–22.

Flickinger, G., and H. Ratcliffe. 1961. The effect of grouping on the adrenals and gonads of chickens. *Proceedings of the Federation of American Societies for Experimental Biology* 20:176.

Flynn, C. B. 1981. Local public opinion. *Annals of the New York Academy of Sciences* 146–58.

Foege, W. 1985. Public health and preventive medicine. *Journal of the American Medical Association* 254:2330–32.

Folkman, S. 1984. Personal control and stress and coping processes: A theoretical analysis. *Journal of Personality and Social Psychology* 46:839–52.

Folkman, S., and R. S. Lazarus. 1980. An analysis of coping in a middle-aged community sample. *Journal of Health and Social Behavior* 21:219–39.

Folkman, S., and R. S. Lazarus. 1985. If it changes it must be a process: Study of emotion and coping during the three stages of a college examination. *Journal of Personality and Social Psychology* 48:150–70.

Folkman, S., and R. S. Lazarus. 1986. Stress processes and depressive symptomatology. *Journal of Abnormal Psychology* 95:107–13.

Folkman, S., and R. S. Lazarus. 1988a. Coping as a mediator of emotion. *Journal of Personality and Social Psychology* 54:466–75.

Folkman, S., and Lazarus, R. S. 1988b. *Manual for the Ways of Coping Questionnaire.* Palo Alto, Calif.: Consulting Psychologists Press.

Folkman, S., and R. S. Lazarus. 1990. Coping and emotion. In N. Stein, B. Leventhal, and T. Trabasso, eds., *Psychological and Biological Approaches to Emotion,* pp. 313–32. Hillsdale, N.J.: Erlbaum.

Folkman, S., R. S. Lazarus, C. Dunkel-Schetter, A. DeLongis, and R. Gruen. 1986a. The dynamics of a stressful encounter: Cognitive appraisal, coping, and encounter outcomes. *Journal of Personality and Social Psychology* 50:992–1003.

Folkman, S., R. S. Lazarus, R. Gruen, and A. DeLongis. 1986b. Appraisal, coping, health status, and psychological symptoms. *Journal of Personality and Social Psychology* 50:571–79.

Folkman, S., R. S. Lazarus, S. Pimley, and J. Novacek. 1987. Age differences in stress and coping processes. *Psychology and Aging* 2:171–84.

Forman, S. 1982. Stress management for teachers: A cognitive-behavioral program. *Journal of School Psychology* 20:180–87.

Fox, B. H. 1978. Premorbid psychological factors as related to cancer incidence. *Journal of Behavioral Medicine* 1:45–134.

Fox, R. 1959. *Experiment Perilous.* New York: Free Press.

Frankel, K. 1986. The social milieu scale: Perceptions of support and stress and relationships to social status. Paper presented at the meetings of the Society for Research in Adolescence, Madison, Wisconsin, March.

Frankenhaeuser, M. 1975. Experimental approaches to the study of catecholamines and emotion. In L. Levi, ed., *Emotions: Their Parameters and Measurements,* pp. 209–34. New York: McGraw-Hill.

Frankenhaeuser, M. 1980. Psychobiological aspects of life stress. In S. Levine and H. Ursin, eds., *Coping and Health.* New York: Plenum.

Frankenhaeuser, M., B. Nordhedin, A. L. Myrsten, and B. Post. 1971. Psychophysiological reactions to understimulation and overstimulation. *Acta Psychologia* 35:298–308.

Frankl, V. 1963. *Man's Search for Meaning.* Boston: Beacon.

Frederick, C. J. 1980. Effects of natural vs. human-induced violence upon victims. In L. Kivens, ed., *Evaluation and Change: Services for Survivors,* pp. 71–75. Minneapolis, Minn.: Minneapolis Medical Research Foundation.

Fredericq, L. 1885. Influence du milieu ambiant sur la composition du sang des animaux aquatiques. *Archives de Zoologie Experimental et Génerale* 3:34.

Freedman, J. L. 1975. *Crowding and Behavior.* San Francisco: W. H. Freeman.

French, S. N. 1978. Electromyographic biofeedback for tension control during gross motor skill acquisition. *Perceptual and Motor Skills* 47:883–89.

Frese, M. 1986. Coping as a moderator and mediator between stress at work and psychosomatic complaints. In M. Appley and R. Trumbull, eds., *Dynamics of Stress.* New York: Plenum.

Freud, A., and D. Burlingham. 1944. War and Children. New York: International Universities Press.

Freud, A., and S. Dann. 1951. An experiment in group upbringing. *Psychoanalytic Study of the Child* 6:127–68.

Freud, S. [1917] 1957. Mourning and melancholia. In J. Strachey, ed., *The Standard Edition of the Complete Original Works of Sigmund Freud,* 14:152–70. London: Hogarth Press.

Freud, S. [1926] 1959. Inhibitions, symptoms, and anxiety. In J. Strachey, ed., *The Standard Edition of the Complete Original Works of Sigmund Freud,* 20:87–175. London: Hogarth Press.

Friedman, H. S., and S. Booth-Kewley. 1987. The "disease-prone personality": A meta-analytic view of the construct. *American Psychologist* 42:539–55.

Friedman, H. S., and S. Booth-Kewley. 1988. Validity of the Type A construct: A reprise. *Psychological Bulletin* 104:381–84.

Friedman, H. S., and M. R. DiMatteo. 1989. *Health Psychology.* Englewood Cliffs, N.J.: Prentice Hall.

Friedman, H. S., J. A. Hall, and M. J. Harris. 1984. Nonverbal expression of emotion: Healthy charisma or coronary-prone behavior? In C. Van Dyke, L. Temoshok, and L. S. Zegans, eds., *Emotions in Health and Illness: Applications to Clinical Practice,* pp. 151–65. Orlando, Fla: Grune & Stratton.

Friedman, M., and R. H. Rosenman. 1974. *Type A Behavior and Your Heart.* New York: Knopf.

Friedman, M., C. E. Thoresen, and J. J. Gill. 1981. Type A behavior: Its possible role, detection, and alteration in patients with ischemic heart disease. In J. W. Hurst, ed., *The Heart: Update V.* Hightstown, N.J.: McGraw-Hill.

Friedman, M., C. E. Thoresen, J. J. Gill, D. Ulmer, L. H. Powell, V. A. Price, B. Brown, L. Thompson, D. D. Rabin, W. S. Breall, E. Bourg, R. Levy, and T. Dixon. 1986. Alteration of Type A behavior and its effect on cardiac recurrences in post-myocardial infarction patients: Summary results of the recurrent coronary prevention project. *American Heart Journal* 112:653–65.

Friedman, M., and D. Ulmer. 1984. *Treating Type A Behavior and Your Heart.* New York: Knopf.

Friedman, S. B., P. Chodoff, J. W. Mason, and D. A. Hamburg. 1963. Behavioral observations on parents anticipating the death of a child. *Pediatrics* 32:610–25.

Fritz, C. E. 1961. Disaster. In R. K. Merton and R. A. Nisbet, eds., *Contemporary Social Problems.* New York: Harcourt, Brace, & World.

Fritz, C. E., and E. S. Marks. 1954. The NORC studies of human behavior in disaster. *Journal of Social Issues* 10:26–41.

Froese, A. P., E. Vasquez, N. H. Cassem, and T. P. Hackett. 1973. Validation of anxiety, depression and denial scales in a coronary care unit. *Journal of Psychosomatic Research* 18:137–41.

Fullerton, D. T., R. F. Harvey, M. H. Klein, and T. Howell. 1981. Psychiatric disorders in patients with spinal cord injury. *Archives of General Psychiatry* 38:1369–71.

Funk, S. C., and B. K. Houston. 1987. A critical analysis of the Hardiness Scale's validity and utility. *Journal of Personality and Social Psychology* 53:572–78.

Funkenstein, D. H., S. H. King, and M. E. Drolette. 1957. *Mastery of Stress.* Cambridge, Mass.: Harvard University Press.

Furman, W., and D. Buhrmester. 1985. Children's perceptions of the personal relationships in their social networks. *Developmental Psychology* 21:1016–22.

Gaines, L. L., B. D. Smith, and B. E. Skolnick. 1977. Psychological differentiation, event uncertainty, and heart rate. *Journal of Human Stress* 3:11–25.

Gal, R., and R. S. Lazarus. 1975. The role of activity in anticipating and confronting stressful situations. *Journal of Human Stress* 1:4–20.

Gans, J. S. 1981. Depression diagnosis in a rehabilitation hospital. *Archives of Physical Medicine and Rehabilitation* 62:386–89.

Gardner, R. W., P. S. Holzman, G. S. Klein, H. B. Linton, and D. P. Spence. 1959. Cognitive control: A study of individual consistencies in cognitive behavior. *Psychological Issues* 1(4).

Garmezy, N. 1982a. Foreword. In E. E. Werner and R. S. Smith, eds., *Vulnerable but Invincible,* pp. xiii–xix. New York: McGraw-Hill.

Garmezy, N. 1982b. Stress resistant children: Research for provocative factors. Paper presented at 10th International Congress of Child and Adolescent Psychiatry and Allied Professions, Dublin, July.

Garrison, J. 1978. Stress management training for the handicapped. *Archives of Physical Medicine and Rehabilitation* 59:580–85.

Gastorf, J. W., J. Suls, and G. S. Sanders. 1980. Type A coronary-prone behavior pattern and social facilitation. *Journal of Personality and Social Psychology* 38:773–80.

Gastorf, J. W., and R. C. Teevan. 1980. Type A coronary-prone behavior and fear of failure. *Motivation and Emotion* 4:71–76.

Gatchel, R. J., M. A. Schaeffer, and A. Baum. 1985. A psychological field study of stress at Three Mile Island. *Psychophysiology* 22:175–81.

Gauron, E. F. 1984. *Mental Training for Peak Performance.* Lancing, New York: Sport Science Associates.

George, J. M., D. S. Scott, S. P. Turner, and J. M. Gregg. 1980. The effects of psychological factors on physical trauma on recovery from oral surgery. *Journal of Behavioral Medicine* 3:291–310.

Gibbs, J., D. Mulvaney, C. Henes, and R. Reed. 1985. Worksite health promotion: Five-year trend in employee health care costs. *Journal of Occupational Medicine* 27:826–30.

Gibbs, M. S. 1986. Psychopathological consequences of exposure to toxins in the water supply. In A. H. Lebovits, A. Baum, and J. Singer, eds., *Advances in Environmental Psychology,* pp. 47–70. Hillsdale, N.J.: Erlbaum.

Gill, J. J., V. A. Price, M. Friedman, C. E. Thoresen, L. H. Powell, D. Ulmer, L. Thompson, B. Brown, and F. R. Drews. 1985. Reduction in Type A behavior in healthy middle-aged American military officers. *American Heart Journal* 110:503–14.

Gilligan, C. 1982. *In A Different Voice.* Cambridge, Mass.: Harvard University Press.

Girdano, D. A., G. S. Everly, Jr., and D. E. Dusek. 1990. *Controlling Stress and Tension: A Holistic Approach.* 3d ed. Englewood Cliffs, N.J.: Prentice-Hall.

Glaser, B. G., and A. L. Strauss. 1967. *The Discovery of Grounded Theory: Strategies for Qualitative Research.* Chicago: Aldine.

Glaser, B. G., and A. L. Strauss. 1968. *Time for Dying.* Chicago: Aldine.

Glass, A. 1959. Psychological considerations in atomic warfare. *U.S. Armed Forces Medical Journal* 7:625–38.

Glass, D. C. 1977a. *Behavior Patterns, Stress, and Coronary Disease.* Hillsdale, N.J.: Erlbaum.

Glass, D. C. 1977b. Stress, behavior patterns, and coronary disease. *American Scientist* 65:177–87.

Glass, D. C., C. R. Lake, R. J. Contrada, K. Kehoe, and L. R. Erlanger. 1983. Stability of individual differences in physiological responses to stress. *Health Psychology* 2:317–41.

Glass, D. C., and J. E. Singer. 1972. *Urban Stress: Experiments on Noise and Social Stressors.* New York: Academic Press.

Gleser, G., and M. Sacks. 1973. Ego defenses and reaction to stress: A validation study of the Defense Mechanisms Inventory. *Journal of Consulting and Clinical Psychology* 40:181–87.

Gleser, G. C., B. L. Green, and C. Winget. 1981. *Prolonged Effects of Disaster.* New York: Academic Press.

Gleser, G. C., and D. Ihilevich. 1969. An objective instrument for measuring defense mechanisms. *Journal of Consulting and Clinical Psychology* 33:51–60.

Glick, I. O., R. S. Weiss, and C. M. Parkes. 1974. *The First Year of Bereavement.* New York: Wiley.

Godkin, M. A., M. J. Krant, and N. J. Doster. 1983–84. The impact of hospice care on families. *International Journal of Psychiatry in Medicine* 13:153–65.

Goffman, E. 1963. *Notes on the Management of Spoiled Identity.* Englewood Cliffs, N.J.: Prentice-Hall.

Goldberger, L. 1983. The concept and mechanisms of denial: A selective overview. In S. Breznitz, ed., *The Denial of Stress,* pp. 83–102. New York: International Universities Press.

Goldfried, M. R. 1977. The use of relaxation and cognitive relabeling as coping skills. In R. Stuart, ed., *Behavioral Self-Management: Strategies, Techniques and Outcomes,* pp. 82–116. New York: Brunner/Mazel.

Goldfried, M. R. 1979. Psychotherapy as coping skills training. In M. J. Mahoney, ed., *Psychotherapy Process: Current Issues and Future Directions,* pp. 89–119. New York: Plenum.

Goldhaber, M. U., S. L. Staub, and G. K. Tokuhata. 1983. Spontaneous abortions after the Three Mile Island nuclear accident: A life table analysis. *American Journal of Public Health* 73:752–59.

Goldiamond, I. 1975. Insider-outsider problems: A constructional approach. *Rehabilitation Psychology* 22:103–16.

Goldsteen, R. L., J. Schorr, and K. S. Goldsteen. 1985. What's the matter with these people: Rethinking TMI. *Mass Emergencies* 2:369–88.

Goldstein, M. J. 1959. The relationship between coping and avoiding behavior and response to fear-arousing propaganda. *Journal of Abnormal and Social Psychology* 58:247–52.

Goldstein, M. J. 1973. Individual differences in response to stress. *American Journal of Community Psychology* 1:113–37.

Golec, J. 1980. Aftermath of disaster: The Teton Dam break. Ph.D. dissertation, Ohio State University, Columbus.

Golin, S., E. O. Herron, R. Lakota, and L. Reineck. 1967. Factor analytic study of the manifest anxiety, extraversion, and repression-sensitization scale. *Journal of Consulting Psychology* 31:564–69.

Goltz, J. D. 1985. Are the news media responsible for the disaster myths? A constant analysis of emergency response imagery. *Mass Emergencies* 2:345–68.

Goodhart, D. 1986. The effects of positive and negative thinking on performance in an achievement situation. *Journal of Personality and Social Psychology* 51:117–24.

Gore, S. 1978. The effect of social support in moderating the health consequences of unemployment. *Journal of Health and Social Behavior* 19:157–65.

Gorton, B. E. 1949. The physiology of hypnosis. *Psychiatric Quarterly* 23:457–85.

Gorzynski, J. G., J. Holland, J. L. Katz, H. Weiner, B. Zumoff, D. Fukushima, and J. Levin. 1980. Stability of ego defenses and endocrine responses in women prior to breast biopsy and ten years later. *Psychosomatic Medicine* 42:323–28.

Gottlieb, B., ed. 1981. *Social Networks and Social Support.* Beverly Hills, Calif.: Sage.

Gould, D. 1983. Developing psychological skills in young athletes. In N. Wood, ed., *Coaching Science Update.* Ottawa, Ontario: Coaching Association of Canada.

Gould, D., R. Weinberg, and A. Jackson. 1980. Mental preparation strategies, cognitions, and strength performance. *Journal of Sport Psychology* 2:329–39.

Green, B. L. 1982. Assessing levels of psychosocial impairment following disaster: Consideration of actual and methodological dimensions. *Journal of Nervous and Mental Diseases* 17:544–52.

Greenberg, J. S. 1990. *Comprehensive Stress Management.* 3d ed. Dubuque, Ia.: Wm. C. Brown.

Greenwood, M. 1935. *Epidemics and Crowd-Diseases.* London: Williams and Norgate.

Greer, D., and V. Mor. 1983. A preliminary final report of the National Hospice Study. Providence, R.I.: Brown University.

Greer, D., and V. Mor. 1986. An overview of National Hospice Study findings. *Journal of Chronic Diseases* 39:5–7.

Greer, D., V. Mor, and R. J. Kastenbaum, eds. In press. *The Hospice Experiment: Is It Working?* Baltimore: Johns Hopkins University Press.

Greer, D., V. Mor, J. Morris, S. Sherwood, D. Kidder, and H. Birnbaum. 1986. An alternative in terminal care: Results of the National Hospice Study. *Journal of Chronic Diseases* 39:9–26.

Greer, S., T. Morris, and K. W. Pettingale. 1979. Psychological response to breast cancer: Effect on outcome. *Lancet* 2:785–87.

Griffin, R. W. 1982. *Task Design: An Integrative Approach.* Glenview, Ill.: Scott, Foresman.

Griffiths, T. J., D. H. Steel, P. Vaccaro, R. Allen, and M. Karpman. 1985. The effects of relaxation and cognitive rehearsal on the anxiety levels and performance of scuba students. *International Journal of Sport Psychology* 16:113–19.

Grinker, R. R., and J. P. Spiegel. 1945. *Men Under Stress.* Philadelphia: Blakiston.

Grof, S., and J. Halifax. 1977. *The Human Encounter with Death.* New York: Dutton.

Gunther, M. S. 1971. Psychiatric consultation in a rehabilitation hospital: A regression hypothesis. *Comprehensive Psychiatry* 12:572–82.

Guthrie, E. R. 1959. *Association by Contiguity.* New York: McGraw-Hill.

Haan, N. 1963. Proposed model of ego functioning: Coping and defense mechanisms in relationship to IQ change. *Psychological Monographs* 77 (8, Whole no. 571).

Haan, N. 1969. A tripartite model of ego functioning: Values and clinical research applications. *Journal of Nervous and Mental Diseases* 148:14–30.

Haan, N. 1977. *Coping and Defending: Processes of Self-Environment Organization.* New York: Academic Press.

Haan, N. 1982. The assessment of coping, defenses, and stress. In L. Goldberger and S. Breznitz, eds., *Handbook of Stress: Theoretical and Clinical Aspects,* pp. 254–69. New York: Free Press.

Hackett, T. P., and N. H. Cassem. 1974. Development of a quantitative rating scale to assess denial. *Journal of Psychosomatic Research* 18:93–100.

Hackett, T. P., and N. H. Cassem. 1975. Psychological management of the myocardial infarction patient. *Journal of Human Stress* 1:25–38.

Hackett, T. P., N. H. Cassem, and H. A. Wishnie. 1968. The coronary-care unit: An appraisal of its psychologic hazards. *New England Journal of Medicine* 279:1365–70.

Hackman, J. R., and G. R. Oldham. 1976. Motivation through the design of work: Test of a theory. *Organizational Behavior and Human Performance* 16:250–79.

Hackman, J. R., and G. R. Oldham. 1980. *Work Redesign.* Reading, Mass.: Addison-Wesley.

Haft, J. I. 1974. Cardiovascular injury induced by sympathetic catecholamines. *Progress in Cardiovascular Disease* 17:73.

Haldane, J. S. 1922. *Respiration.* New Haven, Conn.: Yale University Press.

Hale, B. D. 1982. The effects of internal and external imagery on muscular and ocular concomitants. *Journal of Sport Psychology* 4:379–87.

Hall, E. G., and E. S. Erffmeyer. 1983. The effect of visuo-motor behavior rehearsal with videotaped modeling of free throw accuracy of intercollegiate female basketball players. *Journal of Sport Psychology* 5:343–46.

Hall, E. T. 1959. *The Silent Language.* New York: Doubleday.

Hall, E. T. 1964. Silent assumptions in social communication. In D. Rioch and E. A. Weinstein, eds., *Disorders of Communication,* pp. 41–55. Baltimore: Williams and Wilkins.

Hall, H. K., and A. T. J. Byrne. 1988. Goal setting in sport: Clarifying recent anomalies. *Journal of Sport and Exercise Psychology* 10:184–98.

Hall, H. K., R. S. Weinberg, and A. Jackson. 1987. Effects of goal specificity, goal difficulty, and information feedback on endurance performance. *Journal of Sport Psychology* 9:43–54.

Hall, P. S., and P. W. Landreth. 1975. Assessing some long term consequences of a natural disaster. *Mass Emergencies* 1:55–61.

Hall, S. S. 1989. A molecular code links emotions, mind and health. *Smithsonian* 20:62–71.

Hamburg, D. A., and J. E. Adams. 1967. A perspective on coping behavior: Seeking and utilizing information in major transitions. *Archives of General Psychiatry* 17:277–84.

Hamburg, D. A., G. V. Coelho, and J. E. Adams. 1974. Coping and adaptation: Steps toward a synthesis of biological and social perspectives. In G. V. Coelho, D. A. Hamburg, and J. E. Adams, eds., *Coping and Adaptation,* pp. 403–40. New York: Basic Books.

Hamburg, D. A., B. Hamburg, and S. deGoza. 1953. Adaptive problems and mechanisms in severely burned patients. *Psychiatry* 16:1–20.

Hamburger, E. 1962. A two-stage study of plasma ascorbic acid and its relation to wound healing. *Military Medicine* 127:723–25.

Hanson, J. D., M. E. Larson, and C. T. Snowden. 1976. The effects of control over high intensity noise on plasma cortisol levels in rhesus monkeys. *Behavioral Biology* 16:333–34.

Hanson, S. L., and J. W. Pichert. 1986. Stress and diabetes control in adolescents. *Health Psychology* 5:439–52.

Hansson, R. O., R. Hogan, J. A. Johnson, and D. Schroeder. 1983. Disentangling Type A behavior: The roles of ambition, insensitivity, and anxiety. *Journal of Research in Personality* 17:186–97.

Harburg, E., E. H. Blakelock, and P. J. Roeper. 1979. Resentful and reflective coping with arbitrary authority and blood pressure: Detroit. *Psychosomatic Medicine* 41:189–202.

Hargreaves, A. G. 1980. Coping with disaster. *American Journal of Nursing* 683.

Harlow, H. F. 1958. The nature of love. *American Psychologist* 13:673–85.

Harlow, H. F. 1959. Basic social capacity of primates. In J. N. Spuhler, ed., *The Evolution of Man's Capacity for Culture,* pp. 40–58. Detroit: Wayne State University Press.

Harlow, H. F., and M. K. Harlow. 1965. The affectional systems. In A. M. Schrier, H. F. Harlow, and F. Stollnitz, eds., *Behavior of Nonhuman Primates,* 2:1–27. New York: Academic Press.

Harris, D. V., and B. L. Harris. 1984. *The Athlete's Guide to Sports Psychology: Mental Skills for Physical People.* New York: Leisure Press.

Harris, D. V., and W. J. Robinson. 1986. The effects of skill level on EMG activity during internal and external imagery. *Journal of Sport Psychology* 8:105–11.

Harris, P. L. In press. What children know about the situations that provoke emotion. In M. Lewis and C. Saarni, eds., *The Socialization of Affect.* New York: Plenum.

Harter, S. 1982. The perceived competence scale for children. *Child Development* 53:89–97.

Hartsough, D. M., and J. C. Savitsky. 1984. Three Mile Island: Psychology and environmental policy at a crossroads. *American Psychologist* 39:1113–22.

Hay, D., and S. Oken. 1972. The psychological stresses of intensive care unit nursing. *Psychosomatic Medicine* 34:109–18.

Haynes, S. G., M. Feinleib, and E. D. Eaker. 1983. Type A behavior and the ten-year incidence of coronary heart disease in the Framingham heart study. In

R. H. Rosenman, ed., *Psychosomatic Risk Factors and Coronary Heart Disease.* Berne: Huber.

Haynes, S. G., M. Feinleib, and W. B. Kannel. 1980. The relationship of psychosocial factors to coronary heart disease in the Framingham study: III. Eight-year incidence of coronary heart disease. *American Journal of Epidemiology* 111:37–58.

Hebb, D. O. 1949. *The Organization of Behavior.* New York: Wiley.

Heckhausen, H. 1982. Task-irrelevant cognitions during an exam: Incidence and effects. In H. W. Krohne and L. Laux, eds., *Achievement, Stress, and Anxiety,* pp. 247–74. Washington, D.C.: Hemisphere.

Hediger, H. 1950. *Wild Animals in Captivity.* London: Butterworths.

Heijn, C., and G. Granger. 1974. Understanding motivational patterns—Early identification aids rehabilitation. *Journal of Rehabilitation* 40:26–28.

Heitzmann, C. A., and R. M. Kaplan. 1988. Assessment of methods for measuring social support. *Health Psychology* 7:75–109.

Hellstedt, J. C. 1987a. Sport psychology at a ski academy: Teaching mental skill to young athletes. *Journal of Sport Psychology* 1:56–68.

Hellstedt, J. C. 1987b. The coach/parent/athlete relationship. *Sport Psychologist* 1:151–60.

Helsing, K. J., and M. Szklo. 1981. Mortality after bereavement. *American Journal of Epidemiology* 114:41–52.

Henderson, S., and T. Bostock. 1977. Coping behavior after shipwreck. *British Journal of Psychiatry* 131:15–20.

Herbst, A. L., S. J. Robboy, R. E. Scully, and D. C. Poskanzer. 1974. Clear-cell adenocarcinoma of the vagina and cervix in girls: Analysis of 170 registry cases. *American Journal of Obstetrics and Gynecology* 119:713–24.

Herd, J. A. 1978. Physiological correlates of coronary-prone behavior. In T. M. Dembroski, S. Weiss, J. L. Shields, S. G. Haynes, and M. Feinleib, eds., *Coronary-Prone Behavior.* New York: Springer-Verlag.

Hertzberg, L. J. 1972. Cancer and the dying patient. *American Journal of Psychiatry* 128:7.

Hetherington, E., M. Cox, and R. Cox. 1978. The aftermath of divorce. In J. H. Stevens Jr. and M. Mathews, eds., *Mother-Child Father-Child Relationships.* Washington, D.C.: National Association for the Education of Young Children.

Heyman, S. R. 1987. Research and intervention in sport psychology: Issues encountered in working with an amateur boxer. *The Sport Psychologist* 1:208–23.

Hickman, J. L. 1979. How to elicit supernormal capabilities in athletes. In P. Klavora and J. V. Daniel, eds., *Coach, Athlete, and the Sport Psychologist.* Champaign, Ill.: Human Kinetics.

Hilton, B. 1990. AIDSWEEK. *San Francisco Sunday Examiner and Chronicle,* A-6.

Hinde, R. A. 1960. An ethological approach. In J. M. Tanner, ed., *Stress and Psychiatric Disorder,* pp. 49–58. Oxford: Blackwell.

Hinkle, L. E., Jr. 1974. The effect of exposure to culture change, social change, and changes in interpersonal relationships on health. In B. S. Dohrenwend and B. P. Dohrenwend, eds., *Stressful Life Events: Their Nature and Effects,* pp. 9–44. New York: Wiley.

Hinton, J. M. 1963. The physical and mental distress of the dying. *Quarterly Journal of Medicine* 32:1–21.

Hinton, J. M. 1979. Comparison of places and policies for terminal care. *Lancet* 8106:29–32.

Hirsch, B. J. 1980. Natural support systems and coping with major life changes. *American Journal of Community Psychology* 8:159–72.

Hirsch, B. J. 1981. Social networks and the coping process: Creating personal communities. In B. H. Gottlieb, ed., *Social Networks and Social Support.* Beverly Hills, Calif.: Sage.

Hirsch, J., and J. L. Knittle. 1970. Cellularity of obese and nonobese adipose tissue. *Federation Proceedings* 29:1516–21.

Hitchcock, L. S. 1982. Improving recovery from surgery: The interaction of preoperative interventions, coping processes, and personality variables. Ph.D. dissertation, University of California, Berkeley.

Hodges, W. F., and C. D. Spielberger. 1966. The effects of threat of shock on heart rate for subjects who differ in manifest anxiety and fear of shock. *Psychophysiology* 2:287–94.

Hofer, M. A., C. T. Wolff, S. B. Friedman, and J. W. Mason. 1972. A psychoendocrine study of bereavement: Parts I and II. *Psychosomatic Medicine* 34:481–504.

Hoffman, H. E. 1970. Use of avoidance and vigilance by repressors and sensitizers. *Journal of Consulting and Clinical Psychology* 34:91–96.

Holahan, C. J. 1982. *Environmental Psychology.* New York: Random House.

Holahan, C. J., and R. Moos. 1981. Social support and psychological distress: A longitudinal analysis. *Journal of Abnormal Psychology* 90:365–70.

Holahan, C. J., and R. H. Moos. 1986. Personality, coping, and family resources in stress resistance: A longitudinal analysis. *Journal of Personality and Social Psychology* 51:389–95.

Holahan, C. J., and R. H. Moos. 1987. Personal and contextual determinants of coping strategies. *Journal of Personality and Social Psychology* 52:946–55.

Holahan, C. K., C. J. Holahan, and S. S. Bells. 1984. Adjustment in aging: The roles of life stress, hassles, and self-efficacy. *Health Psychology* 3:315–28.

Holden, C. 1978. Cancer and the mind: How are they connected. *Science* 200:1363–69.

Holden, C. 1981. Cousins' account of self-cure rapped. *Science* 214:892.

Holmes, T. H., and M. Masuda. 1974. Life changes and illness susceptibility. In B. S. Dohrenwend and B. P. Dohrenwend, eds., *Stressful Life Events: Their Nature and Effects,* pp. 47–72. New York: Wiley.

Holmes, T. H., and R. H. Rahe. 1967a. *Schedule of Recent Experiences.* Seattle: School of Medicine, University of Washington.

Holmes, T. H., and R. H. Rahe. 1967b. The social readjustment rating scale. *Journal of Psychosomatic Research* 11:213–18.

Holroyd, K. A., and R. S. Lazarus. 1982. Stress, coping, and somatic adaptation.

In L. Goldberger and S. Breznitz, eds., *Handbook of Stress: Theoretical and Clinical Aspects,* pp. 21–35. New York: Free Press.

Horowitz, M. 1976. *Stress Response Syndromes.* New York: Jason Aronson.

Horowitz, M. J., and N. Wilner. 1980. Life events, stress, and coping. In L. Poon, ed., *Aging in the 1980's: Selected Contemporary Issues,* pp. 363–70. Washington, D.C.: American Psychological Association.

House, J. S., K. R. Landis, and D. Umberson. 1988. Social relationships and health. *Science* 241:540–45.

Houston, B. K. 1988. Division 38 survey: Synopsis of results. *Health Psychologist* 10:2–3.

Houts, P. S., T. W. Hu, R. A. Henderson, P. D. Cleary, and G. Tokuhata. 1984. Utilization of medical care following the Three Mile Island crisis. *American Journal of Public Health* 74:140–42.

Houts, P. S., R. W. Miller, G. K. Tokuhata, and K. S. Ham. 1980. Health related behavioral impact of the Three Mile Island nuclear incident. Manuscript submitted to the TMI Advisory Panel on Health Research Studies of the Pennsylvania Department of Health.

Howell, T., D. T. Fullerton, R. F. Harvey, and M. Klein. 1981. Depression in spinal cord injured patients. *Paraplegia* 19:284–88.

Hoyt, M. F., and B. H. Raven. 1973. Birth order and the 1971 Los Angeles earthquake. *Journal of Personality and Social Psychology* 28:123–28.

Hull, C. L. 1933. *Hypnosis and Suggestibility.* New York: Appleton.

Hull, J. G., R. R. Van-Treuren, and S. Virnelli. 1987. Hardiness and health: A critique and alternative approach. *Journal of Personality and Social Psychology* 53:518–30.

Hunter, F. T., and J. Youniss. 1982. Changes in functions of three relations during adolescence. *Developmental Psychology* 18:806–11.

Hurrell, J. 1987. An overview of organizational stress and health. In L. R. Murphy and T. F. Schoenborn, eds., *Stress Management in Work Settings,* pp. 31–45. Washington, D.C.: National Institute for Occupational Safety and Health.

Husaini, B. A., J. A. Neff, J. R. Newbrough, and M. C. Moore. 1982. The stress-buffering role of social support and personal competence among the rural married. *Journal of Community Psychology* 10:409–26.

Husak, W. S., and D. P. Hemenway. 1986. The influence of competition day practice on the activation and performance of collegiate swimmers. *Journal of Sport Behavior* 9:95–100.

Ikai, M., and A. H. Steinhaus. 1961. Some factors modifying the expression of human strength. *Journal of Applied Physiology* 16:157–63.

Ito, M. 1979. The differential effects of hypnosis and motivational suggestions on muscular strength. *Japanese Journal of Physical Education* 24:93–100.

Jackson, S. 1983. Participation in decision making as a strategy for reducing job-related strain. *Journal of Applied Psychology* 68:3–19.

Jacobs, M. A., and A. Z. Spilken. 1971. Personality patterns associated with heavy cigarette smoking in male college students. *Journal of Consulting and Clinical Psychology* 37:428.

Jacobs, S., and L. Douglas. 1979. Grief: A mediating process between a loss and illness. *Comprehensive Psychiatry* 20:165–76.

Jacobson, E. 1929. *Progressive Relaxation.* Chicago: University of Chicago Press.

Jacobson, E. 1931. Electrical measurements of neuromuscular states during mental activities. *American Journal of Physiology* 96:115–21.

Jacobson, E. 1976. *You Must Relax.* New York: McGraw-Hill.

Jaffe, D., C. Scott, and E. Orioli. 1986. Stress Management in the Workplace. Washington Business Group on Health, Worksite Wellness Series, Washington, D.C.

Jaffe, L., and A. Jaffe. 1976. Terminal candor and the coda syndrome. *American Journal of Nursing* 76:1938–40.

James, W. 1948. *Psychology.* New York: World.

Jameson, J., L. Shuman, and W. Young. 1978. The effects of outpatient psychiatric utilization on the cost of providing third-party coverage: A study sponsored by Blue Cross of Western Pennsylvania, a research series 18. *Medical Care* 16:383–99.

Janis, I. L. 1958. *Psychological Stress: Psychoanalytic and Behavioral Studies of Surgical Patients.* New York: Wiley.

Janis, I. L. 1983. Stress inoculation in health care: Theory and research. In D. Meichenbaum and M. E. Jaremko, eds., *Stress Reduction and Prevention,* pp. 67–99. New York: Plenum.

Janis, I. L., and L. Mann. 1977. *Decision Making: A Psychological Analysis of Conflict, Choice, and Commitment.* New York: Free Press.

Janoff-Bulman, R. 1979. Characterological versus behavioral self-blame: Inquiries into depression and rape. *Journal of Personality and Social Psychology* 37:1798–1809.

Janoff-Bulman, R., and I. H. Frieze. 1983. A theoretical perspective for understanding reactions to victimization. *Journal of Social Issues* 39:1–17.

Janz, N. K., and M. H. Becker. 1984. The health belief model: A decade later. *Health Education Quarterly* 11:1–47.

Jemmott, J. B., III. 1985. Psychoneuroimmunology. *American Behavioral Scientist* 28:497–509.

Jemmott, J. B., III, R. T. Croyle, and P. H. Ditto. 1988. Commonsense epidemiology: Self-based judgments from laypersons and physicians. *Health Psychology* 7:55–73.

Jenkins, C. D. 1971. Psychologic and social precursors of coronary disease. *New England Journal of Medicine* 284:244–55; 307–17.

Jenkins, C. D. 1976. Recent evidence supporting psychological and social risk factors for coronary disease. *New England Journal of Medicine* 294:987–94; 1033–38.

Jenkins, C. D. 1979. Psychosocial modifiers of response to stress. *Journal of Human Stress* 5:3–15.

Jenkins, C. D., S. J. Zyzanski, and R. H. Rosenman. 1971. Progress toward validation of a computer-scored test for the type A coronary-prone behavior pattern. *Psychosomatic Medicine* 33:193–202.

Jenkins, C. D., S. J. Zyzanski, T. J. Ryan, A. Flessas, and S. I. Tannenbaum.

1977. Social insecurity and coronary-prone Type A responses as identifiers of severe atherosclerosis. *Journal of Consulting and Clincial Psychology* 45:1060–67.

Jennings, J. R., and S. Choi. 1981. Type A components and psychophysiological responses to an attention-demanding performance task. *Psychosomatic Medicine* 43:475–87.

Jessor, R., and S. L. Jessor. 1982. Adolescence to young adulthood: A twelve year prospective study of problem behavior and psychosocial development. In A. A. Mednick and M. Harway, eds., *Longitudinal Research in the United States,* pp. 34–61. Boston: Martinus Nijhoff.

Jette, S. H. 1983. Nursing the person with loss. In J. Lindbergh, M. Hunter, and A. Kruszewski, eds., *Introduction to Person-Centered Nursing,* pp. 641–57. Philadelphia: Lippincott.

Joffe, P. E., and B. A. Bast. 1978. Coping and defense in relation to accommodation among a sample of blind men. *Journal of Nervous and Mental Diseases* 166:537–52.

Joffe, P. E., and M. Naditch. 1977. Paper and pencil measures of coping and defense processes. In N. Haan, ed., *Coping and Defending: Processes of Self-Environment Organization,* pp. 280–97. New York: Academic Press.

Johnson, J. 1986. *Life Events as Stressors in Childhood and Adolescence.* Beverly Hills, Calif.: Sage.

Johnson, J. E., and H. Leventhal. 1974. Effects of accurate expectations and behavioral instructions on reactions during a noxious medical examination. *Journal of Personality and Social Psychology* 29:710–18.

Johnson, W. R. 1961. Hypnosis and muscular performance. *Journal of Sports Medicine and Physical Fitness* 1:71–79.

Jones, J., and J. Dosedel. 1986. The impact of corporate stress management on insurance losses. *Legal Insight* 1:24–27.

Jones, K., and T. Vischi. 1979. Impact of alcohol, drug abuse and mental health treatment on medical care utilization: A review of the research literature. *Medical Care* (supplement) 17:ii–82.

Jose, W., and D. Anderson. 1986. Control data: The stay well program. *Corporate Commentary* 2:1–13.

Jourard, S. 1971. Some lethal aspects of the male role. In J. Pleck and J. Sawyer, eds., *Men and Masculinity.* Englewood Cliffs, N.J.: Prentice-Hall.

Julius, S. A. 1977. Borderline hypertension: Epidemiologic and clinical implication. In J. Genest, E. Koiw, and O. Kuchel, eds., *Hypertension Physiopathology and Treatment,* pp. 630–40. New York: McGraw-Hill.

Juni, S. 1982. The composite measure of the Defense Mechanism Inventory. *Journal of Research in Personality* 16:193–200.

Juni, S., and J. Masling. 1980. Reaction to aggression and the Defense Mechanism Inventory. *Journal of Personality Assessment* 44:484–86.

Kahn, J. P., D. S. Kornfeld, D. K. Blood, R. B. Lynn, S. S. Heller, and K. A. Frank. 1982. Type A behavior and the thallium stress test. *Psychosomatic Medicine* 44:431–36.

Kahn, J. P., D. S. Kornfeld, K. A. Frank, S. S. Heller, and P. F. Hoar. 1980. Type A behavior and blood pressure during coronary artery bypass surgery. *Psychosomatic Medicine* 42:407–13.

Kahn, R. L., D. M. Wolfe, R. P. Quinn, J. D. Snoek, and R. A. Rosenthal. 1964. *Organizational Stress: Studies in Role Conflict and Ambiguity.* New York: Wiley.

Kalish, R. A. 1981a. *Death, Grief, and Caring Relationships.* Monterey, Calif.: Brooks/Cole.

Kalish, R. A. 1981b. Services for the dying. In A. Monk, ed., *Handbook of Gerontological Services.* New York: Van Nostrand Reinhold.

Kaloupek, D. G., H. White, and M. Wong. 1984. Multiple assessment of coping strategies used by volunteer blood donors: Implications for preparatory training. *Journal of Behavioral Medicine* 7:35–60.

Kandel, D. B., and G. S. Lesser. 1972. *Youth in Two Worlds: U.S. and Denmark.* San Francisco: Jossey-Bass.

Kane, R. L., L. Berstein, J. Wales, and R. Rothenberg. 1985a. Hospice effectiveness in controlling pain. *Journal of the American Medical Association* 253:2683–86.

Kane, R. L., S. J. Klein, L. Berstein, R. Rothenberg, and J. Wales. 1985b. Hospice role in alleviating the emotional stress of terminal patients and their families. *Medical Care* 23:189–97.

Kane, R. L., J. Wales, L. Berstein, A. Leibowitz, and S. Kaplan. 1984. A randomized controlled trial of hospice care. *Lancet* 890–94.

Kanner, A. D. 1981. Specificity of the impact of daily hassles and uplifts on adaptational outcomes: An analysis of gender, employment status and Type A behavior. Ph.D. dissertation, University of California, Berkeley.

Kanner, A. D., J. C. Coyne, C. Schaefer, and R. S. Lazarus. 1981. Comparison of two modes of stress measurement: Daily hassles and uplifts versus major life events. *Journal of Behavioral Medicine* 4:1–39.

Kanner, A. D., and S. S. Feldman. (n.d.) Control over uplifts and hassles and its relationship to adaptational outcomes. Manuscript.

Kanner, A. D., S. S. Feldman, D. A. Weinberger, and M. E. Ford. 1987. Uplifts, hassles, and adaptational outcomes in early adolescents. *Journal of Early Adolescence* 7:371–94.

Kanner, A. D., A. Harrison, and D. Wertlieb. 1985. Development of the children's hassles and uplifts scales. Poster session presentation at the meeting of the American Psychological Association, Los Angeles, California, August.

Kanner, A. D., D. Kafry, and A. Pines. 1978. Conspicuous in its absence: The lack of positive conditions as a source of stress. *Journal of Human Stress* 4:33–39.

Kaplan, R. M. 1984. The connection between clinical health promotion and health status: A critical overview. *American Psychologist* 39:755–65.

Kardiner, A., R. Linton, L. DuBois, and J. West. 1945. *The Psychological Frontiers of Society.* New York: Columbia University Press.

Karney, R. J. 1976. Psychosocial aspects of the spinal cord injured: The psychologist's approach. In W. M. Jenkins, R. M. Anderson, and W. L. Deitrich, eds., *Rehabilitation of the Severely Disabled*, pp. 201–5. Dubuque, Ia.: Kendall/Hunt.

Karoly, P. 1985. The assessment of pain: Concepts and procedures. In P. Karoly, ed., *Measurement Strategies in Health Psychology*. New York: Wiley.

Kasl, S. V. 1983. Pursuing the link between stressful life experiences and disease: A time for reappraisal. In C. L. Cooper, ed., *Stress Research*, pp. 79–102. New York: Wiley.

Kasl, S. V., and C. L. Cooper, eds. 1987. *Stress and Health: Issues in Research Methodology*. Chichester, Great Britain: John Wiley & Sons.

Kastenbaum, R. J. 1975a. Towards standards of care for the terminally ill, Part I: That a need exists. *Omega* 6:77–80.

Kastenbaum, R. J. 1975b. Towards standards of care for the terminally ill, Part II: What standards exist today? *Omega* 6:289–90.

Kastenbaum, R. J. 1977. *Death, Society, and Human Experience*. St. Louis: Mosby.

Kastenbaum, R. J., and A. D. Weisman. 1972. The psychological autopsy as a research procedure in gerontology. In D. Kent, R. J. Kastenbaum, and S. Sherwood, eds., *Research, Planning, and Action for the Elderly*. New York: Behavioral Publications.

Kates, R. W., J. E. Haas, D. J. Amaral, R A. Olson, R. Ramos, and R. Olson. 1973. Human impact of the Managua earthquake: Transitional societies are peculiarly vulnerable to natural disasters. *Science* 182:981–89.

Katz, J. L., H. Weiner, T. G. Gallagher, and L. Hellman. 1970. Stress, distress, and ego defenses. *Archives of General Psychiatry* 23:131–42.

Katz, R. 1980. Time and work: Toward an integrative perspective. In B. Staw and L. Cummings, eds., *Research in Organizational Behavior*, vol. 2. Greenwich, Conn.: JAI Press.

Kavenaugh, R. 1974. *Facing Death*. Baltimore: Penguin.

Keeley, K. 1962. Prenatal influence on behavior of offspring of crowded mice. *Science* 135:44–45.

Kemeny, M. E. 1985. Psychological and immunological predictors of genital herpes recurrence. Ph.D. dissertation, University of California, San Francisco.

Kemeny, M. E., H. Weiner, S. E. Taylor, S. Schneider, B. Visscher, and J. L. Fahey. 1989. Repeated bereavement, depressed mood, and immune parameters in HIV seropositive and seronegative homosexual men. Manuscript.

Kerr, W., and M. Thompson. 1972. Acceptance of disability of sudden onset in paraplegia. *Paraplegia* 10:94–102.

Kessler, R. C., and J. D. McLeod. 1984. Sex differences in vulnerability to undesirable life events. *American Sociological Review* 49:620–31.

Kessler, R. C., R. H. Price, and C. B. Wortman. 1985. Social factors in psychopathology: Stress, social support, and coping processes. *Annual Review of Psychology* 36:531–72.

Kiecolt-Glaser, J. K., and R. Glaser. In press. Behavioral influences on immune function: Evidence for the interplay between stress and health. In T. Field, P. McCabe, and N. Schneiderman, eds., *Stress and Coping,* vol. 2. Hillsdale, N. J.: Erlbaum.

Kiecolt-Glaser, J. K., R. Glaser, E. C. Shuttleworth, C. S. Dyer, P. Ogrocki, and C. E. Speicher. 1987. Chronic stress and immunity in family caregivers of Alzheimer's disease victims. *Psychosomatic Medicine* 49:523–35.

Kinderlehrer, J. 1974. Vitamin C: The best thing that ever happened to antibiotics. *Prevention* 26:71–75.

Kirschenbaum, D. S., J. Sherman, and J. D. Penrod. 1987. Promoting self-directed hemodialysis: Measurement and cognitive-behavioral intervention. *Health Psychology* 6:373–85.

Kirschenbaum, D. S., D. A. Wittrock, R. J. Smith, and W. Monson. 1984. Criticism inoculation training: Concept in search of a strategy. *Journal of Sport Psychology* 6:77–93.

Klas, L. D. 1970. A study of the relationship between depression and factors in the rehabilitation process of the hospitalized spinal cord injured patient. Ph.D. dissertation, University of Utah, Salt Lake City.

Klenner, F. R. 1971. Observations on the dose and administration of ascorbic acid when employed beyond the range of a vitamin in human pathology. *Journal of Applied Nutrition* 23:61–87.

Klerman, G. L., and J. E. Izen. 1977. The effects of bereavement and grief on physical health and general well-being. *Advances in Psychosomatic Medicine* 9:63–104.

Klinger, E. 1975. Consequences of commitment to and disengagement from incentives. *Psychological Review* 82:1–25.

Klinger, E. 1977. *Meaning and Void: Inner Experience and the Incentives in People's Lives.* Minneapolis: University of Minnesota Press.

Knight, R. B., A. Atkins, C. J. Eagle, N. Evans, J. W. Finkelstein, D. Fukushima, J. Katz, and H. Weiner. 1979. Psychological stress, ego defenses, and cortisol productions in children hospitalized for elective surgery. *Psychosomatic Medicine* 41:40–49.

Knorr, N. J., and J. C. Bull. 1970. Spinal cord injury: Psychiatric considerations. *Maryland State Medical Journal* 19:105–8.

Knudson, A. G., and J. M. Natterson. 1960. Participation of parents in the hospital care of their fatally ill children. *Pediatrics* 26:482–90.

Kobasa, S. C. 1979. Stressful events, personality, and health: An inquiry into hardiness. *Journal of Personality and Social Psychology* 37:1–11.

Kobasa, S. C., S. R. Maddi, and S. Courington. 1981. Personality and constitution as mediators in the stress-illness relationship. *Journal of Health and Social Behavior* 22:368–78.

Kobasa, S. C., S. R. Maddi, and S. Kahn. 1982. Hardiness and health: A prospective study. *Journal of Personality and Social Psychology* 42:168–77.

Kobasa, S. C., S. R. Maddi, and M. C. Puccetti. 1982. Personality and exercise as buffers in the stress-illness relationship. *Journal of Behavioral Medicine* 4:391–404.

Kobasa, S. C., S. R. Maddi, M. C. Puccetti, and M. A. Zola. 1983. Effectiveness of hardiness, exercise, and social support as resources against illness. Manuscript.

Kobasa, S. C., S. R. Maddi, and M. A. Zola. 1983. Type A and hardiness. *Journal of Behavioral Medicine* 6:41–51.

Kobasa, S. C., and M. C. Puccetti. 1983. Personality and social resources in stress-resistance. *Journal of Personality and Social Psychology* 45:839–50.

Koford, C. B. 1963. Rank of mothers and sons in bands of rhesus monkeys. *Science* 141:356–57.

Kohl, R. M., D. L. Roenker, and P. E. Turner. 1985. Clarification of competent imagery as a prerequisite for effective skill imagery. *International Journal of Sport Psychology* 16:37–45.

Kohn, M. L., and C. Schooler. 1978. The reciprocal effects of substantive complexity of work and intellectual flexibility: A longitudinal assessment. *American Journal of Sociology* 84:24–52.

Kohn, M. L., and C. Schooler. 1982. Job conditions and personality: A longitudinal assessment of their reciprocal effects. *American Journal of Sociology* 87:1257–86.

Kolonay, B. J. 1977. The effects of visual-motor behavior rehearsal on athletic performance. Master's thesis, Hunter College, New York.

Kon, I. S., and V. A. Losenkov. 1978. Friendship in adolescence: Values and behavior. *Journal of Marriage and the Family* 40:143–55.

Korman, A. K. 1980. *Career Success and Personal Failure.* Englewood Cliffs, N.J.: Prentice-Hall.

Kornhauser, A. 1965. *Mental Health and the Industrial Worker.* New York: Wiley.

Kosslyn, S. M., S. Pinker, G. E. Smith, and S. P. Schwartz. 1981. On the demystification of mental imagery. In N. Block, ed., *Imagery.* Cambridge, Mass.: MIT Press.

Kosten, T. R., S. C. Jacobs, and S. V. Kasl. 1984. Terminal illness, bereavement, and the family. In D. C. Turk and R. D. Kerns, eds., *Health, Illness, and Families,* pp. 311–37. New York: Wiley.

Kovacs, M. 1980. Rating scales to assess depression in school-aged children. *Acta Paedopsychiatrica* 46:305–15.

Krantz, D. S., J. M. Arabian, J. E. Davia, and J. S. Parker. 1982. Type A behavior and coronary artery bypass surgery: Intraoperative blood pressure and perioperative complications. *Psychosomatic Medicine* 44:273–84.

Krantz, D. S., D. C. Glass, R. Contrada, and N. E. Miller. 1981. Behavior and health. In *National Science Foundation's Second Five-Year Outlook on Science and Technology.* Washington, D.C.: U. S. Government Printing Office.

Krantz, D. S., N. E. Grunberg, and A. Baum. 1985. Health psychology. *Annual Review of Psychology,* 36:349–83. Palo Alto, Calif.: Annual Reviews.

Krantz, D. S., and S. B. Manuck. 1984. Acute psychophysiologic reactivity and risk of cardiovascular disease: A review and methodologic critique. *Psychological Bulletin* 96:435–64.

Krantz, D. S., and R. Schulz. 1980. A model of life crisis, control, and health outcomes: Cardiac rehabilitation and relocation of the elderly. In A. Baum and J. E. Singer, eds., *Advances in Environmental Psychology: Applications of Personal Control,* 2:25–60. Hillsdale, N. J.: Erlbaum.

Kroeber, T. C. 1963. The coping functions of ego mechanism. In R. W. White, ed., *The Study of Lives,* pp. 178–98. Englewood Cliffs, N.J.: Prentice-Hall.

Kroger, W. 1963. *Clinical and Experimental Hypnosis.* Philadelphia: Lippincott.

Krohne, H. W., and L. Laux, eds. 1982. *Achievement, Stress and Anxiety.* Washington, D.C.: Hemisphere.

Krohne, H. W., and J. Rogner. 1982. Repression-sensitization as a central construct in coping research. In H. W. Krohne and L. Laux, eds., *Achievement, Stress, and Anxiety.* Washington, D.C.: Hemisphere.

Kübler-Ross, E. 1969. *On Death and Dying.* New York: Macmillan.

Lacey, J. I., J. Kagan, B. C. Lacey, and H. A. Moss. 1963. The visceral level: Situational determinants and behavioral correlates of autonomic response patterns. In P. H. Knapp, ed., *Expression of the Emotions in Man,* pp. 161–96. New York: International Universities Press.

LaMontagne, L. L. 1982. Children's locus of control beliefs as predictors of their preoperative coping behavior. Ph.D. dissertation, University of California, San Francisco.

Landers, D. M., S. H. Boutcher, and M. Q. Wang. 1986. A psychobiological study of archery performance. *Research Quarterly for Exercise and Sport* 57:236–44.

Langer, E. J., and J. Rodin. 1976. The effects of choice and enhanced personal responsibility for the aged: A field experiment in an institutional setting. *Journal of Personality and Social Psychology* 34:191–98.

LaRocco, J. M., J. S. House, and J. R. P. French, Jr. 1980. Social support, occupational stress, and health. *Journal of Health and Social Behavior* 21:202–18.

LaRocco, J. M., and A. P. Jones. 1978. Co-worker and leader support as moderators of stress-strain relationships in work situations. *Journal of Applied Psychology* 63:629–34.

Lasagna, L. 1962. Some explored and unexplored psychological variables in therapeutics. *Proceedings of the Royal Society of Medicine (London)* 55:773–76.

Lau, R. R., T. M. Bernard, and K. A. Hartman. 1989. Further explorations of common sense representations of common illnesses. *Health Psychology* 8:195–219.

Lau, R. R., R. Kane, S. Berry, J. Ware, and D. Roy. 1980. Channeling health: A review of televised health campaigns. *Health Education Quarterly* 7:56–89.

Laudenslager, M. L., S. M. Ryan, R. C. Drugan, R. L. Hyson, and S. F. Maier. 1983. Coping and immunosuppression: Inescapable but not escapable shock suppresses lymphocyte proliferation. *Science* 231:568–70.

Lawler, K. A., M. T. Allen, E. C. Critcher, and B. A. Standard. 1981. The relationship of physiological responses to the coronary-prone behavior pattern in children. *Journal of Behavioral Medicine* 4:203–16.

Lawson, N. C. 1976. Depression after spinal cord injury: A multimeasure longitudinal study. Ph.D. dissertation, University of Houston, Houston, Texas.

Layman, E. M. 1980. Meditation and sports performance. In W. F. Straub, ed., *Sport Psychology: An Analysis of Athlete Behavior.* Ithaca, N.Y.: Mouvement Publications.

Layne, O. L., Jr., and S. C. Yudofsky. 1971. Postoperative psychosis in cardiotomy patients. *New England Journal of Medicine* 284:518–20.

Lazarus, R. S. 1966. *Psychological Stress and the Coping Process.* New York: McGraw-Hill.

Lazarus, R. S. 1974. Psychological stress and coping in adaptation and illness. *International Journal of Psychiatry in Medicine* 5:321–33.

Lazarus, R. S. 1975. A cognitively oriented psychologist looks at biofeedback. *American Psychologist* 30:553–61.

Lazarus, R. S. 1975. The self-regulation of emotion. In L. Levi, ed., *Emotions—Their Parameters and Measurement,* pp. 47–67. New York: Raven Press.

Lazarus, R. S. 1983. The costs and benefits of denial. In S. Breznitz, ed., *The Denial of Stress,* pp. 1–30. New York: International Universities Press.

Lazarus, R. S. 1984a. Puzzles in the study of daily hassles. *Journal of Behavioral Medicine* 7:375–89.

Lazarus, R. S. 1984b. The trivialization of distress. In B. L. Hammonds and C. J. Scheirer, eds., *Psychology and Health,* 3:121–144. Washington, D. C.: American Psychological Association.

Lazarus, R. S. 1990. Theory-based stress measurement with peer commentaries and rejoinders. *Psychology Inquiry* 1:3–53.

Lazarus, R. S., and E. Alfert. 1964. The short-circuiting of threat. *Journal of Abnormal and Social Psychology* 69:195–205.

Lazarus, R. S., J. R. Averill, and E. M. Opton, Jr. 1970. Toward a cognitive theory of emotion. In M. Arnold, ed., *Feelings and Emotions,* pp. 207–31. New York: Academic Press.

Lazarus, R. S., J. R. Averill, and E. M. Opton, Jr. 1974. The psychology of coping: Issues of research and assessment. In G. V. Coelho, D. A. Hamburg, and J. E. Adams, eds., *Coping and Adaptation,* pp. 249–315. New York: Basic Books.

Lazarus, R. S., and J. B. Cohen. 1977. Environmental stress. In L. Altman and J. F. Wohlwill, eds., *Human Behavior and the Environment: Current Theory and Research,* 2:89–127. New York: Plenum.

Lazaurs, R. S., A. DeLongis, S. Folkman, and R. Gruen. 1985. Stress and adaptational outcomes: The problem of confounded measures. *American Psychologist* 40:770–79.

Lazarus, R. S., and S. Folkman. 1984a. Coping and adaptation. In W. D. Gentry, ed., *The Handbook of Behavioral Medicine,* pp. 282–325. New York: Guilford.

Lazarus, R. S., and S. Folkman. 1984b. *Stress, Appraisal, and Coping.* New York: Springer.

Lazarus, R. S., and S. Folkman. 1984c. The concept of coping. In R. S. Lazarus and S. Folkman, *Stress, Appraisal, and Coping,* pp. 117–40. New York: Springer.

Lazarus, R. S., and S. Folkman. 1989. *Manual for the Study of Daily Hassles and Uplifts Scales.* Palo Alto, Calif.: Consulting Psychologists Press.

Lazarus, R. S., A. D. Kanner, and S. Folkman. 1980. Emotions: A cognitive-phenomenological analysis. In R. Plutchik and H. Kellerman, eds., *Theories of Emotion,* pp. 189–217. New York: Academic Press.

Lazarus, R. S., and R. Launier. 1978. Stress-related transactions between person and environment. In L. A. Pervin and M. Lewis, eds., *Perspective in Interactional Psychology,* pp. 287–327. New York: Plenum.

Lefcourt, H. M. 1966. Repression-sensitization: A measure of the evaluation of emotional expression. *Journal of Consulting Psychology* 30:444–49.

Lefcourt, H. M., R. A. Martin, and W. E. Saleh. 1984. Locus of control and social support: Interactive moderators of stress. *Journal of Personality and Social Psychology* 47:378–89.

Lehman, D. R., C. B. Wortman, and A. F. Williams. 1987. Long-term effects of losing a spouse or child in a motor vehicle crash. *Journal of Personality and Social Psychology* 52:218–31.

Leik, R. K., S. A. Leik, K. Euker, and G. A. Gifford. 1982. *Under the Threat of Mount St. Helens: A Study of Chronic Family Stress.* Minneapolis: University of Minnesota, Family Study Center.

Leopold, R. L., and H. Dillon. 1963. Psychoanatomy of a disaster: A long-term study of post-traumatic neurosis in survivors of a marine explosion. *American Journal of Psychiatry* 119:913–21.

Leventhal, H. 1970. Findings and theory in the study of fear communications. In L. Berkowitz, ed., *Advances in Experimental Social Psychology.* 5:120–86. New York: Academic Press.

Leventhal, H., and P. D. Cleary. 1980. The smoking problem: A review of the research and theory in behavioral risk modification. *Psychological Bulletin* 88:370–405.

Leventhal, H., D. Meyers, and D. Nerenz. 1980. The commonsense representation of illness danger. In S. Rachman, ed., *Contributions to Medical Psychology,* pp. 7–30. Oxford, England: Pergamon Press.

Lever, J. 1976. Sex differences in the games children play. *Social Problems* 23:478–87.

Levine, A. 1982. *Love Canal: Science, Politics, and People.* New York: Lexington Books.

Levine, J., and E. Zigler. 1975. Denial and self-image in stroke, lung cancer, and heart disease victims. *Journal of Consulting and Clinical Psychology* 43:751–57.

Levine, M., and G. Spivack. 1964. *The Rorschach Index of Repressive Style.* Springfield, Ill.: Thomas.

Levinson, D. J. 1977. The mid-life transition: A period in adult psychological development. *Psychiatry* 40:99–112.

Levinson, D. J., et al. 1978. *The Seasons of a Man's Life.* New York: Ballantine Books.

Levy, S., R. Herberman, M. Lippman, and T. d'Angelo. 1987. Correlation of stress factors with sustained depression of natural killer cell activity and predicted prognosis in patients with breast cancer. *Journal of Clinical Oncology* 5:348–53.

Levy, S., R. Herberman, A. Maluish, B. Schlien, and M. Lippman. 1985. Prognostic risk assessment in primary breast cancer by behavioral and immunological parameters. *Health Psychology* 4:99–113.

Lewinsohn, P. M., and J. Talkington. 1979. Studies of the measurement of unpleasant events and relations with depression. *Applied Psychological Measures* 3:83–101.

Lewis, C. E., H. E. Freeman, and C. R. Corey. 1987. AIDS-related competence of California's primary care physicians. *American Journal of Public Health* 77:795–800.

Lewis, S., F. T. Horton, and S. Armstrong. 1981–82. Distress in fatally and chronically ill children: Methodological note. *Omega* 12:293–306.

Lidz, T. 1946. Nightmares and the combat neuroses. *Psychiatry* 9:37–49.

Lifton, R. J. 1976. *Death in Life.* New York: Touchstone.

Lilliston, B. A. 1985. Psychosocial responses to traumatic physical disability. *Social Work in Health Care* 10:1–13.

Lindemann, E. 1944. Symptomatology and management of acute grief. *American Journal of Psychiatry* 101:141–48.

Lipman, R. S., K. Rickles, L. Covi, L. R. Derogatis, and E. H. Uhlenhuth. 1969. Factors of symptom distress. *Archives of General Psychiatry* 21:328–38.

Lipowski, Z. J. 1970–1971. Physical illness, the individual and the coping process. *International Journal of Psychiatry in Medicine* 1:91–102.

Livingston, I. L. 1988. Co-factors, host susceptibility, and AIDS: An argument for stress. *Journal of the National Medical Association* 80:49–59.

Llewellyn, J. H., and J. A. Blucker. 1982. *Psychology of Coaching: Theory and Application.* Minneapolis, Minnesota: Burgess.

Locke, A. A., D. Sirota, and A. D. Wolfson. 1976. An experimental case study of the successes and failures of job enrichment in a government agency. *Journal of Applied Psychology* 61:701–11.

Locke, E. A. 1968. Toward a theory of task motivation and incentives. *Organizational Behavior and Human Performance* 3:157–89.

Locke, E. A. 1976. The nature and causes of job satisfaction. In M. Dunette, ed., *Handbook of Industrial and Organizational Psychology.* New York: Rand McNally.

Locke, E. A., and D. Henne. 1986. Work motivation theories. In C. Cooper and L. Robertson, eds., *International Review of Industrial and Organizational Psychology.* Chichester, England: Wiley.

Locke, E. A., and G. P. Latham. 1985. The application of goal setting to sports. *Journal of Sports Psychology* 7:205–22.

Locke, E. A., K. M. Shaw, L. M. Saari, and G. P. Latham. 1981. Goal setting and task performance: 1969–1980. *Psychological Bulletin* 90:125–52.

Locke, E. A., and M. S. Taylor. 1990. Stress, coping, and the meaning of work. In W. Nord and A. Brief, eds., *The Meaning of Work.* Lexington, Mass.: D. C. Heath.

Loevinger, J. 1976. *Ego Development.* San Francisco: Jossey-Bass.

Loewenstein, S. F. 1984. Fathers and mothers in midlife. Presentation to the

Family Track Seminar of the Boston University Department of Psychology, Boston.

Logue, J. N., and H. Hansen. 1980. A case-control study of hypertensive women in a post-disaster community: Wyoming Valley, Pennsylvania. *Journal of Human Stress* 6:28–34.

Logue, J. N., F. Hansen, and E. Struening. 1979. Emotional and physical distress following Hurricane Agnes in the Wyoming Valley of Pennsylvania. *Public Health Reports* 9:495–502.

Long, B. S. 1980. Stress management for the athlete: A cognitive behavioral model. In C. H. Nadeau, ed., *Psychology of Motor Behavior and Sport, 1979.* Champaign, Ill.: Human Kinetics.

Longfellow, C., P. Zelkowitz, E. Saunders, and D. Belle. 1979. The role of support in moderating the effects of stress and depression. Paper presented at the biennial meeting of the Society for Research in Child Development, San Francisco.

Loomis, C. P. 1960. *Social Systems: Essays and Their Persistence and Change.* New York: Van Nostrand.

Lorig, K., R. Kraines, B. Brown Jr., and N. Richardson. 1985. A workplace health education program that reduces outpatient visits. *Medical Care* 23:1044–54.

Lovallo, W. R., and V. Pishkin. 1980. A psychophysiological comparison of Type A and B men exposed to failure and uncontrollable noise. *Psychophysiology* 17:29–36.

Lowenthal, M. J., and C. Haven. 1968. Interaction and adaptation: Intimacy as a critical variable. *American Sociological Review* 33:20–30.

Lund, D. A., M. S. Caserta, and M. F. Dimond. 1986. Gender differences through two years of bereavement among the elderly. *Gerontologist* 26:314–19.

Lund, D. A., M. F. Dimond, M. S. Caserta, R. J. Johnson, J. L. Poulton, and J. R. Connelly. 1985–1986. Identifying elderly with coping difficulties after two years of bereavement. *Omega* 16:213–24.

Lundberg, U. 1982. Type A behavior and its relation to personality variables in Swedish male and female university students. *Scandinavian Journal of Psychology* 21:133–38.

Luthe, W. 1965. *Autogenic Training.* New York: Grune and Stratton.

McAdoo, H. 1980. Black mothers and the extended family support network. In L. Rodgers-Rose, ed., *The Black Woman.* Beverly Hills, Calif.: Sage.

McClelland, D. C. 1958. Risk-taking in children with high and low need for achievement. In J. W. Atkinson, ed., *Motives in Fantasy, Action, and Society.* New York: Van Nostrand Reinhold.

McClelland, D. C. [1951] 1976. *The Achieving Society.* New York: Irvington.

Maccoby, M. 1976. *The Gamesmen.* New York: Simon & Schuster.

McCrae, R. R. 1982. Age differences in the use of coping mechanisms. *Journal of Gerontology* 37:454–60.

McCrae, R. R. 1984. Situational determinants of coping responses: Loss, threat, and challenge. *Journal of Personality and Social Psychology* 46:919–28.

McCranie, E. W., M. E. Simpson, and J. S. Stevens. 1981. Type A behavior, field

dependence, and serum lipids. *Psychosomatic Medicine* 43:107–16.
McCurdy, S., and L. Wright. 1986. A test for time urgency. Manuscript.
McDonald, D. G., J. Stern, and W. Hahn. 1963. Effects of differential housing and stress on diet selection, water intake, and body weight in the rat. *Journal of Applied Physiology* 18:937–42.
Mace, R. D., and D. Carroll. 1985. The control of anxiety in sport: Stress inoculation training prior to abseiling. *International Journal of Sport Psychology* 16:165–75.
McGrath, J. E. 1970. Settings, measures, and themes: An integrative review of some research on social-psychological factors in stress. In J. E. McGrath, ed., *Social and Psychological Factors in Stress,* pp. 76–83. New York: Holt, Rinehart, and Winston.
McIntosh, J. 1976. Patients' awareness and desire for information about diagnosed but undisclosed malignant disease. *Lancet* 2:300–3.
Mackintosh, J. H. 1962. Effect of strain and group size on the response of mice to "seconal" anaesthesia. *Nature* 194:1304.
McKissick, G. E., G. L. Flickinger, and H. L. Ratcliffe. 1961. Coronary arteriosclerosis in isolated, paired, and grouped chickens. *Proceedings of the Federation of American Societies for Experimental Biology* 20:91.
McLanahan, S. S., N. V. Wedemeyer, and T. Adelberg. 1981. Network structure, social support, and psychological well-being in the single-parent family. *Journal of Marriage and the Family* 43:601–12.
McLeroy, K., L. Green, K. Mullen, and V. Foshee. 1984. Assessing the effects of health promotion in worksites: A review of the stress program evaluations. *Health Education Quarterly* 11:379–401.
McLuckie, B. F. 1975. Centralization and natural disaster response: A preliminary hypothesis and interpretations. *Mass Emergencies* 1:1–9.
McMullen, P. A., and A. E. Gross. 1983. Sex differences, sex roles, and health-related help-seeking. In B. DePaulo, A Nadler, and J. Fisher, eds., *New Directions in Helping,* vol. 2. New York: Academic Press.
Maddi, S. R., and S. C. Kobasa. 1984a. The development of hardiness. In S. R. Maddi and S. C. Kobasa, *The Hardy Executive: Health Under Stress,* pp. 46–58. Homewood, Ill.: Dow Jones-Irwin.
Maddi, S. R., and S. C. Kobasa. 1984b. *The Hardy Executive: Health Under Stress.* Homewood, Ill.: Dow Jones-Irwin.
Maddison, D., and W. L. Walker. 1967. Factors affecting the outcome of conjugal bereavement. *British Journal of Psychiatry* 113:1057–67.
Mages, N. L., and G. A. Mendelsohn. 1979. Effects of cancer on patients' lives: A personological approach. In G. C. Stone, F. Cohen, and N. E. Adler, eds., *Health Psychology: A Handbook,* pp. 255–84. San Francisco: Jossey-Bass.
Mahoney, M. J., ed. 1980. *Psychotherapy Process: Current Issues and Future Directions.* New York: Plenum.
Mahoney, M. J., and M. Avener. 1977. Psychology of the elite athlete: An exploratory study. *Cognitive Therapy and Research* 1:135–41.
Mahoney, M. J., T. J. Gabriel, and T. S. Perkins. 1987. Psychological skills and exceptional athletic performance. *Sport Psychologist* 1:181–99.

Makosky, V. 1980. Stress and the mental health of women: A discussion of research and issues. In M. Guttentag, S. Salasin, and D. Belle, eds., *The Mental Health of Women.* New York: Academic Press.

Malec, J., and R. Neimeyer. 1983. Psychological prediction of duration of inpatient spinal cord injury rehabilitation and performance of self-care. *Archives of Physical Medicine and Rehabilitation* 64:359–63.

Malinowski, B. [1926] 1948. *Magic, Science, and Religion and Other Essays.* Boston: Beacon.

Mandler, G. 1975. *Mind and Emotion.* New York: Wiley.

Mann, G. V. 1977. Diet-heart: End of an era. *New England Journal of Medicine* 297:646–50.

Mannes, M. 1973. *Last Rights.* New York: New American Library.

Manuso, J. 1983. The Equitable Life Assurance Society program. *Preventive Medicine* 12:658–62.

Margaret, S. M. 1977. A psychological study of the aged in the last stages of terminal illness. Ph.D. dissertation, University of California, Berkeley.

Mark, E. W., and T. G. Alper. 1985. Women, men, and intimacy motivation. *Psychology of Women Quarterly* 9:81–88.

Markus, H. 1986. Possible selves. *American Psychologist* 14:954–69.

Marlatt, G. A. 1983. The controlled-drinking controversy: A commentary. *American Psychologist* 38:1097–1110.

Marlatt, G. A. 1985. Relapse prevention: Theoretical rationale and overview of the model. In G. A. Marlatt and J. Gordon, eds., *Relapse Prevention: Maintenance Strategies in Addictive Behavior Change.* New York: Guilford.

Marlatt, G. A., B. Demming, and J. B. Reid. 1973. Loss of control drinking in alcoholics: An experimental analogue. *Journal of Abnormal Psychology* 81:223–41.

Marlatt, G. A., and J. R. Gordon, eds. 1985. *Relapse Prevention: Maintenance Strategies in the Treatment of Addictive Behaviors.* New York: Guilford.

Marris, P. 1958. *Widows and Their Families.* London: Routledge and Kegan Paul.

Martens, R. 1987. *Coaches Guide to Sport Psychology.* Champaign, Ill.: Human Kinetics.

Marx, J. L., and G. B. Kolata. 1978. *Combating the #1 Killer: The SCIENCE Report on Heart Research.* Washington, D.C.: American Association for the Advancement of Science.

Mason, J. W. 1959. Psychological influences on the pituitary-adrenal cortical system. *Recent Progress in Hormone Research* 15:345–89.

Mason, J. W. 1968. Organization of psychoendocrine mechanisms. *Psychosomatic Medicine* 30:565–791.

Mason, J. W. 1971. A re-evaluation of the concept of "non-specificity" in stress theory. *Journal of Psychiatric Research* 8:323–33.

Mason, J. W. 1974. Specificity in the organization of neuro-endocrine response profiles. In P. Seeman and G. M. Brown, eds., *Frontiers in Neurology and Neuroscience Research. First International Symposium of the Neuroscience Institute.* Tornoto: University of Toronto.

Mason, J. W. 1975a. A historical view of the stress field. Part I. *Journal of Human Stress* 1:6–12.

Mason, J. W. 1975b. A historical view of the stress field. Part II. *Journal of Human Stress* 1:22–36.

Mason, J. W. 1975c. Emotion as reflected in patterns of endocrine integration. In L. Levi, ed., *Emotions: Their Parameters and Measurement,* pp. 143–81. New York: Raven Press.

Mason, L., and A. Muhlenkamp. 1976. Patients' self-reported affective states following loss and caregivers' expectations of patients' affective states. *Rehabilitation Psychology* 23:72–76.

Massong, S. R., A. L. Dickson, and B. A. Ritzler. 1982. A correlational comparison of Defense Mechanism measures: The Defense Mechanism Inventory and the Blacky Defense Preference Inventory. *Journal of Personality Assessment* 46:477–80.

Matarazzo, J. D. 1980. Behavioral health and behavioral medicine: Frontiers for a new health psychology. *American Psychologist* 35:807–17.

Matarazzo, J. D. 1982. Behavioral health's challenge to academic, scientific, and professional psychology. *American Psychologist* 37:1–14.

Matarazzo, J. D. 1984. Behavioral health: A 1990 challenge for the health sciences professions. In J. D. Matarazzo, S. M. Weiss, J. A. Herd, N. E. Miller, and S. M. Weiss, eds., *Behavioral Health: A Handbook of Health Enhancement and Disease Prevention,* pp. 3–40. New York: Wiley.

Matarazzo, J. D., S. M. Weiss, J. A. Herd, N. E. Miller, and S. M. Weiss, eds. 1984. *Behavioral Health: A Handbook of Health Enhancement and Disease Prevention.* New York: Wiley.

Matheny, K. B., and P. Cupp. 1983. Control, desirability, and anticipation as moderating variables between life change and illness. *Journal of Human Stress* 9:14–23.

Matthews, K. A. 1982. Psychological perspectives on the Type A behavior pattern. *Psychological Bulletin* 91:293–323.

Matthews, K. A. 1988. Coronary heart disease and Type A behavior: Update on and alternative to the Booth-Kewley and Friedman (1987) quantitative review. *Psychological Bulletin* 104:373–80.

Matthews, K. A., D. C. Glass, R. H. Rosenman, and R. W. Bortner. 1977. Competitive drive, pattern A, and coronary heart disease: A further analysis of some data from the Western Collaborative Group Study. *Journal of Chronic Diseases* 30:489–98.

Matthews, K. A., R. L. Helmreich, W. E. Beane, and G. W. Lucker. 1980. Pattern A, achievement-striving, and scientific merit: Does pattern A help or hinder? *Journal of Personality and Social Psychology* 39:962–67.

Matthews, K. A., and J. R. Jennings. 1984. Cardiovascular responses of boys exhibiting the Type A behavior pattern. *Psychosomatic Medicine* 46:484–97.

Matthews, K. A., and J. M. Siegel. 1983. Type A behaviors by children, social comparison, and standards for self-evaluation. *Developmental Psychology* 19:135–40.

Matthews, K. A., and J. I. Volkin. 1981. Efforts to excel and the Type A behavior pattern in children. *Child Development* 52:1283–89.

Mechanic, D. 1978a. *Medical Sociology.* 2d ed. New York: Free Press.

Mechanic, D. [1962] 1978b. *Students Under Stress: A Study in the Social Psychology of Adaptation.* Madison: University of Wisconsin Press.

Mechanic, D. 1979. The stability of health and illness behavior: Results from a 16-year follow-up. *American Journal of Public Health* 69:1142–45.

Meeks, S., D. B. Arnkoff, C. R. Glass, and C. I. Notarius. 1985. Wives' employment status, hassles, communication, and relational efficacy: Intra- versus extra-relationship factors and marital adjustment. *Family Relations* 34:249–55.

Meichenbaum, D. 1977. *Cognitive-Behavior Modification: An Integrative Approach.* New York: Plenum.

Meichenbaum, D. 1985. *Stress Inoculation Training.* New York: Pergamon.

Meichenbaum, D., and D. C. Turk. 1987. *Facilitating Treatment Adherence.* New York: Plenum.

Melamed, B. G. 1986. Special issue on child health psychology. *Health Psychology* 5(3).

Melick, M. E. 1976. Social psychological and medical aspects of stress-related illness in the recovery period of a natural disaster. Ph.D. dissertation, State University of New York at Albany.

Menaghan, E. 1982. Measuring coping effectiveness: A panel analysis of marital problems and efforts. *Journal of Health and Social Behavior* 23:220–34.

Mendelsohn, G. A. 1979. The psychological consequences of cancer: A study of adaptation to somatic illness. *Cahiers d'Anthropologie* 2:53–92.

Menninger, K. A. 1963. *The Vital Balance: The Life Process in Mental Health and Illness.* New York: Viking.

Menninger, W. C. 1952. Psychological reactions in an emergency. *American Journal of Psychiatry* 109:128–30.

Mikhail, A. 1981. Stress: A psychophysiological conception. *Journal of Human Stress* 7:9–15.

Miles, M. S., and E. K. B. Crandall. 1983. The search for meaning and its potential for affecting growth in bereaved parents. *Health Values: Achieving High Level Wellness* 7:19–23.

Mileti, D. S., D. M. Hartsough, and P. Madson. 1982. The Three Mile Island Incident: A Study of Behavioral Indicators of Human Stress. Report prepared for Shaw, Pittman, Potts, & Trowbridge, Washington, D.C.

Miller, D. T., and C. A. Porter. 1983. Self-blame in victims of violence. *Journal of Social Issues* 39:139–52.

Miller, J. 1976. *Toward a New Psychology of Women.* Boston: Beacon.

Miller, M. 1979. *Suicide after Sixty: The Final Alternative.* New York: Haworth Press.

Miller, N. E. 1980. Applications of learning and biofeedback to psychiatry and medicine. In H. I. Kaplan, A. M. Freedman, and B. J. Sadock, eds., *Comprehensive Textbook of Psychiatry, III,* pp. 468–84. Baltimore, Md.: Williams and Wilkins.

Miller, N. E. 1980. A perspective on the effects of stress and coping on disease health. In S. Levine and H. Ursin, eds., *Coping and Health (NATO Conference Series III: Human Factors)*. New York: Plenum.

Miller, P. M., and J. G. Ingham. 1976. Friends, confidants, and symptoms. *Social Psychiatry* 11:51–58.

Miller, S. M. 1980. When is a little information a dangerous thing? Coping with stressful events by monitoring vs. blunting. In S. Levine and H. Ursin, eds., *Coping and Health*. New York: Plenum.

Miller, S. M., and C. E. Mangan.1983. Interacting effects of information and coping style in adapting to gynecologic stress: Should the doctor tell all? *Journal of Personality and Social Psychology* 45:223–36.

Millstein, S. G., and C. E. Irwin, Jr. 1987. Concepts of health and illness: Different constructs of variations on a theme? *Health Psychology* 6:515–24.

Milne, G. 1977. Cyclone Tracy: Some consequences of the evacuation for adult victims. *Australian Psychologist* 12:39–54.

Mischel, W. 1968. *Personality and Assessment*. New York: Wiley.

Mishel, M. H. 1984. Perceived uncertainty and stress in illness. *Research in Nursing and Health* 7:163–71.

Mishel, M. H., T. Hostetter, B. King, and V. Graham. 1984. Predictors of psychosocial adjustment in patients newly diagnosed with gynecological cancer. *Cancer Nursing* 7:291–99.

Mitchell, R., and C. Hodson. 1986. Coping and social support among battered women: An ecological perspective. In S. Hobfoll, ed., *Stress, Social Support and Women*. New York: Hemisphere.

Mitchell, R. E., R. C. Cronkite, and R. H. Moos. 1983. Stress, coping, and depression among married couples. *Journal of Abnormal Psychology* 92:433–48.

Molleman, E., P. J. Krabbendam, A. A. Annyas, H. S. Koops, D. T. Sleijfer, and A. Vermey. 1984. The significance of the doctor-patient relationship in coping with cancer. *Social Science and Medicine* 18:475–80.

Monat, A. 1976. Temporal uncertainty, anticipation time, and cognitive coping under threat. *Journal of Human Stress* 2:32–43.

Monat, A., J. R. Averill, and R. S. Lazarus. 1972. Anticipatory stress and coping reactions under various conditions of uncertainty. *Journal of Personality and Social Psychology* 24:237–53.

Monat, A., and R. S. Lazarus, eds. 1977. *Stress and Coping: An Anthology*. New York: Columbia University Press.

Monat, A., and R. S. Lazarus, eds. 1985. *Stress and Coping: An Anthology*. 2d ed. New York: Columbia University Press.

Monroe, S. M. 1983. Major and minor life events as predictors of psychological distress: Further issues and findings. *Journal of Behavioral Medicine* 6:189–205.

Moore, H. 1982. As quoted by C. Chandler in *The Ultimate Seduction*. Garden City: New York.

Moos, R. H. 1974. Psychological techniques in the assessment of adaptive behavior. In G. V. Coelho, D. A. Hamburg, and J. E. Adams, eds., *Coping and Adaptation,* pp. 334–97. New York: Basic Books.

Moos, R. H., ed. 1976. *Human Adaptation: Coping with Life Crises.* Lexington, Mass.: D. C. Heath.

Moos, R. H., ed. 1977. *Coping with Physical Illness.* New York: Plenum.

Moos, R. H., and A. G. Billings. 1982. Conceptualizing and measuring coping resources and processes. In L. Goldberger and S. Breznitz, eds., *Handbook of Stress: Theoretical and Clinical Aspects,* pp. 212–30. New York: Free Press.

Moos, R. H., P. M. Insel, and B. Humphrey. 1974. *Family, Work and Group Environment Scales Manual.* Palo Alto, Calif.: Consulting Psychologists Press.

Moos, R. H., and J. A. Schaefer. 1986. Life transitions and crises: A conceptual overview. In R. H. Moos, ed., *Coping with Life Crisis: An Integrated Approach,* pp. 3–28. New York: Plenum Press.

Moos, R. H., and V. D. Tsu. 1977. The crisis of physical illness: An overview. In R. H. Moos, ed., *Coping with Physical Illness.* New York: Plenum.

Mor, V., T. J. Wachtel, and D. Kidder. 1985. Patient predictors of hospice choice: Hospital versus home care programs. *Medical Care* 23:1115–19.

Morgan, W. P. 1972. Hypnosis and muscular performance. In W. P. Morgan, ed., *Ergogenic Aids in Muscular Performance.* New York: Academic Press.

Morgan, W. P., and D. R. Brown. 1983. Hypnosis. In M. H. Williams, ed., *Ergogenic Aids in Sport.* Champaign, Ill.: Human Kinetics.

Morris, J. N., V. Mor, R. J. Goldberg, S. Sherwood, D. S. Greer, and J. Hiris. 1986. The effect of treatment setting and patient characteristics on pain in terminal cancer patients: A report from the National Hospice Study. *Journal of Chronic Diseases* 39:27–35.

Morrissey, J. R. 1965. Death anxiety in children with a fatal illness. In H. J. Parad, ed., *Crisis Intervention,* pp. 324–38. New York: Family Service Association of America.

Morse, N. C., and R. S. Weiss. 1955. The function and meaning of work and the job. *The American Sociological Review* 191–98.

Mortimer, J. T., and J. Lorence. 1979. Work experience and occupational value socialization: A longitudinal study. *American Journal of Sociology* 84:1361–85.

Moskowitz, D. S. 1982. Coherence and cross-situational generality in personality: A new analysis of old problems. *Journals of Personality and Social Psychology* 43:754–68.

Moulton, J. M. 1985. Adjustment to a diagnosis of AIDS or ARC in gay men. Ph.D. dissertation, California School of Professional Psychology, Berkeley.

Mullen, B., and J. Suls. 1982. The effectiveness of attention and rejection as coping styles: A meta-analysis of temporal differences. *Journal of Psychosomatic Research* 26:43–49.

Multiple Risk Factor Intervention Trial Research Group (MRFIT). 1982. Multiple risk factor intervention trial: Risk factor changes and mortality results. *Journal of the American Medical Association* 248:1465–77.

Mumford, E., H. Schlesinger, and G. Glass. 1982. The effects of psychological intervention on recovery from surgery and heart attacks: An analysis of the literature. *American Journal of Public Health* 72:141–51.

Murphy, L. 1982. Worksite stress management programs. *Employee Assistance Programs Digest* 2:22–25.

Murphy, L. 1983. A comparison of relaxation methods for reducing stress in nursing personnel. *Human Factors* 25:431–40.

Murphy, L. B. 1962. *The Widening World of Childhood.* New York: Basic Books.

Murphy, L. B. 1974. Coping, vulnerability, and resilience in childhood. In G. V. Coelho, D. A. Hamburg, and J. E. Adams, eds., *Coping and Adaptation,* pp. 69–100. New York: Basic Books.

Murphy, L. R. 1984. Occupational stress management: A review and appraisal. *Journal of Occupational Psychology* 57:1–15.

Murphy, S. 1985. Conceptual bases for disaster research and intervention. In J. Laube and S. A. Murphy, eds., *Perspectives on Disaster Recovery.* New York: Appleton-Century-Crofts.

Murphy, S. M., and R. L. Woolfolk. 1987. The effects of cognitive interventions on competitive anxiety and performance on a fine motor skill accuracy task. *International Journal of Sport Psychology* 18:152–66.

Myers, G. C. 1985. Demographics of the aging populations—Key issues. In B. J. Jaeger, ed., *Graying Americans and Our Health System.* Durham, N.C.: Duke University Press.

Myers, J. K., J. J. Lindenthal, M. P. Pepper, and D. R. Ostrander. 1972. Life events and mental status: A longitudinal study. *Journal of Health and Social Behavior* 13:398–406.

Nakell, L. 1985. Family adaptation to the stress of having a premature baby cared for in the intensive care nursery. Ph.D. dissertation, University of California, San Francisco.

National Institutes of Health Review Panel on Coronary-Prone Behavior and Coronary Heart Disease. 1981. Coronary-prone behavior and coronary heart disease: A critical review. *Circulation* 63:1199–1215.

National Research Council. 1982. *Risk and Decision Making.* Washington, D.C.: National Academy Press.

Natterson, J. M., and A. G. Knudson. 1960. Observations concerning fear of death in fatally ill children and their mothers. *Psychosomatic Medicine* 22:445–65.

Neal, D. 1984. Blame assignment in a diffuse disaster situation: A case example of the role of an emergent citizen group. *Mass Emergencies* 2:251–66.

Neal, D. M., and J. B. Perry. 1980. A note on blame and disasters: A case of the winter of 1976–1977. Paper presented at the North Central Association Meeting in Dayton, Ohio.

Near, J. P., R. W. Rice, and R. J. Hunt. 1980. The relationship between work and nonwork domains: A review of empirical research. *Academy of Management Review* 5:415–29.

Nelson-LeGall, S., R. A. Gumerman, and D. Scott-Jones. 1983. Instrumental help-seeking and everyday problem-solving: A developmental perspective. In B. DePaulo, A. Nadler, and J. Fisher, eds., *New Directions in Helping,* vol. 2. New York: Academic Press.

Nemiah, J. C. 1957. The psychiatrist and rehabilitation. *Archives of Physical Medicine and Rehabilitation* 38:143–47.

Neugarten, B. L. 1969. Continuities and discontinuities of psychological issues into adult life. *Human Development* 12:121–30.

Neugarten, B. L., J. W. Moore, and J. C. Lowe. 1965. Age norms, age constraints, and adult socialization. *American Journal of Sociology* 70:710–17.

Newman, C. J. 1976. Children of disaster: Clincial observations at Buffalo Creek. *American Journal of Psychiatry* 133:206–312.

Newsweek. 1988. Body and soul.

Nideffer, R. M. 1976. *The Inner Athlete: Mind Plus Muscle for Winning.* New York: Crowell.

Nideffer, R. M. 1981. *The Ethics and Practice of Applied Sport Psychology.* Ithaca, N. Y.: Mouvement Publications.

Nideffer, R. M. 1985. *Athlete's Guide to Mental Training.* Champaign, Ill.: Human Kinetics.

Nideffer, R. M., and C. W. Deckner. 1970. A case study of improved athletic performance following use of relaxation procedures. *Perceptual and Motor Skills* 30:821–22.

Nisbett, R. E., and L. D. Ross. 1980. *Human Inference: Strategies and Shortcomings of Social Judgment.* Englewood Cliffs, N.J.: Prentice-Hall.

Noel, R. C. 1980. The effect of visual-motor behavior rehearsal on tennis performance. *Journal of Sport Psychology* 2:221–26.

Nomikos, M. S., E. M. Opton, Jr., J. R. Averill, and R. S. Lazarus. 1968. Surprise versus suspense in the production of stress reaction. *Journal of Personality and Social Psychology* 8:204–8.

Nuckolls, K. B., J. Cassel, and B. H. Kaplan. 1972. Psychosocial assets, life crisis and the prognosis of pregnancy. *American Journal of Epidemiology* 95:431–41.

Obrist, P. A. 1981. *Cardiovascular Psychophysiology: A Perspective.* New York: Plenum.

Orlick, T. 1986. *Psyching for Sport Mental Training for Athletes.* Champaign, Ill.: Leisure Press.

Orne, M. T. 1959. The nature of hypnosis: Artifact and essence. *Journal of Abnormal and Social Psychology* 58:277–99.

O'Rourke, D. F., B. K. Houston, J. K. Harris, and C. R. Snyder. 1988. The Type A behavior pattern: Summary, conclusions and implications. In B. K. Houston and C. R. Snyder, eds., *Type A Behavior Pattern: Research, Theory, and Intervention,* pp. 1–7. New York: Wiley.

Ortony, A., and G. L. Clore. 1981. Disentangling the affective lexicon. In *Proceedings of the Third Annual Conference of the Cognitive Science Society,* Berkeley, Calif.

Ossip-Klein, D. J., R. M. Shapiro, and J. Stiggins. 1984. Brief report: Freedom line: Increasing utilization of a telephone support service for ex-smokers. *Addictive Behaviors* 9:227–30.

Osterweis, M., F. Solomon, and M. Green, eds. 1984. *Bereavement: Reactions, Consequences, and Care.* Washington, D.C.: National Academy Press.

Oxendine, J. B. 1970. Emotional arousal and motor performance. *Quest* 13:23–30.

Packer, E. 1984. The psychological requirements of a free society. *Objectivist Forum* 5:1–11.

Page, J. D. 1971. *Psychopathology: The Science of Understanding Deviance.* Chicago: Aldine-Atherton.

Pahnke, W. A. 1969. The psychedelic mystical experience in human encounters with death. *Harvard Theological Review* 62:1–32.

Parker, G. 1977. Cyclone Tracy and Darwin evacuees. On the restoration of the species. *British Journal of Psychiatry* 130:548–55.

Parkes, C. M. 1972. *Bereavement: Studies of Grief in Adult Life.* New York: International Universities Press.

Parkes, C. M. 1979a. Terminal care: Evaluation of in-patient service at St. Christopher's Hospice, Part 1: Views of surviving spouse on effects of the service on the patient. *Postgraduate Medical Journal* 55:517–22.

Parkes, C. M. 1979b. Terminal care: Evaluation of in-patient service at St. Christopher's Hospice, Part 2: Self-assessments of effects of the service on surviving spouses. *Postgraduate Medical Journal* 55:523–27.

Parkes, C. M. 1980. Terminal care: Evaluation of an advisory domiciliary service at St. Christopher's Hospice. *Postgraduate Medical Journal* 56:685–89.

Parkes, C. M. 1985. Terminal care: Home, hospital, or hospice? *Lancet* 155–57.

Parkes, C. M., and J. Parkes. 1984. "Hospice" versus "hospital" care: Re-evaluation after 10 years as seen by surviving spouses. *Postgraduate Medical Journal* 60:120–24.

Parkes, C. M., and R. S. Weiss. 1983. *Recovery from Bereavement.* New York: Basic Books.

Parkes, K. R. 1984. Locus of control, cognitive appraisal, and coping in stressful episodes. *Journal of Personality and Social Psychology* 46:655–68.

Parsell, S., and E. M. Tagliareni. 1974. Cancer patients help each other. *American Journal of Nursing* 74:650–51.

Parsons, T., and R. Bales. 1955. *Family, Socialization, and Interaction Process.* New York: Free Press.

Patterson, G. R. 1983. Stress: A change agent for family process. In N. Garmezy and M. Rutter, eds., *Stress, Coping and Development in Children,* pp. 235–64. New York: McGraw-Hill.

Paykel, E. S., B. A. Prusoff, and E. H. Uhlenhuth. 1971. Scaling of life events. *Archives of General Psychiatry* 25:340–47.

Pearlin, L. I. 1959. Social and personal stress and escape television viewing. *Public Opinion Quarterly* 23:255–59.

Pearlin, L. I. 1975a. Sex roles and depression. In N. Datan and L. Ginsberg, eds.,

Life-Span Developmental Psychology Conference: Normative Life Crises, pp. 191–207. New York: Academic Press.

Pearlin, L. I. 1975b. Status inequality and stress in marriage. *American Sociological Review* 40:344–57.

Pearlin, L. I. 1980. Life strains and psychological distress among adults. In N. J. Smelser and E. H. Erikson, eds., *Themes of Work and Love in Adulthood,* pp. 174–92. Cambridge, Mass.: Harvard University Press.

Pearlin, L. I., and J. Johnson. 1977. Marital status, life-strains, and depression. *American Sociological Review* 42:704–15.

Pearlin, L. I., and M. A. Lieberman. 1979. Social sources of emotional distress. In R. Simmons, ed., *Research in Community and Mental Health.* Greenwich, Conn.: JAI Press.

Pearlin, L. I., and C. Radabaugh. 1976. Economic strains and the coping functions of alcohol. *American Journal of Sociology* 82:652–63.

Pearlin, L. I., and C. Schooler. 1978. The structure of coping. *Journal of Health and Social Behavior* 19:2–21.

Peele, S. 1983. Out of the habit trap. *American Health* (September/October):42–47.

Pelletier, K. 1977. *Mind as Healer, Mind as Slayer: A Holistic Approach to Preventing Stress Disorders.* New York: Delacorte and Delta/Seymour Lawrence.

Pelletier, K. 1984. *Healthy People in Unhealthy Places: Stress and Fitness at Work.* New York: Delacorte and Delta/Seymour Lawrence.

Pelletier, K. 1985. White-collar health: The hidden hazards of the modern office. *New York Times,* Sunday, September 8.

Pelletier, K. 1986. Healthy people in healthy places: Health promotion programs in the workplace. In M. Cataldo and T. Coates, eds., *Health and Industry: Behavioral Medicine in Perspective.* New York: Wiley.

Pelletier, K., and D. Herzing. In press. Psychoneuroimmunology: Toward a mindbody model—a critical review. *Advances: Journal of the Institute for the Advancement of Health.*

Pelletier, K., N. Klehr, and S. McPhee. 1987. Town and gown collaboration: Development of workplace health promotion programs. Manuscript.

Pettetier, K., R. Lutz, and N. Klehr. 1987. That's life!: A self-help stress management program. State of California Department of Mental Health.

Pelletier, K. R., and R. Lutz. 1988. Healthy people—healthy business: A critical review of stress management programs in the workplace. *American Journal of Health Promotion* 5–12, 19.

Penick, E. E., B. J. Powell, and W. A. Sieck. 1976. Mental health problems and natural disaster: Tornado victims. *Journal of Community Psychology* 4:64–67.

Perrow, C. 1981. Normal accident at Three Mile Island. *Society* 18:17–26.

Pervin, L. A. 1963. The need to predict and control under conditions of threat. *Journal of Personality* 31:570–85.

Peterson, C., and M. E. P. Seligman. 1984. Causal explanations as a risk factor for depression: Theory and evidence. *Psychological Review* 91:347–74.

Peterson, C., M. E. P. Seligman, and G. E. Vaillant. 1988. Pessimistic explanatory style is a risk factor for physical illness: A thirty-five-year longitudinal study. *Journal of Personality and Social Psychology* 55:23–27.

Peterson, E. A. 1979. Some issues and investigations concerning extraauditory effects of noise. Paper presented at the annual meeting of the American Psychological Association, New York, August.

Pflüger, E. 1877. Die teleologische Mechanik der Lebendigen. *Natur. Pflügers Archiv für die gesamte Physiologie des Menschen und der Tiere* 15:57.

Phares, E. J. 1976. *Locus of Control in Personality.* Morristown, N.J.: General Learning Press.

Piaget, J. 1952. *The Origins of Intelligence in Children.* New York: International Universities Press.

Pittner, M. S., and B. K. Houston. 1980. Response to stress, cognitive coping strategies and the Type A behavior pattern. *Journal of Personality and Social Psychology* 39:145–57.

Pittner, M. S., B. K. Houston, and G. Spiridigliozzi. 1983. Control over stress, Type A behavior pattern, and response to stress. *Journal of Personality and Social Psychology* 44:627–37.

Ploeger, A. 1972. A 10-year follow-up of miners trapped for 2 weeks under threatening circumstances. In C. D. Spielberger and I. G. Sarason, eds., *Stress and Anxiety,* vol. 4. Washington, D.C.: Hemisphere.

Poulshock, S. W., and E. S. Cohen. 1975. The elderly in the aftermath of a disaster. *Gerontologist* 15:357–61.

Pressman, M. D. 1980. Psychological techniques for the advancement of sports potential. In R. M. Suinn, ed., *Psychology in Sports: Methods and Applications.* Minneapolis: Burgess.

Price, E. E., and W. G. Meacci. 1985. Acquisition and retention of golf putting skill through the relaxation, visualization, and body rehearsal intervention. *Research Quarterly for Exercise and Sport* 56:176–79.

Price, J. 1978. Some age-related effects of the 1974 Brisbane floods. *Australian and New Zealand Journal of Psychiatry* 12:55–58.

Price, V. A. 1982. *Type A Behavior Pattern: A Model for Research and Practice.* New York: Academic Press.

Pulos, L. 1979. Athletes and self-hypnosis. In P. Klavora and J. V. Daniel, eds., *Coach, Athlete, and the Sport Psychologist.* Champaign, Ill.: Human Kinetics.

Pynoos, R. S., and S. Eth. 1986. Witness to violence. *Journal of the American Academy of Child Psychiatry* 25:306–19.

Quarantelli, E. L. 1985. What is disaster? The need for clarification in definition and conceptualization in research. In B. J. Sowder, ed., *Disasters and Mental Health: Selected Contemporary Perspectives,* pp. 41–73. Rockville, Md.: U. S. Department of Health and Human Services.

Quarantelli, E. L., and R. R. Dynes. 1972. When disaster strikes. *Psychology Today* (September): 66–70.

Quarantelli, E. L., and R. R. Dynes. 1976. Community conflict: Its absence and its presence in natural disasters. *Mass Emergencies* 1:134–52.

Raab, W., J. P. Chaplin, and E. Bajusz. 1969. Myocardial necroses produced in domesticated rats and in wild rats by sensory and emotional stresses. *Proceedings of the Society of Experimental Biology and Medicine* 116:665–69.

Rabkin, J. G., and E. L. Struening. 1976. Life events, stress, and illness. *Science* 194:1013–20.

Rahe, R. H. 1972. Subjects' recent life changes and their near-future illness susceptibility. *Advances in Psychosomatic Medicine* 8:2–19.

Rahe, R. H. 1974. The pathway between subjects' recent life changes and their near-future illness reports: Representative results and methodological issues. In B. S. Dohrenwend and B. P. Dohrenwend, eds., *Stressful Life Events: Their Nature and Effects,* pp. 73–86. New York: Wiley.

Rahe, R. H. 1975. Life changes and near-future illness reports. In L. Levi, ed., *Emotions: Their Parameters and Measurements,* pp. 511–29. New York: Raven Press.

Rahe, R. H., J. D. McKean, and R. J. Arthur. 1967. A longitudinal study of life-change and illness patterns. *Journal of Psychosomatic Research* 10:355–66.

Rand, A. 1964. The Objectivist ethics. In A. Rand, ed., *The Virtue of Selfishness.* New York: Signet.

Rando, T. A. 1984. *Grief, Dying and Death: Clinical Interventions for Caregivers.* Champaign, Ill.: Research Press.

Rangell, L. 1976. Discussion of the Buffalo Creek disaster: The course of psychic trauma. *American Journal of Psychiatry* 133:313–16.

Raphael, B. 1983. *The Anatomy of Bereavement.* New York: Basic Books.

Ravizza, K., and R. Rotella. 1982. Cognitive somatic behavioral interventions in gymnastics. In L. D. Zaichkowsky and W. E. Sime, eds., *Stress Management for Sport.* Reston, VA.: AAHPERD Publications.

Reddy, J. K., A. J. L. Bai, and V. R. Rao. 1976. The effects of the transcendental meditation program on athletic performance. In D. J. Orme-Johnson and I. Farrow, eds., *Scientific Research on the Transcendental Meditation Program* (collected papers, vol. 1). Weggis, Switzerland: MERU Press.

Reich, J., and A. Zautra. 1981. Life events and personal causation: Some relationships with satisfaction and distress. *Journal of Personality and Social Psychology* 41:1002–12.

Review Panel on Coronary-Prone Behavior and Coronary Heart Disease. 1981. Coronary-prone behavior and coronary heart disease: Critical review. Circulation 63, No. 6. Bethesda, Md.: National Institute of Heart, Lung, and Blood Institute, National Institutes of Health.

Rhodewalt, F., and J. Davison, Jr. 1983. Reactance and the coronary-prone behavior pattern: The role of self-attribution in responses to reduced behavioral freedom. *Journal of Personality and Social Psychology* 44:220–28.

Ribble, M. A. 1944. Infantile experience in relation to personality development. In J. M. Hunt, ed., *Personality and the Behavior Disorders,* 2:621–51. New York: Ronald Press.

Rice, P. L. 1987. *Stress and Health: Principles and Practice for Coping and Wellness.* Monterey, Calif.: Brooks/Cole.

Richmond, J. B., and H. A. Waisman. 1955. Psychologic aspects of management of children with malignant diseases. *American Journal of Diseases of the Child* 89:42–47.

Riley, D., and J. Eckenrode. 1986. Social ties: Subgroup differences in costs and benefits. *Journal of Personality and Social Psychology* 51:770–78.

Rissler, A. 1977. Stress reactions at work and after work during a period of quantitative overload. *Ergonomics* 20:13.

Rivenbark, W. H. 1971. Self-disclosure patterns among adolescents. *Psychological Reports* 28:35–42.

Robins, L. N., R. L. Fischbach, E. M. Smith, L. B. Cotler, and S D. Solomon. 1986. Impact of disaster on previously assessed mental health. In J. Shore, ed., *Disaster Stress Studies: New Methods and Findings.* Washington, D.C.: American Psychiatric Press.

Rokeach, M. 1960. *The Open and Closed Mind.* New York: Basic Books.

Rokeach, M. 1973. *The Nature of Human Values.* New York: Free Press.

Rodin, J. 1985. The application of social psychology. In G. Lindzey and E. Aronson, eds., *Handbook of Social Psychology,* vol. 2. New York: Random House.

Rodin, J. 1986. Aging and health: Effects of the sense of control. *Science* 233:1271–76.

Rodin, J., and P. Salovey. 1989. Health psychology. *Annual Review of Psychology* 40:533–79.

Rodin, J., C. Timko, and S. Harris. 1985. The construct of control: Biological and psychological correlates. In C. Eisdorfer, M. P. Lawton, and G. L. Maddos, eds., *Annual Review of Gerontology and Geriatrics,* vol. 5. New York: Springer.

Rogers, C. R. 1951. *Client-Centered Therapy.* Boston: Houghton Mifflin.

Rogers, G. O., and J. Nehnevajsa. 1984. *Behavior and Attitudes Under Crisis Conditions: Selected Issues and Findings.* Washington, D.C.: Federal Emergency Management Agency.

Rogers, R. W. 1984. Changing health-related attitudes and behavior: The role of preventive health psychology. In R. P. McGlynn and C. D. Stoltenberg, eds., *Social Perception in Clinical and Consulting Psychology,* 2:91–112. Lubbock, Tex.: Texas Tech University Press.

Rollin, B. 1976. *First You Cry.* New York: New American Library.

Rook, K. S. 1984. The negative side of social interaction: Impact on psychological well-being. *Journal of Personality and Social Psychology* 46:1097–1108.

Rosenberg, M., and H. B. Kaplan, eds. 1982. *Social Psychology of the Self-Concept.* Arlington Heights, Ill.: Harlan Davidson.

Rosenberg, M., and L. I. Pearlin. 1978. Social class and self-esteem among children and adults. *American Journal of Sociology* 84:53–77.

Rosenman, R. H. 1978. The interview method of assessment of the coronary-prone behavior pattern. In T. M. Dembroski, S. G. Haynes, and M. Feinleib, eds., *Coronary-Prone Behavior,* pp. 55–69. New York: Springer-Verlag.

Rosenman, R. H., R. J. Brand, C. D. Jenkins, M. Friedman, R. Strauss, and M. Wurm. 1975. Coronary heart disease in the Western Collaborative Group

Study: Final follow-up experience of 8½ years. *Journal of the American Medical Association* 233:872–77.

Rosenman, R. H., M. Friedman, R. Strauss, M. Wurm, R. Kositchek, W. Hahn, and N. T. Werthessen. 1964. A predictive study of coronary heart disease. *Journal of the American Medical Association* 189:15–22.

Rosenstiel, A., and S. Roth. 1981. Relationship between cognitive activity and adjustment in four spinal-cord-injured individuals: A longitudinal investigation. *Journal of Human Stress* March:35–43.

Roskies, E. 1972. *Abnormality and Normality: The Mothering of Thalidomide Children.* Ithaca, N.Y.: Cornell University Press.

Roskies, E. 1983. Stress management: Averting the evil eye. *Contemporary Psychology* 28:542–44.

Roskies, E. 1987. A new approach to managing stress. In E. Roskies, *Stress Management for the Healthy Type A,* pp. 27–46. New York: Guilford Press.

Roskies, E., and R. S. Lazarus. 1980. Coping theory and the teaching of coping skills. In P. O. Davidson and S. M. Davidson, eds., *Behavioral Medicine: Changing Health Lifestyles,* pp. 38–69. New York: Brunner/Mazel.

Ross, H., and I. Sawhill. 1975. *Time of Transition: The Growth of Families Headed by Women.* Washington, D.C.: Urban Institute.

Rotella, R. J., B. Gansneder, D. Ojala, and J. Billings. 1980. Cognitive and coping strategies of elite skiers: An exploratory study of young developing athletes. *Journal of Sport Psychology* 2:350–54.

Rotella, R. J., C. Malone, and D. Ojala. 1985. Facilitating athletic performance through the use of mastery and coping tapes. In L. K. Bunker, R. J. Rotella, and A. S. Reilly, eds., *Sport Psychology.* Charlottesville: University of Virginia Press.

Roth, J. A. 1963. *Timetables.* Indianapolis: Bobbs-Merrill.

Rothbaum, F., J. R. Weisz, and S. S. Snyder. 1982. Changing the world and changing the self: A two-process model of perceived control. *Journal of Personality and Social Psychology* 42:5–37.

Rotter, J. B. 1966. Generalized expectancies for internal versus external control of reinforcement. *Psychological Monographs* 80 (1, whole no. 609).

Rowe, J. W., and R. L. Kahn. 1987. Human aging: Usual and successful. *Science* 237:143–49.

Rowlison, R. T., and R. D. Felner. 1988. Major life events, hassles, and adaptation in adolescence: Confounding in the conceptualization and measurement of life stress and adjustment revisited. *Journal of Personality and Social Psychology* 55:432–44.

Rubenstein, J., and C. Rubin. 1987. The Adolescent Friendship. Manuscript.

Ryan, E. D., and J. Simons. 1981. Cognitive demand, imagery, and frequency of mental rehearsal as factors influencing acquisition of motor skills. *Journal of Sport Psychology* 3:35–45.

Sackheim, H. A. In press. Self-deception, self-esteem, and depression: The adaptive value of lying to oneself. In J. Masling, ed., *Empirical Studies of Psychoanalytic Theory.* Hillsdale, N.J.: Erlbaum.

Sahud, M. A., and R. J. Cohen. 1971. Effect of aspirin ingestion on ascorbic-acid levels in rheumatoid arthritis. *Lancet* 1:937–38.

Sandler, I. N., and B. Lakey. 1982. Locus of control as a stress moderator: The role of control perceptions and social support. *American Journal of Community Psychology* 10:65–80.

Sandler, J. 1960. The background of safety. *International Journal of Psychoanalysis* 41:352–56.

Sandman, C. C. 1972. Psychophysiological parameters of emotional expression. *Dissertation Abstracts International* 33:2356–57.

Sarason, I. G. 1975. Test anxiety, attention, and the general problem of anxiety. In C. D. Spielberger and I. G. Sarason, eds., *Stress and Anxiety,* 1:165–87. Washington, D.C.: Hemisphere.

Sarason, I. G., C. de Monchaux, and T. Hunt. 1975. Methodological issues in the assessment of life stress. In L. Levi, ed., *Emotions: Their Parameters and Measurement,* pp. 499–509. New York: Raven Press.

Sarason, I. G., and B. R. Sarason, eds. 1984. *Social Support: Theory, Research and Applications.* The Hague, Netherlands: Martinus Nijhof.

Sarason, S. B., G. Mandler, and P. C. Craighill. 1952. The effect of differential instructions on anxiety and learning. *Journal of Abnormal and Social Psychology* 47:561–65.

Schachter, S., and J. E. Singer. 1962. Cognitive, social, and physiological determinants of emotional state. *Psychological Review* 69:379–99.

Schafer, R. 1954. *Psychoanalytic Interpretation in Rorschach Testing: Theory and Application.* New York: Grune and Stratton.

Schafer, W. 1987. *Stress Management for Wellness.* New York: Holt, Rinehart and Winston.

Scheier, M. F., and C. S. Carver. 1985. Optimism, coping, and health: Assessment and implications of generalized outcome expectancies. *Health Psychology* 4:219–47.

Scheier, M. F., K. A. Matthews, J. Owens, G. J. Magovern, Sr., R. C. Lefebvre, R. A. Abbott, and C. S. Carver. In press. Dispositional optimism and recovery from coronary artery bypass surgery: The beneficial effects of physical and psychological well-being. *Journal of Personality and Social Psychology.*

Scherwitz, L., K. Berton, and H. Leventhal. 1978. Type A behavior, self-involvement, and cardiovascular response. *Psychosomatic Medicine* 40:593–609.

Scherwitz, L., R. McKelvain, C. Laman, J. Patterson, L. Duttons, S. Yusim, J. Lester, I. Kraft, D. Rochelle, and R. Leachmen. 1983. Type A behavior, self-involvement, and coronary atherosclerosis. *Psychosomatic Medicine* 45:47–57.

Schlesinger, H., E. Mumford, G. Glass, C. Patrick, and S. Sharfstein. 1983. Mental health treatment and medical care utilization in a fee-for-service system. *American Journal of Public Health* 73:422–29.

Schmale, A. H., Jr. 1972. Giving up as a final common pathway to changes in health. *Advances in Psychosomatic Medicine* 8:20–40.

Schneider, J. W., and P. Conrad. 1983. *Having Epilepsy: The Experience and Control of Illness.* Philadelphia: Temple University Press.

Schoenberg, B. B., A. C. Carr, D. Peretz, and A. H. Kutscher. 1969. Physicians and the bereaved. *General Practitioner* 40:105–8.

Schönpflug, W. 1983. Coping efficiency and situational demands. In G. R. J. Hockey, ed., *Stress and Fatigue in Human Performance,* pp. 299–330. New York: Wiley.

Schore, L. 1984. Occupational stress: A union-based approach. In B. G. F. Cohen, ed., *Human Aspects in Office Automation,* pp. 297–302. Amsterdam: Elsevier.

Schottenfeld, R. S., and M. R. Cullen. 1985. Occupation-induced posttraumatic stress disorders. *American Journal of Psychiatry* 142:198–202.

Schultz, J. H., and W. Luthe. 1959. *Autogenic Training: A Psychophysiological Approach to Psychotherapy.* New York: Grune and Stratton.

Schulz, R. 1978. *The Psychology of Death, Dying, and Bereavement.* Reading, Mass.: Addison-Wesley.

Schulz, R., and D. Aderman. 1974. Clinical research and the stages of dying. *Omega* 5:137–43.

Schulz, R., and S. Decker. 1985. Long-term adjustment to physical disability: The role of social support, perceived control and self-blame. *Journal of Personality and Social Psychology* 48:1162–72.

Schulz, R., and B. H. Hanusa. 1980. Experimental social gerontology: A social psychological perspective. *Journal of Social Issues* 36:30–47.

Schulz, R., and J. Schlarb. 1987–88. Two decades of research on dying: What do we know about the patient? *Omega* 18:299–317.

Schulz, R., C. T. Tompkins, and M. T. Rau. 1987. A longitudinal study of the impact of stroke on patients and support persons. *Journal of Applied Social Psychology* 17:401–28.

Schulz, R., C. T. Tompkins, D. Wood, and S. Decker. 1987. The social psychology of caregiving: The physical and psychological costs of providing support to the disabled. *Journal of Applied Social Psychology* 17:401–28.

Schutz, W. C. 1967. *The FIRO Scales Manual.* Palo Alto, Calif.: Consulting Psychologists Press.

Schwartz, G. E. 1982. Testing the biopsychosocial model: The ultimate challenge facing behavioral medicine? *Journal of Consulting and Clinical Psychology* 50:1040–52.

Schwartz, M. S. 1987. *Biofeedback: A Practitioner's Guide.* New York: Guilford Press.

Seabourne, T. G., R. S. Weinberg, and A. Jackson. 1982. Effect of visuo-motor behavior rehearsal in enhancing karate performance. Manuscript, North Texas State University, Denton, Tex.

Seabourne, T. G., R. S. Weinberg, and A. Jackson. 1984. The effect of individualized practice and training of visuo-motor behavior rehearsal in enhancing karate performance. *Journal of Sport Behavior* 7:58–67.

Seabourne, T. G., R. S. Weinberg, A. Jackson, and R. M. Suinn. 1985. Effect of individualized, nonindividualized, and package intervention strategies on karate performance. *Journal of Sport Psychology* 7:40–50.

Seamonds, B. 1982. Stress factors and their effect on absenteeism in a corporate employee group. *Journal of Occupational Medicine* 24:393–97.

Seamonds, B. 1983. Extension of research into stress factors and their effect on illness absenteeism. *Journal of Occupational Medicine* 25:821–22.

Seligman, M. E. P. 1975. *Helplessness: On Depression, Development, and Death.* San Francisco: Freeman.

Selye, H. 1936. A syndrome produced by diverse nocuous agents. *Nature* 138:32.

Selye, H. 1946. The general adaptation syndrome and the diseases of adaptation. *Journal of Clinical Endocrinology* 6:117–20.

Selye, H. 1974. *Stress Without Distress.* Philadelphia: Lippincott.

Selye, H. 1976a. *Stress in Health and Disease.* Reading, MA.: Buttersworth.

Selye, H. [1956] 1976b. *The Stress of Life.* New York: McGraw-Hill.

Selye, H. 1982. History and present status of the stress concept. In L. Goldberger and S. Breznitz, eds., *Handbook of Stress: Theoretical and Clinical Aspects,* pp. 7–17. New York: Free Press.

Shadish, W. R., D. Hickman, and M. C. Arrick. 1981. Psychological problems of spinal cord injury patients: Emotional distress as a function of time and locus of control. *Journal of Consulting and Clinical Psychology* 49:297.

Shannon, T. X., and G. M. Isbell. 1963. Stress in dental patients: Effects of local anesthetic procedures. Technical Report No. SAM-TDR-63-29. Brooks Air Force Base, Tex.: United States Air Force School of Aerospace Medicine.

Shapiro, A. K. 1964. Factors contributing to the placebo effect: Their implications for psychotherapy. *American Journal of Psychotherapy* 18 (Supplement 1):73–88.

Shapiro, D. 1965. *Neurotic Styles.* New York: Basic Books.

Shapiro, D., J. Stoyuva, J. Kamrya, T. Barber, N. Miller, and G. Schwartz, eds. 1979/80. *Biofeedback and Behavioral Medicine.* Chicago: Aldine.

Shapiro, D., and R. Walsh, eds. 1984. *Medication: Classic and Contemporary Perspectives.* Chicago: Aldine.

Shaver, K. G., and D. Drown. 1986. On causality, responsibility, and self-blame: A theoretical note. *Journal of Personality and Social Psychology* 50:697–702.

Shaw, R. E. 1984. the impact of coping, anxiety and social support on information, medical and rehabilitation outcomes in patients undergoing coronary angioplasty. Ph.D. dissertation, University of California, San Francisco.

Shaw, R. E. 1985. Personal communication.

Shaw, R. E., F. Cohen, B. Doyle, and J. Palesky. 1985. The impact of denial and repressive style on information gain and rehabilitation outcomes in myocardial infarction patients. *Psychosomatic Medicine* 47:262–73.

Shaw, R. E., F. Cohen, J. Fishman-Rosen, M. C. Murphy, S. H. Stertzer, D. A. Clark, and R. K. Myler. In press. Psychological predictors of psychosocial and medical outcomes in patients undergoing coronary angioplasty. *Psychosomatic Medicine.*

Shelton, T. O., and M. J. Mahoney. 1978. The content and effect of "psyching-up" strategies in weight lifters. *Cognitive Therapy and Research* 2:275–84.

Shephard, R., P. Corey, P. Ruezland, and M. Cox. 1982. The influence of an employee fitness program and lifestyle modification program upon medical care costs. *Canadian Journal of Public Health* 73:259–63.

Shipley, R. H., J. H. Butt, and E. A. Horwitz. 1979. Preparation to reexperience a stressful medical examination: Effect of repetitious videotape exposure and coping style. *Journal of Consulting and Clinical Psychology* 47:485–92.

Shipley, R. H., J. H. Butt, B. Horwitz, and J. E. Farbry. 1978. Preparation for a stressful medical procedure: Effect of amount of stimulus preexposure and coping style. *Journal of Consulting and Clinical Psychology* 46:499–507.

Shneidman, E. S. 1973. *Death of Man.* New York: Quadrangle New York Times.

Shore, J. H., E. Tatum, and W. M. Vollmer. 1986. Evaluation of mental health effects of disaster. *American Journal of Public Health* 76:76–83.

Shrauger, J. S., and T. M. Osberg. 1981. The relative accuracy of self-predictions and judgments by others in psychological assessment. *Psychological Bulletin* 90:322–51.

Siegal, H. S. 1959. The relation between crowding and weight of adrenal glands in chickens. *Ecology* 40:495–98.

Siegel, K., and P. Tuckel. 1984–85. Rational suicide and the terminally ill cancer patient. *Omega* 15:263–69.

Siller, J. 1969. Psychological situation of the disabled with spinal cord injuries. *Rehabilitation Literature* 30:290–96.

Silver, M. J. 1970. Hypnotizability as a function of adaptive regression, repression, and mood. Ph.D. dissertation, Boston University.

Silver, R. C., C. Boon, and M. H. Stones. 1983. Searching for meaning in misfortune: Making sense of incest. *Journal of Social Issues* 39:81–102.

Silver, R. C., and C. B. Wortman. 1980. Coping with undesirable life events. In J. Garber and M. E. P. Seligman, eds., *Human Helplessness: Theory and Applications,* pp. 279–340. New York: Academic Press.

Silver, R. C., and C. B. Wortman. 1988. Is "Processing" a Loss Necessary for Adjustment? A Study of Parental Reactions to Death of an Infant. Manuscript.

Simons, R. C., ed. 1985. *Understanding Human Behavior in Health and Illness.* 3d ed. Baltimore, Md.: Williams & Wilkins.

Simonton, D. C., S. Matthews-Simonton, and J. Creighton. 1978. *Getting Well Again.* Los Angeles: Tarcher.

Sims, J. H., and D. D. Baumann. 1974. The tornado threat: Coping styles of the north and the south. In J. H. Sims and D. D. Baumann, eds., *Human Behavior and the Environment: Interactions Between Man and His Physical World.* Chicago: Maarovifa Press.

Singer, J. E., and L. M. Davidson. 1986. Specificity and stress research. In M. H. Appley and R. Trumbull, eds., *Dynamics of Stress: Physiological, Psychological, and Social Perspectives,* pp. 47–61. New York: Plenum Press.

Singer, J. E., U. Lundberg, and M. Frankenhaeuser. 1978. Stress on the train: A study of urban commuting. In A. Baum, J. E. Singer, and S. Valins, eds., *Advances in Environmental Psychology: Vol. 1. The Urban Environment*, pp. 21–57. Hillsdale, N.J.: Erlbaum.

Slovic, P., B. Fischhoff, and S. Lichtenstein. 1977. Behavioral decision theory. *Annual Review of Psychology* 28:1–39.

Smelser, N. J. 1963. *Theory of Collective Behavior.* New York: Free Press.

Smith, A. 1975. *Powers of the Mind*, pp. 11–14. New York: Random House.

Smith, C. A. 1989. Dimensions of appraisal and physiological response in emotion. *Journal of Personality and Social Psychology* 56:339–53.

Smith, D. 1987. Conditions that facilitate the development of sport imagery training. *Sport Psychologist* 1:237–47.

Smith, M. B. 1961. "Mental health" reconsidered: A special case of the problem of values in psychology. *American Psychologist* 16:299–306.

Smith, R. E. 1980. A cognitive-affective approach to stress management training for athletes. In C. H. Nadeau, ed., *Psychology of Motor Behavior and Sport.* Champaign, Ill.: Human Kinetics.

Sobel, H. J., ed. 1981. *Behavior Therapy in Terminal Care.* Cambridge, Mass.: Ballinger.

Sobell, M. B., and L. C. Sobell. 1976. Second-year treatment outcome of alcoholics treated by individualized behavior therapy: Results. *Behavior Research and Therapy* 14:195–215.

Sobell, M. B., and L. C. Sobell. 1978. *Behavioral Treatment of Alcohol Problems: Individualized Therapy and Controlled Drinking.* New York: Plenum.

Sofer, C. 1970. *Men in Mid-Career.* London: Cambridge University Press.

Soloff, P. H. 1980. Effects of denial of mood, compliance, and quality of functioning after cardiovascular rehabilitation. *General Hospitals and Psychiatry* 2:134–40.

Spielberger, C. D., ed. 1966. *Anxiety and Behavior.* New York: Academic Press.

Spielberger, C. D., ed. 1972. *Anxiety: Current Trends in Theory and Research*, vols. 1 and 2. New York: Academic Press.

Spielberger, C. D. 1973. *State-Trait Anxiety for Children: Preliminary Manual.* Palo Alto, Calif.: Consulting Psychologists Press.

Spielberger, C. D., G. A. Jacobs, R. S. Crane, S. F. Russell, L. Westberry, L. Barker, E. H. Johnson, J. Knight, and E. Marks. 1979. *Preliminary Manual for the State-Trait Personality Inventory (STPI).* Tampa: University of South Florida Human Resources Institute.

Spielberger, C. D., G. A. Jacobs, S. F. Russell, and R. S. Crane. 1983. Assessment of anger: The State-Trait Anger Scale. In J. N. Butcher and C. D. Spielberger, eds., *Advances in Personality Assessment*, 2:159–87. Hillsdale, N.J.: Erlbaum.

Spielberger, C. D., E. H. Johnson, S. F. Russell, R. S. Crane, G. A. Jacobs, and T. J. Worder. 1985. The experience and expression of anger: Construction and validation of an anger expression scale. In M. A. Chesney and R. H. Rosenman, eds., *Anger and Hostility in Cardiovascular and Behavioral Disorders*, pp. 5–30. New York: Hemisphere/McGraw-Hill.

Spielberger, C. D., S. S. Krasner, and E. P. Solomon. 1988. The experience, expression, and control of anger. In M. P. Janisse, ed., *Health Psychology: Individual Differences and Stress,* pp. 89–108. New York: Springer Verlag.

Spigolon, L., and D. Annalisa. 1985. Autogenic training in frogmen. *International Journal of Sport Psychology* 16:312–20.

Spilman, M., A. Goetz, J. Schultz, R. Bellingham, and D. Johnson. 1986. Effects of a corporate health promotion program. *Journal of Occupational Medicine* 28:285–89.

Spinetta, J. J. 1972. Death anxiety in leukemic children. Ph.D. dissertation, University of Southern California.

Spinetta, J. J., and L. J. Maloney, 1978. The child with cancer: Pattern of communication and denial. *Journal of Consulting and Clinical Psychology* 46:1540–41.

Spinetta, J. J., D. Rigler, and M. Karon. 1973. Anxiety in the dying child. *Pediatrics* 52:841–45.

Spitz, R. A. 1945. Hospitalism. In *The Psychoanalytic Study of the Child,* 1:53–74. New York: International Universities Press.

Spitz, R. A. 1946. Anaclitic depression. In *The Psychoanalytic Study of the Child,* 2:313–42. New York: International Universities Press.

Stack, C. 1974. *All Our Kin: Strategies for Survival in a Black Community.* New York: Harper & Row.

Staudenmeyer, H., R. A. Kinsman, J. F. Dirks, S. L. Spector, and C. Wangaard. 1979. Medical outcome in asthmatic patients: Effects of airways hyperactivity and symptom-focused anxiety. *Psychosomatic Medicine* 41:109–18.

Steffy, B., J. Jones, L. Murphy, and L. A. Kunz. 1986. A demonstration of the impact of stress abatement programs on reducing employees' accidents and their costs. *American Journal of Health Promotion* 1:25–32.

Stein, M., S. E. Keller, and S. J. Schleifer. 1985. Stress and immunomodulation: The role of depression and neuroendocrine function. *Journal of Immunology* 135:827s–833s.

Steinberger, L. 1986. Stability (and instability) of Type A behavior from childhood to young adulthood. *Developmental Psychology* 22:393–402.

Steinmetz, J., J. Blankenship, L. Brown, D. Hall, and G. Miller. 1980. *Managing Stress: Before It Manages You.* Palo Alto, Calif.: Bull Publishing.

Stern, M. J., L. Pascale, and A. Ackerman. 1977. Life adjustment post myocardial infarction: Determining predictive variables. *Archives of Internal Medicine* 137:1680–85.

Stern, M. J., L. Pascale, and J. B. McLoone. 1976. Psychosocial adaptation following an acute myocardial infarction. *Journal of Chronic Diseases* 29:513–26.

Sternbach, R. A. 1966. *Principles of Psychophysiology.* New York: Academic Press.

Stewart, D. C., and T. J. Sullivan. 1982. Illness behavior and the sick role in chronic disease: The case of multiple sclerosis. *Social Science and Medicine* 16:1397–1404.

Stewart, T. D. 1977–1978. Coping behaviour and the moratorium following spinal cord injury. *Paraplegia* 15:338–42.

Stokols, D. 1978. Environmental psychology. *Annual Review of Psychology* 29:253–95.

Stone, A. A. 1985. Assessment of coping efficacy: A comment. *Journal of Behavioral Medicine* 8:115–17.

Stone, A. A., and J. M. Neale. 1984. A new measure of daily coping: Development and preliminary results. *Journal of Personality and Social Psychology* 46:892–906.

Stroebe, M. S., and W. Stroebe. 1983. Who suffers more? Sex differences in health risks of the widowed. *Psychological Bulletin* 93:279–301.

Strumpfer, D. J. W. 1970. Fear and affiliation during a disaster. *Journal of Social Psychology* 82:263–68.

Suinn, R. M. 1972. Removing emotional obstacles to learning and performance by visuo-motor behavior rehearsal. *Behavioral Therapy* 31:308–10.

Suinn, R. M. 1976. Body thinking: Psychology for Olympic champs. *Psychology Today* (July):38–43.

Suinn, R. M. 1980. Body thinking: Psychology for Olympic champs. In R. M. Suinn, ed., *Psychology in Sports: Methods and Applications.* Minneapolis: Burgess.

Suinn, R. M. 1982. Intervention with Type A behaviors. *Journal of Consulting and Clinical Psychology* 50:797–803.

Suinn, R. M. 1983. *The Seven Steps to Peak Performance: Mental Training Manual for Athletes.* Fort Collins, Colo. Rocky Mountain Behavioral Sciences Institute.

Suls, J., and B. Fletcher. 1985. The relative efficacy of avoidant and nonavoidant coping strategies: A meta-analysis. *Health Psychology* 4:249–88.

Super, D. E. 1986. Life career roles: Self-realization in work and leisure. In D. T. Hall, ed., *Career Development in Organizations,* pp. 95–119. San Francisco: Dorsey Press.

Tait, R., and R. C. Silver. 1989. Coming to terms with major negative life events. In J. S. Uleman and J. A. Bargh, eds., *Unintended Thought: The Limits of Awareness, Intention, and Control,* pp. 351–82. New York: Guilford Press.

Taylor, G. P. 1967. Predicted versus actual response to spinal cord injury: A psychological study. Ph.D. dissertation, University of Minnesota, Minneapolis.

Taylor, S. E. 1983. Adjustment to threatening events: A theory of cognitive adaptation. *American Psychologist* 38:1161–73.

Taylor, S. E. 1984. Issues in the study of coping: A commentary. *Cancer* 53:2313–15.

Taylor, S. E. 1986. *Health Psychology.* New York: Random House.

Taylor, S. E. 1990. Health psychology: The science and the field. *American Psychologist* 45:40–50.

Taylor, S. E., and L. F. Clark. 1986. Does information improve adjustment to noxious events? In M. J. Saks and L. Saxe, eds., *Advances in Applied Social Psychology,* 3:1–28. Hillsdale, N.J.: Erlbaum.

Taylor, S. E., R. R. Lichtman, and J. V. Wood. 1984a. Attributions, beliefs about control, and adjustment to breast cancer. *Journal of Personality and Social Psychology* 46:489–502.

Taylor, S. E., R. R. Lichtman, and J. V. Wood. 1984b. Compliance with chemotherapy among breast cancer patients. *Health Psychology* 3:553–62.

Taylor, S. E., and S. K. Schneider. 1989. Coping and the simulation of events. *Social Cognition* 7:176–96.

Taylor, S. E., J. V. Wood, and R. R. Lichtman. 1983. It could be worse: Selective evaluation as a response to victimization. *Journal of Social Issues* 39:19–40.

Taylor, V., G. A. Ross, and E. L. Quarantelli. 1976. *Delivery of Mental Health Services in Disasters: The Xenia Tornado and Some Implications.* Columbus: Ohio State University, Disaster Research Center (Book and Monograph Series No. 11).

Temkin, N. K., and G. R. Davis. 1984. Stress as a risk factor for seizures among adults with epilepsy. *Epilepsia* 25:450–56.

Terkel, S. 1972. *Working: People Talk About What They Do All Day and How They Feel About What They Do.* New York: Avon.

Terr, L. 1979. Children of Chowchilla. *Psychoanalytic Study of the Child* 24:552–623.

Terwogt, M. M., J. Schene, and P. L. Harris. 1985. Self-control of emotional reactions by young children. Presented at meetings of the International Society for Research on Emotion, Cambridge, Mass., June 23–26.

Thiessen, D. D. 1963. Varying sensitivity of C^{57}BL/Crgl mice to grouping. *Science* 141:827–28.

Thoits, P. A. 1983. Dimensions of life events as influences upon the genesis of psychological distress and associated conditions: An evaluation and synthesis of the literature. In H. B. Kaplan, ed., *Psychological Stress: Trends in Theory and Research,* pp. 33–103. New York: Academic Press.

Thomas, L. 1983. *The Youngest Science.* New York: Viking.

Thompson, S. C. 1981. Will it hurt less if I can control it? A complex answer to a simple question. *Psychological Bulletin* 90:89–101.

Thompson, W. R., and T. Schaefer, Jr. 1961. Early environmental stimulation. In D. W. Fiske and S. R. Maddi, eds., *Functions of Varied Experience.* Homewood, Ill.: Dorsey Press.

Thoresen, C. E., M. Friedman, J. K. Gill, and D. Ulmer. 1982. Recurrent coronary prevention project: Some preliminary findings. *Acta Medica Scandinavica* (Supplement) 660:172–92.

Tietjen, A. 1982. The social networks of preadolescent children in Sweden. *International Journal of Behavioral Development* 5:111–30.

Tinbergen, N. 1953. *Social Behaviour in Animals.* London: Methuen.

Titchener, J. L., and F. T. Kapp. 1976. Family and character change at Buffalo Creek. *American Journal of Psychiatry* 133:295–99.

Titley, R. W. 1980. The loneliness of a long-distance kicker. In R. M. Suinn, ed., *Psychology in Sports: Methods and Applications.* Minneapolis: Burgess.

Tomkins, S. S. 1965. Affect and the psychology of knowledge. In S. S. Tomkins and C. E. Izard, eds., *Affect, Cognition, and Personality,* pp. 72–97. New York: Springer.

Trainer, P., and R. Bolin. 1976. Persistent effects of disasters on daily activities: A cross-cultural comparison. *Mass Emergencies* 2:279–90.

Trieschmann, R. B. 1978. The psychological, social, and vocational adjustment in spinal cord injury: A strategy for future research. Report No. 13-P-59011/9-01. Washington, D. C.: Rehabilitation Services Administration.

Trieschmann, R. B. 1980. *Spinal Cord Injuries: Psychological, Social and Vocational Adjustment.* New York: Pergamon Press.

Turk, D. C., and K. Rennert. 1981. Pain and the terminally ill cancer patient: A cognitive-social learning perspective. In H. J. Sobel, ed., *Behavior Therapy in Terminal Care.* Cambridge, Mass.: Ballinger.

Turk, D. C., T. E. Rudy, and P. Salovey. 1984. Health protection: Attitudes and behaviors of LPNs, teachers, and college students. *Health Psychology* 3:189–210.

Turk, D. C., T. E. Rudy, and P. Salovey. 1985. Implicit models of illness. *Journal of Behavioral Medicine* 9:453–74.

Turner, J. A., and C. R. Chapman. 1982a. Psychological interventions for chronic pain: A critical review. I. Relaxation training and biofeedback. *Pain* 12:1–21.

Turner, J. A., and C. R. Chapman. 1982b. Psychological interventions for chronic pain: A critical review. II. Operant conditioning, hypnosis, and cognitive-behavioral therapy. *Pain* 12:23–46.

Turner, R., and L. M. Killian. 1972. *Collective Behavior.* 2d ed. Englewood Cliffs, N.J.: Prentice-Hall.

Turner, R. H., J. M. Nigg, D. H. Paz, and B. S. Young. 1979. *Earthquake Threat: The Human Response in Southern California.* Los Angeles: University of California at Los Angeles, Institute for Social Service Research.

Turner, R. J., and S. Noh. 1982. Psychological distress in women: A longitudinal analysis of the roles of social support and life stress. Paper presented at the National Conference on Social Stress, University of New Hampshire.

Tyhurst, J. S. 1951. Individual reactions to community disaster. *American Journal of Psychiatry* 107:764–69.

U.S. Department of Health, Education, and Welfare. 1978. *Facts of Life and Death.* Publication number (PHS) 79-1222.

Ulett, G. A., and D. B. Peterson. 1965. *Applied Hypnosis and Positive Suggestion.* St. Louis: C. V. Mosby.

Ulrich, R. P. 1973. The effect of hypnotic and non-hypnotic suggestions on archery performance. Ph.D. dissertation, University of Utah, Salt Lake City.

Upton, A. L. 1981. Health impact on the Three Mile Island accident. *Annals of the New York Academy of Sciences* 63–75.

Ursin, A., E. Baude, and S. Levine, eds. 1978. *Psychobiology of Stress: A Study of Coping Men.* New York: Academic Press.

Ursin, H. 1980. Personality, activation, and somatic health: A new psychosomatic theory. In S. Levine and H. Ursin, eds., *Coping and Health* (NATO Conference Series III: Human Factors), pp. 259–79. New York: Plenum.

Vachon, M. L. S., J. Rogers, W. A. L. Lyall, and W. J. Lancee. 1982a. Predictors and correlates of adaptation to conjugal bereavement. *American Journal of Psychiatry* 139:998–1002.

Vachon, M. L. S., A. R. Sheldon, W. J. Lancee, W. A. L. Lyall, J. Rogers, and S. J. J. Freeman. 1982b. Correlates of enduring stress patterns following bereavement: Social network, life situation and personality. *Psychological Medicine* 12:783–88.

Vaillant, G. E. 1976. Natural history of male psychological health: V. The relation of choice of ego mechanisms of defense to adult adjustment. *Archives of General Psychiatry* 33:535–45.

Vaillant, G. E. 1977. *Adaptation to Life.* Boston: Little, Brown.

van der Ploeg, H. M., R. Schwarzer, and C. D. Spielberger, eds. 1984. *Advances in Test Anxiety Research.* Vol. 3. Hillsdale, N.J.: Erlbaum.

Van Egeren, L. F., H. Fabrega, Jr., and D. W. Thornton. 1983. Electocardiographic effects of social stress on coronary-prone (Type A) individuals. *Psychosomatic Medicine* 45:195–203.

Vanek, M., and B. J. Cratty. 1970. *Psychology and the Superior Athlete.* London: Macmillan.

Vanfossen, B. E. 1981. Sex differences in the mental health effects of spouse support and equity. *Journal of Health and Social Behavior* 22:130–43.

Vaux, A., P. Burda, and D. Stewart. In press. Orientation towards utilizing support resources. *Journal of Community Psychology.*

Veltfort, H. R., and G. F. Lee. 1943. The Cocoanut Grove fire: A study in scapegoating. *Journal of Abnormal and Social Psychology* 38 (Clinical suppl.):138–54.

Venables, P. H., and I. Martin, eds. 1967. *A Manual of Psychophysiological Methods.* Amsterdam: North-Holland.

Veroff, J., E. Douvan, and R. Kulka. 1981. *The Inner American: A Self-Portrait From 1957–1976.* New York: Basic Books.

Veroff, J., R. Kulka, and E. Douvan. 1981. *Mental Health in America: Patterns of Help-Seeking From 1957 to 1976.* New York: Basic Books.

Vickers, R. R., T. L. Conway, and M. A. Haight. 1983. Association between Levenson's dimensions of locus of control and measures of coping and defense mechanisms. *Psychological Reports* 52:323–33.

Vickers, R. R., and L. K. Hervig. 1981. Comparison of three psychological defense mechanism questionnaires. *Journal of Personality Assessment* 45:630–38.

Vickers, R. R., L. K. Hervig, R. H. Rahe, and R. H. Rosenman. 1981. Type A behavior pattern and coping and defense. *Psychosomatic Medicine* 43:381–96.

Visotsky, H. M., D. A. Hamburg, M. E. Goss, and B. B. Lebovitz. 1961. Coping behavior under extreme stress: Observations of patients with severe poliomyelitis. *Archives of General Psychiatry* 5:423–48.

Vitaliano, P. P., J. Russo, J. E. Carr, R. D. Maiuro, and J. Becker. 1985. The Ways of Coping checklist: Revision and psychometric properties. *Multivariate Behavioral Research* 20:3–26.

Voelz, C. 1982. *Motivation in Coaching a Team Sport.* Reston, Va.:AAHPERD Publications.

Volkan, V. 1966. Normal and pathological grief reactions: A guide for the family physician. *Virginia Medical Monthly* 93:651–56.

Waddell, C. 1982. The process of neutralisation and the uncertainties of cystic fibrosis. *Sociology of Health and Illness* 4:210–20.

Waechter, E. H. 1968. Death anxiety in children with fatal illness. Ph.D. dissertation, Stanford University.

Waechter, E. H. 1971. Children's awareness of fatal illness. *American Journal of Nursing* 71:1168–72.

Wahler, R. 1980. The insular mother: Her problems in parent-child treatment. *Journal of Applied Behavior Analysis* 13:207–19.

Waldrop, M., and C. Halverson. 1975. Intensive and extensive peer behavior: Longitudinal and cross-sectional analysis. *Child Development* 46:19–26.

Wales, J., R. Kane, S. Robbins, L. Berstein, and R. Krasnow. 1983. UCLA Hospice Evaluation Study: Methodology and instrumentation. *Medical Care* 21:734–44.

Wallace, R. K., and H. Benson. 1972. The physiology of meditation. *Scientific American* 226:85–90.

Wallis, C. 1983. Diabetics' new gospel of control. *Time* (December):75.

Wallston, B. S., S. W. Alagna, B. McE. DeVellis, and R. F. DeVellis. 1983. Social support and physical health. *Health Psychology* 2:367–91.

Walsh, J. A. 1972. Defense Mechanism Inventory. In O. K. Buros, ed., *The Seventh Mental Measurements Yearbook,* 1:63–64. Highland Park, N.J.: Gryphon Press.

Wang, P. 1987. A cure for stress? *Newsweek* (October 12) 64–65.

Wankel, L. M., and R. McEwan. 1976. The effect of privately and publicly set goals upon athletic performance. In K. F. Landry and W. A. R. Arban, eds., *Motor Learning, Sport Psychology, Pedagogy, and Didactics of Physical Activity.* Miami: Symposia Specialists.

Warheit, G. J. 1976. A note on natural disasters and civil disturbances: Similarities and differences. *Mass Emergencies* 1:131–37.

Warheit, G. J. 1985. A propositional paradigm for estimating the impact of disasters on mental health. In B. J. Sowder, ed., *Disasters and Mental Health: Selected Contemporary Perspectives,* pp. 196–214. Rockville, Md.: U.S. Department of Health and Human Services.

Warren, R. 1975. The work role and problem coping: Sex differentials in the use of helping systems in urban communities. Paper presented to the annual meeting of the American Sociological Association, San Franciso.

Washburn, S. L., and L. Devore. 1961. The social life of baboons. *Scientific American* 204:62–71.

Waterhouse, G., and H. Strupp. 1984. The patient-therapist relationship: Research from the psychodynamic perspective. *Clinical Psychology Review* 4:77–92.

Watkins, P. L. 1986. Behavior assessment of interpersonal skill among Type A and B college students. Ph.D. dissertation, Virginia Polytechnic Institute and State University, Blacksburg, Va.

Watzlawick, P. 1976. *How Real is Real?* New York: Random House.

Watzlawick, P. 1978. *The Language of Change.* New York: Basic Books.

Weil, R. J., and F. A. Dunsworth. 1958. Psychiatric aspects of disaster—a case history. Some experiences during the Springhill, Nova Scotia mining disaster. *Canadian Psychiatric Association Journal* 3:11–17.

Weinberg, R. S., L. D. Bruya, and A. Jackson. 1985. The effects of goal proximity and goal specificity on endurance performance. *Journal of Sport Psychology* 7:296–305.

Weinberg, R. S., L. D. Bruya, J. Longino, and A. Jackson. 1988. Effect of goal proximity and specificity on endurance performance of primary-grade children. *Journal of Sport and Exercise Psychology* 10:81–91.

Weinberg, R. S., D. Gould, and A. Jackson. 1980. Expectations and performance: An empirical test of Bandura's self-efficacy theory. *Journal of Sport Psychology* 1:320–31.

Weinberg, R. S., and A. Jackson. 1985. The effects of specific vs. nonspecific mental preparation strategies on strength and endurance performance. *International Journal of Sport Psychology* 8:175–80.

Weinberg, R. S., T. G. Seabourne, and A. Jackson. 1981. Effects of visuomotor behavior rehearsal, relaxation, and imagery on karate performance. *Journal of Sport Psychology* 3:228–38.

Weinberger, D. A. 1985. Summary of recent research and current plans. Manuscript.

Weinberger, D. A. In press. The construct validity of the repressive coping style. In J. L. Singer, ed., *Repression and Association: Defense Mechanisms and Personality Style.* Chicago: University of Chicago Press.

Weinberger, D. A., S. S. Feldman, M. E. Ford, and R. L. Chastain. 1987. Construct validation of the Weinberger Adjustment Inventory. Manuscript.

Weinberger, D. A., G. E. Schwartz, and J. R. Davidson. 1979. Low anxious, high anxious and repressive coping styles: Psychometric patterns and behavioral physiological responses to stress. *Journal of Abnormal Psychology* 88:369–80.

Weinberger, M., S. L. Hiner, and W. M. Tierney. 1987. In support of hassles as a measure of stress in predicting health outcomes. *Journal of Behavioral Medicine* 10:19–31.

Weiner, M. A. 1987. *Maximum Immunity.* New York: Pocket Books.

Weinraub, M., and B. M. Wolf. 1983. Effects of stress and social supports on mother-child interactions in single- and two-parent families. *Child Development* 54:1297–1311.

Weinstein, J., J. R. Averill, E. M. Opton, Jr., and R. S. Lazarus. 1968. Defensive style and discrepancy between self-report and physiological indexes of stress. *Journal of Personality and Social Psychology* 10:406–13.

Weisman, A. D. 1972. *On Dying and Denying: A Psychiatric Study of Terminality.* New York: Behavioral Publications.

Weisman, A. D., and R. J. Kastenbaum. 1968. The psychological autopsy: A study of the terminal phase of life. *Community Mental Health Journal Monograph* (Whole No. 4).

Weisman, A. D., and J. W. Worden. 1976–77. The existential plight in cancer: Significance of the first 100 days. *International Journal of Psychiatry and Medicine* 7:1–15.

Weiss, J. M., E. A. Stone, and N. Harrell. 1972. Coping behavior and brain norepinephrine in rats. *Journal of Comparative and Physiological Psychology* 72:153–60.

Weiss, L., and M. Lowenthal. 1975. Life-course perspectives on friendship. In M. L. Lowenthal, M. Thurnher, and D. Chiriboga, eds., *Four Stages of Life.* San Francisco: Jossey-Bass.

Weiss, R. S. 1985. Men and the family. *Family Process* 24:49–58.

Weissman, H. N., K. Ritter, and R. M. Gordon. 1971. Reliability study of the Defense Mechanism Inventory. *Psychological Reports* 29:1237–38.

Weitz, R. 1989. Uncertainty and the lives of persons with AIDS. *Journal of Health and Social Behavior* 30:270–81.

Weitzenhoffer, A. M. 1963. *Hypnotism: An Objective Study in Suggestibility.* New York: Wiley.

Welch, B. L. 1979. *Extra-Auditory Health Effects of Industrial Noise: Surveys of Foreign Literature.* Dayton, Ohio: Wright-Patterson, Aerospace Medical Research Division, Air Force Systems Command.

Welsh, G. G. 1956. Factor dimensions A and R. In G. S. Welsh and W. G. Dahlstrom, eds., *Basic Reading on the MMPI in Psychology and Medicine,* pp. 264–81. Minneapolis: University of Minnesota Press.

Welty, C. 1957. The geography of birds. *Scientific American* 197:118–28.

Wengner, D. E., J. D. Dykes, T. D. Sebock, and J. L Neff. 1975. It's a matter of myths—empirical examination of individual insight into disaster response. *Mass Emergencies* 1:33–46.

Wenz, B. J., and D. J. Strong. 1980. An application of biofeedback and self-regulation procedures with superior athletes: The fine tuning effect. In R. M. Suinn, ed., *Psychology in Sports: Methods and Applications.* Minneapolis: Burgess.

Wethington, E., J. D. McLeod, and R. C. Kessler. 1987. The importance of life events for explaining sex differences in psychological distress. In R. C. Barnett, L. Biener, and G. K. Baruch, eds., *Gender and Stress,* pp. 144–56. New York: Free Press.

Wheaton, B. 1983. Stress, personal coping resources, and psychiatric symptoms: An investigation of interactive models. *Journal of Health and Social Behavior* 24:208–29.

Wheeler, L., H. Reis, and J. Nezlek. 1983. Loneliness, social interaction, and sex roles. *Journal of Personality and Social Psychology* 45:943–53.

Whelan, E. 1978. *Preventing Cancer.* New York: Norton.

Wherry, R. J., and D. H. Fryer. 1949. Buddy ratings: Popularity contest or leadership criterion? *Personnel Psychology* 2:147–59.

White, E. B., and K. S. White. 1962. *A Subtreasury of American Humor.* New York: Capricorn Books.

White, G. F., and J. E. Haas. 1975. *Assessment of Research on Natural Hazards.* Cambridge, Mass.: MIT Press.

White House Conference on Food, Nutrition and Health: Final Report. 1969. Washington, D.C.: U.S. Government Printing Office.

White, R. W. 1974. Strategies of adaptation: An attempt at systematic description. In G. V. Coelho, D. A. Hamburg, and J. E. Adams, eds., *Coping and Adaptation,* pp. 47–68. New York: Basic Books.

Whiting, B., and J. Whiting. 1975. *Children of Six Cultures.* Cambridge, Mass.: Harvard University Press.

Wiener, C. L. 1975. The burden of rheumatoid arthritis. In A. L. Strauss, ed., *Chronic Illness and the Quality of Life,* pp. 1–88. St. Louis: Mosby.

Wikler, L., M. Wasow, and E. Hatfield. 1981. Chronic sorrow revisited: Parent vs. professional depiction of the adjustment of parents of mentally retarded children. *American Journal of Orthopsychiatry* 51:63–70.

Wilkes, R. L., and J. J. Summers. 1984. Cognitions, mediating variables, and strength performance. *Journal of Sport Psychology* 6:351–59.

Wilkins, W. 1974. Social stress and illness in industrial society. In E. Gunderson and R. Rahe, eds., *Life Stress and Illness.* Springfield, Ill.: Charles C. Thomas.

Williams, L. R. T. 1978. Transcendental meditation and mirror tracing. *Perceptual and Motor Skills* 46:371–78.

Williams, L. R. T., and P. G. Herbert. 1976. Transcendental meditation and fine perceptual motor skill. *Perceptual and Motor Skills* 43:303–09.

Williams, L. R. T., B. Lodge, and P. S. Reddish. 1977. Effects of transcendental meditation on rotary pursuit skill. *Research Quarterly* 48:196–201.

Williams, L. R. T., and B. L. Vickerman. 1976. Effects of transcendental meditation on fine motor skill. *Perceptual and Motor Skills* 43:607–13.

Williams, M. H. 1983. *Ergogenic Aids in Sport.* Champaign, Ill.: Human Kinetics.

Williams, R. B., Jr. 1984. An untrusting heart. *The Sciences* 24:31–36.

Williams, R. B., Jr. 1989. *The Trusting Heart: Great News About Type A Behavior.* New York: Random House.

Williams, R. B., Jr., T. L. Haney, K. L. Lee, Y. Yi-Hong Kong, J. A. Blumenthal, and R. E. Whalen. 1980. Type A behavior, hostility, and coronary atherosclerosis. *Psychosomatic Medicine* 42:539–49.

Williams, R. B., Jr., J. D. Lane, C. M. Kuhn, W. Melosh, A. D. White, and S. M. Schanberg. 1982. Type A behavior and elevated physiological and neuroendocrine responses to cognitive tasks. *Science* 218:483–85.

Wills, T. A. 1986. Stress and coping in early adolescence: Relationships to substance use in urban school samples. *Health Psychology* 5:503–29.

Windom, R., J. McGinnus, and J. Fielding. 1987. Examining worksite health promotion programs. *Business and Health* 4:26–37.

Winnicott, D. W. 1958. Anxiety associated with insecurity. In *Collected Papers,* pp. 97–100. London: Tavistock.

Winter, B. 1982. Relax and win. *Sports and Athlete* (May):72–78.

Witkin, H. A., R. B. Dyk, H. F. Faterson, D. R. Goodenough, and S. A. Karp. 1962. *Psychological Differentiation.* New York: Wiley.

Witkin, H. A., D. R. Goodenough, and P. K. Oltman. 1979. Psychological differentiation: Current status. *Journal of Personality and Social Psychology* 37:1127–45.

Wolchik, S. A., I. N. Sandler, and S. L. Braver. 1984. The social support networks of children of divorce. Paper presented at the American Psychological Association meeting, Toronto.

Wolfe, V. V., A. J. Finch, Jr., C. F. Saylor, R. L. Blount, T. P. Pallmeyer, and D. J. Carek. 1987. Negative affectivity in children: A multitrait-multimethod investigation. *Journal of Consulting and Clinical Psychology* 55:245–50.

Wolfenstein, M. 1957. *Disaster.* London: Routledge.

Wolff, C. T., S. B. Friedman, M. A. Hofer, and J. W. Mason. 1964. Relationship between psychological defenses and mean urinary 17-hydroxycorticosteroid excretion rates: Parts I and II. *Psychosomatic Medicine* 26:576–609.

Wolpe, J. 1958. *Psychotherapy by Reciprocal Inhibition.* Stanford, Calif.: Stanford University Press.

Wong, P. T. P. In press. Stress measurement. *Stress Medicine* (special issue).

Woodrow, J. Z. 1973. A factor analysis and revision of the Defense Mechanism Inventory. Ph.D. dissertation, Ohio University.

Woolfolk, R. L., S. M. Murphy, D. Gottesfeld, and D. Aitken. 1985. Effects of mental rehearsal of task motor activity and mental depiction of task outcome on motor skill performance. *Journal of Sport Psychology* 7:191–97.

Work in America: Report of a Special Task Force to the Secretary of Health, Education, and Welfare. 1971. Cambridge, Mass.: MIT Press.

Wortman, C. B. 1976. Causal attributions and personal control. In J. H. Harvey, W. J. Ickes, and R. F. Kidd, eds., *New Directions in Attribution Research.* Vol. 1. Hillsdale, N.J.: Erlbaum.

Wortman, C. B., and J. W. Brehm. 1975. Responses to uncontrollable outcomes: An integration of reactance theory and the learned helplessness model. In L. Berkowitz, ed., *Advances in Experimental Social Psychology.* Vol. 8. New York: Academic Press.

Wortman, C. B., and C. Dunkel-Schetter. 1979. Interpersonal relationships and cancer: A theoretical analysis. *Journal of Social Issues* 35:120–55.

Wortman, C. B., and R. C. Silver. 1987. Coping with irrevocable loss. In G. R. VandenBos and B. K. Bryant, eds., *Cataclysms, Crises, and Catastrophes: Psychology in Action,* pp. 189–235. Washington, D.C.: American Psychological Association.

Wortman, C. B., and R. C. Silver. 1989. The myths of coping with loss. *Journal of Consulting and Clinical Psychology* 57:349–57.

Wortman, C. B., and R. C. Silver. In press. Effective mastery of bereavement and widowhood: Longitudinal research. In P. B. Baltes and M. M. Baltes, eds., *Successful Aging: Research and Theory.* London: Cambridge University Press.

Wright, B. A. 1983. *Physical Disability—A Psychosocial Approach.* 2d ed. New York: Harper & Row.

Wright, L. 1984. A possible biochemical mechanism for explaining Type A-related coronary artery disease. Speech presented at the Michael Dinoff Memorial Lecture, University of Alabama, Tuscaloosa, April.

Wright, L. 1985. The Way of Life (WOL) scale. Manuscript.

Wright, L. 1987. Type-A behavior pattern and measures of control: A replication. Manuscript.

Wright. L. 1988. The Type A behavior pattern and coronary artery disease: Quest for the active ingredients and the elusive mechanism. *American Psychologist* 43:2–14.

Wright, L., and K. Schmidt-Walker. 1986. An expanded structured interview for measuring time urgency and chronic activation. Manuscript.

Wulf, S. 1987. World Series. *Sports Illustrated* (November 2):28–41.

Yamamoto, K., and H. M. Felsenthal. 1982. Stressful experience of children: Professional judgements. *Psychological Reports* 50:1087–93.

Yanagida, E. H., J. Streltzer, and A. Siemsen. 1981. Denial in dialysis patients: Relationship to compliance and other variables. *Psychosomatic Medicine* 43:271–80.

Yankelovich, D., and J. Immerwahr. 1983. *Putting the Work Ethic to Work: A Public Agenda Report on Restoring America's Competitive Vitality.* New York: Public Agenda Foundation.

Yarnold, P. R., and L. G. Grim. 1982. Time urgency among coronary-prone individuals. *Journal of Abnormal Psychology* 91:175–77.

Yerkes, R. M., and J. D. Dodson. 1908. The relation of strength of stimulus to rapidity of habit-formation. *Journal of Comparative and Neurological Psychology* 18:459–82.

Young, M., and P. Willmott. 1957. *Family and Kinship in East London.* London: Routledge and Kegan Paul.

Zaichkowsky, L. D., and W. E. Sime. 1982. *Stress Management for Sport.* Reston, Va.: AAHPERD Publications.

Zarski, J. J. 1984. Hassles and health: A replication. *Health Psychology* 3:243–51.

Zborowski, M. 1969. *People in Pain.* San Francisco: Jossey-Bass.

Zedeck, S. 1971. Problem with the use of "moderator" variables. *Psychological Bulletin* 76:295–310.

Zeuner, F. E. 1963. *A History of Domesticated Animals.* London: Hutchinson.

Ziegler, S. G., J. Klinzing, and K. Williamson. 1982. The effects of two stress management training programs on cardiorespiratory efficiency. *Journal of Sport Psychology* 4:280–89.

Zisook, S., and S. R. Shuchter. 1986. The first four years of widowhood. *Psychiatric Annals* 15:288–94.

Zuckerman, M. 1979. *Sensation Seeking: Beyond the Optimal Level of Arousal.* Hillsdale, N.J.: Erlbaum.

Zuehlke, T. E. 1975. Psychotherapy with terminally ill patients. Ph.D. dissertation, University of South Dakota.

INDEX

Abeloff, M. D., 67, 377
Abernethy, V., 260
Abrahams, M. J., 110
Abrahamson, L. Y., 131, 132
Absenteeism, and stress, 484–85, 490, 494, 496
Academy of Behavioral Medicine Research, 276
Achievement: and Type A behavior, 281; and work, 149–51
Achte, K. A., 373
Ackerman, A., 240
ACTH, *see* Adrenocorticotrophic hormone
Adams, G. R., 112
Adams, J. E., 5, 7, 206*n*1, 228, 305*n*2
Adams, P. R., 112
Adaptation, 4, 23, 302, 430; diseases of, 30; and hassles, 416; students' use of, 337–51
Addiction, 408; breaking of, 475–82; genetic aspects of, 476–79; relapses in, 481; self-cure of, 479–81; therapy for, 482; and will to change, 480–81
Adelberg, T., 260
Ader, R., 10, 414
Aderman, D., 373
Adler, A., 115, 134, 287
Adolescent Hassles Inventory, 162
Adolescent Perceived Events Scale, 162
Adolescents: hassles among, 178; health habits of, 65; uplifts among, 178
Adrenal cortex: in alarm reaction, 25, 310; and dominance, 92
Adrenal exhaustion, 51–52; *see also* Cousins, Norman
Adrenalin, 28; and coronary heart disease, 286, 288; and Type A behavior, 279, 297
Adrenocorticotrophic hormone (ACTH), 26, 28, 31
Affleck, G., 69
Aggression: and cancer, 11; in Type A behavior, 279
Aging, and health psychology, 79
AIDS: cost of, 77; diagnosis of, 358–59; fear of, 356; psychosocial factors in, 67; role of stress in, 305*n*6; uncertainty in, 303, 352–69; *see also* PWAs
AIDS-related complex (ARC), 303, 354, 369*n*3
Air raids, children in, 314
Alarm reaction (in general adaptation syndrome), 24, 30, *see also* Stress reactions
Alcohol, use of, 10, 78, 420, 429; among disaster victims, 111, 117, 119; and cancer, 11; and stress, 39, 270, 331, 408; and stress in the

Alcohol *(Continued)*
workplace, 484; and terminal illness, 380
Alcoholics Anonymous, 409
Alcoholism, 476, 477–78; recovery from, 479–80
Aldag, J., 142
Aldwin, C., 215, 226, 241
Alexander, Franz, 66
Alfert, E., 4, 235
Ali, Muhammad, 433, 454
Alienation: and coping, 154; and hardiness, 249–50, 253–54
Allen, M. T., 79
Allport, G. W., 284, 285
Allred, K. D., 185
Alper, T. G., 264
Alpert, R., 208
Alsop, Stewart, 376
Ambiguity, and stress, 20
American Heart Association, 64
American Psychiatric Association, 301
Anatomy of An Illness as Perceived by the Patient (Cousins), 19
Anchorage, Alaska, earthquake, 108
Anderson, D., 487
Anderson, J. L., 372, 385–86
Andrew, J. M., 205*n*1, 229, 231, 235, 239
Andrew 1970 Sentence-Completion Test, 239
Anger: among AIDS patients, 361; and cancer, 11; among terminally ill patients, 376; and Type A behavior, 186, 280, 287, 288, 291, 295
Annalisa, D., 439
Anthony, E. J., 301; on overwhelming stress in children, 307–18
Antonoff, S. R., 373
Antonovsky, A., 417
Antonucci, T., 258
Anxiety, 215; among AIDS patients, 356–57, 359, 363, 365; among athletes, 432, 463–64, 466, 468–69; and cancer, 11; among children, 164–65, 315; correlates with uplifts, 173–74, 176, 179; and development of illness, 66; among disaster victims, 116; among the dying, 373, 378–79, 382, 383; among dying children, 375; in Freud, 208; and life events, 335; among students, 350; and workplace stress, 491
Anxiety-stress spiral, 436
Apathy: among disaster victims, 117
Appley, M. H., 1, 18, 42
Appraisal process (in coping), 72
Arizona AIDS Project, 355
Arizona Department of Health Services, 354
Armstrong, S., 375
Arrick, M. C., 398
Arthur, R. J., 83
Asendorpf, J. B., 236
Ashley, F., 64
Aslan, Ana, 60
Aspirin, toxicity of, 53, 54, 58, 61*n*1
Assertiveness, and stress in the workplace, 14, 490
Asterita, M. F., 10
Auerbach, S. M., 205*n*1
Austin, S. H., 230
Autogenic training, 14, 433, 436, 438–39, 473; and stress in the workplace, 485
Autohypnosis, *see* Hypnosis, self-
Automatized adaptive behavior, 197–200
Avener, M., 447
Averill, J. R., 4, 5, 209, 216, 229, 235, 419
Avoidance: as coping mechanism, 72, 75, 190, 196, 215, 225, 235, 239; humor as, 344, 347–49
Azidothymidine (AZT), *see* AIDS; Zidovudine

Bachrach, K. M., 233
Backett, E. M., 316
Baer, L., 458
Bai, A. J. L., 441
Bailyn, L., 144
Bajusz, E., 286
Baker, E., 105
Bales, R., 265, 268
Balls, P., 258, 260
Baluk, U., 403
Bandura, A., 64–65, 68, 225, 283, 384, 423
Barber, T. X., 452, 453

Barkun, M., 102
Baron, R., 45
Barrera, M., 258, 260
Barry, J., 235
Bartolome, F., 144–45
Barton, A. H., 103, 113, 114
Bass, D. M., 377, 381
Bast, B. A., 238
Baude, E., 414
Baugher, R. J., 374
Baum, Andrew, 4, 5, 8, 10, 46, 71, 81, 82, 120, 121, 124, 125, 126, 129, 131, 132, 134, 135, 136, 210, 216, 241, 305*n*1; on toxins, technology and natural disasters, 97–139
Baumann, D. D., 126
Baumann, L. J., 69
Baun, W., 487
Baylor, Don, 446
Bean, G., 205*n*1
Beary, J. F., 436, 441, 442
Beck, A. T., 212. 431*n*1
Beck Depression Inventory, 391
Becker, J., 259
Becker, M. H., 64, 354
Beecher, Henry K., 59
Beeson, D., 357
Beisser, A. R. 206*n*1
Bell, P. A., 236
Belle, D., 258, 259, 260, 263, 266, 272, 273; on gender differences, 258–74
Belle, P. A., 185
Bells, S. S., 159, 160
Benedek, E., 314, 315
Benner, P., 215
Bennet, G., 110
Bennett, B. K., 438
Benson, H., 436, 441, 442
Bereavement, 310, 388–89, 395, 415
Bereavement syndrome, 310
Beres, D., 253
Berkman, L. F., 45, 270, 271
Bernacki, E., 487
Bernard, C., 23
Bernard, J., 267, 268
Bernard, M. E., 212
Bernard, T. M., 68
Bernstein, D. A., 486
Berton, K., 296
Bhrolchain, M., 258, 260
Biernacki, Patrick, 479
Billing, E., 206*n*1
Billings, A. G., 72, 159, 178, 228, 232, 233, 241, 242, 244
Billings and Moos Coping Measures, 232, 241–42, 244
Biobehavioral responses, 36, 46–47, 67
Biofeedback, 14, 32, 411, 425; in sports, 442–45, 473; and stress in the workplace, 485, 490, 493; and Type A behavior, 298
Biologic stress syndrome, *see* General adaptation syndrome
Biopsychosocial model (in health psychology), 20, 63
Birnbaum, H. G., 379
Birnbaum, R. M., 4
Bjork, J. P., 162, 176, 177
Blacky Defense Preference Inventory, 237
Blair, S., 487
Blake, K., 59
Blakelock, E. H., 193
Blame, psychology of, 131–32
Blanchard, E. B., 78
Bleuler, Manfred, 317
Bloch, D. A., 312
Block, N., 446–47
Blucker, J. A., 462
Bluebond-Langner, M., 375–76
Bly, J., 487
Bobo, J. K., 159, 160, 162, 178
Bolin, R., 98, 106, 113, 114
Bonaccorsi, M., 444
Bonica, J., 484
Boon, C., 398
Booth, A., 262
Booth-Kewley, S., 66, 68
Borkovec, T. A., 486
Bornstein, P. E., 393
Borysenko, J., 486
Bostock, T., 115
Botvin, G. J., 65
Boutcher, S. H., 449, 466
Bowlby, J., 305, 310, 390, 391, 393, 394, 395
Bowman, U., 108
Bowne, D., 487
Bracken, M. B., 390, 404
Bradburn, N. M., 159, 160, 177

Bradley, L. A., 76
Brannon, L., 10
Braukmann, W., 212
Braver, S. L., 263
Brehm, J. W., 131, 136
Breznitz, S., 4, 203, 216
Bridge, T. P., 306*n*6
Brief, A. P., 142
Britton, S., 402, 404
Brock, D. B., 386
Brodsky, C., 484
Bromet, E., 119–20
Brousseau, K. R., 145
Brown, B. A., 442
Brown, C. C., 4
Brown, D. R., 451, 455, 459
Brown, G., 258, 260
Brown, G. W., 324
Brown, J. T., 394, 399, 400, 401
Brown, P., 261, 263, 264
Brownell, K. D., 65
Bruya, L. D., 461
Bryant, B., 261, 266, 268
Bucher, R., 129, 130
Buchholz, R. A., 141
Buell, J. C., 285
Buffalo Creek flood (West Virginia), 116–18, 127, 133, 134, 135; children in, 313, 318; chronic effects of, 137
Buhrmeister, D., 266
Bull, J. C., 390
Bulletin boards, in sport psychology, 471
Bulman, R. J., 69, 132, 218
Burda, P. 264
Burger, J. M., 75, 289
Burish, T. G., 75, 76
Burke, R. J., 263, 265
Burlingham, D., 314
Burt, C. E., 162, 176, 177
Bury, M., 358, 359
Bussman, K., 289
Butcher, J. N., 9
Butehorn, L., 260
Butt, J. H., 193
Byrne, A. T. J., 461
Byrne, D., 7, 184, 196, 211, 229, 231, 235, 236, 417
Caldwell, M. A., 262, 267
Calhoun, J. B., 81
California Department of Mental Health: stress management program of, 497
California Psychological Inventory, 238
Campbell, A., 265, 308
Cameron, J., 381
Cancer: coping by patients, 199, 218, 230; denial of, 202–3; and the immune system, 11–12; and personality, 67; and stress, 41; terminal, 374; and toxic substances, 129
Candy, S. G., 262
Cannon, W. B., 2, 23, 52, 56, 69, 414
Caplan, G., 309
Caplan, R. D., 45
Cardiovascular disease: behavioral aspects of, 10; effect on the workplace, 484–85; prevention of, 79; psychological factors in, 46; and Type A behavior, 66
Cardiovascular patients: and social support, 260; and Type A behavior, 291–92
Carol, M. P., 436, 441, 442
Carroll, D., 466
Carson, R. C., 9
Carter Center of Emory University, 486
Cartwright, A., 372, 385–86
Carver, C. S., 68, 72
Caserta, M. S., 391
Cassel, J., 45, 258, 260
Cassem, N. H., 10, 202, 204, 205*n*1, 232, 234, 240
Cassileth, B. R., 377
Catastrophes, technological, *see* Disasters, humanmade
Catatoxic responses, 28–29
Catecholamines, role of in stress, 13, 279, 286, 414
Cauce, A. M., 263
Caudill, D., 468, 469
Centering, 449
Centers for Attitudinal Healing, 382
Chabot, J. A., 235
Challenges, 420; in early childhood, 248–49; and hardiness, 245, 255–56
Chalmers, Thomas C., 59

Chamberlain, B. C., 133
Change, in adulthood, 320
Chaplin, J. P., 286
Chapman, C. R., 75, 78
Charlesworth, E. A., 1
Charmaz, K., 362
Chaves, J. F., 452, 453
Chernobyl accident, 127, 136, 139
Child, I. L., 208
Children: bereaved, 397; death of, 329; dying, 375–76; entry of into school, 324, 329; kidnapping of, 313; nurturing of, 266; social support of, 268–69; stress among, 162, 301, 307–18; stress-resistant, 314; success among, 247–48; as victims, 312–15, 317
Children's Depression Inventory, 165
Children's Hassles Scale (CHS), 85, 163–64, 167, 168–69, 175, 177, 180
Children's Uplifts Scale (CUS), 85, 164, 169–70, 175, 177, 181
Chiriboga, D. A., 263, 264
Chodorow, N., 260
Choi, S., 296
Cholesterol, 275
Christians, fundamentalist: and AIDS, 359–61
Chronic activation, in Type A behavior, 186, 278, 280, 286, 288, 291, 292–95
CHS, *see* Children's Hassles Scale
Cigarette smoking, *see* Tobacco, use of
Cinciripini, P. M., 76
Clark, L. F., 72, 74
Clark, L. V., 448, 463
Clarke, J. C., 451
Clayton, P. J., 390, 393
Cleary, P. D., 65, 121
Clore, G. L., 211
"Closing the Gap" (Carter Center report), 486
Cobb, S., 45, 134, 151, 258
Cocoanut Grove fire (1943), 133, 396; blame for, 130; chronic effects of, 134
Coehlo, G. B., 5, 228, 305*n*2
Cofer, C. N., 18
Cognition, 333; in appraisal of stress, 42–44, 46; comforting, 339–43; and coping, 184, 193–95, 199–200, 209–13, 216; and denial, 203; and emotion, 209–13; in illness, 68–69; measurements of, 240
Cognitive-affective stress management training, 464
Cognitive appraisal, 210–11; of stress, 418–20
Cognitive behavior therapy, 407–8, 422; goals of, 423–24; methods of treatment in, 424–27; role of therapist in, 428–29; therapist-client relationship in, 427–29
Cognitive intervention programs, for athletes, 461–62
Cognitive strategies, 330; for athletes, 445–61
Cohen, E. S., 111, 134
Cohen, F., 5, 6, 7, 8, 9, 184, 196, 205*n*1, 212, 228, 229, 230, 232, 233, 234, 235, 239, 240, 243, 308, 368, 417; on measurement of coping, 228–44
Cohen, J. B., 38, 125, 204, 415
Cohen, L. H., 162, 176, 177, 263
Cohen, R. J., 53, 54, 58, 61*n*2
Cohen, S., 41, 45, 70, 73, 74, 159, 243
Cohler, B. M., 259, 266, 272
Cohn, R. M., 151
Cole, R., 484
Coleman, J. C., 9
Coleman, T. R., 453
Colletta, N., 260
Collins, D. L., 8, 46, 121, 132, 216
Collins, R. L., 73
Colson, S., 292
Colton, J. A., 162
Comaroff, J., 353
Commitment: and hardiness, 245, 253–54; and health, 184; and parent-child relationships, 246–47
Compas, B. E., 159, 160, 162, 163
Conditioning, classical: and Type A behavior, 286
Conflict, 4, 5
Conrad, P., 353, 358, 359
Contrada, R. J., 289
Controllability, 308; among AIDS patients, 357–58, 362–65; and coping, 74–75, 77, 205; and course of ill-

Controllability *(Continued)*
ness, 70; in disasters, 103; among the dying, 384d early childhood experience, 247–48; and hardiness, 245, 250, 254–55; and health, 184; of humanmade disasters, 127, 132; and stress, 20; and Type A behavior, 289–90; and uncertainty, 367–68; and work, 149–51
Converse, P. E., 265, 308
Conway, T. L., 238
Cook, D. W., 392
Cook, W., 291
Cooper, C., 237
Cooper, C. L., 1
Cooper, H. M., 289
Cooper, R. M, 256
COPES (self-report measure), 162
Coping: among adolescents, 178; among AIDS patients, 365; and alienation, 154; animal models of, 190, 200, 207–9; anticipatory, 226, 332–33; behavioral methods of, 150–53, 157*n*1; and cardiovascular response, 190; among children, 178d cognition, 209–13; and cognitive behavior therapy, 424–27; cognitive methods of, 150–53, 157*n*1, 183, 190, 193–95; concept of, 5–9; confrontive, 220–21, 225, 241; and controllability, 205; creativity in, 317; definition of, 71; and development of illness, 65–66, 67–68, 71, 228; dimensions of, 231–32; among disaster victims, 117, 121, 128, 138; emotion-focused, 6–7, 184, 210–12, 221, 223–26; episodic, 229–30; flexibility in, 242–43; hierarchies of, 200; impact of on emotions, 222–23; and life strains, 330–36; and major loss, 388–405, 400–1, 403; measurements of, 9, 72, 184, 228–29, 230–33, 241–44; as mediator of emotions, 213–15; in Menninger, 191; orthodox approaches to, 183, 189–92, 195, 207–9; outcomes of, 6–7, 200–5; palliative, 6, 425; parental, 238; popular views of, 189; problem-focused, 6, 210–12, 219–22, 223, 409, 425; processes of, 5, 211–13; psychological aspects of, 6, 9; psychophysiology of, 190; regressive, 185, 187*n*4; regulatory devices in, 191–92; research on, 1, 71–72, 73, 330; retrospective accounts of, 234–35; and self-concept, 155–56; self-reporting of, 234; situation-specific measures of, 233; sociological aspects of, 6; strategies for, 7–9, 331; styles of, 7–9, 44–45, 65, 67–68, 192–95, 229; taxonomy of, 6; teaching of, 422, 428; traits of, 192–95, 229; transformational, 185, 187*n*4; and work, 145
Coping-Defense Scales (Joffe and Naditch), 184, 238
Coping Operations Preference Enquiry, 238
Coppel, C. B., 259
Corbin, C. B., 448, 449
Cordes, R. S., 202
Corey, C. R., 358
Coronary artery disease, and Type A behavior, 275–99
Coronary heart disease (CHD): mechanism-related research in, 296–97; prediction of, 293–96; and repression, 236; risk factors in, 276, 277, 294; and Type A behavior, 285–88
Corticoids, 27–29, 52, 414
Corticotrophic hormone releasing factor (CRF), 26
Coser, R. L., 343
Costa, A., 444
Costa, P. T., 66, 159, 177
Countertransferences (of stress), 315
Cousins, Norman, 19; hospitalization of, 49–50, 55; medication of, 52–53; recovery of, 56–58; on own illness, 48–61
Cowie, B., 353, 358
Cox, D. J., 159, 160
Cox, M., 261
Cox, R. H., 261, 408, 410*n*2; on intervention strategies, 432–74
Coyne, J. C., 74, 215, 220, 226
Craig, Y., 397
Craighill, P. C., 208
Crandall, E. K. B., 397
Cratty, B. J., 439
Crawshaw, R., 107

Creativity, and will to live, 60
Creighton, J., 381, 382
Crnic, K. A., 260
Crockenberg, S. B., 260
Cronkite, R. C., 8
Crow, M. A., 442, 443
Crowding, 87–91; effect of on humans, 92; among experimental animals, 90–92; social determinants of, 95
Croyle, R. T., 68
Cullen, M. R., 121
Culpability, in natural disasters, 124
Cummings, K. M., 75
Cummings, N., 483, 489
Cupp, P., 160, 178, 179
CUS, *see* Children's Uplifts Scale
"CustomCare" (health management program), 497
Cyclone Tracy (Australia, 1974), 112

Dalton, G. W., 143, 151
D'Amato, M. E., 4
Dancing manias, 95
Daniels, F. S., 445
Dann, S., 314
Dansak, D. A., 202
Danskin, D. G., 442, 443
Danzig, E. R., 102
Davenport, P. R., 151
Davidson, A., 312
Davidson, J. R., 231, 235, 236, 240
Davidson, L. M., 5, 18, 19, 20, 46, 104, 105, 121, 124, 125, 126, 132, 410*n*1; on specificity and stress research, 36–47
Davis, F., 415
Davis, M., 14, 407
Davison, G. C., 13, 302
Death: and coping, 303, 304; demographic aspects of, 370; fear of among AIDS patients, 362–64; preventability of, 486; psychological distress of, 370; warning of, 371
Death imprint, 318
DeBerry, S., 412
Deci, E., 150
Decker, S., 384
Deckner, C. W., 438
Deegan, M. J., 390
Deevey, E. S., 90
Defense Mechanism Inventory (DMI), 232, 237–38
Defense mechanisms, 7, 10, 183, 193, 199; need for, 338–43; among students, 303; students' use of, 337–51; in Vaillant, 200
deGoza, S., 338, 343
Delong, D. R., 205*n*1
DeLongis, A., 159, 177, 416
Dembo, T., 403
Dembroski, T. M., 66, 277, 278, 286, 287
Demming, B., 409
de Monchaux, D., 83
Demographic Yearbook, 371
Denial, 7, 10, 201–6, 218–19, 235, 308, 338; among AIDS patients, 357–58; among cancer patients, 11, 377, 378; among cardiac patients, 240; and death, 303; effect of on emotions, 216–17; and major loss, 392, 400; measurements of, 240; as palliative, 425; positive aspects of, 203; timing of, 204
DePaulo, B., 260, 264
Depner, C., 258, 262
Depression, 212; absence of after loss, 399–401; and avoidance of problems, 215; and cancer, 11; among children, 165; coping strategies in, 226; correlates with uplifts, 176; and development of illness, 66; among disaster victims, 116; among the dying, 373, 376, 383, 386; and grieving, 304; among hospice patients, 381; and life events, 158, 335; and major loss, 390–94; necessity of, 393–94; and physical disability, 390–91, 393; and recovery from loss, 392; among retirees, 321; and social support, 260; and stress, 258; among students, 349–50; therapeutic aspects of, 392; among widows, 390–91, 396; among women, 160, 272; and workplace stress, 491
Derogatis, L. R., 67, 323, 377, 394
Descriptionist theory of cognition, 446
Desensitization, in phobias, 462
Deutsch, H., 391, 392, 400
Dew, M. A., 119

Dewitt, D. J., 444
DiCara, L. V., 442
Dickson, A. L., 237
Diener, E., 159, 160
Diet: and cancer, 11; and stress, 10
Dillon, H., 115, 134
DiMatteo, M. R., 63
Dimond, M. F., 391
Dimond, R. E., 262
Dimsdale, J. E., 240
Dinardo, Q., 392, 393
Disasters, 415; agents of, 101; blame for, 129–33; characteristics of, 124–33; children in, 312–15; chronic consequences of, 133–37; definition of, 100–4, 138; and illness, 110–12; individual responses to, 107–8; nature of, 99–100, 104–6; positive effects of, 106; psychological aspects of, 106, 110–12, 124–33; research on, 97–99, 137–38, 317; responses of organizations to, 108–9; responses to, 106–9; social aspects of, 113–14, 118; as type of crisis, 103; warnings of, 105
Disasters, humanmade, 82, 115–17, 352; characteristics of, 122, 124, 126–28, 135; chronic effects of, 133–37; compared to natural disasters, 122–24; predictability of, 136; uncertainty in, 128
Disasters, natural, 82; characteristics of, 123, 125–26, 135; chronic effects of, 113–14; compared to humanmade disasters, 122–24; effects of, 109–13
Disaster syndrome, 107
Disease, *see* Illness
Distancing, 241; as coping mechanism, 217, 218–19, 221, 223, 225
Distress, and major loss, 390–94
Ditto, P. H., 68
Divorce, 325, 327, 328, 335, 336, 415; and mobilization of support, 263–65
Dmitrova, S., 459
Dodson, J. D., 221, 410*n*2
Dohrenwend, B. P., 83, 119
Dohrenwend, B. S., 71, 83, 269
Dominance: among animals, 92–93; and crowding, 91–95
Donovon, M. I., 399
Dosedel, J., 484
Doster, N. J., 381
Douglas, L., 402
Douglas, M., 352
Douvan, E., 263, 264, 266
Doyle, P., 394, 401
Drabek, T. E., 97, 103, 105, 113, 114, 126, 129, 130–31
"Dream" (sense of self), 144, 157
Drolette, M. E., 193
Dubos, Rene, 81; on the living world, 87–96
Dunbar, F., 65
Dunkel-Schetter, C., 74, 220
Dunsworth, F. A., 109
Dusek, D. E., 13, 14, 407
Dying: in hospices, 376–77; interventions for patients, 378–84; personal accounts of, 376; research on, 370–87; socio-emotional aspects of, 385; stress of, 373–78
Dynes, R. R., 101, 109, 113, 114

Eaker, E. D., 186
Easterbrook, J. A., 208, 221
Eating disorders, 10
Eckenrode, J., 159, 259, 269, 273
Edmonston, W. E., 452, 454
Ego processes, in coping, 191–92
Einstein, A., 412
Eisdorfer, C., 228, 415, 418
Ekman, P., 311
Electroencephalograms (EEG), 443
Electromyography (EMG), 443, 444–45; and imagery, 448
Elias, W., 487
Eliot, R. S., 285
Elite, A., 483
Elizur, E., 397
Elliott, G. R., 228, 415, 418
Elliott, R., 4
Ellis, A., 212, 381, 431*n*1
Emotions: adaptive functions of, 208; cognitive principles of, 209–13; coping as mediator of, 184, 207, 213–15, 223–24; impact of coping on, 222–23; positive, 52, 55; processes of, 211–13

Emotions, negative, 66–68, 320; and dying, 304, 374
Endorphins, 31, 310; role of in addiction, 478–79
Eng, A., 65
Engel, G. L., 63
Environment, stresses in, 81
Epidemiology, 88, 91; of crowd diseases, 95
Epstein, M. L., 212, 448
Epstein, S., 4, 231, 235, 239
Erdelyi, M. H., 201
Erffmeyer, E. S., 464
Ergogenic aids (to performance), 433
Erikson, Erik, 329
Erikson, K., 113, 118, 129, 312, 316
Escape-avoidance, 226, 241
Eshelman, E. R., 14, 407
Eth, S., 314
Eustress, 33
Evans, P. A., 144–45
Evans, R. I., 65, 79
Everly, G. S., 13, 14, 407
Eysenck, H. J., 11

Falek, A., 402, 404
Families: and hassles, 171–72; support systems of, 266
Fan support, in sport psychology, 471–72
Farberow, N., 383
Feather, N. T., 151
Federal Emergency Management Agency, 101
Feigenberg, L., 381, 382
Feinleib, M., 186
Feiring, C., 260
Feist, J., 10
Feldman, S. S., 86*n*2; on uplifts and hassles, 158–81
Felner, R. D., 83, 263
Felsenthal, H. M., 162
Felson, R. B., 352
Felton, J., 484
Feltz, D. L., 449
Fenichel, O., 202
Fenker, R. M., 447
Fenz, W. D., 231, 235, 239
Festinger, L., 337
Feynman, R., 150
Field, T. M., 1
Field dependence-independence (coping mechanism), 194–95, 309
Fielding, J., 485, 497
"Fight or flight response," 279, 286, 287, 311, 414, 436
Fine, S. A., 144
Finlayson, A., 260
Fiore, J., 259
Fischer, C., 259, 262, 265, 272
Fisher, A. C., 443, 447
Fisher, R. H., 386
Fleishman, J. A., 238
Fleming, I. C., 70, 121
Fleming, R., 70, 82, 121, 124, 125, 126, 129, 132, 134, 210, 241
Fletcher, B., 72
Floods, 126; victims of, 107, 110, 111, 114, 116–18
Flynn, C. B., 120
Foege, William H., 486
Folkman, S., 4, 5, 8, 69, 71, 72, 73, 74, 85, 161, 183, 184, 187*n*4, 209, 210, 211, 212, 215, 216, 217, 218, 220, 222, 225, 226, 228, 230, 232, 233, 234–35, 240, 241, 244, 305*n*3, 410*n*1, 418, 419, 420; on concept of coping, 189–206; on coping and emotion, 207–27
Ford, M. E.: on uplifts and hassles, 158–81
Forman, S., 412
Fox, B. H., 66, 67
Fox, H., 261, 263, 264
Fox, R., 343
Frankenhaeuser, M., 46
Frankl, V., 199
Frederick, C. J., 114, 115–16
Fredericq, L., 23
Freedman, J. L., 81
Freeman, H. E., 358
French, J. R., 45, 260
French, S. N., 444
Frese, M., 213
Freud, A., 314
Freud, S., 208, 305, 390
Friedman, H. S., 63, 66, 68, 279
Friedman, M., 1, 67, 186, 280, 283, 295, 298, 299
Friedman, S. B., 199, 417–18

Friendship Support Scale, 165–66
Friesen, W. V., 311
Frieze, I. H., 132
Fritz, C. E., 105–6, 107, 114
Froese, A. P., 240
Frustration, 3
Fryer, D. H., 292
Fullerton, D. T., 391
Funk, S. C., 185
Funkenstein, D. H., 193
Funt, Allen, 55
Furman, W., 266

Gabriel, T. J., 434
Gaines, L. L., 195
Gal, R., 216
Galanter, L. R., 102
Galvanic skin response (GSR), 444
Gans, J. S., 401, 403
Gardner, R. W., 194, 199, 231, 235
Garland, T. N., 377
Garmezy, Norman, 313–14, 400
Garrison, J., 412
Gatchel, R. J., 46, 120, 131, 132, 136
Gauron, E. F., 433
Gender differences: changes in, 266; and hassles, 171, 172, 176–77, 178–79; in social support, 185, 263–69, 273–74; and stress, 259–61; in supportiveness, 271; in uplifts, 178–79
General adaptation syndrome, 11, 18, 24–25, 30, 31, 37–38, 71, 310, 414
General Health Questionnaire (GHQ), 391
General Self-Worth Scale, 166
George, J. M., 205*n*1
Gibbs, J., 487
Gibbs, M. S., 121
Gill, J. J., 293, 411
Gilligan, C., 260, 265
Girdano, D. A., 13, 14, 407
Girton, S. E., 399
Glaser, B. G., 353, 356
Glaser, R., 67
Glass, A., 113
Glass, D. C., 45, 70, 287
Glass, G., 488, 492
Gleser, G., 98, 116, 117, 126, 133, 134, 231, 237
Glick, I. O., 390, 404
Gmelch, G., 352
Goal setting, 152, 433, 434, 459–61; in sports, 470, 473; strategies for, 460–61
Godkin, M. A., 381
Goffman, E., 415
Goldberger, L., 308
Goldfried, M. R., 431*n*1
Goldhaber, M. U., 120
Goldiamond, I., 403
Goldsteen, K. S., 113
Goldsteen, R. L., 113
Goldstein, M. J., 7, 193, 196, 202, 231, 235, 417
Golec, J., 102
Golin, S., 235
Goltz, J. D., 109
Goodenough, D. R., 194, 195
Goodhart, D., 221
Goodwin, F. K., 305*n*6
Gordon, J. R., 65
Gordon, R. M., 237
Gore, S., 258, 259, 260, 269
Gorton, B. E., 457
Gorzynski, J. G., 197
Gottlieb, B., 260
Gould, D., 459, 469
Granger, G., 396
Green, B. L., 98, 99, 116, 117, 126, 133, 134
Green, M., 371, 372, 390, 391–92, 393, 395, 399, 402
Greenberg, J. S., 13, 14, 407
Greer, D., 371, 372, 377, 379, 380
Greer, S., 377
Grieving, 309; absence of, 391–93, 399–401, 403; and depression, 304; psychodynamic models of, 390; psychological aspects of, 402; social expectations for, 404
Griffin, Merv, 475
Griffin, R. W., 142
Griffiths, T. J., 438
Grinker, R. R., 342
Grof, S., 381
Gross, A. E., 264, 265
Gross motor skills: arousal of, 469; and stress reduction, 441
Grunberg, N. E., 5, 10, 71
Guillemin, Roger, 31

Gumenik, W. E., 4
Gumerman, R. A., 263
Gunther, M. S., 390
Guthrie, E. R., 284, 285

Haan, N., 5, 190–92, 200, 204, 209, 228, 238, 244
Haas, J. E., 103, 114
Haber, R. N., 208
Habits, breaking of, 475–82
Hackett, T. P., 10, 202, 204, 205*n*1, 232, 234, 240
Hackett and Cassem Denial Scale, 232, 234, 236, 240
Hackman, J. R., 142
Haft, J. I., 286
Haight, M. A., 238
Haldane, J. S., 23
Hale, B. D., 447–48
Halifax, J., 381
Halikas, J. A., 390
Hall, E. G., 464
Hall, H. K., 461
Hall, J. A., 279
Hall, P. S., 114
Hall, S. S., 10
Halverson, C., 261, 269
Hamburg, B., 338, 343
Hamburg, David, 5, 7, 205–6*n*1, 228, 305*n*2, 338, 343
Hamburger, E., 54
Hansen, F., 134
Hansen, H., 111
Hanson, J. D., 70
Hanson, S. L., 162
Hansson, R. O., 278, 285, 291
Hanusa, B. H., 384
Harburg, E., 193
Hardiness: among adult males, 250; conditions leading to, 249; development of, 245–57; socioeconomic aspects of, 251–53; teaching of, 257
Hargreaves, A. G., 133
Harlow, H. F., 253, 254, 316
Harlow, M. K., 316
Harm, *see* Threats
Harrell, N., 289
Harris, B. L., 434, 439
Harris, D. V., 434, 439, 448
Harris, M. J., 279
Harris, P. L., 226
Harris, S., 384
Harris, T., 258, 260
Harrison, A., 159, 163, 164
Harrison, D., 265
Harter, S., 166
Hartman, K. A., 68
Hartsough, D. M., 119, 139
Hassles, 415, 416, 417; among adolescents, 83, 159, 162–64, 167; among children, 162–64, 167, 169, 171; defined, 159; ethnic differences in, 172–73; evaluation of, 166–67; and family structure, 171–72; gender differences in, 171, 172, 176–77, 178–79; outcome of, 173, 174–75; patterns of, 176–77; psychological correlates of, 173–76, *see also* Stress
Hassles Scales (Kanner), 162, 167
Hatfield, E., 403
Haven, C., 258, 260, 262, 264, 265
Hay, D., 217
Haynes, S., 186
Hazardous waste, 138, 317; psychological effects of, 121, 125, 128–29, 134
Health: modification of habits and, 64–65
Health care: cost of, 77–78; prevention in, 78–79
Health maintenance organizations (HMOs), 488, 489
Health promotion programs: in the workplace, 486–87
Health psychology, 19–20, 74; definition of, 10, 62; recent developments in, 63; research in, 71; trends in, 77–80
Heart rhythm, in stress, 311
Hebb, D. O., 284, 285
Heckhausen, H., 221
Heijn, C., 396
Heitzmann, C. A., 74
Hellstedt, J. C., 434, 472
Helsing, K. J., 270
Hemenway, D. P., 473
Hemoconcentration, in alarm reaction, 25
Henderson, S., 115
Henne, D. A., 141
Herbert, P. G., 441

Herbst, A. L., 41
Herd, J. A., 286
Heroin, addiction to, 476–78, 479, 481–82
Hertzberg, L. J., 381–82
Hervig, L. K., 237, 238
Herzing, D., 483–84
Hess, E., 262
Hetherington, E., 261
Heyman, S. R., 451
Hickman, D., 398
Hickman, J. L., 450
Hiner, S. L., 160
Hinkle, L. E., 3
Hinrichsen, G. A., 212
Hinton, J. M., 280–81, 373, 378, 380
Hippocrates, 22
Hiroshima, 133
Hirsch, B. J., 258, 260
Hirsch, J., 40
Hitchcock, L. S., 205*n*1, 234
Hitzig, W., 49–50, 54–55, 56
Hockey, L., 372, 385–86
Hodges, W. F., 4
Hodson, C., 260
Hofer, M. A., 7, 206*n*1, 230
Hoffman, H. E., 230
Holahan, C. J., 72, 73, 81, 159, 160, 271
Holahan, C. K., 159, 160
Holden, C., 19, 377
Holistic health movement, 19
Holmes, T. H., 83, 85, 158, 159, 160, 324, 386, 416
Holmes and Rahe Life Events Scale, 386
Holroyd, K. A., 9
Homeostasis, 23, 52, 412; social, 93
Hopelessness, 310; among cancer patients, 377; and stress, 308
Hormones: and coronary heart disease, 286–88, 297–98; in stress, 9–10, 13, 26–28, 197, 310, 413
Horowitz, M., 216, 218, 219, 230, 234
Horton, F. T., 375
Horwitz, E. A., 193
Hospices, 376–77, 379–81
Hostility, and development of illness, 66
House, J. S., 73, 260
Houston, B. K., 74, 185
Houts, P. S., 119
Howell, T., 391
Hoyt, M. F., 107
Hull, C. L., 457
Hull, J. G., 185
Humor: as defense mechanism, 343–45; "sick," 347
Hunt, R. J., 140
Hunt, T., 83
Hunter, F. T., 261, 266
Hurrell, B. A., 270
Husaini, B. A., 270
Husak, W. S., 473
Hypnosis, 433, 451–55; for athletes, 433, 454, 456–59, 469, 473; cognitive-behavioral theory of, 452–53; and motor performance, 457; neutral, 454; self-, 438–39, 455–56; waking, 454
Hypothalamus, in alarm reaction, 26

Ihilevich, D., 231, 237
Illness: behavioral factors in, 64; and cognitive coping strategies, 218; coping in, 9–11, 228, 243; and crowding, 88–91; and disasters, 110–12; emotional response to, 377–78; etiology of, 18; prediction of, 416; psychological causes of, 65–68; psychosocial factors in, 70; and stress, 9–11, 13, 17, 30–31, 69–71, 184, 258; and uncertainty, 352–69
Illness, terminal: awareness of, 372; definition of, 371; final stages of, 374, 376–77; length of survival in, 378; psychotherapeutic approaches to, 381–83
Illness behavior, 70
Imagery, 433, 434, 456; development of skills in, 450–51; internal and external, 447–48; and stress in the workplace, 486; use of in athletics, 445–47, 448–51, 462, 464, 467, 468, 473
Immerwahr, J., 143
Immune system, psychological aspects of, 10–12
Indiana State Fairgrounds disaster (1963), 130–31
Industrial Revolution, 87, 94

Inflammatory potential (of alarm reaction), 28
Ingersoll, B., 262
Ingham, J. G., 258, 262, 269
Inoculation effect, *see* Stress inoculation
Institute of Medicine, 390, 393, 415; report on bereavement, 402
International Work Group and Death, Dying and Bereavement, 379
Interventions, 412; and coping, 74–76; corporations participating in, 487; cost of, 78; definition of, 433; in sports, 473; strategies for, 432–33; for terminally ill patients, 383–84; in the workplace, 485; *see also* Stress management
Irwin, C. E., 68
Isbell, G. M., 4
Isolation, psychological effects of, 92
Ito, M., 458, 459
Izen, J. E., 402

Jackson, A., 438, 461, 463–64, 468, 469, 472
Jackson, J. A., 451
Jackson, S., 490
Jacobs, M. A., 113
Jacobs, S., 402
Jacobs, S. C., 372
Jacobson, Edmond, 436–37, 438, 447, 462
Jaffe, A., 376
Jaffe, D., 495
Jaffe, L., 376
James, William, 60
Jameson, J., 488
Janis, I. L., 4, 74, 201–2, 215, 309, 352, 368
Janoff-Bulman, R., 132
Janz, N. K., 64
Jemmott, J. B., 10, 68
Jenkins, C. D., 228, 276, 277
Jenkins Activity Scale (JAS), 277, 278, 290, 292, 296
Jennings, J. R., 282, 296
Jessor, R., 65
Jessor, S. L., 65
Jette, S. H., 399
Job/task demands (in the workplace), 82
Joffe, P. E., 184, 231, 238
Johnson, J., 162
Johnson, J. E., 75
Johnson, T., 258
Johnson, W. R., 457, 458
Johnston, A. M., 316
Joking: as avoidance device, 347–49; as defense mechanism, 343–45; as tension release, 345–47
Jones, A. P., 260
Jones, J., 484
Jones, K., 488–89
Jones, R., 487
Jose, W., 487
Joseph, J. G., 354
Jourard, S., 260
Julius, S. A., 41
Jung, Carl, 287
Juni, S., 237

Kaffman, M., 397
Kafry, D., 176
Kahn, R. L., 79, 201
Kaiser-Permanente Health Plan, 489
Kalish, R. A., 381, 382, 383, 384
Kaloupek, D. G., 230, 234, 242
Kandel, D. B., 266
Kane, R. L., 380
Kannel, W., 64, 186
Kanner, A. D., 71, 83, 85, 86*n*2, 159, 160, 161, 162, 163, 164, 167, 173, 175, 176, 177, 178, 179, 209, 416; on uplifts and hassles, 158–81
Kaplan, B. H., 258, 260
Kaplan, H. B., 384
Kaplan, R. M., 74, 78
Kaposi's sarcoma, 355, 362
Kapp, F. T., 116
Kardiner, A., 106
Karney, R. J., 392
Karoly, P., 384
Karon, M., 375
Kasl, S. V., 1, 70, 151, 372
Kastenbaum, R. J., 371, 372, 373, 374, 379
Kates, R. W., 108
Katz, J. L., 7, 8, 197, 223
Katz, R., 151
Kavenaugh, R., 376
Keller, S. E., 67

Kemeny, M. E., 232, 243
Kerr, W., 392
Kessler, R. C., 259, 270, 400, 401
Key, W. H., 113
Kidder, D., 379, 381
Kiecolt-Glaser, J. K., 67, 74
Killian, L. M., 129
Kinderlehrer, J., 54
King, S. H., 193
Kirschenbaum, D. S., 78, 461
Klas, L. D., 403
Klehr, N., 495, 497
Klein, G. S., 199
Klenner, F. R., 54
Klerman, G. L., 402
Kline, P., 237
Klinger, E., 395
Klinzing, J., 466
Knight, R. B., 206*n*1
Knittle, J., 40
Knorr, N. J., 390
Knudson, A. G., 375
Kobasa, S. C., 4, 184–85, 187*n*4, 197, 305*n*4; on development of hardiness, 245–57
Kohl, R. M., 449
Kohn, M. L., 145
Kolata, G. B., 286
Kolonay, B. J., 450, 462–63
Kon, I. S., 261, 266
Korman, A. K., 147, 152, 154
Kornhauser, A., 155
Kosten, T. R., 372
Kovacs, M., 165
Krant, M. J., 381
Krantz, D. S., 5, 10, 46, 71, 75, 76
Krasner, S. S., 186
Krohne, H. W., 193, 208
Kübler-Ross, Elizabeth, 304, 373, 374, 395
Kulka, R., 263, 264, 266

Lacey, J. I., 4
Lakey, B., 259, 273
Lambiotte, J. G., 447
LaMontagne, L. L., 234, 239
Landers, D. M., 445, 449
Landis, K. R., 73
Landreth, P. W., 114
Langer, E. J., 68
LaRocco, J. M., 260
Larson, M. E., 70
Latham, G. P., 461, 474*n*1
Lau, R. R., 65, 68
Laudenslager, M. L., 67, 70
Laughter, as therapy, 55, 58
Launier, R., 44, 71, 419, 425
Laux, L., 208
Lawson, N. C., 391, 393, 400
Layman, E. M., 440
Lazarus, Richard S., 1, 2, 3, 4, 5, 7, 8, 9, 14, 17, 18, 37, 38, 42, 44, 74, 85, 159, 161, 208, 209, 210, 212, 216, 225, 228, 229, 230, 232, 234, 235, 305*n*3, 308, 367, 368, 410*n*1, 412; on concept of coping, 189–206; on coping and emotion, 207–27; and coping process, 71, 72, 183, 184, 187*n*4, 211, 218, 233, 244, 420, 425; definition of stress, 3, 415, 418–20; on denial, 204, 205*n*1, 215, 223, 240; on disasters, 125; human research by, 69, 196, 220, 222, 226, 239, 241, 416, 417
Lee, G. F., 129, 130
Lefcourt, H. M., 235, 236, 259, 273
Lehman, D. R., 74, 397, 398, 402
Leik, R. K., 112
Leopold, R. L., 115, 134
Lesser, G. S., 266
Levenson, R. W., 311
Leventhal, H., 37, 65, 68, 69, 75, 296
Lever, J., 261
Levine, A., 121, 129, 134
Levine, J., 206*n*1
Levine, M., 231, 235
Levine, S., 414
Levinson, D. J., 144
Leviton, G. L., 403
Levy, S., 67, 262
Lewinsohn, P. M., 176
Lewis, C. E., 358
Lewis, S., 375
Lichtenstein, S., 352
Lichtman, R. R., 69, 75, 217
Lidz, T., 134
Lieberman, M. A., 259, 266, 272, 320, 326, 328
Life events, 20, 158, 416; among adolescents, 177; among adults, 319;

among children, 161; and physical illness, 83; scheduled and nonscheduled, 324–27, 332–35; self-reporting of, 162
Life strains, 302; among adults, 319–36; definition of, 325; at different age levels, 326–30; and psychological distress, 329; and society, 333; and work, 326–27; among young adults, 327–28
Lifestyle, and health, 486, 496
Lifton, R. J., 318
Lilliston, B. A., 402
Lindemann, E., 134, 201, 205*n*1, 305, 309, 396
Lipman, R. S., 323
Lipowski, Z. J., 203, 204–5, 218
Livingston, I. L., 305*n*6
Llewellyn, J. H., 462
Locke, A. A., 142
Locke, Edwin A., 82–83, 141, 153, 157*n*1 460, 461, 474*n*1; on meaning of work, 140–57
Lodge, B., 441
Loevinger, J., 192
Loewenstein, S. F., 266
Logue, J. N., 111, 134
Loneliness, gender differences in, 271
Long, B. S., 465
Longfellow, C. P., 260, 263, 266
Loomis, C. P., 108
Lorence, J., 142, 145
Loris, K., 487
Losenkov, V. A., 261, 266
Loss events, 388–405; failure to recover from, 401–2; intervention in, 401; long-term impact of, 398; recovery from, 396–97; research in, 399; resolution of, 397–99; "working through," 394–96
Lovallo, W. R., 296
Love Canal disaster, 122, 128, 134
Low points (in natural disasters), 126, 128
Lowe, J. C., 334
Lowenthal, M. J., 258, 260, 262, 264, 265
LSD, use of for cancer patients, 383
Lund, D. A., 391, 392, 397, 400
Luthe, W., 439, 486
Lutz, R., 86*n*1, 409, 410, 410*n*3, 495, 497; on stress management in the workplace, 483–98
Lyles, J. N., 75

McAdoo, H., 266
McCabe, P. M., 1
McClelland, David, 247, 254, 255, 479
Maccoby, M., 147
McCrae, R. R., 159, 177, 210, 241
McCurdy, S., 292
Mace, R. D., 466
McEnroe, John, 279
McEwan, R., 459
McGinnus, J., 485
McGrath, J. E., 2
McIntosh, J., 353
McKay, G., 45, 73
McKay, M., 14, 407
McKean, J. D., 83
McLanahan, S. S., 260
McLeod, J. D., 270
McLeroy, K., 484, 490, 493, 494, 495
McLoone, J. B., 206*n*1
McLuckie, B. F., 101
McMullen, P. A., 264, 265
McPhee, S., 497
Maddi, S. R., 184–85, 187*n*4, 305*n*4; on development of hardiness, 245–57
Maddison, D., 404
Madson, P., 119
Mages, N. L., 199, 230
Maguire, P., 353
Mahoney, M. J., 431*n*1, 434, 447, 469
Make Today Count (organization), 382
Makovsky, V., 260
Malec, J., 391, 393
Malinowski, B., 352
Malone, C., 439
Maloney, L. J., 206*n*1
Managua earthquake (1972), 113, 114
Mandler, G., 208
Mangan, C. E., 242
Mann, G. V., 46, 215
Mann, L., 4, 352
Mannes, M., 383
Mantras, 440
Manuck, S. B., 76
Manuso, J., 490, 493, 494

Man with the Golden Arm, The (film), 476
Margaret, S. M., 376
Marital stress, 238, 323, 327–29
Mark, E. W., 264
Marks, E. S., 105–6, 107
Markus, H., 144
Marlatt, G. A., 65, 409, 478
Marris, P., 391, 393, 394, 397
Martens, R., 434
Martin, I., 4
Martin, R. A., 259, 273
Marx, J. L., 286
"M*A*S*H" (television program), 217
Masling, J., 237
Mason, J. W., 2, 3, 17, 18, 38, 46, 71, 414
Mason, L., 403
Massong, S. R., 237
Mastectomy, 331
Masuda, M., 83, 416
Matarazzo, J. D., 62, 64, 65, 79, 371
Material values, 155; and social relationships, 147–48; and stress, 145–49
Matheny, K. B., 160, 178, 179
Matthews, K. A., 66, 68, 277, 278, 282, 285, 287, 291, 293
Matthews-Simonton, S., 381, 382
Maurice, W. L., 390
Meacci, W. G., 449
Mechanic, D., 5, 10, 65, 196, 217, 302–3; on modes of adaptation, 337–51
Mediators: in alarm reaction, 26, 31; in coping, 213–15; of life strains, 330; and social support, 45
Medication, toxicity of, 53, 54
Meditation, 14, 411, 425, 440–41; and stress in the workplace, 485, 490; and Type A behavior, 298
Medley, D., 291
Meeks, S., 159, 160
Meichenbaum, D., 424, 425, 428, 429, 431*n*1, 464
Melamed, B. G., 75
Melick, M. E., 110
Melisaratos, N., 67, 377
Men: bisexual, 366; and emotional intimacy, 268–70; emotional support of, 185–86, 262; mobilization of support for, 263–71; as providers of support, 265, 271–74
Menaghan, E., 212
Mendelsohn, G. A., 199
Menninger, K. A., 5, 107, 190–91, 200, 204, 208, 209
Mental health services, and medical care utilization, 488–89
Meyers, D., 65, 68, 69
Mikhail, A., 5
Miles, M. S., 397
Mileti, D. S., 119
Miller, D. T., 132
Miller, J., 260, 267
Miller, M., 383
Miller, N. E., 190
Miller, P. M., 258, 262, 269
Miller, S. M., 193, 204, 207, 242
Millstein, S. J., 68
Milne, G., 112, 134
Minnesota Multiphasic Personality Inventory (MMPI), 229, 238, 291
Mirsky, A. F., 305*n*6
Mischel, W., 8
Mishel, M. H., 353
Mitchell, R., 8, 260
Molleman, E., 353
Monat, A., 1, 4
Monroe, S. M., 159, 160, 175, 177, 179
Moore, J. W., 334
Moos, R. H., 5, 8, 72, 73, 159, 178, 193, 196, 218, 228, 232, 233, 241, 242, 244, 271, 397
Mor, V., 371, 372, 377, 380, 381
Morgan, W. P., 451, 455, 457, 458, 459
Morris, J. N., 380
Morris, T., 377
Morrissey, J. R., 375
Morse, N. C., 140, 142, 143, 144
Mortimer, J. T., 142, 145
Moskowitz, D. S., 197
Moulton, J. M., 357
Mt. St. Helens eruption, 112
Mourning, disordered, 391–93
Muhlenkamp, A., 403
Multiphasia, in Type A behavior, 278
Multiple Risk Factor Intervention Trial Research Group, 65
Mumford, E., 488, 492
Munz, D. C., 262

Murphy, L., 492, 493
Murphy, L. B., 5, 196, 198
Murphy, L. R., 411
Murphy, R., 487
Murphy, S., 112
Murphy, S. M., 461–62
Myers, G. C., 371
Myers, J. K., 324

Naditch, M., 184, 231, 238
Nadon, G. W., 386
Nakell, L., 233, 241
Nathan, E. A., 1
National Hospice Organization, 371–72, 379
National Hospice Study, 379–80, 386
National Institute for Occupational Safety and Health (NIOSH), 82
National Institute on Aging (NIA), 386
National Research Council, 352
Natterson, J. M., 375
Natural disasters, causes of, 122
Neal, D., 129
Neale, J. M., 8, 13, 72, 234, 242, 302
Near, J. P., 140
Nehnevajsa, J., 123
Neimeyer, A., 391, 393
Nelson, D., 235
Nelson-LeGall, S., 263
Nemiah, J. C., 392, 401
Nerenz, D., 65, 68, 69
Nervous system, 11, 310, 408, 473; and biofeedback, 442, 444; effect of crowding on, 90; stimulation of, 23; and stress, 26; and Type A behavior, 286
Neugarten, Bernice, 319, 334
Neuroendocrine system, 46, 279
Neurohumoral system, 32, 311
Neuroticism, and cancer, 11
New Look Movement (1950s), 201
New Madrid earthquake (1811–12), 102
Newman, C. J., 313, 318
Newsweek, 10
New York Longitudinal Study (of Type A behavior), 282
Nezlek, J., 266, 267
Nideffer, R. M., 434, 437, 438, 439, 440, 455
Nisbett, R. E., 403
Noel, R. C., 463
Noise, as stressor, 41
Nomikos, M. S., 4
Nonmutuality, and Type A behavior, 289–90
Nonspecificity (in alarm response), 18, 19, 22–24, 37–39, 310, 413; *see also* Specificity (in alarm response)
Norton, Ken, 433, 454
Nuclear accidents, 127
Nuclear Regulatory Commission, 127, 138
Nuckolls, K. B., 258, 260
Nye, J., 357

Obers, S. J., 253
Obesity, 476, 477; and stress, 270
Obrist, P. A., 190
Obsessive-compulsive behavior, 192, 284–85; in Type A behavior, 299
O'Donnell, John, 477
Ojala, D., 439
Oken, S., 217
Oldham, G. R., 142
Oltman, P. K., 194, 195
O'Neill, P. 403
Optimism, and development of illness, 68
Opton, E. M., 4, 5, 209, 229, 235, 419
Orioli, E., 495
Orlick, T., 434, 439
Orne, M. T., 452
O'Rourke, D. F., 186
Ortony, A., 211
Osberg, T. M., 234
Ossip-Klein, D. J., 75
Osterweis, M., 371, 372, 390, 391–92, 393, 395, 399, 402
Otto, M. E., 377
Overpopulation, 81, 87–91, 92–94; and social organization, 93
Oxendine, J. B., 469

Packer, E., 155
Page, J. D., 253
Pain: attitudes toward, 54, 196; management of, 75; and terminal illness, 378, 384, 386
Parent-child interactions, 245–47
Parenthood, single, 260

Parents, of dying children, 199, 206*n*1, 229, 325, 417–18
Parents Without Partners (support group), 263
Parker, G., 112, 134
Parkes, C. M., 230, 241, 380, 381, 390, 393, 394, 395, 396, 397, 398, 402, 404, 405*n*2
Parkes, J., 381
Parsell, S., 381, 382
Parsons, T., 265
Pascale, L., 206*n*1
Pathogen reaction model, 39, 42, 46; and appraisal of stress, 43
Patterson, G. R., 160
Paykell, E. S., 324
Pearlin, L. I., 86*n*1, 113, 217, 238, 239, 244, 258, 302, 320, 321, 322, 326, 328, 330, 331, 425; on life strains, 319–36
Pecking order, 92–93
Peele, S., 408, 409; on the habit trap, 475–82
Pelletier, K. R., 86*n*1, 409, 410, 410*n*3, 483–84, 485, 495, 497, 498; on stress management in the workplace, 483–98
Penick, E. E., 111–12
Penrod, J. D., 78
Peplau, L. A., 262, 267
Pep talks, for athletes, 434–35, 470–71
Perceived Social Competence Scale, 166
Perkins, T. S., 434
Perrow, C., 127
Perry, J. B., 129
Perry, S. E., 312
Personality, 337; and cancer, 67; and development of illness, 65–66; and health, 184; and stress, 185, 418
Person-environment transactions, 216–22, 424, 431
Persons with AIDS, *see* PWAs
Pervin, L. A., 4
Peterson, C., 68, 367
Peterson, D. B., 438, 452, 455
Peterson, E. A., 41
Pettingale, K. W., 377
Pflger, E., 23
Phares, E. J., 254, 255
Physical disability, 388–89; emotional recovery from, 398
Physiological tradition (of stress research), 18–19
Piaget, J., 199
Pichert, J. W., 162
Pictorial theory of cognition, 446
Pines, A., 176
Pishkin, V., 296
Pituitary-adrenal cortical system, 18, 414
Placebos, 59–60
Ploeger, A., 116
Populations of animals, crashes in, 88–90
Porter, C. A., 132
Posthypnotic suggestion, 456
Post-traumatic stress disorder (PTSD), 302, 312; in childhood, 309
Poulshock, S. W., 111, 134
Poverty, and stress, 148–49
Powell, B. J., 111–12
Powerlessness: and disasters, 132; and hardiness, 249–50, 254–55
Powers of the Mind (Smith), 48, 58
Predictability: in natural disasters, 124; in stress, 20, 353, 416
Pregnancy: and social support, 260; stress in, 258
Pressman, M. D., 452
Price, E. E., 449
Price, J., 110
Price, R. H., 400, 401
Price, V. A., 283
Primavera, J., 263
Prince, J. B., 145
Problem-solving: as coping mechanism, 72, 220–21, 223, 225; emotion-focused, 241
Professionals, career stages of, 143
Profile of Mood States (POM), 467
Prusoff, B. A., 324
Psyching-up strategies (in athletics), 468–70
Psychoanalytic ego psychology model (of coping), 190, 192, 193, 200, 207–9
Psychoimmunology, 67
Psychological autopsy, 374

Psychological Skills Education Program (PSEP), 466–68, 474
Psychological Skills Inventory for Sports (PSIS), 434
Psychoneuroimmunology, 10–11
Psychosomatic illness, and life events, 158
Psychotherapy, brief, 409, 491–92, 497
Publicity, in sport psychology, 471
Pulos, L., 455
PWAs (Persons with AIDS), 353–69; in Arizona study, 354–56; asymptomatic, 357–58; coping processes of, 360–62, 365; diagnosis of, 358–59, 366; guilt among, 366–68; support networks for, 355
Pynoos, R. S., 314

Quarantelli, E. L., 102, 103, 105, 109, 112, 113, 114, 130–31

Raab, W., 286
Rabkin, J. G., 83, 324, 416
Radabaugh, C., 331
Rahe, R. H., 41, 83, 85, 158, 159, 160, 324, 386, 416
Rand, A., 141
Rando, T. A., 379, 393, 394, 401
Rangell, L., 117–18, 316
Rao, V. R., 441
Raphael, B., 392, 396
Rapid City, South Dakota, flood, 114
Rau, M. T., 384
Raven, B. H., 107
Ravizza, K., 445
Reddish, P. S., 441
Reddy, J. K., 441
Reich, J., 159
Reid, J. B., 409
Reis, H., 266, 267
Relaxation, 424, 425; and stress in the workplace, 490, 493, 495
Relaxation, progressive, 411; in sports, 436–38, 462; and stress in the workplace, 486
Relaxation response, 14, 408, 425, 441; in hypnosis, 452, 453, 454; and stress in the workplace, 486
Relaxation techniques, 32, 426, 427; among cancer patients, 382; in coping, 75, 77; in sports, 434–45, 464, 467, 473; and Type A behavior, 298
Rennert, K., 384
Repression, and development of illness, 66
Repression-sensitization (coping mechanism), 193, 235–36, 417
Repression-Sensitization (R-S) Scale (Byrne), 184, 196, 235–36, 239
Retirement, 324, 328, 332, 335
Revenson, A., 212
Review Panel on Coronary Prone Behavior and Coronary Disease (National Institutes of Health), 276
Ribble, M. A., 253, 254
Rice, P. L., 12
Rice, R. W., 140
Richardson, J., 487
Richmond, J. B., 375
Rigler, D., 375
Riley, D., 259, 273
Ritter, K., 237
Ritzler, B. A., 237
Rivenbark, W. H., 262, 266
Rivers, William Halse, 60
Robins, Lee, 97, 477, 481
Robinson, W. J., 448
Rodgers, W. L., 265, 308
Rodin, J., 45, 63, 68, 75, 76, 384
Roenker, D. L., 449
Roeper, P. J., 193
Rogers, C. R., 284, 285
Rogers, G. O., 123
Rogers, R. W., 64–65
Rogner, J., 193
Rokeach, M., 141–42
Role-playing, and social support, 267
Rollin, Betty, 331
Rook, K. S., 259
Rosenberg, M., 321, 384
Rosenman, R. H., 186, 276, 277, 283, 293, 294, 295
Rosenman and Friedman TABP, 294–95
Rosenn, M., 4
Rosenstiel, A., 206*n*1
Roskies, E., 13, 187, 199, 407, 410*nn*1, 3, 411, 412; on stress management, 411–31

Ross, G. A., 112
Ross, H., 261
Ross, L. D., 403
Rotella, Robert J., 433, 439, 445, 448, 466
Roth, J. A., 353
Roth, S., 206*n*1
Rothbaum, F., 216
Rotter, J. B., 289, 308
Rowe, J. W., 79
Rowlison, R. T., 83
Rubenstein, J., 165
Rubin, C., 165
Rudy, T. E., 68, 69
Ryan, E. D., 449

Sackheim, H. A., 206*n*1
Sacks, M., 237
Sahud, M. A., 53, 54, 58, 61*n*2
Saleh, W. E., 259, 273
Salovey, P., 63, 68, 69, 75, 76
Sandler, I. N., 259, 263, 273
Sandler, J., 316
Sandman, C. C., 309
Sarason, B. R., 73
Sarason, I. G., 73, 83, 221
Sarason, S. B., 208
Savitsky, J. C., 139
Sawhill, I., 261
Schachter, Stanley, 44, 131, 477
Schaefer, J. A., 397
Schaefer, T., 254, 256
Schaeffer, M. A., 46, 120
Schafer, R., 235
Schafer, W., 14
Schedule of Affective Disorders and Schizophrenia, 391
Scheier, M. F., 68, 72
Schene, J., 226
Scherer, K. R., 236
Scherwitz, L., 296
Schlarb, J., 304; on research on dying, 370–87
Schleifer, S. J., 67
Schlesinger, H., 488, 492
Schmale, A. H., 417
Schmidt-Walker, K., 293
Schneider, J. W., 353, 358, 359
Schneider, S. K., 73
Schneiderman, N., 1
Schoenberg, B. B., 403
Schönpflug, W., 208
Schooler, C., 113, 145, 217, 238, 239, 244, 321, 322, 330, 425
Schore, L., 409–10
Schorr, J., 113
Schottenfeld, R. S., 121
Schulberg, H. C., 119
Schultz, Johannes H., 439
Schulz, R., 74, 75, 304, 373, 378, 384; on research on dying, 370–87
Schutz, W. A., 238
Schwartz, G. E., 63, 231, 235, 236, 240
Schwartz, M. S., 443
Schwarzer, R., 208
Scott, C., 495
Scott-Jones, D., 263
Scrimali, T., 444
Seabourne, T. G., 438, 461, 463–64
Seamonds, B., 484, 490, 494
Self-activation, in sport psychology, 472
Self-concept: in marriage, 327; and Type A behavior, 285; and work, 155–56
Self-esteem: and material values, 148; measurements of, 166; and social position, 321; and stress, 258–59, 321; and Type A behavior, 281–82; and work, 144
Self-help, 75, 78, 408–9, 479–82
Self-reports, in Type A behavior, 295
Seligman, M. E. P., 68, 131, 132, 255, 367
Selye, Hans, 11, 17–18, 24, 33, 37–39, 52, 71, 310, 410*n*1 413–14; on history and status of stress concept, 21–35
Sensitivity, and stress, 308, 317
Shadish, W. R., 398
Shannon, T. X., 4
Shapiro, Arthur K., 59, 60
Shapiro, D., 192, 485
Shapiro, R. M., 75
Shaw, R. E., 232, 234, 236, 239, 240
Shedletsky, R., 386
Shelton, T. O., 469
Shepard, M. J., 390, 404
Shepard, R., 487
Sherman, J., 78
Shipley, R. H., 193

Shneidman, E. S., 373
Shore, J. H., 112
Shrauger, J.S., 234
Shuchter, S. R., 396, 404
Shuman, L., 488
Sieck, W. A., 111–12
Siegel, K., 383
Siemsen, A., 206*n*1
Silber, E., 312
Siller, J., 392
Silver, M. J., 235
Silver, R. C., 218, 304–5, 388, 389, 394, 395, 396, 398, 399, 401, 403, 404; on myths of coping with loss, 388–405
Sime, W. E., 433
Simons, J., 449
Simons, R. C., 399
Simonton, D. C., 381, 382–83
Sims, J. H., 126
Singer, J. E., 4, 5, 8, 18, 19, 20, 44, 45, 121, 126, 129, 131, 132, 210, 216, 241, 410*n*1; on specificity and stress research, 36–47
Sirota, D., 142
16 Personality Factor Questionnaire, 467
Skin temperature, in biofeedback, 443
Skokan, L. A., 73
Skolnick, B. E., 194
Slovic, P., 352
Smelser, N. J., 2
Smith, Adam, 48, 58
Smith, B. D., 195
Smith, C. A., 71
Smith, Dan, 433, 447
Smith, M. B., 6
Smith, R. E., 464, 465
Smith, T. W., 185
Snowden, C. T., 70
Snyder, S. S., 216
Sobel, H. J., 381
Sobell, L. C., 409
Sobell, M. B., 409
Social comparison, as defense mechanism, 341–43
Social Desirability Scale (SD), 236
Social networks: participation in, 261–62, 268; response of to stress, 265–68; and work, 153–54
Social position, and self-esteem, 321
Social Readjustment Rating Scale (SRRS), 83, 84–85, 324, 416
Social roles, stress in, 238
Social structure: and adult development, 320–23; and coping, 330–31
Social support, 226, 241; for AIDS patients, 355; in coping, 73–74, 321; among disaster victims, 121; and recovery from loss, 401–2; and social status, 302; and stress reduction, 45, 159, 185, 258–59; among students, 349; and terminal illness, 377; women's expectations of, 273
Social values, and coping, 330–32
Sociodemographic groups: and coping, 239; and hardiness, 251–53
Sofer, C., 143
Soloff, P. H., 240
Solomon, E. P., 186
Solomon, F., 371, 372, 390, 391–92, 393, 395, 399, 402
Spanos, N. P., 453
Specificity (in alarm response), 36, 41, 66; physiological aspects of, 71; *see also* Nonspecificity (in alarm response)
Spiegel, J. P., 342
Spielberger, C. D., 4, 164, 186, 208, 287, 290, 291
Spielberger state/trait measures, 290, 291
Spielberger Trait Anxiety Inventory for Children, 164–65
Spigolon, L., 439
Spilka, B., 373
Spilken, A. Z., 113
Spilman, M., 487
Spinetta, J. J., 206*n*1, 375
Spitz, R. A., 253, 254
Spivack, G., 231, 235
Sport Competition Anxiety Test (SCAT), 467
Sport psychology, 408, 432–33, 434, 461, 467, 470–73
Sports, closed and open skill, 466–67
Stack, C., 259, 260, 266
Stage of exhaustion (in general adaptation syndrome), 25, 30, 38, 310, 413
Stage of resistance (in general adaptation syndrome), 25, 30, 310, 413

Staub, S. L., 120
Staudemeyer, H., 205*n*1
Stay of Execution (Alsop), 376
Steffy, B., 494, 496
Stein, M., 67
Steinberger, L., 282
Steinmetz, J., 14
Stephenson, J. J., 105, 126
Stern, M. J., 206*n*1, 240
Sternbach, R. A., 4
Steroids, role of in stress, 13
Stewart, D., 264, 353, 358, 359
Stewart, T. D., 402
Stiggins, J., 75
Stimulus and response, 2, 24, 227, 413, 417, 418
Stokols, D., 79
Stone, A. A., 8, 72, 213, 234, 242
Stone, E. A., 289
Stones, M. H., 398
Stothart, C. M., 438
Stoudemire, G. A., 394, 399, 400, 401
Strauss, A. L., 353, 356
Streltzer, J., 206*n*1
Stress: among adolescents, 178; among AIDS patients, 305*n*6, 365; appraisal of, 418–20; biology of, 310–11; among children, 161, 178; concept of, 2–3; contagiousness of, 272; and coronary heart disease, 285; cost of to workplace, 484–85; cumulative effects of, 38–39, 40, 41; definition of, 157*n*1, 412; among disaster victims, 119–21; early concepts of, 22–23; effects of, 17–20; as external stimulus, 414–17; and illness, 9–11, 17, 30–31, 69–71, 184, 258; and loss, 388–405; and material values, 145–49; measurement of, 70; mechanisms of, 26–28; models of, 41, 420–21; overwhelming, 312–13, 315–16, 318; and personality, 185; physiological aspects of, 2–3, 4, 9–10, 37, 413–14, 483; popular opinions on, 21, 411; and poverty, 148–49; psychological aspects of, 2, 4, 418–20, 484; reexperience of, 310; research in, 1, 17–20, 31–32, 37, 430; responses to, 4, 315–16; seeking of, 43–44; social moderators of, 261; and social position, 320; and social support, 159; sociological aspects of, 3, 418; systemic, 2, 18; terminology of, 2–3; and uncertainty, 353; vulnerability to, 308, 417–18; in the workplace, 145, 156; among women, 179; *see also* Hassles
Stress and Human Health (Institute of Medicine), 415
Stress inoculation, 309, 368, 411, 425, 464–66; among cancer patients, 420; training for, 428, 429
Stress inoculation training (SIT), 432, 465–66, 474
Stress management, 13–14, 215, 407–10, 431; for athletes, 433; fads in, 411; popularization of, 14; roots of, 410*n*1; use of imagery in, 450; and visual-motor behavior rehearsal, 463–64; in the workplace, 409; *see also* Interventions
Stress management programs: assumptions concerning, 492–95; for athletes, 461–62; clinical, 488–89; cost-effectiveness of, 485, 487, 491, 493–97; individualized, 494; successful components of, 495–96; in the workplace, 483–98
Stress management training (SMT), 464–66, 474
Stress of Life, The (Selye), 52
Stressors, 17–18; accumulation of, 416; acute, 420; among the dying, 373; appraisal of, 42–44; chronic, 415; in disasters, 103, 124, 137; in everyday life, 83; and heart rate, 195; physical, 413; in Selye, 29; universal, 310; in the workplace, 409, 491
Stress reactions, 4, 17, 24–25, 26–28, 414; *see also* Alarm reaction (in general adaptation syndrome)
Stroebe, M. S., 270, 402
Stroebe, W., 270, 402
Strong, D. J., 444
Structured Interview (SI, for Type A behavior), 277, 278, 290, 292, 295, 296
Struening, E. L., 83, 111, 134, 324, 416
Strumpfer, D. J. W., 107

Strupp, H., 427
Students: perception of stress among, 338–43; use of humor, 343–49
Substance abuse, 13
Sudden Infant Death Syndrome (SIDS), depression following, 394, 395, 398
Suicide, 385; among disaster victims, 119; "rational," 383
Suinn, R. M., 67, 75, 450, 461, 462, 465
Sullivan, T. J., 353, 358, 359
Suls, J., 72
Summer, J. J., 469
Super, D. E., 143
Support systems, mobilization of, 263–65
Surgical patients: coping among, 196–97, 202, 239, 417; interventions for, 488
Syme, S. L., 45, 270, 271
Syntoxic responses, 28–29
Szklo, M., 270

Tagliareni, E. M., 381, 382
Tait, R., 389, 396, 404
Talkington, J., 176
Tatum, E., 112
Taylor, G. P., 403
Taylor, J., 260
Taylor, M. Susan, 82–83, 157*n*1, 187*n*3; on meaning of work, 140–57
Taylor, S. E., 7, 19, 20, 69, 71, 72, 73, 74, 75, 217; on health psychology, 62–80
Taylor, V., 112
Taylor Manifest Anxiety Scale, 235–36
Teasdale, J., 131, 132
Terkel, S., 140
Terr, L., 313
Territoriality: biological aspects of, 94–95; and crowding, 91–95
Terror, in disasters, 104
Terwogt, M. M., 226
Thayer, P. W., 102
Thoits, P. A., 158, 416
Thomas, L., 216
Thompson, M., 392
Thompson, P. H., 151
Thompson, S. C., 74
Thompson, W. R., 254, 256
Thoresen, C. E., 67, 298
Thought stopping, 449
Threats, 3, 5, 196; appraisal of, 217–18, 418–19; coping mechanisms for, 3–4; and denial, 203; and hardiness, 255–56; measurement of, 4; and work, 146
Three Mile Island catastrophe, 70, 100, 103, 118–21, 124–25, 128, 138–39; chronic effects of, 134; predictability of, 136; stress reactions to, 82, 138; victims of, 119–21, 132
Tierney, W. M., 160
Tietjen, A., 261
Time urgency, and Type A behavior, 186, 278, 280, 288, 292–95
Timko, C., 384
Titchener, J. L., 116, 316
Titley, R. W., 462
Tobacco, use of, 10, 78, 476, 477; and cancer, 11; among disaster victims, 117; and stress, 408; and stress in the workplace, 484; and will to change, 480
Tokuhata, G. K., 120
Tomkins, S. S., 208
Tompkins, C. T., 384
Topeka, Kansas, flood, 107
Toxicity, as stressor, 39–40
Trainer, P., 98, 106, 113, 114
Trance, in hypnosis, 452–55
Tranquilizers, 31, 349; use of in grief, 401
Transactional tradition (of stress research), 18–19, 37, 42–44, 46
Transcendental meditation, 32, 436, 439–41
Trauma, in disasters, 106
Trieschmann, R. B., 392
Troll, L. W., 262
"True repressors" (of anxiety), 236
Trumbull, R., 1
Tsai, S., 487
Tsu, V. D., 196
Tuchfeld, Barry, 479, 480
Tuckel, P., 383
Tucson AIDS Project, 355
Tudor, John, 446
Turk, D. C., 68, 69, 76, 384

Turner, J. A., 75, 78
Turner, P. E., 449
Turner, R., 129
Turner, R. H., 109
Turner, R. J., 260
Tyhurst, J. S., 107
Type A behavior, 10, 66–67, 68, 410*n*1, 422; and aggression, 279; characteristics of, 186; components of, 289–91; and coronary artery disease, 275–99; and coronary heart disease, 186, 285–88; and failure, 282; measurements of, 291–93; research goals in, 297–98; research strategies for, 288–97; self-monitoring of, 299; social learning in, 283; stress management for, 430; underlying mechanisms of, 285–88; in the workplace, 493
Type A behavior pattern (TABP), 276–77; active ingredients of, 278–81; ontogeny of, 281–82; physical manifestations of, 279–80; psychological theories of, 283–85

Uhlenhuth, E. H., 324
Ulett, G. A., 438, 452, 455
Ulmer, D., 1, 280, 299
Ulrich, R. P., 458
Umberson, D., 73
Uncertainty: and AIDS, 352–69; and control, 367–68
Uplifts: among adolescents, 83, 85, 160–64, 167; among adults, 160–64; among children, 162–64, 167, 169, 171; correlates with anxiety, 173–74, 176; defined, 159; evaluation of, 166–67; function of, 161; gender differences in, 160–61, 178–79; outcome of, 173, 174–75; patterns of, 176–77; psychological correlates of, 173–76
Uprooting and dislocation syndrome, 310
Ursin, A., 414
Ursin, H., 190, 207
U.S. Department of Health, Education and Welfare, 371
U.S. Office of Disease Prevention and Health Promotion, 485

Vachon, M. L. S., 390–91, 392, 393, 396
Vaillant, George E., 68, 190–91, 192, 193, 200, 204, 208, 228, 477–78, 480
Valins, S., 81
VandenBos, G., 483, 489
van der Ploeg, H. M., 208
Vanek, M., 439
Vanfossen, B. E., 265, 271
Van-Treuren, R. R., 185
Vascular system, and stress, 26
Vauhkonen, M. L., 373
Vaux, A., 264
Veltfort, H. R., 129, 130
Venables, P. H., 4
Veroff, J., 263, 264, 266
Vickerman, B. L., 441
Vickers, R. R., 237, 238
Victimization, 426; legal aspects of, 139; long-term effects of, 99
Victims, of disasters, 107–12, 113–18, 129–33, 312
Vigilance: as coping mechanism, 215, 216, 235, 239; and uncertainty, 353
Virnelli, S., 185
Vischi, T., 488–89
Visotsky, H. M., 7, 196
Visual-motor behavior rehearsal (VMBR), 450, 462–64, 474
Vitaliano, P. P., 212, 215, 241
Vitamin C, 19, 56–57, 59
Voelz, C., 470
Volkan, V., 403
Volkin, J. I., 282
Vollmer, W. M., 112

Wachtel, T. J., 381
Waddell, C., 359
Waechter, E. H., 375
Wahler, R., 259
Waisman, H. A., 375
Waldorf, Dan, 479
Waldrop, M., 261, 269
Wales, J., 380
Walker, W. L., 404
Wallace, R. K., 441
Wallis, C., 297
Wallstein, B. S., 73
Walsh, J. A., 237
Walsh, R., 485
Wang, M. Q., 449

Wang, P., 485
Wankel, L. M., 459
Warheit, G. J., 104, 106, 122–23
Warning, in natural disasters, 123
Warren, J., 265
Washington Business Group on Health, 495
Wasow, M., 403
Waterhouse, G., 427
Waterhouse, I. K., 208
Watkins, P. L., 277
Watzlawick, P., 201, 452
Way of Life (WOL) scale, 290, 291
"Ways of Coping Questionnaire" (Folkman and Lazarus), 8, 72, 184, 212, 213, 222–23, 232, 233, 240–41
Wedemeyer, N. V., 260
Weil, R. J., 109
Weinberg, R. S., 438, 461, 463–64, 468, 469, 472
Weinberger, D. A., 66, 231, 235, 236, 240; on uplifts and hassles, 158–81
Weinberger, M. 160, 165, 176
Weinberger Adjustment Inventory, 165
Weinraub, M., 260
Weinstein, J., 4
Weintraub, J. K., 72
Weir, T., 263, 265
Weisman, A. D., 203, 233, 374
Weiss, J. M., 289
Weiss, L., 262, 265
Weiss, R. S., 140, 142, 143, 144, 264, 390, 393, 394, 395, 396, 397, 398, 402, 404, 405*n*2
Weissman, H. N., 237
Weisz, J. R., 216
Weitz, R., 303; on uncertainty and AIDS, 352–69
Weitzenhoffer, A. M., 457
Welch, B. L., 41
Welsh, G. G., 196, 417
Wengner, D. E., 109
Wenz, B. J., 444
Wertlieb, D., 159, 163, 164
Wethington, E., 270
Wheaton, B., 211
Wheeler, L., 266, 267
Whelan, E., 11
Wherry, R. J., 292
White, G. F., 114
White, H., 230, 234, 242
White, R. W., 5
Whiting, B., 262, 267
Whiting, J., 262, 267
Widowhood, 324, 328, 334, 335; and social support, 260
Widows: depression among, 390–93; mortality of, 270; recovery of from grief, 396
Wiener, C. L., 353
Wikler, L., 403
Wildavsky, A., 352
Wiley, W. A., 144
Wilkes, R. L., 469
Wilkins, W., 259
Williams, A. F., 397, 398, 402
Williams, L. R. T., 441
Williams, M. H., 433
Williams, Redford, 186, 277, 278, 286, 297
Williamson, K., 466
Willmott, P., 266
Wills, T. A., 72, 73, 159
Wilner, N., 234
Windom, R., 485
Winget, C., 98, 116, 117, 126, 133, 134
Winick, Charles, 477, 482
Winnicott, D. W., 318
Winter, B., 438
Wishnie, H. A., 204, 205*n*1
Wisdom of the Body, The (Cannon), 52
Witkin, H. A., 194, 195
Wolchik, S. A., 263
Wolf, B. M., 260
Wolfe, V. V., 176
Wolfenstein, M., 312–13
Wolff, C. T., 7, 8, 206*n*1, 229
Wolfson, A. D., 143
Wolpe, J., 462
Women: divorced, 263; and emotional intimacy, 268–70; emotional support of, 185–86; mobilization of support for, 263–71; as providers of support, 265–68, 271–74; socialization of, 267; stress among, 179; support networks for, 259, 260, 261–62
Wong, M., 230, 234, 242
Wong, P. T. P., 4
Wood, J. V., 69, 75, 217
Woodrow, J. Z., 237, 238

Woolfolk, R. L., 449, 461–62
Worden, J. W., 233
Work: and achievement, 142–43, 149–51; effect of on home life, 145; and life strains, 326–27; loss of, 147; material rewards of, 142; meaning of, 140–45; role of stress in, 33–34, 82; and self-concept, 155–56; and self-esteem, 82–83; and sense of purpose, 143, 151–53; and social relationships, 153–54, 336; and social support, 143–44; values of, 141–45, 146, 156–57
Workaholics, 284
Work in America Report (1971), 142
Workplace: conditions affecting stress in, 82; cost of stress to, 484–85; hazards in, 497–98; health promotion programs in, 486–87; stress management in, 483–98
Wortman, C. B., 69, 74, 131, 132, 136, 218, 304–5, 388, 389, 394, 395, 396, 397, 398, 399, 400, 401, 402, 403, 404; on myths of coping with loss, 388–405
Wright, B. A., 393, 403, 404
Wright, L., 186, 286, 289, 290, 292, 293; on type A behavior and coronary artery disease, 275–99
Wulf, S., 446

Yamamoto, K., 162
Yanagida, E. H., 206*n*1
Yankelovich, D., 142
Yerkes, R. M., 221, 410*n*2
Yoga, 439
Yogi, Maharishi Mahesh, 440
Young, M., 266
Young, W., 488
Youniss, J., 261, 266

Zaichkowsky, L. D., 433
Zarski, J. J., 159
Zautra, A., 159, 233
Zborowski, M., 10
Zedeck, S., 213
Zidovudine (AZT), 363–64
Ziegler, S. G., 466
Zigler, E., 206*n*1
Zinberg, Norman, 478
Zisook, S., 396, 404
Zones, J. S., 357
Zubek, J. P., 256
Zuckerman, M., 44
Zuehlke, T. E., 381, 382
Zung Depression Scale, 391
Zyzanski, S. J., 277